Case Studies in Contemporary Criticism

BRAM STOKER

Dracula

Case Studies in Contemporary Criticism
SERIES EDITOR: Ross C Murfin

Case Studies in Contemporary Criticism

SERIES EDITOR: Ross C Murfin, *Southern Methodist University*

BRAM STOKER
Dracula

Complete, Authoritative Text with
Biographical, Historical, and Cultural Contexts,
Critical History, and Essays from
Contemporary Critical Perspectives

EDITED BY

John Paul Riquelme
Boston University

Bedford/St. Martin's
BOSTON ♦ NEW YORK

For Bedford/St. Martin's

Executive Editor: Stephen A. Scipione
Editorial Assistant: Emily Goodall
Production Supervisor: Tina Cameron
Marketing Manager: Richard Cadman
Project Management: Stratford Publishing Services, Inc.
Cover Design: Zenobia Rivetna
Cover Art: Caspar David Friedrich, *Epitaph for Johann Emanuel Bremer,*
c. 1817. Schloss Charlottenburg, West Berlin.
Composition: Stratford Publishing Services, Inc.
Printing and Binding: Haddon Craftsmen, an RR Donnelley & Sons Company

President: Charles H. Christensen
Editorial Director: Joan E. Feinberg
Editor in Chief: Karen S. Henry
Director of Marketing: Karen R. Melton
Director of Editing, Design, and Production: Marcia Cohen
Manager, Publishing Services: Emily Berleth

Library of Congress Control Number: 2001092563

11 10 9 8
j i

For information, write: Bedford/St. Martin's,
75 Arlington Street, Boston, MA 02116   (617-399-4000)

ISBN-10: 0-312-24170-4 (paperback)
          0-312-23710-3 (hardcover)
ISBN-13: 978-0-312-24170-4 (paperback)
          978-0-312-23710-3 (hardcover)

Published and distributed outside North America by:
PALGRAVE
Houndmills, Basingstoke, Hampshire RG21 6XS and London.
Companies and representatives throughout the world.
PALGRAVE is the new global academic imprint of St. Martin's Press LLC Scholarly
and Reference Division and Palgrave Publishers Ltd. (formerly Macmillan Press Ltd.).
ISBN: 0-333-94712-6
A catalogue record for this book is available from the British Library.

Acknowledgments

"Vampiric Typewriting: *Dracula* and Its Media" by Jennifer Wicke originally appeared in *ELH* 59, 1992, pp. 467–93. Copyright © 1992 by the Johns Hopkins University. The essay has been slightly revised for this edition.

About the Series

Volumes in the *Case Studies in Contemporary Criticism* series introduce college students to the current critical and theoretical ferment in literary studies. Each volume reprints the complete text of a significant literary work, together with critical essays that approach the work from different theoretical perspectives and editorial matter that introduces both the literary work and the critics' theoretical perspectives.

The volume editor of each *Case Study* has selected and prepared an authoritative text of a classic work, written introductions (sometimes supplemented by cultural documents) that place the work in biographical and historical context, and surveyed the critical responses to the work since its original publication. Thus situated biographically, historically, and critically, the work is subsequently examined in several critical essays that have been prepared especially for students. The essays show theory in practice; whether written by established scholars or exceptional young critics, they demonstrate how current theoretical approaches can generate compelling readings of great literature.

As series editor, I have prepared introductions to the critical essays and to the theoretical approaches they entail. The introductions, accompanied by bibliographies, explain and historicize the principal concepts, major figures, and key works of particular theoretical approaches as a prelude to discussing how they pertain to the critical essays that follow. It is my hope that the introductions will reveal to students that effective criticism — including their own — is informed by a set of coherent assumptions that can be not only articulated but also modified and extended through comparison of different theoretical approaches. Finally, I have included a glossary of key terms that recur in these volumes and in the discourse of contemporary theory and criticism.

I hope that the *Case Studies in Contemporary Criticism* series will reaffirm the richness of its literary works, even as it presents invigorating new ways to mine their apparently inexhaustible wealth.

I would like to thank Supriyia M. Ray, with whom I wrote *The Bedford Glossary of Critical and Literary Terms,* for her invaluable help in revising introductions to the critical approaches represented in this volume.

Ross C Murfin
Provost, Southern Methodist University
Series Editor

About This Volume

Part One reprints the text of the 1897 first edition of *Dracula,* with annotations, preceded by a biographical and historical introduction and followed by documents, including political cartoons, that pertain to the book's cultural contexts. Part Two opens with a history of critical commentary about *Dracula* and includes five essays that exemplify in their readings various theoretical perspectives: new historical (Gregory Castle), gender-oriented (Sos Eltis), psychoanalytic (Dennis Foster), deconstructive (myself), and blended approaches (Jennifer Wicke). All the essays, which have been written or revised specifically for this volume, approach *Dracula* through interpretive concepts and strategies that are of contemporary concern to teachers, scholars, and students of literature. The five scholar-teachers who have contributed commentaries are committed to teaching and interpreting Stoker's unusual tale in their classrooms and to exploring its cultural relevance in their essays and in related projects. We welcome your participation in our attempt to evoke the complexities and the revelations of this seminal modern narrative.

Acknowledgments

Any editor who attempts to annotate *Dracula,* a tale that has appeared in many editions, makes decisions about what and how to gloss with an eye on earlier attempts to clarify for readers the text's potential obscurities. In writing the glosses for *Dracula,* I consulted various editions but primarily those by Nina Auerbach, Maud Ellmann, Marjorie Howes, and Leonard Wolf, whose efforts I acknowledge with thanks. My primary debt concerning the annotations, however, is to Theodora Goss, my research assistant during the project of editing *Dracula.* She contributed substantially to every aspect of our work in common, but especially to the annotations. The resulting text is more accurate and more useful to readers than I could have produced without her thorough, tenacious research. I wish to thank as well Anna Gilpin and Sara Sullivan, both doctoral students at Boston University, who worked carefully through the proofs with me.

The staff at several libraries provided needed books and information: The British Library, Houghton Library and Widener Library (Harvard University), Mugar Library (Boston University), Princeton University Library, and the Rosenbach Museum and Library (Philadelphia). Rhoda Bilansky of interlibrary loan at the Mugar Library obtained numerous volumes for me from other institutions, several of them difficult to locate on the American side of the Atlantic. Michael J. Barsanti at the Rosenbach shared his knowledge of the notes and outlines of *Dracula.* Mary Doran, curator of Irish materials at the British Library, answered queries and pointed me in helpful directions. Joanna Finegan of the Prints and Drawings department at the National Library of Ireland clarified the publishing history of one of the political cartoons. Richard Dalby of Yorkshire, who knows more about the publishing history of Stoker's works than anyone reasonably could, kindly provided me with a copy of his invaluable *Bram Stoker: A Bibliography of First Editions: Illustrated* (London: Dracula Press, 1983). Timely assistance and advice concerning annotations and my introductions came from Tamar Heller, Ognyan Kovachev, Jonathan Mulrooney, and Joseph Valente. Brittain Smith and William Waters helped me improve my translations from Marx and Nietzsche.

Generous quantities of needed advice, guidance, and patience came from Ross Murfin, the general editor of the series, and Steve Scipione at Bedford/St. Martin's. Steve has my special thanks for suggesting the art for the cover. I am grateful to Steve's assistant Emily Goodall, who pitched in to make sure all the pieces of the manuscript made it safely into production. At Bedford/St.Martin's I would also like to thank the president, Charles Christensen; the editorial director, Joan Feinberg; the manager of publishing services, Emily Berleth; and from Stratford Publishing Services, Leslie Connor and Cathy Jewell.

Victor and Louis, who will read Stoker's narrative in a few years, allowed me time for the necessary work when I pursued the editing at home. Marie-Anne Verougstraete provided expert help in reproducing the cartoons and gave more encouragement and support than I can adequately acknowledge here or anywhere.

John Paul Riquelme
Boston University

About the Text

The text of *Dracula* reprinted here is the first edition published in London by Archibald Constable and Company in 1897. During the remaining fifteen years of Bram Stoker's life, Constable kept the book in print through eight editions, with the paperback edition appearing in 1901. Publication of a reset *Dracula* was undertaken by another publisher only after Stoker's death in 1912. The Constable edition, then, has the authority of Stoker's having seen it through the press and having allowed its reprinting in his lifetime. In the case of at least one other book by Stoker, *The Jewel of Seven Stars* (1903), brought out by a different publisher, he made significant changes after the first edition, apparently at the publisher's request. There were no such alterations in the Constable reprintings of *Dracula*. Curiously, the contract between Stoker and Constable to publish *Dracula* is dated May 20, 1897, though the book appeared in June. Since Constable had published two of Stoker's works in 1895, they may well have had an oral agreement about the new volume. The contract gives the title as *The Un-Dead*. The choice of the actual title seems to have been a last-minute decision. In our edition, some minor typographical errors have been silently corrected, and a few ambiguities about textual matters have been pointed out in the annotations. Works that I consulted while preparing the text and that are cited in the annotations include:

Baedeker, Karl. *London and Its Environs: Handbook for Travellers.* London: Dulau, 1896. (Cited as *Baedeker* 1896.)

Baedeker, Karl. *Austria, Including Hungary, Transylvania, Dalmatia, and Bosnia: Handbook for Travellers.* Leipsic: Baedeker, 1896. (Cited as *Baedeker Austria* 1896.)

Baedeker, Karl. *Great Britain: Handbook for Travellers.* Leipsic: Baedeker, 1897. (Cited as *Baedeker* 1897.)

Black's Guide to London and Its Environs. 8th ed. Edinburgh: Adam & Charles Black, 1885. (Cited as Black.)

Black, Henry Campbell. *A Dictionary of Law.* St. Paul, MN: West, 1891. (Cited as Black's Law.)

The Complete Works of Shakespeare. Ed. David Bevington. Updated 4th ed. New York: Harper, 1997.

The Encyclopædia Britannica. 11th ed. London: Encyclopædia Britannica Company and New York: Encyclopædia Britannica, 1910. (Cited as *Enc. Brit.* 11th.)

The Encyclopædia Britannica On-Line. http://www.britannica .com (Cited as *Enc. Brit.* OL.)

The Essential Dracula. Ed. Leonard Wolf. New York: Plume, 1993. (Cited as Wolf.)

Gerard, Emily. *The Land Beyond the Forest: Facts, Figures, and Fancies from Transylvania.* New York: Harper, 1888. (Cited as Gerard.)

Nevill, Ralph. *London Clubs: Their History and Treasures.* London: Chatto, 1911. (Cited as Nevill.)

The Oxford English Dictionary. 2nd ed. (ed. J. A. Simpson and E. S. C. Weiner). Oxford: Clarendon, 1989. (Cited as *OED.*)

The Oxford English Dictionary On-Line. http://oed.com (Cited as *OED* OL.)

Pope, Alexander. *The Odyssey of Homer, Books XIII–XXIV. The Poems of Alexander Pope, Volume X. Translations of Homer.* Ed. Maynard Mack. London: Methuen and New Haven: Yale UP, 1967. (Cited as Pope.)

Robinson, F. K. *A Glossary of Words Used in the Neighbourhood of Whitby.* Pt. 1, 1875; Pt. 2, 1876. London: Trübner, 1876.

Wilkinson, William. *An Account of the Principalities of Wallachia and Moldavia.* 1820. New York: Arno and the New York Times, 1971. (Cited as Wilkinson.)

Contents

PART TWO

Dracula:

A Case Study in Contemporary Criticism

Case Studies in Contemporary Criticism

BRAM STOKER

Dracula

PART ONE

Dracula:
The Complete Text
in Cultural Context

Introduction:
Biographical and
Historical Contexts

Born in Dublin in November 1847, Abraham Stoker, known as Bram, was the contemporary of Thomas Hardy (1840–1928) and Oscar Wilde (1854–1900). Like them, he was an active member of the community of artists and writers in London in the 1880s and 1890s, when Victorian tendencies in poetry, fiction, and drama were beginning to be challenged and transformed into what eventually became literary modernism. In that transformation, *Dracula* (1897) arguably holds as important a place as Hardy's *Tess of the d'Urbervilles* (1891) or Wilde's *Salomé* (1893). During his lifetime, however, Stoker was known not primarily as a writer but as someone involved centrally in the career of the charismatic English actor Henry Irving (1838–1905), the most important actor on the English-speaking stage in the final decades of the nineteenth century and the first member of his profession to be knighted (1895). A statue commemorating Irving's contribution to the theater stands in a prominent location in the West End of London not far from Trafalgar Square near the Lyceum Theatre. Stoker managed the Lyceum starting in 1878, when Irving became its proprietor under a long-term lease. He and his famous employer would both surely have laughed had anyone predicted that the fame of *Dracula* and its author would eventually exceed Irving's. The obituary that appeared in the *Times* of London (April 22,1912) mentioned his writing only briefly, referring to it as "a particularly lurid and creepy kind of fiction."

The story of how Bram Stoker came to work with a celebrated actor and to write an important literary text is the tale of an energetic Irishman who pursued three careers in Ireland and England and while traveling in North America: as a civil servant for more than a decade, then as the manager of an important theater troupe for over twenty-five years, and as a writer for four decades that included and extended beyond his more public, day-to-day careers. Stoker clearly possessed extraordinary energy and gifts that he exercised in a variety of ways. He had the unusual ability to pursue different work and different interests simultaneously and to make sharp changes in course, virtually to live different lives. Although he never practiced law, when he was thirty-nine, Stoker decided to study to become a lawyer, and four years later, in 1890, was called to the bar (Belford 193). In his writing, Stoker emphasizes doubling, "dual consciousness" (*PR* 2: 21) or "dual existence," as he calls it in *The Jewel of Seven Stars* (1903), and imposture to suggest that identity is neither stable not singular. His own life has a chameleonic character because of its variegated, multiple quality.

THE IRISH YEARS: FAMILY, EARLY LIFE, AND YOUNG ADULTHOOD (1847–1878)

Bram Stoker's early life was not auspicious. Until the age of seven, he was bedridden with an illness that has not been convincingly identified, but from which he appears to have recovered completely. As Stoker indicates in *Personal Reminiscences of Henry Irving* (1906), memoirs focusing primarily on Irving's career, he eventually grew up to be the largest person in his family. Six feet two inches tall, strongly built, with red hair, he made a vivid impression physically from his university years on. Stoker was born at the time of the Great Famine in Ireland (1845–49), a period of severe hardship for the Irish that contributed substantially to emigration and to anti-English sentiment. Disease, including cholera (1848–50), was widespread among rich and poor alike. Reasonable estimates of mortality indicate that at least one million inhabitants of Ireland died as a result of the famine in excess of the deaths that would normally be expected. The eviction of tenants from the land increased dramatically, and the flow of emigration to England, Australia, and North America accelerated. As a result of the deaths and emigration, Ireland's population declined by twenty percent between 1845 and 1851. There was much resentment among the Irish that

England, the richest country in the world, did not do more to relieve the suffering in a neighboring country over which it had dominion.

During his childhood illness, while Stoker was an invalid, his mother, Charlotte Thornley Stoker, told him fantastic tales of Ireland. These included stories about the first deadly epidemic of cholera in Ireland (1832–33) when she was a child in the west of the country and about Irish supernatural myths, such as that of the banshee, the female spirit of Gaelic folklore that announces a coming death by its wailing. Some of her narratives affect his later writing. His first collection of fiction, *Under the Sunset* (1882), consists of fairy tales written for his son, one of which, "The Invisible Giant," deals with a shadowy plague sweeping over the land. His mother's work on behalf of the poor, which included writing for Dublin newspapers about the rights and dignity of women, must also have made an impression on Stoker while he was growing up.

The third child of seven born to Abraham and Charlotte Stoker — who were Protestants but not part of the ruling elite in Ireland — Bram Stoker was only one among several children to achieve success. His older brother, W. Thornley Stoker, became a noted surgeon who was awarded a knighthood at the same time as Henry Irving, and two of his younger brothers also became physicians. Stoker remained close to several family members. In 1878, he worked with another brother, George, on *With "the Unspeakables"; or, Two Years' Campaigning in European and Asiatic Turkey* (1878), an account of his brother's experiences as a medical officer during the last of the Russo-Turkish Wars (1877–78). After establishing his connection with the theater in London, Stoker maintained an active social life that involved many people of accomplishment, including his older brother, Thornley. Through Bram Stoker's influence, George became a consulting physician for the Lyceum Theatre.

Although Stoker's parents were Protestants, they were neither socially prominent nor wealthy. His mother, Charlotte, who grew up in the rural west of Ireland, was Anglo-Celtic rather than Anglo-Saxon, since her mother was from a native Irish family (Haining and Tremayne 44). She and her husband supported their large family on his income as a civil servant at Dublin Castle, the seat of Irish government. When Stoker was in his twenties, his parents moved to France with his sisters to reduce expenses because their income proved insufficient after his father's retirement. By that time, he had completed a degree in science at Trinity College, Dublin, where he excelled as an athlete and became a leader of intellectual organizations. He was president of the Philo-sophical Society and auditor, or president, of the Historical Society, posts that gave him the opportunity to speak in public regularly. In 1866, two years after entering Trinity, Stoker was named University Athlete, the school champion, because of his prowess. In the same year, he first saw Henry Irving, then under thirty with his reputation yet to make, performing in Dublin.

Apparently for financial reasons Stoker's studies at Trinity were dis-rupted after his second year at the university and his progress toward graduation was slowed when he began working in the Irish Civil Ser-vice at Dublin Castle.[1] Over the next dozen years he was promoted from clerk of Petty Sessions to Inspector of Petty Sessions in Ireland. The term *petty sessions* refers to the meeting of two or more justices of the peace or magistrates for the summary trial of minor legal offenses in a particular district. Stoker's term as Inspector of Petty Sessions indi-cates that he was meticulous, well organized, and motivated to write. His first lengthy publication was not a literary text but a detailed guide to the administrative procedures for which he was responsible, *The Duties of Clerks of Petty Sessions in Ireland* (1879), a book of over two-hundred-fifty pages, published under the "official sanction" of the Registrar of Petty Sessions Clerks' Office, Dublin Castle. In his intro-duction to the volume, Stoker refers to the "excessive labour" that went into it, including the consulting of "thousands of documents" (v). His goal was to establish "uniformity of method" for the "several hun-dred men performing daily a multitude of acts" and to develop "a great and effective system of procedure which must sooner or later be adopted for the whole British Empire" (vi). This ambition changed form but did not disappear in later life: to create something of Irish ori-gin that would have a lasting effect internationally and not just in an insular setting. He shared that ambition with other successful modern Irish writers, including Wilde, W. B. Yeats, James Joyce, and Samuel Beckett, who redirected the literary tradition in English by writing works with an Irish inflection that, in time, attracted an international audience. In *Personal Reminiscenes,* Stoker refers to that early volume as

---

[1] The details concerning Stoker's graduation from Trinity are not entirely clear. As W. N. Osborough points out in "The Dublin Castle Career (1866–78) of Bram Stoker," gradu-ation records show a degree awarded in March 1870 but do not support Stoker's own claim that he received "an honours degree in Pure Mathematics" (223). Osborough's article makes it evident that our knowledge of Stoker's life before his move to London is less than certain and that some of the information given by Stoker in *Personal Reminis-cences* cannot be readily verified.

"a dry-as-dust book" (1: 32). His decision to leave his secure administrative position in Dublin in order to pursue a career in the arts in London obviously reflects the secondary importance he assigned to his governmental duties, though he had performed them assiduously for more than a decade.

From his university days, Stoker was fascinated by poetry and the theater. While he was at Trinity College, Walt Whitman's poetry stirred controversy, largely because of its implications for personal attachments between men. When Edward Dowden (1843–1913), a prominent professor of literature at Trinity, championed Whitman's writing at the Philosophical Society in 1871, Stoker was centrally involved in the debate (*PR* 2: 95). At a meeting of the Fortnightly Club in Dublin in 1876, Stoker spoke after Dowden in defense of Whitman (*PR* 2: 95–96), and he wrote to Whitman, who responded. In his memoirs, Stoker includes in the long chapter on Whitman a facsimile of the poet's letter to him of March 6, 1876, which folds out of the book to twice the size of a normal page (*PR* 2: 96bis). In the ardency of his admiration for Whitman, Stoker had written him a lengthy letter in which the devotion of a passionate reader was unmistakable. He visited Whitman in the 1880s when Henry Irving's company was on tour in North America, and the poet gave him signed copies of his work. Like some later modernist writers, including D. H. Lawrence, Stoker was influenced by Whitman's unconventional attitudes and style.

Stoker became an avid theater-goer while he worked in Dublin Castle, and he pursued a writing career through drama reviews and fiction. His interest in the theater may have been sparked by the enthusiasm for drama shown by his father, an admirer of Edmund Kean (1789?–1833), one of Henry Irving's predecessors among English actors who memorably portrayed Shakespeare's tragic characters. The younger Stoker's devotion to drama led him to become the unpaid drama critic for a newspaper, the *Dublin Mail,* in 1871. He volunteered to write his reviews immediately after the performances largely out of frustration that plays were not being brought to public attention in a timely way. When Henry Irving read Stoker's account of his performance in *Hamlet* in Dublin during his tour there in 1876, he invited the young reviewer to dine with him. When Stoker broke down after dinner in response to Irving's moving, late-night recitation of Thomas Hood's "The Dream of Eugene Aram" (1828) an intense friendship began that changed both their lives. As soon as Irving was able to secure control of the Lyceum Theatre in 1878, he offered Stoker the post of business manager, second only to himself in the organization.

Stoker, who was just finishing work on *The Duties of Clerks,* resigned his civil service position and within weeks had relocated to London. His decision to move virtually without notice reflects both his attachment to Irving and his determination to make a life in the arts and continue writing in a larger arena than Dublin provided.

THE LONDON YEARS THROUGH *DRACULA* (1878–1897): MANAGING THE LYCEUM THEATRE

The subsequent transformation in Bram Stoker's life was swift. After receiving Irving's offer in late November, 1878, Stoker, who was engaged to be married to Florence Balcomb, a young woman living in Dublin, coordinated his resignation from the Irish Civil Service with an acceleration of their marriage plans. They chose to live in London, where Stoker arrived in mid-December, after spending a few days in Birmingham, where Irving was on tour (*PR* 1: 60–61). Oscar Wilde had been one of Florence Balcomb's suitors, but there is no evidence that he and Bram Stoker were on anything but cordial terms in the years after the marriage. Within a year, Florence Stoker gave birth to their only child, Noel. From the moment he arrived in London, Stoker was faced with the daunting task of overseeing the organizing work for the first season of the Lyceum Theatre under Henry Irving. Renovation of the Theatre was already in progress, and the first production was in preparation for performance at the end of December. Irving was actor-manager, with ultimate say over hiring, firing, and the choice of productions. Stoker was normally identified on playbills as "acting manager," in effect the business manager. In his memoirs, he refers to himself half-jokingly as "Chancellor of the Exchequer," the governmental official responsible for financial matters, under Henry Irving's "Absolute Monarchy" (*PR* 1: 275). Irving was the king, but Stoker had much influence. He was, in fact, the practical, resourceful manager who turned Irving's plans into realities and who kept Irving from damaging mistakes until late in the actor's career.

Stoker was employed by Henry Irving, but in fact their working relationship was so close that it amounted in its first two decades to a collaboration, despite the fact that Irving's behavior to Stoker in their business relations was regularly high-handed. Out of friendship, personal loyalty, and commitment not just to Irving but to drama, Stoker worked on behalf of Irving and their Theatre, as is clear from the hours that he spent on business matters and from the kind of work he did. As the chief financial officer, Stoker kept the Theatre's books for his own eyes and Irving's only. He was frequently Irving's representative at public functions, his stand-in with reporters, his agent in many practical and personal matters, and his confidential secretary, regularly writing fifty or more letters a day on Irving's behalf, or well over a quarter of a million during the quarter-century of their partnership (*PR* 1: 62). Many of these would have been short notes, but some were longer, more complicated responses, and the number of letters is staggering. Stoker also evaluated manuscripts that came to Irving and gave advice about what would succeed. In this regard, he was influential in mounting the first play by Arthur Conan Doyle, the creator of Sherlock Holmes.

Although Stoker's duties at the Lyceum Theatre were demanding and time-consuming, he found himself in a social, intellectual, and artistic situation that was substantially more stimulating than his previous life in Dublin. Stoker came to know and work closely with talented performers and writers besides Henry Irving and Ellen Terry (1847–1928), Irving's costar in many plays. Arthur Wing Pinero (1855–1934), for example, later an influential playwright, was a young actor in the Lyceum troupe when Stoker became manager. For over two decades, Stoker spent many late-night hours after performances with Irving and with accomplished, prominent guests in the Lyceum's Beefsteak Room, a suite for receptions and dining large enough to seat thirty-six. The discussions regularly dealt with plays in performance at the Lyceum and elsewhere, future productions, and other matters concerning the art world of London.

The Lyceum's repertory was ambitious and successful. The list of productions published in the memoirs (reproduced at the end of this essay) includes over forty plays, twelve by Shakespeare. As a consequence, Stoker would have seen and heard Shakespearean plays and many popular melodramas and comedies night after night and in rehearsal, acted by the most accomplished performers of his day. Continuous engagement with drama in performance provided fuel for his literary sensibility. Passages, scenes, gestures, and effects in these plays became part of the repertoire he brought to his own literary projects, to be drawn on consciously or unconsciously. Contributing to Stoker's intimate knowledge of literature was the type of formal education he received and the traditions in the arts community he was part of in London, both of which encouraged the reciting of passages from literary texts. From time to time, Stoker recited for others during late nights in the Beefsteak Room or during more private encounters, including an unusual meeting with the poet laureate, Alfred Lord Tennyson, in which Stoker recited some of Tennyson's works to the poet while visiting him at home to discuss a production involving Tennyson and Irving.

The immersion in literature that Stoker's work at the Lyceum required and enabled furthered his intention to continue writing when he moved to London. Although he made good on that intention, he could not have anticipated how his responsibilities at the Theatre and the experience he gained there would affect both his rate of production and its character. In Dublin, Stoker's writing that was not administrative had consisted largely of drama reviews and some short fiction, which he was able to produce in spite of daytime work that was not literary in character. The new situation required a shift in emphasis. In the memoirs, Stoker describes a meeting in London that Henry Irving arranged for him in 1877 to discuss his ambitions as a writer with a well-known editor, who later solicited from him an essay dealing with drama (*PR* 1: 44–47). He declined the invitation because his views on the theater might have been attributed to Henry Irving. During his association with Irving, Stoker wrote about the theater only when he was sure that he and Irving were in agreement. Although this decision has the look of a subservient act, it was based on professional and personal tact. Continuing to write on drama without openly coordinating his views with Irving might well have been disruptive for Stoker's work and his friendship. Neither Stoker nor Irving would have wanted him to be perceived always as speaking for Irving, whose views might differ. Nor would he have wanted to be thought of as Irving's echo, deriving his ideas from his master when they were in fact his own. Because of his association with Irving, Bram Stoker shared in the actor's glory and his power. But he also established himself in his own right through his work and his friendships, the intensity and character of which neither came from Irving nor centered on him. Until Henry Irving's death, Stoker found outlets for writing independent of drama, primarily in fiction. Besides *Dracula* he published eight volumes of fiction between 1882 and 1905, including *Under the Sunset* (1882), a collection of fiction, *The Snake's Pass* (1890), his well-received first novel, and *The Jewel of Seven Stars* (1903), an occult mystery narrative. He waited until after 1905 to write at length about the drama and about his disagreement with Irving over Home Rule for the Irish.

Stoker's career as a writer gave him a life as an author separate from Irving, one that was nurtured by his work for the theater, compatible with it, and sufficiently limited not to be a distraction from it. Considering Stoker's massive responsibilities at the Lyceum Theatre, it is surprising that he was able to make time for any significant writing. But, like many other administrators with interests beyond management, he must have developed ways to save time once he grew used to the demands of his work. He also took some of the time he needed during vacations out of London between seasons, one spent near Whitby, where part of *Dracula* is set, and others spent at Cruden Bay on the eastern coast of Scotland. In London, Stoker continuously collected material for writing. He was in the habit of taking notes in a pocket notebook about events, ideas, and stories, which he drew on later. He was also able in London to use the resources of the British Library and, after he became a barrister, the Library of the Inner Temple, the Inn of Court, or legal society, with which he was associated.

Before *Dracula* Stoker published four volumes of fiction, including *Under the Sunset*, which, like the fairy tales and children's stories Yeats and Wilde published early in their careers, was an antirealistic work with an Irish flavor. The other books were two novels, *The Snake's Pass* (1890) and *The Shoulder of Shasta* (1895), and a novella *The Watter's Mou* (1894). Although *The Snake's Pass* concerns a young Englishman, who narrates the story, it is set in the west of Ireland and involves centrally Irish legends and the Irish landscape. The shifting bog, with its ability to swallow up people, houses, and the possessions of invaders, suggests the elusive, resistant qualities of Ireland and its inhabitants, which other Irish writers have also associated with the bog, including Seamus Heaney in his poem, "Bogland." The positive reception accorded to *The Snake's Pass* must have added to Stoker's confidence, though he appears never to have been lacking in that.

In the wake of that book, as Stoker approached fifty, he undertook the complex, ambitious project that became *Dracula,* while he continued finishing and publishing other narratives. Taking as some of his models Mary Shelley's *Frankenstein* (1818), Wilkie Collins's *The Woman in White* (1860), and Sheridan Le Fanu's "Carmilla" (1872), Stoker invented the vampire in the form of Count Dracula that would become a pervasive image for our times. The writing involved considerable research concerning the geography and superstitions of Eastern Europe, which he was able to pursue in the British Library. Drawing on many sources and cultural anxieties, Stoker produced a narrative combining the menace of Gothic writing with the fascination for the exotic that was strong at the end of the nineteenth century. Like Joseph Conrad in *The Heart of Darkness* (1899), who also combines a dark menace with exotic materials, he evoked important issues concerning home and homeland and concerning anthropological questions about the definition of the human. Those issues, which are still with us, became urgent for Western culture from contact with little-known peoples and customs as part of the expansion of empire. The intensified situation required new perspectives. Samuel Beckett, who was born around the time that Bram Stoker died, responded once to astonishingly new artwork by saying "I don't know what it is, having never seen anything like it before" (Beckett 126). Stoker's mother responded similarly on reading *Dracula* when she wrote "I have read much but I never met a book like it at all" (quoted from Stoker family papers in Belford 274). Many later readers have reacted similarly to the book's character and originality.

THE LATER LONDON YEARS:
AFTER *DRACULA* (1897–1912)

It was fortunate that Stoker completed *Dracula*, the book he worked on the longest and the only one continuously in print since its publication, before having to face the distracting difficulties of Henry Irving's late career and his own failing health. These difficulties began with the disastrous fire in 1898 that destroyed the stage sets for forty-four productions that were stored outside the city center because of their size. To reduce expenses, Irving had decided soon before the fire to decrease the amount of insurance, already much lower than the replacement value of the sets, which turned out to be irreplaceable. This event hobbled the future of the Lyceum Theatre. In the next few years there were further problems, including an accident and deteriorating health that kept Irving from acting at times, Stoker's own uneven health, and Irving's ill-considered business judgments, over which Stoker had little influence. In 1898 Irving relinquished control of the Lyceum to a syndicate, whose business ventures did not flourish. As a consequence of the syndicate's financial losses, Irving's acting troupe lost its London base in 1902. Within a year, Ellen Terry stopped acting with Irving.

Frequent tours abroad and in the British Isles to offset financial difficulties in the last fifteen years of Irving's life had taken their toll on Stoker as well as Irving. He suffered increasingly from health problems, including two strokes and kidney disease. Nevertheless, Stoker kept up an energetic pace in his writing after *Dracula*, completing four novels before 1905, the year Irving died during a provincial tour, and six books in the six years after Irving's death, including three novels, a volume of tales, and two substantial nonfictional works, his memoirs and *Famous Impostors* (1910). With its combination of mystery, adventure, and archaeology, *The Jewel of Seven Stars* (1903) anticipates the narratives about Indiana Jones that are popular today. Stoker's productivity was probably motivated by a combination of financial necessity and the desire to complete projects before it was too late.

Personal Reminiscences of Henry Irving, consisting of two volumes totaling over seven hundred pages, is Stoker's longest published work. Together with Stoker's collection of material concerning productions at the Lyceum Theatre and the company's tours, the *Reminiscences* makes a significant contribution to theater history. Stoker also published a volume of fifteen framed tales, *Snowbound* (1908), set on a train stranded in the snow during a provincial tour by a professional theater troupe. The tales almost certainly draw on stories that Stoker heard from other members of the company, and the details of the situation provide information about an aspect of theater — the tour — that was once not unusual but that no longer exists. Stoker's scrapbooks for the Lyceum Theatre from 1879–1904 provide detailed information about what was produced, who the actors and managers were, and when and where the productions took place. There are six volumes devoted just to the provincial and foreign tours dating from 1883 to 1904. They provide a record of extensive travel, at times under arduous conditions, throughout the British Isles and North America. The playbills for the regular seasons fill more than twenty-five bound volumes representing a quarter-century of performances. Stoker's carefully kept collection became part of the British Library's archives soon after his death. The date stamped in the bound volumes, "17 June 1913," suggests that they were sold by Sotheby's at the same auction as were the notes for *Dracula* (now in the collection of the Rosenbach Foundation in Philadelphia).

The narrative of *Personal Reminiscences* is not strictly chronological. It would have been a simple matter for Stoker to turn his diaries and memories into a sequential account. Instead, by shifting at times from chronological organization to commentaries about individuals he considered important and to anecdotes whose relevance emerges indirectly through juxtaposition, Stoker shapes the memoirs in ways that reveal his own interests and attitudes. Although he does not devote much space to himself, he is by no means invisible in the *Personal Reminiscences*. The book's sometimes fragmented, disjointed character recalls various autobiographical works by Stoker's younger, modernist contemporaries, including Yeats's *Autobiography,* Joyce's *A Portrait of the Artist as a Young Man,* and Virginia Woolf's *Moments of Being.*

Stoker's own enthusiasms, allegiances, and friendships are most visible in the longer chapters devoted to individuals: Walt Whitman (2: 92–112), Hall Caine (2: 115–31), and Ellen Terry (2: 190–208). The strongest and most numerous of Stoker's friendships and personal attachments involved male writers and performers. But he also had long-standing friendships with Ellen Terry and Genevieve Ward, an American actress whom Stoker met first in Dublin and then helped to theatrical success in London. Stoker writes admiringly in the memoirs about Terry, Irving's counterpart in the Lyceum troupe and one of the greatest actresses on the English stage at the end of the nineteenth century. Although she and Stoker were born in the same year, she sometimes called him "mama" and inscribed a photograph of herself for him "*To my 'Ma'* — I am her dutiful child" (*PR* 2: 206–206bis) because he took care of so many things for her. He advised her, for example, about compressing a five-act play into a single act and one scene (*PR* 1: 194). Terry praises Stoker in her autobiography, *The Story of My Life* (1908). Stoker's closest friend was probably the prolific novelist Hall Caine (1853–1931), who like Irving, became a prominent public figure. In 1893 Caine dedicated a volume of long tales to Stoker, *Capt'n Davy's Honeymoon, The Last Confession, The Blind Mother.* The dedication includes a lengthy tribute to his friend in which Caine refers to their friendship as part of "a deep stream that buoys me up." He compares Stoker to the protagonist in one of the stories for his unselfishness and honor. Stoker's dedication of *Dracula* to Caine, whom he refers to by his nickname, Hommy-Beg, returns the favor. Stoker drew on Caine's knowledge of Egyptology for *The Jewel of Seven Stars,* and after Irving's death he acted for a time as Caine's literary agent.

Although he has become known as the author of a horror narrative, Bram Stoker had a well-developed sense of humor, evident at various points in his memoirs, especially in the closing of chapter eleven when he presents his response to a complaint about the lack of realism in one of the Lyceum's productions. The conjunction of humor with the issue of realism bears on *Dracula,* a book containing comic elements and many antirealistic effects. The letter writer had complained that the end of *Henry VIII* was not sufficiently realistic, because the king kisses a china doll and not a real infant during the christening of baby Elizabeth, the future queen. He proposed " 'the hire of our real baby' " (*PR* 1: 116) to remedy the situation. Stoker replied that to achieve the effect of complete reality demanded by the letter writer, the real father would have to play the part of the king, and his wife would need to play the queen, with potentially disagreeable results, since, in reality, the king eventually decapitated her. The murder would leave Irving as the Theatre's proprietor open to criminal charges for being an accessory. In addition, if the play ran for many performances, the parents might have to produce another baby to replace the one that had grown too old. Jonathan Swift could not have written a more amusingly ironic response.

The issue of realism is, however, a serious one aesthetically that Stoker reflects on in his memoirs. Earlier in the same chapter he mentions that he learned from the production of *Henry VIII* various lessons about creating effects on an audience without resorting to the real. When one of the actors wore real diamonds instead of stage jewelry, the illusion of jewelry was undermined because the real diamonds were not sufficiently brilliant. When fabrics were being compared without regard to cost for costumes that would look on stage like cloth of gold, the hugely expensive real cloth of gold was discarded in favor of inexpensive cloth stenciled in the Theatre's property room. In effect, Stoker learned from this and other plays he worked on that realism is an artistic convention, not to be confused with the real. Elsewhere in the memoirs, Stoker evokes vividly the uncanny swerve from realism and the unpredictable, proliferating possibilities for humor that can arise in dramas that require one actor to play more than one character. He mentions in this regard Irving's roles in Charles Reade's *The Lyons Mail* (*PR* 1: 134–35) but devotes considerably more attention to *The Corsican Brothers* by the Irish playwright Dion Boucicault (1820–1890), one of the most influential dramatists of the nineteenth century.

Stoker points out that such plays require the actor to have a double, since they regularly include scenes in which both characters played by the actor have to appear together. Because Boucicault's play includes a scene "where one of the two" brothers "*sees the other seeing his brother*" (*PR* 1: 170), more than one double for Irving was required. He explains that Irving's primary double, who was considerably smaller than Irving, appeared to believe that he really was in some sense Henry Irving. As a consequence, the company regularly invented jokes around the situation, including having Irving's small children address the double as "Papa." Stoker describes with delight the hilarity of a burlesque at the Gaiety Theatre focusing on Irving's well-known performances. The send-up involved centrally the size difference, since "about twenty doubles of all sizes and conditions — giants, dwarfs, skinny, fat —" performed the scene requiring multiple doubling and then took a curtain call all together. Stoker's openness to exaggerated effects, his humorous streak, and his interest in doubling find their conjoined place in the excessive aspects of *Dracula,* which, like many other Gothic narratives, regularly veers from realism, becomes at times self-parodic or nearly so, and includes pairings in which various characters and groups of characters are virtually doubles for each other. The exaggerations, which derive in part from the theatrical traditions that Stoker knew well, contribute to an unusual literary style, especially in *Dracula,* that is compatible with modernist writings by later authors and with important Gothic narratives by Stoker's precursors.

Personal Reminiscences also throws light on the political differences between Irving and Stoker concerning Home Rule for Ireland. Home Rule was an important, widely discussed political issue during the whole of Stoker's adult life, which spanned the period from the initial support for the idea by the Irish politician, Isaac Butt (1813–1879), to the more aggressive advocacy by Charles Stewart Parnell (1846–1891), the Irish nationalist politician who convinced William Gladstone (1809–1898), the British prime minister, to support Home Rule, through Gladstone's defeated Home Rule bills of 1886 and 1893 and the continuing debate that followed their defeat. Had Home Rule been put into effect, it would have created an Irish parliament to handle domestic matters but would have maintained British sovereignty concerning foreign affairs, the military, currency, and major taxation. By referring to himself as a "philosophical" supporter of Home Rule (*PR* 2: 31), Stoker indicated that he supported Irish autonomy but not the revolutionary goals of the Fenians, who advocated the creation, by violence if necessary, of an Irish republic independent of England.

Stoker's enthusiastic comments about Henry Irving's accomplishments as "a part of the nation's glory" (*PR* 1: 124) give the impression that he supported and admired not just Irving but England and the British Empire. His admiration for Irving and England was not, however, blind. Because he was Irish, the "nation" for Stoker was not England narrowly considered but English-speaking peoples, including the Irish, Americans, English-speaking Canadians, and others. Stoker's irony about the permanence and rightness of the British Empire, which emerges at times in *Personal Reminiscences,* reflects his recognition of significant historical shifts in the position of colonial peoples at the end of the nineteenth century. Not surprisingly, as an Irish writer in London during a period of transition for England and her colonies, Stoker stood in ambivalent, ambiguous relation to the empire to whose capital he had moved.[2] Like Wilde, George Bernard Shaw, and Yeats, whose time in London overlapped with his own, Stoker would have been sensitive to his difference from the English, about which he was frequently reminded. However assimilated to English society even a Protestant from Ireland became in the latter part of the nineteenth century, the effects of differential treatment, prejudicial attitudes, and contrasting accents would have been impossible to ignore. Because of English anti-Catholicism, an Irish Catholic might well have felt the effects to a greater degree, but not in a radically different way. Like all the other Protestant Irish, Stoker occupied a position that was in-between. Like many Irish Catholics, his family, with roots in the west, were not wealthy landholders with close ties to England. He would have been treated as Irish by the English, while some, perhaps many, Irish would have thought him a "West Briton," or English sympathizer. Stoker's admiring rhetoric concerning Irving as a figure whose glory was the nation's and his in-between situation give rise together to questions about Stoker's political allegiances in matters concerning Irish autonomy and the freedom of other groups under British rule.

Stoker's irony about empire becomes clear when he juxtaposes two events late in the memoirs. Near the end of chapter thirty-six, he describes in vivid detail the energy and work that went into an officially sanctioned and publicized reception hosted by Irving at the Lyceum Theatre as part of the celebration surrounding the coronation of Edward VII in 1902. Stoker presents the glory of the occasion as a crowning moment for the actor and the empire. The coronation reception followed on Irving's earlier receptions for visiting troops and dignitaries during the Queen's Jubilee (1887) and the Diamond Jubilee a decade later. But, as Stoker comments, by the time of the Diamond Jubilee "much more attention was paid to the Colonial and Indian guests than had ever been done before": "The Nation had waked to the importance of the 'Dependencies'. . . ." (334). The use of quotation marks around "Dependencies" is telling, especially considering the chapter's closing and the next chapter's sharp shift in focus. Stoker describes the Theatre's extravagant imperial decorations and the attention paid to so many colonial dignitaries from various cultures as

---

[2]Joseph Valente discusses the complexity of Stoker's position as an Irish Protestant in " 'Double Born': Bram Stoker and the Metrocolonial Gothic" and at greater length in his forthcoming book, *Dracula's Crypt: Bram Stoker, Irishness, and the Question of Blood.*

manifesting "the spirit mastering the heartbeat of that great Empire on which the sun never sets" (342). He adds immediately, however, that the reception was the "swan-song of the old Lyceum": "Two weeks later the old Lyceum as a dramatic theatre closed its doors — for ever." The institution representing the supposedly undying sun of Empire went under; its heartbeat stopped.

The brief chapter thirty-seven, "The Voice of England," punctures the imperial bubble a second time. Stoker shifts to a holiday he and Irving took together in 1880, during the "early days of the Home Rule movement," commenting that "as I was a believer in it Irving was always chaffing me about it" (343). During one of their disagreements about Home Rule, Irving turned to a policemen who was walking by and, calling him "the Voice of England," asked for his opinion. The policeman's response was "stern and full of pent-up feeling," in a "brogue" that, like a piece of Irish turf, "might have been cut with a hatchet." The "Voice of England" that Irving had triggered belonged to an Irishman who talked like "an out and out Fenian" (344). Stoker was no Fenian, but his commitment to Home Rule in 1880 was as strong as his related recognition in 1902 that the sun was going down on the British Empire.

Among the other five books that Stoker published after Irving's death, *Famous Impostors,* a work of historical research and speculation rather than fiction, holds a special place as the most surprising of Stoker's writings besides *Dracula.* In it, people turn out to be other than they seem, and challenges are posed to existing hierarchies, determinate knowledge about history, and conventional wisdom. The book suggests that the boundary between truth and illusion is porous. Stoker explores the history of various impostors, including pretenders to thrones and legacies, witches, persecutors of witches, and women who lived as men. Acting, or pretense, is essential to the book's subject. The narratives about witch-hunting are especially illuminating concerning the vampire hunters in *Dracula,* since Stoker says flatly that the "one thing more evil than oppression in the shape of wrong-doing" "is oppression in the guise of good" (190). The witch-hunters in *Famous Impostors* are self-serving, savage, and destructive. In the long, speculative closing chapter, Stoker suggests that Queen Elizabeth was actually a male, the Bisley Boy, who had been substituted for her when she died as a child. However surprising the speculation may seem, following as it does on the book's previous chapters about the successes and failures of pretense, it raises questions about our certainty concerning what we think we know of history. If various women without substantial resources who lived as men were able to succeed in the manner that Stoker describes, it is possible that the British Queen, whose life is in many ways strange and opaque to us, was an impostor of some kind.

Stoker implicitly questions the history and the legitimacy of the English monarchy, a crucial element in British national identity. Read with the final chapter in mind, the book's opening chapter, which begins vividly with images of blood, carries related implications. The story of Perkin Warbeck's unsuccessful challenge of Henry VII for his throne is for Stoker also the tale of Henry's predecessor, Richard III, who, in Stoker's words "waded" to the throne of England "through blood" (3). In so doing, he "left behind him a legacy of evil consequences" for later rulers. Blood and fraud taint the history of the English monarchy. Other Irish writers of Stoker's time, including Wilde and Joyce, posed challenges to the conventional wisdom about Shakespeare as an icon of British values concerning nationhood and identity. Those challenges included insinuations about Shakespeare's masculinity. Their older contemporary, Bram Stoker, practiced Irish iconoclasm by taking on the British monarchy instead. When we honor Elizabeth, we do not know who the Queen "may have been," he concludes, not even whether she was "boy or girl" (345). Like later modernist writers, Stoker implies that duplicity and ambiguities about gender stand behind the way things came to be as they are. The empire and its history rest not on bedrock but on shifting ground, like the bog in *The Snake's Pass*.

At the time of his death, Bram Stoker was known for having worked in the shadow of Henry Irving. After his death, Stoker became the almost invisible author of a single well-known book, whose importance and influence have continued to grow. His achievements deserve neither shadow nor invisibility. *Dracula,* the most memorable of Stoker's varied and numerous publications, has left an indelible mark on literature, film, and popular culture. With the assistance of Stoker and others, Henry Irving became for a time the preeminent actor on the English stage, one of the important voices of England. But Bram Stoker's writing, with its Irish inflections, projects its own distinctive voice that has attracted an international audience, for whom it continues to speak.

Chronological List of Bram Stoker's Main Works (1879–1914)

The Duties of Clerks of Petty Sessions in Ireland. 1879.
Under the Sunset. 1882.
The Snake's Pass. 1890.
The Watter's Mou. 1894.
The Shoulder of Shasta. 1895.
Dracula. 1897.
Miss Betty. 1898.
The Mystery of the Sea. 1902.
The Jewel of Seven Stars. 1903.
The Man. 1905.
Personal Reminiscences of Henry Irving. 2 vols. 1906.
Snowbound: The Record of a Theatrical Touring Party. 1908
Lady Athlyne. 1908.
The Lady of the Shroud. 1909.
Famous Impostors. 1910.
The Lair of the White Worm. 1911.
Dracula's Guest and Other Weird Stories. 1914. (Collected and published by Florence Stoker after her husband's death.)

Biographies

Belford, Barbara. *Bram Stoker.* New York: Knopf, 1996.
Farson, Daniel. *The Man Who Wrote Dracula: A Biography of Bram Stoker.* New York: St. Martin's, 1976.
Ludlam, Harry. *A Biography of Dracula: The Life Story of Bram Stoker.* London: Foulsham, 1962.

Other Works Cited and Sources

Beckett, Samuel. *Proust and Three Dialogues with Georges Duthuit.* 1965. London: John Calder, 1987.
Caine, Hall. *Capt'n Davy's Honeymoon, The Last Confession, The Blind Mother.* London: William Heinemann, 1893.
Connolly, S. J., ed. *The Oxford Companion to Irish History.* Oxford: Oxford UP, 1998.
Haining, Peter, and Peter Tremayne. *The Undead: The Legend of Bram Stoker and Dracula.* London: Constable, 1997.
Heaney, Seamus. "Bogland." *Door into Darkness.* 1969. London: Faber, 1990. 56.

Osborough, W. N. "The Dublin Castle Career (1866–78) of Bram Stoker." *Gothic Studies* 1.2 (December 1999): 222–40.

Stoker, George. *With "the Unspeakables"; or, Two Years' Campaigning in European and Asiatic Turkey.* London: Chapman and Hall, 1878.

Terry, Ellen. *The Story of My Life.* 1908. New York: Schocken, 1982.

Valente, Joseph. " 'Double Born': Bram Stoker and the Metrocolonial Gothic." *Modern Fiction Studies* 46.3 (Fall 2000): 632–45.

Productions of the Lyceum Theatre (1878–1904)

[Titles and categories from "The Lyceum Productions," chapter seven of *Personal Reminiscences* (1: 70–71).]

By Shakespeare (in the order of production): *Hamlet, The Merchant of Venice, Othello, Romeo and Juliet, Much Ado About Nothing, Twelfth Night, Macbeth, Henry VIII, King Lear, Cymbeline, Richard III, Coriolanus.*

Repeated from the theatre's repertory before 1878: *Eugene Aram, Richelieu, Louis XI, The Lyons Mail, Charles I, The Bells.*

Older plays not previously in the theatre's repertory: *The Lady of Lyon, The Iron Chest, The Corsican Brothers, The Belle's Stratagem, Two Roses, Olivia, The Dead Heart, Robert Macaire,* and various "curtain-raisers."

New plays: *Faust, Werner, Ravenswood, Iolanthe* (one act), *The Cup, The Amber Heart, Beckett, King Arthur, Madame Sans-Gêne, Peter the Great, The Medicine Man, Robespierre, Dante;* one-act plays: *Waterloo, Nance Oldfield, Don Quixote.*

Dracula

BY

BRAM STOKER

To

My Dear Friend

HOMMY-BEG°

HOMMY-BEG: Nickname, meaning "Little Tommy," given by his Manx grandmother to the novelist (Sir Thomas Henry) Hall Caine (1853–1931), who had dedicated one of his books to Stoker.

CONTENTS

How these papers have been placed in sequence will be made manifest in the reading of them. All needless matters have been eliminated, so that a history almost at variance with the possibilities of later-day belief may stand forth as simple fact. There is throughout no statement of past things wherein memory may err, for all the records chosen are exactly contemporary, given from the standpoints and within the range of knowledge of those who made them.

CHAPTER I. JONATHAN HARKER'S JOURNAL

(Kept in shorthand °)

3 *May. Bistritz.*° — Left Munich at 8.35 p.m. on 1st May, arriving at Vienna early next morning; should have arrived at 6.46, but train was an hour late. Buda-Pesth seems a wonderful place, from the glimpse which I got of it from the train and the little I could walk through the

---

shorthand: Stenography, a method of writing speedily by substituting symbols for letters, words, or phrases that dates back to classical Greece and Rome. Modern systems of shorthand were introduced by Sir Isaac Pitman in 1837 and by John Robert Greg in 1888 (*OED* OL; *Enc. Brit.* OL). See About the Text, pp. xi–xii, for a list of works consulted in preparing this volume.   **Bistritz:** A town in northern Transylvania.

streets. I feared to go very far from the station, as we had arrived late and would start as near the correct time as possible. The impression I had was that we were leaving the West and entering the East; the most Western of splendid bridges over the Danube, which is here of noble width and depth, took us among the traditions of Turkish rule.

We left in pretty good time, and came after nightfall to Klausenburgh. Here I stopped for the night at the Hotel Royale. I had for dinner, or rather supper, a chicken done up some way with red pepper, which was very good but thirsty. (*Mem.*, get recipe for Mina.) I asked the waiter, and he said it was called "paprika hendl," and that, as it was a national dish, I should be able to get it anywhere along the Carpathians.° I found my smattering of German very useful here; indeed, I don't know how I should be able to get on without it.

Having some time at my disposal when in London, I had visited the British Museum, and made search among the books and maps in the library° regarding Transylvania°; it had struck me that some foreknowledge of the country could hardly fail to have some importance in dealing with a noble of that country. I find that the district he named is in the extreme east of the country, just on the borders of three states, Transylvania, Moldavia, and Bukovina, in the midst of the Carpathian mountains; one of the wildest and least known portions of Europe. I was not able to light on any map or work giving the exact locality of the Castle Dracula, as there are no maps of this country as yet to compare with our own Ordnance Survey maps°; but I found that Bistritz, the post town° named by Count Dracula, is a fairly well-known place. I

Carpathians: A major mountain system of Central Europe that links the Alps with the Balkan Mountains.   *British Museum . . . library:* In Stoker's time, the national museum of Britain held important archaeological artifacts and housed a library with a large collection of ancient manuscripts and of books, especially those published in Great Britain. In 1896 it contained an estimated 1,800,000 volumes. The library's reading room, a circular hall with seats for three hundred readers under a dome of glass and iron, was opened in 1857 (*Enc. Brit.* OL; *Baedeker* 1896).   *Transylvania:* A region in eastern Europe, now part of Romania but at the time *Dracula* was written a part of Hungary. Its name means "beyond the forest." The region has had a turbulent history. It formed the nucleus of the Dacian kingdom until incorporated by Rome in 106. After the withdrawal of Roman legions in 207, the region was overrun by barbarian tribes. In 1003 it was incorporated into Hungary, but after 1526 it became an autonomous province controlled by the Turks. By 1699 the influence of the Turks had waned, and over the next century and a half Transylvania became variously a part of Hungarian and Austrian crown lands, and an autonomous province under Austrian control. It was reabsorbed by Hungary in 1867 (*Enc. Brit.* OL; *Enc. Brit.* 11th).   *Ordnance Survey maps:* Maps of the United Kingdom made for taxation purposes by military engineers.   *post town:* A town in which horses are stationed for carrying the mail (*OED*).

shall enter here some of my notes, as they may refresh my memory when I talk over my travels with Mina.

In the population of Transylvania there are four distinct nationalities: Saxons in the south, and mixed with them the Wallachs, who are the descendants of the Dacians; Magyars in the west, and Szekelys in the east and north. I am going among the latter, who claim to be descended from Attila and the Huns.° This may be so, for when the Magyars conquered the country in the eleventh century they found the Huns settled in it. I read that every known superstition in the world is gathered into the horseshoe of the Carpathians, as if it were the centre of some sort of imaginative whirlpool; if so my stay may be very interesting. (*Mem.*, I must ask the Count all about them.)

I did not sleep well, though my bed was comfortable enough, for I had all sorts of queer dreams. There was a dog howling all night under my window, which may have had something to do with it; or it may have been the paprika, for I had to drink up all the water in my carafe, and was still thirsty. Towards morning I slept and was wakened by the continuous knocking at my door, so I guess I must have been sleeping soundly then. I had for breakfast more paprika, and a sort of porridge of maize flour which they said was "mamaliga," and egg-plant stuffed with forcemeat,° a very excellent dish; which they call "impletata." (*Mem.*, get recipe for this also.) I had to hurry breakfast, for the train started a little before eight, or rather it ought to have done so, for after rushing to the station at 7.30 I had to sit in the carriage for more than an hour before we began to move. It seems to me that the further East you go the more unpunctual are the trains. What ought they to be in China?

All day long we seemed to dawdle through a country which was full of beauty of every kind. Sometimes we saw little towns or castles on the top of steep hills such as we see in old missals; sometimes we ran by rivers and streams which seemed from the wide stony margin on each side of them to be subject to great floods. It takes a lot of water, and running strong, to sweep the outside edge of a river clear. At every station there were groups of people, sometimes crowds, and in all sorts of attire. Some of them were just like the peasants at home or those I saw

---

Attila and the Huns: The Huns, a tribe of nomadic warriors famous for their prowess in battle, first invaded Europe in 370. After defeating other barbarian tribes, they launched campaigns against the Eastern and Western Roman Empires. From 434–453 they were led by Attila, who was nicknamed the "Scourge of God" because of his ferocity (*Enc. Brit.* OL).   **forcemeat:** Meat that is "chopped fine, spiced, and highly seasoned," generally used for stuffing or as a garnish (*OED*).

coming through France and Germany, with short jackets and round hats and homemade trousers; but others were very picturesque. The women looked pretty, except when you got near them, but they were very clumsy about the waist. They had all full white sleeves of some kind or other, and most of them had big belts with a lot of strips of something fluttering from them like the dresses in a ballet, but of course petticoats under them. The strangest figures we saw were the Slovaks, who are more barbarian than the rest, with their big cowboy hats, great baggy dirty-white trousers, white linen shirts, and enormous heavy leather belts, nearly a foot wide, all studded over with brass nails. They wore high boots, with their trousers tucked into them, and had long black hair and heavy black moustaches. They are very picturesque, but do not look prepossessing. On the stage they would be set down at once as some old Oriental band of brigands. They are, however, I am told, very harmless and rather wanting in natural self-assertion.

It was on the dark side of twilight when we got to Bistritz, which is a very interesting old place. Being practically on the frontier — for the Borgo Pass leads from it into Bukovina — it has had a very stormy existence, and it certainly shows marks of it. Fifty years ago a series of great fires took place, which made terrible havoc on five separate occasions. At the very beginning of the seventeenth century it underwent a siege of three weeks and lost 13,000 people, the casualties of war proper being assisted by famine and disease.

Count Dracula had directed me to go to the Golden Krone Hotel, which I found, to my great delight, to be thoroughly old-fashioned, for of course I wanted to see all I could of the ways of the country. I was evidently expected, for when I got near the door I faced a cheery-looking elderly woman in the usual peasant dress — white undergarment with long double apron, front, and back, of coloured stuff fitting almost too tight for modesty. When I came close she bowed, and said, "The Herr Englishman?" "Yes," I said, "Jonathan Harker." She smiled, and gave some message to an elderly man in white shirt-sleeves, who had followed her to the door. He went, but immediately returned with a letter: —

"My Friend, — Welcome to the Carpathians. I am anxiously expecting you. Sleep well to-night. At three to-morrow the diligence° will start for Bukovina; a place on it is kept for you. At the Borgo Pass my

diligence: A public stagecoach (*OED* OL).

carriage will await you and will bring you to me. I trust that your journey from London has been a happy one, and that you will enjoy your
stay in my beautiful land.

"Your friend,
"DRACULA."

4 *May.* — I found that my landlord had got a letter from the
Count, directing him to secure the best place on the coach for me; but
on making inquiries as to details he seemed somewhat reticent, and pretended that he could not understand my German. This could not be
true, because up to then he had understood it perfectly; at least, he
answered my questions exactly as if he did. He and his wife, the old lady
who had received me, looked at each other in a frightened sort of way.
He mumbled out that the money had been sent in a letter, and that was
all he knew. When I asked him if he knew Count Dracula, and could tell
me anything of his castle, both he and his wife crossed themselves, and,
saying that they knew nothing at all, simply refused to speak further. It
was so near the time of starting that I had no time to ask any one else,
for it was all very mysterious and not by any means comforting.

Just before I was leaving, the old lady came up to my room and said
in a very hysterical way:

"Must you go? Oh! young Herr, must you go?" She was in such an
excited state that she seemed to have lost her grip of what German she
knew, and mixed it all up with some other language which I did not
know at all. I was just able to follow her by asking many questions.
When I told her that I must go at once, and that I was engaged on
important business, she asked again:

"Do you know what day it is?" I answered that it was the fourth of
May. She shook her head as she said again:

"Oh, yes! I know that, I know that! but do you know what day it
is?" On my saying that I did not understand, she went on:

"It is the eve of St. George's Day.° Do you not know that to-night,
when the clock strikes midnight, all the evil things in the world will
have full sway? Do you know where you are going, and what you are
going to?" She was in such evident distress that I tried to comfort her,
but without effect. Finally she went down on her knees and implored

---

eve of St. George's Day: The evening before May 5 by the Eastern calendar and before
April 23, by the Western calendar, which was changed by Pope Gregory XIII in 1582. In
Romanian superstition, the eve of St. George's day is linked to occult practices. Stoker's
British readers would have known that St. George, the chivalrous dragon slayer, was the
patron saint of England (*Enc. Brit.* 11th; Gerard).

me not to go; at least to wait a day or two before starting. It was all very ridiculous, but I did not feel comfortable. However, there was business to be done, and I could allow nothing to interfere with it. I therefore tried to raise her up, and said, as gravely as I could, that I thanked her, but my duty was imperative, and that I must go. She then rose and dried her eyes, and taking a crucifix from her neck offered it to me. I did not know what to do, for, as an English Churchman,° I have been taught to regard such things as in some measure idolatrous, and yet it seemed so ungracious to refuse an old lady meaning so well and in such a state of mind. She saw, I suppose, the doubt in my face, for she put the rosary round my neck, and said, "For your mother's sake," and went out of the room. I am writing up this part of the diary whilst I am waiting for the coach, which is, of course, late; and the crucifix is still round my neck. Whether it is the old lady's fear, or the many ghostly traditions of this place, or the crucifix itself, I do not know, but I am not feeling nearly as easy in my mind as usual. If this book should ever reach Mina before I do, let it bring my good-bye. Here comes the coach!

5 *May. The Castle.* — The grey of the morning has passed, and the sun is high over the distant horizon, which seems jagged, whether with trees or hills I know not, for it is so far off that big things and little are mixed. I am not sleepy, and, as I am not to be called till I awake, naturally I write till sleep comes. There are many odd things to put down, and, lest who reads them may fancy that I dined too well before I left Bistritz, let me put down my dinner exactly. I dined on what they call "robber steak" — bits of bacon, onion, and beef, seasoned with red pepper, and strung on sticks and roasted over the fire, in the simple style of the London cat's-meat°! The wine was Golden Mediasch, which produces a queer sting on the tongue, which is, however, not disagreeable. I had only a couple of glasses of this, and nothing else.

When I got on the coach the driver had not taken his seat, and I saw him talking with the landlady. They were evidently talking of me, for every now and then they looked at me, and some of the people who were sitting on the bench outside the door — which they call by a name meaning "word-bearer" — came and listened, and then looked at me, most of them pityingly. I could hear a lot of words often repeated, queer words, for there were many nationalities in the crowd; so I quietly got my polyglot dictionary° from my bag and looked them out. I must

English Churchman: A Protestant, specifically, a member of the Church of England, which separated from the Roman Catholic Church in the sixteenth century.   *cat's-meat:* Horse flesh prepared by street dealers as food for domestic cats (*OED*).   *polyglot dictionary:* A dictionary containing several languages.

say they were not cheering to me, for amongst them were "Ordog" — Satan, "pokol" — hell, "stregoica" — witch, "vrolok" and "vlkoslak" — both of which mean the same thing, one being Slovak and the other Servian° for something that is either were-wolf or vampire. (*Mem.*, I must ask the Count about these superstitions.)

When we started, the crowd round the inn door, which had by this time swelled to a considerable size, all made the sign of the cross and pointed two fingers towards me. With some difficulty I got a fellow-passenger to tell me what they meant; he would not answer at first, but on learning that I was English he explained that it was a charm or guard against the evil eye. This was not very pleasant for me, just starting for an unknown place to meet an unknown man; but every one seemed so kind-hearted, and so sorrowful, and so sympathetic that I could not but be touched. I shall never forget the last glimpse which I had of the inn-yard, and its crowd of picturesque figures, all crossing themselves, as they stood round the wide archway, with its background of rich foliage of oleander and orange trees in green tubs clustered in the centre of the yard. Then our driver, whose wide linen drawers covered the whole front of the box-seat — "gotza" they call them — cracked his big whip over his four small horses, which ran abreast, and we set off on our journey.

I soon lost sight and recollection of ghostly fears in the beauty of the scene as we drove along, although had I known the language, or rather languages, which my fellow-passengers were speaking, I might not have been able to throw them off so easily. Before us lay a green sloping land full of forests and woods, with here and there steep hills, crowned with clumps of trees or with farmhouses, the blank gable end to the road. There was everywhere a bewildering mass of fruit blossom — apple, plum, pear, cherry; and as we drove by I could see the green grass under the trees spangled with the fallen petals. In and out amongst these green hills of what they call here the "Mittel Land"° ran the road, losing itself as it swept round the grassy curve, or was shut out by the straggling ends of pine woods, which here and there ran down the hillsides like tongues of flame. The road was rugged, but still we seemed to fly over it with a feverish haste. I could not understand then what the haste meant, but the driver was evidently bent on losing no time in reaching Borgo Prund. I was told that this road is in summer-time excellent, but that it had not yet been put in order after the winter

Servian: Serbian.   *Mittel Land:* Middle land (German).

snows. In this respect it is different from the general run of roads in the Carpathians, for it is an old tradition that they are not to be kept in too good order. Of old the Hospadars° would not repair them, lest the Turk should think that they were preparing to bring in foreign troops, and so hasten the war which was always really at loading point.

Beyond the green swelling hills of the Mittel Land rose mighty slopes of forest up to the lofty steeps of the Carpathians themselves. Right and left of us they towered, with the afternoon sun falling full upon them and bringing out all the glorious colours of this beautiful range, deep blue and purple in the shadows of the peaks, green and brown where grass and rock mingled, and an endless perspective of jagged rock and pointed crags, till these were themselves lost in the distance, where the snowy peaks rose grandly. Here and there seemed mighty rifts in the mountains, through which, as the sun began to sink, we saw now and again the white gleam of falling water. One of my companions touched my arm as we swept round the base of a hill and opened up the lofty, snow-covered peak of a mountain, which seemed, as we wound on our serpentine way, to be right before us: —

"Look! Isten szek!" — "God's seat!" — and he crossed himself reverently. As we wound on our endless way, and the sun sank lower and lower behind us, the shadows of the evening began to creep round us. This was emphasized by the fact that the snowy mountain-top still held the sunset, and seemed to glow out with a delicate cool pink. Here and there we passed Cszeks and Slovaks, all in picturesque attire, but I noticed that goitre was painfully prevalent. By the roadside were many crosses, and as we swept by, my companions all crossed themselves. Here and there was a peasant man or woman kneeling before a shrine, who did not even turn round as we approached, but seemed in the self-surrender of devotion to have neither eyes nor ears for the outer world. There were many things new to me: for instance, hay-ricks in the trees, and here and there very beautiful masses of weeping birch, their white stems shining like silver through the delicate green of the leaves. Now and again we passed a leiter-wagon — the ordinary peasant's cart, with its long, snake-like vertebra, calculated to suit the inequalities of the road. On this were sure to be seated quite a group of home-coming peasants, the Cszeks with their white, and the Slovaks with their coloured, sheepskins, the latter carrying lance-fashion their long staves,

Hospadars: Rulers of Wallachia and Moldavia from the fifteenth century until 1866 (Wolf 12n44).

with axe at end. As the evening fell it began to get very cold, and the growing twilight seemed to merge into one dark mistiness the gloom of the trees, oak, beech, and pine, though in the valleys which ran deep between the spurs of the hills, as we ascended through the Pass, the dark firs stood out here and there against the background of late-lying snow. Sometimes, as the road was cut through the pine woods that seemed in the darkness to be closing down upon us, great masses of greyness, which here and there bestrewed the trees, produced a peculiarly weird and solemn effect, which carried on the thoughts and grim fancies engendered earlier in the evening, when the falling sunset threw into strange relief the ghost-like clouds which amongst the Carpathians seem to wind ceaselessly through the valleys. Sometimes the hills were so steep that, despite our driver's haste, the horses could only go slowly. I wished to get down and walk up them, as we do at home, but the driver would not hear of it. "No, no," he said; "you must not walk here; the dogs are too fierce;" and then he added, with what he evidently meant for grim pleasantry — for he looked round to catch the approving smile of the rest — "and you may have enough of such matters before you go to sleep." The only stop he would make was a moment's pause to light his lamps.

When it grew dark there seemed to be some excitement amongst the passengers, and they kept speaking to him, one after the other, as though urging him to further speed. He lashed the horses unmercifully with his long whip, and with wild cries of encouragement urged them on to further exertions. Then through the darkness I could see a sort of patch of grey light ahead of us, as though there were a cleft in the hills. The excitement of the passengers grew greater: the crazy coach rocked on its great leather springs, and swayed like a boat tossed on a stormy sea. I had to hold on. The road grew more level, and we appeared to fly along. Then the mountains seemed to come nearer to us on each side and to frown down upon us; we were entering on the Borgo Pass. One by one several of the passengers offered me gifts, which they pressed upon me with an earnestness which would take no denial; these were certainly of an odd and varied kind, but each was given in simple good faith, with a kindly word, and a blessing, and that strange mixture of fear-meaning movements which I had seen outside the hotel at Bistritz — the sign of the cross and the guard against the evil eye. Then, as we flew along, the driver leaned forward, and on each side the passengers, craning over the edge of the coach, peered eagerly into the darkness. It was evident that something very exciting was either happening or expected, but though I asked each passenger, no one would give me the slightest explanation. This state of excitement kept on for some little time; and at last we saw before us the Pass opening out on the eastern side. There were dark, rolling clouds overhead, and in the air the heavy, oppressive sense of thunder. It seemed as though the mountain range had separated two atmospheres, and that now we had got into the thunderous one. I was now myself looking out for the conveyance which was to take me to the Count. Each moment I expected to see the glare of lamps through the blackness; but all was dark. The only light was the flickering rays of our own lamps, in which the steam from our hard-driven horses rose in a white cloud. We could now see the sandy road lying white before us, but there was on it no sign of a vehicle. The passengers drew back with a sigh of gladness, which seemed to mock my own disappointment. I was already thinking what I had best do, when the driver, looking at his watch, said to the others something which I could hardly hear, it was spoken so quietly and in so low a tone; I thought it was "An hour less than the time." Then turning to me, he said in German worse than my own: —

"There is no carriage here. The Herr is not expected after all. He will now come on to Bukovina, and return to-morrow or the next day; better the next day." Whilst he was speaking the horses began to neigh and snort and plunge wildly, so that the driver had to hold them up. Then, amongst a chorus of screams from the peasants and a universal crossing of themselves, a calèche,° with four horses, drove up behind us, overtook us, and drew up beside the coach. I could see from the flash of our lamps, as the rays fell on them, that the horses were coal-black and splendid animals. They were driven by a tall man, with a long brown beard and a great black hat, which seemed to hide his face from us. I could only see the gleam of a pair of very bright eyes, which seemed red in the lamplight, as he turned to us. He said to the driver: —

"You are early to-night, my friend." The man stammered in reply: —

"The English Herr was in a hurry," to which the stranger replied: —

"That is why, I suppose, you wished him to go on to Bukovina. You cannot deceive me, my friend; I know too much, and my horses are swift." As he spoke he smiled, and the lamplight fell on a hard-looking

---

calèche: "A kind of light carriage with low wheels, having a removable folding hood or top" (*OED* OL).

mouth, with very red lips and sharp-looking teeth, as white as ivory. One of my companions whispered to another the line from Burger's "Lenore:"° —

> "Denn die Todten reiten schnell" —
> ("For the dead travel fast.")

The strange driver evidently heard the words, for he looked up with a gleaming smile. The passenger turned his face away, at the same time putting out his two fingers and crossing himself. "Give me the Herr's luggage," said the driver; and with exceeding alacrity my bags were handed out and put in the calèche. Then I descended from the side of the coach, as the calèche was close alongside, the driver helping me with a hand which caught my arm in a grip of steel; his strength must have been prodigious. Without a word he shook his reins, the horses turned, and we swept into the darkness of the Pass. As I looked back I saw the steam from the horses of the coach by the light of the lamps, and projected against it the figures of my late companions crossing themselves. Then the driver cracked his whip and called to his horses, and off they swept on their way to Bukovina.

As they sank into the darkness I felt a strange chill, and a lonely feeling came over me; but a cloak was thrown over my shoulders, and a rug across my knees, and the driver said in excellent German: —

"The night is chill, mein Herr, and my master the Count bade me take all care of you. There is a flask of slivovitz [the plum brandy of the country] underneath the seat, if you should require it." I did not take any, but it was a comfort to know it was there all the same. I felt a little strangely, and not a little frightened. I think had there been any alternative I should have taken it, instead of prosecuting that unknown night journey. The carriage went at a hard pace straight along, then we made a complete turn and went along another straight road. It seemed to me that we were simply going over and over the same ground again; and so I took note of some salient point, and found that this was so. I would have liked to have asked the driver what this all meant, but I really feared to do so, for I thought that, placed as I was, any protest would

---

Burger's "Lenore": From the ballad "Lenore," by the German writer Gottfried August Bürger (1748–1794), published in 1773 and well known throughout the nineteenth century in Germany and England. In this poem of "the weird and supernatural," Lenore laments her lover William's failure to return from the war. He suddenly appears and asks her to ride off with him to become his bride; however, when they reach their destination she realizes that it is a cemetery and that William is dead. (*Enc. Brit.* 11th 4: 812).

have had no effect in case there had been an intention to delay. By-and-by, however, as I was curious to know how time was passing, I struck a match, and by its flame looked at my watch; it was within a few minutes of midnight. This gave me a sort of shock, for I suppose the general superstition about midnight was increased by my recent experiences. I waited with a sick feeling of suspense.

Then a dog began to howl somewhere in a farmhouse far down the road — a long, agonised wailing, as if from fear. The sound was taken up by another dog, and then another and another, till, borne on the wind which now sighed softly through the Pass, a wild howling began, which seemed to come from all over the country, as far as the imagination could grasp it through the gloom of the night. At the first howl the horses began to strain and rear, but the driver spoke to them soothingly, and they quieted down, but shivered and sweated as though after a run-away from sudden fright. Then, far off in the distance, from the mountains on each side of us began a louder and a sharper howling — that of wolves — which affected both the horses and myself in the same way — for I was minded to jump from the calèche and run, whilst they reared again and plunged madly, so that the driver had to use all his great strength to keep them from bolting. In a few minutes, however, my own ears got accustomed to the sound, and the horses so far became quiet that the driver was able to descend and to stand before them. He petted and soothed them, and whispered something in their ears, as I have heard of horse-tamers doing, and with extraordinary effect, for under his caresses they became quite manageable again, though they still trembled. The driver again took his seat, and shaking his reins, started off at a great pace. This time, after going to the far side of the Pass, he suddenly turned down a narrow roadway which ran sharply to the right.

Soon we were hemmed in with trees, which in places arched right over the roadway till we passed as through a tunnel; and again great frowning rocks guarded us boldly on either side. Though we were in shelter, we could hear the rising wind, for it moaned and whistled through the rocks, and the branches of the trees crashed together as we swept along. It grew colder and colder still, and fine, powdery snow began to fall, so that soon we and all around us were covered with a white blanket. The keen wind still carried the howling of the dogs, though this grew fainter as we went on our way. The baying of the wolves sounded nearer and nearer, as though they were closing round on us from every side. I grew dreadfully afraid, and the horses shared my fear; but the driver was not in the least disturbed. He kept turning his head to left and right, but I could not see anything through the darkness.

Suddenly, away on our left, I saw a faint flickering blue flame. The driver saw it at the same moment; he at once checked the horses and, jumping to the ground, disappeared into the darkness. I did not know what to do, the less as the howling of the wolves grew closer; but while I wondered the driver suddenly appeared again, and without a word took his seat, and we resumed our journey. I think I must have fallen asleep and kept dreaming of the incident, for it seemed to be repeated endlessly, and now looking back, it is like a sort of awful nightmare. Once the flame appeared so near the road, that even in the darkness around us I could watch the driver's motions. He went rapidly to where the blue flame arose — it must have been very faint, for it did not seem to illumine the place around it at all — and gathering a few stones, formed them into some device. Once there appeared a strange optical effect: when he stood between me and the flame he did not obstruct it, for I could see its ghostly flicker all the same. This startled me, but as the effect was only momentary, I took it that my eyes deceived me straining through the darkness. Then for a time there were no blue flames, and we sped onwards through the gloom, with the howling of the wolves around us, as though they were following in a moving circle.

At last there came a time when the driver went further afield than he had yet gone, and during his absence the horses began to tremble worse than ever and to snort and scream with fright. I could not see any cause for it, for the howling of the wolves had ceased altogether; but just then the moon, sailing through the black clouds, appeared behind the jagged crest of a beetling, pine-clad rock, and by its light I saw around us a ring of wolves, with white teeth and lolling red tongues, with long, sinewy limbs and shaggy hair. They were a hundred times more terrible in the grim silence which held them than even when they howled. For myself, I felt a sort of paralysis of fear. It is only when a man feels himself face to face with such horrors that he can understand their true import.

All at once the wolves began to howl as though the moonlight had had some peculiar effect on them. The horses jumped about and reared, and looked helplessly round with eyes that rolled in a way painful to see; but the living ring of terror encompassed them on every side, and they had perforce to remain within it. I called to the coachman to come, for it seemed to me that our only chance was to try to break out through the ring and to aid his approach. I shouted and beat the side of the calèche, hoping by the noise to scare the wolves from that side, so as to give him a chance of reaching the trap.° How he came there, I know not, but I heard his voice raised in a tone of imperious command, and looking towards the sound, saw him stand in the roadway. As he swept his long arms, as though brushing aside some impalpable obstacle, the wolves fell back and back further still. Just then a heavy cloud passed across the face of the moon, so that we were again in darkness.

When I could see again the driver was climbing into the calèche, and the wolves had disappeared. This was all so strange and uncanny that a dreadful fear came upon me, and I was afraid to speak or move. The time seemed interminable as we swept on our way, now in almost complete darkness, for the rolling clouds obscured the moon. We kept on ascending, with occasional periods of quick descent, but in the main always ascending. Suddenly I became conscious of the fact that the driver was in the act of pulling up the horses in the courtyard of a vast ruined castle, from whose tall black windows came no ray of light, and whose broken battlements showed a jagged line against the moonlit sky.

CHAPTER II. JONATHAN HARKER'S JOURNAL

(Continued)

5 *May.* — I must have been asleep, for certainly if I had been fully awake I must have noticed the approach to such a remarkable place. In the gloom the courtyard looked of considerable size, and as several dark ways led from it under great round arches it perhaps seemed bigger than it really is. I have not yet been able to see it by daylight.

When the calèche stopped the driver jumped down, and held out his hand to assist me to alight. Again I could not but notice his prodigious strength. His hand actually seemed like a steel vice that could have crushed mine if he had chosen. Then he took out my traps,° and placed them on the ground beside me as I stood close to a great door, old and studded with large iron nails, and set in a projecting doorway of massive stone. I could see even in the dim light that the stone was massively carved, but that the carving had been much worn by time and

---

trap: "A small carriage on springs," usually with two wheels (*OED* OL).   *traps:* Baggage (*OED*).

weather. As I stood, the driver jumped again into his seat and shook the reins; the horses started forward, and trap and all disappeared down one of the dark openings.

I stood in silence where I was, for I did not know what to do. Of bell or knocker there was no sign; through these frowning walls and dark window openings it was not likely that my voice could penetrate. The time I waited seemed endless, and I felt doubts and fears crowding upon me. What sort of place had I come to, and among what kind of people? What sort of grim adventure was it on which I had embarked? Was this a customary incident in the life of a solicitor's clerk sent out to explain the purchase of a London estate to a foreigner? Solicitor's clerk! Mina would not like that. Solicitor, — for just before leaving London I got word that my examination was successful; and I am now a full-blown solicitor!° I began to rub my eyes and pinch myself to see if I were awake. It all seemed like a horrible nightmare to me, and I expected that I should suddenly awake, and find myself at home, with the dawn struggling in through the windows, as I had now and again felt in the morning after a day of overwork. But my flesh answered the pinching test, and my eyes were not to be deceived. I was indeed awake and among the Carpathians. All I could do now was to be patient, and to wait the coming of the morning.

Just as I had come to this conclusion I heard a heavy step approaching behind the great door, and saw through the chinks the gleam of a coming light. Then there was the sound of rattling chains and the clanking of massive bolts drawn back. A key was turned with the loud grating noise of long disuse, and the great door swung back.

Within, stood a tall old man, clean shaven save for a long white moustache, and clad in black from head to foot, without a single speck of colour about him anywhere. He held in his hand an antique silver lamp, in which the flame burned without chimney or globe of any kind, throwing long quivering shadows as it flickered in the draught of the open door. The old man motioned me in with his right hand with a courtly gesture, saying in excellent English, but with a strange intonation: —

"Welcome to my house! Enter freely and of your own will!" He

---

solicitor's clerk. . . . full-blown solicitor: In Stoker's time, anyone wishing to be a solicitor had to serve a three-to-five-year apprenticeship, pass the necessary examinations, and be formally admitted and entered on a roll of solicitors kept by the Incorporated Law Society. Solicitors were officially permitted to engage in "conveyancing," or the transfer of property, by the Conveyancing Act of 1881 (*Enc. Brit.* 11th).

made no motion of stepping to meet me, but stood like a statue, as though his gesture of welcome had fixed him into stone. The instant, however, that I had stepped over the threshold, he moved impulsively forward, and holding out his hand grasped mine with a strength which made me wince, an effect which was not lessened by the fact that it seemed as cold as ice — more like the hand of a dead than a living man. Again he said: —

"Welcome to my house. Come freely. Go safely; and leave something of the happiness you bring!" The strength of the handshake was so much akin to that which I had noticed in the driver, whose face I had not seen, that for a moment I doubted if it were not the same person to whom I was speaking; so to make sure, I said interrogatively: —

"Count Dracula?" He bowed in a courtly way as he replied: —

"I am Dracula; and I bid you welcome, Mr. Harker, to my house. Come in; the night air is chill, and you must need to eat and rest." As he was speaking he put the lamp on a bracket on the wall, and stepping out, took my luggage; he had carried it in before I could forestall him. I protested but he insisted: —

"Nay, sir, you are my guest. It is late, and my people are not available. Let me see to your comfort myself." He insisted on carrying my traps along the passage, and then up a great winding stair, and along another great passage, on whose stone floor our steps rang heavily. At the end of this he threw open a heavy door, and I rejoiced to see within a well-lit room in which a table was spread for supper, and on whose mighty hearth a great fire of logs flamed and flared.

The Count halted, putting down my bags, closed the door, and crossing the room, opened another door, which led into a small octagonal room lit by a single lamp, and seemingly without a window of any sort. Passing through this, he opened another door, and motioned me to enter. It was a welcome sight; for here was a great bedroom well lighted and warmed with another log fire, which sent a hollow roar up the wide chimney. The Count himself left my luggage inside and withdrew, saying, before he closed the door: —

"You will need, after your journey, to refresh yourself by making your toilet. I trust you will find all you wish. When you are ready come into the other room, where you will find your supper prepared."

The light and warmth and the Count's courteous welcome seemed to have dissipated all my doubts and fears. Having then reached my normal state, I discovered that I was half famished with hunger; so making a hasty toilet, I went into the other room.

I found supper already laid out. My host, who stood on one side of the great fireplace, leaning against the stonework, made a graceful wave of his hand to the table, and said: —

"I pray you, be seated and sup how you please. You will, I trust, excuse me that I do not join you; but I have dined already, and I do not sup."

I handed to him the sealed letter which Mr. Hawkins had entrusted to me. He opened it and read it gravely; then, with a charming smile, he handed it to me to read. One passage of it, at least, gave me a thrill of pleasure:

"I must regret that an attack of gout, from which malady I am a constant sufferer, forbids absolutely any travelling on my part for some time to come; but I am happy to say I can send a sufficient substitute, one in whom I have every possible confidence. He is a young man, full of energy and talent in his own way, and of a very faithful disposition. He is discreet and silent, and has grown into manhood in my service. He shall be ready to attend on you when you will during his stay, and shall take your instructions in all matters."

The Count himself came forward and took off the cover of a dish, and I fell to at once on an excellent roast chicken. This, with some cheese and a salad and a bottle of old Tokay,° of which I had two glasses, was my supper. During the time I was eating it the Count asked me many questions as to my journey, and I told him by degrees all I had experienced.

By this time I had finished my supper, and by my host's desire had drawn up a chair by the fire and begun to smoke a cigar which he offered me, at the same time excusing himself that he did not smoke. I had now an opportunity of observing him, and found him of a very marked physiognomy.

His face was a strong — a very strong — aquiline, with high bridge of the thin nose and peculiarly arched nostrils; with lofty domed forehead, and hair growing scantily round the temples, but profusely elsewhere. His eyebrows were very massive, almost meeting over the nose, and with bushy hair that seemed to curl in its own profusion. The mouth, so far as I could see it under the heavy moustache, was fixed and rather cruel-looking, with peculiarly sharp white teeth; these protruded over the lips, whose remarkable ruddiness showed astonishing vitality in a man of his years. For the rest, his ears were pale and at the tops

---

Tokay: A sweet white wine made in the Tokay district of Hungary, from which it derives its name (*Enc. Brit.* OL).

extremely pointed; the chin was broad and strong, and the cheeks firm though thin. The general effect was one of extraordinary pallor.

Hitherto I had noticed the backs of his hands as they lay on his knees in the firelight, and they had seemed rather white and fine; but seeing them now close to me, I could not but notice that they were rather coarse — broad, with squat fingers. Strange to say, there were hairs in the centre of the palm. The nails were long and fine, and cut to a sharp point. As the Count leaned over me and his hands touched me, I could not repress a shudder. It may have been that his breath was rank, but a horrible feeling of nausea came over me, which, do what I would, I could not conceal. The Count, evidently noticing it, drew back; and with a grim sort of smile, which showed more than he had yet done his protuberant teeth, sat himself down again on his own side of the fireplace. We were both silent for a while; and as I looked towards the window I saw the first dim streak of the coming dawn. There seemed a strange stillness over everything; but as I listened I heard as if from down below in the valley the howling of many wolves. The Count's eyes gleamed, and he said: —

"Listen to them — the children of the night. What music they make!" Seeing, I suppose, some expression in my face strange to him, he added: —

"Ah, sir, you dwellers in the city cannot enter into the feelings of the hunter." Then he rose and said: —

"But you must be tired. Your bedroom is all ready, and to-morrow you shall sleep as late as you will. I have to be away till the afternoon; so sleep well and dream well!" and, with a courteous bow, he opened for me himself the door to the octagonal room, and I entered my bed-room. . . . .

I am all in a sea of wonders. I doubt; I fear; I think strange things which I dare not confess to my own soul. God keep me, if only for the sake of those dear to me!

7 *May*. — It is again early morning, but I have rested and enjoyed the last twenty-four hours. I slept till late in the day, and awoke of my own accord. When I had dressed myself I went into the room where we had supped, and found a cold breakfast laid out, with coffee kept hot by the pot being placed on the hearth. There was a card on the table, on which was written: —

"I have to be absent for a while. Do not wait for me. — D." So I set to and enjoyed a hearty meal. When I had done, I looked for a bell, so that I might let the servants know I had finished; but I could not find one. There are certainly odd deficiencies in the house, considering the extraordinary evidences of wealth which are round me. The table service is of gold, and so beautifully wrought that it must be of immense value. The curtains and upholstery of the chairs and sofas and the hangings of my bed are of the costliest and most beautiful fabrics, and must have been of fabulous value when they were made, for they are centuries old, though in excellent order. I saw something like them in Hampton Court,° but there they were worn and frayed and moth-eaten. But still in none of the rooms is there a mirror. There is not even a toilet glass on my table, and I had to get the little shaving glass from my bag before I could either shave or brush my hair. I have not yet seen a servant anywhere, or heard a sound near the castle except the howling of wolves. When I had finished my meal — I do not know whether to call it breakfast or dinner, for it was between five and six o'clock when I had it — I looked about for something to read, for I did not like to go about the castle until I had asked the Count's permission. There was absolutely nothing in the room, book, newspaper, or even writing materials; so I opened another door in the room and found a sort of library. The door opposite mine I tried, but found it locked.

In the library I found, to my great delight, a vast number of English books, whole shelves full of them, and bound volumes of magazines and newspapers. A table in the centre was littered with English magazines and newspapers, though none of them were of very recent date. The books were of the most varied kind — history, geography, politics, political economy, botany, geology, law — all relating to England and English life and customs and manners. There were even such books of reference as the London Directory,° the "Red" and "Blue" books,° Whitaker's Almanack,° the Army and Navy Lists,° and — it somehow gladdened my heart to see it — the Law List.°

Hampton Court: In Stoker's time, this palace was already a popular tourist attraction. Located on the north bank of the Thames, it had been inhabited by British royalty from the time of Henry VIII (1526) until the time of George II, who reigned until 1760 (*Enc. Brit.* OL; *Enc. Brit.* 11th).   *London Directory:* A directory that listed merchants and manufacturers.   *"Red" and "Blue" books:* The Red books were directories of the nobility and those serving or pensioned by the government; the Blue books were government publications, including parliamentary ones, bound in blue.   *Whitaker's Almanack:* An almanac begun in 1868 by Joseph Whitaker and published annually thereafter containing information on the British Empire, including lists of persons in the nobility, government offices, the church, and the universities; a record of statutes passed that year; information concerning financial institutions, such as banks and insurance companies; crime statistics; and even a summary of the year's sporting events (*Enc. Brit.* 11th).   *Army and Navy Lists:* Two annual publications of military records, one for each service, containing information on personnel and pay, garrisons, ships in the navy, British dockyards, and naval regulations.   *Law List:* An annual publication listing members of the legal profession in Great Britain and the colonies, including judges, lawyers, officers of the court, and notaries public (Black's Law).

Whilst I was looking at the books, the door opened, and the Count entered. He saluted me in a hearty way, and hoped that I had had a good night's rest. Then he went on: —

"I am glad you found your way in here, for I am sure there is much that will interest you. These friends" — and he laid his hand on some of the books — "have been good friends to me, and for some years past, ever since I had the idea of going to London, have given me many, many hours of pleasure. Through them I have come to know your great England; and to know her is to love her. I long to go through the crowded streets of your mighty London, to be in the midst of the whirl and rush of humanity, to share its life, its change, its death, and all that makes it what it is. But alas! as yet I only know your tongue through books. To you, my friend, I look that I know it to speak."

"But, Count," I said, "you know and speak English thoroughly!" He bowed gravely.

"I thank you, my friend, for your all too flattering estimate, but yet I fear that I am but a little way on the road I would travel. True, I know the grammar and the words, but yet I know not how to speak them."

"Indeed," I said, "you speak excellently."

"Not so," he answered. "Well I know that, did I move and speak in your London, none there are who would not know me for a stranger. That is not enough for me. Here I am noble; I am *boyar*°; the common people know me, and I am master. But a stranger in a strange land,° he is no one; men know him not — and to know not is to care not for. I am content if I am like the rest, so that no man stops if he see me, or pause in his speaking if he hear my words, to say, 'Ha, ha! a stranger!' I have been so long master that I would be master still — or at least that none other should be master of me. You come to me not alone as agent of my friend, Peter Hawkins, of Exeter, to tell me all about my new estate in London. You shall, I trust, rest here with me a while, so that by our talking I may learn the English intonation; and I would that you tell me when I make error, even of the smallest, in my speaking. I am sorry that I had to be away so long to-day; but you will, I know, forgive one who has so many important affairs in hand."

Of course I said all I could about being willing, and asked if I might come into that room when I chose. He answered: "Yes, certainly," and added: —

"You may go anywhere you wish in the castle, except where the

---

boyar: Member of the nobility (Wilkinson; *Enc. Brit.* 11th).　**stranger *in a strange* land:** In the Old Testament, after fleeing from Egypt to the land of Midian, Moses refers to himself as having been "a stranger in a strange land" (Exod. 2.22).

doors are locked, where of course you will not wish to go. There is reason that all things are as they are, and did you see with my eyes and know with my knowledge, you would perhaps better understand." I said I was sure of this, and then he went on: —

"We are in Transylvania; and Transylvania is not England. Our ways are not your ways, and there shall be to you many strange things. Nay, from what you have told me of your experiences already, you know something of what strange things here may be."

This led to much conversation; and as it was evident that he wanted to talk, if only for talking's sake, I asked him many questions regarding things that had already happened to me or come within my notice. Sometimes he sheered off the subject, or turned the conversation by pretending not to understand; but generally he answered all I asked most frankly. Then as time went on, and I had got somewhat bolder, I asked him of some of the strange things of the preceding night, as, for instance, why the coachman went to the places where we had seen the blue flames. Was it indeed true that they showed where gold was hidden? He then explained to me that it was commonly believed that on a certain night of the year — last night, in fact, when all evil spirits are supposed to have unchecked sway — a blue flame is seen over any place where treasure has been concealed. "That treasure has been hidden," he went on, "in the region through which you came last night, there can be but little doubt; for it was the ground fought over for centuries by the Wallachian,° the Saxon, and the Turk. Why, there is hardly a foot of soil in all this region that has not been enriched by the blood of men, patriots or invaders. In old days there were stirring times, when the Austrian and the Hungarian came up in hordes, and the patriots went out to meet them — men and women, the aged and the children too — and waited their coming on the rocks above the passes, that they might sweep destruction on them with their artificial avalanches. When the invader was triumphant he found but little, for whatever there was had been sheltered in the friendly soil."

"But how," said I, "can it have remained so long undiscovered, when there is a sure index to it if men will but take the trouble to look?" The Count smiled, and as his lips ran back over his gums, the long, sharp, canine teeth showed out strangely; he answered: —

"Because your peasant is at heart a coward and a fool! Those flames only appear on one night; and on that night no man of this land will, if

---

Wallachian: Inhabitants of the independent principality of Wallachia, established in the fourteenth century south of the Transylvanian Alps in what later became Romania.

he can help it, stir without his doors. And, dear sir, even if he did he would not know what to do. Why, even the peasant that you tell me of who marked the place of the flame would not know where to look in daylight even for his own work. You would not, I dare be sworn, be able to find these places again?'

"There you are right," I said. "I know no more than the dead where even to look for them." Then we drifted into other matters.

"Come," he said at last, "tell me of London and of the house which you have procured for me." With an apology for my remissness, I went into my own room to get the papers from my bag. Whilst I was placing them in order I heard a rattling of china and silver in the next room, and as I passed through, noticed that the table had been cleared and the lamp lit, for it was by this time deep into the dark. The lamps were also lit in the study or library, and I found the Count lying on the sofa, reading, of all things in the world, an English Bradshaw's Guide.° When I came in he cleared the books and papers from the table; and with him I went into plans and deeds and figures of all sorts. He was interested in everything, and asked me a myriad questions about the place and its surroundings. He clearly had studied before-hand all he could get on the subject of the neighbourhood, for he evidently at the end knew very much more than I did. When I remarked this, he answered: —

"Well, but, my friend, is it not needful that I should? When I go there I shall be all alone, and my friend Harker Jonathan — nay, pardon me, I fall into my country's habit of putting your patronymic° first — my friend Jonathan Harker will not be by my side to correct and aid me. He will be in Exeter, miles away, probably working at papers of the law with my other friend, Peter Hawkins. So!"

We went thoroughly into the business of the purchase of the estate at Purfleet.° When I had told him the facts and got his signature to the necessary papers, and had written a letter with them ready to post to Mr. Hawkins, he began to ask me how I had come across so suitable a place. I read to him the notes which I had made at the time, and which I inscribe here: —

"At Purfleet, on a by-road, I came across just such a place as seemed to be required, and where was displayed a dilapidated notice that the place was for sale. It is surrounded by a high wall, of ancient structure,

Bradshaw's Guide: A railway guide containing a map of all the railways in Great Britain, departure and arrival times, and train fares (Black).   *patronymic:* Family name, derived from the father.   *Purfleet:* A town located on the Thames east of London in Essex county; in Stoker's day, one of the principal docks for ships traveling along the river (*Enc. Brit.* 11th).

built of heavy stones, and has not been repaired for a large number of years. The closed gates were of heavy old oak and iron, all eaten with rust.

"The estate is called Carfax, no doubt a corruption of the old *Quatre Face,* as the house is four-sided, agreeing with the cardinal points of the compass. It contains in all some twenty acres, quite surrounded by the solid stone wall above mentioned. There are many trees on it, which make it in places gloomy, and there is a deep, dark-looking pond or small lake, evidently fed by some springs, as the water is clear and flows away in a fair-sized stream. The house is very large and of all periods back, I should say, to mediæval times, for one part is of stone immensely thick, with only a few windows high up and heavily barred with iron. It looks like part of a keep,° and is close to an old chapel or church. I could not enter it, as I had not the key of the door leading to it from the house, but I have taken with my kodak° views of it from various points. The house has been added to, but in a very straggling way, and I can only guess at the amount of ground it covers, which must be very great. There are but few houses close at hand, one being a very large house only recently added to and formed into a private lunatic asylum. It is not, however, visible from the grounds."

When I had finished, he said: —

"I am glad that it is old and big. I myself am of an old family, and to live in a new house would kill me. A house cannot be made habitable in a day; and, after all, how few days go to make up a century. I rejoice also that there is a chapel of old times. We Transylvanian nobles love not to think that our bones may be amongst the common dead. I seek not gaiety nor mirth, not the bright voluptuousness of much sunshine and sparkling waters which please the young and gay. I am no longer young; and my heart, through weary years of mourning over the dead, is not attuned to mirth. Moreover, the walls of my castle are broken; the shadows are many, and the wind breathes cold through the broken battlements and casements. I love the shade and the shadow, and would be alone with my thoughts when I may."

Somehow his words and his look did not seem to accord, or else it was that his cast of face made his smile look malignant and saturnine.

Presently, with an excuse, he left me, asking me to put all my papers together. He was some little time away, and I began to look at some of the books around me. One was an atlas, which I found opened natu-

---

keep: The strongest part of a medieval castle, which serves as its last defense (*OED* OL).
kodak: The Kodak camera, introduced in 1888, was a new technological innovation, the first camera simple and portable enough to be used by amateur photographers, including, in this case, an estate agent interested in selling property (*Enc. Brit.* OL).

rally at England, as if that map had been much used. On looking at it I found in certain places little rings marked, and on examining these I noticed that one was near London on the east side, manifestly where his new estate was situated; the other two were Exeter, and Whitby° on the Yorkshire coast.

It was the better part of an hour when the Count returned. "Aha!" he said; "still at your books? Good! But you must not work always. Come; I am informed that your supper is ready." He took my arm, and we went into the next room, where I found an excellent supper ready on the table. The Count again excused himself, as he had dined out on his being away from home. But he sat as on the previous night, and chatted whilst I ate. After supper I smoked, as on the last evening, and the Count stayed with me, chatting and asking questions on every conceivable subject, hour after hour. I felt that it was getting very late indeed, but I did not say anything, for I felt under obligation to meet my host's wishes in every way. I was not sleepy, as the long sleep yesterday had fortified me; but I could not help experiencing that chill which comes over one at the coming of the dawn, which is like, in its way, the turn of the tide. They say that people who are near death die generally at the change to the dawn or at the turn of the tide; any one who has when tired, and tied as it were to his post, experienced this change in the atmosphere can well believe it. All at once we heard the crow of a cock coming up with preternatural shrillness through the clear morning air; Count Dracula, jumping to his feet, said: —

"Why, there is the morning again! How remiss I am to let you stay up so long. You must make your conversation regarding my dear new country of England less interesting, so that I may not forget how time flies by us," and, with a courtly bow, he left me.

I went into my own room and drew the curtains, but there was little to notice; my window opened into the courtyard, all I could see was the warm grey of quickening sky. So I pulled the curtains again, and have written of this day.

8 *May.* — I began to fear as I wrote in this book that I was getting too diffuse; but now I am glad that I went into detail from the first, for there is something so strange about this place and all in it that I cannot but feel uneasy. I wish I were safe out of it, or that I had never come. It may be that this strange night-existence is telling on me; but would that that were all! If there were any one to talk to I could bear it, but there is

---

Whitby: A port town in Yorkshire. At the time of the novel, Whitby was a resort town with a fishing industry (*Enc. Brit.* OL).

no one. I have only the Count to speak with, and he! — I fear I am myself the only living soul within the place. Let me be prosaic so far as facts can be; it will help me to bear up, and imagination must not run riot with me. If it does I am lost. Let me say at once how I stand — or seem to.

I only slept a few hours when I went to bed, and feeling that I could not sleep any more, got up. I had hung my shaving glass by the window, and was just beginning to shave. Suddenly I felt a hand on my shoulder, and heard the Count's voice saying to me, "Good-morning." I started, for it amazed me that I had not seen him, since the reflection of the glass covered the whole room behind me. In starting I had cut myself slightly, but did not notice it at the moment. Having answered the Count's salutation, I turned to the glass again to see how I had been mistaken. This time there could be no error, for the man was close to me, and I could see him over my shoulder. But there was no reflection of him in the mirror! The whole room behind me was displayed; but there was no sign of a man in it, except myself. This was startling, and, coming on the top of so many strange things, was beginning to increase that vague feeling of uneasiness which I always have when the Count is near; but at the instant I saw that the cut had bled a little, and the blood was trickling over my chin. I laid down the razor, turning as I did so half round to look for some sticking plaster.° When the Count saw my face, his eyes blazed with a sort of demoniac fury, and he suddenly made a grab at my throat. I drew away, and his hand touched the string of beads which held the crucifix. It made an instant change in him, for the fury passed so quickly that I could hardly believe that it was ever there.

"Take care," he said, "take care how you cut yourself. It is more dangerous than you think in this country." Then seizing the shaving glass, he went on: "And this is the wretched thing that has done the mischief. It is a foul bauble of man's vanity. Away with it!" and opening the heavy window with one wrench of his terrible hand, he flung out the glass, which was shattered into a thousand pieces on the stones of the courtyard far below. Then he withdrew without a word. It is very annoying, for I do not see how I am to shave, unless in my watch-case or the bottom of the shaving-pot, which is fortunately of metal.

When I went into the dining-room, breakfast was prepared; but I could not find the Count anywhere. So I breakfasted alone. It is strange that as yet I have not seen the Count eat or drink. He must be a very peculiar man! After breakfast I did a little exploring in the castle. I went out on the stairs and found a room looking towards the south. The view

---

sticking plaster: Fabric spread with an adhesive for covering superficial wounds (*OED*).

was magnificent, and from where I stood there was every opportunity of seeing it. The castle is on the very edge of a terrible precipice. A stone falling from the window would fall a thousand feet without touching anything! As far as the eye can reach is a sea of green tree-tops, with occasionally a deep rift where there is a chasm. Here and there are silver threads where the rivers wind in deep gorges through the forests.

But I am not in heart to describe beauty, for when I had seen the view I explored further; doors, doors, doors everywhere, and all locked and bolted. In no place save from the windows in the castle walls is there an available exit.

The castle is a veritable prison, and I am a prisoner!

CHAPTER III. JONATHAN HARKER'S JOURNAL

(Continued)

WHEN I found that I was a prisoner a sort of wild feeling came over me. I rushed up and down the stairs, trying every door and peering out of every window I could find; but after a little the conviction of my help-lessness overpowered all other feelings. When I look back after a few hours I think I must have been mad for the time, for I behaved much as a rat does in a trap. When, however, the conviction had come to me that I was helpless I sat down quietly — as quietly as I have ever done any-thing in my life — and began to think over what was best to be done. I am thinking still, and as yet have come to no definite conclusion. Of one thing only am I certain: that it is no use making my ideas known to the Count. He knows well that I am imprisoned; and as he has done it him-self, and has doubtless his own motives for it, he would only deceive me if I trusted him fully with the facts. So far as I can see, my only plan will be to keep my knowledge and my fears to myself, and my eyes open. I am, I know, either being deceived, like a baby, by my own fears, or else I am in desperate straits; and if the latter be so, I need, and shall need, all my brains to get through. I had hardly come to this conclusion when I heard the great door below shut, and knew that the Count had returned. He did not come at once into the library, so I went cautiously to my own room and found him making the bed. This was odd, but only con-firmed what I had all along thought — that there were no servants in the house. When later I saw him through the chink of the hinges of the door laying the table in the dining-room, I was assured of it; for if he does himself all these menial offices, surely it is proof that there is no one else to do them. This gave me a fright, for if there is no one else in the castle, it must have been the Count himself who was the driver of the coach that brought me here. This is a terrible thought; for if so, what does it mean that he could control the wolves, as he did, by only holding up his hand in silence. How was it that all the people at Bistritz and on the coach had some terrible fear for me? What meant the giving of the crucifix, of the garlic, of the wild rose, of the mountain ash? Bless that good, good woman who hung the crucifix round my neck! for it is a comfort and a strength to me whenever I touch it. It is odd that a thing which I have been taught to regard with disfavor and as idolatrous should in a time of loneliness and trouble be of help. Is it that there is something in the essence of the thing itself, or that it is a medium, a tangible help, in conveying memories of sympathy and comfort? Some time, if it may be, I must examine this matter and try to make up my mind about it. In the meantime I must find out all I can about Count Dracula, as it may help me to understand. To-night he may talk of himself, if I turn the conversation that way. I must be very careful, however, not to awake his suspicion.

Midnight. — I have had a long talk with the Count. I asked him a few questions on Transylvanian history, and he warmed up to the subject wonderfully. In his speaking of things and people, and especially of battles, he spoke as if he had been present at them all. This he afterwards explained by saying that to a *boyar* the pride of his house and name is his own pride, that their glory is his glory, that their fate is his fate. Whenever he spoke of his house he always said "we," and spoke almost in the plural, like a king speaking. I wish I could put down all he said exactly as he said it, for to me it was most fascinating. It seemed to have in it a whole history of the country. He grew excited as he spoke, and walked about the room pulling his great white moustache and grasping anything on which he laid his hands as though he would crush it by main strength. One thing he said which I shall put down as nearly as I can; for it tells in its way the story of his race: —

"We Szekelys° have a right to be proud, for in our veins flows the blood of many brave races who fought as the lion fights, for lordship. Here, in the whirlpool of European races, the Ugric tribe° bore down from Iceland the fighting spirit which Thor and Wodin° gave them,

Szekelys: A tribe settled in Transylvania to guard the frontier whose name means "frontier guards." Tribe members trace their ancestry to Attila's Huns (*Enc. Brit.* OL; *Baedeker Austria* 1896).   **Ugric tribe:** The Magyars, who eventually formed the principal ethnic group of Hungary (*Enc. Brit.* 11th).   **Thor and Wodin:** Two Germanic gods. Thor is a warrior god associated with thunder. Wodin (or Odin) is the leader of the gods and the father of Thor. He is also the god of the dead and specifically a protector of slain warriors (*Enc. Brit.* OL; *Enc. Brit.* 11th).

which their Berserkers° displayed to such fell intent on the seaboards of
Europe, ay, and of Asia and Africa too, till the peoples thought that the
were-wolves themselves had come. Here, too, when they came, they
found the Huns, whose warlike fury had swept the earth like a living
flame, till the dying peoples held that in their veins ran the blood of
those old witches, who, expelled from Scythia° had mated with the devils in the desert. Fools, fools! What devil or what witch was ever so great
as Attila, whose blood is in these veins?" He held up his arms. "Is it a
wonder that we were a conquering race; that we were proud; that when
the Magyar, the Lombard, the Avar, the Bulgar, or the Turk° poured
his thousands on our frontiers, we drove them back? Is it strange that
when Arpad° and his legions swept through the Hungarian fatherland
he found us here when he reached the frontier; that the Honfoglalas°
was completed there? And when the Hungarian flood swept eastward,
the Szekelys were claimed as kindred by the victorious Magyars, and to
us for centuries was trusted the guarding of the frontier of Turkey-land;
ay and more than that, endless duty of the frontier guard, for, as the
Turks say, 'water sleeps, and enemy is sleepless.' Who more gladly than
we throughout the Four Nations° received the 'bloody sword,'° or at
its warlike call flocked quicker to the standard of the King? When was
redeemed that great shame of my nation, the shame of Cassova,° when
the flags of the Wallach and the Magyar went down beneath the Crescent,° who was it but one of my own race who as Voivode° crossed the
Danube and beat the Turk on his own ground? This was a Dracula
indeed! Woe was it that his own unworthy brother, when he had fallen,
sold his people to the Turk and brought the shame of slavery on them!

Berserkers: From the Old Norse *beserkr* ("bearskin"). Warriors who worshiped Odin,
famous for their ferocity in battle. Their animal-skin battle attire contributed to the development of the werewolf legend (*Enc. Brit.* OL).   **Scythia:** The regions to the north and
northeast of the Black Sea, home of a primarily nomadic group of tribes, probably of
Iranian descent. Herodotus describes the invasion of Scythia by Darius in 512 B.C.E. The
region was finally overrun by the Huns (*Enc. Brit.* 11th).   **the Magyar, the Lombard,
the Avar, the Bulgar, or the Turk:** Tribes that, at various times, invaded Transylvania
(*Enc. Brit.* 11th).   **Arpad:** A semimythical Hungarian ruler (d. 907) chosen to lead his
tribe westward on its migration into the Hungarian plains. He founded the Arpad dynasty
that ruled Hungary until 1301 (*Enc. Brit.* OL; *Enc. Brit.* 11th).   **Honfoglalas:** Arpad's
conquest of the Hungarian homeland for the Magyars, which involved crossing the
Carpathians into what became Hungary (Wolf 41n14).   **Four Nations:** The three
"privileged nations" of Transylvania were the Magyars, the Szekelys, and the Saxons. The
native Romanians were recognized as a fourth nation in 1863 (*Enc. Brit.* 11th).
'bloody sword': Call to battle.   **Cassova:** In 1448, the Hungarian general János Hun-
yadi, a prince of Transylvania, lost a battle against the Turks at Kossovo through the
treachery of his Wallachian ally. Ransomed by the Magyars, he later routed the Turks
from Europe (*Enc. Brit.* 11th).   **Crescent:** Emblem of the Turkish Empire (*Enc. Brit.*
OL).   **Voivode:** Prince (Wilkinson).

Was it not this Dracula, indeed, who inspired that other of his race who in a later age again and again brought his forces over the great river into Turkey-land; who, when he was beaten back, came again, and again, and again, though he had to come alone from the bloody field where his troops were being slaughtered, since he knew that he alone could ultimately triumph? They said that he thought only of himself. Bah! what good are peasants without a leader? Where ends the war without a brain and heart to conduct it? Again, when, after the battle of Mohacs,° we threw off the Hungarian yoke, we of the Dracula blood were amongst their leaders, for our spirit would not brook that we were not free. Ah, young sir, the Szekelys — and the Dracula as their heart's blood, their brains, and their swords — can boast a record that mushroom growths like the Hapsburgs and the Romanoffs° can never reach. The warlike days are over. Blood is too precious a thing in these days of dishonourable peace; and the glories of the great races are as a tale that is told."

It was by this time close on morning, and we went to bed. (*Mem.* this diary seems horribly like the beginning of the "Arabian Nights,"° for everything has to break off at cock-crow — or like the ghost of Hamlet's father.°)

12 *May.* — Let me begin with facts — bare, meagre facts, verified by books and figures, and of which there can be no doubt. I must not confuse them with experiences which will have to rest on my own observation or my memory of them. Last evening when the Count came from his room he began by asking me questions on legal matters and on the doing of certain kinds of business. I had spent the day wearily over books, and, simply to keep my mind occupied, went over some of the matters I had been examined in at Lincoln's Inn.° There

---

battle of Mohacs: Battle of 1526 in which the Turks defeated Hungary and Transylvania became a Turkish principality (*Enc. Brit.* OL).   **the Hapsburgs and the Romanoffs:** The ruling dynasties of Austria and Russia. The Hapsburgs gained control of Austria in 1282 and the Romanoffs began to reign in Russia in 1613. At the time *Dracula* was written, both dynasties were still in power (*Enc. Brit.* 11th).   **"Arabian Nights":** *The Arabian Nights' Entertainment,* a collection of Oriental stories translated into English by Stoker's friend Sir Richard Burton (1821–1890) as *The Thousand Nights and a Night,* published in sixteen volumes (1885–88). The stories are told by Scheherazade, the wife of the Caliph Harun al-Rashid. Having been betrayed by his first wife, the Caliph vows to behead every subsequent wife on the morning after their wedding night. Scheherazade avoids this fate by telling him a new story every night but breaking off at dawn. Eager to hear the end of the story, the Caliph allows her to live for one more day. Burton also translated a vampire story, *Vikram and the Vampire* (1870), which he called the "rude beginnings" of the *Arabian Nights.*   **ghost of Hamlet's father:** In *Hamlet,* the ghost of the dead king of Denmark fades "on the crowing of the cock" (*Hamlet* 1.1.163).   **Lincoln's Inn:** One of the four Inns of Court, the British institutions responsible for legal education (*Enc. Brit.* OL).

was a certain method in the Count's inquiries, so I shall try to put them down in sequence; the knowledge may somehow or some time be useful to me.

First, he asked if a man in England might have two solicitors, or more. I told him he might have a dozen if he wished, but that it would not be wise to have more than one solicitor engaged in one transaction, as only one could act at a time, and that to change would be certain to militate against his interest. He seemed thoroughly to understand, and went on to ask if there would be any practical difficulty in having one man to attend, say, to banking and another to look after shipping, in case local help were needed in a place far from the home of the banking solicitor. I asked him to explain more fully so that I might not by any chance mislead him, so he said: —

"I shall illustrate. Your friend and mine, Mr. Peter Hawkins, from under the shadow of your beautiful cathedral at Exeter, which is far from London, buys for me through your good self my place at London. Good! Now here let me say frankly, lest you should think it strange that I have sought the services of one so far off from London instead of some one resident there, that my motive was that no local interest might be served save my wish only; and as one of London resident might, perhaps, have some purpose of himself or friend to serve, I went thus afield to seek my agent, whose labours should be only to my interest. Now, suppose I, who have much of affairs, wish to ship goods, say, to Newcastle, or Durham, or Harwich, or Dover, might it not be that it could with more ease be done by consigning to one in these ports?" I answered that certainly it would be most easy, but that we solicitors had a system of agency one for the other, so that local work could be done locally on instruction from any solicitor, so that the client, simply placing himself in the hands of one man, could have his wishes carried out by him without further trouble.

"But," said he, "I could be at liberty to direct myself. Is it not so?"

"Of course," I replied; "and such is often done by men of business, who do not like the whole of their affairs to be known by any one person."

"Good!" he said, and then went on to ask about the means of making consignments and the forms to be gone through, and of all sorts of difficulties which might arise, but by forethought could be guarded against. I explained all these things to him to the best of my ability, and he certainly left me under the impression that he would have made a wonderful solicitor, for there was nothing that he did not think of or foresee. For a man who was never in the country, and who did not evidently do much in the way of business, his knowledge and acumen were wonderful. When he had satisfied himself on these points of which he had spoken, and I had verified all as well as I could by the books available, he suddenly stood up and said: —

"Have you written since your first letter to our friend Mr. Peter Hawkins, or to any other?" It was with some bitterness in my heart that I answered that I had not, that as yet I had not seen any opportunity of sending letters to anybody.

"Then write now, my young friend," he said, laying a heavy hand on my shoulder; "write to our friend and to any other; and say, if it will please you, that you shall stay with me until a month from now."

"Do you wish me to stay so long?" I asked, for my heart grew cold at the thought.

"I desire it much; nay, I will take no refusal. When your master, employer, what you will, engaged that some one should come on his behalf, it was understood that my needs only were to be consulted. I have not stinted. Is it not so?"

What could I do but bow acceptance? It was Mr. Hawkins's interest, not mine, and I had to think of him, not myself; and besides, while Count Dracula was speaking, there was that in his eyes and in his bearing which made me remember that I was a prisoner, and that if I wished it I could have no choice. The Count saw his victory in my bow, and his mastery in the trouble of my face, for he began at once to use them, but in his own smooth, resistless way: —

"I pray you, my good young friend, that you will not discourse of things other than business in your letters. It will doubtless please your friends to know that you are well, and that you look forward to getting home to them. Is it not so?" As he spoke he handed me three sheets of note-paper and three envelopes. They were all of the thinnest foreign post, and looking at them, then at him, and noticing his quiet smile, with the sharp, canine teeth lying over the red under-lip, I understood as well as if he had spoken that I should be careful what I wrote, for he would be able to read it. So I determined to write only formal notes now, but to write fully to Mr. Hawkins in secret, and also to Mina, for to her I could write in shorthand, which would puzzle the Count, if he did see it. When I had written my two letters I sat quiet, reading a book whilst the Count wrote several notes, referring as he wrote them to some books on his table. Then he took up my two and placed them with his own, and put by his writing materials, after which, the instant the door had closed behind him, I leaned over and looked at the letters, which were face down on the table. I felt no compunction in doing so, for under the circumstances I felt that I should protect myself in every way I could.

One of the letters was directed to Samuel F. Billington, No. 7, The Crescent, Whitby, another to Herr Leutner, Varna; the third was to Coutts & Co., London, and the fourth to Herren Klopstock & Bill-reuth, bankers, Buda-Pesth. The second and fourth were unsealed. I was just about to look at them when I saw the door-handle move. I sank back in my seat, having just had time to replace the letters as they had been and to resume my book before the Count, holding still another letter in his hand, entered the room. He took up the letters on the table and stamped them carefully, and then turning to me, said: —

"I trust you will forgive me, but I have much work to do in private this evening. You will, I hope, find all things as you wish." At the door he turned, and after a moment's pause said: —

"Let me advise you, my dear young friend — nay, let me warn you with all seriousness, that should you leave these rooms you will not by any chance go to sleep in any other part of the castle. It is old, and has many memories, and there are bad dreams for those who sleep unwisely. Be warned! Should sleep now or ever overcome you, or be like to do, then haste to your own chamber or to these rooms, for your rest will then be safe. But if you be not careful in this respect, then" — He finished his speech in a gruesome way, for he motioned with his hands as if he were washing them. I quite understood; my only doubt was as to whether any dream could be more terrible than the unnatural, horrible net of gloom and mystery which seemed closing round me.

Later. — I endorse the last words written, but this time there is no doubt in question. I shall not fear to sleep in any place where he is not. I have placed the crucifix over the head of my bed — I imagine that my rest is thus freer from dreams; and there it shall remain.

When he left me I went to my room. After a little while, not hearing any sound, I came out and went up the stone stair to where I could look out towards the south. There was some sense of freedom in the vast expanse, inaccessible though it was to me, as compared with the narrow darkness of the courtyard. Looking out on this, I felt that I was indeed in prison, and I seemed to want a breath of fresh air, though it were of the night. I am beginning to feel this nocturnal existence tell on me. It is destroying my nerve. I start at my own shadow, and am full of all sorts of horrible imaginings. God knows that there is ground for any terrible fear in this accursed place! I looked out over the beautiful expanse, bathed in soft yellow moonlight till it was almost as light as day. In the soft light the distant hills became melted, and the shadows in the valleys and gorges of velvety blackness. The mere beauty seemed to cheer me; there was peace and comfort in every breath I drew. As I leaned from the window my eye was caught by something moving a storey below me, and somewhat to my left, where I imagined, from the lie of the rooms, that the windows of the Count's own room would look out. The window at which I stood was tall and deep, stone-mullioned,° and though weather-worn, was still complete; but it was evidently many a day since the case° had been there. I drew back behind the stonework, and looked carefully out.

What I saw was the Count's head coming out from the window. I did not see the face, but I knew the man by the neck and the movement of his back and arms. In any case I could not mistake the hands which I had had so many opportunities of studying. I was at first interested and somewhat amused, for it is wonderful how small a matter will interest and amuse a man when he is a prisoner. But my very feelings changed to repulsion and terror when I saw the whole man slowly emerge from the window and begin to crawl down the castle wall over that dreadful abyss, *face down,* with his cloak spreading out around him like great wings. At first I could not believe my eyes. I thought it was some trick of the moonlight, some weird effect of shadow; but I kept looking, and it could be no delusion. I saw the fingers and toes grasp the corners of the stones, worn clear of the mortar by the stress of years, and by thus using every projection and inequality move downwards with consider-able speed, just as a lizard moves along a wall.

What manner of man is this, or what manner of creature is it in the semblance of man? I feel the dread of this horrible place overpowering me; I am in fear — in awful fear — and there is no escape for me; I am encompassed about with terrors that I dare not think of. . . . .

15 *May.* — Once more have I seen the Count go out in his lizard fashion. He moved downwards in a sidelong way, some hundred feet down, and a good deal to the left. He vanished into some hole or win-dow. When his head had disappeared I leaned out to try and see more, but without avail — the distance was too great to allow a proper angle of sight. I knew he had left the castle now, and thought to use the opportunity to explore more than I had dared to do as yet. I went back to the room, and taking a lamp, tried all the doors. They were all locked, as I had expected, and the locks were comparatively new; but I went down the stone stairs to the hall where I had entered originally. I

---

stone-mullioned: A window divided by a vertical bar, in this instance made of stone (*OED* OL).   *case:* Window frame (*OED* OL).

found I could pull back the bolts easily enough and unhook the great chains; but the door was locked, and the key was gone! That key must be in the Count's room; I must watch should his door be unlocked, so that I may get it and escape. I went on to make a thorough examination of the various stairs and passages, and to try the doors that opened from them. One or two small rooms near the hall were open, but there was nothing to see in them except old furniture, dusty with age and moth-eaten. At last, however, I found one door at the top of a stairway which, though it seemed to be locked, gave a little under pressure. I tried it harder, and found that it was not really locked, but that the resistance came from the fact that the hinges had fallen somewhat, and the heavy door rested on the floor. Here was an opportunity which I might not have again, so I exerted myself, and with many efforts forced it back so that I could enter. I was now in a wing of the castle further to the right than the rooms I knew and a storey lower down. From the windows I could see that the suite of rooms lay along to the south of the castle, the windows of the end room looking out both west and south. On the latter side, as well as to the former, there was a great precipice. The castle was built on the corner of a great rock, so that on three sides it was quite impregnable, and great windows were placed here where sling, or bow, or culverin° could not reach, and consequently light and comfort, impossible to a position which had to be guarded, were secured. To the west was a great valley, and then, rising far away, great jagged mountain fastnesses, rising peak on peak, the sheer rock studded with mountain ash and thorn, whose roots clung in cracks and crevices and crannies of the stone. This was evidently the portion of the castle occupied in bygone days, for the furniture had more air of comfort than any I had seen. The windows were curtainless, and the yellow moonlight, flooding in through the diamond panes, enabled one to see even colours, whilst it softened the wealth of dust which lay over all and disguised in some measure the ravages of time and the moth. My lamp seemed to be of little effect in the brilliant moonlight, but I was glad to have it with me, for there was a dread loneliness in the place which chilled my heart and made my nerves tremble. Still, it was better than living alone in the rooms which I had come to hate from the presence of the Count, and after trying a little to school my nerves, I found a soft quietude come over me. Here I am, sitting at a little oak table where in old times possibly some fair lady sat to pen, with much thought and many blushes, her ill-spelt love-letter, and writing in my diary in shorthand all that has

---

culverin: A large cannon (*OED* OL).

happened since I closed it last. It is nineteenth century up-to-date with a vengeance. And yet, unless my senses deceive me, the old centuries had, and have, powers of their own which mere "modernity" cannot kill.

Later: the Morning of 16 *May.* — God preserve my sanity, for to this I am reduced. Safety and the assurance of safety are things of the past. Whilst I live on here there is but one thing to hope for: that I may not go mad, if, indeed, I be not mad already. If I be sane, then surely it is maddening to think that of all the foul things that lurk in this hateful place the Count is the least dreadful to me; that to him alone I can look for safety, even though this be only whilst I can serve his purpose. Great God! merciful God! Let me be calm, for out of that way lies madness indeed.° I begin to get new lights on certain things which have puzzled me. Up to now I never quite knew what Shakespeare meant when he made Hamlet say: —

"My tablets! quick, my tablets!
'Tis meet that I put it down," etc.,°

for now, feeling as though my own brain were unhinged or as if the shock had come which must end in its undoing, I turn to my diary for repose. The habit of entering accurately must help to soothe me.

The Count's mysterious warning frightened me at the time; it frightens me more now when I think of it, for in future he has a fearful hold upon me. I shall fear to doubt what he may say!

When I had written in my diary and had fortunately replaced the book and pen in my pocket I felt sleepy. The Count's warning came into my mind, but I took a pleasure in disobeying it. The sense of sleep was upon me, and with it the obstinacy which sleep brings as outrider. The soft moonlight soothed, and the wide expanse without gave a sense of freedom which refreshed me. I determined not to return to-night to the gloom-haunted rooms, but to sleep here, where of old ladies had sat and sung and lived sweet lives whilst their gentle breasts were sad for their menfolk away in the midst of remorseless wars. I drew a great couch out of its place near the corner, so that, as I lay, I could look at the lovely view to east and south, and unthinking of and uncaring for the dust, composed myself for sleep.

---

out of that way lies madness indeed: Thinking of the unkindness of his daughters Regan and Goneril, King Lear rages, "O, that way madness lies; let me shun that!" (*King Lear* 3.4.21).   **My tablets!... etc.:** Learning that his uncle has killed his father, Prince Hamlet says bitterly, "My tablets — meet it is I set it down / That one may smile, and smile, and be a villain" (*Hamlet* 1.5.108–09).

I suppose I must have fallen asleep; I hope so, but I fear, for all that followed was startlingly real — so real that now, sitting here in the broad, full sunlight of the morning, I cannot in the least believe that it was all sleep.

I was not alone. The room was the same, unchanged in any way since I came into it; I could see along the floor, in the brilliant moonlight, my own footsteps marked where I had disturbed the long accumulation of dust. In the moonlight opposite me were three young women, ladies by their dress and manner. I thought at the time that I must be dreaming when I saw them, for, though the moonlight was behind them, they threw no shadow on the floor. They came close to me and looked at me for some time, and then whispered together. Two were dark, and had high aquiline noses, like the Count, and great dark, piercing eyes, that seemed to be almost red when contrasted with the pale yellow moon. The other was fair, as fair as can be, with great, wavy masses of golden hair and eyes like pale sapphires. I seemed somehow to know her face, and to know it in connection with some dreamy fear, but I could not recollect at the moment how or where. All three had brilliant white teeth, that shone like pearls against the ruby of their voluptuous lips. There was something about them that made me uneasy, some longing and at the same time some deadly fear. I felt in my heart a wicked, burning desire that they would kiss me with those red lips. It is not good to note this down, lest some day it should meet Mina's eyes and cause her pain; but it is the truth. They whispered together, and then they all three laughed — such a silvery, musical laugh, but as hard as though the sound never could have come through the softness of human lips. It was like the intolerable, tingling sweetness of water-glasses when played on by a cunning hand. The fair girl shook her head coquettishly, and the other two urged her on. One said: —

"Go on! You are first, and we shall follow; yours is the right to begin." The other added: —

"He is young and strong; there are kisses for us all." I lay quiet, looking out under my eyelashes in an agony of delightful anticipation. The fair girl advanced and bent over me till I could feel the movement of her breath upon me. Sweet it was in one sense, honey-sweet, and sent the same tingling through the nerves as her voice, but with a bitter underlying the sweet, a bitter offensiveness, as one smells in blood.

I was afraid to raise my eyelids, but looked out and saw perfectly under the lashes. The fair girl went on her knees, and bent over me, fairly gloating. There was a deliberate voluptuousness which was both thrilling and repulsive, and as she arched her neck she actually licked her lips like an animal, till I could see in the moonlight the moisture shining on the scarlet lips and on the red tongue as it lapped the white sharp teeth. Lower and lower went her head as the lips went below the range of my mouth and chin and seemed about to fasten on my throat. Then she paused, and I could hear the churning sound of her tongue as it licked her teeth and lips, and could feel the hot breath on my neck. Then the skin of my throat began to tingle as one's flesh does when the hand that is to tickle it approaches nearer — nearer. I could feel the soft, shivering touch of the lips on the supersensitive skin of my throat, and the hard dents of two sharp teeth, just touching and pausing there. I closed my eyes in a languorous ecstacy and waited — waited with beating heart.

But at that instant another sensation swept through me as quick as lightning. I was conscious of the presence of the Count, and of his being as if lapped in a storm of fury. As my eyes opened involuntarily I saw his strong hand grasp the slender neck of the fair woman and with giant's power draw it back, the blue eyes transformed with fury, the white teeth champing with rage, and the fair cheeks blazing red with passion. But the Count! Never did I imagine such wrath and fury, even to the demons of the pit. His eyes were positively blazing. The red light in them was lurid, as if the flames of hell-fire blazed behind them. His face was deathly pale, and the lines of it were hard like drawn wires; the thick eyebrows that met over the nose now seemed like a heaving bar of white-hot metal. With a fierce sweep of his arm, he hurled the woman from him, and then motioned to the others, as though he were beating them back; it was the same imperious gesture that I had seen used to the wolves. In a voice which, though low and almost in a whisper, seemed to cut through the air and then ring round the room as he said: —

"How dare you touch him, any of you? How dare you cast eyes on him when I had forbidden it? Back, I tell you all! This man belongs to me! Beware how you meddle with him, or you'll have to deal with me."
The fair girl, with a laugh of ribald coquetry, turned to answer him: —

"You yourself never loved; you never love!" On this the other women joined, and such a mirthless, hard, soulless laughter rang through the room that it almost made me faint to hear; it seemed like the pleasure of fiends. Then the Count turned, after looking at my face attentively, and said in a soft whisper: —

"Yes, I too can love; you yourselves can tell it from the past. Is it not so? Well, now I promise you that when I am done with him you shall kiss him at your will. Now go! go! I must awaken him, for there is work to be done."

"Are we to have nothing to-night?" said one of them, with a low laugh, as she pointed to the bag which he had thrown upon the floor, and which moved as though there were some living thing within it. For answer he nodded his head. One of the women jumped forward and opened it. If my ears did not deceive me there was a gasp and a low wail, as of a half-smothered child. The women closed round, whilst I was aghast with horror; but as I looked they disappeared, and with them the dreadful bag. There was no door near them, and they could not have passed me without my noticing. They simply seemed to fade into the rays of the moonlight and pass out through the window, for I could see outside the dim, shadowy forms for a moment before they entirely faded away.

Then the horror overcame me, and I sank down unconscious.

CHAPTER IV. JONATHAN HARKER'S JOURNAL

(Continued)

I AWOKE in my own bed. If it be that I had not dreamt, the Count must have carried me here. I tried to satisfy myself on the subject, but could not arrive at any unquestionable result. To be sure, there were certain small evidences, such as that my clothes were folded and laid by in a manner which was not my habit. My watch was still unwound, and I am rigorously accustomed to wind it the last thing before going to bed, and many such details. But these things are no proof, for they may have been evidences that my mind was not as usual, and, from some cause or another, I had certainly been much upset. I must watch for proof. Of one thing I am glad: if it was that the Count carried me here and undressed me, he must have been hurried in his task, for my pockets are intact. I am sure this diary would have been a mystery to him which he would not have brooked. He would have taken or destroyed it. As I look round this room, although it has been to me so full of fear, it is now a sort of sanctuary, for nothing can be more dreadful than those awful women, who were — who *are* — waiting to suck my blood.

18 *May.* — I have been down to look at that room again in day-light, for I *must* know the truth. When I got to the doorway at the top of the stairs I found it closed. It had been so forcibly driven against the

jamb that part of the woodwork was splintered. I could see that the bolt of the lock had not been shot, but the door is fastened from the inside. I fear it was no dream, and must act on this surmise.

19 May. — I am surely in the toils.° Last night the Count asked me in the suavest tones to write three letters, one saying that my work here was nearly done, and that I should start for home within a few days, another that I was starting on the next morning from the time of the letter, and the third that I had left the castle and arrived at Bistritz. I would fain have rebelled, but felt that in the present state of things it would be madness to quarrel openly with the Count whilst I am so absolutely in his power; and to refuse would be to excite his suspicion and to arouse his anger. He knows that I know too much, and that I must not live, lest I be dangerous to him; my only chance is to prolong my opportunities. Something may occur which will give me a chance to escape. I saw in his eyes something of that gathering wrath which was manifest when he hurled that fair woman from him. He explained to me that posts were few and uncertain, and that my writing now would ensure ease of mind to my friends; and he assured me with so much impressiveness that he would countermand the later letters, which would be held over at Bistritz until due time in case chance would admit of my prolonging my stay, that to oppose him would have been to create new suspicion. I therefore pretended to fall in with his views, and asked him what dates I should put on the letters. He calculated a minute, and then said: —

"The first should be June 12, the second June 19, and the third June 29."

I know now the span of my life. God help me!

28 May. — There is a chance of escape, or at any rate of being able to send word home. A band of Szgany° have come to the castle, and are encamped in the courtyard. These Szgany are gypsies; I have notes of them in my book. They are peculiar to this part of the world, though allied to the ordinary gypsies all the world over. There are thousands of them in Hungary and Transylvania, who are almost outside all law. They attach themselves as a rule to some great noble or *boyar,* and call themselves by his name. They are fearless and without religion, save superstition, and they talk only their own varieties of the Romany tongue.°

---

toils: "A trap or snare for wild beasts" (*OED* OL, obsolete usage).   *band of Szgany:* Usually spelled Tsigane. Hungarian Gypsies (*OED*). Like other imperial European powers, as early as 1544 the English forcibly exiled Gypsies who came to England by transporting them to their colonies.   *varieties of the Romany tongue:* The language of the Gypsies, related to Sanskrit and Hindi, varies regionally because of the incorporation of

I shall write some letters home, and shall try to get them to have them posted. I have already spoken to them through my window to begin an acquaintanceship. They took their hats off and made obeisance and many signs, which, however, I could not understand any more than I could their spoken language. . . . .

I have written the letters. Mina's is in shorthand, and I simply ask Mr. Hawkins to communicate with her. To her I have explained my situation, but without the horrors which I may only surmise. It would shock and frighten her to death were I to expose my heart to her. Should the letters not carry, then the Count shall not yet know my secret or the extent of my knowledge. . . . .

I have given the letters; I threw them through the bars of my window with a gold piece, and made what signs I could to have them posted. The man who took them pressed them to his heart and bowed, and then put them in his cap. I could do no more. I stole back to the study, and began to read. As the Count did not come in, I have written here. . . . .

The Count has come. He sat down beside me, and said in his smoothest voice as he opened two letters: —

"The Szgany has given me these, of which, though I know not whence they come, I shall, of course, take care. See!" — he must have looked at it — "one is from you, and to my friend Peter Hawkins; the other" — here he caught sight of the strange symbols as he opened the envelope, and the dark look came into his face, and his eyes blazed wickedly — "the other is a vile thing, an outrage upon friendship and hospitality! It is not signed. Well! so it cannot matter to us." And he calmly held letter and envelope in the flame of the lamp till they were consumed. Then he went on: —

"The letter to Hawkins — that I shall, of course, send on, since it is yours. Your letters are sacred to me. Your pardon, my friend, that unknowingly I did break the seal. Will you not cover it again?" He held out the letter to me, and with a courteous bow handed me a clean envelope. I could only re-direct it and hand it to him in silence. When he went out of the room I could hear the key turn softly. A minute later I went over and tried it, and the door was locked.

When, an hour or two after, the Count came quietly into the room; his coming wakened me, for I had gone to sleep on the sofa. He was

words and features from different languages. Harker may have heard them speaking only Romany among themselves, but normally they speak other languages in order to communicate with their neighbors. Speaking English and some German, he may not have been able to communicate with them.

very courteous and very cheery in his manner, and seeing that I had been sleeping, he said: —

"So, my friend, you are tired? Get to bed. There is the surest rest. I may not have the pleasure to talk to-night, since there are many labours to me; but you will sleep, I pray." I passed to my room and went to bed, and, strange to say, slept without dreaming. Despair has its own calms.

31 *May*. — This morning when I woke I thought I would provide myself with some paper and envelopes from my bag and keep them in my pocket, so that I might write in case I should get an opportunity; but again a surprise, again a shock!

Every scrap of paper was gone, and with it all my notes, my memoranda relating to railways and travel, my letter of credit, in fact all that might be useful to me were I once outside the castle. I sat and pondered a while, and then some thought occurred to me, and I made search of my portmanteau and in the wardrobe where I had placed my clothes.

The suit in which I had travelled was gone, and also my overcoat and rug; I could find no trace of them anywhere. This looked like some new scheme of villainy. . . . .

17 *June*. — This morning, as I was sitting on the edge of my bed cudgelling my brains, I heard without a cracking of whips and pounding and scraping of horses' feet up the rocky path beyond the courtyard. With joy I hurried to the window, and saw drive into the yard two great leiter-wagons, each drawn by eight sturdy horses, and at the head of each pair a Slovak, with his wide hat, great, nail-studded belt, dirty sheepskin, and high boots. They had also their long staves in hand. I ran to the door, intending to descend and try and join them through the main hall, as I thought that way might be opened for them. Again a shock: my door was fastened on the outside.

Then I ran to the window and cried to them. They looked up at me stupidly and pointed, but just then the "hetman"° of the Szgany came out, and seeing them pointing to my window, said something, at which they laughed. Henceforth no effort of mine, no piteous cry or agonised entreaty, would make them even look at me. They resolutely turned away. The leiter-wagons contained great, square boxes, with handles of thick rope; these were evidently empty by the ease with which the Slovaks handled them, and by their resonance as they were roughly moved. When they were all unloaded and packed in a great heap in one corner of the yard, the Slovaks were given some money by the Szgany, and

hetman: Captain or commander (from Polish) (*OED*).

spitting on it for luck, lazily went each to his horse's head. Shortly afterwards I heard the cracking of their whips die away in the distance.

24 *June, before morning.* — Last night the Count left me early, and locked himself into his own room. As soon as I dared I ran up the winding stair, and looked out of the window, which opened south. I thought I would watch for the Count, for there is something going on. The Szgany are quartered somewhere in the castle, and are doing work of some kind. I know it, for now and then I hear a far-away, muffled sound as of mattock and spade, and, whatever it is, it must be to the end of some ruthless villainy.

I had been at the window somewhat less than half an hour, when I saw something coming out of the Count's window. I drew back and watched carefully, and saw the whole man emerge. It was a new shock to me to find that he had on the suit of clothes which I had worn whilst travelling here, and slung over his shoulder the terrible bag which I had seen the women take away. There could be no doubt as to his quest, and in my garb, too! Thus, then, is his new scheme of evil: that he will allow others to see me, as they think, so that he may both leave evidence that I have been seen in the towns or villages posting my own letters, and that any wickedness which he may do shall by the local people be attributed to me.

It makes me rage to think that this can go on, and whilst I am shut up here, a veritable prisoner, but without that protection of the law which is even a criminal's right and consolation.

I thought I would watch for the Count's return, and for a long time sat doggedly at the window. Then I began to notice that there were some quaint little specks floating in the rays of the moonlight. They were like the tiniest grains of dust, and they whirled round and gathered in clusters in a nebulous sort of way. I watched them with a sense of soothing, and a sort of calm stole over me. I leaned back in the embrasure in a more comfortable position, so that I could enjoy more fully the aerial gambolling.

Something made me start up, a low, piteous howling of dogs somewhere far below in the valley, which was hidden from my sight. Louder it seemed to ring in my ears, and the floating motes of dust to take new shapes to the sound as they danced in the moonlight. I felt myself struggling to awake to some call of my instincts; nay, my very soul was struggling, and my half-remembered sensibilities were striving to answer the call. I was becoming hypnotised! Quicker and quicker danced the dust, and the moonbeams seemed to quiver as they went by me into the mass of gloom beyond. More and more they gathered till they seemed to take dim phantom shapes. And then I started, broad awake and in full possession of my senses, and ran screaming from the place. The phantom shapes, which were becoming gradually materialised from the moonbeams, were those of the three ghostly women to whom I was doomed. I fled, and felt somewhat safer in my own room, where there was no moonlight and where the lamp was burning brightly.

When a couple of hours had passed I heard something stirring in the Count's room, something like a sharp wail quickly suppressed; and then there was silence, deep, awful silence, which chilled me. With a beating heart, I tried the door; but I was locked in my prison, and could do nothing. I sat down and simply cried.

As I sat I heard a sound in the courtyard without — the agonised cry of a woman. I rushed to the window, and throwing it up, peered out between the bars. There, indeed, was a woman with dishevelled hair, holding her hands over her heart as one distressed with running. She was leaning against a corner of the gateway. When she saw my face at the window she threw herself forward, and shouted in a voice laden with menace: —

"Monster, give me my child!"

She threw herself on her knees, and raising up her hands, cried the same words in tones which wrung my heart. Then she tore her hair and beat her breast, and abandoned herself to all the violences of extravagant emotion. Finally, she threw herself forward, and, though I could not see her, I could hear the beating of her naked hands against the door.

Somewhere high overhead, probably on the tower, I heard the voice of the Count calling in his harsh, metallic whisper. His call seemed to be answered from far and wide by the howling of wolves. Before many minutes had passed a pack of them poured, like a pent-up dam when liberated, through the wide entrance into the courtyard.

There was no cry from the woman, and the howling of the wolves was but short. Before long they streamed away singly, licking their lips.

I could not pity her, for I knew now what had become of her child, and she was better dead.

What shall I do? what can I do? How can I escape from this dreadful thrall of night and gloom and fear?

25 *June, morning.* — No man knows till he has suffered from the night how sweet and how dear to his heart and eye the morning can be. When the sun grew so high this morning that it struck the top of the great gateway opposite my window, the high spot which it touched

seemed to me as if the dove from the ark° had lighted there. My fear fell from me as if it had been a vaporous garment which dissolved in the warmth. I must take action of some sort whilst the courage of the day is upon me. Last night one of my post-dated letters went to post, the first of that fatal series which is to blot out the very traces of my existence from the earth.

Let me not think of it. Action!

It has always been at night-time that I have been molested or threatened, or in some way in danger or in fear. I have not yet seen the Count in the daylight. Can it be that he sleeps when others wake, that he may be awake whilst they sleep? If I could only get into his room! But there is no possible way. The door is always locked, no way for me.

Yes, there is a way, if one dares to take it. Where his body has gone why may not another body go? I have seen him myself crawl from his window; why should not I imitate him, and go in by his window? The chances are desperate, but my need is more desperate still. I shall risk it. At the worst it can only be death; and a man's death is not a calf's, and the dreaded Hereafter may still be open to me. God help me in my task! Good-bye, Mina, if I fail; good-bye, my faithful friend and second father; good-bye, all, and last of all Mina!

Same day, later. — I have made the effort, and, God helping me, have come safely back to this room. I must put down every detail in order. I went whilst my courage was fresh straight to the window on the south side, and at once got outside on the narrow ledge of stone which runs round the building on this side. The stones were big and roughly cut, and the mortar had by process of time been washed away between them. I took off my boots, and ventured out on the desperate way. I looked down once, so as to make sure that a sudden glimpse of the awful depth would not overcome me, but after that kept my eyes away from it. I knew pretty well the direction and distance of the Count's window, and made for it as well as I could, having regard to the opportunities available. I did not feel dizzy — I suppose I was too excited — and the time seemed ridiculously short till I found myself standing on the window-sill and trying to raise up the sash. I was filled with agitation, however, when I bent down and slid feet foremost in through the window. Then I looked around for the Count, but, with surprise and gladness, made a discovery. The room was empty! It was barely furnished with odd things, which seemed to have never been used; the

---

dove from the ark: When the dove that Noah sends out from the ark fails to return, he knows that the flood has ended (Gen. 8.8–13).

furniture was something the same style as that in the south rooms, and was covered with dust. I looked for the key, but it was not in the lock, and I could not find it anywhere. The only thing I found was a great heap of gold in one corner — gold of all kinds, Roman, and British, and Austrian, and Hungarian, and Greek and Turkish money, covered with a film of dust, as though it had lain long in the ground. None of it that I noticed was less than three hundred years old. There were also chains and ornaments, some jewelled, but all of them old and stained.

At one corner of the room was a heavy door. I tried it, for, since I could not find the key of the room or the key of the outer door, which was the main object of my search, I must make further examination, or all my efforts would be in vain. It was open, and led through a stone passage to a circular stairway, which went steeply down. I descended, minding carefully where I went, for the stairs were dark, being only lit by loopholes in the heavy masonry. At the bottom there was a dark, tunnel-like passage, through which came a deathly, sickly odour, the odour of old earth newly turned. As I went through the passage the smell grew closer and heavier. At last I pulled open a heavy door which stood ajar, and found myself in an old, ruined chapel, which had evidently been used as a graveyard. The roof was broken, and in two places were steps leading to vaults, but the ground had recently been dug over, and the earth placed in great wooden boxes, manifestly those which had been brought by the Slovaks. There was nobody about, and I made search for any further outlet, but there was none. Then I went over every inch of the ground, so as not to lose a chance. I went down even into the vaults, where the dim light struggled, although to do so was a dread to my very soul. Into two of these I went, but saw nothing except fragments of old coffins and piles of dust; in the third, however, I made a discovery.

There, in one of the great boxes, of which there were fifty in all, on a pile of newly dug earth, lay the Count! He was either dead or asleep, I could not say which — for the eyes were open and stony, but without the glassiness of death — and the cheeks had the warmth of life through all their pallor, and the lips were as red as ever. But there was no sign of movement, no pulse, no breath, no beating of the heart. I bent over him, and tried to find any sign of life, but in vain. He could not have lain there long, for the earthy smell would have passed away in a few hours. By the side of the box was its cover, pierced with holes here and there. I thought he might have the keys on him, but when I went to search I saw the dead eyes, and in them, dead though they were, such a look of hate, though unconscious of me or my presence, that I fled from the place, and leaving the Count's room by the window, crawled again up the castle wall. Regaining my own chamber, I threw myself panting upon the bed and tried to think. . . . .

29 *June.* — To-day is the date of my last letter, and the Count has taken steps to prove that it was genuine, for again I saw him leave the castle by the same window, and in my clothes. As he went down the wall, lizard fashion, I wished I had a gun or some lethal weapon, that I might destroy him; but I fear that no weapon wrought alone by man's hand would have any effect on him. I dared not wait to see him return, for I feared to see those weird sisters.° I came back to the library, and read there till I fell asleep.

I was awakened by the Count, who looked at me as grimly as a man can look as he said: —

"To-morrow, my friend, we must part. You return to your beautiful England, I to some work which may have such an end that we may never meet. Your letter home has been despatched; to-morrow I shall not be here, but all shall be ready for your journey. In the morning come the Szgany, who have some labours of their own here, and also come some Slovaks. When they have gone, my carriage shall come for you, and shall bear you to the Borgo Pass to meet the diligence from Bukovina to Bistritz. But I am in hopes that I shall see more of you at Castle Dracula." I suspected him, and determined to test his sincerity. Sincerity! It seems like a profanation of the word to write it in connection with such a monster, so asked him point-blank: —

"Why may I not go to-night?"

'Because, dear sir, my coachman and horses are away on a mission."

"But I would walk with pleasure. I want to get away at once." He smiled, such a soft, smooth, diabolical smile that I knew there was some trick behind his smoothness. He said: —

"And your baggage?"

"I do not care about it. I can send for it some other time."

The Count stood up, and said, with a sweet courtesy which made me rub my eyes, it seemed so real: —

"You English have a saying which is close to my heart, for its spirit is that which rules our *boyars:* 'Welcome the coming, speed the parting guest.'° Come with me, my dear young friend. Not an hour shall you

---

weird sisters: The three witches that prophesy to Macbeth identify themselves as "Weird Sisters" (*Macbeth* 1.3.32).   ***'Welcome the coming, speed the parting guest':*** From *The Odyssey* as translated by Alexander Pope (1688–1744). Menelaus says to Telemachus, who wishes to return to Ithaca, "True friendship's laws are by this rule express'd, / Welcome the coming, speed the parting guest" (bk. 15, ll.83–84).

wait in my house against your will, though sad am I at your going, and that you so suddenly desire it. Come!" With a stately gravity, he, with the lamp, preceded me down the stairs and along the hall. Suddenly he stopped.

"Hark!"

Close at hand came the howling of many wolves. It was almost as if the sound sprang up at the raising of his hand, just as the music of a great orchestra seems to leap under the bâton of the conductor. After a pause of a moment, he proceeded, in his stately way, to the door, drew back the ponderous bolts, unhooked the heavy chains, and began to draw it open.

To my intense astonishment I saw that it was unlocked. Suspiciously I looked all round, but could see no key of any kind.

As the door began to open, the howling of the wolves without grew louder and angrier; their red jaws, with champing teeth, and their blunt-clawed feet as they leaped, came in through the opening door. I knew then that to struggle at the moment against the Count was useless. With such allies as these at his command, I could do nothing. But still the door continued slowly to open, and only the Count's body stood in the gap. Suddenly it struck me that this might be the moment and the means of my doom; I was to be given to the wolves, and at my own instigation. There was a diabolical wickedness in the idea great enough for the Count, and as a last chance I cried out: —

"Shut the door; I shall wait till morning!" and covered my face with my hands to hide my tears of bitter disappointment. With one sweep of his powerful arm, the Count threw the door shut, and the great bolts clanged and echoed through the hall as they shot back into their places.

In silence we returned to the library, and after a minute or two I went to my own room. The last I saw of Count Dracula was his kissing his hand to me; with a red light of triumph in his eyes, and with a smile that Judas in hell might be proud of.

When I was in my room and about to lie down, I thought I heard a whispering at my door. I went to it softly and listened. Unless my ears deceived me, I heard the voice of the Count: —

"Back, back, to your own place! Your time is not yet come. Wait. Have patience. To-morrow night, to-morrow night, is yours!" There was a low, sweet ripple of laughter, and in a rage I threw open the door, and saw without the three terrible women licking their lips. As I appeared they all joined in a horrible laugh, and ran away.

I came back to my room and threw myself on my knees. It is then so near the end? To-morrow! to-morrow! Lord, help me, and those to whom I am dear!

30 *June, morning.* — These may be the last words I ever write in this diary. I slept till just before the dawn, and when I woke threw myself on my knees, for I determined that if Death came he should find me ready.

At last I felt that subtle change in the air, and knew that the morning had come. Then came the welcome cock-crow, and I felt that I was safe. With a glad heart, I opened my door and ran down to the hall. I had seen that the door was unlocked, and now escape was before me. With hands that trembled with eagerness, I unhooked the chains and drew back the massive bolts.

But the door would not move. Despair seized me. I pulled, and pulled, at the door, and shook it till, massive as it was, it rattled in its casement. I could see the bolt shot. It had been locked after I left the Count.

Then a wild desire took me to obtain that key at any risk, and I determined then and there to scale the wall again and gain the Count's room. He might kill me, but death now seemed the happier choice of evils. Without a pause I rushed up to the east window, and scrambled down the wall, as before, into the Count's room. It was empty, but that was as I expected. I could not see a key anywhere, but the heap of gold remained. I went through the door in the corner and down the winding stair and along the dark passage to the old chapel. I knew now well enough where to find the monster I sought.

The great box was in the same place, close against the wall, but the lid was laid on it, not fastened down, but with the nails ready in their places to be hammered home. I knew I must search the body for the key, so I raised the lid, and laid it back against the wall; and then I saw something which filled my very soul with horror. There lay the Count, but looking as if his youth had been half renewed, for the white hair and moustache were changed to dark iron-grey; the cheeks were fuller, and the white skin seemed ruby-red underneath; the mouth was redder than ever, for on the lips were gouts of fresh blood, which trickled from the corners of the mouth and ran over the chin and neck. Even the deep, burning eyes seemed set amongst swollen flesh, for the lids and pouches underneath were bloated. It seemed as if the whole awful creature were simply gorged with blood; he lay like a filthy leech, exhausted with his repletion. I shuddered as I bent over to touch him, and every sense in me revolted at the contact; but I had to search, or I was lost.

The coming night might see my own body a banquet in a similar way to those horrid three. I felt all over the body, but no sign could I find of the key. Then I stopped and looked at the Count. There was a mocking smile on the bloated face which seemed to drive me mad. This was the being I was helping to transfer to London, where, perhaps, for centuries to come he might, amongst its teeming millions, satiate his lust for blood, and create a new and ever-widening circle of semi-demons to batten° on the helpless. The very thought drove me mad. A terrible desire came upon me to rid the world of such a monster. There was no lethal weapon at hand, but I seized a shovel which the workmen had been using to fill the cases, and lifting it high struck, with the edge downward, at the hateful face. But as I did so the head turned, and the eyes fell full upon me, with all their blaze of basilisk° horror. The sight seemed to paralyse me, and the shovel turned in my hand and glanced from the face, merely making a deep gash above the forehead. The shovel fell from my hand across the box, and as I pulled it away the flange of the blade caught the edge of the lid, which fell over again, and hid the horrid thing from my sight. The last glimpse I had was of the bloated face, blood-stained and fixed with a grin of malice which would have held its own in the nethermost hell.

I thought and thought what should be my next move, but my brain seemed on fire, and I waited with a despairing feeling growing over me. As I waited I heard in the distance a gypsy song sung by merry voices coming closer, and through their song the rolling of heavy wheels and the cracking of whips; the Szgany and the Slovaks of whom the Count had spoken were coming. With a last look around and at the box which contained the vile body, I ran from the place and gained the Count's room, determined to rush out at the moment the door should be opened. With strained ears, I listened, and heard downstairs the grinding of the key in the great lock and the falling back of the heavy door. There must have been some other means of entry, or some one had a key for one of the locked doors. Then there came the sound of many feet tramping and dying away in some passage which sent up a clanging echo. I turned to run down again towards the vault, where I might find the new entrance; but at the moment there seemed to come a violent puff of wind, and the door to the winding stair blew to with a shock

---

batten: To feed gluttonously; to prosper at the expense of another (*OED*). Though linguistically not related to *bat,* the word Harker uses contains within it, unbeknownst to him, one of Dracula's primary manifestations.　　**basilisk:** A mythical reptile whose gaze is deadly.

that set the dust from the lintels flying. When I ran to push it open, I found that it was hopelessly fast. I was again a prisoner, and the net of doom was closing round me more closely.

As I write there is in the passage below a sound of many tramping feet and the crash of weights being set down heavily, doubtless the boxes, with their freight of earth. There is a sound of hammering; it is the box being nailed down. Now I can hear the heavy feet tramping again along the hall, with many other idle feet coming behind them.

The door is shut, and the chains rattle; there is a grinding of the key in the lock; I can hear the key withdrawn: then another door opens and shuts; I hear the creaking of lock and bolt.

Hark! in the courtyard and down the rocky way the roll of heavy wheels, the crack of whips, and the chorus of the Szgany as they pass into the distance.

I am alone in the castle with those awful women. Faugh!° Mina is a woman, and there is nought in common. They are devils of the Pit!

I shall not remain alone with them; I shall try to scale the castle wall farther than I have yet attempted. I shall take some of the gold with me, lest I want it later. I may find a way from this dreadful place.

And then away for home! away to the quickest and nearest train! away from this cursed spot, from this cursed land, where the devil and his children still walk with earthly feet!

At least God's mercy is better than that of these monsters, and the precipice is steep and high. At its foot a man may sleep — as a man. Good-bye, all! Mina!

CHAPTER V. LETTER FROM MISS MINA MURRAY TO MISS LUCY WESTENRA

"*9 May*

"My dearest Lucy, —

"Forgive my long delay in writing, but I have been simply over-whelmed with work. The life of an assistant schoolmistress is sometimes trying. I am longing to be with you, and by the sea, where we can talk together freely and build our castles in the air. I have been working very hard lately, because I want to keep up with Jonathan's studies, and I have been practising shorthand very assiduously. When we are married I shall be able to be useful to Jonathan, and if I can stenograph well

Faugh: Exclamation of disgust.

enough I can take down what he wants to say in this way and write it out for him on the typewriter,° at which also I am practising very hard. He and I sometimes write letters in shorthand, and he is keeping a stenographic journal of his travels abroad. When I am with you I shall keep a diary in the same way. I don't mean one of those two-pages-to-the-week-with-Sunday-squeezed-in-a-corner diaries, but a sort of journal which I can write in whenever I feel inclined. I do not suppose there will be much of interest to other people; but it is not intended for them. I may show it to Jonathan some day if there is in it anything worth sharing, but it is really an exercise book. I shall try to do what I see lady journalists do: interviewing and writing descriptions and trying to remember conversations. I am told that, with a little practice, one can remember all that goes on or that one hears said during a day. However, we shall see. I shall tell you all my little plans when we meet. I have just had a few hurried lines from Jonathan from Transylvania. He is well, and will be returning in about a week. I am longing to hear all his news. It must be so nice to see strange countries. I wonder if we — I mean Jonathan and I — shall ever see them together. There is the ten o'clock bell ringing. Good-bye.

"Your loving
"MINA.

"Tell me all the news when you write. You have not told me anything for a long time. I hear rumours, and especially of a tall, handsome, curly-haired man???"

Letter, Lucy Westenra to Mina Murray

"17, *Chatham Street,*
"*Wednesday*

"My dearest Mina, —

"I must say you tax me *very* unfairly with being a bad correspondent. I wrote to you *twice* since we parted, and your last letter was only your *second*. Besides, I have nothing to tell you. There is really nothing to interest you. Town is very pleasant just now, and we go a good deal to picture-galleries and for walks and rides in the park. As to the tall,

---

typewriter: A writing machine that produces characters resembling those printed by a press. The first mass-produced typewriters were manufactured by the American gunmaker Remington starting in 1875 (*Enc. Brit.* 11th 27: 501).

curly-haired man, I suppose it was the one who was with me at the last Pop.° Some one has evidently been telling tales. That was Mr. Holmwood. He often comes to see us, and he and mamma get on very well together; they have so many things to talk about in common. We met some time ago a man that would just *do for you,* if you were not already engaged to Jonathan. He is an excellent *parti,°* being handsome, well off, and of good birth. He is a doctor and really clever. Just fancy! He is only nine-and-twenty, and he has an immense lunatic asylum all under his own care. Mr. Holmwood introduced him to me, and he called here to see us, and often comes now. I think he is one of the most resolute men I ever saw, and yet the most calm. He seems absolutely imperturbable. I can fancy what a wonderful power he must have over his patients. He has a curious habit of looking one straight in the face, as if trying to read one's thoughts. He tries this on very much with me, but I flatter myself he has got a tough nut to crack. I know that from my glass. Do you ever try to read your own face? *I do,* and I can tell you it is not a bad study, and gives you more trouble than you can well fancy if you have never tried it. He says that I afford him a curious psychological study, and I humbly think I do. I do not, as you know, take sufficient interest in dress to be able to describe the new fashions. Dress is a bore. That is slang again, but never mind; Arthur says that every day. There, it is all out. Mina, we have told all our secrets to each other since we were *children;* we have slept together and eaten together, and laughed and cried together; and now, though I have spoken, I would like to speak more. Oh, Mina, couldn't you guess? I love him. I am blushing as I write, for although I *think* he loves me, he has not told me so in words. But oh, Mina, I love him; I love him; I love him! There, that does me good. I wish I were with you, dear, sitting by the fire undressing, as we used to sit; and I would try to tell you what I feel. I do not know how I am writing this even to you. I am afraid to stop, or I should tear up the letter, and I don't want to stop, for I *do so* want to tell you all. Let me hear from you *at once,* and tell me all that you think about it. Mina, I must go. Good-night. Bless me in your prayers; and, Mina, pray for my happiness.

"Lucy.

"P.S. — I need not tell you this is a secret. Good-night again.

"L."

Pop: A popular concert.   *parti:* A marriageable person (*OED* OL).

Letter, Lucy Westenra to Mina Murray

"24 May

"My dearest Mina, —

"Thanks, and thanks, and thanks again for your sweet letter! It was so nice to be able to tell you and to have your sympathy.

"My dear, it never rains but it pours. How true the old proverbs are. Here am I, who shall be twenty in September, and yet I never had a proposal till to-day, not a real proposal, and to-day I have had three. Just fancy! THREE proposals in one day! Isn't it awful! I feel sorry, really and truly sorry, for two of the poor fellows. Oh, Mina, I am so happy that I don't know what to do with myself. And three proposals! But, for goodness' sake, don't tell any of the girls, or they would be getting all sorts of extravagant ideas and imagining themselves injured and slighted if in their very first day at home they did not get six at least. Some girls are so vain. You and I, Mina dear, who are engaged and are going to settle down soon soberly into old married women, can despise vanity. Well, I must tell you about the three, but you must keep it a secret, dear, from *every one*, except, of course, Jonathan. You will tell him, because I would, if I were in your place, certainly tell Arthur. A woman ought to tell her husband everything — don't you think so, dear? — and I must be fair. Men like women, certainly their wives, to be quite as fair as they are; and women, I am afraid, are not always quite as fair as they should be. Well, my dear, number One came just before lunch. I told you of him, Dr. John Seward, the lunatic-asylum man, with the strong jaw and the good forehead. He was very cool out-wardly, but was nervous all the same. He had evidently been schooling himself as to all sorts of little things, and remembered them; but he almost managed to sit down on his silk hat, which men don't generally do when they are cool, and then when he wanted to appear at ease he kept playing with a lancet in a way that made me nearly scream. He spoke to me, Mina, very straightforwardly. He told me how dear I was to him, though he had known me so little, and what his life would be with me to help and cheer him. He was going to tell me how unhappy he would be if I did not care for him, but when he saw me cry he said that he was a brute and would not add to my present trouble. Then he broke off and asked if I could love him in time; and when I shook my head his hands trembled and then with some hesitation he asked me if I cared already for any one else. He put it very nicely, saying that he did not want to wring my confidence from me, but only to know, because if a woman's heart was free a man might have hope. And then, Mina, I felt it a sort of duty to tell him that there was some one. I only told him that much, and then he stood up, and he looked very strong and very grave as he took both my hands in his and said he hoped I would be happy, and that if I ever wanted a friend I must count him one of my best. Oh, Mina dear, I can't help crying; and you must excuse this letter being all blotted. Being proposed to is all very nice and all that sort of thing, but it isn't at all a happy thing when you have to see a poor fellow, whom you know loves you honestly, going away and looking all broken-hearted, and to know that, no matter what he may say at the moment, you are passing quite out of his life. My dear, I must stop here at present, I feel so miserable, though I am so happy.

> "*Evening*.

"Arthur has just gone, and I feel in better spirits than when I left off, so I can go on telling you about the day. Well, my dear, number two came after lunch. He is such a nice fellow, an American from Texas, and he looks so young and so fresh that it seems almost impossible that he has been to so many places and has had such adventures. I sympathise with poor Desdemona when she had such a dangerous stream poured in her ear, even by a black man.° I suppose that we women are such cowards that we think a man will save us from fears, and we marry him. I know now what I would do if I were a man and wanted to make a girl love me. No, I don't, for there was Mr. Morris telling us his stories, and Arthur never told any, and yet — My dear, I am somewhat previous. Mr. Quincey P. Morris found me alone. It seems that a man always does find a girl alone. No, he doesn't, for Arthur tried twice to *make* a chance, and I helping him all I could; I am not ashamed to say it now. I must tell you beforehand that Mr. Morris doesn't always speak slang — that is to say, he never does so to strangers or before them, for he is really well educated and has exquisite manners — but he found out that it amused me to hear him talk American slang, and whenever I was present, and there was no one to be shocked, he said such funny things. I am afraid, my dear, he has to invent it all, for it fits exactly into whatever else he has to say. But this is a way slang has. I do not know myself if I shall ever speak slang; I do not know if Arthur likes it, as I have never heard him use any as yet. Well, Mr. Morris sat down beside me and looked as happy and jolly as he could, but I could see all the

---

poor Desdemona . . . black man: In Shakespeare's *Othello*, the Moor Othello woos Desdemona by telling her stories of his adventures. The "dangerous stream," however, calls up the murder of Hamlet's father by poison poured into his ear.

same that he was very nervous. He took my hand in his, and said ever so sweetly: —

"'Miss Lucy, I know I ain't good enough to regulate the fixin's of your little shoes, but I guess if you wait till you find a man that is you will go join them seven young women with the lamps° when you quit. Won't you just hitch up alongside of me and let us go down the long road together, driving in double harness?'

"Well, he did look so good-humoured and so jolly that it didn't seem half so hard to refuse him as it did poor Dr. Seward, so I said, as lightly as I could, that I did not know anything of hitching, and that I wasn't broken to harness at all yet. Then he said that he had spoken in a light manner, and he hoped that if he had made a mistake in doing so on so grave, so momentous, an occasion for him, I would forgive him. He really did look serious when he was saying it, and I couldn't help feeling a bit serious too — I know, Mina, you will think me a horrid flirt — though I couldn't help feeling a sort of exultation that he was number two in one day. And then, my dear, before I could say a word he began pouring out a perfect torrent of love-making, laying his very heart and soul at my feet. He looked so earnest over it that I shall never again think that a man must be playful always, and never earnest, because he is merry at times. I suppose he saw something in my face which checked him, for he suddenly stopped, and said with a sort of manly fervour that I could have loved him for if I had been free: —

"'Lucy, you are an honest-hearted girl, I know. I should not be here speaking to you as I am now if I did not believe you clean grit, right through to the very depths of your soul. Tell me, like one good fellow to another, is there any one else that you care for? And if there is I'll never trouble you a hair's breadth again, but will be, if you let me, a very faithful friend.'

My dear Mina, why are men so noble when we women are so little worthy of them? Here was I almost making fun of this great-hearted, true gentleman. I burst into tears — I am afraid, my dear, you will think this a very sloppy letter in more ways than one — and I really felt very badly. Why can't they let a girl marry three men, or as many as want her, and save all this trouble? But this is heresy, and I must not say it. I am glad to say that, though I was crying, I was able to look into Mr. Morris's brave eyes, and I told him out straight: —

---

seven young women with the lamps: Morris is probably referring in a confused way to the parable of the five wise and five foolish virgins, who are, respectively, accepted and turned away by the bridegroom (Matt. 25.1–12).

" 'Yes, there is some one I love, though he has not told me yet that he even loves me.' I was right to speak to him so frankly, for quite a light came into his face, and he put out both his hands and took mine — I think I put them into his — and said in a hearty way: —

" 'That's my brave girl. It's better worth being late for a chance of winning you than being in time for any other girl in the world. Don't cry, my dear. If it's for me, I'm a hard nut to crack; and I take it standing up. If that other fellow doesn't know his happiness, well, he'd better look for it soon, or he'll have to deal with me. Little girl, your honesty and pluck have made me a friend, and that's rarer than a lover; it's more unselfish anyhow. My dear, I'm going to have a pretty lonely walk between this and Kingdom Come. Won't you give me one kiss? It'll be something to keep off the darkness now and then. You can, you know, if you like, for that other good fellow — he must be a good fellow, my dear, and a fine fellow, or you could not love him — hasn't spoken yet.' That quite won me, Mina, for it *was* brave and sweet of him, and noble, too, to a rival — wasn't it? — and he so sad; so I leant over and kissed him. He stood up with my two hands in his, and as he looked down into my face — I am afraid I was blushing very much — he said: —

" 'Little girl, I hold your hand, and you've kissed me, and if these things don't make us friends nothing ever will. Thank you for your sweet honesty to me, and good-bye.' He wrung my hand, and taking up his hat, went straight out of the room without looking back, without a tear or a quiver or a pause; and I am crying like a baby. Oh, why must a man like that be made unhappy when there are lots of girls about who would worship the very ground he trod on? I know I would if I were free — only I don't want to be free. My dear, this quite upset me, and I feel I cannot write of happiness just at once, after telling you of it; and I don't wish to tell of the number three till it can be all happy.
"Ever your loving
"LUCY.

"P.S. — Oh, about number three — I needn't tell you of number three, need I? Besides, it was all so confused; it seemed only a moment from his coming into the room till both his arms were round me, and he was kissing me. I am very, very happy, and I don't know what I have done to deserve it. I must only try in the future to show that I am not ungrateful for all His goodness to me in sending to me such a lover, such a husband, and such a friend.
"Good-bye."

Dr. Seward's Diary
(Kept in phonograph°)

25 April.° — Ebb tide in appetite to-day. Cannot eat, cannot rest, so diary instead. Since my rebuff of yesterday I have a sort of empty feeling; nothing in the world seems of sufficient importance to be worth the doing. . . . . As I knew that the only cure for this sort of thing was work, I went down amongst the patients. I picked out one who has afforded me a study of much interest. He is so quaint in his ideas, and so unlike the normal lunatic, that I have determined to understand him as well as I can. To-day I seemed to get nearer than ever before to the heart of his mystery.

I questioned him more fully than I had ever done, with a view to making myself master of the facts of his hallucination. In my manner of doing it there was, I now see, something of cruelty. I seemed to wish to keep him to the point of his madness — a thing which I avoid with the patients as I would the mouth of hell. (*Mem.,* under what circumstances would I *not* avoid the pit of hell?) *Omnia Romæ venalia sunt.°* Hell has its price! *verb. sap.°* If there be anything behind this instinct it will be valuable to trace it afterwards *accurately,* so I had better commence to do so, therefore —

R. M. Renfield, ætat 59.° — Sanguine° temperament; great physical strength; morbidly excitable; periods of gloom ending in some fixed idea which I cannot make out. I presume that the sanguine temperament itself and the disturbing influence end in a mentally-accomplished finish; a possibly dangerous man, probably dangerous if unselfish. In selfish men caution is as secure an armour for their foes as for themselves. What I think of on this point is, when self is the fixed point the centripetal force is balanced with the centrifugal; when duty, a cause, etc., is the fixed point, the latter force is paramount, and only accident or a series of accidents can balance it.

---

phonograph: An instrument for reproducing sounds that stores them as grooves on a surface, such as wax. The first phonograph was invented by Thomas Edison in 1877, but his improved wax-cylinder machine came over a decade later (*Enc. Brit.* 11th 21: 467). *25 April:* The error in the dating (the month is May) could be Seward's mistake, Stoker's slip, or one introduced during Mina's transcribing. Similar errors of indeterminate origin occur in Chapters 9 and 12.   *Omnia Romæ venalia sunt:* All Romans are venal (Latin).   *verb. sap.:* An abbreviation of *verbum sapienti sat est* (Latin); a word is enough for a wise person.   *ætat 59:* Aged 59 (Latin).   *Sanguine:* Often used to refer to the hopeful, confident temperament and the ruddy complexion of a person whose controlling humor, or bodily fluid, is blood. Seward is mistaken in applying the term to Renfield's temperament, which is choleric, that is, irascible or angry (*OED*).

Letter, Quincey P. Morris to Hon. Arthur Holmwood

"*25 May*

"My dear Art, —

"We've told yarns by the camp-fire in the prairies; and dressed one another's wounds after trying a landing at the Marquesas°; and drunk healths on the shore of Titicaca.° There are more yarns to be told, and other wounds to be healed, and another health to be drunk. Won't you let this be at my camp-fire to-morrow night? I have no hesitation in asking you, as I know a certain lady is engaged to a certain dinner-party, and that you are free. There will only be one other, our old pal at the Korea,° Jack Seward. He's coming, too, and we both want to mingle our weeps over the wine-cup, and to drink a health with all our hearts to the happiest man in all the wide world, who has won the noblest heart that God has made and the best worth winning. We promise you a hearty welcome, and a loving greeting, and a health as true as your own right hand. We shall both swear to leave you at home if you drink too deep to a certain pair of eyes. Come!

"Yours, as ever and always,
"QUINCEY P. MORRIS."

Telegram from Arthur Holmwood to Quincey P. Morris

"*26 May*

"Count me in every time. I bear messages which will make both your ears tingle.

"ART."

CHAPTER VI. MINA MURRAY'S JOURNAL

24 July. Whitby. — Lucy met me at the station, looking sweeter and lovelier than ever, and we drove up to the house at the Crescent in which they have rooms. This is a lovely place. The little river, the Esk, runs through a deep valley, which broadens out as it comes near the harbour. A great viaduct runs across, with high piers, through which the view seems somehow further away than it really is. The valley is

---

Marquesas: Islands in the South Pacific annexed by the French in 1842 (*Enc. Brit.* 11th). *Titicaca:* The second largest lake in South America, located in the Andes Mountains (*Enc. Brit.* OL).   *Korea:* The Asian country may have been another exotic place the correspondents visited; or it could be the name of a club or other establishment, probably fictitious, where the three men have socialized.

beautifully green, and it is so steep that when you are on the high land on either side you look right across it, unless you are near enough to see down. The houses of the old town — the side away from us — are all red-roofed, and seem piled up one over the other anyhow, like the pictures we see of Nuremberg. Right over the town is the ruin of Whitby Abbey,° which was sacked by the Danes, and which is the scene of part of "Marmion," where the girl was built up in the wall.° It is a most noble ruin, of immense size, and full of beautiful and romantic bits; there is a legend that a white lady is seen in one of the windows. Between it and the town there is another church, the parish one, round which is a big graveyard, all full of tombstones. This is to my mind the nicest spot in Whitby, for it lies right over the town, and has a full view of the harbour and all up the bay to where the headland called Kettleness stretches out into the sea. It descends so steeply over the harbour that part of the bank has fallen away, and some of the graves have been destroyed. In one place part of the stonework of the graves stretches out over the sandy pathway far below. There are walks, with seats beside them, through the churchyard; and people go and sit there all day long looking at the beautiful view and enjoying the breeze. I shall come and sit here very often myself and work. Indeed, I am writing now, with my book on my knee, and listening to the talk of three old men who are sitting beside me. They seem to do nothing all day but sit up here and talk.

The harbour lies below me, with, on the far side, one long granite wall stretching out into the sea, with a curve outwards at the end of it, in the middle of which is a lighthouse. A heavy sea-wall runs along outside of it. On the near side, the sea-wall makes an elbow crooked inversely, and its end too has a lighthouse. Between the two piers there is a narrow opening into the harbour, which then suddenly widens.

It is nice at high tide; but when the tide is out it shoals away to nothing, and there is merely the stream of the Esk, running between banks of sand, with rocks here and there. Outside the harbour on this side there rises for about half a mile a great reef, the sharp edge of which runs straight out from behind the south lighthouse. At the end of it is a buoy with a bell, which swings in bad weather, and sends in a mournful sound on the wind. They have a legend here that when a ship is lost bells are heard out at sea. I must ask the old man about this; he is coming this way. . . . .

Whitby Abbey: Founded by Oswy, King of Northumbria, in 658. In Stoker's time the ruins of the abbey were one of Whitby's tourist attractions (*Enc. Brit.* 11th).   ***"Marmion," where the girl was built in the wall:*** In Sir Walter Scott's poem "Marmion," the nun Constance de Beverly is bricked up alive in the dungeon of Whitby Abbey as punishment for breaking her holy vows by leaving the abbey to follow her lover, Marmion.

He is a funny old man. He must be awfully old, for his face is all gnarled and twisted like the bark of a tree. He tells me that he is nearly a hundred, and that he was a sailor in the Greenland fishing fleet when Waterloo° was fought. He is, I am afraid, a very sceptical person, for when I asked him about the bells at sea and the White Lady at the abbey he said very brusquely: —

"I wouldn't fash masel'° about them, miss. Them things be all wore out. Mind, I don't say that they never was, but I do say that they wasn't in my time. They be all very well for comers and trippers an' the like, but not for a nice young lady like you. Them feet-folks° from York and Leeds that be always eatin' cured herrin's an' drinkin' tea an' lookin' out to buy cheap jet° would creed aught.° I wonder masel' who'd be bothered tellin' lies to them — even the newspapers, which is full of fool-talk." I thought he would be a good person to learn interesting things from, so I asked him if he would mind telling me something about the whale-fishing in the old days. He was just settling himself to begin when the clock struck six, whereupon he laboured to get up, and said: —

"I must gang ageeanwards° home now, miss. My grand-daughter doesn't like to be kept waitin' when the tea is ready, for it takes me time to crammle aboon the grees,° for there be a many of 'em; an', miss, I lack belly-timber° sairly° by the clock."

He hobbled away, and I could see him hurrying, as well as he could, down the steps. The steps are a great feature of the place. They lead from the town up to the church; there are hundreds of them — I do not know how many — and they wind up in a delicate curve; the slope is so gentle that a horse could easily walk up and down them. I think they must originally have had something to do with the Abbey. I shall go home too. Lucy went out visiting with her mother, and as they were only duty calls, I did not go. They will be home by this.

1 *August.* — I came up here an hour ago with Lucy, and we had a most interesting talk with my old friend and the two others who always come and join him. He is evidently the Sir Oracle° of them, and I

Waterloo: The town in Belgium where Napoleon suffered his final defeat in 1815.   ***fash masel':*** Trouble or inconvenience myself (dialect).   ***feet-folks:*** Walkers, that is, tourists (dialect).   ***jet:*** A black stone that is cut and polished for use in jewelry making. In Stoker's time the manufacture of jet was one of Whitby's principal industries (*Enc. Brit.* 11th).   ***creed aught:*** Believe anything (dialect).   ***ageeanwards:*** Toward (dialect).   ***crammle aboon the grees:*** Hobble up the stairs (dialect).   ***belly-timber:*** Food (dialect).   ***sairly:*** Sorely (dialect).   ***Sir Oracle:*** In *The Merchant of Venice,* Gratiano mocks men who wish to appear wise and grave, describing them as ones who say, "I am Sir Oracle, / And when I ope my lips let no dog bark" (*The Merchant of Venice* 1.1.93–94).

should think must have been in his time a most dictatorial person. He will not admit anything, and downfaces everybody. If he can't out-argue them he bullies them, and then takes their silence for agreement with his views. Lucy was looking sweetly pretty in her white lawn frock°; she has got a beautiful colour since she has been here. I noticed that the old men did not lose any time in coming up and sitting near her when we sat down. She is so sweet with old people; I think they all fell in love with her on the spot. Even my old man succumbed and did not contradict her, but gave me double share instead. I got him on the subject of the legends, and he went off at once into a sort of sermon. I must try to remember it and put it down: —

"It be all fool-talk, lock, stock, and barrel; that's what it be, an' nowt else. These bans° an' wafts an' boh-ghosts an' bar-guests an' bogles° an' all anent° them is only fit to set bairns° an' dizzy women a-belderin'.° They be nowt but air-blebs!° They, an' all grims° an signs an' warnin's, be all invented by parsons an' illsome beuk-bodies° an' railway touters° to skeer an' scunner° hafflin's,° an' to get folks to do somethin' that they don't other incline to. It makes me ireful° to think o' them. Why, it's them that, not content with printin' lies on paper an' preachin' them out of pulpits, does want to be cuttin' them on the tombsteans. Look here all around you in what airt° ye will; all them steans, holdin' up their heads as well as they can out of their pride, is acant° — simply tumblin' down with the weight o' the lies wrote on them, 'Here lies the body' or 'Sacred to the memory' wrote on all of them, an' yet in nigh half of them there bean't no bodies at all; an' the memories of them bean't cared a pinch of snuff about, much less sacred. Lies all of them, nothin' but lies of one kind or another! My gog,° but it'll be a quare scowderment° at the Day of Judgment when they come tumblin' up here in their deathsarks,° all jouped° together an' tryin' to drag their tombsteans with them to prove how good they was; some of them trimmlin' and ditherin',° with their hands that

---

lawn frock: A dress made of fine linen (*OED*).   *bans:* Curses (dialect).   *wafts . . .* *bogles:* Types of specters, ghosts, or hobgoblins (dialect).   *anent:* In company with, on par with (dialect).   *bairns:* Children (dialect).   *a-belderin':* Crying, making a commotion (dialect).   *air-blebs:* Air bubbles (dialect).   *grims:* Apparitions (dialect). *beuk-bodies:* "Book-bodies," learned persons (dialect).   *touters:* One who canvasses for customers or clients (*OED* OL).   *scunner:* To frighten (dialect).   *hafflin's:* Halflings, people not fully grown (dialect).   *ireful:* Full of ire, angry (*OED* OL). *airt:* Direction, quarter of the compass (dialect).   *acant:* Leaning to one side (dialect). *gog:* God (dialect).   *quare scowderment:* Queer confusion, peculiar turmoil (dialect). *deathsarks:* Shrouds (dialect).   *jouped:* Splashed (dialect).   *trimmlin' and ditherin':* Trembling and shaking (dialect).

dozzened an' slippy° from lyin' in the sea that they can't even keep their grup° o' them."

I could see from the old fellow's self-satisfied air and the way in which he looked round for the approval of his cronies that he was "showing off," so I put in a word to keep him going: —

"Oh, Mr. Swales, you can't be serious. Surely these tombstones are not all wrong?"

"Yabblins!° There may be a poorish few not wrong, savin' where they make out the people too good; for there be folk that do think a balm-bowl° be like the sea, if only it be their own. The whole thing be only lies. Now look you here; you come here a stranger, an' you see this kirk-garth.'° I nodded, for I thought it better to assent, though I did not quite understand his dialect. I knew it had something to do with the church. He went on: "And you consate° that all these steans be aboon° folk that be happed° here, snod an' snog?"° I assented again. "Then that be just where the lie comes in. Why, there be scores of these lay-beds° that be toom° as old Dun's 'bacca-box° on Friday night." He nudged one of his companions, and they all laughed. "And my gog! how could they be otherwise? Look at that one, the aftest abaft the bier-bank°; read it!" I went over and read: —

"Edward Spencelagh, master mariner, murdered by pirates off the coast of Andres, April, 1854, æt. 30." When I came back Mr. Swales went on: —

"Who brought him home, I wonder, to hap him here? Murdered off the coast of Andres! an' you consated his body lay under! Why, I could name ye a dozen whose bones lie in the Greenland seas above" — he pointed northwards — "or where the currents may have drifted them. There be the steans around ye. Ye can, with your young eyes, read the small-print of the lies from here. This Braithwaite Lowrey — I knew his father, lost in the *Lively* off Greenland in '20; or Andrew Woodhouse, drowned in the same seas in 1777; or John Paxton, drowned off Cape Farewell a year later; or old John Rawlings, whose grandfather sailed with me, drowned in the Gulf of Finland in '50. Do ye think that all these men will have to make a rush to Whitby

---

dozzened an' slippy: Shriveled (dialect) and slippery.   *grup:* Grip (dialect).   *Yabblins:* Gabblings, jabberings, rapid and incoherent speech (dialect).   *balm-bowl:* Chamber pot (dialect).   *kirk-garth:* Churchyard (dialect).   *consate:* Think, conceive a notion or thought (dialect).   *aboon:* Above (dialect).   *happed:* Covered (dialect).   *snod an' snog:* Snug and tidy (dialect).   *lay-beds:* Graves (dialect).   *toom:* Empty (dialect). *'bacca-box:* Tobacco box (dialect).   *aftest abaft the bier-bank:* Furthest past the churchyard path along which a bier and coffin can be carried (dialect).

when the trumpet sounds? I have me antherums° aboot it! I tell ye that
when they got here they'd be jommlin' an' jostlin' one another that
way that it ud be like a fight up on the ice in the old days, when we'd be
at one another from daylight to dark, an' tryin' to tie up our cuts by the
light of the aurora borealis." This was evidently local pleasantry, for the
old man cackled over it, and his cronies joined in with gusto.

"But," I said, "surely you are not quite correct, for you start on the
assumption that all the poor people, or their spirits, will have to take
their tombstones with them on the Day of Judgment. Do you think
that will be really necessary?"

"Well, what else be they tombsteans for? Answer me that, miss!"

"To please their relatives, I suppose."

"To please their relatives, you suppose!" This he said with intense
scorn. "How will it pleasure their relatives to know that lies is wrote
over them, and that everybody in the place knows that they be lies?" He
pointed to a stone at our feet which had been laid down as a slab, on
which the seat was rested, close to the edge of the cliff. "Read the lines
on that thruff-stean,"° he said. The letters were upside down to me
from where I sat, but Lucy was more opposite to them, so she leant
over and read: —

"Sacred to the memory of George Canon, who died, in the hope of
a glorious resurrection, on July 29, 1873, falling from the rocks at Kettleness. This tomb is erected by his sorrowing mother to her dearly
beloved son. 'He was the only son of his mother, and she was a
widow.'" "Really, Mr. Swales, I don't see anything very funny in that!"
She spoke her comment very gravely and somewhat severely.

"Ye don't see aught funny! Ha! ha! But that's because ye don't
gawm° the sorrowin' mother was a hell-cat that hated him because he
was acrewk'd° — a regular lamiter° he was — an' he hated her so that
he committed suicide in order that she mightn't get an insurance she
put on his life. He blew nigh the top of his head off with an old musket
that they had for scarin' the crows with. 'Twarn't for crows then, for it
brought the clegs° and the dowps° to him. That's the way he fell off the
rocks. And, as to hopes of a glorious resurrection, I've often heard him
say masel' that he hoped he'd go to hell, for his mother was so pious
that she'd be sure to go to heaven, an' he didn't wan't to addle° where
she was. Now isn't that stean at any rate" — he hammered it with his

antherums: Doubts (dialect).   ***thruff-stean:*** Flat gravestone (dialect).   ***gawm:***
Understand (dialect).   *acrewk'd:* Crooked or twisted (dialect).   *lamiter:* Cripple
(dialect).   *clegs:* Horseflies (dialect).   *dowps:* Carion crows (dialect).   *addle:* To
acquire or gain as one's own (dialect).

stick as he spoke — "a pack of lies? and won't it make Gabriel keckle°
when Geordie comes pantin' up the grees° with the tombstean balanced
on his hump, and asks it to be took as evidence!"

I did not know what to say, but Lucy turned the conversation as she
said, rising up: —

"Oh, why did you tell us of this? It is my favourite seat, and I cannot
leave it; and now I find I must go on sitting over the grave of a suicide."

"That won't harm ye, my pretty; an' it may make poor Geordie
gladsome to have so trim a lass sittin' on his lap. That won't hurt ye.
Why, I've sat here off an' on for nigh twenty years past, an' it hasn't
done me no harm. Don't ye fash about them as lies under ye, or that
doesn' lie there either! It'll be time for ye to be getting scart when ye
see the tombsteans all run away with, and the place as bare as a stubble-
field. There's the clock, an' I must gang.° My service to ye, ladies!" And
off he hobbled.

Lucy and I sat a while, and it was all so beautiful before us that we
took hands as we sat; and she told me all over again about Arthur and
their coming marriage. That made me just a little heart-sick, for I
haven't heard from Jonathan for a whole month.

The same day. — I came up here alone, for I am very sad. There was
no letter for me. I hope there cannot be anything the matter with
Jonathan. The clock has just struck nine. I see the lights scattered all
over the town, sometimes in rows where the streets are, and sometimes
singly; they run right up the Esk and die away in the curve of the valley.
To my left the view is cut off by a black line of roof of the old house
next the Abbey. The sheep and lambs are bleating in the fields away
behind me, and there is a clatter of a donkey's hoofs up the paved road
below. The band on the pier is playing a harsh waltz in good time, and
further along the quay there is a Salvation Army meeting in a back
street. Neither of the bands hears the other, but up here I hear and see
them both. I wonder where Jonathan is and if he is thinking of me! I
wish he were here.

Dr. Seward's Diary

5 *June.* — The case of Renfield grows more interesting the more I
get to understand the man. He has certain qualities very largely developed: selfishness, secrecy, and purpose. I wish I could get at what is
the object of the latter. He seems to have some settled scheme of his

---

keckle: Chuckle or giggle (dialect).   *grees:* Stairs (dialect).   *gang:* Go (dialect).

own, but what it is I do not yet know. His redeeming quality is a love of animals, though, indeed, he has such curious turns in it that I sometimes imagine he is only abnormally cruel. His pets are of odd sorts. Just now his hobby is catching flies. He has at present such a quantity that I have had myself to expostulate. To my astonishment, he did not break out into a fury, as I expected, but took the matter in simple seriousness. He thought for a moment, and then said: "May I have three days? I shall clear them away." Of course, I said that would do. I must watch him.

18 *June.* — He has turned his mind now to spiders, and has got several very big fellows in a box. He keeps feeding them with his flies, and the number of the latter is becoming sensibly diminished, although he has used half his food in attracting more flies from outside to his room.

1 *July.* — His spiders are now becoming as great a nuisance as his flies, and to-day I told him that he must get rid of them. He looked very sad at this, so I said that he must clear out some of them, at all events. He cheerfully acquiesced in this, and I gave him the same time as before for reduction. He disgusted me much while with him, for when a horrid blow-fly, bloated with some carrion food, buzzed into the room, he caught it, held it exultingly for a few moments between his finger and thumb, and, before I knew what he was going to do, put it in his mouth and ate it. I scolded him for it, but he argued quietly that it was very good and very wholesome; that it was life, strong life, and gave life to him. This gave me an idea, or the rudiment of one. I must watch how he gets rid of his spiders. He has evidently some deep problem in his mind, for he keeps a little note-book in which he is always jotting down something. Whole pages of it are filled with masses of figures, generally single numbers added up in batches, and then the totals added in batches again, as though he were "focussing" some account, as the auditors put it.

8 *July.* — There is a method in his madness, and the rudimentary idea in my mind is growing. It will be a whole idea soon, and then, oh, unconscious cerebration!° you will have to give the wall to° your conscious brother. I kept away from my friend for a few days, so that I might notice if there were any change. Things remain as they were except that he has parted with some of his pets and got a new one. He

---

unconscious cerebration: The process of thinking without being conscious of thought (*OED* OL). **give the wall to:** Yield deferentially to someone; allow someone to walk on the inner side of the pavement, next to the wall, where the person is more protected (*OED*).

has managed to get a sparrow, and has already partially tamed it. His means of taming is simple, for already the spiders have diminished. Those that do remain, however, are well fed, for he still brings in the flies by tempting them with his food.

19 *July* — We are progressing. My friend has now a whole colony of sparrows, and his flies and spiders are almost obliterated. When I came in he ran to me and said he wanted to ask me a great favour — a very, very great favour; and as he spoke he fawned on me like a dog. I asked him what it was, and he said, with a sort of rapture in his voice and bearing: —

"A kitten, a nice little, sleek, playful kitten, that I can play with, and teach, and feed — and feed — and feed!" I was not unprepared for this request, for I had noticed how his pets went on increasing in size and vivacity, but I did not care that his pretty family of tame sparrows should be wiped out in the same manner as the flies and the spiders; so I said I would see about it, and asked him if he would not rather have a cat than a kitten. His eagerness betrayed him as he answered: —

"Oh yes, I would like a cat! I only asked for a kitten lest you should refuse me a cat. No one would refuse me a kitten, would they?" I shook my head, and said that at present I feared it would not be possible, but that I would see about it. His face fell, and I could see a warning of danger in it, for there was a sudden fierce, sidelong look which meant killing. The man is an undeveloped homicidal maniac. I shall test him with his present craving and see how it will work out; then I shall know more.

10 *p.m.* — I have visited him again and found him sitting in a corner brooding. When I came in he threw himself on his knees before me and implored me to let him have a cat; that his salvation depended upon it. I was firm, however, and told him that he could not have it, whereupon he went without a word, and sat down, gnawing his fingers, in the corner where I had found him. I shall see him in the morning early.

20 *July.* — Visited Renfield very early, before the attendant went his rounds. Found him up and humming a tune. He was spreading out his sugar, which he had saved, in the window, and was manifestly beginning his fly-catching again; and beginning it cheerfully and with a good grace. I looked around for his birds, and not seeing them, asked him where they were. He replied, without turning round, that they had all flown away. There were a few feathers about the room and on his pillow a drop of blood. I said nothing, but went and told the keeper to report to me if there were anything odd about him during the day.

11 *a.m.* — The attendant has just been to me to say that Renfield has been very sick and has disgorged a whole lot of feathers. "My belief is, doctor," he said, "that he has eaten his birds, and that he just took and ate them raw!"

11 *p.m.* — I gave Renfield a strong opiate to-night, enough to make even him sleep, and took away his pocket-book° to look at it. The thought that has been buzzing about my brain lately is complete, and the theory proved. My homicidal maniac is of a peculiar kind. I shall have to invent a new classification for him, and call him a zoophagous (life-eating) maniac; what he desires is to absorb as many lives as he can, and he has laid himself out to achieve it in a cumulative way. He gave many flies to one spider and many spiders to one bird, and then wanted a cat to eat the many birds. What would have been his later steps? It would almost be worth while to complete the experiment. It might be done if there were only a sufficient cause. Men sneered at vivisection, and yet look at its results to-day! Why not advance science in its most difficult and vital aspect — the knowledge of the brain? Had I even the secret of one such mind — did I hold the key to the fancy of even one lunatic — I might advance my own branch of science to a pitch compared with which Burdon-Sanderson's physiology or Ferrier's brain-knowledge° would be as nothing. If only there were a sufficient cause! I must not think too much of this, or I may be tempted; a good cause might turn the scale with me, for may not I too be of an exceptional brain, congenitally?

How well the man reasoned; lunatics always do within their own scope. I wonder at how many lives he values a man, or if at only one. He has closed the account most accurately, and to-day begun a new record. How many of us begin a new record with each day of our lives?

To me it seems only yesterday that my whole life ended with my new hope, and that truly I began a new record. So it will be until the Great Recorder sums me up and closes my ledger account with a balance to profit or loss. Oh, Lucy, Lucy, I cannot be angry with you, nor

---

pocket-book: A small notebook (*OED* OL).   **Burdon-Sanderson's physiology or Ferrier's brain-knowledge:** Sir John Scott Burdon-Sanderson (1828–1905), English physiologist, investigated the cause of diseases such as diphtheria, cattle plague, and cholera. He was criticized by antivivisectionists for supporting medical research on animals. Sir David Ferrier (1843–1928), Scottish physician and first professor of neuropathology at King's College, London, also experimented on live animals, including monkeys, to identify by means of electrical stimulation and other methods the function of different areas of the brain (*Enc. Brit.* 11th). Seward is expressing his temptation to go beyond even these controversial experimenters by using a human subject.

can I be angry with my friend whose happiness is yours; but I must only wait on hopeless and work. Work! work!

If I only could have as strong a cause as my poor mad friend there, a good, unselfish cause to make me work, that would be indeed happiness.

Mina Murray's Journal

26 *July.* — I am anxious, and it soothes me to express myself here; it is like whispering to one's self and listening at the same time. And there is also something about the shorthand symbols that makes it different from writing. I am unhappy about Lucy and about Jonathan. I had not heard from Jonathan for some time, and was very concerned; but yesterday dear Mr. Hawkins, who is always so kind, sent me a letter from him. I had written asking him if he had heard, and he said the enclosed had just been received. It is only a line dated from Castle Dracula, and says that he is just starting for home. That is not like Jonathan; I do not understand it, and it makes me uneasy. Then, too, Lucy, although she is so well, has lately taken to her old habit of walking in her sleep. Her mother has spoken to me about it, and we have decided that I am to lock the door of our room every night. Mrs. Westenra has got an idea that sleep-walkers always go out on roofs of houses and along the edges of cliffs, and then get suddenly wakened and fall over with a despairing cry that echoes all over the place. Poor dear, she is naturally anxious about Lucy, and she tells me that her husband, Lucy's father, had the same habit; that he would get up in the night and dress himself and go out, if he were not stopped. Lucy is to be married in the autumn, and she is already planning out her dresses and how her house is to be arranged. I sympathise with her, for I do the same, only Jonathan and I will start in life in a very simple way, and shall have to try to make both ends meet. Mr. Holmwood — he is the Hon. Arthur Holmwood, only son of Lord Godalming — is coming up here very shortly — as soon as he can leave town, for his father is not very well, and I think dear Lucy is counting the moments till he comes. She wants to take him up to the seat on the churchyard cliff and show him the beauty of Whitby. I daresay it is the waiting which disturbs her; she will be all right when he arrives.

27 *July.* — No news from Jonathan. I am getting quite uneasy about him, though why I should I do not know; but I *do* wish that he would write, if it were only a single line. Lucy walks more than ever, and each night I am awakened by her moving about the room. Fortunately,

the weather is so hot that she cannot get cold; but still the anxiety and the perpetually being wakened is beginning to tell on me, and I am getting nervous and wakeful myself. Thank God, Lucy's health keeps up. Mr. Holmwood has been suddenly called to Ring to see his father, who has been taken seriously ill. Lucy frets at the postponement of seeing him, but it does not touch her looks; she is a trifle stouter, and her cheeks are a lovely rose pink. She has lost that anæmic look which she had. I pray it will all last.

3 *August.* — Another week gone, and no news from Jonathan, not even to Mr. Hawkins, from whom I have heard. Oh, I do hope he is not ill. He surely would have written. I look at that last letter of his, but somehow it does not satisfy me. It does not read like him, and yet it is his writing. There is no mistake of that. Lucy has not walked much in her sleep the last week, but there is an odd concentration about her which I do not understand; even in her sleep she seems to be watching me. She tries the door, and finding it locked, goes about the room searching for the key.

6 *August.* — Another three days, and no news. This suspense is getting dreadful. If I only knew where to write to or where to go to, I should feel easier; but no one has heard a word of Jonathan since that last letter. I must only pray to God for patience. Lucy is more excitable than ever, but is otherwise well. Last night was very threatening, and the fishermen say that we are in for a storm. I must try to watch it and learn the weather signs. To-day is a grey day, and the sun as I write is hidden in thick clouds, high over Kettleness. Everything is grey — except the green grass, which seems like emerald amongst it; grey earthy rock; grey clouds, tinged with the sunburst at the far edge, hang over the grey sea, into which the sand-points stretch like grey fingers. The sea is tumbling in over the shallows and the sandy flats with a roar, muffled in the sea-mists drifting inland. The horizon is lost in a grey mist. All is vastness; the clouds are piled up like giant rocks, and there is a "brool"° over the sea that sounds like some presage of doom. Dark figures are on the beach here and there, sometimes half shrouded in the mist, and seem "men like trees walking."° The fishing-boats are racing for home, and rise and dip in the ground swell as they sweep into the harbour, bending to the scuppers.° Here comes old Mr. Swales. He is making straight for me, and I can see, by the way he lifts his hat, that he wants to talk. . . . .

---

brool: A low humming or murmur (*OED* OL).   *men like trees walking:* In Mark 8.24, a blind man healed by Jesus sees "men as trees, walking."   *scuppers:* "An opening in a ship's side on a level with the deck to allow water to run away" (*OED* OL).

I have been quite touched by the change in the poor old man. When he sat down beside me, he said in a very gentle way: —

"I want to say something to you, miss." I could see he was not at ease, so I took his poor old wrinkled hand in mine and asked him to speak fully; so he said, leaving his hand in mine: —

"I'm afraid, my deary, that I must have shocked you by all the wicked things I've been sayin' about the dead, and such-like, for weeks past; but I didn't mean them, and I want ye to remember that when I'm gone. We aud folks that be daffled, and with one foot abaft the krok-hooal,° don't altogether like to think of it, and we don't want to feel scart of it; an' that's why I've took to makin' light of it, so that I'd cheer up my own heart a bit. But, Lord love ye, miss, I ain't afraid of dyin', not a bit; only I don't want to die if I can help it. My time must be nigh at hand now, for I be aud, and a hundred years is too much for any man to expect; and I'm so nigh it that the Aud Man is already whettin' his scythe. Ye see, I can't get out o' the habit of caffin'° about it all at once; the chafts° will wag as they be used to. Some day soon the Angel of Death will sound his trumpet for me. But don't ye dooal an' greet,° my deary!" — for he saw that I was crying — "if he should come this very night I'd not refuse to answer his call. For life be, after all, only a waitin' for somethin' else than what we're doin'; and death be all that we can rightly depend on. But I'm content, for it's comin' to me, my deary, and comin' quick. It may be comin' while we be lookin' and wonderin'. Maybe it's in that wind out over the sea that's bringin' with it loss and wreck, and sore distress, and sad hearts. Look! look!" he cried suddenly. "There's something in that wind and in the hoast beyont that sounds, and looks, and tastes, and smells like death. It's in the air; I feel it comin'. Lord, make me answer cheerful when my call comes!" He held up his arms devoutly, and raised his hat. His mouth moved as though he were praying. After a few minutes' silence, he got up, shook hands with me, and blessed me, and said good-bye, and hobbled off. It all touched me, and upset me very much.

I was glad when the coastguard came along, with his spy-glass under his arm. He stopped to talk with me, as he always does, but all the time kept looking at a strange ship.

"I can't make her out," he said; "she's a Russian, by the look of her; but she's knocking about in the queerest way. She doesn't know her

---

daffled, and with one foot abaft the krok-hooal: Faltering, and with one foot above the grave (dialect).   ***caffin':*** Chaffing, fretting (dialect).   ***chafts:*** Jaws (dialect).   ***dooal an' greet:*** Show any grief and weep (dialect).

mind a bit; she seems to see the storm coming, but can't decide whether to run up north in the open, or to put in here. Look there again! She is steered mighty strangely, for she doesn't mind the hand on the wheel; changes about with every puff of wind. We'll hear more of her before this time to-morrow."

CHAPTER VII. CUTTING FROM "THE DAILYGRAPH," 8 AUGUST

(Pasted in Mina Murray's Journal)

FROM A CORRESPONDENT

Whitby.

ONE of the greatest and suddenest storms on record has just been experienced here, with results both strange and unique. The weather had been somewhat sultry, but not to any degree uncommon in the month of August. Saturday evening was as fine as was ever known, and the great body of holiday-makers laid out yesterday for visits to Mulgrave Woods, Robin Hood's Bay, Rig Mill, Runswick, Staithes, and the various trips in the neighbourhood of Whitby.° The steamers *Emma* and *Scarborough* made trips up and down the coast, and there was an unusual amount of "tripping" both to and from Whitby. The day was unusually fine till the afternoon, when some of the gossips who frequent the East Cliff churchyard, and from that commanding eminence watch the wide sweep of sea visible to the north and east, called attention to a sudden show of "mares'-tails"° high in the sky to the northwest. The wind was then blowing from the south-west in the mild degree which in barometrical language is ranked "No. 2: light breeze." The coastguard on duty at once made report, and one old fisherman, who for more than half a century has kept watch on weather signs from the East Cliff, foretold in an emphatic manner the coming of a sudden storm. The approach of sunset was so very beautiful, so grand in its masses of splendidly-coloured clouds, that there was quite an assemblage on the walk along the cliff in the old churchyard to enjoy the beauty. Before the sun dipped below the black mass of Kettleness, standing boldly athwart the western sky, its downward way was marked by myriad clouds of every sunset-colour — flame, purple, pink, green, violet, and all the tints of gold; with here and there masses not large,

Mulgrave Woods . . . Whitby: Tourist attractions and villages around Whitby (*Baedeker* 1897).   *mares'-tails:* Cirrus clouds.

but of seemingly absolute blackness, in all sorts of shapes, as well out-lined as colossal silhouettes. The experience was not lost on the painters, and doubtless some of the sketches of the "Prelude to the Great Storm" will grace the R.A. and R.I.° walls in May next. More than one captain made up his mind then and there that his "cobble" or his "mule," as they term the different classes of boats, would remain in the harbour till the storm had passed. The wind fell away entirely dur-ing the evening, and at midnight there was a dead calm, a sultry heat, and that prevailing intensity which, on the approach of thunder, affects persons of a sensitive nature. There were but few lights in sight at sea, for even the coasting steamers, which usually "hug" the shore so closely, kept well to seaward, and but few fishing-boats were in sight. The only sail noticeable was a foreign schooner with all sails set, which was seemingly going westwards. The foolhardiness or ignorance of her officers was a prolific theme for comment whilst she remained in sight, and efforts were made to signal her to reduce sail in face of her danger. Before the night shut down she was seen with sails idly flapping as she gently rolled on the undulating swell of the sea,

"As idle as a painted ship upon a painted ocean."°

Shortly before ten o'clock the stillness of the air grew quite oppres-sive, and the silence was so marked that the bleating of a sheep inland or the barking of a dog in the town was distinctly heard, and the band on the pier, with its lively French air, was like a discord in the great har-mony of nature's silence. A little after midnight came a strange sound from over the sea, and high overhead the air began to carry a strange, faint, hollow booming.

Then without warning the tempest broke. With a rapidity which, at the time, seemed incredible, and even afterwards is impossible to realise, the whole aspect of nature at once became convulsed. The waves rose in growing fury, each overtopping its fellow, till in a very few

---

R.A. and R.I.: The R.A., the Royal Academy of Arts in London, and the R.I., the Royal Institute of Painters in Water-Colours (*Enc. Brit.* 11th; *Baedeker* 1896), both of which held exhibitions in May annually.   **"As idle as a painted ship upon a painted ocean":** After the Mariner kills the Albatross in "The Rime of the Ancient Mariner" by Samuel Taylor Coleridge (1772–1834), the ship is becalmed; as the Mariner tells the Wedding-Guest, "Day after day, day after day, / We stuck, nor breath nor motion; / As idle as a painted ship / Upon a painted ocean" (ll. 116–18). The Mariner also describes a vam-pirelike, undead apparition who comes to the beleaguered vessel: "*Her* lips were red, *her* looks were free, / Her locks were yellow as gold: / Her skin was white as leprosy, / The nightmare LIFE-IN-DEATH was she, / Who thicks man's blood with cold" (ll. 190–94).

minutes the lately glassy sea was like a roaring and devouring monster. White-crested waves beat madly on the level sands and rushed up the shelving cliffs; others broke over the piers, and with their spume swept the lanthorns° of the lighthouses which rise from the end of either pier of Whitby Harbour. The wind roared like thunder, and blew with such force that it was with difficulty that even strong men kept their feet, or clung with grim clasp to the iron stanchions. It was found necessary to clear the entire piers from the mass of onlookers, or else the fatalities of the night would have been increased manifold. To add to the difficulties and dangers of the time, masses of sea-fog came drifting inland — white, wet clouds, which swept by in ghostly fashion, so dank and damp and cold that it needed but little effort of imagination to think that the spirits of those lost at sea were touching their living brethren with the clammy hands of death, and many a one shuddered as the wreaths of sea-mist swept by. At times the mist cleared, and the sea for some distance could be seen in the glare of the lightning, which now came thick and fast, followed by such sudden peals of thunder that the whole sky overhead seemed trembling under the shock of the footsteps of the storm. Some of the scenes thus revealed were of immeasurable grandeur and of absorbing interest — the sea, running mountains high, threw skywards with each wave mighty masses of white foam, which the tempest seemed to snatch at and whirl away into space; here and there a fishing-boat, with a rag of sail, running madly for shelter before the blast; now and again the white wings of a storm-tossed sea-bird. On the summit of the East Cliff the new searchlight was ready for experiment, but had not yet been tried. The officers in charge of it got it into working order, and in the pauses of the inrushing mist swept with it the surface of the sea. Once or twice its service was most effective, as when a fishing-boat, with gunwale under water, rushed into the harbour, able, by the guidance of the sheltering light, to avoid the danger of dashing against the piers. As each boat achieved the safety of the port there was a shout of joy from the mass of people on shore, a shout which for a moment seemed to cleave the gale and was then swept away in its rush. Before long the searchlight discovered some distance away a schooner with all sails set, apparently the same vessel which had been noticed earlier in the evening. The wind had by this time backed to the east, and there was a shudder amongst the watchers on the cliff as they realised the terrible danger in which she now was. Between her and the port lay the great flat reef on which so many good ships have from time to time

lanthorns: Lanterns (*OED* OL).

suffered, and, with the wind blowing from its present quarter, it would be quite impossible that she should fetch the entrance of the harbour. It was now nearly the hour of high tide, but the waves were so great that in their troughs the shallows of the shore were almost visible, and the schooner, with all sails set, was rushing with such speed that, in the words of one old salt, "she must fetch up somewhere, if it was only in hell." Then came another rush of sea-fog, greater than any hitherto — a mass of dank mist, which seemed to close on all things like a grey pall, and left available to men only the organ of hearing, for the roar of the tempest, and the crash of the thunder, and the booming of the mighty billows came through the damp oblivion even louder than before. The rays of the searchlight were kept fixed on the harbour mouth across the East Pier, where the shock was expected, and men waited breathless. The wind suddenly shifted to the north-east, and the remnant of the sea-fog melted in the blast; and then, *mirabile dictu,*° between the piers, leaping from wave to wave as it rushed at headlong speed, swept the strange schooner before the blast, with all sail set, and gained the safety of the harbour. The searchlight followed her, and a shudder ran through all who saw her, for lashed to the helm was a corpse, with drooping head, which swung horribly to and fro at each motion of the ship. No other form could be seen on deck at all. A great awe came on all as they realised that the ship, as if by a miracle, had found the harbour, unsteered save by the hand of a dead man! However, all took place more quickly than it takes to write these words. The schooner paused not, but rushing across the harbour, pitched herself on that accumulation of sand and gravel washed by many tides and many storms into the south-east corner of the pier jutting under the East Cliff, known locally as Tate Hill Pier.

There was of course a considerable concussion as the vessel drove up on the sand heap. Every spar, rope, and stay was strained, and some of the "top-hamper"° came crashing down. But, strangest of all, the very instant the shore was touched, an immense dog sprang up on deck from below, as if shot up by the concussion, and running forward, jumped from the bow on the sand. Making straight for the steep cliff, where the churchyard hangs over the laneway to the East Pier so steeply that some of the flat tombstones — "thruff-steans" or "through-stones," as they call them in the Whitby vernacular — actually project over where the sustaining cliff has fallen away, it disappeared

---

mirabile dictu: Wonderful to relate (Latin).   *top-hamper:* A "weight or encumbrance aloft" such as the "upper masts, sails, and riggings of a ship" (*OED*).

in the darkness, which seemed intensified just beyond the focus of the searchlight.

It so happened that there was no one at the moment on Tate Hill Pier, as all those whose houses are in close proximity were either in bed or were out on the heights above. Thus the coastguard on duty on the eastern side of the harbour, who at once ran down to the little pier, was the first to climb on board. The men working the searchlight, after scouring the entrance of the harbour without seeing anything, then turned the light on the derelict and kept it there. The coastguard ran aft, and when he came beside the wheel, bent over to examine it, and recoiled at once as though under some sudden emotion. This seemed to pique general curiosity, and quite a number of people began to run. It is a good way round from the West Cliff by the Drawbridge to Tate Hill Pier, but your correspondent is a fairly good runner, and came well ahead of the crowd. When I arrived, however, I found already a-ssembled on the pier a crowd, whom the coastguard and police refused to allow to come on board. By the courtesy of the chief boat-man, I was, as your correspondent, permitted to climb on deck, and was one of a small group who saw the dead seaman whilst actually lashed to the wheel.

It was no wonder that the coastguard was surprised, or even awed, for not often can such a sight have been seen. The man was simply fastened by his hands, tied one over the other, to a spoke of the wheel. Between the inner hand and the wood was a crucifix, the set of beads on which it was fastened being around both wrists and wheel, and all kept fast by the binding cords. The poor fellow may have been seated at one time, but the flapping and buffeting of the sails had worked through the rudder of the wheel and dragged him to and fro, so that the cords with which he was tied had cut the flesh to the bone. Accurate note was made of the state of things, and a doctor — Surgeon J. M. Caffyn, of 33, East Elliot Place — who came immediately after me, declared, after making examination, that the man must have been dead for quite two days. In his pocket was a bottle, carefully corked, empty save for a little roll of paper, which proved to be the addendum to the log. The coastguard said the man must have tied up his own hands, fastening the knots with his teeth. The fact that a coastguard was the first on board may save some complications, later on, in the Admiralty Court; for coastguards cannot claim the salvage which is the right of the first civilian entering on a derelict. Already, however, the legal tongues are wagging, and one young law student is loudly asserting that the rights of the owner are already completely sacrificed, his property being held in contravention of the statutes of mortmain,° since the tiller, as emblemship, if not proof, of delegated possession, is held in a *dead hand*. It is needless to say that the dead steersman has been reverently removed from the place where he held his honourable watch and ward till death — a steadfastness as noble as that of the young Casabianca° — and placed in the mortuary to await inquest.

Already the sudden storm is passing, and its fierceness is abating; the crowds are scattering homeward, and the sky is beginning to redden over the Yorkshire wolds.° I shall send, in time for your next issue, further details of the derelict ship which found her way so miraculously into harbour in the storm.

Whitby.

9 *August.* — The sequel to the strange arrival of the derelict in the storm last night is almost more startling than the thing itself. It turns out that the schooner is a Russian from Varna,° and is called the *Demeter.*° She is almost entirely in ballast of silver sand, with only a small amount of cargo — a number of great wooden boxes filled with mould.° This cargo was consigned to a Whitby solicitor, Mr. S. F. Billington, of 7, The Crescent, who this morning went aboard and formally took possession of the goods consigned to him. The Russian consul, too, acting for the charter-party, took formal possession of the ship, and paid all harbour dues, etc. Nothing is talked about here to-day except the strange coincidence; the officials of the Board of Trade have been most exacting in seeing that every compliance has been made with existing regulations. As the matter is to be a "nine days' wonder," they are evidently determined that there shall be no cause of after complaint. A good deal of interest was abroad concerning the dog which landed when the ship struck, and more than a few of the members of the S.P.C.A., which is very strong in Whitby, have tried to befriend the animal. To the general disappointment, however, it was not to be found; it seems to have disappeared entirely from the town. It may be that it was frightened and made its way on to the moors, where it is still hiding in

---

statutes of mortmain: Laws preventing the church or other institutions from declaring that certain lands and properties may never be sold. Stoker's pun depends upon the literal meaning of *mortmain,* "dead hand" (Latin; *OED*).   *Casabianca:* In the poem "Casabianca" by Felicia Hemans (1793–1835), the young boy of that name remains at his post on a burning ship and dies when the vessel explodes.   *wolds:* Hilly, open countryside (*OED* OL).   *Varna:* A port city in Bulgaria located on the Bay of Varna, an inlet of the Black Sea.   *Demeter:* The ship is named after the Greek goddess of grain and agriculture, also associated with the underworld, the land of the dead, through the myth of her daughter Persephone, who was abducted by Hades, ruler of the underworld. *mould:* British spelling of "mold," or topsoil, rich in organic matter; in British usage, the word also refers to the earth of the grave.

terror. There are some who look with dread on such a possibility, lest later on it should in itself become a danger, for it is evidently a fierce brute. Early this morning a large dog, a half-bred mastiff belonging to a coal merchant close to Tate Hill Pier, was found dead in the roadway opposite its master's yard. It had been fighting, and manifestly had had a savage opponent, for its throat was torn away, and its belly was slit open as if with a savage claw.

Later. — By the kindness of the Board of Trade inspector, I have been permitted to look over the log-book of the *Demeter*, which was in order up to within three days, but contained nothing of special interest except as to facts of missing men. The greater interest, however, is with regard to the paper found in the bottle, which was to-day produced at the inquest; and a more strange narrative than the two between them unfold it has not been my lot to come across. As there is no motive for concealment, I am permitted to use them, and accordingly send you a rescript, simply omitting technical details of seamanship and supercargo. It almost seems as though the captain had been seized with some kind of mania before he had got well into blue water, and that this had developed persistently throughout the voyage. Of course my statement must be taken *cum grano,*° since I am writing from the dictation of a clerk of the Russian consul, who kindly translated for me, time being short.

Log of the "Demeter"

(Varna to Whitby)

Written 18 *July, things so strange happening, that I shall keep accurate note henceforth till we land.*

On 6 July we finished taking in cargo, silver sand and boxes of earth. At noon set sail. East wind, fresh. Crew, five hands, ... two mates, cook, and myself (captain).

On 11 July at dawn entered Bosphorus.° Boarded by Turkish Customs officers. Backsheesh.° All correct. Under way at 4 p.m.

On 12 July through Dardanelles.° More Customs officers and flag-boat of guarding squadron. Backsheesh again. Work of officers thorough, but quick. Want us off soon. At dark passed into Archipelago.°

---

cum grano: *Cum grano salis,* with a grain of salt, that is, with skepticism (Latin). **Bosphorus:** A strait between the Black Sea and the Sea of Marmora. **Backsheesh:** A present of money, a tip or a bribe (*OED* OL). **Dardanelles:** A strait between the Sea of Marmora and the Aegean, once called the Hellespont. **Archipelago:** The Aegean Sea (Italian: *Arcipelago*).

On 13 July passed Cape Matapan.° Crew dissatisfied about something. Seemed scared, but would not speak out.

On 14 July was somewhat anxious about crew. Men all steady fellows, who sailed with me before. Mate could not make out what was wrong; they only told him there was *something*, and crossed themselves. Mate lost temper with one of them that day and struck him. Expected fierce quarrel, but all was quiet.

On 16 July mate reported in the morning that one of crew, Petrofsky, was missing. Could not account for it. Took larboard watch eight bells last night; was relieved by Abramoff, but did not go to bunk. Men more downcast than ever. All said they expected something of the kind, but would not say more than that there was *something* aboard. Mate getting very impatient with them; feared some trouble ahead.

On 17 July, yesterday, one of the men, Olgaren, came to my cabin, and in an awestruck way confided to me that he thought there was a strange man aboard the ship. He said that in his watch he had been sheltering behind the deck-house, as there was a rain-storm, when he saw a tall, thin man, who was not like any of the crew, come up the companion-way, and go along the deck forward, and disappear. He followed cautiously, but when he got to bows found no one, and the hatchways were all closed. He was in a panic of superstitious fear, and I am afraid the panic may spread. To allay it, I shall to-day search entire ship carefully from stem to stern.

Later in the day I got together the whole crew, and told them, as they evidently thought there was some one in the ship, we would search from stem to stern. First mate angry; said it was folly, and to yield to such foolish ideas would demoralise the men; said he would engage to keep them out of trouble with a handspike.° I let him take the helm, while the rest began thorough search, all keeping abreast, with lanterns; we left no corner unsearched. As there were only the big wooden boxes, there were no odd corners where a man could hide. Men much relieved when search over, and went back to work cheerfully. First mate scowled, but said nothing.

22 *July.* — Rough weather last three days, and all hands busy with sails — no time to be frightened. Men seem to have forgotten their dread. Mate cheerful again, and all on good terms. Praised men for

---

Cape Matapan: Located at one of the southern tips of the Peloponnesus, the peninsula forming the southern part of Greece, south of the Gulf of Corinth.   **handspike:** A wooden bar used as a lever (*OED* OL).

work in bad weather. Passed Gibraltar and out through Straits.° All well.

24 *July.* — There seems some doom over this ship. Already a hand short, and entering on the Bay of Biscay° with wild weather ahead, and yet last night another man lost — disappeared. Like the first, he came off his watch and was not seen again. Men all in a panic of fear; sent a round robin,° asking to have double watch, as they fear to be alone. Mate violent. Fear there will be some trouble, as either he or the men will do some violence.

28 *July.* — Four days in hell, knocking about in a sort of maelstrom, and the wind a tempest. No sleep for any one. Men all worn out. Hardly know how to set a watch, since no one fit to go on. Second mate volunteered to steer and watch, and let men snatch a few hours' sleep. Wind abating; seas still terrific, but feel them less, as ship is steadier.

29 *July.* — Another tragedy. Had single watch to-night, as crew too tired to double. When morning watch came on deck could find no one except steersman. Raised outcry, and all came on deck. Thorough search, but no one found. Are now without second mate, and crew in a panic. Mate and I agreed to go armed henceforth and wait for any sign of cause.

30 *July.* — Last night. Rejoiced we are nearing England. Weather fine, all sails set. Retired worn out; slept soundly; awaked by mate telling me that both man of watch and steersman missing. Only self and mate and two hands left to work ship.

1 *August.* — Two days of fog, and not a sail sighted. Had hoped when in the English Channel to be able to signal for help or get in somewhere. Not having power to work sails, have to run before wind. Dare not lower, as could not raise them again. We seem to be drifting to some terrible doom. Mate now more demoralised than either of men. His stronger nature seems to have worked inwardly against himself. Men are beyond fear, working stolidly and patiently, with minds made up to worst. They are Russian, he Roumanian.

2 *August, midnight.* — Woke up from few minutes' sleep by hearing a cry, seemingly outside my port. Could see nothing in fog. Rushed on deck, and ran against mate. Tells me heard cry and ran, but no sign

---

Gibraltar ... *Straits:* The Straits of Gibraltar, off Spain's southern coast, provide the only outlet from the Mediterranean Sea to the Atlantic Ocean.   *Bay of Biscay:* An inlet of the Atlantic Ocean bounded by France and Spain, well known for its storms.   *round robin:* A document, especially a complaint or petition, "having the names of the subscribers arranged in a circle so as to disguise the order in which they have signed" (*OED* OL).

of man on watch. One more gone. Lord, help us! Mate says we must be past Straits of Dover,° as in a moment of fog lifting he saw North Foreland,° just as he heard the man cry out. If we are now off in the North Sea, and only God can guide us in the fog, which seems to move with us; and God seems to have deserted us.

3 *August*. — At midnight I went to relieve the man at the wheel, but when I got to it found no one there. The wind was steady, and as we ran before it there was no yawing.° I dared not leave it, so shouted for the mate. After a few seconds he rushed up on deck in his flannels. He looked wild-eyed and haggard, and I greatly fear his reason has given way. He came close to me and whispered hoarsely, with his mouth to my ear, as though fearing the very air might hear: "*It* is here; I know it, now. On the watch last night I saw It, like a man, tall and thin, and ghastly pale. It was in the bows, and looking out. I crept behind It, and gave It my knife; but the knife went through It, empty as the air." And as he spoke he took his knife and drove it savagely into space. Then he went on: "But It is here, and I'll find It. It is in the hold, perhaps, in one of those boxes. I'll unscrew them one by one and see. You work the helm." And, with a warning look and his finger on his lip, he went below. There was springing up a choppy wind, and I could not leave the helm. I saw him come out on deck again with a tool-chest and a lantern, and go down the forward hatchway. He is mad, stark, raving mad, and it's no use my trying to stop him. He can't hurt those big boxes: they are invoiced as "clay," and to pull them about is as harmless a thing as he can do. So here I stay, and mind the helm, and write these notes. I can only trust in God and wait till the fog clears. Then, if I can't steer to any harbour with the wind that is, I shall cut down sails and lie by, and signal for help. . . . .

It is nearly all over now. Just as I was beginning to hope that the mate would come out calmer — for I heard him knocking away at something in the hold, and work is good for him — there came up the hatchway a sudden, startled scream, which made my blood run cold, and up on the deck he came as if shot from a gun — a raging madman, with his eyes rolling and his face convulsed with fear. "Save me! save me!" he cried, and then looked round on the blanket of fog. His horror turned to despair, and in a steady voice he said: "You had better come too, captain, before it is too late. *He* is there. I know the secret now. The sea will save me from Him, and it is all that is left!" Before I could

Straits of Dover: A strait between the English Channel and the North Sea.   ***North Foreland:*** A headland on the southeast coast of England south of Margate and north of Ramsgate.   ***yawing:*** Momentary swerving off course.

say a word, or move forward to seize him, he sprang on the bulwark and deliberately threw himself into the sea. I suppose I know the secret too, now. It was this madman who had got rid of the men one by one, and now he has followed them himself. God help me! How am I to account for all these horrors when I get to port? *When* I get to port! Will that ever be?

4 *August.* — Still fog, which the sunrise cannot pierce. I know there is sunrise because I am a sailor, why else I know not. I dared not go below, I dared not leave the helm; so here all night I stayed, and in the dimness of the night I saw It — Him! God forgive me, but the mate was right to jump overboard. It is better to die like a man; to die like a sailor in blue water no man can object. But I am captain, and I must not leave my ship. But I shall baffle° this fiend or monster, for I shall tie my hands to the wheel when my strength begins to fail, and along with them I shall tie that which He — It! — dare not touch; and then, come good wind or foul, I shall save my soul, and my honour as a captain. I am growing weaker, and the night is coming on. If He can look me in the face again, I may not have time to act. . . . . If we are wrecked, may-hap this bottle may be found, and those who find it may understand; if not, ... well, then all men shall know that I have been true to my trust. God and the Blessed Virgin and the saints help a poor ignorant soul trying to do his duty. . . . .'

Of course the verdict was an open one. There is no evidence to adduce; and whether or not the man himself committed the murders there is now none to say. The folk hold almost universally here that the captain is simply a hero, and he is to be given a public funeral. Already it is arranged that his body is to be taken with a train of boats up the Esk for a piece and then brought back to Tate Hill Pier and up the Abbey steps; for he is to be buried in the churchyard on the cliff. The owners of more than a hundred boats have already given in their names as wishing to follow him to the grave.

No trace has ever been found of the great dog; at which there is much mourning, for, with public opinion in its present state, he would, I believe, be adopted by the town. Tomorrow will see the funeral; and so will end this one more "mystery of the sea."

Mina Murray's Journal

8 *August.* — Lucy was very restless all night, and I, too, could not sleep. The storm was fearful, and as it boomed loudly among the

baffle: Frustrate; stop.

chimney-pots, it made me shudder. When a sharp puff came it seemed to be like a distant gun. Strangely enough, Lucy did not wake; but she got up twice and dressed herself. Fortunately, each time I awoke in time, and managed to undress her without waking her, and got her back to bed. It is a very strange thing, this sleep-walking, for as soon as her will is thwarted in any physical way, her intention, if there be any, disappears, and she yields herself almost exactly to the routine of her life.

Early in the morning we both got up and went down to the harbour to see if anything had happened in the night. There were very few people about, and though the sun was bright, and the air clear and fresh, the big, grim-looking waves, that seemed dark themselves because the foam that topped them was like snow, forced themselves in through the narrow mouth of the harbour — like a bullying man going through a crowd. Somehow I felt glad that Jonathan was not on the sea last night, but on land. But, oh, is he on land or sea? Where is he, and how? I am getting fearfully anxious about him. If I only knew what to do, and could do anything!

10 *August.* — The funeral of the poor sea-captain to-day was most touching. Every boat in the harbour seemed to be there, and the coffin was carried by captains all the way from Tate Hill Pier up to the church-yard. Lucy came with me, and we went early to our old seat, whilst the cortège of boats went up the river to the Viaduct and came down again. We had a lovely view, and saw the procession nearly all the way. The poor fellow was laid to rest quite near our seat, so that we stood on it when the time came and saw everything. Poor Lucy seemed much upset. She was restless and uneasy all the time, and I cannot but think that her dreaming at night is telling on her. She is quite odd in one thing: she will not admit to me that there is any cause for restlessness; or if there be, she does not understand it herself. There is an additional cause in that poor old Mr. Swales was found dead this morning on our seat, his neck being broken. He had evidently, as the doctor said, fallen back in the seat in some sort of fright, for there was a look of fear and horror on his face that the men said made them shudder. Poor dear old man! Perhaps he had seen Death with his dying eyes! Lucy is so sweet and sensitive that she feels influences more acutely than other people do. Just now she was quite upset by a little thing which I did not much heed, though I am myself very fond of animals. One of the men who come up here often to look for the boats was followed by his dog. The dog is always with him. They are both quiet persons, and I never saw the man angry, nor heard the dog bark. During the service the dog

would not come to its master, who was on the seat with us, but kept a few yards off, barking and howling. Its master spoke to it gently, and then harshly, and then angrily; but it would neither come nor cease to make a noise. It was in a sort of fury, with its eyes savage, and all its hairs bristling out like a cat's tail when puss is on the war-path. Finally the man, too, got angry, and jumped down and kicked the dog, and then took it by the scruff of the neck and half dragged and half threw it on the tombstone on which the seat is fixed. The moment it touched the stone the poor thing became quiet and fell all into a tremble. It did not try to get away, but crouched down, quivering and cowering, and was in such a pitiable state of terror that I tried, though without effect, to comfort it. Lucy was full of pity, too, but she did not attempt to touch the dog, but looked at it in an agonised sort of way. I greatly fear that she is of too super-sensitive a nature to go through the world without trouble. She will be dreaming of this to-night, I am sure. The whole agglomeration of things — the ship steered into port by a dead man; his attitude, tied to the wheel with a crucifix and beads; the touching funeral; the dog, now furious and now in terror — will all afford material for her dreams.

I think it will be best for her to go to bed tired out physically, so I shall take her for a long walk by the cliffs to Robin Hood's Bay and back. She ought not to have much inclination for sleep-walking then.

CHAPTER VIII. MINA MURRAY'S JOURNAL

Same day, 11 *o'clock p.m.* — Oh, but I am tired! If it were not that I have made my diary a duty I should not open it to-night. We had a lovely walk. Lucy, after a while, was in gay spirits, owing, I think, to some dear cows who came nosing towards us in a field close to the lighthouse, and frightened the wits out of us. I believe we forgot everything, except, of course, personal fear, and it seemed to wipe the slate clean and give us a fresh start. We had a capital "severe tea" at Robin Hood's Bay in a sweet little old-fashioned inn, with a bow-window right over the seaweed-covered rocks of the strand. I believe we should have shocked the "New Woman"° with our appetites. Men are more tolerant, bless them! Then we walked home with some, or rather many,

New Woman: The new generation of women at the end of the nineteenth century who believed in the Suffrage movement, education for women, and doing away with sexual double standards. The New Woman was regularly the subject of ridicule for unconventional, supposedly unfeminine behavior.

stoppages to rest, and with our hearts full of a constant dread of wi̇
bulls. Lucy was really tired, and we intended to creep off to bed as soon
as we could. The young curate came in, however, and Mrs. Westenra
asked him to stay for supper. Lucy and I had both a fight for it with the
dusty miller°; I know it was a hard fight on my part, and I am quite
heroic. I think that some day the bishops must get together and see
about breeding up a new class of curates, who don't take supper, no
matter how they may be pressed to, and who will know when girls are
tired. Lucy is asleep and breathing softly. She has more colour in her
cheeks than usual, and looks, oh, so sweet. If Mr. Holmwood fell in
love with her seeing her only in the drawing-room, I wonder what he
would say if he saw her now. Some of the "New Women" writers° will
some day start an idea that men and women should be allowed to see
each other asleep before proposing or accepting. But I suppose the
New Woman won't condescend in future to accept; she will do the
proposing herself. And a nice job she will make of it, too! There's some
consolation in that. I am so happy to-night, because dear Lucy seems
better. I really believe she has turned the corner, and that we are over
her troubles with dreaming. I should be quite happy if I only knew if
Jonathan . . . . God bless and keep him.

11 *August, 3 a.m.* — Diary again. No sleep now, so I may as well
write. I am too agitated to sleep. We have had such an adventure,
such an agonising experience. I fell asleep as soon as I had closed my
diary. . . . . Suddenly I became broad awake, and sat up, with a horrible
sense of fear upon me, and of some feeling of emptiness around me.
The room was dark, so I could not see Lucy's bed; I stole across and felt
for her. The bed was empty. I lit a match, and found that she was not in
the room. The door was shut, but not locked, as I had left it. I feared to
wake her mother, who has been more than usually ill lately, so threw on
some clothes and got ready to look for her. As I was leaving the room it
struck me that the clothes she wore might give me some clue to her
dreaming intention. Dressing-gown would mean house; dress, outside.
Dressing-gown and dress were both in their places. "Thank God," I
said to myself, "she cannot be far, as she is only in her nightdress." I ran
downstairs and looked in the sitting-room. Not there! Then I looked in
all the other open rooms of the house, with an ever-growing fear chill-
ing my heart. Finally I came to the hall-door and found it open. It was
not wide open, but the catch of the lock had not caught. The people of

---

dusty miller: Sandman; in England, the dustman is the bringer of sleep (*OED*).   ***New Women writers:*** Term applied to writers such as the novelist Sarah Grand (1854–1943), who is usually credited with the initial published use of the term "New Woman."

eful to lock the door every night, so I feared that Lucy
out as she was. There was no time to think of what
vague, overmastering fear obscured all details. I took a
l and ran out. The clock was striking one as I was in the
Crescent, ... there was not a soul in sight. I ran along the North Terrace, but could see no sign of the white figure which I expected. At the
edge of the West Cliff above the pier I looked across the harbour to the
East Cliff, in the hope or fear — I don't know which — of seeing Lucy
in our favourite seat. There was a bright full moon, with heavy black,
driving clouds, which threw the whole scene into a fleeting diorama° of
light and shade as they sailed across. For a moment or two I could see
nothing, as the shadow of a cloud obscured St. Mary's Church and all
around it. Then as the cloud passed I could see the ruins of the Abbey
coming into view; and as the edge of a narrow band of light as sharp as
a sword-cut moved along, the church and the churchyard became gradually visible. Whatever my expectation was, it was not disappointed, for
there, on our favourite seat, the silver light of the moon struck a half-
reclining figure, snowy white. The coming of the cloud was too quick
for me to see much, for shadow shut down on light almost immediately; but it seemed to me as though something dark stood behind the
seat where the white figure shone, and bent over it. What it was,
whether man or beast, I could not tell; I did not wait to catch another
glance, but flew down the steep steps to the pier and along by the fish-
market to the bridge, which was the only way to reach the East Cliff.
The town seemed as dead, for not a soul did I see; I rejoiced that it was
so, for I wanted no witness of poor Lucy's condition. The time and distance seemed endless, and my knees trembled and my breath came
laboured as I toiled up the endless steps to the Abbey. I must have
gone fast, and yet it seemed to me as if my feet were weighted with
lead, and as though every joint in my body were rusty. When I got
almost to the top I could see the seat and the white figure, for I was
now close enough to distinguish it even through the spells of shadow.
There was undoubtedly something, long and black, bending over the
half-reclining white figure. I called in fright, "Lucy! Lucy!" and some-

---

diorama: "A mode of scenic representation in which a picture, some portions of which
are translucent, is viewed through an aperture, the sides of which are continued towards
the picture; the light, which is thrown upon the picture from the roof, may be diminished or increased at pleasure, so as to represent the change from sunshine to cloudy
weather." First presented in London in 1823 in a building constructed in Regent's Park
(*OED*).

thing raised a head, and from where I was I could see a white face and red, gleaming eyes. Lucy did not answer, and I ran on to the entrance of the churchyard. As I entered, the church was between me and the seat, and for a minute or so I lost sight of her. When I came in view again the cloud had passed, and the moonlight struck so brilliantly that I could see Lucy half reclining with her head lying over the back of the seat. She was quite alone, and there was not a sign of any living thing about.

When I bent over her I could see that she was still asleep. Her lips were parted, and she was breathing — not softly, as usual with her, but in long, heavy gasps, as though striving to get her lungs full at every breath. As I came closer, she put up her hand in her sleep and pulled the collar of her nightdress close round her throat. Whilst she did so there came a little shudder through her, as though she felt the cold. I flung the warm shawl over her, and drew the edges tight round her neck, for I dreaded lest she should get some deadly chill from the night air, unclad as she was. I feared to wake her all at once, so, in order to have my hands free that I might help her, I fastened the shawl at her throat with a big safety-pin; but I must have been clumsy in my anxiety and pinched or pricked her with it, for by-and-by, when her breathing became quieter, she put her hand to her throat again and moaned. When I had her carefully wrapped up I put my shoes on her feet, and then began very gently to wake her. At first she did not respond; but gradually she became more and more uneasy in her sleep, moaning and sighing occasionally. At last, as time was passing fast, and, for many other reasons, I wished to get her home at once, I shook her more forcibly, till finally she opened her eyes and awoke. She did not seem surprised to see me, as, of course, she did not realise all at once where she was. Lucy always wakes prettily, and even at such a time, when her body must have been chilled with cold, and her mind somewhat appalled at waking unclad in a churchyard at night, she did not lose her grace. She trembled a little, and clung to me; when I told her to come at once with me home she rose without a word, with the obedience of a child. As we passed along, the gravel hurt my feet, and Lucy noticed me wince. She stopped and wanted to insist upon my taking my shoes; but I would not. However, when we got to the pathway outside the churchyard, where there was a puddle of water remaining from the storm, I daubed my feet with mud, using each foot in turn on the other, so that as we went home no one, in case we should meet any one, should notice my bare feet.

Fortune favoured us, and we got home without meeting a soul.

Once we saw a man, who seemed not quite sober, passing along a street in front of us; but we hid in a door till he had disappeared up an opening such as there are here, steep little closes, or "wynds,"° as they call them in Scotland. My heart beat so loud all the time that sometimes I thought I should faint. I was filled with anxiety about Lucy, not only for her health, lest she should suffer from the exposure, but for her reputation in case the story should get wind. When we got in, and had washed our feet, and had said a prayer of thankfulness together, I tucked her into bed. Before falling asleep she asked — even implored — me not to say a word to any one, even her mother, about her sleep-walking adventure. I hesitated at first to promise; but on thinking of the state of her mother's health, and how the knowledge of such a thing would fret her, and thinking, too, of how such a story might become distorted — nay, infallibly would — in case it should leak out, I thought it wiser to do so. I hope I did right. I have locked the door, and the key is tied to my wrist, so perhaps I shall not be again disturbed. Lucy is sleeping soundly; the reflex of the dawn is high and far over the sea. . . . .

Same day, noon. — All goes well. Lucy slept till I woke her, and seemed not to have even changed her side. The adventure of the night does not seem to have harmed her; on the contrary, it has benefited her, for she looks better this morning than she has done for weeks. I was sorry to notice that my clumsiness with the safety-pin hurt her. Indeed, it might have been serious, for the skin of her throat was pierced. I must have pinched up a piece of loose skin and have transfixed it, for there are two little red points like pin-pricks, and on the band of her night-dress was a drop of blood. When I apologised and was concerned about it, she laughed and petted me, and said she did not even feel it. Fortunately it cannot leave a scar, as it is so tiny.

Same day, night. — We passed a happy day. The air was clear, and the sun bright, and there was a cool breeze. We took our lunch to Mulgrave Woods, Mrs. Westenra driving by the road and Lucy and I walking by the cliff-path and joining her at the gate. I felt a little sad myself, for I could not but feel how *absolutely* happy it would have been had Jonathan been with me. But there! I must only be patient. In the evening we strolled in the Casino Terrace, and heard some good music by Spohr and Mackenzie,° and went to bed early. Lucy seems more restful than she has been for some time, and fell asleep at once. I shall

---

closes, or wynds: Narrow lanes or alleys turning off from the main street (*OED* OL).
Spohr and Mackenzie: Louis Spohr (1784–1859), German composer and violinist, and Sir Alexander Campbell MacKenzie (1847–1935), Scottish violinist and composer.

lock the door and secure the key the same as before, though I do not expect any trouble to-night.

12 *August.* — My expectations were wrong, for twice during the night I was wakened by Lucy trying to get out. She seemed, even in her sleep, to be a little impatient at finding the door shut, and went back to bed under a sort of protest. I woke with the dawn, and heard the birds chirping outside of the window. Lucy woke, too, and I was glad to see, was even better than on the previous morning. All her old gaiety of manner seemed to have come back, and she came and snuggled in beside me, and told me all about Arthur; I told her how anxious I was about Jonathan, and then she tried to comfort me. Well, she succeeded somewhat, for, though sympathy can't alter facts, it can help to make them more bearable.

13 *August.* — Another quiet day, and to bed with the key on my wrist as before. Again I awoke in the night, and found Lucy sitting up in bed, still asleep, pointing to the window. I got up quietly, and pulling aside the blind, looked out. It was brilliant moonlight, and the soft effect of the light over the sea and sky — merged together in one great, silent mystery — was beautiful beyond words. Between me and the moonlight flitted a great bat, coming and going in great, whirling circles. Once or twice it came quite close, but was, I suppose, frightened at seeing me, and flitted away across the harbour towards the Abbey. When I came back from the window Lucy had lain down again, and was sleeping peacefully. She did not stir again all night.

14 *August.* — On the East Cliff, reading and writing all day. Lucy seems to have become as much in love with the spot as I am, and it is hard to get her away from it when it is time to come home for lunch or tea or dinner. This afternoon she made a funny remark. We were coming home for dinner, and had come to the top of the steps up from the West Pier and stopped to look at the view, as we generally do. The setting sun, low down in the sky, was just dropping behind Kettleness; the red light was thrown over on the East Cliff and the old Abbey, and seemed to bathe everything in a beautiful rosy glow. We were silent for a while, and suddenly Lucy murmured as if to herself: —

"His red eyes again! They are just the same." It was such an odd expression, coming *apropos* of nothing, that it quite startled me. I slewed round a little, so as to see Lucy well without seeming to stare at her, and saw that she was in a half-dreamy state, with an odd look on her face that I could not quite make out; so I said nothing, but followed her eyes. She appeared to be looking over at our own seat, whereon was a dark figure seated alone. I was a little startled myself, for it seemed for an instant as if the stranger had great eyes like burning flames; but a second look dispelled the illusion. The red sunlight was shining on the windows of St. Mary's Church behind our seat, and as the sun dipped there was just sufficient change in the refraction and reflection to make it appear as if the light moved. I called Lucy's attention to the peculiar effect, and she became herself with a start, but she looked sad all the same; it may have been that she was thinking of that terrible night up there. We never refer to it; so I said nothing, and we went home to dinner. Lucy had a headache and went early to bed. I saw her asleep, and went out for a little stroll myself; I walked along the cliffs to the westward, and was full of sweet sadness, for I was thinking of Jonathan. When coming home — it was then bright moonlight, so bright that, though the front of our part of the Crescent was in shadow, everything could be well seen — I threw a glance up at our window, and saw Lucy's head leaning out. I thought that perhaps she was looking out for me, so I opened my handkerchief and waved it. She did not notice or make any movement whatever. Just then, the moonlight crept round an angle of the building, and the light fell on the window. There distinctly was Lucy with her head lying up against the side of the window-sill and her eyes shut. She was fast asleep, and by her, seated on the window-sill, was something that looked like a good-sized bird. I was afraid she might get a chill, so I ran upstairs, but as I came into the room she was moving back to her bed, fast asleep, and breathing heavily; she was holding her hand to her throat, as though to protect it from cold.

I did not wake her, but tucked her up warmly; I have taken care that the door is locked and the window securely fastened.

She looks so sweet as she sleeps; but she is paler than is her wont, and there is a drawn, haggard look under her eyes which I do not like. I fear she is fretting about something. I wish I could find out what it is.

15 *August.* — Rose later than usual. Lucy was languid and tired, and slept on after we had been called. We had a happy surprise at breakfast. Arthur's father is better, and wants the marriage to come off soon. Lucy is full of quiet joy, and her mother is glad and sorry at once. Later on in the day she told me the cause. She is grieved to lose Lucy as her very own, but she is rejoiced that she is soon to have some one to protect her. Poor dear, sweet lady! She confided to me that she has got her death-warrant. She has not told Lucy, and made me promise secrecy; her doctor told her that within a few months, at most, she must die, for her heart is weakening. At any time, even now, a sudden shock would

be almost sure to kill her. Ah, we were wise to keep from her the affair of the dreadful night of Lucy's sleep-walking.

17 *August.* — No diary for two whole days. I have not had the heart to write. Some sort of shadowy pall seems to be coming over our happiness. No news from Jonathan, and Lucy seems to be growing weaker, whilst her mother's hours are numbering to a close. I do not understand Lucy's fading away as she is doing. She eats well and sleeps well, and enjoys the fresh air; but all the time the roses in her cheeks are fading, and she gets weaker and more languid day by day; at night I hear her gasping as if for air. I keep the key of our door always fastened to my wrist at night, but she gets up and walks about the room, and sits at the open window. Last night I found her leaning out when I woke up, and when I tried to wake her I could not; she was in a faint. When I managed to restore her she was as weak as water, and cried silently between long, painful struggles for breath. When I asked her how she came to be at the window she shook her head and turned away. I trust her feeling ill may not be from that unlucky prick of the safety pin. I looked at her throat just now as she lay asleep, and the tiny wounds seem not to have healed. They are still open, and, if anything, larger than before, and the edges of them are faintly white. They are like little white dots with red centres. Unless they heal within a day or two, I shall insist on the doctor seeing about them.

Letter, Samuel F. Billington & Son, Solicitors, Whitby, to Messrs. Carter, Paterson & Co., London

"17 *August*

"Dear Sirs, —

"Herewith please receive invoice of goods sent by Great Northern Railway. Same are to be delivered at Carfax, near Purfleet, immediately on receipt at goods station King's Cross. The house is at present empty, but enclosed please find keys, all of which are labelled.

"You will please deposit the boxes, fifty in number, which form the consignment, in the partially ruined building forming part of the house and marked 'A' on rough diagram enclosed. Your agent will easily recognise the locality, as it is the ancient chapel of the mansion. The goods leave by the train at 9.30 to-night, and will be due at King's Cross at 4.30 to-morrow afternoon. As our client wishes the delivery made as soon as possible, we shall be obliged by your having teams ready at King's Cross at the time named and forthwith conveying the goods to destination. In order to obviate any delays possible through any routine requirements as to payment in your departments, we enclose cheque herewith for ten pounds (£10), receipt of which please acknowledge. Should the charge be less than this amount, you can return balance; if greater, we shall at once send cheque for difference on hearing from you. You are to leave the keys on coming away in the main hall of the house, where the proprietor may get them on his entering the house by means of his duplicate key.

"Pray do not take us as exceeding the bounds of business courtesy in pressing you in all ways to use the utmost expedition.

"We are, dear Sirs,

"Faithfully yours,

"SAMUEL F. BILLINGTON & SON."

Letter, Messrs. Carter, Paterson & Co., London, to Messrs. Billington & Son, Whitby

"21 *August*

"Dear Sirs, —

"We beg to acknowledge £ 10 received and to return cheque £1 17*s*. 9*d*., amount of overplus, as shown in receipted account herewith. Goods are delivered in exact accordance with instructions, and keys left in parcel in main hall, as directed.

"We are, dear Sirs,

"Yours respectfully,

"*PRO* CARTER, PATTERSON & CO."

Mina Murray's Journal

18 *August*. — I am happy to-day, and write sitting on the seat in the churchyard. Lucy is ever so much better. Last night she slept well all night, and did not disturb me once. The roses seem coming back already to her cheeks, though she is still sadly pale and wan-looking. If she were in any way anæmic I could understand it, but she is not. She is in gay spirits and full of life and cheerfulness. All the morbid reticence seems to have passed from her, and she has just reminded me, as if I needed any reminding, of *that* night, and that it was here, on this very seat, I found her asleep. As she told me she tapped playfully with the heel of her boot on the stone slab and said: —

"My poor little feet didn't make much noise then! I daresay poor old Mr. Swales would have told me that it was because I didn't want to wake up Geordie." As she was in such a communicative humour, I asked her if she had dreamed at all that night. Before she answered, that sweet, puckered look came into her forehead, which Arthur — I call him Arthur from her habit — says he loves; and, indeed, I don't wonder that he does. Then she went on in a half-dreaming kind of way, as if trying to recall it to herself: —

"I didn't quite dream; but it all seemed to be real. I only wanted to be here in this spot — I don't know why, for I was afraid of something — I don't know what. I remember, though I suppose I was asleep, passing through the streets and over the bridge. A fish leaped as I went by, and I leaned over to look at it, and I heard a lot of dogs howling — the whole town seemed as if it must be full of dogs all howling at once — as I went up the steps. Then I have a vague memory of something long and dark with red eyes, just as we saw in the sunset, and something very sweet and very bitter all around me at once; and then I seemed sinking into deep green water, and there was a singing in my ears, as I have heard there is to drowning men; and then everything seemed passing away from me; my soul seemed to go out from my body and float about the air. I seem to remember that once the West Lighthouse was right under me, and then there was a sort of agonising feeling, as if I were in an earthquake, and I came back and found you shaking my body. I saw you do it before I felt you."

Then she began to laugh. It seemed a little uncanny to me, and I listened to her breathlessly. I did not quite like it, and thought it better not to keep her mind on the subject, so we drifted on to other subjects, and Lucy was like her old self again. When we got home the fresh breeze had braced her up, and her pale cheeks were really more rosy. Her mother rejoiced when she saw her, and we all spent a very happy evening together.

19 *August.* — Joy, joy, joy! although not all joy. At last, news of Jonathan. The dear fellow has been ill; that is why he did not write. I am not afraid to think it or to say it, now that I know. Mr. Hawkins sent me on the letter, and wrote himself, oh, so kindly. I am to leave in the morning and to go over to Jonathan, and to help to nurse him if necessary, and to bring him home. Mr. Hawkins says it would not be a bad thing if we were to be married out there. I have cried over the good Sister's letter till I can feel it wet against my bosom, where it lies. It is of Jonathan, and must be next my heart, for he is *in* my heart. My journey is all mapped out, and my luggage ready. I am only taking one change of dress; Lucy will bring my trunk to London and keep it till I send for it, for it may be that . . . . I must write no more; I must keep it to say to Jonathan, my husband. The letter that he has seen and touched must comfort me till we meet.

**Letter, Sister Agatha, Hospital of St. Joseph and Ste. Mary,
Buda-Pesth, to Miss Wilhelmina Murray**

"12 *August*

"Dear Madam, —

"I write by desire of Mr. Jonathan Harker, who is himself not strong enough to write, though progressing well, thanks to God and St. Joseph and Ste. Mary. He has been under our care for nearly six weeks, suffering from a violent brain fever. He wishes me to convey his love, and to say that by this post I write for him to Mr. Peter Hawkins, Exeter, to say, with his dutiful respects, that he is sorry for his delay, and that all his work is completed. He will require some few weeks' rest in our sanatorium in the hills, but will then return. He wishes me to say that he has not sufficient money with him, and that he would like to pay for his staying here, so that others who need shall not be wanting for help.

"Believe me,
"Yours, with sympathy and all blessings,
"SISTER AGATHA

"P.S. — My patient being asleep, I open this to let you know something more. He has told me all about you, and that you are shortly to be his wife. All blessings to you both! He has had some fearful shock — so says our doctor — and in his delirium his ravings have been dreadful; of wolves and poison and blood; of ghosts and demons; and I fear to say of what. Be careful with him always that there may be nothing to excite him of this kind for a long time to come; the traces of such an illness as his do not lightly die away. We should have written long ago, but we knew nothing of his friends, and there was on him nothing that any one could understand. He came in the train from Klausenburg, and the guard was told by the station-master there that he rushed into the station shouting for a ticket for home. Seeing from his violent demeanour that he was English, they gave him a ticket for the furthest station on the way thither that the train reached.

"Be assured that he is well cared for. He has won all hearts by his sweetness and gentleness. He is truly getting on well, and I have no doubt will in a few weeks be all himself. But be careful of him for safety's sake. There are, I pray God and St. Joseph and Ste. Mary, many, many happy years for you both."

Dr. Seward's Diary

19 *August*. — Strange and sudden change in Renfield last night. About eight o'clock he began to get excited and to sniff about as a dog does when setting. The attendant was struck by his manner, and knowing my interest in him, encouraged him to talk. He is usually respectful to the attendant, and at times servile; but to-night, the man tells me, he was quite haughty. Would not condescend to talk with him at all. All he would say was: —

"I don't want to talk to you: you don't count now; the Master is at hand."

The attendant thinks it is some sudden form of religious mania which has seized him. If so, we must look out for squalls, for a strong man with homicidal and religious mania at once might be dangerous. The combination is a dreadful one. At nine o'clock I visited him myself. His attitude to me was the same as that to the attendant; in his sublime self-feeling the difference between myself and attendant seemed to him as nothing. It looks like religious mania, and he will soon think that he himself is God. These infinitesimal distinctions between man and man are too paltry for an Omnipotent Being. How these madmen give themselves away! The real God taketh heed lest a sparrow fall; but the God created from human vanity sees no difference between an eagle and a sparrow.° Oh, if men only knew!

For half an hour or more Renfield kept getting excited in greater and greater degree. I did not pretend to be watching him, but I kept strict observation all the same. All at once that shifty look came into his eyes which we always see when a madman has seized an idea, and with it the shifty movement of the head and back which asylum attendants come to know so well. He became quite quiet, and went and sat on the edge of his bed resignedly, and looked into space with lack-lustre eyes. I thought I would find out if his apathy were real or only assumed, and tried to lead him to talk of his pets, a theme which had never failed to excite his attention. At first he made no reply, but at length said testily: —

"Bother them all! I don't care a pin about them."

"What?" I said. "You don't mean to tell me you don't care about spiders?" (Spiders at present are his hobby, and the note-book is filling up with columns of small figures.) To this he answered enigmatically: —

The real God . . . an eagle and a sparrow: Seward draws on the parable Jesus tells about God's awareness of even the death of a sparrow (Matthew 10.29–31; Luke 12.6–7), but his elaboration concerning the hierarchical difference between eagle and sparrow, like Renfield's statement about the bride that soon follows, has no biblical counterpart.

"The bride-maidens rejoice the eyes that wait the coming of the bride; but when the bride draweth nigh, then the maidens shine not to the eyes that are filled."°

He would not explain himself, but remained obstinately seated on his bed all the time I remained with him.

I am weary to-night and low in spirits. I cannot but think of Lucy, and how different things might have been. If I don't sleep at once, chloral, the modern Morpheus° — $C_2HCl_3O \cdot H_2O$! I must be careful not to let it grow into a habit. No, I shall take none to-night! I have thought of Lucy, and I shall not dishonour her by mixing the two. If need be, to-night shall be sleepless. . . . .

Glad I made the resolution; gladder that I kept to it. I had lain tossing about, and had heard the clock strike only twice, when the night-watchman came to me, sent up from the ward, to say that Renfield had escaped. I threw on my clothes and ran down at once; my patient is too dangerous a person to be roaming about. Those ideas of his might work out dangerously with strangers. The attendant was waiting for me. He said he had seen him not ten minutes before, seemingly asleep in his bed, when he had looked through the observation-trap in the door. His attention was called by the sound of the window being wrenched out. He ran back and saw his feet disappear through the window, and had at once sent up for me. He was only in his night-gear, and cannot be far off. The attendant thought it would be more useful to watch where he should go than to follow him, as he might lose sight of him whilst getting out of the building by the door. He is a bulky man, and couldn't get through the window. I am thin, so, with his aid, I got out, but feet foremost, and, as we were only a few feet above ground, landed unhurt. The attendant told me the patient had gone to the left and had taken a straight line, so I ran as quickly as I could. As I got through the belt of trees I saw a white figure scale the high wall which separates our grounds from those of the deserted house.

I ran back at once, and told the watchman to get three or four men immediately and follow me into the grounds of Carfax, in case our friend might be dangerous. I got a ladder myself, and crossing the wall, dropped down on the other side. I could see Renfield's figure just disappearing behind the angle of the house, so I ran after him. On the far side of the house I found him pressed close against the old iron-bound

bride-maidens . . . are filled: Although Renfield's language sounds biblical in character, no passage has been convincingly identified as a source.   chloral, the modern Morpheus: Chloral hydrate, a common sedative, is compared to the classical god of dreams, the son of Hypnos, god of sleep.

oak door of the chapel. He was talking, apparently to some one, but I was afraid to go near enough to hear what he was saying, lest I might frighten him, and he should run off. Chasing an errant swarm of bees is nothing to following a naked lunatic when the fit of escaping is upon him! After a few minutes, however, I could see that he did not take note of anything around him, and so ventured to draw nearer to him — the more so as my men had now crossed the wall and were closing him in. I heard him say: —

"I am here to do Your bidding, Master. I am Your slave, and You will reward me, for I shall be faithful. I have worshipped You long and afar off. Now that You are near, I await Your commands, and You will not pass me by, will You, dear Master, in Your distribution of good things?"

He *is* a selfish old beggar anyhow. He thinks of the loaves and fishes even when he believes he is in a Real Presence. His manias make a startling combination. When we closed in on him he fought like a tiger. He is immensely strong, and he was more like a wild beast than a man. I never saw a lunatic in such a paroxysm of rage before; and I hope I shall not again. It is a mercy that we have found out his strength and his danger in good time. With strength and determination like his, he might have done wild work before he was caged. He is safe now at any rate. Jack Sheppard° himself couldn't get free from the strait-waistcoat° that keeps him restrained, and he's chained to the wall in the padded room. His cries are at times awful, but the silences that follow are more deadly still, for he means murder in every turn and movement.

Just now he spoke coherent words for the first time: —

"I shall be patient, Master. It is coming — coming — coming!"

So I took the hint, and came too. I was too excited to sleep, but this diary has quieted me, and I feel I shall get some sleep to-night.

CHAPTER IX. LETTER, MINA HARKER TO LUCY WESTENRA

"Buda-Pesth, 24 *August*

"My dearest Lucy, —

"I know you will be anxious to hear all that has happened since we parted at the railway station at Whitby. Well, my dear, I got to Hull all right, and caught the boat to Hamburg, and then the train on here. I

Jack Sheppard: John Sheppard (1702–1724), a notorious criminal known for his many prison escapes, including one from Newgate, where he had been chained to the floor of his cell (*Enc. Brit.* 11th).   *strait-waistcoat:* Straitjacket.

feel that I can hardly recall anything of the journey, except that I knew I
was coming to Jonathan, and, that as I should have to do some nursing,
I had better get all the sleep I could. . . . . I found my dear one, oh, so
thin and pale and weak-looking. All the resolution has gone out of his
dear eyes, and that quiet dignity which I told you was in his face has
vanished. He is only a wreck of himself, and he does not remember anything that has happened to him for a long time past. At least, he wants
me to believe so, and I shall never ask. He has had some terrible shock,
and I fear it might tax his poor brain if he were to try to recall it. Sister
Agatha, who is a good creature and a born nurse, tells me that he raved
of dreadful things whilst he was off his head. I wanted her to tell me
what they were; but she would only cross herself, and say she would
never tell; that the ravings of the sick were the secrets of God, and that
if a nurse through her vocation should hear them, she should respect
her trust. She is a sweet, good soul, and the next day, when she saw I
was troubled, she opened up the subject again, and after saying that she
could never mention what my poor dear raved about, added: 'I can tell
you this much, my dear: that it was not about anything which he has
done wrong himself; and you, as his wife to be, have no cause to be
concerned. He has not forgotten you or what he owes to you. His fear
was of great and terrible things, which no mortal can treat of.' I do
believe the dear soul thought I might be jealous lest my poor dear
should have fallen in love with any other girl. The idea of *my* being jealous about Jonathan! And yet, my dear, let me whisper, I felt a thrill of
joy through me when I *knew* that no other woman was a cause of
trouble. I am now sitting by his bedside, where I can see his face while
he sleeps. He is waking! . . . . When he woke he asked me for his coat,
as he wanted to get something from the pocket; I asked Sister Agatha,
and she brought all his things. I saw that amongst them was his note-
book, and was going to ask him to let me look at it — for I knew then
that I might find some clue to his trouble — but I suppose he must
have seen my wish in my eyes, for he sent me over to the window, saying he wanted to be quite alone for a moment. Then he called me back,
and when I came he had his hand over the note-book, and he said to
me very solemnly: —

   " 'Wilhelmina' — I knew then that he was in deadly earnest, for he
has never called me by that name since he asked me to marry him —
'you know, dear, my ideas of the trust between husband and wife: there
should be no secret, no concealment. I have had a great shock, and
when I try to think of what it is I feel my head spin round, and I do not
know if it was all real or the dreaming of a madman. You know I have

had brain fever, and that is to be mad. The secret is here, and I do not want to know it. I want to take up my life here, with our marriage.' For, my dear, we had decided to be married as soon as the formalities are complete. 'Are you willing, Wilhelmina, to share my ignorance? Here is the book. Take it and keep it, read it if you will, but never let me know; unless, indeed, some solemn duty should come upon me to go back to the bitter hours, asleep or awake, sane or mad, recorded here.' He fell back exhausted, and I put the book under his pillow, and kissed him. I have asked Sister Agatha to beg the Superior to let our wedding be this afternoon, and am waiting her reply. . . . .

"She has come and told me that the chaplain of the English mission church has been sent for. We are to be married in an hour, or as soon after as Jonathan awakes. . . . .

"Lucy, the time has come and gone. I feel very solemn, but very, very happy. Jonathan woke a little after the hour, and all was ready, and he sat up in bed, propped up with pillows. He answered his 'I will' firmly and strongly. I could hardly speak; my heart was so full that even those words seemed to choke me. The dear Sisters were so kind. Please God, I shall never, never forget them, nor the grave and sweet responsibilities I have taken upon me. I must tell you of my wedding present. When the chaplain and the Sisters had left me alone with my husband — oh, Lucy, it is the first time I have written the words 'my husband' — left me alone with my husband, I took the book from under his pillow, and wrapped it up in white paper, and tied it with a little bit of pale blue ribbon which was round my neck, and sealed it over the knot with sealing-wax, and for my seal I used my wedding ring. Then I kissed it and showed it to my husband, and told him that I would keep it so, and then it would be an outward and visible sign for us all our lives that we trusted each other; that I would never open it unless it were for his own dear sake or for the sake of some stern duty. Then he took my hand in his, and oh, Lucy, it was the first time he took *his wife's* hand, and said that it was the dearest thing in all the wide world, and that he would go through all the past again to win it, if need be. The poor dear meant to have said a part of the past; but he cannot think of time yet, and I shall not wonder if at first he mixes up not only the month, but the year.

"Well, my dear, what could I say? I could only tell him that I was the happiest woman in all the wide world, and that I had nothing to give him except myself, my life, and my trust, and that with these went my love and duty for all the days of my life. And, my dear, when he kissed me, and drew me to him with his poor weak hands, it was like a very solemn pledge between us. . . . .

"Lucy dear, do you know why I tell you all this? It is not only because it is all sweet to me, but because you have been, and are, very dear to me. It was my privilege to be your friend and guide when you came from the schoolroom to prepare for the world of life. I want you to see now, and with the eyes of a very happy wife, whither duty has led me; so that in your own married life you too may be all happy as I am. My dear, please Almighty God, your life may be all it promises: a long day of sunshine, with no harsh wind, no forgetting duty, no distrust. I must not wish you no pain, for that can never be; but I do hope you will be *always* as happy as I am *now*. Good-bye, my dear. I shall post this at once, and, perhaps, write you very soon again. I must stop, for Jonathan is waking — I must attend to my husband!

"Your ever-loving
"MINA HARKER"

Letter, Lucy Westenra to Mina Harker

"*Whitby*, 30 *August*°

"My dearest Mina, —

"Oceans of love and millions of kisses, and may you soon be in your own home with your husband. I wish you could be coming home soon enough to stay with us here. This strong air would soon restore Jonathan; it has quite restored me. I have an appetite like a cormorant,° am full of life, and sleep well. You will be glad to know that I have quite given up walking in my sleep. I think I have not stirred out of my bed for a week, that is when I once got into it at night. Arthur says I am getting fat. By the way, I forgot to tell you that Arthur is here. We have such walks and drives, and rides, and rowing, and tennis, and fishing together; and I love him more than ever. He *tells me* that he loves me more, but I doubt that, for at first he told me that he couldn't love me more than he did then. But this is nonsense. There he is, calling to me. So no more just at present from your loving

"LUCY

"P.S. — Mother sends her love. She seems better, poor dear.
"P.P.S. — We are to be married on 28 September."

---

30 August: The correct date is probably August 20; here and once in Chapter 12 the apparent discrepancy could be due to a printer's error or Stoker's mistake, or it could be part of the book's realistic detail, either Lucy's misdating of her letter or Mina's later mistranscribing of the document.   **cormorant:** Large dark sea-bird with a hooked bill, known for its voracious appetite.

Dr. Seward's Diary

20 *August*. — The case of Renfield grows even more interesting. He has now so far quieted that there are spells of cessation from his passion. For the first week after his attack he was perpetually violent. Then one night, just as the moon rose, he grew quiet, and kept murmuring to himself: "Now I can wait; now I can wait." The attendant came to tell me, so I ran down at once to have a look at him. He was still in the strait-waistcoat and in the padded room, but the suffused look had gone from his face, and his eyes had something of their old pleading — I might almost say, "cringing" — softness. I was satisfied with his present condition, and directed him to be relieved. The attendants hesitated, but finally carried out my wishes without protest. It was a strange thing that the patient had humour enough to see their distrust, for, coming close to me, he said in a whisper, all the while looking furtively at them: —

"They think I could hurt you! Fancy *me* hurting *you!* The fools!"

It was soothing, somehow, to the feelings to find myself dissociated even in the mind of this poor madman from the others; but all the same I do not follow his thought. Am I to take it that I have anything in common with him, so that we are, as it were, to stand together; or has he to gain from me some good so stupendous that my well-being is needful to him? I must find out later on. To-night he will not speak. Even the offer of a kitten or even a full-grown cat will not tempt him. He will only say: "I don't take any stock in cats. I have more to think of now, and I can wait; I can wait."

After a while I left him. The attendant tells me that he was quiet until just before dawn, and that then he began to get uneasy, and at length violent, until at last he fell into a paroxysm which exhausted him so that he swooned into a sort of coma.

. . . . . Three nights has the same thing happened — violent all day, then quiet from moonrise to sunrise. I wish I could get some clue to the cause. It would almost seem as if there was some influence which came and went. Happy thought! We shall to-night play sane wits against mad ones. He escaped before without our help; to-night he shall escape with it. We shall give him a chance, and have the men ready to follow in case they are required. . . . .

23 *August*. — "The unexpected always happens." How well Disraeli knew life.° Our bird when he found the cage open would not fly, so

---

"The unexpected always happens." . . . *Disraeli knew life:* Benjamin Disraeli, Earl of Beaconsfield (1804–1881), was both a Conservative prime minister and a well-known novelist. Seward seems to be associating this proverb, which has a long history, with Disraeli.

all our subtle arrangements went for nought. At any rate, we have proved one thing: that the spells of quietness last a reasonable time. We shall in future be able to ease his bonds for a few hours each day. I have given orders to the night attendant merely to shut him in the padded room, when once he is quiet, until an hour before sunrise. The poor soul's body will enjoy the relief even if his mind cannot appreciate it. Hark! The unexpected again! I am called; the patient has once more escaped.

Later. — Another night adventure. Renfield artfully waited until the attendant was entering the room to inspect. Then he dashed out past him and flew down the passage. I sent word for the attendants to follow. Again he went into the grounds of the deserted house, and we found him in the same place, pressed against the old chapel door. When he saw me he became furious, and had not the attendants seized him in time, he would have tried to kill me. As we were holding him a strange thing happened. He suddenly redoubled his efforts, and then as suddenly grew calm. I looked round instinctively, but could see nothing. Then I caught the patient's eye and followed it, but could trace nothing as it looked into the moonlit sky except a big bat, which was flapping its silent and ghostly way to the west. Bats usually wheel and flit about, but this one seemed to go straight on, as if it knew where it was bound for or had some intention of its own. The patient grew calmer every instant, and presently said: —

"You needn't tie me; I shall go quietly!" Without trouble we came back to the house. I feel there is something ominous in his calm, and shall not forget this night. . . . .

Lucy Westenra's Diary

Hillingham, 24 *August.* — I must imitate Mina, and keep writing things down. Then we can have long talks when we do meet. I wonder when it will be. I wish she were with me again, for I feel so unhappy. Last night I seemed to be dreaming again just as I was at Whitby. Perhaps it is the change of air, or getting home again. It is all dark and horrid to me, for I can remember nothing; but I am full of vague fear, and I feel so weak and worn out. When Arthur came to lunch he looked quite grieved when he saw me, and I hadn't the spirit to try to be cheerful. I wonder if I could sleep in mother's room to-night. I shall make an excuse and try.

25 *August.* — Another bad night. Mother did not seem to take to my proposal. She seems not too well herself, and doubtless she fears to worry me. I tried to keep awake, and succeeded for a while; but when

the clock struck twelve it waked me from a doze, so I must have been falling asleep. There was a sort of scratching or flapping at the window, but I did not mind it, and as I remember no more, I suppose I must then have fallen asleep. More bad dreams. I wish I could remember them. This morning I am horribly weak. My face is ghastly pale, and my throat pains me. It must be something wrong with my lungs, for I don't seem ever to get air enough. I shall try to cheer up when Arthur comes, or else I know he will be miserable to see me so.

Letter, Arthur Holmwood to Dr. Seward

"Albermarle Hotel,° 31 *August*

"My dear Jack, —

"I want you to do me a favour. Lucy is ill; that is, she has no special disease, but she looks awful, and is getting worse every day. I have asked her if there is any cause; I do not dare to ask her mother, for to disturb the poor lady's mind about her daughter in her present state of health would be fatal. Mrs. Westenra has confided to me that her doom is spoken — disease of the heart — though poor Lucy does not know it yet. I am sure that there is something preying on my dear girl's mind. I am almost distracted when I think of her; to look at her gives me a pang. I told her I should ask you to see her, and though she demurred at first — I know why, old fellow — she finally consented. It will be a painful task for you, I know, old friend, but it is for *her* sake, and I must not hesitate to ask, or you to act. You are to come to lunch at Hillingham to-morrow, two o'clock, so as not to arouse any suspicion in Mrs. Westenra, and after lunch Lucy will take an opportunity of being alone with you. I shall come in for tea, and we can go away together; I am filled with anxiety, and want to consult with you alone as soon as I can after you have seen her. Do not fail!

"ARTHUR."

Telegram, Arthur Holmwood to Seward

"1 *September*

"Am summoned to see my father, who is worse. Am writing. Write me fully by to-night's post to Ring. Wire me if necessary."

Albemarle Hotel: An expensive and fashionable hotel at the corner of Albemarle Street and Piccadilly; patronized by royalty, the nobility, and diplomats, it was noted for excellent wine and cuisine (*Baedeker* 1896).

Letter from Dr. Seward to Arthur Holmwood

"*2 September*

"My dear old fellow, —

"With regard to Miss Westenra's health, I hasten to let you know at once that in my opinion there is not any functional disturbance or any malady that I know of. At the same time, I am not by any means satisfied with her appearance; she is woefully different from what she was when I saw her last. Of course you must bear in mind that I did not have full opportunity of examination such as I should wish; our very friendship makes a little difficulty which not even medical science or custom can bridge over. I had better tell you exactly what happened, leaving you to draw, in a measure, your own conclusions. I shall then say what I have done and propose doing.

"I found Miss Westenra in seemingly gay spirits. Her mother was present, and in a few seconds I made up my mind that she was trying all she knew to mislead her mother and prevent her from being anxious. I have no doubt she guesses, if she does not know, what need of caution there is. We lunched alone, and as we all exerted ourselves to be cheerful, we got, as some kind of reward for our labours, some real cheerfulness amongst us. Then Mrs. Westenra went to lie down, and Lucy was left with me. We went into her boudoir, and till we got there her gaiety remained, for the servants were coming and going. As soon as the door was closed, however, the mask fell from her face, and she sank down into a chair with a great sigh, and hid her eyes with her hand. When I saw that her high spirits had failed, I at once took advantage of her reaction to make a diagnosis. She said to me very sweetly: —

" 'I cannot tell you how I loathe talking about myself.' I reminded her that a doctor's confidence was sacred, but that you were grievously anxious about her. She caught on to my meaning at once, and settled that matter in a word. 'Tell Arthur everything you choose. I do not care for myself, but all for him!' So I am quite free.

"I could easily see that she is somewhat bloodless, but I could not see the usual anæmic signs, and by a chance I was actually able to test the quality of her blood, for in opening a window which was stiff a cord gave way, and she cut her hand slightly with broken glass. It was a slight matter in itself, but it gave me an evident chance, and I secured a few drops of the blood and have analysed them. The qualitative analysis gives a quite normal condition, and shows, I should infer, in itself a vigorous state of health. In other physical matters I was quite satisfied that there is no need for anxiety; but as there must be a cause somewhere, I have come to the conclusion that it must be something mental. She complains of difficulty in breathing satisfactorily at times, and of heavy, lethargic sleep, with dreams that frighten her, but regarding which she can remember nothing. She says that as a child she used to walk in her sleep, and that when in Whitby the habit came back, and that once she walked out in the night and went to the East Cliff, where Miss Murray found her; but she assures me that of late the habit has not returned. I am in doubt, and so have done the best thing I know of; I have written to my old friend and master, Professor Van Helsing, of Amsterdam, who knows as much about obscure diseases as any one in the world. I have asked him to come over, and as you told me that all things were to be at your charge, I have mentioned to him who you are and your relations to Miss Westenra. This, my dear fellow, is only in obedience to your wishes, for I am only too proud and happy to do anything I can for her. Van Helsing would, I know, do anything for me for a personal reason. So, no matter on what ground he comes, we must accept his wishes. He is a seemingly arbitrary man, but this is because he knows what he is talking about better than any one else. He is a philosopher and a metaphysician, and one of the most advanced scientists of his day; and he has, I believe, an absolutely open mind. This, with an iron nerve, a temper of the ice-brook,° an indomitable resolution, self-command and toleration exalted from virtues to blessings, and the kindliest and truest heart that beats — these form his equipment for the noble work that he is doing for mankind — work both in theory and practice, for his views are as wide as his all-embracing sympathy. I tell you these facts that you may know why I have such confidence in him. I have asked him to come at once. I shall see Miss Westenra to-morrow again. She is to meet me at the Stores,° so that I may not alarm her mother by too early a repetition of my call.

"Yours always,
"JOHN SEWARD."

---

temper of the ice-brook: In *Othello,* Othello says, "I have another weapon in this chamber; / It was a sword of Spain, the ice-brook's temper —" (5.2.261–62). Seward uses "temper" differently from Othello, who refers to the sword's having been hardened in a process involving cold water. Seward implies that Van Helsing has a composed, or even icy, temperament (*OED*).   *the Stores:* This could be either "one of the larger London co-operative societies, consisting of a number of departments, each dealing in a separate class of goods," or the trading establishments who adopted the name to indicate their resemblance to "The Stores" "in extent and in multifariousness of business" (*OED* 16: 789). The fashionable Harrod's was one such establishment and could be meant here.

Letter, Abraham Van Helsing, M.D., D.Ph., D. Lit., etc., etc., to Dr. Seward

"*2 September*

"My good Friend, —

"When I have received your letter I am already coming to you. By good fortune I can leave just at once, without wrong to any of those who have trusted me. Were fortune other, then it were bad for those who have trusted, for I come to my friend when he call me to aid those he holds dear. Tell your friend that when that time you suck from my wound so swiftly the poison of the gangrene from that knife that our other friend, too nervous, let slip, you did more for him when he wants my aids and you call for them than all his great fortune could do. But it is pleasure added to do for him, your friend; it is to you that I come. Have then rooms for me at the Great Eastern Hotel,° so that I may be near to hand, and please it so arrange that we may see the young lady not too late on to-morrow, for it is likely that I may have to return here that night. But if need be I shall come again in three days and stay longer if it must. Till then good-bye, my friend John.

"VAN HELSING."

Letter, Dr. Seward to Hon. Arthur Holmwood

"*3 September*

"My dear Art, —

"Van Helsing has come and gone. He came on with me to Hilling-ham, and found that, by Lucy's discretion, her mother was lunching out, so that we were alone with her. Van Helsing made a very careful examination of the patient. He is to report to me, and I shall advise you, for of course I was not present all the time. He is, I fear, much concerned, but says he must think. When I told him of our friendship and how you trust to me in the matter, he said: 'You must tell him all you think. Tell him what I think, if you can guess it, if you will. Nay, I am not jesting. This is no jest, but life and death, perhaps more.' I asked what he meant by that, for he was very serious. This was when we had come back to town, and he was having a cup of tea before starting on his return to Amsterdam. He would not give me any further clue. You must not be angry with him, Art, because his very reticence means that all his brains are working for her good. He will speak plainly enough

---

Great Eastern Hotel: A large railway hotel in central London, generally frequented by Germans staying in London for business purposes (*Baedeker* 1896).

when the time comes, be sure. So I told him I would simply write an account of our visit, just as if I were doing a descriptive special article for *The Daily Telegraph*. He seemed not to notice, but remarked that the smuts° in London were not quite so bad as they used to be when he was a student here. I am to get his report to-morrow if he can possibly make it. In any case I am to have a letter.

"Well, as to the visit. Lucy was more cheerful than on the day I first saw her, and certainly looked better. She had lost something of the ghastly look that so upset you, and her breathing was normal. She was very sweet to the Professor (as she always is), and tried to make him feel at ease; though I could see that the poor girl was making a hard struggle for it. I believe Van Helsing saw it, too, for I saw the quick look under his bushy brows that I knew of old. Then he began to chat of all things, except ourselves and diseases, and with such an infinite geniality that I could see poor Lucy's pretence of animation merge into reality. Then, without any seeming change, he brought the conversation gently round to his visit, and suavely said: —

" 'My dear young miss, I have the so great pleasure because you are much beloved. That is much, my dear, even were there that which I do not see. They told me you were down in the spirit, and that you were of a ghastly pale. To them I say: "Pouf!" ' And he snapped his fingers at me and went on: 'But you and I shall show them how wrong they are. How can he' — and he pointed at me with the same look and gesture as that with which once he pointed me out to his class, on, or rather after, a particular occasion which he never fails to remind me of — 'know anything of a young ladies? He has his madmans to play with, and to bring them back to happiness and to those that love them. It is much to do, and, oh, but there are rewards, in that we can bestow such happiness. But the young ladies! He has no wife nor daughter, and the young do not tell themselves to the young, but to the old, like me, who have known so many sorrows and the causes of them. So, my dear, we will send him away to smoke the cigarette in the garden, whiles you and I have little talk all to ourselves.' I took the hint, and strolled about, and presently the Professor came to the window and called me in. He looked grave, but said: 'I have made careful examination, but there is no functional cause. With you I agree that there has been much blood lost; it has been, but is not. But the conditions of her are in no way anæmic. I have asked her to send me her maid, that I may ask just one or two question, that so I may not chance to miss nothing. I know well

smuts: Soot (*OED* OL).

what she will say. And yet there is cause; there is always cause for everything. I must go back home and think. You must send to me the telegram every day; and if there be cause I shall come again. The disease — for not to be all well is a disease — interest me, and the sweet young dear, she interest me too. She charm me, and for her, if not for you or disease, I come.'

"As I tell you, he would not say a word more, even when we were alone. And so now, Art, you know all I know. I shall keep stern watch. I trust your poor father is rallying. It must be a terrible thing to you, my dear old fellow, to be placed in such a position between two people who are both so dear to you. I know your idea of duty to your father, and you are right to stick to it; but, if need be, I shall send you word to come at once to Lucy; so do not be over-anxious unless you hear from me."

Dr. Seward's Diary

4 *September.* — Zoophagous patient still keeps up our interest in him. He had only one outburst, and that was yesterday at an unusual time. Just before the stroke of noon he began to grow restless. The attendant knew the symptoms, and at once summoned aid. Fortunately the men came at a run, and were just in time, for at the stroke of noon he became so violent that it took all their strength to hold him. In about five minutes, however, he began to get more and more quiet, and finally sank into a sort of melancholy, in which state he has remained up to now. The attendant tells me that his screams whilst in the paroxysm were really appalling; I found my hands full when I got in, attending to some of the other patients who were frightened by him. Indeed, I can quite understand the effect, for the sounds disturbed even me, though I was some distance away. It is now after the dinner-hour of the asylum, and as yet my patient sits in a corner brooding, with a dull, sullen, woebegone look in his face, which seems rather to indicate than to show something directly. I cannot quite understand it.

Later. — Another change in my patient. At five o'clock I looked in on him, and found him seemingly as happy and contented as he used to be. He was catching flies and eating them, and was keeping note of his capture by making nail-marks on the edge of the door between the ridges of padding. When he saw me, he came over and apologised for his bad conduct, and asked me in a very humble, cringing way to be led back to his own room and to have his note-book again. I thought it well to humour him; so he is back in his room, with the window open.

He has the sugar of his tea spread out on the window-sill, and is reaping quite a harvest of flies. He is not now eating them, but putting them into a box, as of old, and is already examining the corners of his room to find a spider. I tried to get him to talk about the past few days, for any clue to his thoughts would be of immense help to me; but he would not rise. For a moment or two he looked very sad, and said in a sort of far-away voice, as though saying it rather to himself than to me: —

"All over! all over! He has deserted me. No hope for me now unless I do it for myself!" Then suddenly turning to me in a resolute way, he said: "Doctor, won't you be very good to me and let me have a little more sugar? I think it would be good for me."

"And the flies?" I said.

"Yes! The flies like it, too, and I like the flies; therefore I like it." And there are people who know so little as to think that madmen do not argue. I procured him a double supply, and left him as happy a man as, I suppose, any in the world. I wish I could fathom his mind.

Midnight. — Another change in him. I had been to see Miss Westenra, whom I found much better, and had just returned, and was standing at our own gate looking at the sunset, when once more I heard him yelling. As his room is on this side of the house, I could hear it better than in the morning. It was a shock to me to turn from the wonderful smoky beauty of a sunset over London, with its lurid lights and inky shadows and all the marvellous tints that come on foul clouds even as on foul water, and to realise all the grim sternness of my own cold stone building, with its wealth of breathing misery, and my own desolate heart to endure it all. I reached him just as the sun was going down, and from his window saw the red disc sink. As it sank he became less and less frenzied; and just as it dipped he slid from the hands that held him, an inert mass, on the floor. It is wonderful, however, what intellectual recuperative power lunatics have, for within a few minutes he stood up quite calmly and looked around him. I signalled to the attendants not to hold him, for I was anxious to see what he would do. He went straight over to the window and brushed out the crumbs of sugar; then he took his fly-box and emptied it outside, and threw away the box; then he shut the window, and crossing over, sat down on his bed. All this surprised me, so I asked him: "Are you not going to keep flies any more?"

"No," said he; "I am sick of all that rubbish!" He certainly is a wonderfully interesting study. I wish I could get some glimpse of his mind or of the cause of his sudden passion. Stop; there may be a clue after all, if we can find why to-day his paroxysms came on at high noon and at sunset.

Can it be that there is a malign influence of the sun at periods which affects certain natures — as at times the moon does others? We shall see.

Telegram, Seward, London to Van Helsing, Amsterdam

"4 *September.* — Patient still better to-day."

Telegram, Seward, London, to Van Helsing, Amsterdam

"5 *September.* — Patient greatly improved. Good appetite; sleeps naturally; good spirits; colour coming back."

Telegram, Seward, London, to Van Helsing, Amsterdam

"6 *September.* — Terrible change for the worse. Come at once; do not lose an hour. I hold over telegram to Holmwood till have seen you."

CHAPTER X. LETTER, DR. SEWARD TO HON. ARTHUR HOLMWOOD

"6 *September*

"My dear Art, —

"My news to-day is not so good. Lucy this morning had gone back a bit. There is, however, one good thing which has arisen from it: Mrs. Westenra was naturally anxious concerning Lucy, and has consulted me professionally about her. I took advantage of the opportunity, and told her that my old master, Van Helsing, the great specialist, was coming to stay with me, and that I would put her in his charge conjointly with myself; so now we can come and go without alarming her unduly, for a shock to her would mean sudden death, and this, in Lucy's weak condition, might be disastrous to her. We are hedged in with difficulties, all of us, my poor old fellow; but, please God, we shall come through them all right. If any need I shall write, so that, if you do not hear from me, take it for granted that I am simply waiting for news. In haste,

"Yours ever,
"JOHN SEWARD."

Dr. Seward's Diary

7 *September.* — The first thing Van Helsing said to me when we met at Liverpool Street was: —

"Have you said anything to our young friend the lover of her?"

"No," I said. "I waited till I had seen you, as I said in my telegram. I wrote him a letter simply telling him that you were coming, as Miss Westenra was not so well, and that I should let him know if need be."

"Right, my friend," he said, "quite right! Better he not know as yet; perhaps he shall never know. I pray so; but if it be needed, then he shall know all. And, my good friend John, let me caution you. You deal with the madmen. All men are mad in some way or the other; and inasmuch as you deal discreetly with your madmen, so deal with God's madmen, too — the rest of the world. You tell not your madmen what you do nor why you do it; you tell them not what you think. So you shall keep knowledge in its place, where it may rest — where it may gather its kind around it and breed. You and I shall keep as yet what we know here, and here." He touched me on the heart and on the forehead, and then touched himself the same way. "I have for myself thoughts at the present. Later I shall unfold to you."

"Why not now?" I asked. "It may do some good; we may arrive at some decision." He stopped and looked at me, and said: —

"My friend John, when the corn° is grown, even before it has ripened — while the milk of its mother-earth is in him, and the sunshine has not yet begun to paint him with his gold, the husbandman he pull the ear and rub him between his rough hands, and blow away the green chaff, and say to you: 'Look! he's good corn; he will make good crop when the time comes.'" I did not see the application, and told him so. For reply he reached over and took my ear° in his hand and pulled it playfully, as he used long ago to do at lectures, and said: "The good husbandman tell you so then because he knows, but not till then. But you do not find the good husbandman dig up his planted corn to see if he grow; that is for the children who play at husbandry, and not for those who take it as of the work of their life. See you now, friend John? I have sown my corn, and Nature has her work to do in making it sprout; if he sprout at all, there's some promise; and I wait till the ear begins to swell." He broke off, for he evidently saw that I understood. Then he went on, and very gravely: —

"You were always a careful student, and your case-book was ever more full than the rest. You were only student then; now you are master, and I trust that good habit have not fail. Remember, my friend, that knowledge is stronger than memory, and we should not trust the

---

corn: Not American maize, which this word designates in American English, but one of the grains, such as wheat, rye, oats, or barley (*OED*).   **ear:** Van Helsing's action puns on the double meaning of "ear": an ear, that is, the head or spike, of grain and Seward's ear, which he pulls.

weaker. Even if you have not kept the good practice, let me tell you that this case of our dear miss is one that may be — mind, I say *may be* — of such interest to us and others that all the rest may not make him kick the beam,° as your peoples say. Take then good note of it. Nothing is too small. I counsel you, put down in record even your doubts and surmises. Hereafter it may be of interest to you to see how true you guess. We learn from failure, not from success!"

When I described Lucy's symptoms — the same as before, but infinitely more marked — he looked very grave, but said nothing. He took with him a bag in which were many instruments and drugs, "the ghastly paraphernalia of our beneficial trade," as he once called, in one of his lectures, the equipment of a professor of the healing craft. When we were shown in, Mrs. Westenra met us. She was alarmed, but not nearly so much as I expected to find her. Nature in one of her beneficent moods has ordained that even death has some antidote to its own terrors. Here, in a case where any shock may prove fatal, matters are so ordered that, from some cause or other, the things not personal — even the terrible change in her daughter to whom she is so attached — do not seem to reach her. It is something like the way Dame Nature gathers round a foreign body an envelope of some insensitive tissue which can protect from evil that which it would otherwise harm by contact. If this be an ordered selfishness, then we should pause before we condemn any one for the vice of egoism, for there may be deeper roots for its causes than we have knowledge of.

I used my knowledge of this phase of spiritual pathology, and laid down a rule that she should not be present with Lucy or think of her illness more than was absolutely required. She assented readily, so readily that I saw again the hand of Nature fighting for life. Van Helsing and I were shown up to Lucy's room. If I was shocked when I saw her yesterday, I was horrified when I saw her to-day. She was ghastly, chalkily pale; the red seemed to have gone even from her lips and gums, and the bones of her face stood out prominently; her breathing was painful to see or hear. Van Helsing's face grew set as marble, and his eyebrows converged till they almost touched over his nose. Lucy lay motionless and did not seem to have strength to speak, so for a while we were all silent. Then Van Helsing beckoned to me, and we went gently out of the room. The instant we had closed the door he stepped quickly along

---

not make him kick the beam: Lucy's case may so outweigh others they have looked into, if it were placed on one scale of a balance (consisting of a central pivot, a beam, and two scales) with the other cases on the opposing scale, hers would keep that opposing scale from pushing up Lucy's end of the beam.

the passage to the next door, which was open. Then he pulled me quickly in with him and closed the door. "My God!" he said; "this is dreadful. There is no time to be lost. She will die for sheer want of blood to keep the heart's action as it should be. There must be transfusion of blood at once. Is it you or me?"

"I am younger and stronger, Professor. It must be me."

"Then get ready at once. I will bring up my bag. I am prepared."

I went downstairs with him, and as we were going there was a knock at the hall-door. When we reached the hall the maid had just opened the door, and Arthur was stepping quickly in. He rushed up to me, saying in an eager whisper: —

"Jack, I was so anxious. I read between the lines of your letter, and have been in an agony. The dad was better, so I ran down here to see for myself. Is not that gentleman Dr. Van Helsing? I am so thankful to you, sir, for coming." When first the Professor's eye had lit upon him he had been angry at any interruption at such a time; but now, as he took in his stalwart proportions and recognised the strong young manhood which seemed to emanate from him, his eyes gleamed. Without a pause he said to him gravely as he held out his hand: —

"Sir, you have come in time. You are the lover of our dear miss. She is bad, very, very bad. Nay, my child, do not go like that." For he suddenly grew pale and sat down in a chair almost fainting. "You are to help her. You can do more than any that live, and your courage is your best help."

"What can I do?" asked Arthur hoarsely. "Tell me, and I shall do it. My life is hers, and I would give the last drop of blood in my body for her." The Professor has a strongly humorous side, and I could from old knowledge detect a trace of its origin in his answer: —

"My young sir, I do not ask so much as that — not the last!"

"What shall I do?" There was fire in his eyes, and his open nostril quivered with intent. Van Helsing slapped him on the shoulder. "Come!" he said. "You are a man, and it is a man we want. You are better than me, better than my friend John." Arthur looked bewildered, and the Professor went on by explaining in a kindly way: —

"Young miss is bad, very bad. She wants blood,° and blood she must have or die. My friend John and I have consulted; and we are about to perform what we call transfusion of blood° — to transfer from

wants blood: Is deficient in blood, but ***wants,*** which can mean "desires," anticipates by a pun Lucy's desire for blood once she becomes a vampire (*OED*).   ***transfusion of blood:*** "The process of transferring the blood of a person or animal into the veins of another" (*OED*). Blood transfusions date back to the seventeenth century, but the process was so unsafe that it was outlawed in France, England, and Italy. Blood transfusions did not become safe until blood types were discovered in the twentieth century (*Enc. Brit.* OL).

full veins of one to the empty veins which pine for him. John was to give his blood, as he is the more young and strong than me" — here Arthur took my hand and wrung it hard in silence — "but, now you are here, you are more good than us, old or young, who toil much in the world of thought. Our nerves are not so calm and our blood not so bright than yours!" Arthur turned to him and said: —

"If you only knew how gladly I would die for her you would understand —"

He stopped, with a sort of choke in his voice.

"Good boy!" said Van Helsing. "In the not-so-far-off you will be happy that you have done all for her you love. Come now and be silent. You shall kiss her once before it is done, but then you must go; and you must leave at my sign. Say no word to Madame; you know how it is with her! There must be no shock; any knowledge of this would be one. Come!"

We all went up to Lucy's room. Arthur by direction remained outside. Lucy turned her head and looked at us, but said nothing. She was not asleep, but she was simply too weak to make the effort. Her eyes spoke to us; that was all. Van Helsing took some things from his bag and laid them on a little table out of sight. Then he mixed a narcotic, and coming over to the bed, said cheerily: —

"Now, little miss, here is your medicine. Drink it off, like a good child. See, I lift you so that to swallow is easy. Yes." She had made the effort with success.

It astonished me how long the drug took to act. This, in fact, marked the extent of her weakness. The time seemed endless until sleep began to flicker in her eyelids. At last, however, the narcotic began to manifest its potency; and she fell into a deep sleep. When the Professor was satisfied he called Arthur into the room, and bade him strip off his coat. Then he added: "You may take that one little kiss whiles I bring over the table. Friend John, help to me!" So neither of us looked whilst he bent over her.

Van Helsing turning to me, said: —

"He is so young and strong and of blood so pure that we need not defibrinate° it."

Then with swiftness, but with absolute method, Van Helsing performed the operation. As the transfusion went on something like life seemed to come back to poor Lucy's cheeks, and through Arthur's

---

defibrinate: To remove fibrin, a protein that causes clotting, from the blood (*OED*).

growing pallor the joy of his face seemed absolutely to shine. After a bit I began to grow anxious, for the loss of blood was telling on Arthur, strong man as he was. It gave me an idea of what a terrible strain Lucy's system must have undergone that what weakened Arthur only partially restored her. But the Professor's face was set, and he stood watch in hand and with his eyes fixed now on the patient and now on Arthur. I could hear my own heart beat. Presently he said in a soft voice: "Do not stir an instant. It is enough. You attend him; I will look to her." When all was over I could see how much Arthur was weakened. I dressed the wound and took his arm to bring him away, when Van Helsing spoke without turning round — the man seems to have eyes in the back of his head: —

"The brave lover, I think deserve another kiss, which he shall have presently." And as he had now finished his operation, he adjusted the pillow to the patient's head. As he did so the narrow black velvet band which she seems always to wear round her throat, buckled with an old diamond buckle which her lover had given her, was dragged a little up, and showed a red mark on her throat. Arthur did not notice it, but I could hear the deep hiss of indrawn breath which is one of Van Helsing's ways of betraying emotion. He said nothing at the moment, but turned to me, saying: "Now take down our brave young lover, give him of the port wine, and let him lie down a while. He must then go home and rest, sleep much and eat much, that he may be recruited of what he has so given to his love. He must not stay here. Hold! a moment. I may take it, sir, that you are anxious of result. Then bring it with you that in all ways the operation is successful. You have saved her life this time, and you can go home and rest easy in mind that all that can be is. I shall tell her all when she is well; she shall love you none the less for what you have done. Good-bye."

When Arthur had gone I went back to the room. Lucy was sleeping gently, but her breathing was stronger; I could see the counterpane move as her breast heaved. By the bedside sat Van Helsing, looking at her intently. The velvet band again covered the red mark. I asked the Professor in a whisper: —

"What do you make of that mark on her throat?"

"What do you make of it?"

"I have not seen it yet," I answered, and then and there proceeded to loose the band. Just over the external jugular vein there were two punctures, not large, but not wholesome-looking. There was no sign of disease, but the edges were white and worn-looking, as if by some trituration.° It at once occurred to me that this wound, or whatever it was, might be the means of that manifest loss of blood; but I abandoned the idea as soon as formed, for such a thing could not be. The whole bed would have been drenched to a scarlet with the blood which the girl must have lost to leave such a pallor as she had before the transfusion.

"Well?" said Van Helsing.

"Well," said I, "I can make nothing of it." The Professor stood up. "I must go back to Amsterdam to-night," he said. "There are books and things there which I want. You must remain here all the night, and you must not let your sight pass from her."

"Shall I have a nurse?" I asked.

"We are the best nurses, you and I. You keep watch all night; see that she is well fed, and that nothing disturbs her. You must not sleep all the night. Later on we can sleep, you and I. I shall be back so soon as possible. And then we may begin."

"May begin?" I said. "What on earth do you mean?"

"We shall see!" he answered as he hurried out. He came back a moment later and put his head inside the door, and said, with warning finger held up: —

"Remember, she is your charge. If you leave her, and harm befall, you shall not sleep easy hereafter!"

Dr. Seward's Diary *(Continued)*

8 September. — I sat up all night with Lucy. The opiate worked itself off towards dusk, and she waked naturally; she looked a different being from what she had been before the operation. Her spirits even were good, and she was full of a happy vivacity, but I could see evidences of the absolute prostration which she had undergone. When I told Mrs. Westenra that Dr. Van Helsing had directed that I should sit up with her she almost pooh-poohed the idea, pointing out her daughter's renewed strength and excellent spirits. I was firm, however, and made preparations for my long vigil. When her maid had prepared her for the night I came in, having in the meantime had supper, and took a seat by the bedside. She did not in any way make objection, but looked at me gratefully whenever I caught her eye. After a long spell she seemed sinking off to sleep, but with an effort seemed to pull herself together and

---

trituration: The process of rubbing, grinding, or bruising (*OED*).

shook it off. This was repeated several times, with greater effort and with shorter pauses as the time moved on. It was apparent that she did not want to sleep, so I tackled the subject at once: —

"You do not want to go to sleep?"

"No; I am afraid."

"Afraid to go to sleep! Why so? It is the boon we all crave for."

"Ah, not if you were like me — if sleep was to you a presage of horror!"

"A presage of horror! What on earth do you mean?"

"I don't know; oh, I don't know. And that is what is so terrible. All this weakness comes to me in sleep; until I dread the very thought."

"But, my dear girl, you may sleep to-night. I am here watching you, and I can promise that nothing will happen."

"Ah, I can trust you!" I seized the opportunity, and said: "I promise you that if I see any evidence of bad dreams I will wake you at once."

"You will? Oh, will you really? How good you are to me. Then I will sleep!" And almost at the word she gave a deep sigh of relief, and sank back, asleep.

All night long I watched by her. She never stirred, but slept on and on in a deep, tranquil, life-giving, health-giving sleep. Her lips were slightly parted, and her breast rose and fell with the regularity of a pendulum. There was a smile on her face, and it was evident that no bad dreams had come to disturb her peace of mind.

In the early morning her maid came, and I left her in her care and took myself back home, for I was anxious about many things. I sent a short wire to Van Helsing and to Arthur, telling them of the excellent result of the operation. My own work, with its manifold arrears, took me all day to clear off; it was dark when I was able to inquire about my zoophagous patient. The report was good: he had been quite quiet for the past day and night. A telegram came from Van Helsing at Amsterdam whilst I was at dinner, suggesting that I should be at Hillingham to-night, as it might be well to be at hand, and stating that he was leaving by the night mail and would join me early in the morning.

9 September. — I was pretty tired and worn out when I got to Hillingham. For two nights I had hardly had a wink of sleep, and my brain was beginning to feel that numbness which marks cerebral exhaustion. Lucy was up and in cheerful spirits. When she shook hands with me she looked sharply in my face and said: —

"No sitting up to-night for you. You are worn out. I am quite well again; indeed, I am; and if there is to be any sitting up, it is I who will sit up with you." I would not argue the point, but went and had my supper. Lucy came with me, and, enlivened by her charming presence, I made an excellent meal, and had a couple of glasses of the more than excellent port. Then Lucy took me upstairs, and showed me a room next her own, where a cosy fire was burning. "Now," she said, "you must stay here. I shall leave this door open and my door too. You can lie on the sofa, for I know that nothing would induce any of you doctors to go to bed whilst there is a patient above the horizon. If I want anything I shall call out, and you can come to me at once." I could not but acquiesce, for I was "dog-tired," and could not have sat up had I tried. So, on her renewing her promise to call me if she should want anything, I lay on the sofa, and forgot all about everything.

Lucy Westenra's Diary

9 *September.* — I feel so happy to-night. I have been so miserably weak, that to be able to think and move about is like feeling sunshine after a long spell of east wind out of a steel sky. Somehow Arthur feels very, very close to me. I seem to feel his presence warm about me. I suppose it is that sickness and weakness are selfish things and turn our inner eyes and sympathy on ourselves, whilst health and strength give Love rein, and in thought and feeling he can wander where he wills. I know where my thoughts are. If Arthur only knew! My dear, my dear, your ears must tingle as you sleep, as mine do waking. Oh, the blissful rest of last night! How I slept, with that dear, good Dr. Seward watching me. And to-night I shall not fear to sleep, since he is close at hand and within call. Thank everybody for being so good to me! Thank God! Good-night, Arthur.

Dr. Seward's Diary

10 *September.* — I was conscious of the Professor's hand on my head, and started awake all in a second. That is one of the things that we learn in an asylum, at any rate.

"And how is our patient?"

"Well, when I left her, or rather when she left me," I answered.

"Come, let us see," he said. And together we went into the room.

The blind was down, and I went over to raise it gently, whilst Van Helsing stepped, with his soft, cat-like tread, over to the bed.

As I raised the blind, and the morning sunlight flooded the room, I heard the Professor's low hiss of inspiration, and knowing its rarity, a deadly fear shot through my heart. As I passed over he moved back, and his exclamation of horror, "Gott in Himmel!"° needed no enforcement from his agonised face. He raised his hand and pointed to the bed, and his iron face was drawn and ashen white. I felt my knees begin to tremble. There on the bed, seemingly in a swoon, lay poor Lucy, more horribly white and wan-looking than ever. Even the lips were white, and the gums seemed to have shrunken back from the teeth, as we sometimes see in a corpse after a prolonged illness. Van Helsing raised his foot to stamp in anger, but the instinct of his life and all the long years of habit stood to him, and he put it down again softly. "Quick!" he said. "Bring the brandy." I flew to the dining-room, and returned with the decanter. He wetted the poor white lips with it, and together we rubbed palm and wrist and heart. He felt her heart, and after a few moments of agonising suspense said: —

"It is not too late. It beats, though but feebly. All our work is undone; we must begin again. There is no young Arthur here now; I have to call on you yourself this time, friend John." As he spoke, he was dipping into his bag and producing the instruments for transfusion; I had taken off my coat and rolled up my shirt-sleeve. There was no possibility of an opiate just at present, and no need of one; and so, without a moment's delay, we began the operation. After a time — it did not seem a short time either, for the draining away of one's blood, no matter how willingly it be given, is a terrible feeling — Van Helsing held up a warning finger. "Do not stir," he said, "but I fear that with growing strength she may wake; and that would make danger, oh, so much danger. But I shall precaution take. I shall give hypodermic injection of morphia." He proceeded then, swiftly and deftly, to carry out his intent. The effect on Lucy was not bad, for the faint seemed to merge subtly into the narcotic sleep. It was with a feeling of personal pride that I could see a faint tinge of colour steal back into the pallid cheeks and lips. No man knows till he experiences it, what it is to feel his own life-blood drawn away into the veins of the woman he loves.

The Professor watched me critically. "That will do," he said. "Already?" I remonstrated. "You took a great deal more from Art." To which he smiled a sad sort of smile as he replied: —

"He is her lover, her *fiancé*. You have work, much work, to do for her and for others; and the present will suffice."

Gott in Himmel: God in Heaven (German). That Van Helsing, who is Dutch, uses German expressions would have struck Stoker's initial readers as surprising and laughable. Van Helsing's native language is Flemish, not German, and expressions such as this one come from comic representations of Germans on the nineteenth-century British stage.

When we stopped the operation, he attended to Lucy, whilst I applied digital pressure to my own incision. I laid down, whilst I waited his leisure to attend to me, for I felt faint and a little sick. By-and-by he bound up my wound, and sent me downstairs to get a glass of wine for myself. As I was leaving the room, he came after me, and half whispered: —

"Mind, nothing must be said of this. If our young lover should turn up unexpected, as before, no word to him. It would at once frighten him and enjealous him, too. There must be none. So!"

When I came back he looked at me carefully, and then said: —

"You are not much the worse. Go into the room, and lie on your sofa, and rest awhile; then have much breakfast, and come here to me."

I followed out his orders, for I knew how right and wise they were. I had done my part, and now my next duty was to keep up my strength. I felt very weak, and in the weakness lost something of the amazement at what had occurred. I fell asleep on the sofa, however, wondering over and over again how Lucy had made such a retrograde movement, and how she could have been drained of so much blood with no sign anywhere to show for it. I think I must have continued my wonder in my dreams, for, sleeping and waking, my thoughts always came back to the little punctures in her throat and the ragged, exhausted appearance of their edges — tiny though they were.

Lucy slept well into the day; and when she woke she was fairly well and strong, though not nearly so much so as the day before. When Van Helsing had seen her, he went out for a walk, leaving me in charge, with strict injunctions that I was not to leave her for a moment. I could hear his voice in the hall, asking the way to the nearest telegraph office.

Lucy chatted with me freely, and seemed quite unconscious that anything had happened. I tried to keep her amused and interested. When her mother came up to see her, she did not seem to notice any change whatever, but said to me gratefully: —

"We owe you so much, Dr. Seward, for all you have done, but you really must now take care not to overwork yourself. You are looking pale yourself. You want a wife to nurse and look after you a bit; that you do!" As she spoke, Lucy turned crimson, though it was only momentarily, for her poor wasted veins could not stand for long such an unwonted drain to the head. The reaction came in excessive pallor as she turned imploring eyes on me. I smiled and nodded, and laid my finger on my lips; with a sigh, she sank back amid her pillows.

Van Helsing returned in a couple of hours, and presently said to me: "Now you go home, and eat much and drink enough. Make yourself strong. I stay here to-night, and I shall sit up with little miss myself. You and I must watch the case, and we must have none other to know. I have grave reasons. No, do not ask them; think what you will. Do not fear to think even the most not-probable. Good-night."

In the hall two of the maids came to me, and asked if they or either of them might not sit up with Miss Lucy. They implored me to let them; and when I said it was Dr. Van Helsing's wish that either he or I should sit up, they asked me quite piteously to intercede with the "foreign gentleman." I was much touched by their kindness. Perhaps it is because I am weak at present, and perhaps because it was on Lucy's account, that their devotion was manifested; for over and over again have I seen similar instances of woman's kindness. I got back here in time for a late dinner; went my rounds — all well; and set this down whilst waiting for sleep. It is coming.

11 *September.* — This afternoon I went over to Hillingham. Found Van Helsing in excellent spirits, and Lucy much better. Shortly after I had arrived, a big parcel from abroad came for the Professor. He opened it with much impressment — assumed, of course — and showed a great bundle of white flowers.

"These are for you, Miss Lucy," he said.

"For me? Oh, Dr. Van Helsing!"

"Yes, my dear, but not for you to play with. These are medicines." Here Lucy made a wry face. "Nay, but they are not to take in a decoction° or in nauseous form, so you need not snub that so charming nose, or I shall point out to my friend Arthur what woes he may have to endure in seeing so much beauty that he so loves so much distort. Aha, my pretty miss, that bring the so nice nose all straight again. This is medicinal, but you do not know how. I put him in your window, I make pretty wreath, and hang him round your neck, so that you sleep well. Oh yes! they, like the lotus flower, make your trouble forgotten. It smell so like the waters of Lethe, and of that fountain of youth that the Conquistodores sought for in the Floridas, and find him all too late."°

Whilst he was speaking, Lucy had been examining the flowers and smelling them. Now she threw them down, saying, with half-laughter and half-disgust: —

decoction: A liquid in which a medicinal substance has been boiled (*OED* OL).   *lotus flower. . . . waters of Lethe . . . fountain of youth . . . all too late:* In this jumble of references, Van Helsing compares the garlic and its effect first to the lotus blossoms that make part of Odysseus's crew lose their desire to return home in *The Odyssey,* then to the Lethe, river of forgetfulness in the classical underworld (whose waters the dead drink in order to forget life), and finally to the fountain of youth that Spanish explorers sought for in vain in the New World. None of these references suggests a successful return or recovery.

"Oh, Professor, I believe you are only putting up a joke on me. Why, these flowers are only common garlic."

To my surprise, Van Helsing rose up and said with all his sternness, his iron jaw set and his bushy eyebrows meeting: —

"No trifling with me! I never jest! There is grim purpose in all I do; and I warn you that you do not thwart me. Take care, for the sake of others if not for your own." Then seeing poor Lucy scared, as she might well be, he went on more gently: "Oh, little miss, my dear, do not fear me. I only do for your good; but there is much virtue° to you in those so common flower. See, I place them myself in your room. I make myself the wreath that you are to wear. But hush! no telling to others that make so inquisitive questions. We must obey, and silence is a part of obedience; and obedience is to bring you strong and well into loving arms that wait for you. Now sit still awhile. Come with me, friend John, and you shall help me deck the room with my garlic, which is all the way from Haarlem,° where my friend Vanderpool raise herb in his glass-houses all the year. I had to telegraph yesterday, or they would not have been here."

We went into the room, taking the flowers with us. The Professor's actions were certainly odd and not to be found in any pharmacopœia° that I ever heard of. First he fastened up the windows and latched them securely; next, taking a handful of the flowers, he rubbed them all over the sashes, as though to ensure that every whiff of air that might get in would be laden with the garlic smell. Then with the wisp he rubbed all over the jamb of the door, above, below, and at each side, and round the fireplace in the same way. It all seemed grotesque to me, and presently I said: —

"Well, Professor, I know you always have a reason for what you do, but this certainly puzzles me. It is well we have no sceptic here, or he would say that you were working some spell to keep out an evil spirit."

"Perhaps I am!" he answered quietly as he began to make the wreath which Lucy was to wear round her neck.

We then waited whilst Lucy made her toilet for the night, and when she was in bed he came and himself fixed the wreath of garlic round her neck. The last words he said to her were: —

---

virtue: Van Helsing uses the word here not applied to persons to mean moral excellence but applied to the garlic to mean the power or strength inherent in and derivable from it (*OED*).   **Haarlem:** A city in Holland.   **pharmacopœia:** "A book containing a list of drugs, with directions for their preparation and identification" (*OED* OL).

"Take care you do not disturb it; and even if the room feel close, do not to-night open the window or the door."

"I promise," said Lucy, "and thank you both a thousand times for all your kindness to me! Oh, what have I done to be blessed with such friends?"

As we left the house in my fly,° which was waiting, Van Helsing said: —

"To-night I can sleep in peace, and sleep I want — two nights of travel, much reading in the day between, and much anxiety on the day to follow, and a night to sit up, without to wink. To-morrow in the morning early you call for me, and we come together to see our pretty miss, so much more strong for my 'spell' which I have work. Ho! ho!"

He seemed so confident that I, remembering my own confidence two nights before and with the baneful result, felt awe and vague terror. It must have been my weakness that made me hesitate to tell it to my friend, but I felt it all the more like unshed tears.

CHAPTER XI. LUCY WESTENRA'S DIARY

12 *September.* — How good they all are to me. I quite love that dear Dr. Van Helsing. I wonder why he was so anxious about these flowers. He positively frightened me, he was so fierce. And yet he must have been right, for I feel comfort from them already. Somehow, I do not dread being alone to-night, and I can go to sleep without fear. I shall not mind any flapping outside the window. Oh, the terrible struggle that I have had against sleep so often of late; the pain of the sleepless-ness, or the pain of the fear of sleep, with such unknown horrors as it has for me! How blessed are some people, whose lives have no fears, no dreads; to whom sleep is a blessing that comes nightly, and brings nothing but sweet dreams. Well, here I am to-night hoping for sleep, and lying like Ophelia in the play, with "virgin crants and maiden strewments."° I never liked garlic before, but to-night it is delightful! There is peace in its smell; I feel sleep coming already. Good-night, everybody.°

---

fly: A single-horse covered carriage.   *Ophelia in the play . . . strewments:* In *Hamlet,* the dead Ophelia is allowed a ceremonious funeral, with "her virgin crants, / Her maiden strewments, and the bringing home / Of bell and burial," even though she may have committed suicide (*Hamlet* 5.1.232–34).   *Good-night, everybody:* Lucy echoes Ophelia's mad leave-taking, "Good night, ladies, good night, sweet ladies, good night, good night" (*Hamlet* 4.5.73–74).

Dr. Seward's Diary

13 September. — Called at the Berkeley° and found Van Helsing, as usual, up to time. The carriage ordered from the hotel was waiting. The Professor took his bag, which he always brings with him now.

Let all be put down exactly. Van Helsing and I arrived at Hillingham at eight o'clock. It was a lovely morning; the bright sunshine and all the fresh feeling of early autumn seemed like the completion of nature's annual work. The leaves were turning to all kinds of beautiful colours, but had not yet begun to drop from the trees. When we entered we met Mrs. Westenra coming out of the morning room. She is always an early riser. She greeted us warmly and said: —

"You will be glad to know that Lucy is better. The dear child is still asleep. I looked into her room and saw her, but did not go in, lest I should disturb her." The Professor smiled, and looked quite jubilant. He rubbed his hands together, and said: —

"Aha! I thought I had diagnosed the case. My treatment is working," to which she answered: —

"You must not take all the credit to yourself, doctor. Lucy's state this morning is due in part to me."

"How do you mean, ma'am?" asked the Professor.

"Well, I was anxious about the dear child in the night, and went into her room. She was sleeping soundly — so soundly that even my coming did not wake her. But the room was awfully stuffy. There were a lot of those horrible, strong-smelling flowers about everywhere, and she had actually a bunch of them round her neck. I feared that the heavy odour would be too much for the dear child in her weak state, so I took them all away and opened a bit of the window to let in a little fresh air. You will be pleased with her, I am sure."

She moved off into her boudoir, where she usually breakfasted early. As she had spoken, I watched the Professor's face, and saw it turn ashen grey. He had been able to retain his self-command whilst the poor lady was present, for he knew her state and how mischievous a shock would be; he actually smiled on her as he held open the door for her to pass into her room. But the instant she had disappeared he pulled me, suddenly and forcibly, into the dining-room and closed the door.

Then, for the first time in my life, I saw Van Helsing break down. He raised his hands over his head in a sort of mute despair, and then beat his palms together in a helpless way; finally he sat down on a chair,

---

Berkeley: Like the Albemarle, an expensive and fashionable hotel, located at the corner of Berkeley Street near Piccadilly (*Baedeker* 1896).

and putting his hands before his face, began to sob, with loud, dry sobs that seemed to come from the very racking of his heart. Then he raised his arms again, as though appealing to the whole universe. "God! God! God!" he said. "What have we done, what has this poor thing done, that we are so sore beset? Is there fate amongst us still, sent down from the pagan world of old, that such things must be, and in such way? This poor mother, all unknowing, and all for the best as she think, does such thing as lose her daughter body and soul; and we must not tell her, we must not even warn her, or she die, and then both die. Oh, how we are beset! How are all the powers of the devils against us!" Suddenly he jumped to his feet. "Come," he said, "come, we must see and act. Devils or no devils, or all the devils at once, it matters not; we fight him all the same." He went to the hall-door for his bag; and together we went up to Lucy's room.

Once again I drew up the blind, whilst Van Helsing went towards the bed. This time he did not start as he looked on the poor face with the same awful, waxen pallor as before. He wore a look of stern sadness and infinite pity.

"As I expected," he murmured, with that hissing inspiration of his which meant so much. Without a word he went and locked the door, and then began to set out on the little table the instruments for yet another operation of transfusion of blood. I had long ago recognised the necessity, and begun to take off my coat, but he stopped me with a warning hand. "No!" he said. "To-day you must operate. I shall provide. You are weakened already." As he spoke he took off his coat and rolled up his shirt-sleeve.

Again the operation; again the narcotic; again some return of colour to the ashy cheeks, and the regular breathing of healthy sleep. This time I watched whilst Van Helsing recruited himself° and rested.

Presently he took an opportunity of telling Mrs. Westenra that she must not remove anything from Lucy's room without consulting him; that the flowers were of medicinal value, and that the breathing of their odour was a part of the system of cure. Then he took over the care of the case himself, saying that he would watch this night and the next and would send me word when to come.

After another hour Lucy waked from her sleep, fresh and bright and seemingly not much the worse for her terrible ordeal.

What does it all mean? I am beginning to wonder if my long habit of life amongst the insane is beginning to tell upon my own brain.

recruited himself: Recovered, renewed his strength or vigor (*OED*).

Lucy Westenra's Diary

17 *September.* — Four days and nights of peace. I am getting so strong again that I hardly know myself. It is as if I had passed through some long nightmare, and had just awakened to see the beautiful sunshine and feel the fresh air of the morning around me. I have a dim half-remembrance of long, anxious times of waiting and fearing; darkness in which there was not even the pain of hope to make present distress more poignant; and then long spells of oblivion, and the rising back to life as a diver coming up through a great press of water. Since, however, Dr. Van Helsing has been with me, all this bad dreaming seems to have passed away; the noises that used to frighten me out of my wits — the flapping against the windows, the distant voices which seemed so close to me, the harsh sounds that came from I know not where and commanded me to do I know not what — have all ceased. I go to bed now without any fear of sleep. I do not even try to keep awake. I have grown quite fond of the garlic, and a boxful arrives for me every day from Haarlem. To-night Dr. Van Helsing is going away, as he has to be for a day in Amsterdam. But I need not be watched; I am well enough to be left alone. Thank God for mother's sake, and dear Arthur's, and for all our friends who have been so kind! I shall not even feel the change, for last night Dr. Van Helsing slept in his chair a lot of the time. I found him asleep twice when I awoke; but I did not fear to go to sleep again, although the boughs or bats or something flapped almost angrily against the window-panes.

"The Pall Mall Gazette,"° 18 September

THE ESCAPED WOLF

PERILOUS ADVENTURE OF OUR INTERVIEWER

Interview with the Keeper in the Zoological Gardens

After many inquiries and almost as many refusals, and perpetually using the words "Pall Mall Gazette" as a sort of talisman, I managed to find the keeper of the section of the Zoological Gardens in which the wolf department is included. Thomas Bilder lives in one of the cottages in the enclosure behind the elephant-house, and was just sitting down to his tea when I found him. Thomas and his wife are hospitable folk,

---

The Pall Mall Gazette: One of London's principal daily evening papers, sold at railway stations, newspaper shops, and in the streets by newsboys (*Baedeker* 1896).

elderly, and without children, and if the specimen I enjoyed of their hospitality be of the average kind, their lives must be pretty comfortable. The keeper would not enter on what he called "business" until the supper was over, and we were all satisfied. Then when the table was cleared, and he had lit his pipe, he said: —

"Now, sir, you can go on and arsk me what you want. You'll excoose me refoosin' to talk of perfeshunal subjects afore meals. I gives the wolves and the jackals and the hyenas in all our section their tea afore I begins to arsk them questions."

"How do you mean, ask them questions?" I queried, wishful to get him into a talkative humour.

"'Ittin' of them over the 'ead with a pole is one way; scratchin' of their hears is another, when gents as is flush wants a bit of a show-orf to their gals. I don't so much mind the fust — the 'ittin' with a pole afore I chucks in their dinner; but I waits till they've 'ad their sherry and kawffee, so to speak, afore I tries on with the ear-scratchin'. Mind you," he added philosophically, "there's a deal of the same nature in us as in them theer animiles. Here's you a-comin' and arskin' of me questions about my business, and I that grumpy-like that only for your bloomin' 'arf-quid° I'd 'a' seen you blowed fust 'fore I'd answer. Not even when you arsked me sarcastic-like if I'd like you to arsk the Superintendent if you might arsk me questions. Without offence, did I tell yer to go to 'ell?"

"You did."

"An' when you said you'd report me for usin' of obscene language that was 'ittin' me over the 'ead; but the 'arf-quid made that all right. I weren't a-goin' to fight, so I waited for the food, and did with my 'owl as the wolves, and lions, and tigers does. But, Lor' love yer 'art, now that the old 'ooman has stuck a chunk of her tea-cake in me, an' rinsed me out with her bloomin' old teapot, and I've lit hup, you may scratch my ears for all you're worth, and won't git even a growl out of me. Drive along with your questions. I know what yer a-comin' at, that 'ere escaped wolf."

"Exactly. I want you to give me your view of it. Just tell me how it happened; and when I know the facts I'll get you to say what you consider was the cause of it, and how you think the whole affair will end."

"All right, guv'nor. This 'ere is about the 'ole story. That 'ere wolf what we called Bersicker° was one of three grey ones that came from

---

'arf-quid: Half-quid. *Quid* is slang for a pound sterling.   **Bersicker:** The zookeeper's pronunciation of Berserker (see note, p. 53).

Norway to Jamrach's, which we bought off him four year ago. He was a nice well-behaved wolf, that never gave no trouble to talk of. I'm more surprised at 'im for wantin' to get out nor any other animile in the place. But, there, you can't trust wolves no more nor women."

"Don't you mind him, sir!" broke in Mrs. Tom, with a cheery laugh. " 'E's got mindin' the animiles so long that blest if he ain't like a old wolf 'isself! But there ain't no 'arm in 'im."

"Well, sir, it was about two hours after feedin' yesterday when I first hear any disturbance. I was makin' up a litter in the monkey-house for a young puma which is ill; but when I heard the yelpin' and 'owlin' I kem away straight. There was Bersicker a-tearin' like a mad thing at the bars as if he wanted to get out. There wasn't much people about that day, and close at hand was only one man, a tall, thin chap, with a 'ook nose and a pointed beard, with a few white hairs runnin' through it. He had a 'ard, cold look and red eyes, and I took a sort of mislike to him, for it seemed as if it was 'im as they was hirritated at. He 'ad white kid gloves on 'is 'ands, and he pointed out the animiles to me and says: 'Keeper, these wolves seem upset at something.'

"Maybe it's you, sasys I, for I did not like the airs as he give 'isself. He didn't git angry, as I 'oped he would, but he smiled a kind of insolent smile, with a mouth full of white, sharp teeth. "Oh no, they wouldn't like me," 'e says.

" 'Ow yes, they would,' says I, a-imitatin' of him. 'They always likes a bone or two to clean their teeth on about tea-time, which you 'as a bagful.'

"Well, it was a odd thing, but when the animiles see us a-talkin' they lay down, and when I went over to Bersicker he let me stroke his ears same as ever. That there man kem over, and blessed but if he didn't put in his hand and stroke the old wolf's ears too!

" 'Tyke care,' says I. 'Bersicker is quick.'

" 'Never mind,' he says. 'I'm used to 'em!'

"Are you in the business yourself?' I says, tyking off my 'at, for a man what trades in wolves, anceterer,° is a good friend to keepers.

" 'No,' says he, 'not exactly in the business, but I 'ave made pets of several.' And with that he lifts his 'at as perlite as a lord, and walks away. Old Bersicker kep' a-lookin' arter 'im till 'e was out of sight, and then went and lay down in a corner, and wouldn't come hout the 'ole hevening. Well, larst night, so soon as the moon was hup, the wolves here all began a-'owling. There warn't nothing for them to 'owl at.

anceterer: Etcetera.

There warn't no one near, except some one that was evidently a-callin'
a dog somewheres out back of the gardings in the Park road. Once or
twice I went out to see that all was right, and it was, and then the 'owling stopped. Just before twelve o'clock I just took a look round afore
turnin' in, an', bust me, but when I kem opposite to old Bersicker's
cage I see the rails broken and twisted about and the cage empty. And
that's all I know for certing."

"Did any one else see anything?"

"One of our gard'ners was a-comin' 'ome about that time from a
'armony,° when he sees a big grey dog comin' out through the garding
'edges.° At least, so he says; but I don't give much for it myself, for if he
did 'e never said a word about it to his missis when 'e got 'ome, and it
was only after the escape of the wolf was made known, and we had been
up all night a-huntin' of the Park for Bersicker, that he remembered
seein' anything. My own belief was that the 'armony 'ad got into his
'ead."

"Now, Mr. Bilder, can you account in any way for the escape of the
wolf?"

"Well, sir," he said, with a suspicious sort of modesty, "I think I can;
but I don't know as 'ow you'd be satisfied with the theory."

"Certainly I shall. If a man like you, who knows the animals from
experience, can't hazard a good guess at any rate, who is even to try?"

"Well then, sir, I accounts for it this way; it seems to me that 'ere
wolf escaped — simply because he wanted to get out."

From the hearty way that both Thomas and his wife laughed at the
joke I could see that it had done service before, and that the whole
explanation was simply an elaborate sell. I couldn't cope in badinage
with the worthy Thomas, but I thought I knew a surer way to his heart,
so I said: —

"Now, Mr. Bilder, we'll consider that first half-sovereign worked
off, and this brother of his is waiting to be claimed when you've told me
what you think will happen."

"Right y'are, sir," he said briskly. "Ye'll excoose me, I know, for
a-chaffin' of ye, but the old woman here winked at me, which was as
much as telling me to go on."

"Well, I never!" said the old lady.

"My opinion is this: that 'ere wolf is a-'idin' of, somewheres. The
gard'ner wot didn't remember said he was a-gallopin' northward faster
than a horse could go; but I don't believe him, for, yer see, sir, wolves

don't gallop no more nor dogs does, they not bein' built that way. Wolves is fine things in a story-book, and I dessay when they gets in packs and does be chivyin'° somethin' that's more afeared than they is they can make a devil of a noise and chop it up, whatever it is. But, Lor' bless you, in real life a wolf is only a low creature, not half so clever or bold as a good dog; and not half a quarter so much fight in 'im. This one ain't been used to fightin' or even to providin' for hisself, and more like he's somewhere round the Park a-'idin' an' a-shiverin' of, and, if he thinks at all, wonderin' where he is to get his breakfast from; or maybe he's got down some area and is in a coal-cellar. My eye, won't some cook get a rum start when she sees his green eyes a-shining at her out of the dark! If he can't get food he's bound to look for it, and mayhap he may chance to light on a butcher's shop in time. If he doesn't, and some nursemaid goes a-walkin' orf with a soldier, leavin' of the hinfant in the perambulator — well then I shouldn't be surprised if the census is one babby the less. That's all."

I was handing him the half-sovereign, when something came bobbing up against the window, and Mr. Bilder's face doubled its natural length with surprise.

"God bless me!" he said. "If there ain't old Bersicker come back by 'isself!"

He went to the door and opened it; a most unnecessary proceeding it seemed to me. I have always thought that a wild animal never looks so well as when some obstacle of pronounced durability is between us; a personal experience has intensified rather than diminished that idea.

After all, however, there is nothing like custom, for neither Bilder nor his wife thought any more of the wolf than I should of a dog. The animal itself was as peaceful and well-behaved as that father of all picture-wolves — Red Riding Hood's quondam° friend, whilst moving her confidence in masquerade.

The whole scene was an unutterable mixture of comedy and pathos. The wicked wolf that for half a day had paralysed London and set all the children in the town shivering in their shoes, was there in a sort of penitent mood, and was received and petted like a sort of vulpine prodigal son. Old Bilder examined him all over with most tender solicitude, and when he had finished with his penitent said: —

"There, I knew the poor old chap would get into some kind of trouble; didn't I say it all along? Here's his head all cut and full of broken glass. 'E's been a-gettin' over some bloomin' wall or other. It's a

---

chivyin': Chivying: chasing or harassing.   *quondam:* Former.

shyme that people are allowed to top their walls with broken bottles. This 'ere's what comes of it. Come along, Bersicker."

He took the wolf and locked him up in a cage, with a piece of meat that satisfied, in quantity at any rate, the elementary conditions of the fatted calf,° and went off to report.

I came off, too, to report the only exclusive information that is given to-day regarding the strange escapade at the Zoo.

Dr. Seward's Diary

17 *September.* — I was engaged after dinner in my study posting up my books,° which, through press of other work and the many visits to Lucy, had fallen sadly into arrear. Suddenly the door was burst open, and in rushed my patient, with his face distorted with passion. I was thunder-struck, for such a thing as a patient getting of his own accord into the Superintendent's study is almost unknown. Without an instant's pause he made straight at me. He had a dinner-knife in his hand, and, as I saw he was dangerous, I tried to keep the table between us. He was too quick and too strong for me, however; for before I could get my balance he had struck at me and cut my left wrist rather severely. Before he could strike again, however, I got in my right, and he was sprawling on his back on the floor. My wrist bled freely, and quite a little pool trickled on to the carpet. I saw that my friend was not intent on further effort, and occupied myself binding up my wrist, keeping a wary eye on the prostrate figure all the time. When the attendants rushed in, and we turned our attention to him, his employment positively sickened me. He was lying on his belly on the floor licking up, like a dog, the blood which had fallen from my wounded wrist. He was easily secured, and, to my surprise, went with the attendants quite placidly, simply repeating over and over again: "The blood is the life! the blood is the life!"°

I cannot afford to lose blood just at the present: I have lost too much of late for my physical good, and then the prolonged strain of Lucy's illness and its horrible phases is telling on me. I am over-excited

---

fatted calf: In the New Testament parable of the prodigal son, referred to two paragraphs earlier, the joyful father orders that the fatted calf be slaughtered to celebrate his son's return (Luke 15.23).   *posting up my books:* A bookkeeping term meaning to transfer entries from a daybook or journal into a ledger; generally, to keep one's accounts (*OED*). *the blood is the life:* Renfield's statement echoes one of the Old Testament's dietary prohibitions. Deuteronomy 12.23 states, "Only be sure that thou eat not the blood: for the blood is the life; and thou mayest not eat the life with the flesh." The biblical injunction prohibits exactly what Renfield has been doing: ingesting blood.

and weary, and I need rest, rest, rest. Happily Van Helsing has not summoned me, so I need not forego my sleep; to-night I could not well do without it.

Telegram, Van Helsing, Antwerp, to Seward, Carfax

*(Sent to Carfax, Sussex, as no county given;
delivered late by twenty-two hours.)*

"17 *September.* Do not fail to be at Hillingham to-night. If not watching all the time, frequently visit and see that flowers are as placed; very important; do not fail. Shall be with you as soon as possible after arrival."

Dr. Seward's Diary

18 *September.* — Just off for train to London. The arrival of Van Helsing's telegram filled me with dismay. A whole night lost, and I know by bitter experience what may happen in a night. Of course it is possible that all may be well, but what *may* have happened? Surely there is some horrible doom hanging over us that every possible accident should thwart us in all we try to do. I shall take this cylinder with me, and then I can complete my entry on Lucy's phonograph.

Memorandum left by Lucy Westenra

17 *September. Night.* — I write this and leave it to be seen, so that no one may by any chance get into any trouble through me. This is an exact record of what took place to-night. I feel I am dying of weakness, and have barely strength to write, but it must be done if I die in the doing.

I went to bed as usual, taking care that the flowers were placed as Dr. Van Helsing directed, and soon fell asleep.

I was waked by the flapping at the window, which had begun after that sleep-walking on the cliff at Whitby when Mina saved me, and which now I know so well. I was not afraid, but I did wish that Dr. Seward was in the next room — as Dr. Van Helsing said he would be — so that I might have called him. I tried to go to sleep, but could not. Then there came to me the old fear of sleep, and I determined to keep awake. Perversely sleep would try to come then when I did not want it; so as I feared to be alone, I opened my door and called out: "Is there anybody there?" There was no answer. I was afraid to wake mother, and so closed my door again. Then outside in the shrubbery I heard a sort of howl like a dog's, but more fierce and deeper. I went to the window and looked out, but could see nothing, except a big bat, which had evidently been buffeting its wings against the window. So I went back to bed again, but determined not to go to sleep. Presently the door opened, and mother looked in; seeing by my moving that I was not asleep, came in, and sat by me. She said to me even more sweetly and softly than her wont: —

"I was uneasy about you, darling, and came in to see that you were all right."

I feared she might catch cold sitting there, and asked her to come in and sleep with me, so she came into bed, and lay down beside me; she did not take off her dressing gown, for she said she would only stay a while and then go back to her own bed. As she lay there in my arms, and I in hers, the flapping and buffeting came to the window again. She was startled and a little frightened, and cried out: "What is that?" I tried to pacify her, and at last succeeded, and she lay quiet; but I could hear her poor dear heart still beating terribly. After a while there was the low howl again out in the shrubbery, and shortly after there was a crash at the window, and a lot of broken glass was hurled on the floor. The window blind blew back with the wind that rushed in, and in the aperture of the broken panes there was the head of a great, gaunt grey wolf. Mother cried out in a fright, and struggled up into a sitting posture, and clutched wildly at anything that would help her. Amongst other things, she clutched the wreath of flowers that Dr. Van Helsing insisted on my wearing round my neck, and tore it away from me. For a second or two she sat up, pointing at the wolf, and there was a strange and horrible gurgling in her throat; then she fell over, as if struck with lightning, and her head hit my forehead and made me dizzy for a moment or two. The room and all round seemed to spin round. I kept my eyes fixed on the window, but the wolf drew his head back, and a whole myriad of little specks seemed to come blowing in through the broken window, and wheeling and circling round like the pillar of dust that travellers describe when there is a simoom° in the desert. I tried to stir, but there was some spell upon me, and dear mother's poor body, which seemed to grow cold already — for her dear heart had ceased to beat — weighed me down; and I remembered no more for a while.

simoom: A hot, strong, sandy wind of the Sahara and the Arabian deserts.

The time did not seem long, but very, very awful, till I recovered consciousness again. Somewhere near, a passing bell was tolling; the dogs all round the neighbourhood were howling; and in our shrubbery, seemingly just outside, a nightingale was singing. I was dazed and stupid with pain and terror and weakness, but the sound of the nightingale seemed like the voice of my dead mother come back to comfort me. The sounds seemed to have awakened the maids, too, for I could hear their bare feet pattering outside my door. I called to them, and they came in, and when they saw what had happened, and what it was that lay over me on the bed, they screamed out. The wind rushed in through the broken window, and the door slammed to. They lifted off the body of my dear mother, and laid her, covered up with a sheet, on the bed after I had got up. They were all so frightened and nervous that I directed them to go to the dining-room and have each a glass of wine. The door flew open for an instant and closed again. The maids shrieked, and then went in a body to the dining-room; and I laid what flowers I had on my dear mother's breast. When they were there I remembered what Dr. Van Helsing had told me, but I didn't like to remove them, and, besides, I would have some of the servants to sit up with me now. I was surprised that the maids did not come back. I called them, but got no answer, so I went to the dining-room to look for them.

My heart sank when I saw what had happened. They all four lay helpless on the floor, breathing heavily. The decanter of sherry was on the table half full, but there was a queer, acrid smell about. I was suspicious, and examined the decanter. It smelt of laudanum,° and looking on the sideboard, I found that the bottle which mother's doctor uses for her — oh! did use — was empty. What am I to do? what am I to do? I am back in the room with mother. I cannot leave her, and I am alone, save for the sleeping servants, whom some one has drugged. Alone with the dead! I dare not go out, for I can hear the low howl of the wolf through the broken window.

The air seems full of specks, floating and circling in the draught from the window, and the lights burn blue and dim. What am I to do? God shield me from harm this night! I shall hide this paper in my breast, where they shall find it when they come to lay me out. My dear mother gone! It is time that I go too. Good-bye, dear Arthur, if I should not survive this night. God keep you, dear, and God help me!

laudanum: A medicine in which opium is the main ingredient.

CHAPTER XII. DR. SEWARD'S DIARY

18 *September.* — I drove at once to Hillingham and arrived early. Keeping my cab at the gate, I went up the avenue alone. I knocked gently and rang as quietly as possible, for I feared to disturb Lucy or her mother, and hoped to only bring a servant to the door. After a while, finding no response, I knocked and rang again; still no answer. I cursed the laziness of the servants that they should lie abed at such an hour — for it was now ten o'clock — and so rang and knocked again, but more impatiently, but still without response. Hitherto I had blamed only the servants, but now a terrible fear began to assail me. Was this desolation but another link in the chain of doom which seemed drawing tight around us? Was it indeed a house of death to which I had come, too late? I knew that minutes, even seconds, of delay might mean hours of danger to Lucy, if she had had again one of those frightful relapses; and I went round the house to try if I could find by chance an entry anywhere.

I could find no means of ingress. Every window and door was fastened and locked, and I returned baffled to the porch. As I did so, I heard the rapid pit-pat of a swiftly driven horse's feet. They stopped at the gate, and a few seconds later I met Van Helsing running up the avenue. When he saw me, he gasped out: —

"Then it was you, and just arrived. How is she? Are we too late? Did you not get my telegram?"

I answered as quickly and coherently as I could that I had only got his telegram early in the morning and had not lost a minute in coming here, and that I could not make any one in the house hear me. He paused and raised his hat as he said solemnly: —

"Then I fear we are too late. God's will be done!" With his usual recuperative energy, he went on: "Come. If there be no way open to get in, we must make one. Time is all in all to us now."

We went round to the back of the house, where there was a kitchen window. The Professor took a small surgical saw from his case, and handing it to me, pointed to the iron bars which guarded the window. I attacked them at once and had very soon cut through three of them. Then with a long, thin knife we pushed back the fastening of the sashes and opened the window. I helped the Professor in, and followed him. There was no one in the kitchen or in the servants' rooms, which were close at hand. We tried all the rooms as we went along, and in the dining-room, dimly lit by rays of light through the shutters, found four servant-women lying on the floor. There was no need to think them dead, for their stertorous breathing and the acrid smell of laudanum in the room left no doubt as to their condition. Van Helsing and I looked at each other, and as we moved away he said: "We can attend to them later." Then we ascended to Lucy's room. For an instant or two we paused at the door to listen, but there was no sound that we could hear. With white faces and trembling hands, we opened the door gently, and entered the room.

How shall I describe what we saw? On the bed lay two women, Lucy and her mother. The latter lay farthest in, and she was covered with a white sheet, the edge of which had been blown back by the draught through the broken window, showing the drawn, white face, with a look of terror fixed upon it. By her side lay Lucy, with face white and still more drawn. The flowers which had been round her neck we found upon her mother's bosom, and her throat was bare, showing the two little wounds which we had noticed before, but looking horribly white and mangled. Without a word the Professor bent over the bed, his head almost touching poor Lucy's breast; then he gave a quick turn of his head, as of one who listens, and leaping to his feet, he cried out to me: —

"It is not yet too late! Quick! quick! Bring the brandy!"

I flew downstairs and returned with it, taking care to smell and taste it, lest it, too, were drugged like the decanter of sherry which I found on the table. The maids were still breathing, but more restlessly, and I fancied that the narcotic was wearing off. I did not stay to make sure, but returned to Van Helsing. He rubbed the brandy, as on another occasion, on her lips and gums and on her wrists and the palms of her hands. He said to me: —

"I can do this, all that can be at the present. You go wake those maids. Flick them in the face with a wet towel, and flick them hard. Make them get heat and fire and a warm bath. This poor soul is nearly as cold as that beside her. She will need to be heated before we can do anything more."

I went at once, and found little difficulty in waking three of the women. The fourth was only a young girl, and the drug had evidently affected her more strongly, so I lifted her on the sofa and let her sleep. The others were dazed at first, but as remembrance came back to them they cried and sobbed in a hysterical manner. I was stern with them, however, and would not let them talk. I told them that one life was bad enough to lose, and that if they delayed they would sacrifice Miss Lucy. So, sobbing and crying, they went about their way, half clad as they were, and prepared fire and water. Fortunately, the kitchen and boiler fires were still alive, and there was no lack of hot water. We got a bath, and carried Lucy out as she was° and placed her in it. Whilst we were busy chafing her limbs there was a knock at the hall-door. One of the maids ran off, hurried on some more clothes, and opened it. Then she returned and whispered to us that there was a gentleman who had come with a message from Mr. Holmwood. I bade her simply tell him that he must wait, for we could see no one now. She went away with the message, and, engrossed with our work, I clean forgot all about him.

I never saw in all my experience the Professor work in such deadly earnest. I knew — as he knew — that it was a stand-up fight with death, and in a pause told him so. He answered me in a way that I did not understand, but with the sternest look that his face could wear: —

"If that were all, I would stop here where we are now, and let her fade away into peace, for I see no light in life over her horizon." He went on with his work with, if possible, renewed and more frenzied vigour.

Presently we both began to be conscious that the heat was beginning to be of some effect. Lucy's heart beat a trifle more audibly to the stethoscope, and her lungs had a perceptible movement. Van Helsing's face almost beamed, and as we lifted her from the bath and rolled her in a hot sheet to dry her he said to me: —

"The first gain is ours! Check to the King!"°

We took Lucy into another room, which had by now been prepared, and laid her in bed and forced a few drops of brandy down her throat. I noticed that Van Helsing tied a soft silk handkerchief round her throat. She was still unconscious, and was quite as bad as, if not worse than, we had ever seen her.

Van Helsing called in one of the women, and told her to stay with her and not to take her eyes off her till we returned, and then beckoned me out of the room.

"We must consult as to what is to be done," he said as we descended the stairs. In the hall he opened the dining-room door, and we passed in, he closing the door carefully behind him. The shutters had been opened, but the blinds were already down, with that obedience to the etiquette of death which the British woman of the lower classes always rigidly observes. The room was, therefore, dimly dark. It was, however,

---

as she was: Still only in the nightclothes in which she had been sleeping.   **Check to the King:** The call in chess that gives notice that the opponent's king is being attacked (*OED*).

light enough for our purposes. Van Helsing's sternness was somewhat relieved by a look of perplexity. He was evidently torturing his mind about something, so I waited for an instant, and he spoke: —

"What are we to do now? Where are we to turn for help? We must have another transfusion of blood, and that soon, or that poor girl's life won't be worth an hour's purchase. You are exhausted already; I am exhausted too. I fear to trust those women, even if they would have courage to submit. What are we to do for some one who will open his veins for her?"

"What's the matter with me, anyhow?"

The voice came from the sofa across the room, and its tones brought relief and joy to my heart, for they were those of Quincey Morris. Van Helsing started angrily at the first sound, but his face softened and a glad look came into his eyes as I cried out: "Quincey Morris!" and rushed towards him with outstretched hands.

"What brought you here?" I cried as our hands met.

"I guess Art is the cause."

He handed me a telegram: —

"Have not heard from Seward for three days, and am terribly anxious. Cannot leave. Father still in same condition. Send me word how Lucy is. Do not delay. — Holmwood."

"I think I came just in the nick of time. You know you have only to tell me what to do."

Van Helsing strode forward and took his hand, looking him straight in the eyes as he said: —

"A brave man's blood is the best thing on this earth when a woman is in trouble. You're a man, and no mistake. Well, the devil may work against us for all he's worth, but God sends us men when we want them."

Once again we went through that ghastly operation. I have not the heart to go through with the details. Lucy had got a terrible shock, and it told on her more than before, for though plenty of blood went into her veins, her body did not respond to the treatment as well as on the other occasions. Her struggle back into life was something frightful to see and hear. However, the action of both heart and lungs improved, and Van Helsing made a subcutaneous injection of morphia, as before, and with good effect. Her faint became a profound slumber. The Professor watched whilst I went downstairs with Quincey Morris, and sent one of the maids to pay off one of the cabmen who were waiting. I left Quincey lying down after having a glass of wine, and told the cook to get ready a good breakfast. Then a thought struck me, and I went back to the room where Lucy now was. When I came softly in, I found Van Helsing with a sheet or two of note-paper in his hand. He had evidently read it, and was thinking it over as he sat with his hand to his brow. There was a look of grim satisfaction in his face, as of one who has had a doubt solved. He handed me the paper saying only: "It dropped from Lucy's breast when we carried her to the bath."

When I had read it, I stood looking at the Professor, and after a pause asked him: "In God's name, what does it all mean? Was she, or is she, mad; or what sort of horrible danger is it?" I was so bewildered that I did not know what to say more. Van Helsing put out his hand and took the paper, saying: —

"Do not trouble about it now. Forget it for the present. You shall know and understand it all in good time; but it will be later. And now what is it that you came to me to say?" This brought me back to fact, and I was all myself again.

"I came to speak about the certificate of death. If we do not act properly and wisely, there may be an inquest, and that paper would have to be produced. I am in hopes that we need have no inquest, for if we had it would surely kill poor Lucy, if nothing else did. I know, and you know, and the other doctor who attended her knows, that Mrs. Westenra had disease of the heart, and we can certify that she died of it. Let us fill up the certificate at once, and I shall take it myself to the registrar and go on to the undertaker."

"Good, oh my friend John! Well thought of! Truly Miss Lucy, if she be sad in the foes that beset her, is at least happy in the friends that love her. One, two, three, all open their veins for her, besides one old man. Ah yes, I know, friend John; I am not blind! I love you all the more for it! Now go."

In the hall I met Quincey Morris, with a telegram for Arthur telling him that Mrs. Westenra was dead; that Lucy also had been ill, but was now going on better; and that Van Helsing and I were with her. I told him where I was going, and he hurried me out, but as I was going said: —

"When you come back, Jack, may I have two words with you all to ourselves?" I nodded in reply and went out. I found no difficulty about the registration, and arranged with the local undertaker to come up in the evening to measure for the coffin and to make arrangements.

When I got back Quincey was waiting for me. I told him I would see him as soon as I knew about Lucy, and went up to her room. She was still sleeping, and the Professor seemingly had not moved from his seat at her side. From his putting his finger to his lips, I gathered that he expected her to wake before long and was afraid of forestalling nature. So I went down to Quincey and took him into the breakfast-room, where the blinds were not drawn down, and which was a little more cheerful, or rather less cheerless, than the other rooms. When we were alone, he said to me: —

"Jack Seward, I don't want to shove myself in anywhere where I've no right to be; but this is no ordinary case. You know I loved that girl and wanted to marry her; but, although that's all past and gone, I can't help feeling anxious about her all the same. What is it that's wrong with her? The Dutchman — and a fine old fellow he is; I can see that — said, that time you two came into the room, that you must have *another* transfusion of blood, and that both you and he were exhausted. Now I know well that you medical men speak *in camera*,° and that a man must not expect to know what they consult about in private. But this is no common matter, and, whatever it is, I have done my part. Is not that so?"

"That's so," I said, and he went on: —

"I take it that both you and Van Helsing had done already what I did to-day. Is not that so?"

"That's so."

"And I guess Art was in it too. When I saw him four days ago down at his own place he looked queer. I have not seen anything pulled down so quick since I was on the Pampas° and had a mare that I was fond of go to grass° all in a night. One of those big bats that they call vampires had got at her in the night, and, what with his gorge and the vein left open, there wasn't enough blood in her to let her stand up, and I had to put a bullet through her as she lay. Jack, if you may tell me without betraying confidence, Arthur was the first; is not that so?" As he spoke the poor fellow looked terribly anxious. He was in a torture of suspense regarding the woman he loved, and his utter ignorance of the terrible mystery which seemed to surround her intensified his pain. His very heart was bleeding, and it took all the manhood of him — and there was a royal lot of it, too — to keep him from breaking down. I paused before answering, for I felt that I must not betray anything which the Professor wished kept secret; but already he knew so much, and guessed so much, that there could be no reason for not answering, so I answered in the same phrase: "That's so."

"And how long has this been going on?"

in camera: Literally, in a chamber; generally used to mean in private, that is, confidentially (Latin). **Pampas:** A large, grassy plain in Argentina. **go to grass:** An American expression meaning to be ruined or die (*OED*).

"About ten days."

"Ten days! Then I guess, Jack Seward, that that poor pretty creature that we all love has had put into her veins within that time the blood of four strong men. Man alive, her whole body wouldn't hold it." Then, coming close to me, he spoke in a fierce half-whisper: "What took it out?"

I shook my head. "That," I said, "is the crux. Van Helsing is simply frantic about it, and I am at my wits' end. I can't even hazard a guess. There has been a series of little circumstances which have thrown out all our calculations as to Lucy being properly watched. But these shall not occur again. Here we stay until all be well — or ill." Quincey held out his hand. "Count me in," he said. "You and the Dutchman will tell me what to do, and I'll do it."

When we woke late in the afternoon, Lucy's first movement was to feel in her breast, and, to my surprise, produced the paper which Van Helsing had given me to read. The careful Professor had replaced it where it had come from, lest on waking she should be alarmed. Her eye then lit on Van Helsing and on me too, and gladdened. Then she looked round the room, and seeing where she was, shuddered; she gave a loud cry, and put her poor thin hands before her pale face. We both understood what that meant — that she had realised to the full her mother's death; so we tried what we could to comfort her. Doubtless sympathy eased her somewhat, but she was very low in thought and spirit, and wept silently and weakly for a long time. We told her that either or both of us would now remain with her all the time, and that seemed to comfort her. Towards dusk she fell into a doze. Here a very odd thing occurred. Whilst still asleep she took the paper from her breast and tore it in two. Van Helsing stepped over and took the pieces from her. All the same, however, she went on with the action of tearing, as though the material were still in her hands; finally she lifted her hands and opened them as though scattering the fragments. Van Helsing seemed surprised, and his brows gathered as if in thought, but he said nothing.

19 *September.*° — All last night she slept fitfully, being always afraid to sleep, and something weaker when she woke from it. The Professor and I took it in turns to watch, and we never left her for a moment unattended. Quincey Morris said nothing about his intention, but I knew that all night long he patrolled round and round the house.

---

19 September: The entry seems to have been written after midnight, that is, on 20 September. See note, p. 124 concerning an earlier discrepancy.

When the day came, its searching light showed the ravages in poor Lucy's strength. She was hardly able to turn her head, and the little nourishment which she could take seemed to do her no good. At times she slept, and both Van Helsing and I noticed the difference in her, between sleeping and waking. Whilst asleep she looked stronger, although more haggard, and her breathing was softer; her open mouth showed the pale gums drawn back from the teeth, which thus looked positively longer and sharper than usual; when she woke the softness of her eyes evidently changed the expression, for she looked her own self, although a dying one. In the afternoon she asked for Arthur, and we telegraphed for him. Quincey went off to meet him at the station.

When he arrived it was nearly six o'clock, and the sun was setting full and warm, and the red light streamed in through the window and gave more colour to the pale cheeks. When he saw her, Arthur was simply choking with emotion, and none of us could speak. In the hours that had passed, the fits of sleep, or the comatose condition that passed for it, had grown more frequent, so that the pauses when conversation was possible were shortened. Arthur's presence, however, seemed to act as a stimulant; she rallied a little, and spoke to him more brightly than she had done since we arrived. He too pulled himself together, and spoke as cheerily as he could, so that the best was made of everything.

It is now nearly one o'clock, and he and Van Helsing are sitting with her. I am to relieve them in a quarter of an hour, and I am entering this on Lucy's phonograph. Until six o'clock they are to try to rest. I fear that to-morrow will end our watching, for the shock has been too great; the poor child cannot rally. God help us all.

Letter, Mina Harker to Lucy Westenra

(Unopened by her)

"17 *September*

"My dearest Lucy, —

"It seems *an age* since I heard from you, or indeed since I wrote. You will pardon me, I know, for all my faults when you have read all my budget of news. Well, I got my husband back all right; when we arrived at Exeter there was a carriage waiting for us, and in it, though he had an attack of gout, Mr. Hawkins. He took us to his own house, where there were rooms for us all nice and comfortable, and we dined together. After dinner Mr. Hawkins said: —

" 'My dears, I want to drink your health and prosperity; and may every blessing attend you both. I know you both from children, and have, with love and pride, seen you grow up. Now I want you to make your home here with me. I have left to me neither chick nor child; all are gone, and in my will I have left you everything.' I cried, Lucy dear, as Jonathan and the old man clasped hands. Our evening was a very, very happy one.

"So here we are, installed in this beautiful old house, and from both my bedroom and drawing-room I can see the great elms of the cathedral close, with their great black stems standing out against the old yellow stone of the cathedral; and I can hear the rooks overhead cawing and cawing and chattering and gossiping all day, after the manner of rooks — and humans. I am busy, I need not tell you, arranging things and housekeeping. Jonathan and Mr. Hawkins are busy all day; for, now that Jonathan is a partner,° Mr. Hawkins wants to tell him all about the clients.

"How is your dear mother getting on? I wish I could run up to town for a day or two to see you, dear, but I dare not go yet, with so much on my shoulders; and Jonathan wants looking after still. He is beginning to put some flesh on his bones again, but he was terribly weakened by the long illness; even now he sometimes starts out of his sleep in a sudden way and awakes all trembling until I can coax him back to his usual placidity. However, thank God, these occasions grow less frequent as the days go on, and they will in time pass away altogether, I trust. And now I have told you my news, let me ask yours. When are you to be married, and where, and who is to perform the ceremony, and what are you to wear, and is it to be a public or a private wedding? Tell me all about it, dear; tell me all about everything, for there is nothing which interests you which will not be dear to me. Jonathan asks me to send his 'respectful duty,' but I do not think that is good enough from the junior partner of the important firm of Hawkins & Harker; and so, as you love me, and he loves me, and I love you with all the moods and tenses of the verb, I send you simply his 'love' instead. Good-bye, my dearest Lucy, and all blessings on you.

"Yours,
"MINA HARKER."

---

partner: A partial owner in the legal practice (*OED*).

Report from Patrick Hennessey, M.D., M.R.C.S., L.K.Q.C.P.I., etc., etc.,° to John Seward, M.D.

"20 *September*

"My dear Sir, —

"In accordance with your wishes, I enclose report of the conditions of everything left in my charge. . . . With regard to patient, Renfield, there is more to say. He has had another outbreak which might have had a dreadful ending, but which, as it fortunately happened, was unattended with any unhappy results. This afternoon a carrier's cart with two men made a call at the empty house whose grounds abut on ours — the house to which, you will remember, the patient twice ran away. The men stopped at our gate to ask the porter their way, as they were strangers. I was myself looking out of the study window, having a smoke after dinner, and saw one of them come up to the house. As he passed the window of Renfield's room, the patient began to rate him from within, and called him all the foul names he could lay his tongue to. The man, who seemed a decent fellow enough, contented himself by telling him to 'shut up for a foul-mouthed beggar,' whereon our man accused him of robbing him and wanting to murder him and said that he would hinder him if he were to swing for it. I opened the window and signed to the man not to notice, so he contented himself after looking the place over and making up his mind as to what kind of a place he had got to by saying: 'Lor' bless yer, sir, I wouldn't mind what was said to me in a bloomin' madhouse. I pity ye and the guv'nor for havin' to live in the house with a wild beast like that.' Then he asked his way civilly enough, and I told him where the gate of the empty house was; he went away, followed by threats and curses and revilings from our man. I went down to see if I could make out any cause for his anger, since he is usually such a well-behaved man, and except his violent fits nothing of the kind had ever occurred. I found him, to my astonishment, quite composed and most genial in his manner. I tried to get him to talk of the incident, but he blandly asked me questions as to what I meant, and led me to believe that he was completely oblivious of the affair. It was, I am sorry to say, however, only another instance of his cunning, for within half an hour I heard of him again. This time he had broken out through the window of his room, and was running down

---

M.D. . . . L.K.Q.C.P.I., etc., etc.: Doctor of Medicine, Member of the Royal College of Surgeons, Licentiate of the King's and Queen's College of Physicians of Ireland. The source of the etceteras is unclear. They could be the letter writer's, or they could originate with an impatient transcriber of the document.

the avenue. I called to the attendants to follow me, and ran after him, for I feared he was intent on some mischief. My fear was justified when I saw the same cart which had passed before coming down the road, having on it some great wooden boxes. The men were wiping their foreheads, and were flushed in the face, as if with violent exercise. Before I could get up to him the patient rushed at them, and pulling one of them off the cart, began to knock his head against the ground. If I had not seized him just at the moment I believe he would have killed the man there and then. The other fellow jumped down and struck him over the head with the butt-end of his heavy whip. It was a terrible blow; but he did not seem to mind it, but seized him also, and struggled with the three of us, pulling us to and fro as if we were kittens. You know I am no light weight, and the others were both burly men. At first he was silent in his fighting; but as we began to master him, and the attendants were putting a strait-waistcoat on him, he began to shout: 'I'll frustrate them! They shan't rob me! they shan't murder me by inches! I'll fight for my Lord and Master!' and all sorts of similar incoherent ravings. It was with very considerable difficulty that they got him back to the house and put him in the padded room. One of the attendants, Hardy, had a finger broken. However, I set it all right; and he is going on well.

"The two carriers were at first loud in their threats of actions for damages, and promised to rain all the penalties of the law on us. Their threats were, however, mingled with some sort of indirect apology for the defeat of the two of them by a feeble madman. They said that if it had not been for the way their strength had been spent in carrying and raising the heavy boxes to the cart they would have made short work of him. They gave as another reason for their defeat the extraordinary state of drouth° to which they had been reduced by the dusty nature of their occupation and the reprehensible distance from the scene of their labours of any place of public entertainment. I quite understood their drift, and after a stiff glass of grog,° or rather more of the same, and with each a sovereign° in hand, they made light of the attack, and swore that they would encounter a worse madman any day for the pleasure of meeting so 'bloomin' good a bloke' as your correspondent. I took their names and addresses, in case they might be needed. They are as follows: — Jack Smollet, of Dudding's Rents, King George's Road, Great Walworth, and Thomas Snelling, Peter Parley's Row, Guide Court,

---

state of drouth: Used figuratively to mean thirst.   *grog:* A mixture of rum and water (*OED* OL).   *sovereign:* British gold coin worth one pound sterling.

Bethnal Green. They are both in the employment of Harris & Sons, Moving and Shipment Company, Orange Master's Yard, Soho.

"I shall report to you any matter of interest occurring here, and shall wire you at once if there is anything of importance.

"Believe me, dear Sir,

"Yours faithfully,

"PATRICK HENNESSEY."

Letter, Mina Harker to Lucy Westenra

(Unopened by her)

"18 *September*

"My dearest Lucy, —

"Such a sad blow has befallen us. Mr. Hawkins has died very suddenly. Some may not think it so sad for us, but we had both come to so love him that it really seems as though we had lost a father. I never knew either father or mother, so that the dear old man's death is a real blow to me. Jonathan is greatly distressed. It is not only that he feels sorrow, deep sorrow, for the dear, good man who has befriended him all his life, and now at the end has treated him like his own son and left him a fortune which to people of our modest bringing up is wealth beyond the dream of avarice, but Jonathan feels it on another account. He says the amount of responsibility which it puts upon him makes him nervous. He begins to doubt himself. I try to cheer him up, and *my* belief in *him* helps him to have a belief in himself. But it is here that the grave shock that he experienced tells upon him the most. Oh, it is too hard that a sweet, simple, noble, strong nature such as his — a nature which enabled him by our dear, good friend's aid to rise from clerk to master in a few years — should be so injured that the very essence of its strength is gone. Forgive me, dear, if I worry you with my troubles in the midst of your own happiness; but, Lucy dear, I must tell some one, for the strain of keeping up a brave and cheerful appearance to Jonathan tries me, and I have no one here that I can confide in. I dread coming up to London, as we must do the day after to-morrow; for poor Mr. Hawkins left in his will that he was to be buried in the grave with his father. As there are no relations at all, Jonathan will have to be chief mourner. I shall try to run over to see you, dearest, if only for a few minutes. Forgive me for troubling you. With all blessings,

"Your loving

"MINA HARKER."

Dr. Seward's Diary

20 *September.* — Only resolution and habit can let me make an entry to-night. I am too miserable, too low-spirited, too sick of the world and all in it, including life itself, that I would not care if I heard this moment the flapping of the wings of the angel of death. And he has been flapping those grim wings to some purpose of late — Lucy's mother and Arthur's father, and now . . . . Let me get on with my work.

I duly relieved Van Helsing in his watch over Lucy. We wanted Arthur to go to rest also, but he refused at first. It was only when I told him that we should want him to help us during the day, and that we must not all break down for want of rest, lest Lucy should suffer, that he agreed to go. Van Helsing was very kind to him. "Come, my child," he said; "come with me. You are sick and weak, and have had much sorrow and much mental pain, as well as that tax on your strength that we know of. You must not be alone; for to be alone is to be full of fears and alarms. Come to the drawing-room, where there is a big fire, and there are two sofas. You shall lie on one, and I on the other, and our sympathy will be comfort to each other, even though we do not speak, and even if we sleep." Arthur went off with him, casting back a longing look on Lucy's face, which lay on her pillow, almost whiter than the lawn.° She lay quite still, and I looked round the room to see that all was as it should be. I could see that the Professor had carried out in this room, as in the other, his purpose of using the garlic; the whole of the window-sashes reeked with it, and round Lucy's neck, over the silk handkerchief which Van Helsing made her keep on, was a rough chaplet° of the same odorous flowers. Lucy was breathing somewhat stertorously, and her face was at its worst, for the open mouth showed the pale gums. Her teeth, in the dim, uncertain light, seemed longer and sharper than they had been in the morning. In particular, by some trick of the light, the canine teeth looked longer and sharper than the rest. I sat down by her, and presently she moved uneasily. At the same moment there came a sort of dull flapping or buffeting at the window. I went over to it softly, and peeped out by the corner of the blind. There was a full moonlight, and I could see that the noise was made by a great bat, which wheeled round — doubtless attracted by the light, although so dim — and every now and again struck the window with its wings. When I came back to my seat I found that Lucy had moved slightly, and had torn

---

lawn: Fine linen, probably covering the pillow.   *chaplet:* Necklace (*OED* OL).

away the garlic flowers from her throat. I replaced them as well as I could, and sat watching her.

Presently she woke, and I gave her food, as Van Helsing had prescribed. She took but a little, and that languidly. There did not seem to be with her now the unconscious struggle for life and strength that had hitherto so marked her illness. It struck me as curious that the moment she became conscious she pressed the garlic flowers close to her. It was certainly odd that whenever she got into that lethargic state, with the stertorous breathing, she put the flowers from her; but that when she waked she clutched them close. There was no possibility of making any mistake about this, for in the long hours that followed, she had many spells of sleeping and waking and repeated both actions many times.

At six o'clock Van Helsing came to relieve me. Arthur had then fallen into a doze, and he mercifully let him sleep on. When he saw Lucy's face I could hear the hissing indraw of his breath, and he said to me in a sharp whisper: "Draw up the blind; I want light!" Then he bent down, and, with his face almost touching Lucy's, examined her carefully. He removed the flowers and lifted the silk handkerchief from her throat. As he did so he started back, and I could hear his ejaculation, "Mein Gott!" as it was smothered in his throat. I bent over and looked too, and as I noticed some queer chill came over me.

The wounds on the throat had absolutely disappeared.

For fully five minutes Van Helsing stood looking at her, with his face at its sternest. Then he turned to me and said calmly: —

"She is dying. It will not be long now. It will be much difference, mark me, whether she dies conscious or in her sleep. Wake that poor boy, and let him come and see the last; he trusts us, and we have promised him."

I went to the dining-room and waked him. He was dazed for a moment, but when he saw the sunlight streaming in through the edges of the shutters he thought he was late, and expressed his fear. I assured him that Lucy was still asleep, but told him as gently as I could that both Van Helsing and I feared that the end was near. He covered his face with his hands, and slid down on his knees by the sofa, where he remained, perhaps a minute, with his head buried, praying, whilst his shoulders shook with grief. I took him by the hand and raised him up. "Come," I said, "my dear old fellow, summon all your fortitude; it will be best and easiest for *her*."

When we came into Lucy's room I could see that Van Helsing had, with his usual forethought, been putting matters straight and making everything look as pleasing as possible. He had even brushed Lucy's hair, so that it lay on the pillow in its usual sunny ripples. When we came into the room she opened her eyes, and seeing him, whispered softly: —

"Arthur! Oh, my love, I am so glad you have come!" He was stooping to kiss her, when Van Helsing motioned him back. "No," he whispered, "not yet! Hold her hand; it will comfort her more."

So Arthur took her hand and knelt beside her, and she looked her best, with all the soft lines matching the angelic beauty of her eyes. Then gradually her eyes closed, and she sank to sleep. For a little bit her breast heaved softly, and her breath came and went like a tired child's.

And then insensibly there came the strange change which I had noticed in the night. Her breathing grew stertorous, the mouth opened, and the pale gums, drawn back, made the teeth look longer and sharper than ever. In a sort of sleep-waking, vague, unconscious way she opened her eyes, which were now dull and hard at once, and said in a soft, voluptuous voice, such as I had never heard from her lips: —

"Arthur! Oh, my love, I am so glad you have come! Kiss me!" Arthur bent eagerly over to kiss her; but at that instant Van Helsing, who, like me, had been startled by her voice, swooped upon him, and catching him by the neck with both hands, dragged him back with a fury of strength which I never thought he could have possessed, and actually hurled him almost across the room.

"Not for your life!" he said; "not for your living soul and hers!" And he stood between them like a lion at bay.

Arthur was so taken aback that he did not for a moment know what to do or say; and before any impulse of violence could seize him he realised the place and the occasion, and stood silent, waiting.

I kept my eyes fixed on Lucy, as did Van Helsing, and we saw a spasm as of rage flit like a shadow over her face; the sharp teeth champed together. Then her eyes closed, and she breathed heavily.

Very shortly after she opened her eyes in all their softness, and putting out her poor pale, thin hand, took Van Helsing's great brown one; drawing it to her, she kissed it. "My true friend," she said, in a faint voice, but with untellable pathos, "My true friend, and his! Oh, guard him, and give me peace!"

"I swear it!" said he solemnly, kneeling beside her and holding up his hand, as one who registers an oath. Then he turned to Arthur, and said to him: "Come, my child, take her hand in yours, and kiss her on the forehead, and only once."

Their eyes met instead of their lips; and so they parted.

Lucy's eyes closed; and Van Helsing, who had been watching closely, took Arthur's arm, and drew him away.

And then Lucy's breathing became stertorous again, and all at once it ceased.

"It is all over," said Van Helsing. "She is dead!"

I took Arthur by the arm, and led him away to the drawing-room, where he sat down, and covered his face with his hands, sobbing in a way that nearly broke me down to see.

I went back to the room, and found Van Helsing looking at poor Lucy, and his face was sterner than ever. Some change had come over her body. Death had given back part of her beauty, for her brow and cheeks had recovered some of their flowing lines; even the lips had lost their deadly pallor. It was as if the blood, no longer needed for the working of the heart, had gone to make the harshness of death as little rude as might be.

> "We thought her dying whilst she slept,
> And sleeping when she died."°

I stood beside Van Helsing, and said: —

"Ah well, poor girl, there is peace for her at last. It is the end!"

He turned to me, and said with grave solemnity: —

"Not so; alas! not so. It is only the beginning!"

When I asked him what he meant, he only shook his head and answered: —

"We can do nothing as yet. Wait and see."

CHAPTER XIII. DR. SEWARD'S DIARY

(Continued)

THE funeral was arranged for the next succeeding day, so that Lucy and her mother might be buried together. I attended to all the ghastly formalities, and the urbane undertaker proved that his staff were afflicted — or blessed — with something of his own obsequious suavity. Even the woman who performed the last offices for the dead remarked to me, in a confidential, brother-professional way, when she had come out from the death-chamber: —

"We thought ... died": From the poem "The Death-Bed," by Thomas Hood (1799–1845).

"She makes a very beautiful corpse, sir. It's quite a privilege to attend on her. It's not too much to say that she will do credit to our establishment!"

I noticed that Van Helsing never kept far away. This was possible from the disordered state of things in the household. There were no relatives at hand; and as Arthur had to be back the next day to attend at his father's funeral, we were unable to notify any one who should have been bidden. Under the circumstances, Van Helsing and I took it upon ourselves to examine papers, etc. He insisted upon looking over Lucy's papers himself. I asked him why, for I feared that he, being a foreigner, might not be quite aware of English legal requirements, and so might in ignorance make some unnecessary trouble. He answered me: —

"I know; I know. You forget that I am a lawyer as well as a doctor. But this is not altogether for the law. You knew that, when you avoided the coroner. I have more than him to avoid. There may be papers more — such as this."

As he spoke he took from his pocket-book the memorandum which had been in Lucy's breast, and which she had torn in her sleep.

"When you find anything of the solicitor who is for the late Mrs. Westenra, seal all her papers, and write him to-night. For me, I watch here in the room and in Miss Lucy's old room all night, and I myself search for what may be. It is not well that her very thoughts go into the hands of strangers."

I went on with my part of the work, and in another half-hour had found the name and address of Mrs. Westenra's solicitor and had written to him. All the poor lady's papers were in order; explicit directions regarding the place of burial were given. I had hardly sealed the letter, when, to my surprise, Van Helsing walked into the room, saying: —

"Can I help you, friend John? I am free, and if I may, my service is to you."

"Have you got what you looked for?" I asked, to which he replied: —

"I did not look for any specific thing. I only hoped to find, and find I have, all that there was — only some letters and a few memoranda, and a diary new begun. But I have them here, and we shall for the present say nothing of them. I shall see that poor lad to-morrow evening, and, with his sanction, I shall use some."

When we had finished the work in hand, he said to me: —

"And now, friend John, I think we may to bed. We want sleep, both you and I, and rest to recuperate. To-morrow we shall have much to do, but for the to-night there is no need of us. Alas!"

Before turning in we went to look at poor Lucy. The undertaker had certainly done his work well, for the room was turned into a small *chapelle ardente.*° There was a wilderness of beautiful white flowers, and death was made as little repulsive as might be. The end of the winding-sheet was laid over the face; when the Professor bent over and turned it gently back, we both started at the beauty before us, the tall wax candles showing a sufficient light to note it well. All Lucy's loveliness had come back to her in death, and the hours that had passed, instead of leaving traces of "decay's effacing fingers,"° had but restored the beauty of life, till positively I could not believe my eyes that I was look-ing at a corpse.

The Professor looked sternly grave. He had not loved her as I had, and there was no need for tears in his eyes. He said to me: "Remain till I return," and left the room. He came back with a handful of wild garlic from the box waiting in the hall, but which had not been opened, and placed the flowers amongst the others on and around the bed. Then he took from his neck, inside his collar, a little golden crucifix, and placed it over the mouth. He restored the sheet to its place, and we came away.

I was undressing in my own room, when, with a premonitory tap at the door, he entered, and at once began to speak: —

"To-morrow I want you to bring me, before night, a set of post-mortem knives."

"Must we make an autopsy?" I asked.

"Yes, and no. I want to operate, but not as you think. Let me tell you now, but not a word to another. I want to cut off her head and take out her heart. Ah! you a surgeon, and so shocked! You, whom I have seen with no tremble of hand or heart, do operations of life and death that make the rest shudder. Oh, but I must not forget, my dear friend John, that you loved her; and I have not forgotten it, for it is I that shall operate, and you must only help. I would like to do it to-night, but for Arthur I must not; he will be free after his father's funeral to-morrow, and he will want to see her — to see *it*. Then, when she is coffined ready for the next day, you and I shall come when all sleep. We shall

---

chapelle ardente: A mortuary chapel; literally a "burning chapel" (French), so called because a number of candles are burning around the deceased, who is lying in state. *"decay's effacing fingers":* From the poem "The Giaour" (1814) by George Gordon, Lord Byron (1788–1824). The poem contains a curse uttered by a Turk against the Giaour that condemns him to becoming a vampire and feasting on his own family: ". . . on earth as Vampire sent, / Thy corse shall from its tomb be rent: / Then ghastly haunt thy native place, / And suck the blood of all thy race . . ."

unscrew the coffin-lid, and shall do our operation; and then replace all, so that none know, save we alone."

"But why do it at all? The girl is dead. Why mutilate her poor body without need? And if there is no necessity for a post-mortem and nothing to gain by it — no good to her, to us, to science, to human knowledge — why do it? Without such it is monstrous."

For answer he put his hand on my shoulder, and said, with infinite tenderness: —

"Friend John, I pity your poor bleeding heart; and I love you the more because it does so bleed. If I could, I would take on myself the burden that you do bear. But there are things that you know not, but that you shall know, and bless me for knowing, though they are not pleasant things. John, my child, you have been my friend now many years, and yet did you ever know me to do any without good cause? I may err — I am but man; but I believe in all I do. Was it not for these causes that you send for me when the great trouble came? Yes! Were you not amazed, nay horrified, when I would not let Arthur kiss his love — though she was dying — and snatched him away by all my strength? Yes! And yet you saw how she thanked me, with her so beautiful dying eyes, her voice, too, so weak, and she kiss my rough old hand and bless me? Yes! And did you not hear me swear promise to her, that so she closed her eyes grateful? Yes!

"Well, I have good reason now for all I want to do. You have for many years trust me; you have believe me weeks past, when there be things so strange that you might have well doubt. Believe me yet a little, friend John. If you trust me not, then I must tell what I think; and that is not perhaps well. And if I work — as work I shall, no matter trust or no trust — without my friend trust in me, I work with heavy heart and feel, oh! so lonely when I want all help and courage that may be!" He paused a moment and went on solemnly: "Friend John, there are strange and terrible days before us. Let us not be two, but one, that so we work to a good end. Will you not have faith in me?"

I took his hand, and promised him. I held my door open as he went away, and watched him go into his room and close the door. As I stood without moving, I saw one of the maids pass silently along the passage — she had her back towards me, so did not see me — and go into the room where Lucy lay. The sight touched me. Devotion is so rare, and we are so grateful to those who show it unasked to those we love. Here was a poor girl putting aside the terrors which she naturally had of death to go watch alone by the bier of the mistress whom she loved, so that the poor clay might not be lonely till laid to eternal rest. . . . .

I must have slept long and soundly, for it was broad daylight when Van Helsing waked me by coming into my room. He came over to my bedside and said: —

"You need not trouble about the knives; we shall not do it."

"Why not?" I asked. For his solemnity of the night before had greatly impressed me.

"Because," he said sternly, "it is too late — or too early. See!" Here he held up the little golden crucifix. "This was stolen in the night."

"How, stolen," I asked in wonder, "since you have it now?"

"Because I get it back from the worthless wretch who stole it, from the woman who robbed the dead and the living. Her punishment will surely come, but not through me; she knew not altogether what she did, and thus unknowing, she only stole. Now we must wait."

He went away on the word, leaving me with a new mystery to think of, a new puzzle to grapple with.

The forenoon was a dreary time, but at noon the solicitor came: Mr. Marquand, of Wholeman, Sons, Marquand & Lidderdale. He was very genial and very appreciative of what we had done, and took off our hands all cares as to details. During lunch he told us that Mrs. Westenra had for some time expected sudden death from her heart, and had put her affairs in absolute order; he informed us that, with the exception of a certain entailed property of Lucy's father's which now, in default of direct issue, went back to a distant branch of the family, the whole estate, real and personal, was left absolutely to Arthur Holmwood. When he had told us so much he went on: —

"Frankly we did our best to prevent such a testamentary disposition, and pointed out certain contingencies that might leave her daughter either penniless or not so free as she should be to act regarding a matrimonial alliance. Indeed, we pressed the matter so far that we almost came into collision, for she asked us if we were or were not prepared to carry out her wishes. Of course, we had then no alternative but to accept. We were right in principle, and ninety-nine times out of a hundred we should have proved, by the logic of events, the accuracy of our judgment. Frankly, however, I must admit that in this case any other form of disposition would have rendered impossible the carrying out of her wishes. For by her predeceasing her daughter the latter would have come into possession of the property, and, even had she only survived her mother by five minutes, her property would, in case there were no will — and a will was a practical impossibility in such a case — have been treated at her decease as under intestacy. In which case Lord Godalming,° though so dear a friend, would have had no claim in the world; and the inheritors, being remote, would not be likely to abandon their just rights, for sentimental reasons regarding an entire stranger. I assure you, my dear sirs, I am rejoiced at the result, perfectly rejoiced."

He was a good fellow, but his rejoicing at the one little part — in which he was officially interested — of so great a tragedy, was an object-lesson in the limitations of sympathetic understanding.

He did not remain long, but said he would look in later in the day and see Lord Godalming. His coming, however, had been a certain comfort to us, since it assured us that we should not have to dread hostile criticism as to any of our acts. Arthur was expected at five o'clock, so a little before that time we visited the death-chamber. It was so in very truth, for now both mother and daughter lay in it. The undertaker, true to his craft, had made the best display he could of his goods, and there was a mortuary air about the place that lowered our spirits at once. Van Helsing ordered the former arrangement to be adhered to, explaining that, as Lord Godalming was coming very soon, it would be less harrowing to his feelings to see all that was left of his *fiancée* quite alone. The undertaker seemed shocked at his own stupidity, and exerted himself to restore things to the condition in which we left them the night before, so that when Arthur came such shocks to his feelings as we could avoid were saved.

Poor fellow! He looked desperately sad and broken; even his stalwart manhood seemed to have shrunk somewhat under the strain of his much-tried emotions. He had, I knew, been very genuinely and devotedly attached to his father; and to lose him, and at such a time, was a bitter blow to him. With me he was warm as ever, and to Van Helsing he was sweetly courteous; but I could not help seeing that there was some constraint with him. The Professor noticed it, too, and motioned me to bring him upstairs. I did so, and left him at the door of the room, as I felt he would like to be quite alone with her; but he took my arm and led me in, saying huskily: —

"You loved her too, old fellow; she told me all about it, and there was no friend had a closer place in her heart than you. I don't know how to thank you for all you have done for her. I can't think yet . . . ."

Here he suddenly broke down, and threw his arms round my shoulders and laid his head on my breast, crying: —

Lord Godalming: Arthur Holmwood, who has assumed the title after his father's death.

"Oh, Jack! Jack! What shall I do? The whole of life seems gone from me all at once, and there is nothing in the wide world for me to live for."

I comforted him as well as I could. In such cases men do not need much expression. A grip of the hand, the tightening of an arm over the shoulder, a sob in unison, are expressions of sympathy dear to a man's heart. I stood still and silent till his sobs died away, and then I said softly to him: —

"Come and look at her."

Together we moved over to the bed, and I lifted the lawn from her face. God! how beautiful she was. Every hour seemed to be enhancing her loveliness. It frightened and amazed me somewhat; and as for Arthur, he fell a-trembling, and finally was shaken with doubt as with an ague. At last, after a long pause, he said to me in a faint whisper: —

"Jack, is she really dead?"

I assured him sadly that it was so, and went on to suggest — for I felt that such a horrible doubt should not have life for a moment longer than I could help — that it often happened that after death faces became softened and even resolved into their youthful beauty; that this was especially so when death had been preceded by any acute or pro- longed suffering. It seemed to quite do away with any doubt, and, after kneeling beside the couch for a while and looking at her lovingly and long, he turned aside. I told him that that must be good-bye, as the cof- fin had to be prepared; so he went back and took her dead hand in his and kissed it, and bent over and kissed her forehead. He came away, fondly looking back over his shoulder at her as he came.

I left him in the drawing-room, and told Van Helsing that he had said good-bye; so the latter went to the kitchen to tell the undertaker's men to proceed with the preparations and to screw up the coffin. When he came out of the room again I told him of Arthur's question, and he replied: —

"I am not surprised. Just now I doubted for a moment myself!"

We all dined together, and I could see that poor Art was trying to make the best of things. Van Helsing had been silent all dinner-time, but when we had lit our cigars he said: —

"Lord ——;" but Arthur interrupted him: —

"No, no, not that, for God's sake! not yet at any rate. Forgive me, sir: I did not mean to speak offensively; it is only because my loss is so recent."

The Professor answered very sweetly: —

"I only used that name because I was in doubt. I must not call you 'Mr.,' and I have grown to love you — yes, my dear boy, to love you — as Arthur."

Arthur held out his hand, and took the old man's warmly.

"Call me what you will," he said. "I hope I may always have the title of a friend. And let me say that I am at a loss for words to thank you for your goodness to my poor dear." He paused a moment, and went on: "I know that she understood your goodness even better than I do; and if I was rude or in any way wanting at that time you acted so — you remember" — the Professor nodded — "you must forgive me."

He answered with a grave kindness: —

"I know it was hard for you to quite trust me then, for to trust such violence needs to understand; and I take it that you do not — that you cannot — trust me now, for you do not yet understand. And there may be more times when I shall want you to trust when you cannot — and may not — and must not yet understand. But the time will come when your trust shall be whole and complete in me, and when you shall understand as though the sunlight himself shone through. Then you shall bless me from first to last for your own sake, and for the sake of others, and for her dear sake to whom I swore to protect."

"And, indeed, indeed, sir," said Arthur warmly, "I shall in all ways trust you. I know and believe you have a very noble heart, and you are Jack's friend, and you were hers. You shall do what you like."

The Professor cleared his throat a couple of times, as though about to speak, and finally said: —

"May I ask you something now?"

"Certainly."

"You know that Mrs. Westenra left you all her property?"

"No, poor dear; I never thought of it."

"And as it is all yours, you have a right to deal with it as you will. I want you to give me permission to read all Miss Lucy's papers and letters. Believe me, it is no idle curiosity. I have a motive of which, be sure, she would have approved. I have them all here. I took them before we knew that all was yours, so that no strange hand might touch them — no strange eye look through words into her soul. I shall keep them, if I may; even you may not see them yet, but I shall keep them safe. No word shall be lost; and in the good time I shall give them back to you. It's a hard thing I ask, but you will do it, will you not, for Lucy's sake?"

Arthur spoke out heartily, like his old self: —

"Dr. Van Helsing, you may do what you will. I feel that in saying this I am doing what my dear one would have approved. I shall not trouble you with questions till the time comes."

The old Professor stood up as he said solemnly: —

"And you are right. There will be pain for us all; but it will not be all pain, nor will this pain be the last. We and you too — you most of all, my dear boy — will have to pass through the bitter water before we reach the sweet. But we must be brave of heart and unselfish, and do our duty, and all will be well!"

I slept on a sofa in Arthur's room that night. Van Helsing did not go to bed at all. He went to and fro, as if patrolling the house, and was never out of sight of the room where Lucy lay in her coffin, strewn with the wild garlic flowers, which sent, through the odour of lily and rose, a heavy, overpowering smell into the night.

Mina Harker's Journal

22 *September.* — In the train to Exeter. Jonathan sleeping.

It seems only yesterday that the last entry was made, and yet how much between then, in Whitby and all the world before me, Jonathan away and no news of him; and now, married to Jonathan, Jonathan a solicitor, a partner, rich, master of his business, Mr. Hawkins dead and buried, and Jonathan with another attack that may harm him. Some day he may ask me about it. Down it all goes. I am rusty in my shorthand — see what unexpected prosperity does for us — so it may be as well to freshen it up again with an exercise anyhow. . . . .

The service was very simple and very solemn. There were only ourselves and the servants there, one or two old friends of his from Exeter, his London agent, and a gentleman representing Sir John Paxton, the President of the Incorporated Law Society. Jonathan and I stood hand in hand, and we felt that our best and dearest friend was gone from us. . . . .

We came back to town quietly, taking a 'bus° to Hyde Park Corner.° Jonathan thought it would interest me to go into the Row° for a while, so we sat down; but there were very few people there, and it was sad-looking and desolate to see so many empty chairs. It made us think of the empty chair at home; so we got up and walked down Piccadilly.° Jonathan was holding me by the arm, the way he used to in old days before I went to school. I felt it very improper, for you can't go on for some years teaching etiquette and decorum to other girls without the

---

'bus: An omnibus, a "four-wheeled public vehicle for carrying passengers," in Stoker's day drawn by horses (*OED*).   *Hyde Park Corner:* The southern corner of Hyde Park, a large fashionable park, where Piccadilly and Grosvenor Place intersected (Black).   *the Row:* Rotten Row, the riding ground in Hyde Park.   *Piccadilly:* An important London street beginning at the Haymarket, passing along Green Park, and ending at Hyde Park Corner, lined with fashionable shops (Black, *Enc. Brit.* 11th).

pedantry of it biting into yourself a bit; but it was Jonathan, and he was my husband, and we didn't know anybody who saw us — and we didn't care if they did — so on we walked. I was looking at a very beautiful girl, in a big cart-wheel hat, sitting in a victoria° outside Giuliano's, when I felt Jonathan clutch my arm so tight that he hurt me, and he said under his breath: "My God!" I am always anxious about Jonathan, for I fear that some nervous fit may upset him again; so I turned to him quickly, and asked him what it was that disturbed him.

He was very pale, and his eyes seemed bulging out as, half in terror and half in amazement, he gazed at a tall, thin man, with a beaky nose and black moustache and pointed beard, who was also observing the pretty girl. He was looking at her so hard that he did not see either of us, and so I had a good view of him. His face was not a good face; it was hard, and cruel, and sensual, and his big white teeth, that looked all the whiter because his lips were so red, were pointed like an animal's. Jonathan kept staring at him, till I was afraid he would notice. I feared he might take it ill, he looked so fierce and nasty. I asked Jonathan why he was disturbed, and he answered, evidently thinking that I knew as much about it as he did: "Do you see who it is?"

"No, dear," I said; "I don't know him; who is it?" His answer seemed to shock and thrill me, for it was said as if he did not know that it was to me, Mina, to whom he was speaking: —

"It is the man himself!"

The poor dear was evidently terrified at something — very greatly terrified; I do believe that if he had not had me to lean on and to support him he would have sunk down. He kept staring; a man came out of the shop with a small parcel, and gave it to the lady, who then drove off. The dark man kept his eyes fixed on her, and when the carriage moved up Piccadilly he followed in the same direction, and hailed a hansom.° Jonathan kept looking after him, and said, as if to himself: —

"I believe it is the Count, but he has grown young. My God, if this be so! Oh, my God! my God! If I only knew! if I only knew!" He was distressing himself so much that I feared to keep his mind on the subject by asking him any questions, so I remained silent. I drew him away quietly, and he, holding my arm, came easily. We walked a little further, and then went in and sat for a while in the Green Park.° It was a hot day

---

victoria: A light, four-wheeled carriage with a collapsible hood and seats for two passengers (*OED*).   ***hansom:*** A hansom cab, a low-slung, two-wheeled carriage for hire with a driver perched behind the passengers (*OED*).   ***Greek Park:*** A park by Piccadilly, giving a prospect of Buckingham Palace, Westminster Abbey, and the Houses of Parliament.

for autumn, and there was a comfortable seat in a shady place. After a few minutes' staring at nothing, Jonathan's eyes closed, and he went quietly into a sleep, with his head on my shoulder. I thought it was the best thing for him, so did not disturb him. In about twenty minutes he woke up, and said to me quite cheerfully: —

"Why, Mina, have I been asleep? Oh, do forgive me for being so rude. Come, and we'll have a cup of tea somewhere." He had evidently forgotten all about the dark stranger, as in his illness he had forgotten all that this episode had reminded him of. I don't like this lapsing into forgetfulness; it may make or continue some injury to the brain. I must not ask him, for fear I shall do more harm than good; but I must somehow learn the facts of his journey abroad. The time is come, I fear, when I must open that parcel and know what is written. Oh, Jonathan, you will, I know, forgive me if I do wrong, but it is for your own dear sake.

Later. — A sad home-coming in every way — the house empty of the dear soul who was so good to us; Jonathan still pale and dizzy under a slight relapse of his malady; and now a telegram from Van Helsing, whoever he may be: —

"You will be grieved to hear that Mrs. Westenra died five days ago, and that Lucy died the day before yesterday. They were both buried to-day."

Oh, what a wealth of sorrow in a few words! Poor Mrs. Westenra! poor Lucy! Gone, gone, never to return to us! And poor, poor Arthur, to have lost such sweetness out of his life! God help us all to bear our troubles.

Dr. Seward's Diary

22 September. — It is all over. Arthur has gone back to Ring, and has taken Quincey Morris with him. What a fine fellow is Quincey! I believe in my heart of hearts that he suffered as much about Lucy's death as any of us; but he bore himself through it like a moral Viking. If America can go on breeding men like that, she will be a power in the world indeed. Van Helsing is lying down, having a rest preparatory to his journey. He goes over to Amsterdam to-night, but says he returns to-morrow night; that he only wants to make some arrangements which can only be made personally. He is to stop with me then, if he can; he says he has work to do in London which may take him some time. Poor old fellow! I fear that the strain of the past week has broken down even his iron strength. All the time of the burial he was, I could see, putting some terrible restraint on himself. When it was all over, we were standing beside Arthur, who, poor fellow, was speaking of his part in the operation where his blood had been transfused to his Lucy's veins, I could see Van Helsing's face grow white and purple by turns. Arthur was saying that he felt since then as if they two had been really married, and that she was his wife in the sight of God. None of us said a word of the other operations, and none of us ever shall. Arthur and Quincey went away together to the station, and Van Helsing and I came on here. The moment we were alone in the carriage he gave way to a regular fit of hysterics. He has denied to me since that it was hysterics, and insisted that it was only his sense of humour asserting itself under very terrible conditions. He laughed till he cried, and I had to draw down the blinds lest any one should see us and misjudge; and then he cried till he laughed again; and laughed and cried together, just as a woman does. I tried to be stern with him, as one is to a woman under the circumstances; but it had no effect. Men and women are so different in manifestations of nervous strength or weakness! Then when his face grew grave and stern again I asked him why his mirth, and why at such a time. His reply was in a way characteristic of him, for it was logical and forceful and mysterious. He said: —

"Ah, you don't comprehend, friend John. Do not think that I am not sad, though I laugh. See, I have cried even when the laugh did choke me. But no more think that I am all sorry when I cry, for the laugh he come just the same. Keep it always with you that laughter who knock at your door and say, 'May I come in?' is not the true laughter. No! he is a king, and he come when and how he like. He ask no person; he choose no time of suitability. He say, 'I am here.' Behold, in example I grieve my heart out for that so sweet young girl; I give my blood for her, though I am old and worn; I give my time, my skill, my sleep; I let my other sufferers want that so she may have all. And yet I can laugh at her very grave — laugh when the clay from the spade of the sexton drop upon her coffin and say, 'Thud! thud!' to my heart, till it send back the blood from my cheek. My heart bleed for that poor boy — that dear boy, so of the age of mine own boy had I been so blessed that he live, and with his hair and eyes the same. There, you know now why I love him so. And yet when he say things that touch my husband heart to the quick, and make my father-heart yearn to him as to no other man — not even to you, friend John, for we are more level in experiences than father and son — yet even at such moment King Laugh he come to me and shout and bellow in my ear, 'Here I am! here I am!' till the blood come dance back and bring some of the sunshine that he carry with him to my cheek. Oh, friend John, it is a strange world, a sad world, a world full of miseries, and woes, and troubles; and yet when King Laugh come he make them all dance to the tune he play. Bleeding hearts, and dry bones of the churchyard, and tears that burn as they fall — all dance together to the music that he make with that smileless mouth of him. And believe me, friend John, that he is good to come, and kind. Ah, we men and women are like ropes drawn tight with strain that pull us different ways. Then tears come; and, like the rain on the ropes, they brace us up, until perhaps the strain become too great, and we break. But King Laugh he come like the sunshine, and he ease off the strain again; and we bear to go on with our labour, what it may be."

I did not like to wound him by pretending not to see his idea; but, as I did not yet understand the cause of his laughter, I asked him. As he answered me his face grew stern, and he said in quite a different tone: —

"Oh, it was the grim irony of it all — this so lovely lady garlanded with flowers, that looked so fair as life, till one by one we wondered if she were truly dead; she laid in that so fine marble house in that lonely churchyard, where rest so many of her kin, laid there with the mother who loved her, and whom she loved; and that sacred bell going 'Toll! toll! toll!' so sad and slow; and those holy men, with the white garments of the angel, pretending to read books, and yet all the time their eyes never on the page; and all us with the bowed head. And all for what? She is dead; so! Is it not?"

"Well, for the life of me, Professor," I said, "I can't see anything to laugh at in all that. Why, your explanation makes it a harder puzzle than before. But even if the burial service was comic, what about poor Art and his trouble? Why, his heart was simply breaking."

"Just so. Said he not that the transfusion of his blood to her veins had made her truly his bride?"

"Yes, and it was a sweet and comforting idea for him."

"Quite so. But there was a difficulty, friend John. If so that, then what about the others? Ho, ho! Then this so sweet maid is a poly-andrist,° and me, with my poor wife dead to me, but alive by Church's law, though no wits, all gone — even I, who am faithful husband to this now-no-wife, am bigamist."

"I don't see where the joke comes in there either!" I said; and I did not feel particularly pleased with him for saying such things. He laid his hand on my arm, and said: —

---

polyandrist: "A woman who has several husbands at the same time" (*OED* OL).

"Friend John, forgive me if I pain. I showed not my feeling to others when it would wound, but only to you, my old friend, whom I can trust. If you could have looked into my very heart then when I want to laugh; if you could have done so when the laugh arrived; if you could do so now, when King Laugh have pack up his crown and all that is to him — for he go far, far away from me, and for a long, long time — maybe you would perhaps pity me the most of all."

I was touched by the tenderness of his tone, and asked why.

"Because I know!"

And now we are all scattered; and for many a long day loneliness will sit over our roofs with brooding wings. Lucy lies in the tomb of her kin, a lordly death-house in a lonely churchyard, away from teeming London; where the air is fresh, and the sun rises over Hampstead Hill,° and where wild flowers grow of their own accord.

So I can finish this diary; and God only knows if I shall ever begin another. If I do, or if I ever open this again, it will be to deal with different people and different themes; for here at the end, where the romance of my life is told, ere I go back to take up the thread of my life-work, I say sadly and without hope,

"Finis."

"The Westminster Gazette,"° 25 September

A HAMPSTEAD MYSTERY

The neighbourhood of Hampstead is just at present exercised with a series of events which seem to run on lines parallel to those of what was known to the writers of headlines as "The Kensington Horror," or "The Stabbing Woman," or "The Woman in Black." During the past two or three days several cases have occurred of young children straying from home or neglecting to return from their playing on the Heath. In all these cases the children were too young to give any properly intelligible account of themselves, but the consensus of their excuses is that they had been with a "bloofer lady." It has always been late in the evening when they have been missed, and on two occasions the chil-

---

Hampstead Hill: Stoker may be referring to a part of Hampstead Heath, a broad, open area that in Stoker's day could be reached by railway or omnibus. Although a Hampstead Road did exist, no Hampstead Hill has been identified. In combination with Shooter's Hill in the "Bloofer Lady" article that follows, the unidentifiable reference suggests that the locations are fictitious.   *The Westminster Gazette:* One of London's principal daily evening papers (*Baedeker* 1896).

dren have not been found until early in the following morning. It is generally supposed in the neighbourhood that, as the first child missed gave as his reason for being away that a "bloofer lady" had asked him to come for a walk, the others had picked up the phrase and used it as occasion served. This is the more natural as the favourite game of the little ones at present is luring each other away by wiles. A correspondent writes us that to see some of the tiny tots pretending to be the "bloofer lady"° is supremely funny. Some of our caricaturists might, he says, take a lesson in the irony of grotesque by comparing the reality and the picture. It is only in accordance with general principles of human nature that the "bloofer lady" should be the popular rôle at these *al fresco*° performances. Our correspondent naïvely says that even Ellen Terry° could not be so winningly attractive as some of these grubby-faced little children pretend — and even imagine themselves — to be.

There is, however, possibly a serious side to the question, for some of the children, indeed all who have been missed at night, have been slightly torn or wounded in the throat. The wounds seem such as might be made by a rat or a small dog, and although of not much importance individually, would tend to show that whatever animal inflicts them has a system or method of its own. The police of the division have been instructed to keep a sharp look-out for straying children, especially when very young, in and around Hampstead Heath, and for any stray dog which may be about.

"The Westminster Gazette," 25 September

Extra Special

THE HAMPSTEAD HORROR

ANOTHER CHILD INJURED

The "Bloofer Lady"

We have just received intelligence that another child, missed last night, was only discovered late in the morning under a furze bush at the

---

bloofer lady: The child's pronunciation of what may be an invented word suggests "bloody" or, more distantly, "beautiful." *al fresco:* In open air (Italian). **Ellen Terry:** (1848–1928); a popular English actress most famous for her interpretation of Shakespearean roles. From 1878 for more than twenty years, she was the principal actress of the Lyceum Theater, where Henry Irving was the principal male actor and Stoker was the manager.

Shooter's Hill side of Hampstead Heath,° which is, perhaps, less frequented than the other parts. It has the same tiny wound in the throat
as has been noticed in other cases. It was terribly weak, and looked
quite emaciated. It too, when partially restored, had the common story
to tell of being lured away by the "bloofer lady."

CHAPTER XIV. MINA HARKER'S JOURNAL

23 *September.* — Jonathan is better after a bad night. I am so glad that
he has plenty of work to do, for that keeps his mind off the terrible
things; and oh, I am rejoiced that he is not now weighed down with the
responsibility of his new position. I knew he would be true to himself,
and now how proud I am to see my Jonathan rising to the height of his
advancement and keeping pace in all ways with the duties that come
upon him. He will be away all day till late, for he said he could not
lunch at home. My household work is done, so I shall take his foreign
journal, and lock myself up in my room and read it. . . . .

24 *September.* — I hadn't the heart to write last night; that terrible
record of Jonathan's upset me so. Poor dear! How he must have suffered, whether it be true or only imagination. I wonder if there is any
truth in it at all. Did he get his brain fever, and then write all those
terrible things; or had he some cause for it all? I suppose I shall never
know, for I dare not open the subject to him. . . . . And yet that man we
saw yesterday! He seemed quite certain of him. . . . . Poor fellow! I
suppose it was the funeral upset him and sent his mind back on some
train of thought. . . . . He believes it all himself. I remember how on
our wedding-day he said: "Unless some solemn duty come upon me to
go back to the bitter hours, asleep or awake, mad or sane." There seems
to be through it all some thread of continuity. . . . . That fearful Count
was coming to London. . . . . 'If it should be, and he came to London,
with its teeming millions.' . . . . There may be a solemn duty; and if it
come we must not shrink from it. . . . . I shall be prepared. I shall get
my typewriter this very hour and begin transcribing. Then we shall be
ready for other eyes if required. And if it be wanted; then, perhaps, if I
am ready, poor Jonathan may not be upset, for I can speak for him and

---

the Shooter's Hill side of Hampstead Heath: The description is either an error on the part
of the reporter or Stoker, or it is fictitious. No Shooter's Hill was located close to Hampstead Heath, but a mound of clay capped with gravel drift rising to a height of 412 feet,
located close to Woolwich, southeast of London, was called by that name (Black).

never let him be troubled or worried with it at all. If ever Jonathan quite gets over the nervousness he may want to tell me of it all, and I can ask him questions and find out things, and see how I may comfort him.

Letter, Van Helsing to Mrs. Harker

"24 September
(Confidence)

"Dear Madam, —

"I pray you to pardon my writing, in that I am so far friend as that I sent to you sad news of Miss Lucy Westenra's death. By the kindness of Lord Godalming, I am empowered to read her letters and papers, for I am deeply concerned about certain matters vitally important. In them I find some letters from you, which show how great friends you were and how you love her. Oh, Madam Mina, by that love, I implore you, help me. It is for others' good that I ask — to redress great wrong, and to lift much and terrible troubles — that may be more great than you can know. May it be that I see you? You can trust me. I am friend of Dr. John Seward and of Lord Godalming (that was Arthur of Miss Lucy). I must keep it private for the present from all. I should come to Exeter to see you at once if you tell me I am privilege to come, and where and when. I implore your pardon, madam. I have read your letters to poor Lucy, and know how good you are and how your husband suffer; so I pray you, if it may be, enlighten him not, lest it may harm. Again your pardon, and forgive me.

"VAN HELSING."

Telegram, Mrs. Harker to Van Helsing

"25 *September.* — Come to-day by quarter-past ten train if you can catch it. Can see you any time you call.

"WILHELMINA HARKER."

Mina Harker's Journal

25 *September.* — I cannot help feeling terribly excited as the time draws near for the visit of Dr. Van Helsing, for somehow I expect that it will throw some light upon Jonathan's sad experience; and as he attended poor dear Lucy in her last illness, he can tell me all about her. That is the reason of his coming; it is concerning Lucy and her sleep-walking, and not about Jonathan. Then I shall never know the real

truth now! How silly I am. That awful journal gets hold of my imagination and tinges everything with something of its own colour. Of course it is about Lucy. That habit came back to the poor dear, and that awful night on the cliff must have made her ill. I had almost forgotten in my own affairs how ill she was afterwards. She must have told him of her sleep-walking adventure on the cliff, and that I knew all about it; and now he wants me to tell him about it, so that he may understand. I hope I did right in not saying anything of it to Mrs. Westenra; I should never forgive myself if any act of mine, were it even a negative one, brought harm on poor dear Lucy. I hope, too, Dr. Van Helsing will not blame me; I have had so much trouble and anxiety of late that I feel I cannot bear more just at present.

I suppose a cry does us all good at times — clears the air as other rain does. Perhaps it was reading the journal yesterday that upset me, and then Jonathan went away this morning to stay away from me a whole day and night, the first time we have been parted since our marriage. I do hope the dear fellow will take care of himself, and that nothing will occur to upset him. It is two o'clock, and the doctor will be here soon now. I shall say nothing of Jonathan's journal unless he asks me. I am so glad I have type-written out my own journal, so that, in case he asks about Lucy, I can hand it to him; it will save much questioning.

Later. — He has come and gone. Oh, what a strange meeting, and how it all makes my head whirl round! I feel like one in a dream. Can it be all possible, or even a part of it? If I had not read Jonathan's journal first, I should never have accepted even a possibility. Poor, poor, dear Jonathan! How he must have suffered. Please the good God, all this may not upset him again. I shall try to save him from it; but it may be even a consolation and a help to him — terrible though it be and awful in its consequences — to know for certain that his eyes and ears and brain did not deceive him, and that it is all true. It may be that it is the doubt which haunts him; that when the doubt is removed, no matter which — waking or dreaming — may prove the truth, he will be more satisfied and better able to bear the shock. Dr. Van Helsing must be a good man as well as a clever one if he is Arthur's friend and Dr. Seward's, and if they brought him all the way from Holland to look after Lucy. I feel from having seen him that he *is* good and kind and of a noble nature. When he comes to-morrow I shall ask him about Jonathan; and then, please God, all this sorrow and anxiety may lead to a good end. I used to think I would like to practise interviewing; Jonathan's friend on "The Exeter News" told him that memory was everything in such work — that you must be able to put down exactly almost every word spoken, even if you had to refine some of it afterwards. Here was a rare interview; I shall try to record it *verbatim*.

It was half-past two o'clock when the knock came. I took my courage *à deux mains*° and waited. In a few minutes Mary opened the door, and announced "Dr. Van Helsing."

I rose and bowed, and he came towards me; a man of medium height, strongly built, with his shoulders set back over a broad, deep chest and a neck well balanced on the trunk as the head is on the neck. The poise of the head strikes one at once as indicative of thought and power; the head is noble, well-sized, broad, and large behind the ears. The face, clean-shaven, shows a hard, square chin, a large, resolute, mobile mouth, a good-sized nose, rather straight, but with quick, sensitive nostrils, that seem to broaden as the big, bushy brows come down and the mouth tightens. The forehead is broad and fine, rising at first almost straight and then sloping back above two bumps or ridges wide apart; such a forehead that the reddish hair cannot possibly tumble over it, but falls naturally back and to the sides. Big, dark blue eyes are set widely apart, and are quick and tender or stern with the man's moods. He said to me: —

"Mrs. Harker, is it not?" I bowed assent.

"That was Miss Mina Murray?" Again I assented.

"It is Mina Murray that I came to see that was friend of that poor dear child Lucy Westenra. Madam Mina, it is on account of the dead I come."

"Sir," I said, "you could have no better claim on me than that you were a friend and helper of Lucy Westenra." And I held out my hand. He took it and said tenderly: —

"Oh, Madam Mina, I knew that the friend of that poor lily girl must be good, but I had yet to learn —" He finished his speech with a courtly bow. I asked him what it was that he wanted to see me about, so he at once began: —

"I have read your letters to Miss Lucy. Forgive me, but I had to begin to inquire somewhere, and there was none to ask. I know that you were with her at Whitby. She sometimes kept a diary — you need not look surprised, Madam Mina; it was begun after you had left, and was made in imitation of you — and in that diary she traces by inference certain things to a sleep-walking in which she puts down that you saved her. In great perplexity then I come to you, and ask you out of your so much kindness to tell me all of it that you remember."

à deux mains: In both hands (French).

"I can tell you, I think, Dr. Van Helsing, all about it."

"Ah, then you have good memory for facts, for details? It is not always so with young ladies."

"No, doctor, but I wrote it all down at the time. I can show it to you if you like."

"Oh, Madam Mina, I will be grateful; you will do me much favour." I could not resist the temptation of mystifying him a bit — I suppose it is some of the taste of the original apple that remains still in our mouths — so I handed him the shorthand diary. He took it with a grateful bow, and said: —

"May I read it?"

"If you wish," I answered as demurely as I could. He opened it, and for an instant his face fell. Then he stood up and bowed.

"Oh, you so clever woman!" he said. "I long knew that Mr. Jonathan was a man of much thankfulness; but see, his wife have all the good things. And will you not so much honour me and so help me as to read it for me? Alas! I know not the shorthand." By this time my little joke was over, and I was almost ashamed; so I took the typewritten copy from my workbasket and handed it to him.

"Forgive me," I said: "I could not help it; but I had been thinking that it was of dear Lucy that you wished to ask, and so that you might not have to wait — not on my account, but because I know your time must be precious — I have written it out on the typewriter for you."

He took it, and his eyes glistened. "You are so good," he said. "And may I read it now? I may want to ask you some things when I have read."

"By all means," I said, "read it over whilst I order lunch; and then you can ask me questions whilst we eat." He bowed and settled himself in a chair with his back to the light, and became absorbed in the papers, whilst I went to see after lunch, chiefly in order that he might not be disturbed. When I came back I found him walking hurriedly up and down the room, his face all ablaze with excitement. He rushed up to me and took me by both hands.

"Oh, Madam Mina," he said, "how can I say what I owe to you? This paper is as sunshine. It opens the gate to me. I am daze, I am dazzle, with so much light; and yet clouds roll in behind the light every time. But that you do not, cannot, comprehend. Oh, but I am grateful to you, you so clever woman. Madam" — he said this very solemnly — "if ever Abraham Van Helsing can do anything for you or yours, I trust you will let me know. It will be pleasure and delight if I may serve you as a friend; as a friend, but all I have ever learned, all I can ever do, shall be for you and those you love. There are darknesses in life, and there are lights; you are one of the lights. You will have happy life and good life, and your husband will be blessed in you."

"But, doctor, you praise me too much, and — and you do not know me."

"Not know you — I, who am old, and who have studied all my life men and women; I, who have made my specialty the brain and all that belongs to him and all that follow from him! And I have read your diary that you have so goodly written for me, and which breathes out truth in every line. I, who have read your so sweet letter to poor Lucy of your marriage and your trust, not know you! Oh, Madam Mina, good women tell all their lives, and by day and by hour and by minute, such things that angels can read; and we men who wish to know have in us something of angels' eyes. Your husband is noble nature, and you are noble too, for you trust, and trust cannot be where there is mean nature. And your husband — tell me of him. Is he quite well? Is all that fever gone, and is he strong and hearty?" I saw here an opening to ask him about Jonathan, so I said: —

"He was almost recovered, but he has been greatly upset by Mr. Hawkins's death." He interrupted: —

"Oh yes, I know, I know. I have read your last two letters." I went on: —

"I suppose this upset him, for when we were in town on Thursday last he had a sort of shock."

"A shock, and after brain fever so soon! That was not good. What kind of shock was it?"

"He thought he saw some one who recalled something terrible, something which led to his brain fever." And here the whole thing seemed to overwhelm me in a rush. The pity for Jonathan, the horror which he experienced, the whole fearful mystery of his diary, and the fear that has been brooding over me ever since, all came in a tumult. I suppose I was hysterical, for I threw myself on my knees and held up my hands to him, and implored him to make my husband well again. He took my hands and raised me up, and made me sit on the sofa, and sat by me; he held my hand in his, and said to me with, oh, such infinite sweetness: —

"My life is a barren and lonely one, and so full of work that I have not had much time for friendships; but since I have been summoned to here by my friend John Seward I have known so many good people and seen such nobility that I feel more than ever — and it has grown with my advancing years — the loneliness of my life. Believe me, then, that I come here full of respect for you, and you have given me hope — hope, not in what I am seeking of, but that there are good women still left to make life happy — good women, whose lives and whose truths may make good lesson for the children that are to be. I am glad, glad, that I may here be of some use to you; for if your husband suffer, he suffer within the range of my study and experience. I promise you that I will gladly do *all* for him that I can — all to make his life strong and manly, and your life a happy one. Now you must eat. You are overwrought and perhaps over-anxious. Husband Jonathan would not like to see you so pale; and what he like not where he love, is not to his good. Therefore for his sake you must eat and smile. You have told me all about Lucy, and so now we shall not speak of it, lest it distress. I shall stay in Exeter to-night, for I want to think much over what you have told me, and when I have thought I will ask you questions, if I may. And then, too, you will tell me of husband Jonathan's trouble so far as you can, but not yet. You must eat now; afterwards you shall tell me all."

After lunch, when we went back to the drawing-room, he said to me: —

"And now tell me all about him." When it came to speaking to this great, learned man, I began to fear that he would think me a weak fool, and Jonathan a madman — that journal is all so strange — and I hesitated to go on. But he was so sweet and kind, and he had promised to help, and I trusted him, so I said: —

"Dr. Van Helsing, what I have to tell you is so queer that you must not laugh at me or at my husband. I have been since yesterday in a sort of fever of doubt; you must be kind to me, and not think me foolish that I have even half believed some very strange things." He reassured me by his manner as well as his words when he said: —

"Oh, my dear, if you only knew how strange is the matter regarding which I am here, it is you who would laugh. I have learned not to think little of any one's belief, no matter how strange it be. I have tried to keep an open mind; and it is not the ordinary things of life that could close it, but the strange things, the extraordinary things, the things that make one doubt if they be mad or sane."

"Thank you, thank you, a thousand times! You have taken a weight off my mind. If you will let me, I shall give you a paper to read. It is long, but I have typewritten it out. It will tell you my trouble and Jonathan's. It is the copy of his journal when abroad, and all that happened. I dare not say anything of it; you will read for yourself and judge. And then when I see you, perhaps, you will be very kind and tell me what you think."

"I promise," he said as I gave him the papers; "I shall in the morning, so soon as I can, come to see you and your husband, if I may."

"Jonathan will be here at half-past eleven, and you must come to lunch with us and see him then; you could catch the quick 3.34 train, which will leave you at Paddington° before eight." He was surprised at my knowledge of the trains off-hand, but he does not know that I have made up° all the trains to and from Exeter, so that I may help Jonathan in case he is in a hurry.

So he took the papers with him and went away, and I sit here thinking — thinking I don't know what.

Letter (by hand), Van Helsing to Mrs. Harker

"25 *September*, 6 *o'clock*

"Dear Madam Mina, —

"I have read your husband's so wonderful diary. You may sleep without doubt. Strange and terrible as it is, it is *true*! I will pledge my life on it. It may be worse for others; but for him and you there is no dread. He is a noble fellow; and let me tell you from experience of men, that one who would do as he did in going down that wall and to that room — ay, and going a second time — is not one to be injured in permanence by a shock. His brain and his heart are all right; this I swear, before I have even seen him; so be at rest. I shall have much to ask him of other things. I am blessed that to-day I come to see you, for I have learn all at once so much that again I am dazzle — dazzle more than ever, and I must think.

"Yours the most faithful,
"ABRAHAM VAN HELSING."

Letter, Mrs. Harker to Van Helsing

"25 *September*, 6.30 *p.m.*

"My dear Dr. Van Helsing, —

"A thousand thanks for your kind letter, which has taken a great weight off my mind. And yet, if it be true, what terrible things there are in the world, and what an awful thing if that man, that monster, be really in London! I fear to think. I have this moment, whilst writing, had a wire from Jonathan, saying that he leaves by the 6.25 to-night

---

Paddington: The London terminus for the Great Western Railway, which connected the capital with the west and southwest of England (*Baedeker* 1896).   ***made up:*** Compiled a list of (*OED*).

from Launceston° and will be here at 10.18, so that I shall have no fear to-night. Will you, therefore, instead of lunching with us, please come to breakfast at eight o'clock, if this be not too early for you? You can get away, if you are in a hurry, by the 10.30 train, which will bring you to Paddington by 2.35. Do not answer this, as I shall take it that, if I do not hear, you will come to breakfast.

"Believe me,
"Your faithful and grateful friend,
"MINA HARKER."

Jonathan Harker's Journal

26 *September.* — I thought never to write in this diary again, but the time has come. When I got home last night Mina had supper ready, and when we had supped she told me of Van Helsing's visit, and of her having given him the two diaries copied out, and of how anxious she has been about me. She showed me in the doctor's letter that all I wrote down was true. It seems to have made a new man of me. It was the doubt as to the reality of the whole thing that knocked me over. I felt impotent, and in the dark, and distrustful. But, now that I *know*, I am not afraid, even of the Count. He has succeeded after all, then, in his design in getting to London, and it was he I saw. He has got younger, and how? Van Helsing is the man to unmask him and hunt him out, if he is anything like what Mina says. We sat late, and talked it all over. Mina is dressing, and I shall call at the hotel in a few minutes and bring him over. . . . .

He was, I think, surprised to see me. When I came into the room where he was, and introduced myself, he took me by the shoulder, and turned my face round to the light, and said, after a sharp scrutiny: —

"But Madam Mina told me you were ill, that you had had a shock." It was so funny to hear my wife called "Madam Mina" by this kindly strong-faced old man. I smiled, and said: —

"I *was* ill, I *have* had a shock; but you have cured me already."

"And how?"

"By your letter to Mina last night. I was in doubt, and then every-thing took a hue of unreality, and I did not know what to trust, even the evidence of my own senses. Not knowing what to trust, I did not know what to do; and so had only to keep on working in what had hitherto been the groove of my life. The groove ceased to avail me, and

Launceston: A market town in Cornwall (*Enc. Brit.* 11th).

I mistrusted myself. Doctor, you don't know what it is to doubt everything, even yourself. No, you don't; you couldn't with eye-brows like
yours." He seemed pleased, and laughed as he said: —

"So! You are physiognomist.° I learn more here with each hour. I
am with so much pleasure coming to you to breakfast; and, oh, sir, you
will pardon praise from an old man, but you are blessed in your wife." I
would listen to him go on praising Mina for a day, so I simply nodded
and stood silent.

"She is one of God's women, fashioned by His own hand to show
us men and other women that there is a heaven where we can enter, and
that its light can be here on earth. So true, so sweet, so noble, so little
an egoist — and that, let me tell you, is much in this age, so sceptical
and selfish. And you, sir — I have read all the letters to poor Miss Lucy,
and some of them speak of you, so I know you since some days from
the knowing of others; but I have seen your true self since last night.
You will give me your hand, will you not? And let us be friends for all
our lives."

We shook hands, and he was so earnest and so kind that it made me
quite choky.

"And now," he said, "may I ask you for some more help? I have a
great task to do, and at the beginning it is to know. You can help me
here. Can you tell me what went before your going to Transylvania?
Later on I may ask more help and of a different kind; but at first this
will do."

"Look here, sir," I said, "does what you have to do concern the
Count?"

"It does," he said solemnly.

"Then I am with you heart and soul. As you go by the 10.30 train,
you will not have time to read them; but I shall get the bundle of
papers. You can take them with you and read them in the train."

After breakfast I saw him to the station. When we were parting he
said: —

"Perhaps you will come to town if I send to you, and take Madam
Mina too."

"We shall both come when you will," I said.

I had got him the morning papers and the London papers of the
previous night, and while we were talking at the carriage window,
waiting for the train to start, he was turning them over. His eye sud-

---

physiognomist: Someone who practices physiognomy, which involves reading character or
disposition from a person's face.

denly seemed to catch something in one of them, "The Westminister Gazette" — I knew it by the colour — and he grew quite white. He read something intently, groaning to himself: "Mein Gott! Mein Gott! So soon! so soon!" I do not think he remembered me at the moment. Just then the whistle blew, and the train moved off. This recalled him to himself, and he leaned out of the window and waved his hand, calling out: "Love to Madam Mina; I shall write so soon as ever I can."

Dr. Seward's Diary

26 *September.* — Truly there is no such thing as finality. Not a week since I said "Finis," and yet here I am starting fresh again, or rather going on with the same record. Until this afternoon I had no cause to think of what is done. Renfield had become, to all intents, as sane as he ever was. He was already well ahead with his fly business; and he had just started in the spider line also; so he had not been of any trouble to me. I had a letter from Arthur, written on Sunday, and from it I gather that he is bearing up wonderfully well. Quincey Morris is with him, and that is much of a help, for he himself is a bubbling well of good spirits. Quincey wrote me a line too, and from him I hear that Arthur is beginning to recover something of his old buoyancy; so as to them all my mind is at rest. As for myself, I was settling down to my work with the enthusiasm which I used to have for it, so that I might fairly have said that the wound which poor Lucy left on me was becoming cicatrised.° Everything is, however, now reopened; and what is to be the end God only knows. I have an idea that Van Helsing thinks he knows too, but he will only let out enough at a time to whet curiosity. He went to Exeter yesterday, and stayed there all night. To-day he came back, and almost bounded into the room at about half-past five o'clock, and thrust last night's "Westminster Gazette" into my hand.

"What do you think of that?" he asked as he stood back and folded his arms.

I looked over the paper, for I really did not know what he meant; but he took it from me and pointed out a paragraph about children being decoyed away at Hampstead. It did not convey much to me, until I reached a passage where it described small punctured wounds on their throats. An idea struck me, and I looked up. "Well?" he said.

"It is like poor Lucy's."

"And what do you make of it?"

cicatrised: Healed by forming a scar (*OED* OL).

"Simply that there is some cause in common. Whatever it was that injured her has injured them." I did not quite understand his answer: —

"That is true indirectly, but not directly."

"How do you mean, Professor?" I asked. I was a little inclined to take his seriousness lightly — for, after all, four days of rest and freedom from burning, harrowing anxiety does help to restore one's spirits — but when I saw his face, it sobered me. Never, even in the midst of our despair about poor Lucy, had he looked more stern.

"Tell me!" I said. "I can hazard no opinion. I do not know what to think, and I have no data on which to found a conjecture."

"Do you mean to tell me, friend John, that you have no suspicion as to what poor Lucy died of; not after all the hints given, not only by events, but by me?"

"Of nervous prostration following on great loss or waste of blood."

"And how the blood lost or waste?" I shook my head. He stepped over and sat down beside me, and went on: —

"You are clever man, friend John; you reason well, and your wit is bold; but you are too prejudiced. You do not let your eyes see nor your ears hear, and that which is outside your daily life is not of account to you. Do you not think that there are things which you cannot understand, and yet which are; that some people see things that others cannot? But there are things old and new which must not be contemplate by men's eyes, because they know — or think they know — some things which other men have told them. Ah, it is the fault of our science that it wants to explain all; and if it explain not, then it says there is nothing to explain. But yet we see around us every day the growth of new beliefs, which think themselves new; and which are yet but the old, which pretend to be young — like the fine ladies at the opera. I suppose now you do not believe in corporeal transference.° No? Nor in materialisation.° No? Nor in astral bodies.° No? Nor in the reading of thought. No? Nor in hypnotism ——"

"Yes," I said. "Charcot° has proved that pretty well." He smiled as

---

corporeal transference: Movement of bodies by mental effort only.   *materialisation:* "The appearance of a spirit in bodily form" (*OED*).   *astral bodies:* "The ethereal counterpart or shadow of a human or animal body" (*OED* I: 731). A term from Theosophy, a form of organized occultism important in New York City, London, and Dublin at the end of the nineteenth century.   *Charcot:* Jean Martin Charcot (1825–1893), a French physician, influenced the study of neurology through his research into nervous diseases and conditions such as hysteria. He was best known for his investigations of hypnotism (*Enc. Brit.* 11th).

he went on: "Then you are satisfied as to it. Yes? And of course then you understand how it act, and can follow the mind of the great Charcot — alas that he is no more! — into the very soul of the patient that he influence. No? Then, friend John, am I to take it that you simply accept fact, and are satisfied to let from premise to conclusion be a blank? No? Then tell me — for I am student of the brain — how you accept the hypnotism and reject the thought-reading. Let me tell you, my friend, that there are things done to-day in electrical science which would have been deemed unholy by the very men who discovered electricity — who would themselves not so long before have been burned as wizards. There are always mysteries in life. Why was it that Methuselah° lived nine hundred years, and 'Old Parr'° one hundred and sixty-nine, and yet that poor Lucy, with four men's blood in her poor veins, could not live even one day? For, had she live one more day, we could have save her. Do you know all the mystery of life and death? Do you know the altogether of comparative anatomy, and can say wherefore the qualities of brutes are in some men, and not in others? Can you tell me why, when other spiders die small and soon, that one great spider lived for centuries in the tower of the old Spanish church and grew and grew, till, on descending, he could drink the oil of all the church lamps? Can you tell me why in the Pampas, ay and elsewhere, there are bats that come at night and open the veins of cattle and horses and suck dry their veins; how in some islands of the Western seas there are bats which hang on the trees all day, that those who have seen describe as like giant nuts or pods, and that when the sailors sleep on the deck, because that it is hot, flit down on them, and then — and then in the morning are found dead men, white as even Miss Lucy was?"

"Good God, Professor!" I said, starting up. "Do you mean to tell me that Lucy was bitten by such a bat; and that such a thing is here in London in the nineteenth century?" He waved his hand for silence, and went on: —

"Can you tell me why the tortoise lives more long than generations of men; why the elephant goes on and on till he have seen dynasties; and why the parrot never die only of bite of cat or dog or other complaint? Can you tell me why men believe in all ages and places that there are some few women who cannot die? We all know — because science has vouched for the fact — that there have been toads shut up on rocks

---

Methuselah: An Old Testament patriarch famed for his longevity. (Gen. 5.27). ***Old Parr:*** Thomas Parr, an English farmer, was said to have lived 152 years, from 1483 to 1635. (*Enc. Brit.* 11th).

for thousands of years, shut in one so small hole that only hold him since the youth of the world. Can you tell me how the Indian fakir can make himself to die and have been buried, and his grave sealed and corn sowed on it, and the corn reaped and be cut and sown and reaped and cut again, and then men come and take away the unbroken seal, and that there lie the Indian fakir, not dead, but that rise up and walk amongst them as before?" Here I interrupted him. I was getting bewildered; he so crowded on my mind his list of nature's eccentricities and possible impossibilities that my imagination was getting fired. I had a dim idea that he was teaching me some lesson, as long ago he used to do in his study in Amsterdam; but he used then to tell me the thing, so that I could have the object of thought in mind all the time. But now I was without this help, yet I wanted to follow him, so I said: —

"Professor, let me be your pet student again. Tell me the thesis, so that I may apply your knowledge as you go on. At present I am going in my mind from point to point as a mad man, and not a sane one, follows an idea. I feel like a novice blundering through a bog in a mist, jumping from one tussock to another in the mere blind effort to move on without knowing where I am going."

"That is good image," he said. "Well, I shall tell you. My thesis is this: I want you to believe."

"To believe what?"

"To believe in things that you cannot. Let me illustrate. I heard once of an American who so defined faith: 'that which enables us to believe things which we know to be untrue.'° For one, I follow that man. He meant that we shall have an open mind, and not let a little bit of truth check the rush of a big truth, like a small rock does a railway truck. We get the small truth first. Good! We keep him, and we value him; but all the same we must not let him think himself all the truth in the universe."

"Then you want me not to let some previous conviction injure the receptivity of my mind with regard to some strange matter. Do I read your lesson aright?"

"Ah, you are my favourite pupil still. It is worth to teach you. Now that you are willing to understand, you have taken the first step to

American . . . '. . . untrue': This reflection on belief, the fictitious, and truth is probably a reference to the epigraph for chapter 12 of *Following the Equator,* by Mark Twain (1835–1910): "There are those who scoff at the schoolboy, calling him frivolous and shallow. Yet it was the schoolboy who said 'Faith is believing what you know ain't so.'" Twain attributes the epigraph to *Puddn'head Wilson's New Calendar,* the fictitious sequel to an equally fictitious book of aphorisms created by the title character of Twain's *Puddn'head Wilson,* itself a work of fiction.

understand. You think then that those so small holes in the children's throats were made by the same that made the hole in Miss Lucy?"

"I suppose so." He stood up and said solemnly: —

"Then you are wrong. Oh, would it were so! but alas! no. It is worse, far, far worse."

"In God's name, Professor Van Helsing, what do you mean?" I cried.

He threw himself with a despairing gesture into a chair, and placed his elbows on the table, covering his face with his hands as he spoke: —

"They were made by Miss Lucy!"

CHAPTER XV. DR. SEWARD'S DIARY

(Continued)

FOR a while sheer anger mastered me; it was as if he had during her life struck Lucy on the face. I smote the table hard and rose up as I said to him: —

"Dr. Van Helsing, are you mad?" He raised his head and looked at me, and somehow the tenderness of his face calmed me at once. "Would I were!" he said. "Madness were easy to bear compared with truth like this. Oh, my friend, why, think you, did I go so far round, why take so long to tell you so simple a thing? Was it because I hate you and have hated you all my life? Was it because I wished to give you pain? Was it that I wanted, now so late, revenge for that time when you saved my life, and from a fearful death? Ah no!"

"Forgive me," said I. He went on: —

"My friend, it was because I wished to be gentle in the breaking to you, for I know you have loved that so sweet lady. But even yet I do not expect you to believe. It is so hard to accept at once any abstract truth, that we may doubt such to be possible when we have always believed the 'no' of it; it is more hard still to accept so sad a concrete truth, and of such a one as Miss Lucy. To-night I go to prove it. Dare you come with me?"

This staggered me. A man does not like to prove such a truth; Byron excepted from the category, jealousy.

"And prove the very truth he most abhorred."°

And prove ... abhorred: In the poem *Don Juan* by Lord Byron, Don Alfonso, correctly suspecting that his wife Donna Julia is having a love affair, bursts into her bedroom with his servants "[t]o prove himself the thing he most abhored" — that is, a cuckold (l. 139).

He saw my hesitation, and spoke: —

"The logic is simple, no madman's logic this time, jumping from tussock to tussock in a misty bog. If it be not true, then proof will be relief; at worst it will not harm. If it be true! Ah, there is the dread; yet very dread should help my cause, for in it is some need of belief. Come, I tell you what I propose: first, that we go off now and see that child in the hospital. Dr. Vincent, of the North Hospital, where the papers say the child is, is friend of mine, and I think of yours since you were in class at Amsterdam. He will let two scientists see his case, if he will not let two friends. We shall tell him nothing, but only that we wish to learn. And then ——"

"And then?" He took a key from his pocket and held it up. "And then we spend the night, you and I, in the churchyard where Lucy lies. This is the key that lock the tomb. I had it from the coffin-man to give to Arthur." My heart sank within me, for I felt that there was some fearful ordeal before us. I could do nothing, however, so I plucked up what heart I could and said that we had better hasten, as the afternoon was passing. . . . .

We found the child awake. It had had a sleep and taken some food, and altogether was going on well. Dr. Vincent took the bandage from its throat, and showed us the punctures. There was no mistaking the similarity to those which had been on Lucy's throat. They were smaller, and the edges looked fresher; that was all. We asked Vincent to what he attributed them, and he replied that it must have been a bite of some animal, perhaps a rat; but, for his own part, he was inclined to think that it was one of the bats which are so numerous on the northern heights of London. "Out of so many harmless ones," he said, "there may be some wild specimen from the South of a more malignant species. Some sailor may have brought one home, and it managed to escape; or even from the Zoological Gardens a young one may have got loose, or one be bred there from a vampire. These things do occur, you know. Only ten days ago a wolf got out, and was, I believe, traced up in this direction. For a week after, the children were playing nothing but Red Riding Hood on the Heath and in every alley in the place until this 'bloofer lady' scare came along, since when it has been quite a gala-time with them. Even this poor little mite, when he woke up to-day, asked the nurse if he might go away. When she asked him why he wanted to go, he said he wanted to play with the 'bloofer lady.'"

"I hope," said Van Helsing, "that when you are sending the child home you will caution its parents to keep strict watch over it. These fancies to stray are most dangerous; and if the child were to remain out another night, it would probably be fatal. But in any case I suppose you will not let it away for some days?"

"Certainly not, not for a week at least; longer if the wound is not healed."

Our visit to the hospital took more time than we had reckoned on, and the sun had dipped before we came out. When Van Helsing saw how dark it was, he said: —

"There is no hurry. It is more late than I thought. Come, let us seek somewhere that we may eat, and then we shall go on our way."

We dined at "Jack Straw's Castle"° along with a little crowd of bicyclists and others who were genially noisy. About ten o'clock we started from the inn. It was then very dark, and the scattered lamps made the darkness greater when we were once outside their individual radius. The Professor had evidently noted the road we were to go, for he went on unhesitatingly; but, as for me, I was in quite a mix-up as to locality. As we went further, we met fewer and fewer people, till at last we were somewhat surprised when we met even the patrol of horse police going their usual suburban round. At last we reached the wall of the churchyard, which we climbed over. With some little difficulty — for it was very dark, and the whole place seemed so strange to us — we found the Westenra tomb. The Professor took the key, opened the creaky door, and standing back, politely, but quite unconsciously, motioned me to precede him. There was a delicious irony in the offer, in the courtliness of giving preference on such a ghastly occasion. My companion followed me quickly, and cautiously drew the door to, after carefully ascertaining that the lock was a falling, and not a spring, one. In the latter case we should have been in a bad plight. Then he fumbled in his bag, and taking out a match-box and a piece of candle, proceeded to make a light. The tomb in the day-time, and when wreathed with fresh flowers, had looked grim and gruesome enough; but now, some days afterwards, when the flowers hung lank and dead, their whites turning to rust and their greens to browns; when the spider and the beetle had resumed their accustomed dominance; when time-discoloured stone, and dust-encrusted mortar, and rusty, dank iron, and tarnished brass, and clouded silver-plating gave back the feeble glimmer of a candle, the effect was more miserable and sordid than could have been imagined. It conveyed irresistibly the idea that life — animal life — was not the only thing which could pass away.

Van Helsing went about his work systematically. Holding his candle

Jack Straw's Castle: One of two well-known inns on Hampstead Heath.

so that he could read the coffin plates, and so holding it that the sperm°
dropped in white patches which congealed as they touched the metal,
he made assurance of Lucy's coffin. Another search in his bag, and he
took out a turnscrew.°

"What are you going to do?" I asked.

"To open the coffin. You shall yet be convinced." Straightway he
began taking out the screws, and finally lifted off the lid, showing
the casing of lead beneath. The sight was almost too much for me. It
seemed to be as much an affront to the dead as it would have been to
have stripped off her clothing in her sleep whilst living; I actually took
hold of his hand to stop him. He only said: "You shall see," and again
fumbling in his bag, took out a tiny fret-saw.° Striking the turnscrew
through the lead with a swift downward stab, which made me wince, he
made a small hole, which was, however, big enough to admit the point
of the saw. I had expected a rush of gas from the week-old corpse. We
doctors, who have had to study our dangers, have to become accustomed to such things, and I drew back towards the door. But the Professor never stopped for a moment; he sawed down a couple of feet
along one side of the lead coffin, and then across, and down the other
side. Taking the edge of the loose flange, he bent it back towards the
foot of the coffin, and holding up the candle into the aperture, motioned to me to look.

I drew near and looked. The coffin was empty.

It was certainly a surprise to me, and gave me a considerable shock,
but Van Helsing was unmoved. He was now more sure than ever of his
ground, and so emboldened to proceed in his task. "Are you satisfied
now, friend John?" he asked.

I felt all the dogged argumentativeness of my nature awake within
me as I answered him: —

"I am satisfied that Lucy's body is not in that coffin; but that only
proves one thing."

"And what is that, friend John?"

"That it is not there."

"That is good logic," he said, "so far as it goes. But how do you —
how can you — account for it not being there?"

"Perhaps a body-snatcher," I suggested. "Some of the undertaker's
people may have stolen it." I felt that I was speaking folly, and yet it was

---

sperm: Short for spermaceti, fat from the head of a sperm whale used for making candles
(*OED*).   *turnscrew:* Screwdriver.   *fret-saw:* A saw used to cut out decorative patterns (*OED*).

the only real cause which I could suggest. The Professor sighed. "Ah well!" he said, "we must have more proof. Come with me."

He put on the coffin-lid again, gathered up all his things and placed them in the bag, blew out the light, and placed the candle also in the bag. We opened the door, and went out. Behind us he closed the door and locked it. He handed me the key, saying: "Will you keep it? You had better be assured." I laughed — it was not a very cheerful laugh, I am bound to say — as I motioned him to keep it. "A key is nothing," I said; "there may be duplicates; and anyhow it is not difficult to pick a lock of that kind." He said nothing, but put the key in his pocket. Then he told me to watch at one side of the churchyard whilst he would watch at the other. I took up my place behind a yew-tree, and I saw his dark figure move until the intervening headstones and trees hid it from my sight.

It was a lonely vigil. Just after I had taken my place I heard a distant clock strike twelve, and in time came one and two. I was chilled and unnerved and angry with the Professor for taking me on such an errand and with myself for coming. I was too cold and too sleepy to be keenly observant, and not sleepy enough to betray my trust; so altogether I had a dreary, miserable time.

Suddenly, as I turned round, I thought I saw something like a white streak, moving between two dark yew-trees at the side of the church-yard farthest from the tomb; at the same time a dark mass moved from the Professor's side of the ground, and hurriedly went towards it. Then I too moved; but I had to go round headstones and railed-off tombs, and I stumbled over graves. The sky was overcast, and somewhere far off an early cock crew. A little way off, beyond a line of scattered juniper-trees, which marked the pathway to the church, a white, dim figure flitted in the direction of the tomb. The tomb itself was hidden by trees, and I could not see where the figure disappeared. I heard the rustle of actual movement where I had first seen the white figure, and coming over, found the Professor holding in his arms a tiny child. When he saw me he held it out to me, and said: —

"Are you satisfied now?"

"No," I said, in a way that I felt was aggressive.

"Do you not see the child?"

"Yes, it is a child, but who brought it here? And is it wounded?" I asked.

"We shall see," said the Professor, and with one impulse we took our way out of the churchyard, he carrying the sleeping child.

When we had got some little distance away, we went into a clump of trees, and struck a match, and looked at the child's throat. It was without a scratch or scar of any kind.

"Was I right?" I asked triumphantly.

"We were just in time," said the Professor thankfully.

We had now to decide what we were to do with the child, and so consulted about it. If we were to take it to a police-station we should have to give some account of our movements during the night; at least, we should have had to make some statement as to how we had come to find the child. So finally we decided that we would take it to the Heath, and when we heard a policeman coming, would leave it where he could not fail to find it; we would then seek our way home as quickly as we could. All fell out well. At the edge of Hampstead Heath we heard a policeman's heavy tramp, and laying the child on the pathway, we waited and watched until he saw it as he flashed his lantern to and fro. We heard his exclamation of astonishment, and then we went away silently. By good chance we got a cab near the "Spaniards,"° and drove to town.

I cannot sleep, so I make this entry. But I must try to get a few hours' sleep, as Van Helsing is to call for me at noon. He insists that I shall go with him on another expedition.

27 September. — It was two o'clock before we found a suitable opportunity for our attempt. The funeral held at noon was all completed, and the last stragglers of the mourners had taken themselves lazily away, when, looking carefully from behind a clump of alder-trees, we saw the sexton lock the gate after him. We knew then that we were safe till morning did we desire it; but the Professor told me that we should not want more than an hour at most. Again I felt that horrid sense of the reality of things, in which any effort of imagination seemed out of place; and I realised distinctly the perils of the law which we were incurring in our unhallowed work. Besides, I felt it was all so useless. Outrageous as it was to open a leaden coffin, to see if a woman dead nearly a week were really dead, it now seemed the height of folly to open the tomb again, when we knew, from the evidence of our own eyesight, that the coffin was empty. I shrugged my shoulders, however, and rested silent, for Van Helsing had a way of going on his own road, no matter who remonstrated. He took the key, opened the vault, and again courteously motioned me to precede. The place was not so gruesome as last night, but oh, how unutterably mean-looking when the

---

Spaniards: Like Jack Straw's Castle, an inn on Hampstead Heath.

sunshine streamed in. Van Helsing walked over to Lucy's coffin, and I followed. He bent over and again forced back the leaden flange; and then a shock of surprise and dismay shot through me.

There lay Lucy seemingly just as we had seen her the night before her funeral. She was, if possible, more radiantly beautiful than ever; and I could not believe that she was dead. The lips were red, nay redder than before; and on the cheeks was a delicate bloom.

"Is this a juggle°?" I said to him.

"Are you convinced now?" said the Professor in response, and as he spoke he put over his hand, and in a way that made me shudder, pulled back the dead lips and showed the white teeth.

"See," he went on, "see, they are even sharper than before. With this and this" — and he touched one of the canine teeth and that below it — "the little children can be bitten. Are you of belief now, friend John?" Once more, argumentative hostility woke within me. I *could* not accept such an overwhelming idea as he suggested; so, with an attempt to argue of which I was even at the moment ashamed, I said: —

"She may have been placed here since last night."

"Indeed? That is so, and by whom?"

"I do not know. Some one has done it."

"And yet she has been dead one week. Most peoples in that time would not look so." I had no answer for this, so was silent. Van Helsing did not seem to notice my silence; at any rate, he showed neither chagrin nor triumph. He was looking intently at the face of the dead woman, raising the eyelids and looking at the eyes, and once more opening the lips and examining the teeth. Then he turned to me and said: —

"Here, there is one thing which is different from all recorded: here is some dual life that is not as the common. She was bitten by the vampire when she was in a trance, sleep-walking — oh, you start; you do not know that, friend John, but you shall know it all later — and in trance could he best come to take more blood. In trance she died, and in trance she is Un-Dead, too. So it is that she differ from all other. Usually when the Un-Dead sleep at home" — as he spoke he made a comprehensive sweep of his arm to designate what to a vampire was "home" — "their face show what they are, but this so sweet that-was when she not Un-Dead she go back to the nothings of the common dead. There is no malign there, see, and so it make hard that I must kill her in her sleep." This turned my blood cold, and it began to dawn

---

juggle: A trick, an act of deception or imposture (*OED*).

upon me that I was accepting Van Helsing's theories; but if she were really dead, what was there of terror in the idea of killing her? He looked up at me, and evidently saw the change in my face, for he said almost joyously: —

"Ah, you believe now?"

I answered: "Do not press me too hard all at once. I am willing to accept. How will you do this bloody work?"

"I shall cut off her head and fill her mouth with garlic, and I shall drive a stake through her body." It made me shudder to think of so mutilating the body of the woman whom I had loved. And yet the feeling was not so strong as I had expected. I was, in fact, beginning to shudder at the presence of this being, this Un-Dead, as Van Helsing called it, and to loathe it. Is it possible that love is all subjective, or all objective?

I waited a considerable time for Van Helsing to begin, but he stood as if wrapped in thought. Presently he closed the catch of his bag with a snap, and said: —

"I have been thinking, and have made up my mind as to what is best. If I did simply follow my inclining I would do now, at this moment, what is to be done; but there are other things to follow, and things that are thousand times more difficult in that them we do not know. This is simple. She have yet no life taken, though that is of time; and to act now would be to take danger from her for ever. But then we may have to want Arthur, and how shall we tell him of this? If you, who saw the wounds on Lucy's throat, and saw the wounds so similar on the child's at the hospital; if you, who saw the coffin empty last night and full to-day with a woman who have not change only to be more rose and more beautiful in a whole week after she die — if you know of this and know of the white figure last night that brought the child to the churchyard, and yet of your own senses you did not believe, how, then, can I expect Arthur, who know none of those things, to believe? He doubted me when I took him from her kiss when she was dying. I know he has forgiven me because in some mistaken idea I have done things that prevent him say good-bye as he ought; and he may think that in some more mistaken idea this woman was buried alive; and that in most mistake of all we have killed her. He will then argue back that it is we, mistaken ones, that have killed her by our ideas; and so he will be much unhappy always. Yet he never can be sure; and that is the worst of all. And he will sometimes think that she he loved was buried alive, and that will paint his dreams with horrors of what she must have suffered; and, again, he will think that we may be right, and that his so beloved was, after all, an Un-Dead. No! I told him once, and since then I learn much. Now, since I know it is all true, a hundred thousand times more do I know that he must pass through the bitter waters to reach the sweet. He, poor fellow, must have one hour that will make the very face of heaven grow black to him; then we can act for good all round and send him peace. My mind is made up. Let us go. You return home for to-night to your asylum, and see that all be well. As for me, I shall spend the night here in this churchyard in my own way. To-morrow night you will come to me to the Berkeley Hotel at ten of the clock. I shall send for Arthur to come too, and also that so fine young man of America that gave his blood. Later we shall all have work to do. I come with you so far as Piccadilly and there dine, for I must be back here before the sun set."

So we locked the tomb and came away, and got over the wall of the churchyard, which was not much of a task, and drove back to Piccadilly.

Note left by Van Helsing in his portmanteau, Berkeley Hotel, directed to John Seward, M.D.

(Not delivered)

"*27 September*

"Friend John, —

"I write this in case anything should happen. I go alone to watch in that churchyard. It pleases me that the Un-Dead, Miss Lucy, shall not leave to-night, that so on the morrow night she may be more eager. Therefore I shall fix some things she like not — garlic and a crucifix — and so seal up the door of the tomb. She is young as Un-Dead, and will heed. Moreover, these are only to prevent her coming out; they may not prevail on her wanting to get in; for then the Un-Dead is desperate, and must find the line of least resistance, whatsoever it may be. I shall be at hand all the night from sunset till after the sunrise, and if there be aught that may be learned I shall learn it. For Miss Lucy, or from her, I have no fear: but that other to whom is there that she is Un-Dead, he have now the power to seek her tomb and find shelter. He is cunning, as I know from Mr. Jonathan and from the way that all along he have fooled us when he played with us for Miss Lucy's life, and we lost; and in many ways the Un-Dead are strong. He have always the strength in his hand of twenty men; even we four who gave our strength to Miss Lucy it also is all to him. Besides, he can summon his wolf and I know not what. So if it be that he come thither on this night he shall find me; but none other shall — until it be too late. But it may be that he will not attempt the place. There is no reason why he should; his hunting ground is more full of game than the churchyard where the Un-Dead woman sleep, and one old man watch.

"Therefore I write this in case. . . . . Take the papers that are with this, the diaries of Harker and the rest, and read them, and then find this great Un-Dead, and cut off his head and burn his heart or drive a stake through it, so that the world may rest from him.

"If it be so, farewell.

"VAN HELSING."

Dr. Seward's Diary

28 *September.* — It is wonderful what a good night's sleep will do for one. Yesterday I was almost willing to accept Van Helsing's monstrous ideas; but now they seem to start out lurid before me as outrages on common sense. I have no doubt that he believes it all. I wonder if his mind can have become in any way unhinged. Surely there must be *some* rational explanation of all these mysterious things. Is it possible that the Professor can have done it himself? He is so abnormally clever that if he went off his head he would carry out his intent with regard to some fixed idea in a wonderful way. I am loath to think it, and indeed it would be almost as great a marvel as the other to find that Van Helsing was mad; but anyhow I shall watch him carefully. I may get some light on the mystery.

29 *September, morning.* . . . . . Last night, at a little before ten o'clock, Arthur and Quincey came into Van Helsing's room; he told us all that he wanted us to do, but especially addressing himself to Arthur, as if all our wills were centred in his. He began by saying that he hoped we would all come with him too, "for," he said, "there is a grave duty to be done there. You were doubtless surprised at my letter?" This query was directly addressed to Lord Godalming.

"I was. It rather upset me for a bit. There has been so much trouble around my house of late that I could do without any more. I have been curious, too, as to what you mean. Quincey and I talked it over; but the more we talked, the more puzzled we got, till now I can say for myself that I'm about up a tree as to any meaning about anything."

"Me, too," said Quincey Morris laconically.

"Oh," said the Professor, "then you are nearer the beginning, both of you, than friend John here, who has to go a long way back before he can even get so far as to begin."

It was evident that he recognised my return to my old doubting frame of mind without my saying a word. Then, turning to the other two, he said with intense gravity: —

"I want your permission to do what I think good this night. It is, I know, much to ask; and when you know what it is I propose to do you will know, and only then, how much. Therefore may I ask that you promise me in the dark, so that afterwards, though you may be angry with me for a time — I must not disguise from myself the possibility that such may be — you shall not blame yourselves for anything."

"That's frank anyhow," broke in Quincey. "I'll answer for the Professor. I don't quite see his drift, but I swear he's honest; and that's good enough for me."

"I thank you, sir," said Van Helsing proudly. "I have done myself the honour of counting you one trusting friend, and such endorsement is dear to me." He held out a hand, which Quincey took.

Then Arthur spoke out: —

"Dr. Van Helsing, I don't quite like to 'buy a pig in a poke,' as they say in Scotland, and if it be anything in which my honour as a gentleman or my faith as a Christian is concerned, I cannot make such a promise. If you can assure me that what you intend does not violate either of these two, then I give my consent at once; though, for the life of me, I cannot understand what you are driving at."

"I accept your limitation," said Van Helsing, "and all I ask of you is that if you feel it necessary to condemn any act of mine, you will first consider it well and be satisfied that it does not violate your reservations."

"Agreed!" said Arthur; "that is only fair. And now that the *pourparlers*° are over, may I ask what it is we are to do?"

"I want you to come with me, and to come in secret, to the churchyard at Kingstead."°

Arthur's face fell as he said in an amazed sort of way: —

"Where poor Lucy is buried?" The Professor bowed. Arthur went on: "And when there?"

"To enter the tomb!" Arthur stood up.

"Professor, are you in earnest; or is it some monstrous joke? Pardon me, I see that you are in earnest." He sat down again, but I could see that he sat firmly and proudly, as one who is on his dignity. There was silence until he asked again: —

---

pourparlers: French for "conferences," specifically informal discussions prior to actual negotiations" (*OED*).   *Kingstead:* An apparently fictitious location.

"And when in the tomb?"

"To open the coffin."

"This is too much!" he said, angrily rising again. "I am willing to be patient in all things that are reasonable; but in this — this desecration of the grave — of one who ——" He fairly choked with indignation. The Professor looked pityingly at him.

"If I could spare you one pang, my poor friend," he said, "God knows I would. But this night our feet must tread in thorny paths; or later, and for ever, the feet you love must walk in paths of flame!"

Arthur looked up with set, white face and said: —

"Take care, sir, take care!"

"Would it not be well to hear what I have to say?" said Van Helsing. "And then you will at least know the limit of my purpose. Shall I go on?"

"That's fair enough," broke in Morris.

After a pause Van Helsing went on, evidently with an effort: —

"Miss Lucy is dead; is it not so? Yes! Then there can be no wrong to her. But if she be not dead ——"

Arthur jumped to his feet.

"Good God!" he cried. "What do you mean? Has there been any mistake; has she been buried alive?" He groaned in anguish that not even hope could soften.

"I did not say she was alive, my child; I did not think it. I go no further than to say that she might be Un-Dead."

"Un-Dead! Not alive! What do you mean? Is this all a nightmare, or what is it?"

"There are mysteries which men can only guess at, which age by age they may solve only in part. Believe me, we are now on the verge of one. But I have not done. May I cut off the head of dead Miss Lucy?"

"Heavens and earth, no!" cried Arthur in a storm of passion. "Not for the wide world will I consent to any mutilation of her dead body. Dr. Van Helsing, you try me too far. What have I done to you that you should torture me so? What did that poor, sweet girl do that you should want to cast such dishonour on her grave? Are you mad that speak such things, or am I mad that listen to them? Don't dare to think more of such a desecration; I shall not give my consent to anything you do. I have a duty to do in protecting her grave from outrage; and, by God, I shall do it!"

Van Helsing rose up from where he had all the time been seated, and said, gravely and sternly: —

"My Lord Godalming, I, too, have a duty to do, a duty to others, a duty to you, a duty to the dead; and, by God, I shall do it! All I ask you now is that you come with me, that you look and listen; and if when later I make the same request you do not be more eager for its fulfilment even than I am, then — then I shall do my duty, whatever it may seem to me. And then, to follow of your Lordship's wishes, I shall hold myself at your disposal to render an account to you, when and where you will." His voice broke a little, and he went on with a voice full of pity: —

"But, I beseech you, do not go forth in anger with me. In a long life of acts which were often not pleasant to do, and which sometimes did wring my heart, I have never had so heavy a task as now. Believe me that if the time comes for you to change your mind towards me, one look from you will wipe away all this so sad hour, for I would do what a man can to save you from sorrow. Just think. For why should I give myself so much of labour and so much of sorrow? I have come here from my own land to do what I can of good; at the first to please my friend John, and then to help a sweet young lady, whom, too, I came to love. For her — I am ashamed to say so much, but I say it in kindness — I gave what you gave: the blood of my veins; I gave it, I, who was not, like you, her lover, but only her physician and her friend. I gave to her my nights and days — before death, after death; and if my death can do her good even now, when she is the dead Un-Dead, she shall have it freely." He said this with a very grave, sweet pride, and Arthur was much affected by it. He took the old man's hand and said in a broken voice: —

"Oh, it is hard to think of it, and I cannot understand; but at least I shall go with you and wait."

CHAPTER XVI. DR. SEWARD'S DIARY

(Continued)

IT was just a quarter before twelve o'clock when we got into the church-yard over the low wall. The night was dark, with occasional gleams of moonlight between the rents of the heavy clouds that scudded across the sky. We all kept somehow close together, with Van Helsing slightly in front as he led the way. When we had come close to the tomb I looked well at Arthur, for I feared that the proximity to a place laden with so sorrowful a memory would upset him; but he bore himself well.

I took it that the very mystery of the proceeding was in some way a counteractent to his grief. The Professor unlocked the door, and seeing a natural hesitation amongst us for various reasons, solved the difficulty by entering first himself. The rest of us followed, and he closed the door. He then lit a dark lantern and pointed to the coffin. Arthur stepped forward hesitatingly; Van Helsing said to me: —

"You were with me here yesterday. Was the body of Miss Lucy in that coffin?"

"It was." The Professor turned to the rest, saying: —

"You hear; and yet there is one who does not believe with me." He took his screwdriver and again took off the lid of the coffin. Arthur looked on, very pale but silent; when the lid was removed he stepped forward. He evidently did not know that there was a leaden coffin, or, at any rate, had not thought of it. When he saw the rent in the lead, the blood rushed to his face for an instant, but as quickly fell away again, so that he remained of a ghastly whiteness; he was still silent. Van Helsing forced back the leaden flange, and we all looked in and recoiled.

The coffin was empty!

For several minutes no one spoke a word. The silence was broken by Quincey Morris: —

"Professor, I answered for you. Your word is all I want. I wouldn't ask such a thing ordinarily — I wouldn't so dishonour you as to imply a doubt; but this is a mystery that goes beyond any honour or dishonour. Is this your doing?"

"I swear to you by all that I hold sacred that I have not removed nor touched her. What happened was this: Two nights ago my friend Seward and I came here — with good purpose, believe me. I opened that coffin, which was then sealed up, and we found it, as now, empty. We then waited, and saw something white come through the trees. The next day we came here in day-time, and she lay there. Did she not, friend John?"

"Yes."

"That night we were just in time. One more so small child was missing, and we find it, thank God, unharmed amongst the graves. Yesterday I came here before sundown, for at sundown the Un-Dead can move. I waited here all the night till the sun rose, but I saw nothing. It was most probable that it was because I had laid over the clamps of those doors garlic, which the Un-Dead cannot bear, and other things which they shun. Last night there was no exodus, so to-night before the sundown I took away my garlic and other things. And so it is we find this coffin empty. But bear with me. So far there is much that is strange. Wait you with me outside, unseen and unheard, and things much stranger are yet to be. So" — here he shut the dark slide of his lantern — "now to the outside." He opened the door, and we filed out, he coming last and locking the door behind him.

Oh! but it seemed fresh and pure in the night air after the terror of that vault. How sweet it was to see the clouds race by, and the passing gleams of the moonlight between the scudding clouds crossing and passing — like the gladness and sorrow of a man's life; how sweet it was to breathe the fresh air, that had no taint of death and decay; how humanising to see the red lighting of the sky beyond the hill, and to hear far away the muffled roar that marks the life of a great city. Each in his own way was solemn and overcome. Arthur was silent, and was, I could see, striving to grasp the purpose and the inner meaning of the mystery. I was myself tolerably patient, and half inclined again to throw aside doubt and to accept Van Helsing's conclusions. Quincey Morris was phlegmatic in the way of a man who accepts all things, and accepts them in the spirit of cool bravery, with hazard of all he has to stake. Not being able to smoke, he cut himself a good-sized plug of tobacco and began to chew. As to Van Helsing, he was employed in a definite way. First he took from his bag a mass of what looked like thin, wafer-like biscuit, which was carefully rolled up in a white napkin; next he took out a double-handful of some whitish stuff, like dough or putty. He crumbled the wafer up fine and worked it into the mass between his hands. This he then took, and rolling it into thin strips, began to lay them into the crevices between the door and its setting in the tomb. I was somewhat puzzled at this, and being close, asked him what it was that he was doing. Arthur and Quincey drew near also, as they too were curious. He answered: —

"I am closing the tomb, so that the Un-Dead may not enter."

"And is that stuff you have put there going to do it?" asked Quincey. "Great Scott! Is this a game?"

"It is."

"What is that which you are using?" This time the question was by Arthur. Van Helsing reverently lifted his hat as he answered: —

"The Host.° I brought it from Amsterdam. I have an Indulgence."° It was an answer that appalled the most sceptical of us, and we

---

The Host: A wafer of bread used in celebrating mass, considered to be part of the body of Christ.   **Indulgence:** A remission given by the Roman Catholic Church of the punishment for sin. Although Van Helsing may give the impression to his non-Catholic audience that he has license to use the Host in the way he plans, it is inconceivable that an indulgence would sanction the sacrilegious steps that he takes.

felt individually that in the presence of such earnest purpose as the Professor's, a purpose which could thus use the to him most sacred of things, it was impossible to distrust. In respectful silence we took the places assigned to us close round the tomb, but hidden from the sight of any one approaching. I pitied the others, especially Arthur. I had myself been apprenticed by my former visits to this watching horror; and yet I, who had up to an hour ago repudiated the proofs, felt my heart sink within me. Never did tombs look so ghastly white; never did cypress, or yew, or juniper so seem the embodiment of funereal gloom; never did tree or grass wave or rustle so ominously; never did bough creak so mysteriously; and never did the far-away howling of dogs send such a woeful presage through the night.

There was a long spell of silence, a big, aching void, and then from the Professor a keen "S-s-s-s!" He pointed; and far down the avenue of yews we saw a white figure advance — a dim white figure, which held something dark at its breast. The figure stopped, and at the moment a ray of moonlight fell between the masses of driving clouds and showed in startling prominence a dark-haired woman, dressed in the cerements of the grave. We could not see the face, for it was bent down over what we saw to be a fair-haired child. There was a pause and a sharp little cry, such as a child gives in sleep, or a dog as it lies before the fire and dreams. We were starting forward, but the Professor's warning hand, seen by us as he stood behind a yew-tree, kept us back; and then as we looked the white figure moved forwards again. It was now near enough for us to see clearly, and the moonlight still held. My own heart grew cold as ice, and I could hear the gasp of Arthur, as we recognised the features of Lucy Westenra. Lucy Westenra, but yet how changed. The sweetness was turned to adamantine, heartless cruelty, and the purity to voluptuous wantonness. Van Helsing stepped out, and, obedient to his gesture, we all advanced too; the four of us ranged in a line before the door of the tomb. Van Helsing raised his lantern and drew the slide; by the concentrated light that fell on Lucy's face we could see that the lips were crimson with fresh blood, and that the stream had trickled over her chin and stained the purity of her lawn death-robe.

We shuddered with horror. I could see by the tremulous light that even Van Helsing's iron nerve had failed. Arthur was next to me, and if I had not seized his arm and held him up, he would have fallen.

When Lucy — I call the thing that was before us Lucy because it bore her shape — saw us she drew back with an angry snarl, such as a cat gives when taken unawares; then her eyes ranged over us. Lucy's eyes in form and colour; but Lucy's eyes unclean and full of hell-fire,

instead of the pure, gentle orbs we knew. At th
of my love passed into hate and loathing; had
could have done it with savage delight. As sh
with unholy light, and the face became wre
smile. Oh, God, how it made me shudder
motion, she flung to the ground, callous as a
now she had clutched strenuously to her breast, grow...
dog growls over a bone. The child gave a sharp cry, and lay there moaning. There was a cold-bloodedness in the act which wrung a groan from Arthur; when she advanced to him with outstretched arms and a wanton smile, he fell back and hid his face in his hands.

She still advanced, however, and with a languorous, voluptuous grace, said: —

"Come to me, Arthur. Leave these others and come to me. My arms are hungry for you. Come, and we can rest together. Come, my husband, come!"

There was something diabolically sweet in her tones — something of the tingling of glass when struck — which rang through the brains even of us who heard the words addressed to another. As for Arthur, he seemed under a spell; moving his hands from his face, he opened wide his arms. She was leaping for them, when Van Helsing sprang forward and held between them his little golden crucifix. She recoiled from it, and, with a suddenly distorted face, full of rage, dashed past him as if to enter the tomb.

When within a foot or two of the door, however, she stopped as if arrested by some irresistible force. Then she turned, and her face was shown in the clear burst of moonlight and by the lamp, which had now no quiver from Van Helsing's iron nerves. Never did I see such baffled malice on a face; and never, I trust, shall such ever be seen again by mortal eyes. The beautiful colour became livid, the eyes seemed to throw out sparks of hell-fire, the brows were wrinkled as though the folds of the flesh were the coils of Medusa's snakes,° and the lovely, blood-stained mouth grew to an open square, as in the passion masks of the Greeks and Japanese.° If ever a face meant death — if looks could kill — we saw it at that moment.

Medusa's snakes: In classical mythology, Medusa is the only mortal among the three monstrous Gorgons, whose hair is a mass of snakes. The sight of Medusa turned people to stone. Anthropologists of Stoker's time speculated "that Medusa, whose virtue is really in her head, is derived from the ritual mask common to primitive cults" (*Enc. Brit.* 11th 12: 257). *masks of the Greeks and Japanese:* Our word *mask* comes from Latin *mascus,* meaning specter. Greek and Japanese dramatic traditions both employed masks for the faces of the actors (*Enc. Brit.* 11th 8: 493, 15: 176).

...o for full half a minute, which seemed an eternity, she re-
...between the lifted crucifix and the sacred closing of her means
...try. Van Helsing broke the silence by asking Arthur: —

"Answer me, oh my friend! Am I to proceed in my work?"

Arthur threw himself on his knees, and hid his face in his hands, as
he answered: —

"Do as you will, friend; do as you will. There can be no horror like
this ever any more!" and he groaned in spirit. Quincey and I simultaneously moved towards him, and took his arms. We could hear the click of
the closing lantern as Van Helsing held it down; coming close to the
tomb, he began to remove from the chinks some of the sacred emblem
which he had placed there. We all looked on in horrified amazement as
we saw, when he stood back, the woman, with a corporeal body as real
at the moment as our own, pass in through the interstice where scarce a
knife-blade could have gone. We all felt a glad sense of relief when we
saw the Professor calmly restoring the strings of putty to the edges of
the door.

When this was done, he lifted the child and said: —

"Come now, my friends; we can do no more till to-morrow. There
is a funeral at noon, so here we shall all come before long after that. The
friends of the dead will all be gone by two, and when the sexton lock
the gate we shall remain. Then there is more to do; but not like this of
to-night. As for this little one, he is not much harm, and by to-morrow
night he shall be well. We shall leave him where the police will find him
as on the other night; and then to home." Coming close to Arthur, he
said: —

"My friend Arthur, you have had sore trial; but after, when you will
look back, you will see how it was necessary. You are now in the bitter
waters, my child. By this time to-morrow you will, please God, have
passed them, and have drunk of the sweet waters; so do not mourn
overmuch. Till then I shall not ask you to forgive me."

Arthur and Quincey came home with me, and we tried to cheer
each other on the way. We had left the child in safety, and were tired; so
we all slept with more or less reality of sleep.

29 *September, night.* — A little before twelve o'clock we three —
Arthur, Quincey Morris, and myself — called for the Professor. It was
odd to notice that by common consent we had all put on black clothes.
Of course, Arthur wore black, for he was in deep mourning, but the
rest of us wore it by instinct. We got to the churchyard by half-past one,
and strolled about, keeping out of official observation, so that when the
gravediggers had completed their task and the sexton, under the belief

that every one had gone, had locked the gate, we had the place all to ourselves. Van Helsing, instead of his little black bag, had with him a long leather one, something like a cricketing bag; it was manifestly of fair weight.

When we were alone and had heard the last of the footsteps die out up the road, we silently, and as if by ordered intention, followed the Professor to the tomb. He unlocked the door, and we entered, closing it behind us. Then he took from his bag the lantern, which he lit, and also two wax candles, which, when lighted, he stuck, by melting their own ends, on other coffins, so that they might give light sufficient to work by. When he again lifted the lid off Lucy's coffin we all looked — Arthur trembling like an aspen — and saw that the body lay there in all its death-beauty. But there was no love in my own heart, nothing but loathing for the foul Thing which had taken Lucy's shape without her soul. I could see even Arthur's face grow hard as he looked. Presently he said to Van Helsing: —

"Is this really Lucy's body, or only a demon in her shape?"

"It is her body, and yet not it. But wait a while, and you shall see her as she was, and is."

She seemed like a nightmare of Lucy as she lay there; the pointed teeth, the bloodstained, voluptuous mouth — which it made one shudder to see — the whole carnal and unspiritual appearance, seeming like a devilish mockery of Lucy's sweet purity. Van Helsing, with his usual methodicalness, began taking the various contents from his bag and placing them ready for use. First he took out a soldering iron and some plumbing solder, and then a small oil-lamp, which gave out, when lit in a corner of the tomb, gas which burned at fierce heat with a blue flame; then his operating knives, which he placed to hand; and last a round wooden stake, some two and a half or three inches thick and about three feet long. One end of it was hardened by charring in the fire, and was sharpened to a fine point. With this stake came a heavy hammer, such as in households is used in the coal-cellar for breaking the lumps. To me, a doctor's preparations for work of any kind are stimulating and bracing, but the effect of these things on both Arthur and Quincey was to cause them a sort of consternation. They both, however, kept their courage, and remained silent and quiet.

When all was ready, Van Helsing said: —

"Before we do anything, let me tell you this; it is out of the lore and experience of the ancients and of all those who have studied the powers of the Un-Dead. When they become such, there comes with the change the curse of immortality; they cannot die, but must go on age after age adding new victims and multiplying the evils of the world; for all that die from the preying of the Un-Dead become themselves Un-Dead, and prey on their kind. And so the circle goes on ever widening, like as the ripples from a stone thrown in the water. Friend Arthur, if you had met that kiss which you know of before poor Lucy die; or again, last night when you open your arms to her, you would in time, when you had died, have become *nosferatu*,° as they call it in Eastern Europe, and would all time make more of those Un-Deads that so have fill us with horror. The career of this so unhappy dear lady is but just begun. Those children whose blood she suck are not as yet so much the worse; but if she live on, Un-Dead, more and more they lose their blood, and by her power over them they come to her; and so she draw their blood with that so wicked mouth. But if she die in truth, then all cease; the tiny wounds of the throats disappear, and they go back to their plays unknowing ever of what has been. But of the most blessed of all, when this now Un-Dead be made to rest as true dead, then the soul of the poor lady whom we love shall again be free. Instead of working wickedness by night and growing more debased in the assimilation of it by day, she shall take her place with the other Angels. So that, my friend, it will be a blessed hand for her that shall strike the blow that sets her free. To this I am willing; but is there none amongst us who has a better right? Will it be no joy to think of hereafter in the silence of the night when sleep is not: 'It was my hand that sent her to the stars; it was the hand of him that loved her best; the hand that of all she would herself have chosen, had it been to her to choose'? Tell me if there be such a one amongst us?"

We all looked at Arthur. He saw, too, what we all did, the infinite kindness which suggested that his should be the hand which would restore Lucy to us as a holy, and not an unholy, memory; he stepped forward and said bravely, though his hand trembled, and his face was as pale as snow: —

"My true friend, from the bottom of my broken heart I thank you. Tell me what I am to do, and I shall not falter!" Van Helsing laid a hand on his shoulder, and said: —

"Brave lad! A moment's courage, and it is done. This stake must be driven through her. It will be a fearful ordeal — be not deceived in that — but it will be only a short time, and you will then rejoice more than your pain was great; from this grim tomb you will emerge as though you tread on air. But you must not falter when once you have

---

nosferatu: Vampire (Romanian) (Gerard).

begun. Only think that we, your true friends, are round you, and that we pray for you all the time."

"Go on," said Arthur hoarsely. "Tell me what I am to do."

"Take this stake in your left hand, ready to place the point over the heart, and the hammer in your right. Then when we begin our prayer for the dead — I shall read him, I have here the book, and the others shall follow — strike in God's name, that so all may be well with the dead that we love, and that the Un-Dead pass away."

Arthur took the stake and the hammer, and when once his mind was set on action his hands never trembled nor even quivered. Van Helsing opened his missal and began to read, and Quincey and I followed as well as we could. Arthur placed the point over the heart, and as I looked I could see its dint in the white flesh. Then he struck with all his might.

The Thing in the coffin writhed; and a hideous, blood-curdling screech came from the opened red lips. The body shook and quivered and twisted in wild contortions; the sharp white teeth champed together till the lips were cut, and the mouth was smeared with a crimson foam. But Arthur never faltered. He looked like a figure of Thor° as his untrembling arm rose and fell, driving deeper and deeper the mercy-bearing stake, whilst the blood from the pierced heart welled and spurted up around it. His face was set, and high duty seemed to shine through it; the sight of it gave us courage, so that our voices seemed to ring through the little vault.

And then the writhing and quivering of the body became less, and the teeth ceased to champ, and the face to quiver. Finally it lay still. The terrible task was over.

The hammer fell from Arthur's hand. He reeled and would have fallen had we not caught him. The great drops of sweat sprang out on his forehead, and his breath came in broken gasps. It had indeed been an awful strain on him; and had he not been forced to his task by more than human considerations he could never have gone through with it. For a few minutes we were so taken up with him that we did not look towards the coffin. When we did, however, a murmur of startled surprise ran from one to the other of us. We gazed so eagerly that Arthur rose, for he had been seated on the ground, and came and looked too; and then a glad, strange light broke over his face and dispelled altogether the gloom of horror that lay upon it.

Thor: In Norse mythology, the principal weapon of Thor, god of thunder, is a hammer, which he used to battle the enemies of the gods.

There, in the coffin lay no longer the foul Thing that we had so dreaded and grown to hate that the work of her destruction was yielded as a privilege to the one best entitled to it, but Lucy as we had seen her in her life, with her face of unequalled sweetness and purity. True that there were there, as we had seen them in life, the traces of care and pain and waste; but these were all dear to us, for they marked her truth to what we knew. One and all we felt that the holy calm that lay like sunshine over the wasted face and form was only an earthly token and symbol of the calm that was to reign for ever.

Van Helsing came and laid his hand on Arthur's shoulder, and said to him: —

"And now, Arthur, my friend, dear lad, am I not forgiven?"

The reaction of the terrible strain came as he took the old man's hand in his, and raising it to his lips, pressed it, and said: —

"Forgiven! God bless you that you have given my dear one her soul again, and me peace." He put his hands on the Professor's shoulder, and laying his head on his breast, cried for a while silently, whilst we stood unmoving. When he raised his head Van Helsing said to him: —

"And now, my child, you may kiss her. Kiss her dead lips if you will, as she would have you to, if for her to choose. For she is not a grinning devil now — not any more a foul Thing for all eternity. No longer she is the devil's Un-Dead. She is God's true dead, whose soul is with Him!"

Arthur bent and kissed her, and then we sent him and Quincey out of the tomb; the Professor and I sawed the top off the stake, leaving the point of it in the body. Then we cut off the head and filled the mouth with garlic. We soldered up the leaden coffin, screwed on the coffin-lid, and gathering up our belongings, came away. When the Professor locked the door he gave the key to Arthur.

Outside the air was sweet, the sun shone, and the birds sang, and it seemed as if all nature were tuned to a different pitch. There was gladness and mirth and peace everywhere, for we were at rest ourselves on one account, and we were glad, though it was with a tempered joy.

Before we moved away Van Helsing said: —

"Now, my friends, one step of our work is done, one the most harrowing to ourselves. But there remains a greater task: to find out the author of all this our sorrow and to stamp him out. I have clues which we can follow; but it is a long task, and a difficult, and there is danger in it, and pain. Shall you not all help me? We have learned to believe, all of us — is it not so? And since so, do we not see our duty? Yes! And do we not promise to go on to the bitter end?"

Each in turn, we took his hand, and the promise was made. Then said the Professor as we moved off: —

"Two nights hence you shall meet with me and dine together at seven of the clock with friend John. I shall entreat two others, two that you know not as yet; and I shall be ready to all our work show and our plans unfold. Friend John, you come with me home, for I have much to consult about, and you can help me. To-night I leave for Amsterdam, but shall return to-morrow night. And then begins our great quest. But first I shall have much to say, so that you may know what is to do and to dread. Then our promise shall be made to each other anew; for there is a terrible task before us, and once our feet are on the ploughshare,° we must not draw back."

CHAPTER XVII. DR. SEWARD'S DIARY

(Continued)

WHEN we arrived at the Berkeley Hotel, Van Helsing found a telegram waiting for him: —

"Am coming up by train. Jonathan at Whitby. Important news. — MINA HARKER."

The Professor was delighted. "Ah, that wonderful Madam Mina," he said, "pearl among women! She arrive, but I cannot stay. She must go to your house, friend John. You must meet her at the station. Telegraph her *en route,* so that she may be prepared."

When the wire was despatched he had a cup of tea; over it he told me of a diary kept by Jonathan Harker when abroad, and gave me a typewritten copy of it, as also of Mrs. Harker's diary at Whitby. "Take these," he said, "and study them well. When I have returned you will be master of all the facts, and we can then better enter on our inquisition. Keep them safe, for there is in them much of treasure. You will need all your faith, even you who have had such an experience as that of to-day. What is here told," he laid his hand heavily and gravely on the packet of papers as he spoke, "may be the beginning of the end to you and me and many another; or it may sound the knell of the Un-Dead who walk the earth. Read all, I pray you, with the open mind; and if you can add

---

feet are on the ploughshare: Van Helsing transforms in an unintentionally comic way Luke 9.62, in which Jesus tells a follower, "No man, having put his hand to the plough, and looking back, is fit for the kingdom of God."

in any way to the story here told do so, for it is all-important. You have kept diary of all these so strange things; is it not so? Yes! Then we shall go through all these together when that we meet." He then made ready for his departure, and shortly after drove off to Liverpool Street.° I took my way to Paddington, where I arrived about fifteen minutes before the train came in.

The crowd melted away after the bustling fashion common to arrival platforms; and I was beginning to feel uneasy, lest I might miss my guest, when a sweet-faced, dainty-looking girl stepped up to me, and, after a quick glance, said: "Dr. Seward, is it not?"

"And you are Mrs. Harker!" I answered at once; whereupon she held out her hand.

"I knew you from the description of poor dear Lucy; but —" She stopped suddenly, and a quick blush overspread her face.

The blush that rose to my own cheeks somehow set us both at ease, for it was a tacit answer to her own. I got her luggage, which included a typewriter, and we took the Underground to Fenchurch Street,° after I had sent a wire to my housekeeper to have a sitting-room and bedroom prepared at once for Mrs. Harker.

In due time we arrived. She knew, of course, that the place was a lunatic asylum, but I could see that she was unable to repress a slight shudder when we entered.

She told me that, if she might, she would come presently to my study, as she had much to say. So here I am finishing my entry in my phonograph diary whilst I await her. As yet I have not had the chance of looking at the papers which Van Helsing left with me, though they lie open before me. I must get her interested in something, so that I may have an opportunity of reading them. She does not know how precious time is, or what a task we have in hand. I must be careful not to frighten her. Here she is!

Mina Harker's Journal

29 *September.* — After I had tidied myself, I went down to Dr. Seward's study. At the door I paused a moment, for I thought I heard him

---

Liverpool Street: The location of the Liverpool Street Station, the terminus for the Great Eastern Railway (*Baedeker* 1896).   *Underground to Fenchurch Street:* Fenchurch Street was the site of a station for the Blackwall Railway. The Underground, London's metropolitan rail system, provided rapid transportation between stations in the city and suburbs. (*Baedeker* 1896).

talking with some one. As, however, he had pressed me to be quick, I knocked at the door, and on his calling out, "Come in," I entered.

To my intense surprise, there was no one with him. He was quite alone, and on the table opposite him was what I knew at once from the description to be a phonograph. I had never seen one, and was much interested.

"I hope I did not keep you waiting," I said; "but I stayed at the door as I heard you talking, and thought there was some one with you."

"Oh," he replied, with a smile, "I was only entering my diary."

"Your diary?" I asked him in surprise.

"Yes," he answered. "I keep it in this." As he spoke he laid his hand on the phonograph. I felt quite excited over it, and blurted out: —

"Why, this beats even shorthand! May I hear it say something?"

"Certainly," he replied with alacrity, and stood up to put it in train for speaking. Then he paused, and a troubled look overspread his face.

"The fact is," he began awkwardly, "I only keep my diary in it; and as it is entirely — almost entirely — about my cases, it may be awkward — that is, I mean" —— He stopped, and I tried to help him out of his embarrassment: —

"You helped to attend dear Lucy at the end. Let me hear how she died; for all that I can know of her, I shall be very grateful. She was very, very dear to me."

To my surprise, he answered, with a horrorstruck look in his face: —

"Tell you of her death? Not for the wide world!"

"Why not?" I asked, for some grave, terrible feeling was coming over me. Again he paused, and I could see that he was trying to invent an excuse. At length he stammered out: —

"You see, I do not know how to pick out any particular part of the diary." Even while he was speaking an idea dawned upon him, and he said with unconscious simplicity, in a different voice, and with the naïveté of a child: "That's quite true, upon my honour. Honest Indian!" I could not but smile, at which he grimaced. "I gave myself away that time!" he said. "But do you know that, although I have kept the diary for months past, it never once struck me how I was going to find any particular part of it in case I wanted to look it up?" By this time my mind was made up that the diary of a doctor who attended Lucy might have something to add to the sum of our knowledge of that terrible Being, and I said boldly: —

"Then, Dr. Seward, you had better let me copy it out for you on my typewriter." He grew to a positively deathly pallor as he said: —

"No! no! no! For all the world, I wouldn't let you know that terrible story!"

Then it was terrible; my intuition was right! For a moment I thought, and as my eyes ranged the room, unconsciously looking for something or some opportunity to aid me, they lit on the great batch of typewriting on the table. His eyes caught the look in mine, and, without his thinking, followed their direction. As they saw the parcel he realised my meaning.

"You do not know me." I said. "When you have read those papers — my own diary and my husband's also, which I have typed — you will know me better. I have not faltered in giving every thought of my own heart in this cause; but, of course, you do not know me — yet; and I must not expect you to trust me so far."

He is certainly a man of noble nature; poor dear Lucy was right about him. He stood up and opened a large drawer, in which were arranged in order a number of hollow cylinders of metal covered with dark wax, and said: —

"You are quite right. I did not trust you because I did not know you. But I know you now; and let me say that I should have known you long ago. I know that Lucy told you of me; she told me of you too. May I make the only atonement in my power? Take the cylinders and hear them — the first half-dozen of them are personal to me, and they will not horrify you; then you will know me better. Dinner will by then be ready. In the meantime I shall read over some of these documents, and shall be better able to understand certain things." He carried the phonograph himself up to my sitting-room and adjusted it for me. Now I shall learn something pleasant, I am sure; for it will tell me the other side of a true love episode of which I know one side already. . . . .

Dr. Seward's Diary

29 *September.* — I was so absorbed in that wonderful diary of Jonathan Harker and that other of his wife that I let the time run on without thinking. Mrs. Harker was not down when the maid came to announce dinner, so I said: "She is possibly tired; let dinner wait an hour;" and I went on with my work. I had just finished Mrs. Harker's diary, when she came in. She looked sweetly pretty, but very sad, and her eyes were flushed with crying. This somehow moved me much. Of

late I have had cause for tears, God knows! but the relief of them was denied me; and now the sight of those sweet eyes, brightened with recent tears, went straight to my heart. So I said as gently as I could: —

"I greatly fear I have distressed you."

"Oh no, not distressed me," she replied, "but I have been more touched than I can say by your grief. That is a wonderful machine, but it is cruelly true. It told me, in its very tones, the anguish of your heart. It was like a soul crying out to almighty God. No one must hear them spoken ever again! See, I have tried to be useful. I have copied out the words on my typewriter, and none other need now hear your heart beat, as I did."

"No one need ever know, shall ever know," I said in a low voice. She laid her hand on mine and said very gravely: —

"Ah, but they must!"

"Must! But why?" I asked.

"Because it is a part of the terrible story, a part of poor dear Lucy's death and all that led to it; because in the struggle which we have before us to rid the earth of this terrible monster we must have all the knowledge and all the help which we can get. I think that the cylinders which you gave me contained more than you intended me to know; but I can see that there are in your record many lights to this dark mystery. You will let me help, will you not? I know all up to a certain point; and I see already, though your diary only took me to 7 September, how poor Lucy was beset, and how her terrible doom was being wrought out. Jonathan and I have been working day and night since Professor Van Helsing saw us. He is gone to Whitby to get more information, and he will be here to-morrow to help us. We need have no secrets amongst us; working together and with absolute trust, we can surely be stronger than if some of us were in the dark." She looked at me so appealingly, and at the same time manifested such courage and resolution in her bearing, that I gave in at once to her wishes. "You shall," I said, "do as you like in the matter. God forgive me if I do wrong! There are terrible things yet to learn of; but if you have so far travelled on the road to poor Lucy's death, you will not be content, I know, to remain in the dark. Nay, the end — the very end — may give you a gleam of peace. Come, there is dinner. We must keep one another strong for what is before us; we have a cruel and dreadful task. When you have eaten you shall learn the rest, and I shall answer any questions you ask — if there be anything which you do not understand, though it was apparent to us who were present."

Mina Harker's Journal

29 September. — After dinner I came with Dr. Seward to his study. He brought back the phonograph from my room, and I took my typewriter. He placed me in a comfortable chair, and arranged the phonograph so that I could touch it without getting up, and showed me how to stop it in case I should want to pause. Then he very thoughtfully took a chair, with his back to me, so that I might be as free as possible, and began to read. I put the forked metal to my ears and listened.

When the terrible story of Lucy's death, and — and all that followed, was done, I lay back in my chair powerless. Fortunately I am not of a fainting disposition. When Dr. Seward saw me he jumped up with a horrified exclamation, and hurriedly taking a case-bottle° from a cupboard, gave me some brandy, which in a few minutes somewhat restored me. My brain was all in a whirl, and only that there came through all the multitude of horrors, the holy ray of light that my dear, dear Lucy was at last at peace, I do not think I could have borne it without making a scene. It is all so wild, and mysterious, and strange that if I had not known Jonathan's experience in Transylvania I could not have believed. As it was, I didn't know what to believe, and so get out of my difficulty by attending to something else. I took the cover off my typewriter, and said to Dr. Seward: —

"Let me write this all out now. We must be ready for Dr. Van Helsing when he comes. I have sent a telegram to Jonathan to come on here when he arrives in London from Whitby. In this matter dates are everything, and I think that if we get all our material ready, and have every item put in chronological order, we shall have done much. You tell me that Lord Godalming and Mr. Morris are coming too. Let us be able to tell them when they come." He accordingly set the phonograph at a slow pace, and I began to typewrite from the beginning of the seventh cylinder. I used manifold,° and so took three copies of the diary, just as I had done with all the rest. It was late when I got through, but Dr. Seward went about his work of going his round of the patients; when he had finished he came back and sat near me, reading, so that I did not feel too lonely whilst I worked. How good and thoughtful he is; the world seems full of good men — even if there *are* monsters in it. Before I left him I remembered what Jonathan put in his diary of the Professor's perturbation at reading something in an evening paper at the station at Exeter; so, seeing that Dr. Seward keeps his newspapers, I

---

case-bottle: A bottle, usually square, made to fit into a case (*OED*).   *manifold:* "Carbonized paper used in making several copies of a writing at one time" (*OED*).

borrowed the files of "The Westminster Gazette" and "The Pall Mall Gazette," and took them to my room. I remember how much "The Dailygraph" and "The Whitby Gazette," of which I had made cuttings, helped us to understand the terrible events at Whitby when Count Dracula landed, so I shall look through the evening papers since then, and perhaps I shall get some new light. I am not sleepy, and the work will help to keep me quiet.

Dr. Seward's Diary

30 *September.* — Mr. Harker arrived at nine o'clock. He had got his wife's wire just before starting. He is uncommonly clever, if one can judge from his face, and full of energy. If his journal be true — and judging by one's own wonderful experiences, it must be — he is also a man of great nerve. That going down to the vault a second time was a remarkable piece of daring. After reading his account of it I was prepared to meet a good specimen of manhood, but hardly the quiet, business-like gentleman who came here to-day.

Later. — After lunch Harker and his wife went back to their own room, and as I passed a while ago I heard the click of the typewriter. They are hard at it. Mrs. Harker says that they are knitting together in chronological order every scrap of evidence they have. Harker has got the letters between the consignee of the boxes at Whitby and the carriers in London who took charge of them. He is now reading his wife's typescript of my diary. I wonder what they make out of it. Here he is. . . . .

Strange that it never struck me that the very next house might be the Count's hiding-place! Goodness knows that we had enough clues from the conduct of the patient Renfield! The bundle of letters relating to the purchase of the house were with the typescript. Oh, if we had only had them earlier we might have saved poor Lucy! Stop; that way madness lies! Harker has gone back, and is again collating his material. He says that by dinner-time they will be able to show a whole connected narrative. He thinks that in the meantime I should see Renfield, as hitherto he has been a sort of index to the coming and going of the Count. I hardly see this yet, but when I get at the dates I suppose I shall. What a good thing that Mrs. Harker put my cylinders into type! We never could have found the dates otherwise. . . . .

I found Renfield sitting placidly in his room with his hands folded, smiling benignly. At the moment he seemed as sane as any one I ever saw. I sat down and talked with him on a lot of subjects, all of which he treated naturally. He then, of his own accord, spoke of going home, a subject he has never mentioned to my knowledge during his sojourn here. In fact, he spoke quite confidently of getting his discharge at once. I believe that, had I not had the chat with Harker and read the letters and the dates of his outbursts, I should have been prepared to sign for him after a brief time of observation. As it is, I am darkly suspicious. All those outbreaks were in some way linked with the proximity of the Count. What then does this absolute content mean? Can it be that his instinct is satisfied as to the vampire's ultimate triumph? Stay; he is himself zoophagous, and in his wild ravings outside the chapel door of the deserted house he always spoke of "master." This all seems confirmation of our idea. However, after a while I came away; my friend is just a little too sane at present to make it safe to probe him too deep with questions. He might begin to think, and then —! So I came away. I mistrust these quiet moods of his; so I have given the attendant a hint to look closely after him, and to have a strait-waistcoat ready in case of need.

Jonathan Harker's Journal

29 September, in train to London. — When I received Mr. Billington's courteous message that he would give me any information in his power, I thought it best to go down to Whitby and make, on the spot, such inquiries as I wanted. It was now my object to trace that horrid cargo of the Count's to its place in London. Later, we may be able to deal with it. Billington junior, a nice lad, met me at the station, and brought me to his father's house, where they had decided that I must stay the night. They are hospitable, with true Yorkshire hospitality: give a guest everything, and leave him free to do as he likes. They all knew that I was busy, and that my stay was short, and Mr. Billington had ready in his office all the papers concerning the consignment of boxes. It gave me almost a turn to see again one of the letters which I had seen on the Count's table before I knew of his diabolical plans. Everything had been carefully thought out, and done systematically and with precision. He seemed to have been prepared for every obstacle which might be placed by accident in the way of his intentions being carried out. To use an Americanism, he had "taken no chances," and the absolute accuracy with which his instructions were fulfilled, was simply the logical result of his care. I saw the invoice, and took note of it: "Fifty cases of common earth, to be used for experimental purposes." Also the copy of letter to Carter Paterson, and their reply; of both of these I got copies. This was all the information Mr. Billington could give me, so I went down to the port and saw the coastguards, the Customs officers and the harbour-master. They had all something to say of the strange entry of the ship, which is already taking its place in local tradition; but no one could add to the simple description "Fifty cases of common earth." I then saw the station-master, who kindly put me in communication with the men who had actually received the boxes. Their tally was exact with the list, and they had nothing to add except that the boxes were "main and mortal heavy," and that shifting them was dry work. One of them added that it was hard lines that there wasn't any gentleman "such-like as yourself, squire," to show some sort of appreciation of their efforts in a liquid form; another put in a rider that the thirst then generated was such that even the time which had elapsed had not completely allayed it. Needless to add, I took care before leaving to lift, for ever and adequately, this source of reproach.

30 *September.* — The station-master was good enough to give me a line to his old companion the station-master at King's Cross, so that when I arrived there in the morning I was able to ask him about the arrival of the boxes. He, too, put me at once in communication with the proper officials, and I saw that their tally was correct with the original invoice. The opportunities of acquiring an abnormal thirst had been here limited; a noble use of them had, however, been made, and again I was compelled to deal with the result in an *ex post facto*° manner.

From thence I went on to Carter Paterson's central office, where I met with the utmost courtesy. They looked up the transaction in their day-book and letter-book, and at once telephoned to their King's Cross office for more details. By good fortune, the men who did the teaming were waiting for work, and the official at once sent them over, sending also by one of them the way-bill and all the papers connected with the delivery of the boxes at Carfax. Here again I found the tally agreeing exactly; the carriers' men were able to supplement the paucity of the written words with a few details. These were, I shortly found, connected almost solely with the dusty nature of the job, and of the consequent thirst engendered in the operators. On my affording an opportunity, through the medium of the currency of the realm, of the allaying, at a later period, this beneficent evil, one of the men remarked: —

ex post facto: After the fact (Latin).

"That 'ere 'ouse, guv'nor, is the rummiest° I ever was in. Blyme!°
but it ain't been touched sence a hundred years. There was dust that
thick in the place that you might have slep' on it without 'urtin' of yer
bones; an' the place was that neglected that yer might 'ave smelled ole
Jerusalem in it. But the ole chapel — that took the cike, that did! Me
and my mate, we thort we wouldn't never git out quick enough. Lor', I
wouldn't take less nor a quid° a moment to stay there arter dark."

Having been in the house, I could well believe him; but if he knew
what I know, he would, I think, have raised his terms.

Of one thing I am now satisfied: that *all* the boxes which arrived at
Whitby from Varna in the *Demeter* were safely deposited in the old
chapel of Carfax. There should be fifty of them there, unless any have
since been removed — as from Dr. Seward's diary I fear.

I shall try to see the carter who took away the boxes from Carfax
when Renfield attacked them. By following up this clue we may learn a
good deal.

Later. — Mina and I have worked all day, and we have put all the
papers into order.

Mina Harker's Journal

30 *September.* — I am so glad that I hardly know how to contain
myself. It is, I suppose, the reaction from the haunting fear which I
have had: that this terrible affair and the reopening of his old wound
might act detrimentally on Jonathan. I saw him leave for Whitby with as
brave a face as I could, but I was sick with apprehension. The effort has,
however, done him good. He was never so resolute, never so strong,
never so full of volcanic energy, as at present. It is just as that dear, good
Professor Van Helsing said: he is true grit, and he improves under strain
that would kill a weaker nature. He came back full of life and hope and
determination; we have got everything in order for to-night. I feel
myself quite wild with excitement. I suppose one ought to pity any
thing so hunted as is the Count. That is just it: this Thing is not
human — not even beast. To read Dr. Seward's account of poor Lucy's
death, and what followed, is enough to dry up the springs of pity in
one's heart.

Later. — Lord Godalming and Mr. Morris arrived earlier than we
expected. Dr. Seward was out on business and had taken Jonathan with

---

rummiest: Oddest, strangest (colloquial).   **Blyme:** Blimey; vulgar expression of surprise or contempt, short for "God blind me!"   **less nor a quid:** Less than one pound
sterling.

him, so I had to see them. It was to me a painful meeting, for it brought back all poor dear Lucy's hopes of only a few months ago. Of course they had heard Lucy speak of me, and it seemed that Dr. Van Helsing, too, has been quite "blowing my trumpet," as Mr. Morris expressed it. Poor fellows, neither of them is aware that I know all about the proposals they made to Lucy. They did not quite know what to say or do, as they were ignorant of the amount of my knowledge; so they had to keep on neutral subjects. However, I thought the matter over and came to the conclusion that the best thing I could do would be to post them in affairs right up to date. I knew from Dr. Seward's diary that they had been at Lucy's death — her real death — and that I need not fear to betray any secret before the time. So I told them, as well as I could, that I had read all the papers and diaries, and that my husband and I, having typewritten them, had just finished putting them in order. I gave them each a copy to read in the library. When Lord Godalming got his and turned it over — it does make a pretty good pile — he said: —

"Did you write all this, Mrs. Harker?"

I nodded, and he went on: —

"I don't quite see the drift of it; but you people are all so good and kind, and have been working so earnestly and so energetically, that all I can do is to accept your ideas blindfold and try to help you. I have had one lesson already in accepting facts that should make a man humble to the last hour of his life. Besides, I know you loved my poor Lucy —" Here he turned away and covered his face with his hands. I could hear the tears in his voice. Mr. Morris, with instinctive delicacy, just laid a hand for a moment on his shoulder, and then walked quietly out of the room. I suppose there is something in woman's nature that makes a man free to break down before her and express his feelings on the tender or emotional side without feeling it derogatory to his manhood; for when Lord Godalming found himself alone with me he sat down on the sofa and gave way utterly and openly. I sat down beside him and took his hand. I hope he didn't think it forward of me, and that if he ever thinks of it afterwards he never will have such a thought. There I wrong him; I *know* he never will — he is too true a gentleman. I said to him, for I could see that his heart was breaking: —

"I loved dear Lucy, and I know what she was to you, and what you were to her. She and I were like sisters; and now she is gone, will you not let me be like a sister to you in your trouble? I know what sorrows you have had, though I cannot measure the depth of them. If sympathy and pity can help in your affliction, won't you let me be of some little service — for Lucy's sake?"

In an instant the poor dear fellow was overwhelmed with grief. It seemed to me that all that he had of late been suffering in silence found a vent at once. He grew quite hysterical, and raising his open hands, beat his palms together in a perfect agony of grief. He stood up and then sat down again, and the tears rained down his cheeks. I felt an infinite pity for him, and opened my arms unthinkingly. With a sob he laid his head on my shoulder, and cried like a wearied child, whilst he shook with emotion.

We women have something of the mother in us that makes us rise above smaller matters when the mother-spirit is invoked; I felt this big, sorrowing man's head resting on me, as though it were that of the baby that some day may lie on my bosom, and I stroked his hair as though he were my own child. I never thought at the time how strange it all was.

After a little bit his sobs ceased, and he raised himself with an apology, though he made no disguise of his emotion. He told me that for days and nights past — weary days and sleepless night — he had been unable to speak with any one, as a man must speak in his time of sorrow. There was no woman whose sympathy could be given to him, or with whom, owing to the terrible circumstance with which his sorrow was surrounded, he could speak freely. "I know now how I suffered," he said, as he dried his eyes, "but I do not know even yet — and none other can ever know — how much your sweet sympathy has been to me to-day. I shall know better in time; and believe me that, though I am not ungrateful now, my gratitude will grow with my understanding. You will let me be like a brother, will you not, for all our lives — for dear Lucy's sake?"

"For dear Lucy's sake," I said as we clasped hands. "Ay, and for your own sake," he added, "for if a man's esteem and gratitude are ever worth the winning, you have won mine to-day. If ever the future should bring to you a time when you need a man's help, believe me, you will not call in vain. God grant that no such time may ever come to you to break the sunshine of your life; but if it should ever come, promise me that you will let me know." He was so earnest, and his sorrow was so fresh, that I felt it would comfort him, so I said: —

"I promise."

As I came along the corridor I saw Mr. Morris looking out of a window. He turned as he heard my footsteps. "How is Art?" he said. Then noticing my red eyes, he went on: "Ah, I see you have been comforting him. Poor old fellow! he needs it. No one but a woman can help a man when he is in trouble of the heart; and he had no one to comfort him."

He bore his own trouble so bravely that my heart bled for him. I saw the manuscript in his hand, and I knew that when he read it he would realise how much I knew; so I said to him: —

"I wish I could comfort all who suffer from the heart. Will you let me be your friend, and will you come to me for comfort if you need it? You will know, later on, why I speak." He saw that I was in earnest, and stooping, took my hand, and raising it to his lips, kissed it. It seemed but poor comfort to so brave and unselfish a soul, and impulsively I bent over and kissed him. The tears rose in his eyes, and there was a momentary choking in his throat; he said quite calmly: —

"Little girl, you will never regret that true-hearted kindness, so long as ever you live!" Then he went into the study to his friend.

"Little girl!" — the very words he had used to Lucy, and oh, but he proved himself a friend!

CHAPTER XVIII. DR. SEWARD'S DIARY

30 *September.* — I got home at five o'clock, and found that Godalming and Morris had not only arrived, but had already studied the transcript of the various diaries and letters which Harker and his wonderful wife had made and arranged. Harker had not yet returned from his visit to the carriers' men, of whom Dr. Hennessey had written to me. Mrs. Harker gave us a cup of tea, and I can honestly say that, for the first time since I had lived in it, this old house seemed like *home*. When we had finished, Mrs. Harker said: —

"Dr. Seward may I ask a favour? I want to see your patient, Mr. Renfield. Do let me see him. What you have said of him in your diary interests me so much!" She looked so appealing and so pretty that I could not refuse her, and there was no possible reason why I should; so I took her with me. When I went into the room, I told the man that a lady would like to see him; to which he simply answered: "Why?"

"She is going through the house, and wants to see every one in it," I answered. "Oh, very well," he said; "let her come in, by all means; but just wait a minute till I tidy up the place." His method of tidying was peculiar: he simply swallowed all the flies and spiders in the boxes before I could stop him. It was quite evident that he feared, or was jealous of, some interference. When he had got through his disgusting task, he said cheerfully: "Let the lady come in," and sat down on the edge of his bed with his head down, but with his eyelids raised so that he could see her as she entered. For a moment I thought that he might have some homicidal intent; I remembered how quiet he had been just before he attacked me in my own study, and I took care to stand where I should seize him at once if he attempted to make a spring at her. She came into the room with an easy gracefulness which would at once command the respect of any lunatic — for easiness is one of the qualities mad people most respect. She walked over to him, smiling pleasantly, and held out her hand.

"Good-evening, Mr. Renfield," said she. "You see, I know you, for Dr. Seward has told me of you." He made no immediate reply, but eyed her all over intently with a set frown on his face. This look gave way to one of wonder, which merged in doubt; then, to my intense astonishment, he said: —

"You're not the girl the doctor wanted to marry, are you? You can't be, you know, for she's dead." Mrs. Harker smiled sweetly as she replied: —

"Oh no! I have a husband of my own, to whom I was married before I ever saw Dr. Seward, or he me. I am Mrs. Harker."

"Then what are you doing here?"

"My husband and I are staying on a visit with Dr. Seward."

"Then don't stay."

"But why not?" I thought that this style of conversation might not be pleasant to Mrs. Harker, any more than it was to me, so I joined in: —

"How did you know I wanted to marry any one?" His reply was simply contemptuous, given in a pause in which he turned his eyes from Mrs. Harker to me, instantly turning them back again: —

"What an asinine question!"

"I don't see that at all, Mr. Renfield," said Mrs. Harker, at once championing me. He replied to her with as much courtesy and respect as he had shown contempt to me: —

"You will, of course, understand, Mrs. Harker, that when a man is so loved and honoured as our host is, everything regarding him is of interest in our little community. Dr. Seward is loved not only by his household and his friends, but even by his patients, who, being some of them hardly in mental equilibrium, are apt to distort causes and effects. Since I myself have been an inmate of a lunatic asylum, I cannot but notice that the sophistic tendencies of some of its inmates lean towards the errors of *non causæ* and *ignoratio elenchi*."° I positively opened my eyes at this new development. Here was my own pet lunatic — the

---

non causæ . . . ignoratio elenchi: Two legal terms in Latin. *Non causæ* means "no reason," while *ignoratio elenchi* refers to the logical fallacy of overlooking the adversary's counterposition in an argument (Black's Law).

most pronounced of his type that I had ever met with — talking ele-mental philosophy, and with the manner of a polished gentleman. I wonder if it was Mrs. Harker's presence which had touched some chord in his memory. If this new phase was spontaneous, or in any way due to her unconscious influence, she must have some rare gift or power.

We continued to talk for some time; and, seeing that he was seem-ingly quite reasonable, she ventured, looking at me questioningly as she began, to lead him to his favourite topic. I was again astonished, for he addressed himself to the question with the impartiality of the com-pletest sanity; he even took himself as an example when he mentioned certain things.

"Why, I myself am an instance of a man who had a strange belief. Indeed, it was no wonder that my friends were alarmed, and insisted on my being put under control. I used to fancy that life was a positive and perpetual entity, and that by consuming a multitude of live things, no matter how low in the scale of creation, one might indefinitely prolong life. At times I held the belief so strongly that I actually tried to take human life. The doctor here will bear me out that on one occasion I tried to kill him for the purpose of strengthening my vital powers by the assimilation with my own body of his life through the medium of his blood — relying, of course, upon the Scriptural phrase, 'For the blood is the life.' Though, indeed, the vendor of a certain nostrum has vulgarised the truism to the very point of contempt.° Isn't that true, doctor?" I nodded assent, for I was so amazed that I hardly knew what to either think or say; it was hard to imagine that I had seen him eat up his spiders and flies not five minutes before. Looking at my watch, I saw that I should go to the station to meet Van Helsing, so I told Mrs. Harker that it was time to leave. She came at once, after saying pleasantly to Mr. Ren-field: "Good-bye, and I hope I may see you often, under auspices pleas-anter to yourself," to which, to my astonishment, he replied: —

"Good-bye, my dear. I pray God I may never see your sweet face again. May He bless and keep you!"

When I went to the station to meet Van Helsing I left the boys behind me. Poor Art seemed more cheerful than he has been since Lucy first took ill, and Quincey is more like his own bright self than he has been for many a long day.

Van Helsing stepped from the carriage with the eager nimbleness of a boy. He saw me at once, and rushed up to me, saying: —

---

nostrum . . . contempt: Some version of the biblical phrasing had been used in advertising patent medicines, such as "Hughes's Blood Pills" (Wolf, 284n5).

"Ah, friend John, how goes all? Well? So! I have been busy, for I come here to stay if need be. All affairs are settled with me, and I have much to tell. Madam Mina is with you? Yes. And her so fine husband? And Arthur and my friend Quincey, they are with you, too? Good!"

As I drove to the house I told him of what had passed, and of how my own diary had come to be of some use through Mrs. Harker's suggestion; at which the Professor interrupted me: —

"Ah, that wonderful Madam Mina! She has man's brain — a brain that a man should have were he much gifted — and woman's heart. The good God fashioned her for a purpose, believe me, when He made that so good combination. Friend John, up to now fortune has made that woman of help to us; after to-night she must not have to do with this so terrible affair. It is not good that she run a risk so great. We men are determined — nay, are we not pledged? — to destroy this monster; but it is no part for a woman. Even if she be not harmed, her heart may fail her in so much and so many horrors; and hereafter she may suffer — both in waking, from her nerves, and in sleep, from her dreams. And, besides, she is young woman and not so long married; there may be other things to think of some time, if not now. You tell me she has wrote all, then she must consult with us; but to-morrow she say good-bye to this work, and we go alone." I agreed heartily with him, and then I told him what we had found in his absence: that the house which Dracula had bought was the very next one to my own. He was amazed, and a great concern seemed to come on him. "Oh that we had known it before!" he said, "for then we might have reached him in time to save poor Lucy. However, 'the milk that is spilt cries not out afterwards,' as you say. We shall not think of that, but go on our way to the end." Then he fell into a silence that lasted till we entered my own gateway. Before we went to prepare for dinner he said to Mrs. Harker: —

"I am told, Madam Mina, by my friend John that you and your husband have put up in exact order all things that have been, up to this moment."

"Not up to this moment, Professor," she said impulsively, "but up to this morning."

"But why not up to now? We have seen hitherto how good light all the little things have made. We have told our secrets, and yet no one who has told is the worse for it."

Mrs. Harker began to blush, and taking a paper from her pocket, she said: —

"Dr. Van Helsing, will you read this, and tell me if it must go in. It is my record of to-day. I too have seen the need of putting down at present everything, however trivial; but there is little in this except what is personal. Must it go in?" The Professor read it over gravely, and handed it back, saying: —

"It need not go in if you do not wish it; but I pray that it may. It can but make your husband love you the more, and all us, your friends, more honour you — as well as more esteem and love." She took it back with another blush and a bright smile.

And so now, up to this very hour, all the records we have are complete and in order. The Professor took away one copy to study after dinner, and before our meeting, which is fixed for nine o'clock. The rest of us have already read everything; so when we meet in the study we shall all be informed as to facts, and can arrange our plan of battle with this terrible and mysterious enemy.

Mina Harker's Journal

30 *September.* — When we met in Dr. Seward's study two hours after dinner, which had been at six o'clock, we unconsciously formed a sort of board or committee. Professor Van Helsing took the head of the table, to which Dr. Seward motioned him as he came into the room. He made me sit next to him on his right, and asked me to act as secretary; Jonathan sat next to me. Opposite us were Lord Godalming, Dr. Seward, and Mr. Morris — Lord Godalming being next the Professor, and Dr. Seward in the centre. The Professor said: —

"I may, I suppose, take it that we are all acquainted with the facts that are in these papers." We all expressed assent, and he went on: —

"Then it were, I think good that I tell you something of the kind of enemy with which we have to deal. I shall then make known to you something of the history of this man, which has been ascertained for me. So we then can discuss how we shall act, and can take our measure according.

"There are such beings as vampires; some of us have evidence that they exist. Even had we not the proof of our own unhappy experience, the teachings and the records of the past give proof enough for sane peoples. I admit that at the first I was sceptic. Were it not that through long years I have train myself to keep an open mind, I could not have believe until such time as that fact thunder on my ear. 'See! see! I prove; I prove.' Alas! Had I known at the first what now I know — nay, had I even guess at him — one so precious life had been spared to many of us who did love her. But that is gone; and we must so work, that other poor souls perish not, whilst we can save. The *nosferatu* do not die like the bee when he sting once. He is only stronger; and being stronger, have yet more power to work evil. This vampire which is amongst us is of himself so strong in person as twenty men; he is of cunning more than mortal, for his cunning be the growth of ages; he have still the aids of necromancy, which is, as his etymology imply, the divination by the dead, and all the dead that he can come nigh to are for him at command; he is brute, and more than brute: he is devil in callous, and the heart of him is not; he can, within limitations, appear at will when, and where, and in any of the forms that are to him; he can, within his range, direct the elements: the storm, the fog, the thunder; he can command all the meaner things: the rat, and the owl, and the bat — the moth, and the fox, and the wolf; he can grow and become small; and he can at times vanish and come unknown. How then are we to begin our strife to destroy him? How shall we find his where; and having found it, how can we destroy? My friends, this is much; it is a terrible task that we undertake, and there may be consequence to make the brave shudder. For if we fail in this our fight he must surely win: and then where end we? Life is nothings; I heed him not. But to fail here, is not mere life or death. It is that we become as him; that we henceforward become foul things of the night like him — without heart or conscience, preying on the bodies and the souls of those we love best. To us for ever are the gates of heaven shut; for who shall open them to us again? We go on for all time abhorred by all; a blot on the face of God's sunshine; an arrow in the side of Him who died for man. But we are face to face with duty; and in such case must we shrink? For me, I say, no; but then I am old, and life, with his sunshine, his fair places, his song of birds, his music, and his love, lie far behind. You others are young. Some have seen sorrow; but there are fair days yet in store. What say you?"

Whilst he was speaking Jonathan had taken my hand. I feared, oh so much, that the appalling nature of our danger was overcoming him when I saw his hand stretch out; but it was life to me to feel its touch — so strong, so self-reliant, so resolute. A brave man's hand can speak for itself; it does not even need a woman's love to hear its music.

When the Professor had done speaking my husband looked in my eyes, and I in his; there was no need for speaking between us.

"I answer for Mina and myself," he said.

"Count me in, Professor," said Mr. Quincey Morris, laconically as usual.

"I am with you," said Lord Godalming, "for Lucy's sake, if for no other reason."

Dr. Seward simply nodded. The Professor stood up and, after laying his golden crucifix on the table, held out his hand on either side. I took his right hand, and Lord Godalming his left; Jonathan held my right with his left and stretched across to Mr. Morris. So as we all took hands our solemn compact was made. I felt my heart icy cold, but it did not even occur to me to draw back. We resumed our places, and Dr. Van Helsing went on with a sort of cheerfulness which showed that the serious work had begun. It was to be taken as gravely, and in as businesslike a way, as any other transaction of life: —

"Well, you know what we have to contend against; but we, too, are not without strength. We have on our side power of combination — a power denied to the vampire kind; we have resources of science; we are free to act and think; and the hours of the day and the night are ours equally. In fact, so far as our powers extend, they are unfettered, and we are free to use them. We have self-devotion in a cause, and an end to achieve which is not a selfish one. These things are much.

"Now let us see how far the general powers arrayed against us are restrict, and how the individual cannot. In fine, let us consider the limitations of the vampire in general, and of this one in particular.

"All we have to go upon are traditions and superstitions. These do not at the first appear much, when the matter is one of life and death — nay of more than either life or death. Yet must we be satisfied; in the first place because we have to be — no other means is at our control — and secondly, because, after all, these things — tradition and superstition — are everything. Does not the belief in vampires rest for others — though not, alas! for us — on them? A year ago which of us would have received such a possibility, in the midst of our scientific, sceptical, matter-of-fact nineteenth century? We even scouted a belief that we saw justified under our very eyes. Take it, then, that the vampire, and the belief in his limitations and his cure, rest for the moment on the same base. For, let me tell you, he is known everywhere that men have been. In old Greece, in old Rome; he flourish in Germany all over, in France, in India, even in the Chersonese°; and in China, so far from us in all ways, there even is he, and the peoples fear him at this day. He have follow the wake of the berserker Icelander, the devil-begotten Hun, the Slav, the Saxon, the Magyar. So far, then, we have all we may

Chersonese: Peninsula (Greek). Several areas were known by this name, all of them far from England: the Chersonesus Thracica (Gallipoli peninsula) of the Dardanelles, the Chersonesus Taurica or Scythica of the Crimea, the Chersonesus Cimbrica of Jutland, and the Golden Chersonesus of Malacca (*Enc. Brit.* 11th).

act upon; and let me tell you that very much of the beliefs are justified by what we have seen in our own so unhappy experience. The vampire live on, and cannot die by mere passing of the time; he can flourish when that he can fatten on the blood of the living. Even more, we have seen amongst us that he can even grow younger; that his vital faculties grow strenuous, and seem as though they refresh themselves when his special pabulum is plenty. But he cannot flourish without this diet; he eat not as others. Even friend Jonathan, who lived with him for weeks, did never see him to eat, never! He throws no shadow; he make in the mirror no reflect, as again Jonathan observe. He has the strength of many in his hand — witness again Jonathan when he shut the door against the wolfs, and when he help him from the diligence too. He can transform himself to wolf, as we gather from the ship arrival in Whitby, when he tear open the dog; he can be as bat, as Madam Mina saw him on the window at Whitby, and as friend John saw him fly from this so near house, and as my friend Quincey saw him at the window of Miss Lucy. He can come in mist which he create — that noble ship's captain proved him of this; but, from what we know, the distance he can make this mist is limited, and it can only be round himself. He come on moonlight rays as elemental dust — as again Jonathan saw those sisters in the castle of Dracula. He become so small — we ourselves saw Miss Lucy, ere she was at peace, slip through a hairbreadth space at the tomb door. He can, when once he find his way, come out from anything or into anything, no matter how close it be bound or even fused up with fire — solder you call it. He can see in the dark — no small power this, in a world which is one half shut from the light. Ah, but hear me through. He can do all these things, yet he is not free. Nay; he is even more prisoner than the slave of the galley, than the madman in his cell. He cannot go where he lists; he who is not of nature has yet to obey some of nature's laws — why we know not. He may not enter anywhere at the first, unless there be some one of the household who bid him to come; though afterwards he can come as he please. His power ceases, as does that of all evil things, at the coming of the day. Only at certain times can he have limited freedom. If he be not at the place whither he is bound, he can only change himself at noon or at exact sunrise or sunset. These things are we told, and in this record of ours we have proof by inference. Thus, whereas he can do as he will within his limit, when he have his earth-home, his coffin-home, his hell-home, the place unhallowed, as we saw when he went to the grave of the suicide at Whitby; still at other time he can only change when the time come. It is said, too, that he can only pass running water at the slack or the flood of the tide. Then there are things which so afflict him that he has no power, as the garlic that we know of, and as for things sacred, as the symbol, my crucifix, that was amongst us even now when we resolve, to them he is nothing, but in their presence he take his place far off and silent with respect. There are others, too, which I shall tell you of, lest in our seeking we may need them. The branch of wild rose on his coffin keep him that he move not from it; a sacred bullet fired into the coffin kill him so that he be true dead; and as for the stake through him, we know already of its peace; or the cut-off head that giveth rest. We have seen it with our eyes.

"Thus when we find the habitation of this man-that-was, we can confine him to his coffin and destroy him, if we obey what we know. But he is clever. I have asked my friend Arminius, of Buda-Pesth University,° to make his record; and, from all the means that are, he tell me of what he has been. He must, indeed, have been that Voivode Dracula who won his name against the Turk, over the great river on the very frontier of Turkey-land. If it be so, then was he no common man; for in that time, and for centuries after, he was spoken of as the cleverest and the most cunning, as well as the bravest of the sons of the 'land beyond the forest.'° That mighty brain and that iron resolution went with him to his grave, and are even now arrayed against us. The Draculas were, says Arminius, a great and noble race, though now and again were scions who were held by their coevals to have had dealings with the Evil One. They learned his secrets in the Scholomance, amongst the mountains over Lake Hermanstadt, where the devil claims the tenth scholar as his due.° In the records are such words as 'stregoica' — witch, 'ordog,' and 'pokol' — Satan and hell; and in one manuscript this very Dracula is spoken of as 'wampyr,' which we all understand too well. There have been from the loins of this very one great men and good women, and their graves make sacred the earth where alone this foulness can dwell. For it is not the least of its terrors that this evil thing is rooted deep in all good; in soil barren of holy memories it cannot rest."

Arminius, of Buda-Pesth University: Van Helsing's friend is based on Ármin Vámbéry (1832–1913), whom Stoker met in London in 1890. A professor of Oriental Languages at the University of Budapest, Vámbéry was famous in England and Western Europe for his skills as a linguist, his travels through Asia, and the many books he wrote in various languages about those travels (*Enc. Brit.* 11th 27: 876 and 13th 31: 926).   *land beyond the forest:* Translation of "Transylvania."   *Scholomance ... as his due:* The mythical Scholomance was a school, supposedly in the mountains of Transylvania where the devil taught nature's secrets, animal languages, and magic spells. Only ten scholars were allowed to study at any one time, and the devil kept one of them in payment (Gerard 198).

Whilst they were talking Mr. Morris was looking steadily at the window, and he now got up quietly, and went out of the room. There was a little pause, and then the Professor went on: —

"And now we must settle what we do. We have here much data, and we must proceed to lay out our campaign. We know from the inquiry of Jonathan that from the castle to Whitby came fifty boxes of earth, all of which were delivered at Carfax; we also know that at least some of these boxes have been removed. It seems to me, that our first step should be to ascertain whether all the rest remain in the house beyond that wall where we look to-day; or whether any more have been removed. If the latter, we must trace —"

Here we were interrupted in a very startling way. Outside the house came the sound of a pistol-shot; the glass of the window was shattered with a bullet, which, ricochetting from the top of the embrasure, struck the far wall of the room. I am afraid I am at heart a coward, for I shrieked out. The men all jumped to their feet; Lord Godalming flew over to the window and threw up the sash. As he did so we heard Mr. Morris's voice without: —

"Sorry! I fear I have alarmed you. I shall come in and tell you about it." A minute later he came in and said: —

"It was an idiotic thing of me to do, and I ask your pardon, Mrs. Harker, most sincerely; I fear I must have frightened you terribly. But the fact is that whilst the Professor was talking there came a big bat and sat on the window-sill. I have got such a horror of the damned brutes from recent events that I cannot stand them, and I went out to have a shot, as I have been doing of late of evenings whenever I have seen one. You used to laugh at me for it then, Art."

"Did you hit it?" asked Dr. Van Helsing.

"I don't know; I fancy not, for it flew away into the wood." Without saying any more he took his seat, and the Professor began to resume his statement: —

"We must trace each of these boxes; and when we are ready, we must either capture or kill this monster in his lair; or we must, so to speak, sterilise the earth, so that no more he can seek safety in it. Thus in the end we may find him in his form of man between the hours of noon and sunset, and so engage with him when he is at his most weak.

"And now for you, Madam Mina, this night is the end until all be well. You are too precious to us to have such risk. When we part to-night, you no more must question. We shall tell you all in good time. We are men, and are able to bear; but you must be our star and our hope, and we shall act all the more free that you are not in the danger, such as we are."

All the men, even Jonathan, seemed relieved; but it did not seem to me good that they should brave danger and, perhaps, lessen their safety — strength being the best safety — through care of me; but their minds were made up, and, though it was a bitter pill for me to swallow, I could say nothing, save to accept their chivalrous care of me.

Mr. Morris resumed the discussion: —

"As there is no time to lose, I vote we have a look at his house right now. Time is everything with him; and swift action on our part may save another victim."

I own that my heart began to fail me when the time for action came so close, but I did not say anything, for I had a greater fear that if I appeared as a drag or a hindrance to their work, they might even leave me out of their counsels altogether. They have now gone off to Carfax, with means to get into the house.

Manlike, they have told me to go to bed and sleep; as if a woman can sleep when those she loves are in danger! I shall lie down and pretend to sleep, lest Jonathan have added anxiety about me when he returns.

Dr. Seward's Diary

1 *October,* 4 *a.m.* — Just as we were about to leave the house, an urgent message was brought to me from Renfield to know if I would see him at once, as he had something of the utmost importance to say to me. I told the messenger to say that I would attend to his wishes in the morning; I was busy just at the moment. The attendant added: —

"He seems very importuante, sir. I have never seen him so eager. I don't know but what, if you don't see him soon, he will have one of his violent fits." I knew the man would not have said this without some cause, so I said: "All right; I'll go now;" and I asked the others to wait a few minutes for me, as I had to go and see my "patient."

"Take me with you, friend John," said the Professor. "His case in your diary interested me much, and it had bearing, too, now and again on *our* case. I should much like to see him, and especial when his mind is disturbed."

"May I come also?" asked Lord Godalming.

"Me too?" said Quincey Morris. I nodded, and we all went down the passage together.

We found him in a state of considerable excitement, but far more rational in his speech and manner than I had ever seen him. There was an unusual understanding of himself, which was unlike anything I had ever met with in a lunatic; and he took it for granted that his reasons would prevail with others entirely sane. We all four went into the room, but none of the others at first said anything. His request was that I would at once release him from the asylum and send him home. This he backed up with arguments regarding his complete recovery, and adduced his own existing sanity. "I appeal to your friends," he said; "they will, perhaps, not mind sitting in judgment on my case. By the way, you have not introduced me." I was so much astonished, that the oddness of introducing a madman in an asylum did not strike me at the moment; and, besides, there was a certain dignity in the man's manner, so much of the habit of equality, that I at once made the introduction: "Lord Godalming; Professor Van Helsing; Mr. Quincey Morris, of Texas; Mr. Renfield." He shook hands with each of them, saying in turn: —

"Lord Godalming, I had the honour of seconding your father at the Windham°; I grieve to know, by your holding the title, that he is no more. He was a man loved and honoured by all who knew him; and in his youth was, I have heard, the inventor of a burnt rum punch, much patronised on Derby night.° Mr. Morris, you should be proud of your great state. Its reception into the Union° was a precedent which may have far-reaching effects hereafter, when the Pole and the Tropics may hold allegiance to the Stars and Stripes. The power of Treaty may yet prove a vast engine of enlargement, when the Monroe doctrine° takes its true place as a political fable. What shall any man say of his pleasure at meeting Van Helsing? Sir, I make no apology for dropping all forms of conventional prefix. When an individual has revolutionised therapeutics by his discovery of the continuous evolution of brain-matter, conventional forms are unfitting, since they would seem to limit him to one of a class. You, gentlemen, who by nationality, by heredity, or by the possession of natural gifts, are fitted to hold your respective places in

---

Windham: A club located in St. James' Square founded to bring together gentlemen interested in literature (*Baedeker* 1896). *Derby night:* The Derby is an annual English horse race. *reception into the Union:* Texas joined the Union of American states in 1845 as the twenty-eighth state. *Monroe doctrine:* A statement of United States foreign policy made by President James Monroe in 1823 that carved out a sphere of influence for the United States. It stated that the United States would not interfere in the internal affairs of European nations, but would prevent European nations from establishing any new colonies in the Western Hemisphere or interfering in the internal affairs of Western Hemisphere nations. (*Enc. Brit.* OL).

the moving world, I take to witness that I am as sane as at least the majority of men who are in full possession of their liberties. And I am sure that you, Dr. Seward, humanitarian and medico-jurist as well as scientist, will deem it a moral duty to deal with me as one to be considered as under exceptional circumstances." He made this last appeal with a courtly air of conviction which was not without its own charm.

I think we were all staggered. For my own part, I was under the conviction, despite my knowledge of the man's character and history, that his reason had been restored; and I felt under a strong impulse to tell him that I was satisfied as to his sanity, and would see about the necessary formalities for his release in the morning. I thought it better to wait, however, before making so grave a statement, for of old I knew the sudden changes to which this particular patient was liable. So I contented myself with making a general statement that he appeared to be improving very rapidly; that I would have a longer chat with him in the morning, and would then see what I could do in the direction of meeting his wishes. This did not at all satisfy him, for he said quickly: —

"But I fear, Dr. Seward, that you hardly apprehend my wish. I desire to go at once — here — now — this very hour — this very moment, if I may. Time presses, and in our implied agreement with the old scytheman° it is of the essence of the contract. I am sure it is only necessary to put before so admirable a practitioner as Dr. Seward so simple, yet so momentous a wish, to ensure its fulfilment." He looked at me keenly, and seeing the negative in my face, turned to the others, and scrutinised them closely. Not meeting any sufficient response, he went on: —

"Is it possible that I have erred in my supposition?"

"You have," I said frankly, but at the same time, as I felt, brutally. There was a considerable pause, and then he said slowly: —

"Then I suppose I must only shift my ground of request. Let me ask for this concession — boon, privilege, what you will. I am content to implore in such a case, not on personal grounds, but for the sake of others. I am not at liberty to give you the whole of my reasons; but you may, I assure you, take it from me that they are good ones, sound and unselfish, and springing from the highest sense of duty. Could you look, sir, into my heart, you would approve to the full the sentiments which animate me. Nay, more, you would count me amongst the best and truest of your friends." Again he looked at us all keenly. I had a growing conviction that this sudden change of his entire intellectual method was but yet another form or phase of his madness, and so determined to let

the old scytheman: Time, who is sometimes represented as an old man with a scythe.

him go on a little longer, knowing from experience that he would, like all lunatics, give himself away in the end. Van Helsing was gazing at him with a look of the utmost intensity, his bushy eyebrows almost meeting with the fixed concentration of his look. He said to Renfield in a tone which did not surprise me at the time, but only when I thought of it afterwards — for it was as of one addressing an equal: —

"Can you not tell frankly your real reason for wishing to be free to-night? I will undertake that if you will satisfy even me — a stranger, without prejudice, and with the habit of keeping an open mind — Dr. Seward will give you, at his own risk and on his own responsibility, the privilege you seek." He shook his head sadly, and with a look of poignant regret on his face. The Professor went on: —

"Come, sir, bethink yourself. You claim the privilege of reason in the highest degree, since you seek to impress us with your complete reasonableness. You do this, whose sanity we have reason to doubt, since you are not released from medical treatment for this very defect. If you will not help us in our effort to choose the wisest course, how can we perform the duty which you yourself put upon us? Be wise, and help us; and if we can we shall aid you to achieve your wish." He still shook his head as he said: —

"Dr. Van Helsing, I have nothing to say. Your argument is complete, and if I were free to speak I should not hesitate a moment; but I am not my own master in the matter. I can only ask you to trust me. If I am refused, the responsibility does not rest with me." I thought it was now time to end the scene, which was becoming too comically grave, so I went towards the door, simply saying: —

"Come, my friends, we have work to do. Good-night."

As, however, I got near the door, a new change came over the patient. He moved towards me so quickly that for the moment I feared that he was about to make another homicidal attack. My fears, however, were groundless, for he held up his two hands imploringly, and made his petition in a moving manner. As he saw that the very excess of his emotion was militating against him, by restoring us more to our old relations, he became still more demonstrative. I glanced at Van Helsing, and saw my conviction reflected in his eyes; so I became a little more fixed in my manner, if not more stern, and motioned to him that his efforts were unavailing. I had previously seen something of the same constantly growing excitement in him when he had to make some request of which at the time he had thought much, such, for instance, as when he wanted a cat; and I was prepared to see the collapse into the same sullen acquiescence on this occasion. My expectation was not realised, for, when he found that his appeal would not be successful, he got into quite a frantic condition. He threw himself on his knees, and held up his hands, wringing them in plaintive supplication, and poured forth a torrent of entreaty, with the tears rolling down his cheeks and his whole face and form expressive of the deepest emotion: —

"Let me entreat you, Dr. Seward, oh, let me implore you, to let me out of this house at once. Send me away how you will and where you will; send keepers with me with whips and chains; let them take me in a strait-waistcoat, manacled and leg-ironed, even to a gaol; but let me go out of this. You don't know what you do by keeping me here. I am speaking from the depths of my heart — of my very soul. You don't know whom you wrong, or how; and I may not tell. Woe is me! I may not tell. By all you hold sacred — by all you hold dear — by your love that is lost — by your hope that lives — for the sake of the Almighty, take me out of this and save my soul from guilt! Can't you hear me, man? Can't you understand? Will you never learn? Don't you know that I am sane and earnest now; that I am no lunatic in a mad fit, but a sane man fighting for his soul? Oh, hear me! hear me! Let me go! let me go! let me go!"

I thought that the longer this went on the wilder he would get, and so would bring on a fit; so I took him by the hand and raised him up.

"Come," I said sternly, "no more of this; we have had quite enough already. Get to your bed and try to behave more discreetly."

He suddenly stopped and looked at me intently for several moments. Then, without a word, he rose and moving over, sat down on the side of the bed. The collapse had come, as on former occasions, just as I had expected.

When I was leaving the room, last of our party, he said to me in a quiet, well-bred voice: —

"You will, I trust, Dr. Seward, do me the justice to bear in mind, later on, that I did what I could to convince you to-night."

CHAPTER XIX. JONATHAN HARKER'S JOURNAL

1 *October*, 5 *a.m.* — I went with the party to the search with an easy mind, for I think I never saw Mina so absolutely strong and well. I am so glad that she consented to hold back and let us men do the work. Somehow, it was a dread to me that she was in this fearful business at all; but now that her work is done, and that it is due to her energy and brains and foresight that the whole story is put together in such a way

that every point tells, she may well feel that her part is finished, and that she can henceforth leave the rest to us. We were, I think, all a little upset by the scene with Mr. Renfield. When we came away from his room we were silent till we got back to the study. Then Mr. Morris said to Dr. Seward: —

"Say, Jack, if that man wasn't attempting a bluff, he is about the sanest lunatic I ever saw. I'm not sure, but I believe that he had some serious purpose, and if he had, it was pretty rough on him not to get a chance." Lord Godalming and I were silent, but Dr. Van Helsing added: —

"Friend John, you know more of lunatics than I do, and I'm glad of it, for I fear that if it had been to me to decide I would before that last hysterical outburst have given him free. But we live and learn, and in our present task we must take no chance, as my friend Quincey would say. All is best as they are." Dr. Seward seemed to answer them both in a dreamy kind of way: —

"I don't know but that I agree with you. If that man had been an ordinary lunatic I would have taken my chance of trusting him; but he seems so mixed up with the Count in an indexy° kind of way that I am afraid of doing anything wrong by helping his fads. I can't forget how he prayed with almost equal fervour for a cat, and then tried to tear my throat out with his teeth. Besides, he called the Count 'lord and master,' and he may want to get out to help him in some diabolical way. That horrid thing has the wolves and the rats and his own kind to help him, so I suppose he isn't above trying to use a respectable lunatic. He certainly did seem earnest, though. I only hope we have done what is best. These things, in conjunction with the wild work we have in hand, help to unnerve a man." The Professor stepped over, and laying his hand on his shoulder, said in his grave, kindly way: —

"Friend John, have no fear. We are trying to do our duty in a very sad and terrible case; we can only do as we deem best. What else have we to hope for, except the pity of the good God?" Lord Godalming had slipped away for a few minutes, but he now returned. He held up a little silver whistle as he remarked: —

"That old place may be full of rats, and if so, I've got an antidote on call." Having passed the wall, we took our way to the house, taking care to keep in the shadows of the trees on the lawn when the moonlight shone out. When we got to the porch the Professor opened his bag and

---

indexy: Seward means that Renfield's actions serve as an index, or indicator, of the Count's activities.

took out a lot of things, which he laid on the step, sorting them into four little groups, evidently one for each. Then he spoke: —

"My friends, we are going into a terrible danger, and we need arms of many kinds. Our enemy is not merely spiritual. Remember that he has the strength of twenty men, and that, though our necks or our windpipes are of the common kind — and therefore breakable or crushable — his are not amenable to mere strength. A stronger man, or a body of men more strong in all than him, can at certain times hold him; but yet they cannot hurt him as we can be hurt by him. We must, therefore, guard ourselves from his touch. Keep this near your heart" — as he spoke he lifted a little silver crucifix and held it out to me, I being nearest to him — "put these flowers round your neck" — here he handed to me a wreath of withered garlic blossoms — "for other enemies more mundane, this revolver and this knife; and for aid in all, these so small electric lamps, which you can fasten to your breast; and for all, and above all at the last, this, which we must not desecrate needless." This was a portion of sacred wafer, which he put in an envelope and handed to me. Each of the others was similarly equipped. "Now," he said, "friend John, where are the skeleton keys? If so that we can open the door, we need not break house by the window, as before at Miss Lucy's."

Dr. Seward tried one or two skeleton keys, his mechanical dexterity as a surgeon standing him in good stead. Presently he got one to suit; after a little play back and forward the bolt yielded, and, with a rusty clang, shot back. We pressed on the door, the rusty hinges creaked, and it slowly opened. It was startlingly like the image conveyed to me in Dr. Seward's diary of the opening of Miss Westenra's tomb; I fancy that the same idea seemed to strike the others, for with one accord they shrank back. The Professor was the first to move forward, and stepped into the open door.

"In manus tuas, Domine!"° he said, crossing himself as he passed over the threshold. We closed the door behind us, lest when we should have lit our lamps we should possibly attract attention from the road. The Professor carefully tried the lock, lest we might not be able to open it from within should we be in a hurry making our exit. Then we all lit our lamps and proceeded on our search.

The light from the tiny lamps fell in all sorts of odd forms, as the

---

In manus tuas, Domine: "Into your hands, Lord" (Latin). Van Helsing here echoes Jesus' last words on the cross, "Father, into thy hands I commend my spirit" (Luke 23.46).

rays crossed each other, or the opacity of our bodies threw great shadows. I could not for my life get away from the feeling that there was some one else amongst us. I suppose it was the recollection, so powerfully brought home to me by the grim surroundings, of that terrible experience in Transylvania. I think the feeling was common to us all, for I noticed that the others kept looking over their shoulders, at every sound and every new shadow, just as I felt myself doing.

The whole place was thick with dust. The floor was seemingly inches deep except where there were recent footsteps, in which on holding down my lamp I could see marks of hobnails° where the dust was caked. The walls were fluffy and heavy with dust, and in the corners were masses of spiders' webs, whereon the dust had gathered till they looked like old tattered rags as the weight had torn them partly down. On a table in the hall was a great bunch of keys, with a time-yellowed label on each. They had been used several times, for on the table were several similar rents in the blanket of dust, similar to that exposed when the Professor lifted them. He turned to me and said: —

"You know this place, Jonathan. You have copied maps of it, and you know at least more than we do. Which is the way to the chapel?" I had an idea of its direction, though on my former visit I had not been able to get admission to it; so I led the way, and after a few wrong turnings found myself opposite a low, arched oaken door, ribbed with iron bands. "This is the spot," said the Professor as he turned his lamp on a small map of the house, copied from the file of my original correspondence regarding the purchase. With a little trouble we found the key on the bunch and opened the door. We were prepared for some unpleasantness, for as we were opening the door a faint, malodorous air seemed to exhale through the gaps, but none of us ever expected such an odour as we encountered. None of the others had met the Count at all at close quarters, and when I had seen him he was either in the fasting stage of his existence in his rooms or, when he was gloated with fresh blood,° in a ruined building open to the air; but here the place was small and close, and the long disuse had made the air stagnant and foul. There was an earthy smell, as of some dry miasma, which came through the fouler air. But as to the odour itself, how shall I describe it? It was not alone that it was composed of all the ills of mortality and with the pungent, acrid smell of blood, but it seemed as though corruption had become itself corrupt. Faugh! it sickens me to think of it. Every

---

hobnails: Broad nails used to protect the soles of heavy boots and shoes (*OED* OL).
gloated with fresh blood: A possible misprint for "bloated."

breath exhaled by that monster seemed to have clung to the place and intensified its loathsomeness.

Under ordinary circumstances such a stench would have brought our enterprise to an end; but this was no ordinary case, and the high and terrible purpose in which we were involved gave us a strength which rose above merely physical considerations. After the involuntary shrinking consequent on the first nauseous whiff, we one and all set about our work as though that loathsome place were a garden of roses.

We made an accurate examination of the place, the Professor saying as we began: —

"The first thing is to see how many of the boxes are left; we must then examine every hole and corner and cranny, and see if we cannot get some clue as to what has become of the rest." A glance was sufficient to show how many remained, for the great earth chests were bulky, and there was no mistaking them.

There were only twenty-nine left out of the fifty! Once I got a fright, for, seeing Lord Godalming suddenly turn and look out of the vaulted door into the dark passage beyond, I looked too, and for an instant my heart stood still. Somewhere, looking out from the shadow, I seemed to see the high lights of the Count's evil face, the ridge of the nose, the red eyes, the red lips, the awful pallor. It was only for a moment, for, as Lord Godalming said, "I thought I saw a face, but it was only the shadows," and resumed his inquiry, I turned my lamp in the direction, and stepped into the passage. There was no sign of any one; and as there were no corners, no doors, no aperture of any kind, but only the solid walls of the passage, there could be no hiding-place even for *him*. I took it that fear had helped imagination, and said nothing.

A few minutes later I saw Morris step suddenly back from a corner, which he was examining. We all followed his movements with our eyes, for undoubtedly some nervousness was growing on us, and we saw a whole mass of phosphorescence, which twinkled like stars. We all instinctively drew back. The whole place was becoming alive with rats.

For a moment or two we stood appalled, all save Lord Godalming, who was seemingly prepared for such an emergency. Rushing over to the great iron-bound oaken door, which Dr. Seward had described from the outside, and which I had seen myself, he turned the key in the lock, drew the huge bolts, and swung the door open. Then, taking his little silver whistle from his pocket, he blew a low, shrill call. It was answered from behind Dr. Seward's house by the yelping of dogs, and after about a minute three terriers came dashing round the corner of the house. Unconsciously we had all moved towards the door, and as we moved I noticed that the dust had been much disturbed: the boxes which had been taken out had been brought this way. But even in the minute that had elapsed the number of the rats had vastly increased. They seemed to swarm over the place all at once, till the lamplight, shining on their moving dark bodies and glittering, baleful eyes, made the place look like a bank of earth set with fireflies. The dogs dashed on, but at the threshold suddenly stopped and snarled, and then, simultaneously lifting their noses, began to howl in most lugubrious fashion. The rats were multiplying in thousands, and we moved out.

Lord Godalming lifted one of the dogs, and carrying him in, placed him on the floor. The instant his feet touched the ground he seemed to recover his courage, and rushed at his natural enemies. They fled before him so fast that before he had shaken the life out of a score, the other dogs, who had by now been lifted in in the same manner, had but small prey ere the whole mass had vanished.

With their going it seemed as if some evil presence had departed, for the dogs frisked about and barked merrily as they made sudden darts at their prostrate foes, and turned them over and over and tossed them in the air with vicious shakes. We all seemed to find our spirits rise. Whether it was the purifying of the deadly atmosphere by the opening of the chapel door, or the relief which we experienced by finding ourselves in the open I know not; but most certainly the shadow of dread seemed to slip from us like a robe, and the occasion of our coming lost something of its grim significance, though we did not slacken a whit in our resolution. We closed the outer door and barred and locked it, and bringing the dogs with us, began our search of the house. We found nothing throughout except dust in extraordinary proportions, and all untouched save for my own footsteps when I had made my first visit. Never once did the dogs exhibit any symptom of uneasiness, and even when we returned to the chapel they frisked about as though they had been rabbit-hunting in a summer wood.

The morning was quickening in the east when we emerged from the front. Dr. Van Helsing had taken the key of the hall-door from the bunch, and locked the door in orthodox fashion, putting the key into his pocket when he had done.

"So far," he said, "our night has been eminently successful. No harm has come to us such as I feared might be, and yet we have ascertained how many boxes are missing. More than all do I rejoice that this, our first — and perhaps our most difficult and dangerous — step has been accomplished without the bringing thereinto our most sweet

Madam Mina or troubling her waking or sleeping thoughts with sights and sounds and smells of horror which she might never forget. One lesson, too, we have learned, if it be allowable to argue *a particulari:*° that the brute beasts which are to the Count's command are yet themselves not amenable to his spiritual power; for look, these rats that would come to his call, just as from his castle top he summon the wolves to your going and to that poor mother's cry, though they come to him, they run pell-mell from the so little dogs of my friend Arthur. We have other matters before us, other dangers, other fears; and that monster — he has not used his power over the brute world for the only or the last time to-night. So be it that he has gone elsewhere. Good! It has given us opportunity to cry 'check' in some ways in this chess game, which we play for the stake of human souls. And now let us go home. The dawn is close at hand, and we have reason to be content with our first night's work. It may be ordained that we have many nights and days to follow, if full of peril; but we must go on, and from no danger shall we shrink."

The house was silent when we got back, save for some poor creature who was screaming away in one of the distant wards, and a low, moaning sound from Renfield's room. The poor wretch was doubtless torturing himself, after the manner of the insane, with needless thoughts of pain.

I came tiptoe into our own room, and found Mina asleep, breathing so softly that I had to put my ear down to hear it. She looks paler than usual. I hope the meeting to-night has not upset her. I am truly thankful that she is to be left out of our future work, and even of our deliberations. It is too great a strain for a woman to bear. I did not think so at first, but I know better now. Therefore I am glad that it is settled. There may be things which would frighten her to hear; and yet to conceal them from her might be worse than to tell her if once she suspected that there was any concealment. Henceforth our work is to be a sealed book to her, till at least such time as we can tell her that all is finished, and the earth free from a monster of the nether world. I daresay it will be difficult to begin to keep silence after such confidence as ours; but I must be resolute, and to-morrow I shall keep dark over to-night's doings, and shall refuse to speak of anything that has happened. I rest on the sofa, so as not to disturb her.

1 *October, later.* — I suppose it was natural that we should have all overslept ourselves, for the day was a busy one, and the night had no rest at all. Even Mina must have felt its exhaustion, for though I slept

---

a particulari: An abbreviation of the Latin phrase *a particulari ad universale,* meaning to argue from the particular to the universal or general.

till the sun was high, I was awake before her, and had to call two or three times before she awoke. Indeed, she was so sound asleep that for a few seconds she did not recognise me, but looked at me with a sort of blank terror, as one looks who has been waked out of a bad dream. She complained a little of being tired, and I let her rest till later in the day. We now know of twenty-one boxes having been removed, and if it be that several were taken in any of these removals we may be able to trace them all. Such will, of course, immensely simplify our labour, and the sooner the matter is attended to the better. I shall look up Thomas Snelling to-day.

Dr. Seward's Diary

1 *October.* — It was towards noon when I was awakened by the Professor walking into my room. He was more jolly and cheerful than usual, and it is quite evident that last night's work has helped to take some of the brooding weight off his mind. After going over the adventure of the night he suddenly said: —

"Your patient interests me much. May it be that with you I visit him this morning? Or if that you are too occupy, I can go alone if it may be. It is a new experience to me to find a lunatic who talk philosophy, and reason so sound." I had some work to do which pressed, so I told him that if he would go alone I would be glad, as then I should not have to keep him waiting; so I called an attendant and gave him the necessary instructions. Before the Professor left the room I cautioned him against getting any false impression from my patient. "But," he answered, "I want him to talk of himself and of his delusion as to consuming live things. He said to Madam Mina, as I see in your diary of yesterday, that he had once had such a belief. Why do you smile, friend John?"

"Excuse me," I said, "but the answer is here." I laid my hand on the type-written matter. "When our sane and learned lunatic made that very statement of how he *used* to consume life, his mouth was actually nauseous with the flies and spiders which he had eaten just before Mrs. Harker entered the room." Van Helsing smiled in turn. "Good!" he said. "Your memory is true, friend John. I should have remembered. And yet it is this very obliquity of thought and memory which makes mental disease such a fascinating study. Perhaps I may gain more knowledge out of the folly of this madman than I shall from the teaching of the most wise. Who knows?" I went on with my work, and before long was through that in hand. It seemed that the time had been very short indeed, but there was Van Helsing back in the study. "Do I interrupt?" he asked politely as he stood at the door.

"Not at all," I answered. "Come in. My work is finished, and I am free. I can go with you now, if you like."

"It is needless; I have seen him!"

"Well?"

"I fear that he does not appraise me at much. Our interview was short. When I entered his room he was sitting on a stool in the centre, with his elbows on his knees, and his face was the picture of sullen discontent. I spoke to him as cheerfully as I could, and with such a measure of respect as I could assume. He made no reply whatever. "Don't you know me?" I asked. His answer was not reassuring: "I know you well enough; you are the old fool Van Helsing. I wish you would take yourself and your idiotic brain theories somewhere else. Damn all thick-headed Dutchmen!" Not a word more would he say, but sat in his implacable sullenness as indifferent to me as though I had not been in the room at all. Thus departed for this time my chance of much learning from this so clever lunatic; so I shall go, if I may, and cheer myself with a few happy words with that sweet soul Madam Mina. Friend John, it does rejoice me unspeakable that she is no more to be pained, no more to be worried, with our terrible things. Though we shall much miss her help, it is better so."

"I agree with you with all my heart," I answered earnestly, for I did not want him to weaken in this matter. "Mrs. Harker is better out of it. Things are quite bad enough for us, all men of the world, and who have been in many tight places in our time; but it is no place for a woman, and if she had remained in touch with the affair, it would in time infallibly have wrecked her."

So Van Helsing has gone to confer with Mrs. Harker and Harker; Quincey and Art are all out following up the clues as to the earth-boxes. I shall finish my round of work, and we shall meet to-night.

Mina Harker's Journal

1 *October.* — It is strange to me to be kept in the dark as I am to-day; after Jonathan's full confidence for so many years, to see him manifestly avoid certain matters, and those the most vital of all. This morning I slept late after the fatigues of yesterday, and though Jonathan was late too, he was the earlier. He spoke to me before he went out, never more sweetly or tenderly, but he never mentioned a

word of what had happened in the visit to the Count's house. And yet he must have known how terribly anxious I was. Poor dear fellow! I suppose it must have distressed him even more than it did me. They all agreed that it was best that I should not be drawn further into this awful work, and I acquiesced. But to think that he keeps anything from me! And now I am crying like a silly fool, when I *know* it comes from my husband's great love and from the good, good wishes of those other strong men. . . .

That has done me good. Well, some day Jonathan will tell me all; and lest it should ever be that he should think for a moment that I kept anything from him, I still keep my journal as usual. Then if he has feared of my trust I shall show it to him, with every thought of my heart put down for his dear eyes to read. I feel strangely sad and low-spirited to-day. I suppose it is the reaction from the terrible excitement.

Last night I went to bed when the men had gone, simply because they told me to. I didn't feel sleepy, and I did feel full of devouring anxiety. I kept thinking over everything that has been ever since Jonathan came to see me in London, and it all seems like a horrible tragedy, with fate pressing on relentlessly to some destined end. Everything that one does seems, no matter how right it may be, to bring on the very thing which is most to be deplored. If I hadn't gone to Whitby, perhaps poor dear Lucy would be with us now. She hadn't taken to visiting the churchyard till I came, and if she hadn't come there in the day-time with me she wouldn't have walked there in her sleep; and if she hadn't gone there at night and asleep, that monster couldn't have destroyed her as he did. Oh, why did I ever go to Whitby? There now, crying again! I wonder what has come over me to-day. I must hide it from Jonathan, for if he knew that I had been crying twice in one morning — I, who never cried on my own account, and whom he has never caused to shed a tear — the dear fellow would fret his heart out. I shall put a bold face on, and if I do feel weepy, he shall never see it. I suppose it is one of the lessons that we poor women have to learn. . . .

I can't quite remember how I fell asleep last night. I remember hearing the sudden barking of the dogs and a lot of queer sounds, like praying on a very tumultuous scale, from Mr. Renfield's room, which is somewhere under this. And then there was silence over everything, silence so profound that it startled me, and I got up and looked out of the window. All was dark and silent, the black shadows thrown by the moonlight seeming full of a silent mystery of their own. Not a thing seemed to be stirring, but all to be grim and fixed as death or fate; so that a thin streak of white mist, that crept with almost imperceptible slowness across the grass towards the house, seemed to have a sentience and a vitality of its own. I think that the digression of my thoughts must have done me good, for when I got back to bed I found a lethargy creeping over me. I lay a while, but could not quite sleep, so I got out and looked out of the window again. The mist was spreading, and was now close up to the house, so that I could see it lying thick against the wall, as though it were stealing up to the windows. The poor man was more loud than ever, and though I could not distinguish a word he said, I could in some way recognise in his tones some passionate entreaty on his part. Then there was the sound of a struggle, and I knew that the attendants were dealing with him. I was so frightened that I crept into bed, and pulled the clothes over my head, putting my fingers in my ears. I was not then a bit sleepy, at least so I thought; but I must have fallen asleep, for, except dreams, I do not remember anything until the morning, when Jonathan woke me. I think that it took me an effort and a little time to realise where I was, and that it was Jonathan who was bending over me. My dream was very peculiar, and was almost typical of the way that waking thoughts become merged in, or continued in, dreams.

I thought that I was asleep, and waiting for Jonathan to come back. I was very anxious about him, and I was powerless to act; my feet, and my hands, and my brain were weighted, so that nothing could proceed at the usual pace. And so I slept uneasily and thought. Then it began to dawn upon me that the air was heavy, and dank, and cold. I put back the clothes from my face, and found, to my surprise, that all was dim around me. The gas-light which I had left lit for Jonathan, but turned down, came only like a tiny red spark through the fog, which had evidently grown thicker and poured into the room. Then it occurred to me that I had shut the window before I had come to bed. I would have got out to make certain on the point, but some leaden lethargy seemed to chain my limbs and even my will. I lay still and endured; that was all. I closed my eyes, but could still see through my eyelids. (It is wonderful what tricks our dreams play us, and how conveniently we can imagine.) The mist grew thicker and thicker, and I could see now how it came in, for I could see it like smoke — or with the white energy of boiling water — pouring in, not through the window, but through the joinings of the door. It got thicker and thicker, till it seemed as if it became concentrated into a sort of pillar of cloud in the room, through the top of which I could see the light of the gas shining like a red eye. Things began to whirl through my brain just as the cloudy column was now whirling in the room, and through it all came the scriptural words "a

pillar of cloud by day and of fire by night."° Was it indeed some such
spiritual guidance that was coming to me in my sleep? But the pillar was
composed of both the day and the night-guiding, for the fire was in the
red eye, which at the thought got a new fascination for me; till, as I
looked, the fire divided, and seemed to shine on me through the fog
like two red eyes, such as Lucy told me of in her momentary mental
wandering when, on the cliff, the dying sunlight struck the windows of
St. Mary's Church. Suddenly the horror burst upon me that it was thus
that Jonathan had seen those awful women growing into reality
through the whirling mist in the moonlight, and in my dream I must
have fainted, for all became black darkness. The last conscious effort
which imagination made was to show me a livid white face bending
over me out of the mist. I must be careful of such dreams, for they
would unseat one's reason if there were too much of them. I would get
Dr. Van Helsing or Dr. Seward to prescribe something for me which
would make me sleep, only that I fear to alarm them. Such a dream at
the present time would become woven into their fears for me. To-night
I shall strive hard to sleep naturally. If I do not, I shall to-morrow night
get them to give me a dose of chloral; that cannot hurt me for once,
and it will give me a good night's sleep. Last night tired me more than if
I had not slept at all.

2 *October*, 10 *p.m.* — Last night I slept, but did not dream. I must
have slept soundly, for I was not waked by Jonathan coming to bed; but
the sleep has not refreshed me, for to-day I feel terribly weak and spirit-
less. I spent all yesterday trying to read, or lying down dozing. In the
afternoon Mr. Renfield asked if he might see me. Poor man, he was very
gentle, and when I came away he kissed my hand and bade God bless
me. Some way it affected me much; I am crying when I think of him.
This is a new weakness, of which I must be careful. Jonathan would be
miserable if he knew I had been crying. He and the others were out
until dinner-time, and they all came in tired. I did what I could to
brighten them up, and I suppose that the effort did me good, for I forgot how tired I was. After dinner they sent me to bed, and all went off
to smoke together, as they said, but I knew that they wanted to tell each
other of what had occurred to each during the day; I could see from
Jonathan's manner that he had something important to communicate.
I was not so sleepy as I should have been; so before they went I asked

---

a pillar of cloud by day and of fire by night: God goes before the Israelites as they flee
Egypt "in a pillar of a cloud" during the day and "in a pillar of fire" during the night
(Exod. 13.21–22).

Dr. Seward to give me a little opiate of some kind, as I had not slept well the night before. He very kindly made me up a sleeping draught, which he gave to me, telling me that it would do me no harm, as it was very mild. . . . I have taken it, and am waiting for sleep, which still keeps aloof. I hope I have not done wrong, for as sleep begins to flirt with me, a new fear comes: that I may have been foolish in thus depriving myself of the power of waking. I might want it. Here comes sleep. Good-night.

CHAPTER XX. JONATHAN HARKER'S JOURNAL

1 *October, evening.* — I found Thomas Snelling in his house at Bethnal Green,° but unhappily he was not in a condition to remember anything. The very prospect of beer which my expected coming had opened to him had proved too much, and he had begun too early on his expected debauch. I learned, however, from his wife, who seemed a decent, poor soul, that he was only the assistant to Smollet, who of the two mates was the responsible person. So off I drove to Walworth,° and found Mr. Joseph Smollet at home and in his shirt-sleeves, taking a late tea out of a saucer. He is a decent, intelligent fellow, distinctly a good, reliable type of workman, and with a headpiece of his own. He remembered all about the incident of the boxes, and from a wonderful dog's-eared notebook, which he produced from some mysterious receptacle about the seat of his trousers, and which had hieroglyphical entries in thick, half-obliterated pencil, he gave me the destinations of the boxes. There were, he said, six in the cartload which he took from Carfax and left at 197, Chicksand Street, Mile End New Town, and another six which he deposited at Jamaica Lane, Bermondsey.° If then the Count meant to scatter these ghastly refuges of his over London, these places were chosen as the first of delivery, so that later he might distribute more fully. The systematic manner in which this was done made me think that he could not mean to confine himself to two sides of London. He was now fixed on the far east of the northern shore, on the east of the southern shore, and on the south. The north and west were

---

Bethnal Green: A London borough located in the East End, north of the Thames, principally inhabited by the working classes (Black; *Enc. Brit.* 11th).   *Walworth:* A neighborhood in southeastern London, below the Thames (Black; *Enc. Brit.* 11th).   *Mile End New Town ... Bermondsey:* Mile End is an area of the East End, beyond Whitechapel; Bermondsey is a working-class borough in the south of London, close to Walworth (Black; *Enc. Brit.* 11th).

surely never meant to be left out of his diabolical scheme — let alone the City° itself and the very heart of fashionable London in the southwest and west. I went back to Smollet, and asked him if he could tell us if any other boxes had been taken from Carfax.

He replied: —

"Well, guv'nor, you've treated me wery 'an'some" — I had given him half a sovereign — "an' I'll tell yer all I know. I heeard a man by the name of Bloxam say four nights ago in the 'Are an' 'Ounds, in Pincher's Alley, as 'ow he an' his mate 'ad 'ad a rare dusty job in a old 'ouse at Purfleet. There ain't a-many such jobs as this 'ere, an' I'm thinkin' that maybe Sam Bloxam could tell ye summut." I asked if he could tell me where to find him. I told him that if he could get me the address it would be worth another half-sovereign to him. So he gulped down the rest of his tea and stood up, saying that he was going to begin the search then and there. At the door he stopped, and said: —

"Look 'ere, guv'nor, there ain't no sense in me a-keepin' you 'ere. I may find Sam soon, or I mayn't; but anyhow he ain't like to be in a way to tell ye much to-night. Sam is a rare one when he starts on the booze. If you can give me a envelope with a stamp on it, and put yer address on it, I'll find out where Sam is to be found and post it ye to-night. But ye'd better be up arter 'im soon in the mornin', or maybe ye won't ketch 'im; for Sam gets off main early, never mind the booze the night afore."

This was all practical, so one of the children went off with a penny to buy an envelope and a sheet of paper, and to keep the change. When she came back, I addressed the envelope and stamped it, and when Smollet had again faithfully promised to post the address when found, I took my way to home. We're on the track anyhow. I am tired to-night, and want sleep. Mina is fast asleep, and looks a little too pale; her eyes look as though she had been crying. Poor dear, I've no doubt it frets her to be kept in the dark, and it may make her doubly anxious about me and the others. But it is best as it is. It is better to be disappointed and worried in such a way now than to have her nerve broken. The doctors were quite right to insist on her being kept out of this dreadful business. I must be firm, for on me this particular burden of silence must rest. I shall not ever enter on the subject with her under any circumstances. Indeed, it may not be a hard task, after all, for she herself

---

the City: The oldest part of London, which had been inside the walls of the city in the middle ages, containing London's main financial institutions.

has become reticent on the subject, and has not spoken of the Count or his doings ever since we told her of our decision.

2 October, evening. — A long and trying and exciting day. By the first post I got my directed envelope with a dirty scrap of paper enclosed, on which was written with a carpenter's pencil in a sprawling hand: —

"Sam Bloxam, Korkrans, 4, Poters Cort, Bartel Street, Walworth. Arsk for the depite."

I got the letter in bed, and rose without waking Mina. She looked heavy and sleepy and pale, and far from well. I determined not to wake her, but that, when I should return from this new search, I would arrange for her going back to Exeter. I think she would be happier in our own home, with her daily tasks to interest her, than in being here amongst us and in ignorance. I only saw Dr. Seward for a moment, and told him where I was off to, promising to come back and tell the rest so soon as I should have found out anything. I drove to Walworth and found, with some difficulty, Potter's Court. Mr. Smollet's spelling mis-led me, as I asked for Poter's Court instead of Potter's Court. How-ever, when I had found the court, I had no difficulty in discovering Corcoran's lodging-house. When I asked the man who came to the door for the "depite," he shook his head, and said: "I dunno 'im. There ain't no such a person 'ere; I never 'eard of 'im in all my bloomin' days. Don't believe there ain't nobody of that kind livin' 'ere or anywheres." I took out Smollet's letter, and as I read it it seemed to me that the les-son of the spelling of the name of the court might guide me. "What are you?" I asked.

"I'm the depity," he answered. I saw at once that I was on the right track; phonetic spelling had again misled me. A half-crown tip put the deputy's knowledge at my disposal, and I learned that Mr. Bloxam, who had slept off the remains of his beer on the previous night at Corcoran's, had left for his work at Poplar° at five o'clock that morn-ing. He could not tell me where the place of work was situated, but he had a vague idea that it was some kind of a "new-fangled ware'us;" and with this slender clue I had to start for Poplar. It was twelve o'clock before I got any satisfactory hint of such a building, and this I got at a coffee-shop, where some workmen were having their dinner. One of these suggested that there was being erected at Cross Angel Street a new "cold storage" building; and as this suited the condition of

---

Poplar: A working-class London borough in the East End, north of the Thames and close to the docks of Limehouse (Black; *Enc. Brit.* 11th).

a "new-fangled ware'us," I at once drove to it. An interview with a surly gatekeeper and a surlier foreman, both of whom were appeased with coin of the realm, put me on the track of Bloxam; he was sent for on my suggesting that I was willing to pay his day's wages to his foreman for the privilege of asking him a few questions on a private matter. He was a smart enough fellow, though rough of speech and bearing. When I had promised to pay for his information and given him an earnest, he told me that he had made two journeys between Carfax and a house in Piccadilly, and had taken from this house to the latter nine great boxes — "main heavy ones" — with a horse and cart hired by him for this purpose. I asked him if he could tell me the number of the house in Piccadilly, to which he replied: —

"Well, guv'nor, I forgits the number, but it was only a few doors from a big white church or somethink of the kind, not long built. It was a dusty old 'ouse, too, though nothin' to the dustiness of the 'ouse we tooked the bloomin' boxes from."

"How did you get into the houses if they were both empty?"

"There was the old party what engaged me a-waitin' in the 'ouse at Purfleet. He 'elped me to lift the boxes and put them in the dray. Curse me, but he was the strongest chap I ever struck, an' him a old feller, with a white moustache, one that thin you would think he couldn't throw a shadder."

How this phrase thrilled through me!

"Why, 'e took up 'is end o' the boxes like they was pounds of tea, and me a-puffin' an' a-blowin' afore I could up-end mine anyhow — an' I'm no chicken, neither."

"How did you get into the house in Piccadilly?" I asked.

"He was there too. He must 'a' started off and got there afore me, for when I rung of the bell he kem an' opened the door 'isself an' 'elped me to carry the boxes into the 'all."

"The whole nine?" I asked.

"Yus; there was five in the first load an' four in the second. It was main dry work, an' I don't so well remember 'ow I got 'ome." I interrupted him: —

"Were the boxes left in the hall?"

"Yus; it was a big 'all, an' there was nothin' else in it." I made one more attempt to further matters: —

"You didn't have any key?"

"Never used no key nor nothink. The old gent, he opened the door 'isself an' shut it again when I druv off. I don't remember the last time — but that was the beer."

"And you can't remember the number of the house?"

"No, sir. But ye needn't have no difficulty about that. It's a 'igh 'un with a stone front with a bow on it, an' 'igh steps up to the door. I know them steps, 'avin' 'ad to carry the boxes up with three loafers what come round to earn a copper. The old gent give them shillin's, an' they seein' they got so much, they wanted more; but 'e took one of them by the shoulder and was like to throw 'im down the steps, till the lot of them went away cussin'." I thought that with this description I could find the house, so, having paid my friend for his information, I started off for Piccadilly. I had gained a new painful experience: the Count could, it was evident, handle the earth-boxes himself. If so, time was precious; for, now that he had achieved a certain amount of distribution, he could, by choosing his own time, complete the task unobserved. At Piccadilly Circus° I discharged my cab, and walked westward; beyond the Junior Constitutional° I came across the house described, and was satisfied that this was the next of the lairs arranged by Dracula. The house looked as though it had been long untenanted. The windows were encrusted with dust, and the shutters were up. All the framework was black with time, and from the iron the paint had mostly scaled away. It was evident that up to lately there had been a large notice-board in front of the balcony; it had, however, been roughly torn away, the uprights which had supported it still remaining. Behind the rails of the balcony I saw there were some loose boards, whose raw edges looked white. I would have given a good deal to have been able to see the notice-board intact, as it would, perhaps, have given some clue to the ownership of the house. I remembered my experience of the investigation and purchase of Carfax, and I could not but feel that if I could find the former owner there might be some means discovered of gaining access to the house.

There was at present nothing to be learned from the Piccadilly side, and nothing could be done; so I went round to the back to see if anything could be gathered from this quarter. The mews° were active, the Piccadilly houses being mostly in occupation. I asked one or two of the grooms and helpers whom I saw round if they could tell me anything about the empty house. One of them said that he heard it had lately been taken, but he couldn't say from whom. He told me, however, that up to very lately there had been a notice-board of "For sale" up, and

Piccadilly Circus: Circular area with a traffic rotary at the intersection of Piccadilly and Regent Street.   *Junior Constitutional:* A political club for Conservatives, located on Piccadilly (Nevill; *Baedeker* 1896).   *mews:* Stables grouped together around an open space or yard, where carriage horses and carriages are kept.

that perhaps Mitchell, Sons, & Candy, the house agents, could tell me something, as he thought he remembered seeing the name of that firm on the board. I did not wish to seem too eager, or to let my informant know or guess too much, so, thanking him in the usual manner, I strolled away. It was now growing dusk, and the autumn night was closing in, so I did not lose any time. Having learned the address of Mitchell, Sons, & Candy from a directory at the Berkeley, I was soon at their office in Sackville Street.°

The gentleman who saw me was particularly suave in manner, but uncommunicative in equal proportion. Having once told me that the Piccadilly house — which throughout our interview he called a "mansion" — was sold, he considered my business as concluded. When I asked who had purchased it, he opened his eyes a thought wider, and paused a few seconds before replying: —

"It is sold, sir."

"Pardon me," I said, with equal politeness, "but I have a special reason for wishing to know who purchased it."

Again he paused longer, and raised his eyebrows still more. "It is sold, sir," was again his laconic reply.

"Surely," I said, "you do not mind letting me know so much."

"But I do mind," he answered. "The affairs of their clients are absolutely safe in the hands of Mitchell, Sons, & Candy." This was manifestly a prig of the first water, and there was no use arguing with him. I thought I had best meet him on his own ground, so I said: —

"Your clients, sir are happy in having so resolute a guardian of their confidence. I am myself a professional man." Here I handed him my card. "In this instance I am not prompted by curiosity; I act on the part of Lord Godalming, who wishes to know something of the property which was, he understood, lately for sale." These words put a different complexion on affairs. He said: —

"I would like to oblige you if I could, Mr. Harker, and especially would I like to oblige his lordship. We once carried out a small matter of renting some chambers for him when he was the Honourable Arthur Holmwood. If you will let me have his lordship's address I will consult the House on the subject, and will, in any case, communicate with his lordship by to-night's post. It will be a pleasure if we can so far deviate from our rules as to give the required information to his lordship."

I wanted to secure a friend, and not to make an enemy, so I thanked

Sackville Street: A street running north from Piccadilly, near Regent Street.

him, gave the address at Dr. Seward's, and came away. It was now dark, and I was tired and hungry. I got a cup of tea at the Aërated Bread Company° and came down to Purfleet by the next train.

I found all the others at home. Mina was looking tired and pale, but she made a gallant effort to be bright and cheerful; it wrung my heart to think that I had had to keep anything from her and so caused her inquietude. Thank God, this will be the last night of her looking on at our conferences, and feeling the sting of our not showing our confidence. It took all my courage to hold to the wise resolution of keeping her out of our grim task. She seems somehow more reconciled; or else the very subject seems to have become repugnant to her, for when any accidental allusion is made she actually shudders. I am glad we made our resolution in time, as with such a feeling as this, our growing knowledge would be torture to her.

I could not tell the others of the day's discovery till we were alone; so after dinner — followed by a little music to save appearances even amongst ourselves — I took Mina to her room and left her to go to bed. The dear girl was more affectionate with me than ever, and clung to me as though she would detain me; but there was much to be talked of and I came away. Thank God, the ceasing of telling things has made no difference between us.

When I came down again I found the others all gathered round the fire in the study. In the train I had written my diary so far, and simply read it off to them as the best means of letting them get abreast of my own information; when I had finished Van Helsing said: —

"This has been a great day's work, friend Jonathan. Doubtless we are on the track of the missing boxes. If we find them all in that house, then our work is near the end. But if there be some missing, we must search until we find them. Then shall we make our final *coup,* and hunt the wretch to his real death." We all sat silent awhile and all at once Mr. Morris spoke: —

"Say! how are we going to get into that house?"

"We got into the other" answered Lord Godalming quickly.

"But, Art, this is different. We broke house at Carfax, but we had night and a walled park to protect us. It will be a mighty different thing to commit burglary in Piccadilly, either by day or night. I confess I don't see how we are going to get in unless that agency duck can find us a key of some sort; perhaps we shall know when you get his letter in the

---

Aërated Bread Company: The company had a shop with a tea room (*Baedeker* 1896).

morning." Lord Godalming's brows contracted, and he stood up and walked about the room. By-and-by he stopped and said, turning from one to another of us: —

"Quincey's head is level. This burglary business is getting serious; we got off once all right; but we have now a rare job on hand — unless we can find the Count's key basket."

As nothing could well be done before morning, and as it would be at least advisable to wait till Lord Godalming should hear from Mitchell's, we decided not to take any active step before breakfast time. For a good while we sat and smoked, discussing the matter in its various lights and bearings; I took the opportunity of bringing this diary right up to the moment. I am very sleepy and shall go to bed. . . .

Just a line. Mina sleeps soundly and her breathing is regular. Her forehead is puckered up into little wrinkles, as though she thinks even in her sleep. She is still too pale, but does not look so haggard as she did this morning. To-morrow will, I hope, mend all this; she will be herself at home in Exeter. Oh, but I am sleepy!

Dr. Seward's Diary

1 *October.* — I am puzzled afresh about Renfield. His moods change so rapidly that I find it difficult to keep touch of them, and as they always mean something more than his own well-being, they form a more than interesting study. This morning, when I went to see him after his repulse of Van Helsing, his manner was that of a man commanding destiny. He was, in fact, commanding destiny — subjectively. He did not really care for any of the things of mere earth; he was in the clouds and looked down on all the weaknesses and wants of us poor mortals. I thought I would improve the occasion and learn something, so I asked him: —

"What about the flies these times?" He smiled on me in quite a superior sort of way — such a smile as would have become the face of Malvolio° — as he answered me: —

"The fly, my dear sir, has one striking feature: its wings are typical of the aërial powers of the psychic faculties. The ancients did well when they typified the soul as a butterfly!"

I thought I would push his analogy to its utmost logically, so I said quickly: —

Malvolio: In Shakespeare's *Twelfth Night*, the vain steward Malvolio, tricked by a practical joke into thinking that his mistress Olivia loves him, appears before her smiling.

"Oh, it is a soul you are after now, is it?" His madness foiled his reason, and a puzzled look spread over his face as, shaking his head with a decision which I had but seldom seen in him, he said: —

"Oh no, oh no! I want no souls. Life is all I want." Here he brightened up; "I am pretty indifferent about it at present. Life is all right; I have all I want. You must get a new patient, doctor, if you wish to study zoophagy!"

This puzzled me a little, so I drew him on: —

"Then you command life; you are a god I suppose?" He smiled with an ineffably benign superiority.

"Oh no! far be it from me to arrogate to myself the attributes of the Deity. I am not even concerned in His especially spiritual doings. If I may state my intellectual position I am, so far as concerns things purely terrestrial, somewhat in the position which Enoch occupied spiritually!" This was a poser to me. I could not at the moment recall Enoch's appositeness; so I had to ask a simple question, though I felt that by so doing I was lowering myself in the eyes of the lunatic: —

"And why with Enoch?"

"Because he walked with God."° I could not see the analogy, but did not like to admit it; so I harked back to what he had denied: —

"So you don't care about life and you don't want souls. Why not?" I put my question quickly and somewhat sternly, on purpose to disconcert him. The effort succeeded; for an instant he unconsciously relapsed into his old servile manner, bent low before me, and actually fawned upon me as he replied: —

"I don't want any souls, indeed, indeed! I don't. I couldn't use them if I had them; they would be no manner of use to me. I couldn't eat them or ——" he suddenly stopped and the old cunning look spread over his face, like a wind-sweep on the surface of the water. "And doctor, as to life, what is it after all? When you've got all you require, and you know that you will never want, that is all. I have friends — good friends — like you Dr. Seward;" this was said with a leer of inexpressible cunning, "I know that I shall never lack the means of life!"

I think that through the cloudiness of his insanity he saw some antagonism in me, for he at once fell back on the last refuge of such as

Enoch. . . . walked with God: In the Bible, Enoch, the father of Methuselah, "walked with God" (Gen. 5.22, 24). Renfield aspires to the kind of extended life associated with Enoch's family.

he — a dogged silence. After a short time I saw that for the present it was useless to speak to him. He was sulky, and so I came away.

Later in the day he sent for me. Ordinarily I would not have come without special reason, but just at present I am so interested in him that I would gladly make an effort. Besides, I am glad to have anything to help to pass the time. Harker is out, following up clues; and so are Lord Godalming and Quincey. Van Helsing sits in my study poring over the record prepared by the Harkers; he seems to think that by accurate knowledge of all details he will light upon some clue. He does not wish to be disturbed in the work, without cause. I would have taken him with me to see the patient, only I thought that after his last repulse he might not care to go again. There was also another reason: Renfield might not speak so freely before a third person as when he and I were alone.

I found him sitting out in the middle of the floor on his stool, a pose which is generally indicative of some mental energy on his part. When I came in, he said at once, as though the question had been waiting on his lips: —

"What about souls?" It was evident then that my surmise had been correct. Unconscious cerebration was doing its work, even with the lunatic. I determined to have the matter out. "What about them yourself?" I asked. He did not reply for a moment but looked all round him, and up and down, as though he expected to find some inspiration for an answer.

"I don't want any souls!" he said in a feeble, apologetic way. The matter seemed preying on his mind, and so I determined to use it — to "be cruel only to be kind."° So I said: —

"You like life, and you want life?"

"Oh yes! but that is all right; you needn't worry about that!"

"But," I asked, "how are we to get the life without getting the soul also?" This seemed to puzzle him, so I followed it up: —

"A nice time you'll have some time when you're flying out there, with the souls of thousands of flies and spiders and birds and cats buzzing and twittering and miauing all round you. You've got their lives, you know, and you must put up with their souls!" Something seemed to affect his imagination, for he put his fingers to his ears and shut his eyes, screwing them up tightly just as a small boy does when his

---

"be cruel only to be kind": After reviling his mother, Queen Gertrude, for having married her late husband's murderer, Hamlet tells her that he must "be cruel only to be kind" (*Hamlet* 3.4.185).

face is being soaped. There was something pathetic in it that touched me; it also gave me a lesson, for it seemed that before me was a child — only a child, though the features were worn, and the stubble on the jaws was white. It was evident that he was undergoing some process of mental disturbance, and, knowing how his past moods had interpreted things seemingly foreign to himself, I thought I would enter into his mind as well as I could and go with him. The first step was to restore confidence, so I asked him, speaking pretty loud so that he would hear me through his closed ears: —

"Would you like some sugar to get your flies round again!" He seemed to wake up all at once, and shook his head. With a laugh he replied: —

"Not much! flies are poor things, after all!" After a pause he added "But I don't want their souls buzzing round me, all the same."

"Or spiders" I went on.

"Blow spiders! What's the use of spiders? There isn't anything in them to eat or" — he stopped suddenly, as though reminded of a forbidden topic.

"So, so!" I thought to myself, "this is the second time he has suddenly stopped at the word 'drink'; what does it mean?" Renfield seemed himself aware of having made a lapse, for he hurried on, as though to distract my attention from it: —

"I don't take any stock at all in such matters. 'Rats and mice and such small deer' as Shakespeare has it 'chicken-feed of the larder'° they might be called. I'm past all that sort of nonsense. You might as well ask a man to eat molecules with a pair of chop-sticks, as to try to interest me about the lesser carnivora, when I know of what is before me."

"I see," I said. "You want big things that you can make your teeth meet in? How would you like to breakfast on elephant?"

"What ridiculous nonsense you are talking!" He was getting too wide awake, so I thought I would press him hard. "I wonder," I said reflectively, "what an elephant's soul is like!"

The effect I desired was obtained, for he at once fell from his high-horse and became a child again.

"I don't want an elephant's soul, or, any soul at all!" he said. For a few moments he sat despondently. Suddenly he jumped to his feet, with his eyes blazing and all the signs of intense cerebral excitement. "To

---

°*Rats and mice . . . larder':* In *King Lear,* Edgar, disguised as the madman Poor Tom, tells the king's party that "mice and rats and such small deer / Have been Tom's food for seven long year" (*King Lear* 3.4.137–38).

hell with you and your souls!" he shouted. "Why do you plague me about souls. Haven't I got enough to worry, and pain, and distract me already, without thinking of souls!" He looked so hostile that I thought he was in for another homicidal fit, so I blew my whistle. The instant, however, that I did so he became calm, and said apologetically: —

"Forgive me, Doctor; I forgot myself. You do not need any help. I am so worried in my mind that I am apt to be irritable. If you only knew the problem I have to face, and that I am working out, you would pity, and tolerate, and pardon me. Pray do not put me in a strait-waistcoat. I want to think and I cannot think freely when my body is confined. I am sure you will understand!" He had evidently self-control; so when the attendants came I told them not to mind, and they withdrew. Renfield watched them go; when the door was closed he said, with considerable dignity and sweetness: —

"Dr. Seward you have been very considerate towards me. Believe me that I am very very grateful to you!" I thought it well to leave him in this mood, and so I came away. There is certainly something to ponder over in this man's state. Several points seem to make what the American interviewer calls "a story," if one could only get them in proper order. Here they are: —

Will not mention "drinking."

Fears the thought of being burdened with the "soul" of anything.

Has no dread of wanting "life" in the future.

Despises the meaner forms of life altogether, though he dreads being haunted by their souls.

Logically all these things point one way! he has assurance of some kind that he will acquire some higher life. He dreads the consequence — the burden of a soul. Then it is a human life he looks to!

And the assurance —?

Merciful God! the Count has been to him, and there is some new scheme of terror afoot!

Later. — I went after my round to Van Helsing and told him my suspicion. He grew very grave; and, after thinking the matter over for a while asked me to take him to Renfield. I did so. As we came to the door we heard the lunatic within singing gaily, as he used to do in the time which now seems so long ago. When we entered we saw with amazement that he had spread out his sugar as of old; the flies, lethargic with the autumn, were beginning to buzz into the room. We tried to make him talk of the subject of our previous conversation, but he would not attend. He went on with his singing, just as though we had not been present. He had got a scrap of paper and was folding it into a note-book. We had to come away as ignorant as we went in.

His is a curious case indeed; we must watch him to-night.

Letter, Mitchell, Sons and Candy to Lord Godalming

"1 *October*

"My Lord,

"We are at all times only too happy to meet your wishes. We beg, with regard to the desire of your Lordship, expressed by Mr. Harker on your behalf, to supply the following information concerning the sale and purchase of No. 347, Piccadilly. The original vendors are the executors of the late Mr. Archibald Winter-Suffield. The purchaser is a foreign nobleman, Count de Ville, who effected the purchase himself paying the purchase money in notes 'over the counter,' if your Lordship will pardon us using so vulgar an expression. Beyond this we know nothing whatever of him.

"We are, my Lord,

"Your Lordship's humble servants,

"MITCHELL, SONS & CANDY."

Dr. Seward's Diary

2 *October.* — I placed a man in the corridor last night, and told him to make an accurate note of any sound he might hear from Renfield's room, and gave him instructions that if there should be anything strange he was to call me. After dinner, when we had all gathered round the fire in the study — Mrs. Harker having gone to bed — we discussed the attempts and discoveries of the day. Harker was the only one who had any result, and we are in great hopes that his clue may be an important one.

Before going to bed I went round to the patient's room and looked in through the observation trap. He was sleeping soundly, and his heart rose and fell with regular respiration.

This morning the man on duty reported to me that a little after midnight he was restless and kept saying his prayers somewhat loudly. I asked him if that was all; he replied that it was all he heard. There was something about his manner so suspicious that I asked him point blank if he had been asleep. He denied sleep, but admitted to having "dozed" for a while. It is too bad that men cannot be trusted unless they are watched.

To-day Harker is out following up his clue, and Art and Quincey are looking after horses. Godalming thinks that it will be well to have horses always in readiness, for when we get the information which we seek there will be no time to lose. We must sterilize all the imported earth between sunrise and sunset; we shall thus catch the Count at his weakest, and without a refuge to fly to. Van Helsing is off to the British Museum looking up some authorities on ancient medicine. The old physicians took account of things which their followers do not accept, and the Professor is searching for witch and demon cures which may be useful to us later.

I sometimes think we must be all mad and that we shall wake to sanity in strait-waistcoats.

Later. — We have met again. We seem at last to be on the track, and our work of to-morrow may be the beginning of the end. I wonder if Renfield's quiet has anything to do with this. His moods have so followed the doings of the Count, that the coming destruction of the monster may be carried to him in some subtle way. If we could only get some hint as to what passed in his mind, between the time of my argument with him to-day and his resumption of fly-catching, it might afford us a valuable clue. He is now seemingly quiet for a spell . . . . Is he? —— that wild yell seemed to come from his room . . . .

The attendant came bursting into my room and told me that Renfield had somehow met with some accident. He had heard him yell; and when he went to him found him lying on his face on the floor, all covered with blood. I must go at once. . . . .

CHAPTER XXI. DR. SEWARD'S DIARY

3 *October.* — Let me put down with exactness all that happened, as well as I can remember it, since last I made an entry. Not a detail that I can recall must be forgotten; in all calmness I must proceed.

When I came to Renfield's room I found him lying on the floor on his left side in a glittering pool of blood. When I went to move him, it became at once apparent that he had received some terrible injuries; there seemed none of that unity of purpose between the parts of the body which marks even lethargic sanity. As the face was exposed I could see that it was horribly bruised, as though it had been beaten against the floor — indeed it was from the face wounds that the pool of blood originated. The attendant who was kneeling beside the body said to me as we turned him over: —

"I think, sir, his back is broken. See, both his right arm and leg and the whole side of his face are paralysed." How such a thing could have happened puzzled the attendant beyond measure. He seemed quite bewildered, and his brows were gathered in as he said: —

"I can't understand the two things. He could mark his face like that by beating his own head on the ground. I saw a young woman do it once at the Eversfield Asylum before anyone could lay hands on her. And I suppose he might have broke his back by falling out of bed, if he got in an awkward kink. But for the life of me I can't imagine how the two things occurred. If his back was broke, he couldn't beat his head; and if his face was like that before the fall out of bed, there would be marks of it." I said to him: —

"Go to Dr. Van Helsing, and ask him to kindly come here at once. I want him without an instant's delay." The man ran off, and within a very few minutes the Professor, in his dressing gown and slippers, appeared. When he saw Renfield on the ground, he looked keenly at him a moment and then turned to me. I think he recognized my thought in my eyes, for he said very quietly, manifestly for the ears of the attendant: —

"Ah, a sad accident! He will need very careful watching, and much attention. I shall stay with you myself; but I shall first dress myself. If you will remain I shall in a few minutes join you."

The patient was now breathing stertorously, and it was easy to see that he had suffered some terrible injury. Van Helsing returned with extraordinary celerity, bearing with him a surgical case. He had evidently been thinking and had his mind made up; for, almost before he looked at the patient, he whispered to me: —

"Send the attendant away. We must be alone with him when he becomes conscious, after the operation." So I said: —

"I think that will do now, Simmons. We have done all that we can at present. You had better go your round, and Dr. Van Helsing will operate. Let me know instantly if there be anything unusual anywhere."

The man withdrew, and we went into a strict examination of the patient. The wounds of the face were superficial; the real injury was a depressed fracture of the skull, extending right up through the motor area. The Professor thought a moment and said: —

"We must reduce the pressure and get back to normal conditions, as far as can be; the rapidity of the suffusion shows the terrible nature of his injury. The whole motor area seems affected. The suffusion of the brain will increase quickly, so we must trephine° at once or it may be too late." As he was speaking there was a soft tapping at the door. I went over and opened it and found in the corridor without, Arthur and Quincey in pyjamas and slippers: the former spoke: —

"I heard your man call up Dr. Van Helsing and tell him of an accident. So I woke Quincey, or rather called for him as he was not asleep. Things are moving too quickly and too strangely for sound sleep for any of us these times. I've been thinking that to-morrow night will not see things as they have been. We'll have to look back — and forward a little more than we have done. May we come in?" I nodded, and held the door open till they had entered; then I closed it again. When Quincey saw the attitude and state of the patient, and noted the horrible pool on the floor, he said softly: —

"My God! what has happened to him? Poor, poor devil!" I told him briefly, and added that we expected he would recover consciousness after the operation — for a short time at all events. He went at once and sat down on the edge of the bed, with Godalming beside him; we all watched in patience.

"We shall wait," said Van Helsing, "just long enough to fix the best spot for trephining, so that we may most quickly and perfectly remove the blood clot; for it is evident that the hæmorrhage is increasing."

The minutes during which we waited passed with fearful slowness. I had a horrible sinking in my heart, and from Van Helsing's face I gathered that he felt some fear or apprehension as to what was to come. I dreaded the words that Renfield might speak. I was positively afraid to think; but the conviction of what was coming was on me, as I have read of men who have heard the death-watch.° The poor man's breathing came in uncertain gasps. Each instant he seemed as though he would open his eyes and speak; but then would follow a prolonged stertorous breath, and he would relapse into a more fixed insensibility. Inured as I was to sick beds and death, this suspense grew, and grew upon me. I could almost hear the beating of my own heart; and the blood surging through my temples sounded like blows from a hammer. The silence finally became agonising. I looked at my companions, one after another, and saw from their flushed faces and damp brows that they were enduring equal torture. There was a nervous suspense over us all, as though overhead some dread bell would peal out powerfully when we should least expect it.

---

trephine: To cut out a small piece of bone from the skull, usually in order to remove a clot or tumor.   **death-watch:** Insects that make a noise like the ticking of a clock, thought to foretell death (*OED; Enc. Brit.* 11th).

At last there came a time when it was evident that the patient was sinking fast; he might die at any moment. I looked up at the Professor and caught his eyes fixed on mine. His face was sternly set as he spoke: —

"There is no time to lose. His words may be worth many lives; I have been thinking so, as I stood here. It may be there is a soul at stake! We shall operate just above the ear."

Without another word he made the operation. For a few moments the breathing continued to be stertorous. Then there came a breath so prolonged that it seemed as though it would tear open his chest. Suddenly his eyes opened, and became fixed in a wild, helpless stare. This was continued for a few moments; then it softened into a glad surprise, and from the lips came a sigh of relief. He moved convulsively, and as he did so, said: —

"I'll be quiet, Doctor. Tell them to take off the strait-waistcoat. I have had a terrible dream, and it has left me so weak that I cannot move. What's wrong with my face? it feels all swollen, and it smarts dreadfully." He tried to turn his head; but even with the effort his eyes seemed to grow glassy again, so I gently put it back. Then Van Helsing said in a quiet grave tone: —

"Tell us your dream, Mr. Renfield." As he heard the voice his face brightened through its mutilation, and he said: —

"That is Dr. Van Helsing. How good it is of you to be here. Give me some water, my lips are dry; and I shall try to tell you. I dreamed" — he stopped and seemed fainting, I called quietly to Quincey — "The brandy — it is in my study — quick!" He flew and returned with a glass, the decanter of brandy and a carafe of water. We moistened the parched lips, and the patient quickly revived. It seemed however that his poor injured brain had been working in the interval, for, when he was quite conscious, he looked at me piercingly with an agonised confusion which I shall never forget, and said: —

"I must not deceive myself; it was no dream, but all a grim reality." Then his eyes roved round the room; as they caught sight of the two figures sitting patiently on the edge of the bed he went on: —

"If I were not sure already, I would know from them." For an instant his eyes closed — not with pain or sleep but voluntarily, as though he were bringing all his faculties to bear; when he opened them he said, hurriedly, and with more energy than he had yet displayed: —

"Quick, Doctor, quick. I am dying! I feel that I have but a few minutes; and then I must go back to death — or worse! Wet my lips with brandy again. I have something that I must say before I die; or before my poor crushed brain dies anyhow. Thank you! It was that night after you left me, when I implored you to let me go away. I couldn't speak then, for I felt my tongue was tied; but I was as sane then, except in that way, as I am now. I was in an agony of despair for a long time after you left me; it seemed hours. Then there came a sudden peace to me. My brain seemed to become cool again, and I realized where I was. I heard the dogs bark behind our house, but not where He was!" As he spoke Van Helsing's eyes never blinked, but his hand came out and met mine and gripped it hard. He did not, however, betray himself; he nodded slightly, and said: "Go on," in a low voice. Renfield proceeded: —

"He came up to the window in the mist, as I had seen him often before; but he was solid then — not a ghost, and his eyes were fierce like a man's when angry. He was laughing with his red mouth; the sharp white teeth glinted in the moonlight when he turned to look back over the belt of trees, to where the dogs were barking. I wouldn't ask him to come in at first, though I knew he wanted to — just as he had wanted all along. Then he began promising me things — not in words but by doing them." He was interrupted by a word from the Professor: —

"How?"

"By making them happen; just as he used to send in the flies when the sun was shining. Great big fat ones with steel and sapphire on their wings; and big moths, in the night, with skull and cross-bones on their backs." Van Helsing nodded to him as he whispered to me unconsciously: —

"The *Acherontia atropos of the Sphinges* — what you call the 'Death's-head moth!'" The patient went on without stopping.

"Then he began to whisper: 'Rats, rats, rats! Hundreds, thousands, millions of them, and every one a life; and dogs to eat them, and cats too. All lives! all red blood, with years of life in it; and not merely buzzing flies!' I laughed at him, for I wanted to see what he could do. Then the dogs howled, away beyond the dark trees in His house. He beckoned me to the window. I got up and looked out, and He raised his hands, and seemed to call out without using any words. A dark mass spread over the grass, coming on like the shape of a flame of fire; and then He moved the mist to the right and left, and I could see that there were thousands of rats with their eyes blazing red — like His, only smaller. He held up his hand, and they all stopped; and I thought He seemed to be saying: 'All these lives will I give you, ay, and many more and greater, through countless ages, if you will fall down and worship me!'° And

if you will fall down and worship me: When the devil shows Jesus "all the kingdoms of the world," he says to him, "All these things will I give thee, if thou wilt fall down and worship me" (Matt. 4.8–9; see also Luke 4.5–7).

then a red cloud, like the colour of blood, seemed to close over my eyes; and before I knew what I was doing, I found myself opening the sash and saying to Him: 'Come in, Lord and Master!' the rats were all gone, but He slid into the room through the sash, though it was only open an inch wide — just as the Moon herself has often come in through the tiniest crack, and has stood before me in all her size and splendour."

His voice was weaker, so I moistened his lips with the brandy again, and he continued; but it seemed as though his memory had gone on working in the interval for his story was further advanced. I was about to call him back to the point, but Van Helsing whispered to me: "Let him go on. Do not interrupt him; he cannot go back, and may-be could not proceed at all if once he lost the thread of his thought." He proceeded: —

"All day I waited to hear from him, but he did not send me anything, not even a blow-fly, and when the moon got up I was pretty angry with him. When he slid in through the window, though it was shut, and did not even knock, I got mad with him. He sneered at me, and his white face looked out of the mist with his red eyes gleaming, and he went on as though he owned the whole place, and I was no one. He didn't even smell the same as he went by me. I couldn't hold him. I thought that, somehow, Mrs. Harker had come into the room."

The two men sitting on the bed stood up and came over standing behind him so that he could not see them, but where they could hear better. They were both silent, but the Professor started and quivered; his face, however, grew grimmer and sterner still. Renfield went on without noticing: —

"When Mrs. Harker came in to see me this afternoon she wasn't the same; it was like tea after the teapot had been watered." Here we all moved, but no one said a word; he went on: —

"I didn't know that she was here till she spoke; and she didn't look the same. I don't care for the pale people; I like them with lots of blood in them, and hers had all seemed to have run out. I didn't think of it at the time; but when she went away I began to think, and it made me mad to know that He had been taking the life out of her." I could feel that the rest quivered, as I did; but we remained otherwise still. "So when He came to-night I was ready for Him. I saw the mist stealing in, and I grabbed it tight. I had heard that madmen have unnatural strength; and as I knew I was a madman — at times anyhow — I resolved to use my power. Ay, and He felt it too, for He had to come out of the mist to struggle with me. I held tight; and I thought I was going to win, for I didn't mean Him to take any more of her life, till I saw His eyes. They burned into me, and my strength became like water. He slipped through it, and when I tried to cling to Him, He raised me up and flung me down. There was a red cloud before me, and a noise like thunder, and the mist seemed to steal away under the door." His voice was becoming fainter and his breath more stertorous. Van Helsing stood up instinctively.

"We know the worst now," he said. "He is here, and we know his purpose. It may not be too late. Let us be armed — the same as we were the other night, but lose no time; there is not an instant to spare." There was no need to put our fear, nay our conviction, into words — we shared them in common. We all hurried and took from our rooms the same things that we had when we entered the Count's house. The Professor had his ready, and as we met in the corridor he pointed to them significantly as he said: —

"They never leave me; and they shall not till this unhappy business is over. Be wise also, my friends. It is no common enemy that we deal with. Alas! alas! that that dear Madam Mina should suffer." He stopped; his voice was breaking, and I do not know if rage or terror predominated in my own heart.

Outside the Harkers' door we paused. Art and Quincey held back, and the latter said: —

"Should we disturb her?"

"We must," said Van Helsing grimly. "If the door be locked, I shall break it in."

"May it not frighten her terribly? It is unusual to break into a lady's room!" Van Helsing said solemnly.

"You are always right; but this is life and death. All chambers are alike to the doctor; and even were they not they are all as one to me to-night. Friend John, when I turn the handle, if the door does not open, do you put your shoulder down and shove; and you too, my friends. Now!"

He turned the handle as he spoke, but the door did not yield. We threw ourselves against it; with a crash it burst open, and we almost fell headlong into the room. The Professor did actually fall, and I saw across him as he gathered himself up from hands and knees. What I saw appalled me. I felt my hair rise like bristles on the back of my neck, and my heart seemed to stand still.

The moonlight was so bright that through the thick yellow blind the room was light enough to see. On the bed beside the window lay Jonathan Harker, his face flushed and breathing heavily as though in a stupor. Kneeling on the near edge of the bed facing outwards was the white-clad figure of his wife. By her side stood a tall, thin man, clad in black. His face was turned from us, but the instant we saw we all recognised the Count — in every way, even to the scar on his forehead. With his left hand he held both Mrs. Harker's hands, keeping them away with her arms at full tension; his right hand gripped her by the back of the neck, forcing her face down on his bosom. Her white nightdress was smeared with blood, and a thin stream trickled down the man's bare breast which was shown by his torn-open dress. The attitude of the two had a terrible resemblance to a child forcing a kitten's nose into a saucer of milk to compel it to drink. As we burst into the room, the Count turned his face, and the hellish look that I had heard described seemed to leap into it. His eyes flamed red with devilish passion; the great nostrils of the white aquiline nose opened wide and quivered at the edge; and the white sharp teeth, behind the full lips of the blood-dripping mouth, champed together like those of a wild beast. With a wrench, which threw his victim back upon the bed as though hurled from a height, he turned and sprang at us. But by this time the Professor had gained his feet, and was holding towards him the envelope which contained the Sacred Wafer. The Count suddenly stopped, just as poor Lucy had done outside the tomb, and cowered back. Further and further back he cowered, as we, lifting our crucifixes, advanced. The moonlight suddenly failed, as a great black cloud sailed across the sky; and when the gaslight sprang up under Quincey's match, we saw nothing but a faint vapour. This, as we looked, trailed under the door, which with the recoil from its bursting open, had swung back to its old position. Van Helsing, Art, and I moved forward to Mrs. Harker, who by this time had drawn her breath and with it had given a scream so wild, so ear-piercing, so despairing that it seems to me now that it will ring in my ears till my dying day. For a few seconds she lay in her helpless attitude and disarray. Her face was ghastly, with a pallor which was accentuated by the blood which smeared her lips and cheeks and chin; from her throat trickled a thin stream of blood. Her eyes were mad with terror. Then she put before her face her poor crushed hands, which bore on their whiteness the red mark of the Count's terrible grip, and from behind them came a low desolate wail which made the terrible scream seem only the quick expression of an endless grief. Van Helsing stepped forward and drew the coverlet gently over her body, whilst Art, after looking at her face for an instant despairingly, ran out of the room. Van Helsing whispered to me: —

"Jonathan is in a stupor such as we know the Vampire can produce. We can do nothing with poor Madam Mina for a few moments till she recovers herself; I must wake him!" He dipped the end of a towel in cold water and with it began to flick him on the face, his wife all the while holding her face between her hands and sobbing in a way that was heart-breaking to hear. I raised the blind, and looked out of the window. There was much moonshine; and as I looked I could see Quincey Morris run across the lawn and hide himself in the shadow of a great yew tree. It puzzled me to think why he was doing this; but at the instant I heard Harker's quick exclamation as he woke to partial consciousness, and turned to the bed. On his face, as there might well be, was a look of wild amazement. He seemed dazed for a few seconds, and then full consciousness seemed to burst upon him all at once, and he started up. His wife was aroused by the quick movement, and turned to him with her arms stretched out, as though to embrace him; instantly, however, she drew them in again, and putting her elbows together, held her hands before her face, and shuddered till the bed beneath her shook.

"In God's name what does this mean?" Harker cried out, "Dr. Seward, Dr. Van Helsing, what is it? What has happened? What is wrong? Mina, dear, what is it? What does that blood mean? My God, my God! has it come to this!" and, raising himself to his knees, he beat his hands wildly together. "Good God help us! help her! Oh, help her!" With a quick movement he jumped from bed, and began to pull on his clothes, — all the man in him awake at the need for instant exertion. "What has happened? Tell me all about it?" he cried without pausing. "Dr. Van Helsing, you love Mina, I know. Oh, do something to save her. It cannot have gone too far yet. Guard her while I look for *him!*" His wife, through her terror and horror and distress, saw some sure danger to him; instantly forgetting her own grief, she seized hold of him and cried out: —

"No! no! Jonathan, you must not leave me. I have suffered enough to-night, God knows, without the dread of his harming you. You must stay with me. Stay with these friends who will watch over you!" Her expression became frantic as she spoke; and, he yielding to her, she pulled him down sitting on the bed side, and clung to him fiercely.

Van Helsing and I tried to calm them both. The Professor held up his little golden crucifix, and said with wonderful calmness: —

"Do not fear, my dear. We are here; and whilst this is close to you no foul thing can approach. You are safe for to-night; and we must be calm and take counsel together." She shuddered and was silent, holding down her head on her husband's breast. When she raised it, his white night-robe was stained with blood where her lips had touched, and where the thin open wound in her neck had sent forth drops. The instant she saw it she drew back, with a low wail, and whispered, amidst choking sobs: —

"Unclean, unclean!° I must touch him or kiss him no more. Oh, that it should be that it is I who am now his worst enemy, and whom he may have most cause to fear." To this he spoke out resolutely: —

"Nonsense, Mina. It is a shame to me to hear such a word. I would not hear it of you; and I shall not hear it from you. May God judge me by my deserts, and punish me with more bitter suffering than even this hour, if by any act or will of mine anything ever come between us!" He put out his arms and folded her to his breast; and for a while she lay there sobbing. He looked at us over her bowed head, with eyes that blinked damply above his quivering nostrils; his mouth was set as steel. After a while her sobs became less frequent and more faint, and then he said to me, speaking with a studied calmness which I felt tried his nervous power to the utmost: —

"And now, Dr. Seward, tell me all about it. Too well I know the broad fact; tell me all that has been." I told him exactly what had happened, and he listened with seeming impassiveness; but his nostrils twitched and his eyes blazed as I told how the ruthless hands of the Count had held his wife in that terrible and horrid position, with her mouth to the open wound in his breast. It interested me, even at that moment, to see, that, whilst the face of white set passion worked convulsively over the bowed head, the hands tenderly and lovingly stroked the ruffled hair. Just as I had finished, Quincey and Godalming knocked at the door. They entered in obedience to our summons. Van Helsing looked at me questioningly. I understood him to mean if we were to take advantage of their coming to divert if possible the thoughts of the unhappy husband and wife from each other and from themselves; so on nodding acquiescence to him he asked them what they had seen or done. To which Lord Godalming answered: —

"I could not see him anywhere in the passage, or in any of our rooms. I looked in the study but, though he had been there, he had gone. He had however ——" He stopped suddenly looking at the poor drooping figure on the bed. Van Helsing said gravely: —

"Go on friend Arthur. We want here no more concealments. Our hope now is in knowing all. Tell freely!" So Art went on: —

Unclean, unclean: According to Lev. 13.45, the "leper in whom the plague is, his clothes shall be rent, and his head bare, and he shall put a covering upon his upper lip, and shall cry, Unclean, unclean."

"He had been there, and though it could only have been for a few seconds, he made rare hay of the place. All the manuscript had been burned, and the blue flames were flickering amongst the white ashes; the cylinders of your phonograph too were thrown on the fire, and the wax had helped the flames." Here I interrupted. "Thank God there is the other copy in the safe!" His face lit for a moment, but fell again as he went on: "I ran down stairs then, but could see no sign of him. I looked into Renfield's room; but there was no trace there except —!" Again he paused. "Go on," said Harker hoarsely; so he bowed his head and moistening his lips with his tongue, added: "except that the poor fellow is dead." Mrs. Harker raised her head, looking from one to the other of us as she said solemnly: —

"God's will be done!" I could not but feel that Art was keeping back something; but, as I took it that it was with a purpose, I said nothing. Van Helsing turned to Morris and asked: —

"And you, friend Quincey, have you any to tell?"

"A little," he answered. "It may be much eventually, but at present I can't say. I thought it well to know if possible where the Count would go when he left the house. I did not see him; but I saw a bat rise from Renfield's window, and flap westward. I expected to see him in some shape go back to Carfax; but he evidently sought some other lair. He will not be back to-night; for the sky is reddening in the east, and the dawn is close. We must work to-morrow!"

He said the latter words through his shut teeth. For a space of perhaps a couple of minutes there was silence, and I could fancy that I could hear the sound of our hearts beating; then Van Helsing said, placing his hand very tenderly on Mrs. Harker's head: —

"And now, Madam Mina — poor, dear, dear Madam Mina — tell us exactly what happened. God knows that I do not want that you be pained; but it is need that we know all. For now more than ever has all work to be done quick and sharp, and in deadly earnest. The day is close to us that must end all, if it may so be; and now is the chance that we may live and learn."

The poor, dear lady shivered, and I could see the tension of her nerves as she clasped her husband closer to her and bent her head lower and lower still on his breast. Then she raised her head proudly, and held out one hand to Van Helsing who took it in his, and, after stooping and kissing it reverently, held it fast. The other hand was locked in that of her husband, who held his other arm thrown round her protectingly. After a pause in which she was evidently ordering her thoughts, she began: —

"I took the sleeping draught which you had so kindly given me, but for a long time it did not act. I seemed to become more wakeful, and myriads of horrible fancies began to crowd in upon my mind — all of them connected with death, and vampires; with blood, and pain, and trouble." Her husband involuntarily groaned as she turned to him and said lovingly: "Do not fret, dear. You must be brave and strong, and help me through the horrible task. If you only knew what an effort it is to me to tell of this fearful thing at all, you would understand how much I need your help. Well, I saw I must try to help the medicine to its work with my will, if it was to do me any good, so I resolutely set myself to sleep. Sure enough sleep must soon have come to me, for I remember no more. Jonathan coming in had not waked me, for he lay by my side when next I remember. There was in the room the same thin white mist that I had before noticed. But I forget now if you know of this; you will find it in my diary which I shall show you later. I felt the same vague terror which had come to me before, and the same sense of some presence. I turned to wake Jonathan, but found that he slept so soundly that it seemed as if it was he who had taken the sleeping draught, and not I. I tried, but I could not wake him. This caused me a great fear, and I looked around terrified. Then indeed, my heart sank within me: beside the bed, as if he had stepped out of the mist — or rather as if the mist had turned into his figure, for it had entirely disappeared — stood a tall, thin man, all in black. I knew him at once from the descriptions of the others. The waxen face; the high aquiline nose, on which the light fell in a thin white line; the parted red lips, with the sharp white teeth showing between; and the red eyes that I had seemed to see in the sunset on the windows of St. Mary's Church at Whitby. I knew, too, the red scar on his forehead where Jonathan had struck him. For an instant my heart stood still, and I would have screamed out, only that I was paralysed. In the pause he spoke in a sort of keen, cutting, whisper, pointing as he spoke to Jonathan: —

'"Silence! If you make a sound I shall take him and dash his brains out before your very eyes.' I was appalled and was too bewildered to do or say anything. With a mocking smile, he placed one hand upon my shoulder and, holding me tight, bared my throat with the other, saying as he did so: 'First, a little refreshment to reward my exertions. You may as well be quiet; it is not the first time, or the second, that your veins have appeased my thirst!' I was bewildered, and, strangely enough, I did not want to hinder him. I suppose it is a part of the horrible curse that such is, when his touch is on his victim. And oh, my God, my God, pity me! He placed his reeking lips upon my throat!" Her husband groaned again. She clasped his hand harder, and looked at him pity-ingly, as if he were the injured one, and went on: —

"I felt my strength fading away, and I was in a half swoon. How long this horrible thing lasted I know not; but it seemed that a long time must have passed before he took his foul, awful, sneering mouth away. I saw it drip with the fresh blood!" The remembrance seemed for a while to overpower her, and she drooped and would have sunk down but for her husband's sustaining arm. With a great effort she recovered herself and went on: —

"Then he spoke to me mockingly, 'And so you, like the others, would play your brains against mine. You would help these men to hunt me and frustrate me in my designs! You know now, and they know in part already, and will know in full before long, what it is to cross my path. They should have kept their energies for use closer to home. Whilst they played wits against me — against me who commanded nations, and intrigued for them, and fought for them, hundreds of years before they were born — I was countermining them. And you, their best beloved one, are now to me, flesh of my flesh°; blood of my blood; kin of my kin; my bountiful wine-press for a while; and shall be later on my companion and my helper. You shall be avenged in turn; for not one of them but shall minister to your needs. But as yet you are to be pun-ished for what you have done. You have aided in thwarting me; now you shall come to my call. When my brain says "Come!" to you, you shall cross land or sea to do my bidding; and to that end this!' with that he pulled open his shirt, and with his long sharp nails opened a vein in his breast. When the blood began to spurt out, he took my hands in one of his, holding them tight, and with the other seized my neck and pressed my mouth to the wound, so that I must either suffocate or swallow some of the — Oh my God! my God! what have I done? What have I done to deserve such a fate, I who have tried to walk in meekness and righteous-ness all my days. God pity me! Look down on a poor soul in worse than mortal peril; and in mercy pity those to whom she is dear!" Then she began to rub her lips as though to cleanse them from pollution.

As she was telling her terrible story, the eastern sky began to quicken, and everything became more and more clear. Harker was still and quiet; but over his face, as the awful narrative went on, came a grey look which deepened and deepened in the morning light, till when the

---

flesh of my flesh: In Gen. 2.23, Adam says of the newly created Eve, "this is now bone of my bones, and flesh of my flesh."

first red streak of the coming dawn shot up, the flesh stood darkly out against the whitening hair.

We have arranged that one of us is to stay within call of the unhappy pair till we can meet together and arrange about taking action.

Of this I am sure: the sun rises to-day on no more miserable house in all the great round of its daily course.

CHAPTER XXII. JONATHAN HARKER'S JOURNAL

3 October. — As I must do something or go mad; I write this diary. It is now six o'clock, and we are to meet in the study in half an hour and take something to eat; for Dr. Van Helsing and Dr. Seward are agreed that if we do not eat we cannot work our best. Our best will be, God knows, required to-day. I must keep writing at every chance, for I dare not stop to think. All, big and little, must go down; perhaps at the end the little things may teach us most. The teaching, big or little, could not have landed Mina or me anywhere worse than we are to-day. However, we must trust and hope. Poor Mina told me just now, with the tears running down her dear cheeks, that it is in trouble and trial that our faith is tested — that we must keep on trusting; and that God will aid us up to the end. The end! oh my God! what end? . . . . . To work! To work!

When Dr. Van Helsing and Dr. Seward had come back from seeing poor Renfield, we went gravely into what was to be done. First, Dr. Seward told us that when he and Dr. Van Helsing had gone down to the room below they had found Renfield lying on the floor, all in a heap. His face was all bruised and crushed in, and the bones of the neck were broken.

Dr. Seward asked the attendant who was on duty in the passage if he had heard anything. He said that he had been sitting down — he confessed to half dozing — when he heard loud voices in the room, and then Renfield had called out loudly several times, "God! God! God!" After that there was a sound of falling, and when he entered the room he found him lying on the floor, face down, just as the doctors had seen him. Van Helsing asked if he had heard "voices" or "a voice," and he said he could not say; that at first it had seemed to him as if there were two, but as there was no one in the room it could have been only one. He could swear to it, if required, that the word "God" was spoken by the patient. Dr. Seward said to us, when we were alone, that he did not wish to go into the matter; the question of an inquest had to be considered, and it would never do to put forward the truth, as no one would believe it. As it was, he thought that on the attendant's evidence he could give a certificate of death by misadventure in falling from bed. In case the coroner should demand it, there would be a formal inquest, necessarily to the same result.

When the question began to be discussed as to what should be our next step, the very first thing we decided was that Mina should be in full confidence; that nothing of any sort — no matter how painful — should be kept from her. She herself agreed as to its wisdom, and it was pitiful to see her so brave and yet so sorrowful, and in such a depth of despair. "There must be no more concealment," she said, "Alas!" we have had too much already. And besides there is nothing in all the world that can give me more pain than I have already endured — than I suffer now! Whatever may happen, it must be of new hope or of new courage to me!" Van Helsing was looking at her fixedly as she spoke, and said, suddenly but quietly: —

"But dear Madam Mina are you not afraid; not for yourself, but for others from yourself, after what has happened?" Her face grew set in its lines, but her eyes shone with the devotion of a martyr as she answered: —

"Ah no! for my mind is made up!"

"To what?" he asked gently, whilst we were all very still; for each in our own way we had a sort of vague idea of what she meant. Her answer came with direct simplicity, as though she were simply stating a fact: —

"Because if I find in myself — and I shall watch keenly for it — a sign of harm to any that I love, I shall die!"

"You would not kill yourself?" he asked, hoarsely.

"I would; if there were no friend who loved me, who would save me such a pain, and so desperate an effort!" She looked at him meaningly as she spoke. He was sitting down; but now he rose and came close to her and put his hand on her head as he said solemnly:

"My child, there is such an one if it were for your good. For myself I could hold it in my account with God to find such an euthanasia for you; even at this moment if it were best. Nay, were it safe! But my child —" for a moment he seemed choked, and a great sob rose in his throat; he gulped it down and went on: —

"There are here some who would stand between you and death. You must not die. You must not die by any hand; but least of all by your own. Until the other, who has fouled your sweet life, is true dead you must not die; for if he is still with the quick Un-dead, your death would make you even as he is. No, you must live! You must struggle and strive to live, though death would seem a boon unspeakable. You must fight Death himself, though he come to you in pain or in joy; by the day, or the night; in safety or in peril! On your living soul I charge you that you do not die — nay nor think of death — till this great evil be past." The poor dear grew white as death, and shook and shivered, as I have seen a quicksand shake and shiver at the incoming of the tide. We were all silent; we could do nothing. At length she grew more calm and turning to him said, sweetly, but oh! so sorrowfully, as she held out her hand: —

"I promise you, my dear friend, that if God will let me live, I shall strive to do so; till, if it may be in His good time, this horror may have passed away from me." She was so good and brave that we all felt that our hearts were strengthened to work and endure for her, and we began to discuss what we were to do. I told her that she was to have all the papers in the safe, and all the papers or diaries and phonographs we might hereafter use; and was to keep the record as she had done before. She was pleased with the prospect of anything to do — if "pleased" could be used in connection with so grim an interest.

As usual Van Helsing had thought ahead of everyone else, and was prepared with an exact ordering of our work.

"It is perhaps well" he said "that at our meeting after our visit to Carfax we decided not to do anything with the earth-boxes that lay there. Had we done so, the Count must have guessed our purpose, and would doubtless have taken measures in advance to frustrate such an effort with regard to the others; but now he does not know our intentions. Nay more, in all probability, he does not know that such a power exists to us as can sterilize his lairs, so that he cannot use them as of old. We are now so much further advanced in our knowledge as to their disposition, that, when we have examined the house in Piccadilly, we may track the very last of them. To-day, then, is ours; and in it rests our hope. The sun that rose on our sorrow this morning guards us in its course. Until it sets to-night, that monster must retain whatever form he now has. He is confined within the limitations of his earthly envelope. He cannot melt into thin air nor disappear through cracks or chinks or crannies. If he go through a door-way, he must open the door like a mortal. And so we have this day to hunt out all his lairs and sterilize them. So we shall, if we have not yet catch him and destroy him, drive him to bay in some place where the catching and the destroying shall be, in time, sure." Here I started up for I could not contain myself at the thought that the minutes and seconds so preciously laden with Mina's life and happiness were flying from us, since whilst we talked action was possible.

But Van Helsing held up his hand warningly. "Nay, friend Jonathan," he said, "in this, the quickest way home is the longest way, so your proverb say. We shall all act, and act with desperate quick, when the time has come. But think, in all probable the key of the situation is in that house in Piccadilly. The Count may have many houses which he has bought. Of them he will have deeds of purchase, keys and other things. He will have paper that he write on; he will have his book of cheques. There are many belongings that he must have somewhere; why not in this place so central, so quiet, where he come and go by the front or the back at all hour, when in the very vast of the traffic there is none to notice. We shall go there and search that house; and when we learn what it holds, then we do what our friend Arthur call, in his phrases of hunt 'stop the earths'° and so we run down our old fox — so? is it not?"

"Then let us come at once," I cried, "we are wasting the precious, precious time!" The Professor did not move, but simply said: —

"And how are we to get into that house in Piccadilly?"

"Any way!" I cried. "We shall break in if need be."

"And your police; where will they be, and what will they say?"

I was staggered; but I knew that if he wished to delay he had a good reason for it. So I said, as quietly as I could: —

"Don't wait more than need be; you know, I am sure, what torture I am in."

"Ah, my child, that I do; and indeed there is no wish of me to add to your anguish. But just think, what can we do, until all the world be at movement. Then will come our time. I have thought and thought, and it seems to me that the simplest way is the best of all. Now we wish to get into the house, but we have no key; is it not so?" I nodded.

"Now suppose that you were in truth, the owner of that house, and could not still get in; and think there was to you no conscience of the housebreaker, what would you do?"

"I should get a respectable locksmith, and set him to work to pick the lock for me."

"And your police, they would interfere, would they not?"

"Oh, no! not if they knew the man was properly employed."

"Then," he looked at me keenly as he spoke, "all that is in doubt is the conscience of the employer, and the belief of your policemen as to whether or no that employer has a good conscience or a bad one. Your police must indeed be zealous men and clever — oh so clever! — in

---

stop the earths: In fox hunting, to close up the fox dens before the hunt begins (*Enc. Brit.* OL).

reading the heart, that they trouble themselves in such matter. No, no, my friend Jonathan, you go take the lock off a hundred empty house in this your London, or of any city in the world; and if you do it as such things are rightly done, and at the time such things are rightly done, no one will interfere. I have read of a gentleman who owned a so fine house in your London, and when he went for months of summer to Zwitzerland and lock up his house, some burglar came and broke window at back and got in. Then he went and made open the shutters in front and walk out and in through the door, before the very eyes of the police. Then he have an auction in that house, and advertise it, and put up big notice; and when the day come he sell off by a great auctioneer all the goods of that other man who own them. Then he go to a builder, and he sell him that house, making an agreement that he pull it down and take all away within a certain time. And your police and other authority help him all they can. And when that owner come back from his holiday in Zwitzerland he find only an empty hole where his house had been. This was all done *en règle*°; and in our work we shall be *en règle* too. We shall not go so early that the policeman who have then little to think of, shall deem it strange; but we shall go after ten o'clock when there are many about, and when such things would be done were we indeed owners of the house."

I could not but see how right he was, and the terrible despair of Mina's face became relaxed a thought; there was hope in such good counsel. Van Helsing went on: —

"When once within that house we may find more clues; at any rate some of us can remain there whilst the rest find the other places where there be more earth-boxes — at Bermondsey and Mile End."

Lord Godalming stood up. "I can be of some use here" he said. "I shall wire to my people to have horses and carriages where they will be most convenient."

"Look here, old fellow," said Morris, "it is a capital idea to have all ready in case we want to go horsebacking; but don't you think that one of your snappy carriages with its heraldic adornments in a byeway of Walworth or Mile End would attract too much attention for our purposes? It seems to me that we ought to take cabs when we go south or east; and even leave them somewhere near the neighbourhood we are going to."

"Friend Quincey is right!" said the Professor. "His head is what you call in plane with the horizon. It is a difficult thing that we go to do, and we do not want no peoples to watch us if so it may."

en règle: In an orderly or regular way, conforming to prescriptions (French).

Mina took a growing interest in everything, and I was rejoiced to see that the exigency of affairs was helping her to forget for a time the terrible experience of the night. She was very, very pale — almost ghastly, and so thin that her lips were drawn away, showing her teeth in somewhat of prominence. I did not mention this last, lest it should give her needless pain; but it made my blood run cold in my veins to think of what had occurred with poor Lucy when the Count had sucked her blood. As yet there was no sign of the teeth growing sharper; but the time as yet was short, and there was time for fear.

When we came to the discussion of the sequence of our efforts and of the disposition of our forces, there were new sources of doubt. It was finally agreed that before starting for Piccadilly we should destroy the Count's lair close at hand. In case he should find it out too soon, we should thus be still ahead of him in our work of destruction; and his presence in his purely material shape, and at his weakest, might give us some new clue.

As to the disposal of forces, it was suggested by the Professor that, after our visit to Carfax, we should all enter the house in Piccadilly; that the two doctors and I should remain there, whilst Lord Godalming and Quincey found the lairs at Walworth and Mile End and destroyed them. It was possible, if not likely, the Professor urged, that the Count might appear in Piccadilly during the day, and that if so we might be able to cope with him then and there. At any rate we might be able to follow him in force. To this plan I strenuously objected, in so far as my going was concerned, for I said that I intended to stay and protect Mina. I thought that my mind was made up on the subject; but Mina would not listen to my objection. She said that there might be some law matter in which I could be useful; that amongst the Count's papers might be some clue which I could understand out of my experience in Transylvania; and that, as it was, all the strength we could muster was required to cope with the Count's extraordinary power. I had to give in, for Mina's resolution was fixed; she said that it was the last hope for *her* that we should all work together. "As for me," she said, "I have no fear. Things have been as bad as they can be; and whatever may happen must have in it some element of hope or comfort. Go my husband! God can, if He wishes it, guard me as well alone as with any one present." So I started up crying out: "Then in God's name let us come at once, for we are losing time. The Count may come to Piccadilly earlier than we think."

"Not so!" said Van Helsing holding up his hand.

"But why?" I asked.

"Do you forget," he said, with actually a smile, "that last night he banqueted heavily, and will sleep late?"

Did I forget! shall I ever — can I ever! Can any of us ever forget that terrible scene! Mina struggled hard to keep her brave countenance; but the pain overmastered her and she put her hands before her face, and shuddered whilst she moaned. Van Helsing had not intended to recall her frightful experience. He had simply lost sight of her and her part in the affair in his intellectual effort. When it struck him what he had said, he was horrified at his thoughtlessness and tried to comfort her. "Oh Madam Mina," he said, "dear, dear Madam Mina, alas! that I of all who so reverence you, should have said anything so forgetful. These stupid old lips of mine and this stupid old head do not deserve so; but you will forget it, will you not?" He bent low beside her as he spoke; she took his hands, and looking at him through her tears, said hoarsely: —

"No, I shall not forget, for it is well that I remember; and with it I have so much in memory of you that is sweet, that I take it all together. Now, you must all be going soon. Breakfast is ready, and we must all eat that we may be strong."

Breakfast was a strange meal to us all. We tried to be cheerful and encourage each other, and Mina was the brightest and most cheerful of us. When it was over, Van Helsing stood up and said: —

"Now, my dear friends, we go forth to our terrible enterprise. Are we all armed, as we were on that night when first we visited our enemy's lair; armed against ghostly as well as carnal attack?" We all assured him. "Then it is well. Now Madam Mina, you are in any case *quite* safe here until the sunset; and before then we shall return — if — We shall return! But before we go let me see you armed against personal attack. I have myself, since you came down, prepared your chamber by the placing of things of which we know, so that He may not enter. Now let me guard yourself. On your forehead I touch this piece of Sacred Wafer in the name of the Father, the Son, and —"

There was a fearful scream which almost froze our hearts to hear. As he had placed the Wafer on Mina's forehead, it had seared it — had burned into the flesh as though it had been a piece of white-hot metal. My poor darling's brain told her the significance of the fact as quickly as her nerves received the pain of it; and the two so overwhelmed her that her overwrought nature had its voice in that dreadful scream. But the words to her thought came quickly; the echo of the scream had not ceased to ring on the air when there came the reaction, and she sank on her knees on the floor in an agony of abasement. Pulling her beautiful hair over her face, as the leper of old his mantle, she wailed out: —

"Unclean! Unclean! Even the Almighty shuns my polluted flesh! I must bear this mark of shame upon my forehead until the Judgment Day." They all paused. I had thrown myself beside her in an agony of helpless grief, and putting my arms around held her tight. For a few minutes our sorrowful hearts beat together, whilst the friends around us turned away their eyes that ran tears silently. Then Van Helsing turned and said gravely; so gravely that I could not help feeling that he was in some way inspired, and was stating things outside himself: —

"It may be that you may have to bear that mark till God himself see fit, as He most surely shall, on the Judgment Day to redress all wrongs of the earth and of His children that He has placed thereon. And oh, Madam Mina, my dear, my dear, may we who love you be there to see, when that red scar, the sign of God's knowledge of what has been, shall pass away and leave your forehead as pure as the heart we know. For so surely as we live, that scar shall pass away when God sees right to lift the burden that is hard upon us. Till then we bear our Cross, as His Son did in obedience to His will. It may be that we are chosen instruments of His good pleasure, and that we ascend to His bidding as that other through stripes and shame; through tears and blood; through doubts and fears, and all that makes the difference between God and man."

There was hope in his words, and comfort; and they made for resignation. Mina and I both felt so, and simultaneously we each took one of the old man's hands and bent over and kissed it. Then without a word we all knelt down together, and, all holding hands, swore to be true to each other. We men pledged ourselves to raise the veil of sorrow from the head of her whom, each in his own way, we loved; and we prayed for help and guidance in the terrible task which lay before us.

It was then time to start. So I said farewell to Mina, a parting which neither of us shall forget to our dying day; and we set out.

To one thing I have made up my mind: if we find out that Mina must be a vampire in the end, then she shall not go into that unknown and terrible land alone. I suppose it is thus that in old times one vampire meant many; just as their hideous bodies could only rest in sacred earth, so the holiest love was the recruiting sergeant for their ghastly ranks.

We entered Carfax without trouble and found all things the same as on the first occasion. It was hard to believe that amongst so prosaic surroundings of neglect and dust and decay there was any ground for such fear as already we knew. Had not our minds been made up, and had there not been terrible memories to spur us on, we could hardly have proceeded with our task. We found no papers, or any sign of use in the house; and in the old chapel the great boxes looked just as we had seen them last. Dr. Van Helsing said to us solemnly as we stood before them: —

"And now, my friends, we have a duty here to do. We must sterilise this earth, so sacred of holy memories, that he has brought from a far distant land for such fell use. He has chosen this earth because it has been holy. Thus we defeat him with his own weapon, for we make it more holy still. It was sanctified to such use of man, now we sanctify it to God." As he spoke he took from his bag a screw-driver and a wrench, and very soon the top of one of the cases was thrown open. The earth smelled musty and close; but we did not somehow seem to mind, for our attention was concentrated on the Professor. Taking from his box a piece of the Sacred Wafer he laid it reverently on the earth, and then shutting down the lid began to screw it home, we aiding him as he worked.

One by one we treated in the same way each of the great boxes, and left them as we had found them to all appearance; but in each was a portion of the Host.

When we closed the door behind us, the Professor said solemnly: —

"So much is already done. If it may be that with all the others we can be so successful, then the sunset of this evening may shine on Madam Mina's forehead all white as ivory and with no stain!"

As we passed across the lawn on our way to the station to watch our train we could see the front of the asylum. I looked eagerly, and in the window of my own room saw Mina. I waved my hand to her, and nodded to tell that our work there was successfully accomplished. She nodded in reply to show that she understood. The last I saw, she was waving her hand in farewell. It was with a heavy heart that we sought the station and just caught the train, which was steaming in as we reached the platform.

I have written this in the train.

Piccadilly, 12:30 *o'clock.* — Just before we reached Fenchurch Street Lord Godalming said to me:

"Quincey and I will find a locksmith. You had better not come with us in case there should be any difficulty; for under the circumstances it wouldn't seem so bad for us to break into an empty house. But you are a solicitor and the Incorporated Law Society° might tell you that you

---

Incorporated Law Society: The organization that sets standards for the conduct of solicitors (*Enc. Brit.* OL).

should have known better." I demurred as to my not sharing any danger even of odium, but he went on: "Besides, it will attract less attention if there are not too many of us. My title will make it all right with the locksmith, and with any policeman that may come along. You had better go with Jack and the Professor and stay in the Green Park, somewhere in sight of the house; and when you see the door opened and the smith has gone away, do you all come across. We shall be on the look out for you, and shall let you in."

"The advice is good!" said Van Helsing, so we said no more. Godalming and Morris hurried off in a cab, we following in another. At the corner of Arlington Street our contingent got out and strolled into the Green Park. My heart beat as I saw the house on which so much of our hope was centred, looming up grim and silent in its deserted condition amongst its more lively and spruce-looking neighbours. We sat down on a bench within good view, and began to smoke cigars so as to attract as little attention as possible. The minutes seemed to pass with leaden feet as we waited for the coming of the others.

At length we saw a four-wheeler drive up. Out of it, in leisurely fashion, got Lord Godalming and Morris; and down from the box descended a thick-set working man with his rush-woven basket of tools. Morris paid the cabman, who touched his hat and drove away. Together the two ascended the steps, and Lord Godalming pointed out what he wanted done. The workman took off his coat leisurely and hung it on one of the spikes of the rail, saying something to a policeman who just then sauntered along. The policeman nodded acquiescence, and the man kneeling down placed his bag beside him. After searching through it, he took out a selection of tools which he proceeded to lay beside him in orderly fashion. Then he stood up, looked into the keyhole, blew into it, and, turning to his employers, made some remark. Lord Godalming smiled, and the man lifted a good sized bunch of keys; selecting one of them, he began to probe the lock, as if feeling his way with it. After fumbling about for a bit he tried a second, and then a third. All at once the door opened under a slight push from him, and he and the two others entered the hall. We sat still; my own cigar burnt furiously, but Van Helsing's went cold altogether. We waited patiently as we saw the workman come out and bring in his bag. Then he held the door partly open, steadying it with his knees, whilst he fitted a key to the lock. This he finally handed to Lord Godalming, who took out his purse and gave him something. The man touched his hat, took his bag, put on his coat and departed; not a soul took the slightest notice of the whole transaction.

When the man had fairly gone, we three crossed the street and knocked at the door. It was immediately opened by Quincey Morris, beside whom stood Lord Godalming lighting a cigar.

"The place smells so vilely," said the latter as we came in. It did indeed smell vilely — like the old chapel at Carfax — and with our previous experience it was plain to us that the Count had been using the place pretty freely. We moved to explore the house, all keeping together in case of attack; for we knew we had a strong and wily enemy to deal with, and as yet we did not know whether the Count might not be in the house. In the dining-room, which lay at the back of the hall, we found eight boxes of earth. Eight boxes only out of the nine which we sought! Our work was not over, and would never be until we should have found the missing box. First we opened the shutters of the window which looked out across a narrow stone-flagged yard at the blank face of a stable, pointed to look like the front of a miniature house. There were no windows in it, so we were not afraid of being overlooked. We did not lose any time in examining the chests. With the tools which we had brought with us we opened them, one by one, and treated them as we had treated those others in the old chapel. It was evident to us that the Count was not at present in the house, and we proceeded to search for any of his effects.

After a cursory glance at the rest of the rooms, from basement to attic, we came to the conclusion that the dining-room contained any effects which might belong to the Count; and so we proceeded to minutely examine them. They lay in a sort of orderly disorder on the great dining-room table. There were title deeds of the Piccadilly house in a great bundle; deeds of the purchase of the houses at Mile End and Bermondsey; notepaper, envelopes, and pens and ink. All were covered up in thin wrapping paper to keep them from the dust. There were also a clothes brush, a brush and comb, and a jug and basin — the latter containing dirty water which was reddened as if with blood. Last of all was a little heap of keys of all sorts and sizes, probably those belonging to the other houses. When we had examined this last find, Lord Godalming and Quincey Morris taking accurate notes of the various addresses of the houses in the East and the South, took with them the keys in a great bunch, and set out to destroy the boxes in these places. The rest of us are, with what patience we can, waiting their return — or the coming of the Count.

CHAPTER XXIII. DR. SEWARD'S DIARY

3 *October.* — The time seemed terribly long whilst we were waiting for the coming of Godalming and Quincey Morris. The Professor tried to keep our minds active by using them all the time. I could see his beneficent purpose, by the side glances which he threw from time to time at Harker. The poor fellow is overwhelmed in a misery that is appalling to see. Last night he was a frank, happy-looking man, with strong youthful face, full of energy, and with dark brown hair. To-day he is a drawn, haggard old man, whose white hair matches well with the hollow burning eyes and grief-written lines of his face. His energy is still intact; in fact he is like a living flame. This may yet be his salvation, for, if all go well, it will tide him over the despairing period; he will then, in a kind of way, wake again to the realities of life. Poor fellow, I thought my own trouble was bad enough, but his —! The Professor knows this well enough, and is doing his best to keep his mind active. What he has been saying was, under the circumstances, of absorbing interest. So well as I can remember, here it is: —

"I have studied, over and over again since they came into my hands, all the papers relating to this monster; and the more I have studied, the greater seems the necessity to utterly stamp him out. All through there are signs of his advance; not only of his powers, but of his knowledge of it. As I learned from the researches of my friend Arminius of Buda-Pesth, he was in life a most wonderful man. Soldier, statesman, and alchemist — which latter was the highest development of the science-knowledge of his time. He had a mighty brain, a learning beyond compare, and a heart that knew no fear and no remorse. He dared even to attend the Scholomance, and there was no branch of knowledge of his time that he did not essay. Well, in him the brain powers survived the physical death; though it would seem that memory was not all complete. In some faculties of mind he has been, and is, only a child; but he is growing, and some things that were childish at the first are now of man's stature. He is experimenting, and doing it well; and if it had not been that we have crossed his path he would be yet — he may be yet if we fail — the father or furtherer of a new order of beings, whose road must lead, through Death, not Life."

Harker groaned and said, "And this is all arrayed against my darling! But how is he experimenting? The knowledge may help us to defeat him!"

"He has all along, since his coming, been trying his power, slowly but surely; that big child-brain of his is working. Well for us, it is, as yet, a child-brain; for had he dared, at the first, to attempt certain things he would long ago have been beyond our power. However, he means to succeed, and a man who has centuries before him can afford to wait and to go slow. *Festina lente*° may well be his motto."

"I fail to understand," said Harker wearily. "Oh, do be more plain to me! Perhaps grief and trouble are dulling my brain." The Professor laid his hand tenderly on his shoulder as he spoke: —

"Ah, my child, I will be plain. Do you not see how, of late, this monster has been creeping into knowledge experimentally. How he has been making use of the zoophagous patient to effect his entry into friend John's home; for your Vampire, though in all afterwards he can come when and how he will, must at the first make entry only when asked thereto by an inmate. But these are not his most important experiments. Do we not see how at the first all these so great boxes were moved by others. He knew not then but that must be so. But all the time that so great child-brain of his was growing, and he began to consider whether he might not himself move the box. So he begin to help; and then, when he found that this be all-right, he try to move them all alone. And so he progress, and he scatter these graves of him; and none but he know where they are hidden. He may have intend to bury them deep in the ground. So that he only use them in the night, or at such time as he can change his form, they do him equal well; and none may know these are his hiding place! But, my child, do not despair; this knowledge come to him just too late! Already all of his lairs but one be sterilize as for him; and before the sunset this shall be so. Then he have no place where he can move and hide. I delayed this morning that so we might be sure. Is there not more at stake for us than for him? Then why we not be even more careful than him? By my clock it is one hour, and already, if all be well, friend Arthur and Quincey are on their way to us. To-day is our day, and we must go sure, if slow, and lose no chance. See! there are five of us when those absent ones return."

Whilst he was speaking we were startled by a knock at the hall door, the double postman's knock of the telegraph boy. We all moved out to the hall with one impulse, and Van Helsing, holding up his hand to us to keep silence, stepped to the door and opened it. The boy handed in a despatch. The Professor closed the door again and, after looking at the direction, opened it and read it aloud.

Festina lente: Make haste slowly (Latin).

"Look out for D. He has just now, 12.45, come from Carfax hurriedly and hastened towards the south. He seems to be going the round and may want to see you: Mina."

There was a pause, broken by Jonathan Harker's voice: —

"Now, God be thanked, we shall soon meet!" Van Helsing turned to him quickly and said: —

'God will act in His own way and time. Do not fear, and do not rejoice as yet; for what we wish for at the moment may be our undoings."

"I care for nothing now," he answered hotly, "except to wipe out this brute from the face of creation. I would sell my soul to do it!"

"Oh hush, hush, my child!" said Van Helsing, "God does not purchase souls in this wise; and the Devil, though he may purchase, does not keep faith. But God is merciful and just, and knows your pain and your devotion to that dear Madam Mina. Think you, how her pain would be doubled, did she but hear your wild words. Do not fear any of us; we are all devoted to this cause, and to-day shall see the end. The time is coming for action; to-day this Vampire is limit to the powers of man, and till sunset he may not change. It will take him time to arrive here — see it is twenty minutes past one — and there are yet some times before he can hither come, be he never so quick. What we must hope for is that my Lord Arthur and Quincey arrive first."

About half an hour after we had received Mrs. Harker's telegram, there cam a quiet resolute knock at the hall door. It was just an ordinary knock, such as is given hourly by thousands of gentlemen, but it made the Professor's heart and mine beat loudly. We looked at each other, and together moved out into the hall; we each held ready to use our various armaments — the spiritual in the left hand, the mortal in the right. Van Helsing pulled back the latch, and, holding the door half open, stood back, having both hands ready for action. The gladness of our hearts must have shown upon our faces when on the step, close to the door, we saw Lord Godalming and Quincey Morris. They came quickly in and closed the door behind them, the former saying, as they moved along the hall: —

"It is all right. We found both places; six boxes in each, and we destroyed them all!"

"Destroyed?" asked the Professor.

"For him!" We were silent for a minute, and then Quincey said: —

"There's nothing to do but to wait here. If, however, he doesn't turn up by five o'clock, we must start off; for it won't do to leave Mrs. Harker alone after sunset."

"He will be here before long now," said Van Helsing, who had been consulting his pocket-book. "*Nota bene*,° in Madam's telegram he went south from Carfax, that means he went to cross the river, and he could only do so at slack of tide, which should be something before one o'clock. That he went south has a meaning for us. He is as yet only suspicious; and he went from Carfax first to the place where he would suspect interference least. You must have been at Bermondsey only a short time before him. That he is not here already shows that he went to Mile End next. This took him some time; for he would then have to be carried over the river in some way. Believe me, my friends, we shall not have long to wait now. We should have ready some plan of attack, so that we may throw away no chance. Hush, there is no time now. Have all your arms! Be ready!' He held up a warning hand as he spoke, for we all could hear a key softly inserted in the lock of the hall door.

I could not but admire, even at such a moment, the way in which a dominant spirit asserted itself. In all our hunting parties and adventures in different parts of the world, Quincey Morris had always been the one to arrange the plan of action, and Arthur and I had been accustomed to obey him implicitly. Now, the old habit seemed to be renewed instinctively. With a swift glance round the room, he at once laid out our plan of attack, and, without speaking a word, with a gesture, placed us each in position. Van Helsing, Harker, and I were just behind the door so that when it was opened the Professor could guard it whilst we two stepped between the incomer and the door. Godalming behind and Quincey in front stood just out of sight ready to move in front of the window. We waited in suspense that made the seconds pass with nightmare slowness. The slow, careful steps came along the hall; the Count was evidently prepared for some surprise — at least he feared it.

Suddenly with a single bound he leaped into the room, winning a way past us before any of us could raise a hand to stay him. There was something so panther-like in the movement — something so unhuman, that it seemed to sober us all from the shock of his coming. The first to act was Harker, who, with a quick movement, threw himself before the door leading into the room in the front of the house. As the Count saw us, a horrible sort of snarl passed over his face, showing the eye-teeth long and pointed; but the evil smile as quickly passed into a cold stare of lion-like disdain. His expression again changed, as, with a single impulse, we all advanced upon him. It was a pity that we had not some better organised plan of attack, for even at the moment I

Nota bene: Note well, take notice (Latin).

wondered what we were to do. I did not myself know whether our lethal weapons would avail us anything. Harker evidently meant to try the matter, for he had ready his great Kukri knife,° and made a fierce and sudden cut at him. The blow was a powerful one; only the diabolical quickness of the Count's leap back saved him. A second less and the trenchant blade had shorne through his heart. As it was, the point just cut the cloth of his coat, making a wide gap whence a bundle of banknotes and a stream of gold fell out. The expression of the Count's face was so hellish, that for a moment I feared for Harker, though I saw him throw the terrible knife aloft again for another stroke. Instinctively I moved forward with a protective impulse, holding the crucifix and wafer in my left hand. I felt a mighty power fly along my arm; and it was without surprise I saw that the monster cower back before a similar movement made spontaneously by each one of us. It would be impossible to describe the expression of hate and baffled malignity — of anger and hellish rage — which came over the Count's face. His waxen hue became greenish-yellow by the contrast of his burning eyes, and the red scar on the forehead showed on the pallid skin like a palpitating wound. The next instant, with a sinuous dive he swept under Harker's arm, ere his blow could fall, and, grasping a handful of the money from the floor, dashed across the room, threw himself at the window. Amid the crash and glitter of the falling glass, he tumbled into the flagged area below. Through the sound of the shivering glass I could hear the "ting" of the gold, as some of the sovereigns fell on the flagging.

We ran over and saw him spring unhurt from the ground. He, rushing up the steps, crossed the flagged yard, and pushed open the stable door. There he turned and spoke to us: —

"You think to baffle me, you — with your pale faces all in a row, like sheep in a butcher's. You shall be sorry yet, each one of you! You think you have left me without a place to rest; but I have more. My revenge is just begun! I spread it over centuries, and time is on my side. Your girls that you all love are mine already; and through them you and others shall yet be mine — my creatures, to do my bidding and to be my jackals when I want to feed. Bah!" With a contemptuous sneer, he passed quickly through the door, and we heard the rusty bolt creak as he fastened it behind him. A door beyond opened and shut. The first of us to speak was the Professor, as, realising the difficulty of following him through the stable, we moved towards the hall.

Kukri knife: "A curved knife, broader at the point than at the handle, and usually having the keen edge on the concave side, used by the Gorkas of India" *(OED).*

"We have learnt something — much! Notwithstanding his brave words, he fears us; he fear time, he fear want! For if not, why he hurry so? His very tone betray him, or my ears deceive. Why take that money? You follow quick. You are hunters of wild beast, and understand it so. For me, I make sure that nothing here may be of use to him, if so that he return." As he spoke he put the money remaining into his pocket; took the title-deeds in the bundle as Harker had left them; and swept the remaining things into the open fireplace where he set fire to them with a match.

Godalming and Morris had rushed out into the yard, and Harker had lowered himself from the window to follow the Count. He had, however, bolted the stable door; and by the time they had forced it open there was no sign of him. Van Helsing and I tried to make inquiry at the back of the house; but the mews was deserted and no one had seen him depart.

It was now late in the afternoon, and sunset was not far off. We had to recognise that our game was up; with heavy hearts we agreed with the Professor when he said: —

"Let us go back to Madam Mina — poor, poor, dear Madam Mina. All we can do just now is done; and we can there, at least, protect her! But we need not despair. There is but one more earth-box, and we must try to find it; when that is done all may yet be well." I could see that he spoke as bravely as he could to comfort Harker. The poor fellow was quite broken down; now and again he gave a low groan which he could not suppress — he was thinking of his wife.

With sad hearts we came back to my house, where we found Mrs. Harker waiting us, with an appearance of cheerfulness which did honour to her bravery and unselfishness. When she saw our faces, her own became as pale as death; for a second or two her eyes were closed as if she were in secret prayer; and then she said cheerfully: —

"I can never thank you all enough. Oh, my poor darling!" as she spoke, she took her husband's grey head in her hands and kissed it — "Lay your poor head here and rest it. All will yet be well, dear! God will protect us if He so will it in His good intent." The poor fellow only groaned. There was no place for words in his sublime misery.

We had a sort of perfunctory supper together, and I think it cheered us all up somewhat. It was, perhaps, the mere animal heat of food to hungry people — for none of us had eaten anything since breakfast — or the sense of companionship may have helped us; but anyhow we were all less miserable, and saw the morrow as not altogether without hope. True to our promise, we told Mrs. Harker everything which had passed; and although she grew snowy white at times when danger had seemed to threaten her husband, and red at others when his devotion to her was manifested, she listened bravely and with calmness. When we came to the part where Harker had rushed at the Count so recklessly, she clung to her husband's arm, and held it tight as though her clinging could protect him from any harm that might come. She said nothing, however, till the narration was all done, and matters had been brought right up to the present time. Then without letting go her husband's hand she stood up amongst us and spoke. Oh that I could give any idea of the scene; of that sweet, sweet, good, good woman in all the radiant beauty of her youth and animation, with the red scar on her forehead of which she was conscious, and which we saw with grinding of our teeth — remembering whence and how it came; her loving kindness against our grim hate; her tender faith against all our fears and doubting; and we, knowing that so far as symbols went, she with all her goodness and purity and faith, was outcast from God.

"Jonathan," she said, and the word sounded like music on her lips it was so full of love and tenderness, "Jonathan dear, and you all my true, true friends, I want you to bear something in mind through all this dreadful time. I know that you must fight — that you must destroy even as you destroyed the false Lucy so that the true Lucy might live hereafter; but it is not a work of hate. That poor soul who was wrought all this misery is the saddest case of all. Just think what will be his joy when he too is destroyed in his worser part that his better part may have spiritual immortality. You must be pitiful to him too, though it may not hold your hands from his destruction."

As she spoke I could see her husband's face darken and draw together, as though the passion in him were shrivelling his being to its core. Instinctively the clasp on his wife's hand grew closer, till his knuckles looked white. She did not flinch from the pain which I knew she must have suffered, but looked at him with eyes that were more appealing than ever. As she stopped speaking he leaped to his feet, almost tearing his hand from hers as he spoke: —

"May God give him into my hand just for long enough to destroy that earthy life of him which we are aiming at. If beyond it I could send his soul for ever and ever to burning hell I would do it!"

"Oh, hush! oh hush! in the name of the good God. Don't say such things, Jonathan, my husband; or you will crush me with fear and horror. Just think, my dear — I have been thinking all this long, long day of it — that . . . perhaps . . . some day . . . I too may need such pity; and that some other like you — and with equal cause for anger — may deny it to me! Oh my husband! my husband, indeed I would have spared you such a thought had there been another way; but I pray that God may not have treasured your wild words, except as the heart-broken wail of a very loving and sorely stricken man. Oh God, let these poor white hairs go in evidence of what he has suffered, who all his life has done no wrong, and on whom so many sorrows have come."

We men were all in tears now. There was no resisting them, and we wept openly. She wept too, to see that her sweeter counsels had prevailed. Her husband flung himself on his knees beside her, and putting his arms round her, hid his face in the folds of her dress. Van Helsing beckoned to us and we stole out of the room, leaving the two loving hearts alone with their God.

Before they retired the Professor fixed up the room against any coming of the Vampire, and assured Mrs. Harker that she might rest in peace. She tried to school herself to the belief, and, manifestly for her husband's sake, tried to seem content. It was a brave struggle; and was, I think and believe, not without its reward. Van Helsing had placed at hand a bell which either of them was to sound in case of any emergency. When they had retired, Quincey, Godalming, and I arranged that we should sit up, dividing the night between us, and watch over the safety of the poor stricken lady. The first watch falls to Quincey, so the rest of us shall be off to bed as soon as we can. Godalming has already turned in, for his is the second watch. Now that my work is done I, too, shall go to bed.

Jonathan Harker's Journal

3–4 *October, close to midnight.* — I thought yesterday would never end. There was over me a yearning for sleep, in some sort of blind belief that to wake would be to find things changed, and that any change must now be for the better. Before we parted, we discussed what our next step was to be, but we could arrive at no result. All we knew was that one earth-box remained, and that the Count alone knew where it was. If he chooses to lie hidden, he may baffle us for years; and in the meantime! — the thought is too horrible, I dare not think of it even now. This I know: that if ever there was a woman who was all perfec-tion, that one is my poor wronged darling. I love her a thousand times more for her sweet pity of last night, a pity that made my own hate of the monster seem despicable. Surely God will not permit the world to be the poorer by the loss of such a creature. This is hope to me. We are all drifting reefwards now, and faith is our only anchor. Thank God!

Mina is sleeping, and sleeping without dreams. I fear what her dreams might be like, with such terrible memories to ground them in. She has not been so calm, within my seeing, since the sunset. Then, for a while, there came over her face a repose which was like spring after the blasts of March. I thought at the time that it was the softness of the red sunset on her face, but somehow now I think it has a deeper meaning. I am not sleepy myself, though I am weary — weary to death. However, I must try to sleep; for there is to-morrow to think of, and there is no rest for me until . . . .

Later. — I must have fallen asleep, for I was awakened by Mina, who was sitting up in bed, with a startled look on her face. I could see easily, for we did not leave the room in darkness; she had placed a warning hand over my mouth, and now she whispered in my ear: —

"Hush! there is someone in the corridor!" I got up softly, and, crossing the room, gently opened the door.

Just outside, stretched on a mattress lay Mr. Morris, wide awake. He raised a warning hand for silence as he whispered to me: —

"Hush! go back to bed; it is all right. One of us will be here all night. We don't mean to take any chances!"

His look and gesture forbade discussion, so I came back and told Mina. She sighed, and positively a shadow of a smile stole over her poor, pale face as she put her arms round me and said softly: —

"Oh, thank God for good brave men!" With a sigh she sank back again to sleep. I write this now as I am not sleepy, though I must try again.

4 *October, morning.* — Once again during the night I was wakened by Mina. This time we had all had a good sleep, for the grey of the coming dawn was making the windows into sharp oblongs, and the gas flame was like a speck rather than a disc of light. She said to me hurriedly: —

"Go, call the Professor. I want to see him at once."

"Why?" I asked.

"I have an idea. I suppose it must have come in the night, and matured without my knowing it. He must hypnotise me before the dawn, and then I shall be able to speak. Go quick, dearest; the time is getting close." I went to the door. Dr. Seward was resting on the mattress, and, seeing me, he sprang to his feet.

"Is anything wrong?" he asked, in alarm.

"No," I replied; "but Mina wants to see Dr. Van Helsing at once."

"I will go," he said, and hurried into the Professor's room.

In two or three minutes later Van Helsing was in the room in his dressing-gown, and Mr. Morris and Lord Godalming were with Dr. Seward at the door asking questions. When the Professor saw Mina a smile — a positive smile ousted the anxiety of his face; he rubbed his hands as he said: —

"Oh, my dear Madam Mina, this is indeed a change. See! friend Jonathan, we have got our dear Madam Mina, as of old, back to us to-day!' then turning to her, he said, cheerfully: "And what am I do for you? For at this hour you do not want me for nothings."

"I want you to hypnotise me!" she said. "Do it before the dawn, for I feel that then I can speak, and speak freely. Be quick, for the time is short!" Without a word he motioned her to sit up in bed.

Looking fixedly at her, he commenced to make passes in front of her, from over the top of her head downward, with each hand in turn. Mina gazed at him fixedly for a few minutes, during which my own heart beat like a trip hammer, for I felt that some crisis was at hand. Gradually her eyes closed, and she sat, stock still; only by the gentle heaving of her bosom could one know that she was alive. The Professor made a few more passes and then stopped, and I could see that his forehead was covered with great beads of perspiration. Mina opened her eyes; but she did not seem the same woman. There was a far-away look in her eyes, and her voice had a sad dreaminess which was new to me. Raising his hand to impose silence, the Professor motioned to me to bring the others in. They came on tip-toe, closing the door behind them, and stood at the foot of the bed, looking on. Mina appeared not to see them. The stillness was broken by Van Helsing's voice speaking in a low level tone which would not break the current of her thoughts: —

"Where are you?" The answer came in a neutral way: —

"I do not know. Sleep has no place it can call its own." For several minutes there was silence. Mina sat rigid, and the Professor stood staring at her fixedly; the rest of us hardly dared to breathe. The room was growing lighter; without taking his eyes from Mina's face, Dr. Van Helsing motioned me to pull up the blind. I did so, and the day seemed just upon us. A red streak shot up, and a rosy light seemed to diffuse itself through the room. On the instant the Professor spoke again: —

"Where are you now?" The answer came dreamily, but with intention; it were as though she were interpreting something. I have heard her use the same tone when reading her shorthand notes.

"I do not know. It is all strange to me!"

"What do you see?"

"I can see nothing; it is all dark."

"What do you hear?" I could detect the strain in the Professor's patient voice.

"The lapping water. It is gurgling by, and little waves leap. I can hear them on the outside."

"Then you are on a ship?" We all looked at each other, trying to glean something each from the other. We were afraid to think. The answer came quick: —

"Oh, yes!"

"What else do you hear?"

"The sound of men stamping overhead as they run about. There is the creaking of a chain, and the loud tinkle as the check of the capstan falls into the rachet."°

"What are you doing?"

"I am still — oh, so still. It is like death!" The voice faded away into a deep breath as of one sleeping, and the open eyes closed again.

By this time the sun had risen, and we were all in the full light of day. Dr. Van Helsing placed his hands on Mina's shoulders, and laid her head down softly on her pillow. She lay like a sleeping child for a few moments, and then, with a long sigh, awoke and stared in wonder to see us all around her. "Have I been talking in my sleep?" was all she said. She seemed, however, to know the situation without telling; though she was eager to know what she had told. The Professor repeated the conversation, and she said: —

"Then there is not a moment to lose: it may not be yet too late!" Mr. Morris and Lord Godalming started for the door but the Professor's calm voice called them back: —

"Stay, my friends. That ship wherever it was, was weighing anchor whilst she spoke. There are many ships weighing anchor at the moment in your so great Port of London. Which of them is it that you seek? God be thanked that we have once again a clue, though whither it may lead us we know not. We have been blind somewhat; blind after the manner of men, since when we can look back we see what we might have seen! Alas! but that sentence is a puddle; is it not? We can know now what was in the Count's mind when he seize that money, though Jonathan's

---

the check of the capstan falls into the rachet: A capstan, a "cylinder or barrel revolving on a vertical axis" with bars that can be pushed by men walking in a circle, is used for weighing anchor and hoisting heavy weights. It is held in a particular position by a ratchet (here spelled "rachet"), a "set of angular or saw-like teeth" on the rim of a wheel, into which a cog or tooth can catch to prevent reverse motion *(OED).*

so fierce knife put him in the danger that even he dread. He meant escape. Hear me, ESCAPE! He saw that with but one earth-box left, and a pack of men following like dogs after a fox, this London was no place for him. He have take his last earth-box on board a ship, and he leave the land. He think to escape, but no! we follow him. Tally Ho! as friend Arthur would say when he put on his red frock! Our old fox is wily; oh! so wily and we must follow with wile. I too am wily and I think his mind in a little while. In meantime we may rest and in peace, for there are waters between us which he do not want to pass, and which he could not if he would — unless the ship were to touch the land, and then only at full or slack tide. See, and the sun is just rose, and all day to sunset is to us. Let us take bath, and dress, and have breakfast which we all need, and which we can eat comfortable since he be not in the same land with us." Mina looked at him appealingly as she asked: —

"But why need we seek him further, when he is gone away from us?" He took her hand and patted it as he replied: —

"Ask me nothings as yet. When we have breakfast, then I answer all questions." He would say no more, and we separated to dress.

After breakfast Mina repeated her question. He looked at her gravely for a minute and then said sorrowfully: —

"Because my dear, dear Madam Mina, now more than ever must we find him even if we have to follow him to the jaws of Hell!" She grew paler as she asked faintly: —

"Why?"

"Because," he answered solemnly, "he can live for centuries and you are but mortal woman. Time is now to be dreaded — since once he put that mark upon your throat."

I was just in time to catch her as she fell forward in a faint.

CHAPTER XXIV. DR. SEWARD'S PHONOGRAPH DIARY, SPOKEN BY VAN HELSING

THIS to Jonathan Harker.

You are to stay with your dear Madam Mina. We shall go to make our search — if I can call it so, for it is not search but knowing, and we seek confirmation only. But do you stay and take care of her to-day. This is your best and most holiest office. This day nothing can find him here. Let me tell you that so you will know what we four know already, for I have tell them. He, our enemy, have gone away; he have gone back to his castle in Transylvania. I know it so well, as if a great hand of fire wrote it on the wall. He have prepare for this in some way, and that last earth-box was ready to ship somewheres. For this he took the money; for this he hurry at the last, lest we catch him before the sun go down. It was his last hope, save that he might hide in the tomb that he think poor Miss Lucy, being as he thought like him, keep open to him. But there was not of time. When that fail he make straight for his last resource — his last earthwork I might say did I wish *double entente*.° He is clever, oh so clever! he know that his game here was finish; and so he decide he go back home. He find ship going by the route he came, and he go in it. We go off now to find what ship, and whither bound; when we have discover that, we come back and tell you all. Then we will comfort you and poor dear Madam Mina with new hope. For it will be hope when you think it over: that all is not lost. This very creature that we pursue, he take hundreds of years to get so far as London; and yet in one day, when we know of the disposal of him we drive him out. He is finite, though he is powerful to do much harm and suffers not as we do. But we are strong, each in our purpose; and we are all more strong together. Take heart afresh dear husband of Madam Mina. This battle is but begun, and in the end we shall win — so sure as that God sits on high to watch over His children. Therefore be of much comfort till we return.

VAN HELSING.

Jonathan Harker's Journal

4 *October.* — When I read to Mina, Van Helsing's message in the phonograph, the poor girl brightened up considerably. Already the certainty that the Count is out of the country has given her comfort; and comfort is strength to her. For my own part, now that this horrible danger is not face to face with us, it seems almost impossible to believe in it. Even my own terrible experiences in Castle Dracula seem like a long-forgotten dream. Here in the crisp autumn air in the bright sunlight —

Alas! how can I disbelieve! In the midst of my thought my eye fell on the red scar on my poor darling's white forehead. Whilst that lasts, there can be no disbelief. And afterwards the very memory of it will keep faith crystal clear. Mina and I fear to be idle, so we have been over all the diaries again and again. Somehow, although the reality seems

---

earthwork . . . double entente: By linking *double-entente,* an expression that conveys two meanings (French), with "earthwork," Van Helsing adds the implication of a grave or burial mound to the military meaning of the word, "a bank or mound of earth used as a rampart or fortification" *(OED).*

greater each time, the pain and the fear seem less. There is something of a guiding purpose manifest throughout, which is comforting. Mina says that perhaps we are the instruments of ultimate good. It may be! I shall try to think as she does. We have never spoken to each other yet of the future. It is better to wait till we see the Professor and the others after their investigations.

The day is running by more quickly than I ever thought a day could run for me again. It is now three o'clock.

Mina Harker's Journal

5 *October,* 5 *p.m.* — Our meeting for report. Present: Professor Van Helsing, Lord Godalming, Dr. Seward, Mr. Quincey Morris, Jonathan Harker, Mina Harker.

Dr. Van Helsing described what steps were taken during the day to discover on what boat and whither bound Count Dracula made his escape: —

"As I knew that he wanted to get back to Transylvania, I felt sure that he must go by the Danube mouth; or by somewhere in the Black Sea, since by that way he come. It was a dreary blank that was before us. *Omne ignotum pro magnifico*°; and so with heavy hearts we start to find what ships leave for the Black Sea last night. He was in sailing ship, since Madam Mina tell of sails being set. These not so important as to go in your list of the shipping in the *Times,* and so we go, by suggestion of my Lord Godalming, to your Lloyd's,° where are note of all ships that sail, however so small. There we find that only one Black-Sea-bound ship go out with the tide. She is the *Czarina Catherine,* and she sail from Doolittle's Wharf for Varna, and thence on to other parts and up the Danube. 'Soh!' said I, 'this is the ship whereon is the Count.' So off we go to Doolittle's Wharf, and there we find a man in an office of wood so small that the man look bigger than the office. From him we inquire of the goings of the *Czarina Catherine.* He swear much, and he red face and loud of voice, but he good fellow all the same; and when Quincey give him something from his pocket which crackle as he roll it up, and put it in a so small bag which he have hid deep in his clothing, he still better fellow and humble servant to us. He come with us, and

---

Omne ignotum pro magnifico: "Whatever is unknown is held to be magnificent" (Latin). *Lloyd's:* An association of shipowners, merchants, underwriters, and brokers for providing marine insurance. Lloyd's maintained a registry of all shipping, English or foreign, insured by the corporation, and also published a daily list of shipping movements. (*Enc. Brit.* 11th).

ask many men who are rough and hot; these be better fellows too when they have been no more thirsty. They say much of blood and bloom and of others which I comprehend not,° though I guess what they mean; but nevertheless they tell us all things which we want to know.

"They make known to us among them, how last afternoon at about five o'clock comes a man so hurry. A tall man, thin and pale, with high nose and teeth so white, and eyes that seem to be burning. That he be all in black, except that he have a hat of straw which suit not him or the time. That he scatter his money in making quick inquiry as to what ship sails for the Black Sea and for where. Some took him to the office and then to the ship, where he will not go aboard but halt at shore end of gang-plank, and ask that the captain come to him. The captain come, when told that he will be pay well; and though he swear much at the first he agree to term. Then the thin man go and some one tell him where horse and cart can be hired. He go there, and soon he come again, himself driving cart on which is a great box; this he himself lift down, though it take several to put it on truck for the ship. He give much talk to captain as to how and where his box is to be place; but the captain like it not and swear at him in many tongues, and tell him that if he like he can come and see where it shall be. But he say 'no;' that he come not yet, for that he have much to do. Whereupon the captain tell him that he had better be quick — with blood — for that his ship will leave the place — of blood — before the turn of the tide — with blood. Then the thin man smile, and say that of course he must go when he think fit; but he will be surprise if he go quite so soon. The captain swear again, polyglot, and the thin man make him bow, and thank him, and say that he will so far intrude on his kindness as to come aboard before the sailing. Final the captain, more red than ever, and in more tongues, tell him that he doesn't want no Frenchmen — with bloom upon them and also with blood — in his ship — with blood on her also. And so, after asking where there might be close at hand a shop where he might purchase ship forms, he departed.

"No one knew where he went 'or bloomin' well cared,' as they said, for they had something else to think of — well with blood again; for it soon became apparent to all that the *Czarina Catherine* would not sail as was expected. A thin mist began to creep up from the river, and it grew, and grew; till soon a dense fog enveloped the ship and all around her. The captain swore polyglot — very polyglot — polyglot with

---

They say much ... I comprehend not: Their speech is filled with colloquial phrases and expletives, such as "bloody" and "blooming," some of which Van Helsing does not understand.

bloom and blood; but he could do nothing. The water rose and rose; and he began to fear that he would lose the tide altogether. He was in no friendly mood, when just at full tide, the thin man came up the gang-plank again and asked to see where his box had been stowed. Then the captain replied that he wished that he and his box — old and with much bloom and blood — were in hell. But the thin man did not be offend, and went down with the mate and saw where it was place, and came up and stood awhile on deck in fog. He must have come off by himself, for none notice him. Indeed they thought not of him; for soon the fog begin to melt away, and all was clear again. My friends of the thirst and the language that was of bloom and blood laughed, as they told how the captain's swears exceeded even his usual polyglot, and was more than ever full of picturesque, when on questioning other mariners who were on movement up and down on the river that hour, he found that few of them had seen any of fog at all, except where it lay round the wharf. However the ship went out on the ebb tide; and was doubtless by morning far down the river mouth. She was by then, when they told us, well out to sea.

"And so my dear Madam Mina, it is that we have to rest for a time, for our enemy is on the sea, with the fog at his command, on his way to the Danube mouth. To sail a ship takes time, go she never so quick; and when we start we go on land more quick, and we meet him there. Our best hope is to come on him when in the box between sunrise and sunset; for then he can make no struggle, and we may deal with him as we should. There are days for us, in which we can make ready our plan. We know all about where he go; for we have seen the owner of the ship, who have shown us invoices and all papers that can be. The box we seek is to be landed in Varna, and to be given to an agent, one Ristics who will there present his credentials; and so our merchant friend will have done his part. When he ask if there be any wrong, for that so, he can telegraph and have inquiry made at Varna, we say 'no;' for what is to be done is not for police or of the customs. It must be done by us alone and in our own way."

When Dr. Van Helsing had done speaking, I asked him if it were certain that the Count had remained on board the ship. He replied: "We have the best proof of that: your own evidence, when in the hypnotic trance this morning." I asked him again if it were really necessary that they should pursue the Count, for oh! I dread Jonathan leaving me, and I know that he would surely go if the others went. He answered in growing passion, at first quietly. As he went on, however, he grew more angry and more forceful, till in the end we could not but see wherein was at least some of that personal dominance which made him so long a master amongst men: —

"Yes it is necessary — necessary — necessary! For your sake in the first, and then for the sake of humanity. This monster has done much harm already, in the narrow scope where he find himself, and in the short time when as yet he was only as a body groping his so small measure in darkness and not knowing. All this have I told these others; you, my dear Madam Mina, will learn it in the phonograph of my friend John, or in that of your husband. I have told them how the measure of leaving his own barren land — barren of peoples — and coming to a new land where life of man teems till they are like the multitude of standing corn, was the work of centuries. Were another of the Un-Dead, like him, to try to do what he has done, perhaps not all the centuries of the world that have been, or that will be, could aid him. With this one, all the forces of nature that are occult and deep and strong must have worked together in some wondrous way. The very place, where he have been alive, Un-Dead for all these centuries, is full of strangeness of the geologic and chemical world. There are deep caverns and fissures that reach none know whither. There have been volcanoes, some of whose openings still send out waters of strange properties, and gases that kill or make to vivify. Doubtless, there is something magnetic or electric in some of these combinations of occult forces which work for physical life in strange way; and in himself were from the first some great qualities. In a hard and warlike time he was celebrate that he have more iron nerve, more subtle brain, more braver heart, than any man. In him some vital principle have in strange way found their utmost; and as his body keep strong and grow and thrive, so his brain grow too. All this without that diabolic aid which is surely to him; for it have to yield to the powers that come from, and are, symbolic of good. And now this is what he is to us. He have infect you — oh forgive me, my dear, that I must say such; but it is for good of you that I speak. He infect you in such wise, that even if he do no more, you have only to live — to live in your own old, sweet way; and so in time, death, which is of man's common lot and with God's sanction, shall make you like to him. This must not be! We have sworn together that it must not. Thus are we ministers of God's own wish: that the world, and men for whom His Son die, will not be given over to monsters, whose very existence would defame Him. He have allowed us to redeem one soul already, and we go out as the old knights of the Cross° to redeem more.

old knights of the Cross: Crusaders, that is, warriors who fought in the Crusades (from Latin *crux*, cross), the military expeditions undertaken by European Christians in the eleventh through thirteenth centuries to recover the Holy Land from the Muslims.

Like them we shall travel towards the sunrise; and like them, if we fall, we fall in good cause." He paused and I said: —

"But will not the Count take his rebuff wisely? Since he has been driven from England, will he not avoid it, as a tiger does the village from which he has been hunted?"

"Aha!" he said, "your simile of the tiger good, for me, and I shall adopt him. Your man-eater, as they of India call the tiger who has once taste blood of the human, care no more for other prey, but prowl unceasing till he get him. This that we hunt from our village is a tiger, too, a man-eater, and he never cease to prowl. Nay in himself he is not one to retire and stay afar. In his life, his living life, he go over the Turkey frontier and attack his enemy on his own ground; he be beaten back, but did he stay? No! He come again, and again, and again. Look at his persistence and endurance. With the child-brain that was to him he have long since conceive the idea of coming to a great city. What does he do? He find out the place of all the world most of promise for him. Then he deliberately set himself down to prepare for the task. He find in patience just how is his strength, and what are his powers. He study new tongues. He learn new social life; new environment of old ways, the politic, the law, the finance, the science, the habit of a new land and a new people who have come to be since he was. His glimpse that he have had, whet his appetite only and enkeen his desire. Nay, it help him to grow as to his brain; for it all prove to him how right he was at the first in his surmises. He have done this alone; all alone! from a ruin tomb in a forgotten land. What more may he not do when the greater world of thought is open to him. He that can smile at death, as we know him; who can flourish in the midst of diseases that kill off whole peoples. Oh! if such an one was to come from God, and not the Devil, what a force for good might he not be in this old world of ours. But we are pledged to set the world free. Our toil must be in silence, and our efforts all in secret; for in this enlightened age, when men believe not even what they see, the doubting of wise men would be his greatest strength. It would be at once his sheath and his armour, and his weapons to destroy us, his enemies, who are willing to peril even our own souls for the safety of one we love — for the good of mankind, and for the honour and glory of God."

After a general discussion it was determined that for to-night nothing be definitely settled; that we should all sleep on the facts, and try to think out the proper conclusions. To-morrow at breakfast we are to meet again, and, after making our conclusions known to one another, we shall decide on some definite cause of action.

. . . . . .

I feel a wonderful peace and rest to-night. It is as if some haunting presence were removed from me. Perhaps . . . .

My surmise was not finished, could not be; for I caught sight in the mirror of the red mark upon my forehead; and I knew that I was still unclean.

Dr. Seward's Diary

5 *October.* — We all rose early, and I think that sleep did much for each and all of us. When we met at early breakfast there was more general cheerfulness than any of us had ever expected to experience again. It is really wonderful how much resilience there is in human nature. Let any obstructing cause, no matter what, be removed in any way — even by death — and we fly back to first principles of hope and enjoyment. More than once as we sat around the table, my eyes opened in wonder whether the whole of the past days had not been a dream. It was only when I caught sight of the red blotch on Mrs. Harker's forehead that I was brought back to reality. Even now, when I am gravely revolving the matter, it is almost impossible to realise that the cause of all our trouble is still existent. Even Mrs. Harker seems to lose sight of her trouble for whole spells; it is only now and again, when something recalls it to her mind, that she thinks of her terrible scar. We are to meet here in my study in half an hour and decide on our course of action. I see only one immediate difficulty, I know it by instinct rather than reason: we shall all have to speak frankly; and yet I fear that in some mysterious way poor Mrs. Harker's tongue is tied. I *know* that she forms conclusions of her own, and from all that has been I can guess how brilliant and how true they must be; but she will not, or cannot, give them utterance. I have mentioned this to Van Helsing, and he and I are to talk it over when we are alone. I suppose it is some of that horrid poison which has got into her veins beginning to work. The Count had his own purposes when he gave her what Van Helsing called "the Vampire's baptism of blood." Well, there may be a poison that distils itself out of good things; in an age when the existence of ptomaines° is a mystery we should not wonder at anything! One thing I know: that if my instinct be true regarding poor Mrs. Harker's silences, then there is a terrible difficulty — and unknown danger — in the work before us.

ptomaines: Alkaloids found in putrefying animal and vegetable matter, some of which are poisonous (*OED* OL).

The same power that compels her silence may compel her speech. I dare not think further; for so I should in my thoughts dishonour a noble woman!

Van Helsing is coming to my study a little before the others. I shall try to open the subject with him.

Later. — When the Professor came in, we talked over the state of things. I could see that he had something on his mind he wanted to say, but felt some hesitancy about broaching the subject. After beating about the bush a little, he said suddenly: —

"Friend John, there is something that you and I must talk of alone, just at the first at any rate. Later, we may have to take the others into our confidence;" then he stopped, so I waited; he went on: —

"Madam Mina, our poor, dear Madam Mina is changing." A cold shiver ran through me to find my worst fears thus endorsed. Van Helsing continued: —

"With the sad experience of Miss Lucy, we must this time be warned before things go too far. Our task is now in reality more difficult than ever, and this new trouble makes every hour of the direst importance. I can see the characteristics of the vampire coming in her face. It is now but very, very slight; but it is to be seen if we have eyes to notice without to prejudge. Her teeth are some sharper, and at times her eyes are more hard. But these are not all, there is to her the silence now often; as so it was with Miss Lucy. She did not speak, even when she wrote that which she wished to be known later. Now my fear is this. If it be that she can, by our hypnotic trance, tell what the Count see and hear, is it not more true that he who have hypnotise her first, and who have drink of her blood and make her drink of his, should, if he will, compel her mind to disclose to him that which she know?" I nodded acquiescence; he went on: —

"Then, what we must do is to prevent this; we must keep her ignorant of our intent, and so she cannot tell what she know not. This is a painful task! Oh! so painful that it heartbreak me to think of; but it must be. When to-day we meet, I must tell her that for reason which we will not to speak she must not more be of our council, but be simply guarded by us." He wiped his forehead, which had broken out in profuse perspiration at the thought of the pain which he might have to inflict upon the poor soul already so tortured. I knew that it would be some sort of comfort to him if I told him that I also had come to the same conclusion; for at any rate it would take away the pain of doubt. I told him, and the effect was as I expected.

It is now close to the time of our general gathering. Van Helsing has gone away to prepare for the meeting, and his painful part of it. I really believe his purpose is to be able to pray alone.

Later. — At the very onset of our meeting a great personal relief was experienced by both Van Helsing and myself. Mrs. Harker had sent a message by her husband to say that she would not join us at present, as she thought it better that we should be free to discuss our movements without her presence to embarrass us. The Professor and I looked at each other for an instant, and somehow we both seemed relieved. For my own part, I thought that if Mrs. Harker realised the danger herself, it was much pain as well as much danger averted. Under the circumstances we agreed, by a questioning look and answer, with finger on lip, to preserve silence of our suspicions, until we should have been able to confer alone again. We went at once into our Plan of Campaign. Van Helsing roughly put the facts before us first: —

"The *Czarina Catherine* left the Thames yesterday morning. It will take her at the quickest speed she has ever made at least three weeks to reach Varna; but we can travel overland to the same place in three days. Now, if we allow for two days less for the ship's voyage, owing to such weather influences as we know that the Count can bring to bear; and if we allow a whole day and night for any delays which may occur to us, then we have a margin of nearly two weeks. Thus, in order to be quite safe, we must leave here on 17th at latest. Then we shall at any rate be in Varna a day before the ship arrives, and able to make such preparations as may be necessary. Of course we shall all go armed — armed against evil things, spiritual as well as physical." Here Quincey Morris added: —

"I understand that the Count comes from a wolf country, and it may be that he shall get there before us. I propose that we add Winchesters° to our armament. I have a kind of belief in a Winchester when there is any trouble of that sort around. Do you remember Art, when we had the pack after us at Tobolsk°? What wouldn't we have given then for a repeater apiece!"

"Good!" said Van Helsing, "Winchesters it shall be. Quincey's head is level at all times, but most so when there is to hunt, though my metaphor be more dishonour to science than wolves be of danger to man. In the meantime we can do nothing here; and as I think that

---

Winchesters: American repeating rifles (as opposed to single-shot weapons) made by the Winchester Repeating Arms Company.   *Tobolsk:* A city in northwestern Russia.

Varna is not familiar to any of us, why not go there more soon? It is as long to wait here as there. To-night and to-morrow we can get ready, and then, if all be well, we four can set out on our journey."

"We four?" said Harker interrogatively, looking from one to another of us.

"Of course!' answered the Professor quickly, "You must remain to take care of your so sweet wife!" Harker was silent for awhile and then said in a hollow voice: —

"Let us talk to that part of it in the morning. I want to consult with Mina." I thought that now was the time for Van Helsing to warn him not to disclose our plans to her; but he took no notice. I looked at him significantly and coughed. For answer he put his finger on his lip and turned away.

Jonathan Harker's Journal

5 *October, afternoon.* — For some time after our meeting this morning I could not think. The new phases of things leave my mind in a state of wonder which allows no room for active thought. Mina's determination not to take any part in the discussion set me thinking; and as I could not argue the matter with her, I could only guess. I am as far as ever from a solution now. The way the others received it, too, puzzled me; the last time we talked of the subject we agreed that there was to be no more concealment of anything amongst us. Mina is sleeping now, calmly and sweetly like a little child. Her lips are curved and her face beams with happiness. Thank God there are such moments still for her.

Later. — How strange it all is. I sat watching Mina's happy sleep, and came as near to being happy myself as I suppose I shall ever be. As the evening drew on, and the earth took its shadows from the sun sinking lower, the silence of the room grew more and more solemn to me. All at once Mina opened her eyes, and looking at me tenderly, said: —

"Jonathan, I want you to promise me something on your word of honour. A promise made to me, but made holily in God's hearing, and not to be broken though I should go down on my knees and implore you with bitter tears. Quick, you must make it to me at once."

"Mina," I said, "a promise like that, I cannot make at once. I may have no right to make it."

"But, dear one," she said, with such spiritual intensity that her eyes were like pole stars, "it is I who wish it; and it is not for myself. You can ask Dr. Van Helsing if I am not right; if he disagrees you may do as you will. Nay more, if you all agree, later, you are absolved from the promise."

"I promise!" I said, and for a moment she looked supremely happy; though to me all happiness for her was denied by the red scar on her forehead. She said: —

"Promise me that you will not tell me anything of the plans formed for the campaign against the Count. Not by word, or inference, or implication; not at any time whilst this remains to me!" and she solemnly pointed to the scar. I saw that she was in earnest, and said solemnly: —

"I promise!" and as I said it I felt that from that instant a door had shut between us.

Later, midnight. — Mina has been bright and cheerful all the evening. So much so that all the rest seemed to take courage, as if infected somewhat with her gaiety; as a result even I myself felt as if the pall of gloom which weighs us down were somewhat lifted. We all retired early. Mina is now sleeping like a little child; it is a wonderful thing that her faculty of sleep remains to her in the midst of her terrible trouble. Thank God for it, for then at least she can forget her care. Perhaps her example may affect me as her gaiety did to-night. I shall try it. Oh! for a dreamless sleep.

6 *October, morning.* — Another surprise. Mina woke me early, about the same time as yesterday, and asked me to bring Dr. Van Helsing. I thought that it was another occasion for hypnotism, and without question went for the Professor. He had evidently expected some such call, for I found him dressed in his room. His door was ajar, so that he could hear the opening of the door of our room. He came at once; as he passed into the room, he asked Mina if the others might come too.

"No," she said quite simply, "it will not be necessary. You can tell them just as well. I must go with you on your journey."

Dr. Van Helsing was as startled as I was. After a moment's pause he asked: —

"But why?"

"You must take me with you. I am safer with you, and you shall be safer too."

"But why, dear Madam Mina? You know that your safety is our solemnest duty. We go into danger, to which you are, or may be, more liable than any of us from — from circumstances — things that have been." He paused embarrassed.

As she replied, she raised her finger and pointed to her forehead: —

"I know. That is why I must go. I can tell you now, whilst the sun is coming up; I may not be able again. I know that when the Count wills me I must go. I know that if he tells me to come in secret, I must come by wile; by any device to hoodwink — even Jonathan." God saw the look that she turned on me as she spoke, and if there be indeed a Recording Angel that look is noted to her everlasting honour. I could only clasp her hand. I could not speak; my emotion was too great for even the relief of tears. She went on: —

"You men are brave and strong. You are strong in your numbers, for you can defy that which would break down the human endurance of one who had to guard alone. Besides, I may be of service, since you can hypnotise me and so learn that which even I myself do not know." Dr. Van Helsing said very gravely: —

"Madam Mina you are, as always, most wise. You shall with us come; and together we shall do that which we go forth to achieve." When he had spoken, Mina's long spell of silence made me look at her. She had fallen back on her pillow asleep; she did not even wake when I had pulled up the blind and let in the sunlight which flooded the room. Van Helsing motioned to me to come with him quietly. We went to his room, and within a minute Lord Godalming, Dr. Seward, and Mr. Morris were with us also. He told them what Mina had said, and went on: —

"In the morning we shall leave for Varna. We have now to deal with a new factor: Madam Mina. Oh, but her soul is true. It is to hear an agony to tell us so much as she has done; but it is most right, and we are warned in time. There must be no chance lost, and in Varna we must be ready to act the instant when that ship arrives."

"What shall we do exactly?" asked Mr. Morris laconically. The Professor paused before relying: —

"We shall at the first board that ship; then, when we have identified the box, we shall place a branch of the wild rose on it. This we shall fasten, for when it is there none can emerge; so at least says the superstition. And to superstition must we trust at the first; it was man's faith in the early, and it have its root in faith still. Then, when we get the opportunity that we seek, when none are near to see, we shall open the box, and — and all will be well."

"I shall not wait for any opportunity," said Morris. "When I see the box I shall open it and destroy the monster, though there were a thousand men looking on, and if I am to be wiped out for it the next moment!" I grasped his hand instinctively and found it as firm as a piece of steel. I think he understood my look; I hope he did.

"Good boy ," said Dr. Van Helsing. "Brave boy. Quincey is all man, God bless him for it. My child, believe me none of us shall lag behind or pause from any fear. I do but say what we may do — what we must do. But, indeed, indeed we cannot say what we shall do. There are so many things which may happen, and their ways and their ends are so various that until the moment we may not say. We shall all be armed, in all ways; and when the time for the end has come, our effort shall not be lack. Now let us to-day put all our affairs in order. Let all things which touch on others dear to us, and who on us depend, be complete; for none of us can tell what, or when, or how, the end may be. As for me, my own affairs are regulate; and as I have nothing else to do, I shall go make arrangement for the travel. I shall have all tickets and so forth for our journey."

There was nothing further to be said, and we parted. I shall now settle up all my affairs of earth, and be ready for whatever may come. . . .

Later. — It is all done; my will is made, and all complete. Mina if she survive is my sole heir. If it should not be so, then the others who have been so good to us shall have remainder.

It is now drawing towards the sunset; Mina's uneasiness calls my attention to it. I am sure that there is something on her mind which the time of exact sunset will reveal. These occasions are becoming harrowing times for us all, for each sunrise and sunset opens up some new danger — some new pain, which, however, may in God's will be means to a good end. I write all these things in the diary since my darling must not hear them now; but if it may be that she can see them again, they shall be ready."

She is calling to me.

CHAPTER XXV. DR. SEWARD'S DIARY

11 *October, Evening.* — Jonathan Harker has asked me to note this, as he says he is hardly equal to the task, and he wants an exact record kept.

I think that none of us were surprised when we were asked to see Mrs. Harker a little before the time of sunset. We have of late come to understand that sunrise and sunset are to her times of peculiar freedom; when her old self can be manifest without any controlling force subduing or restraining her, or inciting her to action. This mood or condition begins some half hour or more before actual sunrise or sunset, and lasts till either the sun is high, or whilst the clouds are still aglow with the rays streaming above the horizon. At first there is a sort of negative condition, as if some tie were loosened, and then the absolute freedom quickly follows; when however the freedom ceases the change-back or relapse comes quickly, preceded only by a spell of warning silence.

To-night, when we met she was somewhat constrained, and bore all the signs of an internal struggle. I put it down myself to her making a violent effort at the earliest instant she could do so. A very few minutes, however, gave her complete control of herself; then, motioning her husband to sit beside her on the sofa where she was half reclining, she made the rest of us bring chairs up close. Taking her husband's hand in hers she began: —

"We are all here together in freedom, for perhaps the last time! I know dear; I know that you will always be with me to the end." This was to her husband whose hand had, as we could see, tightened upon hers. "In the morning we go out upon our task, and God alone knows what may be in store for any of us. You are going to be so good to me as to take me with you. I know that all that brave earnest men can do for a poor weak woman, whose soul perhaps is lost — no, no, not yet, but is at any rate at stake — you will do. But you must remember that I am not as you are. There is a poison in my blood, in my soul, which may destroy me; which must destroy me, unless some relief comes to us. Oh, my friends, you know as well as I do, that my soul is at stake; and though I know there is one way out for me, you must not and I must not take it!" She looked appealingly to us all in turn, beginning and ending with her husband.

"What is that way?" asked Van Helsing in a hoarse voice. "What is that way, which we must not — may not — take?"

"That I may die now, either by my own hand or that of another, before the greater evil is entirely wrought. I know and you know, that were I once dead you could and would set free my immortal spirit, even as you did my poor Lucy's. Were death, or the fear of death, the only thing that stood in the way I would not shrink to die here, now, amidst the friends who love me. But death is not all. I cannot believe that to die in such a case, when there is hope before us and a bitter task to be done, is God's will. Therefore, I on my part, give up here the certainty of eternal rest, and go out into the dark where may be the blackest things that the world or the nether world holds!" We were all silent, for we knew instinctively that this was only a prelude. The faces of the others were set, and Harker's grew ashen grey; perhaps he guessed better than any of us what was coming. She continued: —

"This is what I can give into the hotch-pot."° I could not but note the quaint legal phrase which she used in such a place, and with all seriousness. "What will each of you give? Your lives I know," she went on quickly, "that is easy for brave men. Your lives are God's, and you can give them back to Him; but what will you give to me?" She looked again questioningly, but this time avoided her husband's face. Quincey seemed to understand; he nodded, and her fact lit up. "Then I shall tell you plainly what I want, for there must be no doubtful matter in this connection between us now. You must promise me, one and all — even you my beloved husband — that, should the time come, you will kill me."

"What is that time?" The voice was Quincey's, but it was low and strained.

"When you shall be convinced that I am so changed that it is better that I die that I may live. When I am thus dead in the flesh, then you will, without a moment's delay, drive a stake through me and cut off my head; or do whatever else may be wanting to give me rest!"

Quincey was the first to rise after the pause. He knelt down before her and taking her hand in his said solemnly: —

"I'm only a rough fellow, who hasn't, perhaps, lived as a man should to win such a distinction, but I swear to you by all that I hold sacred and dear that, should the time ever come, I shall not flinch from the duty that you have set us. And I promise you, too, that I shall make all certain, for if I am only doubtful I shall take it that the time has come!"

"My true friend!" was all she could say amid her fast-falling tears, as, bending over, she kissed his hand.

"I swear the same, my dear Madam Mina!" said Van Helsing.

"And I!" said Lord Godalming, each of them in turn kneeling to her to take the oath. I followed, myself. Then her husband turned to her, wan-eyed and with a greenish pallor which subdued the snowy whiteness of his hair, and asked: —

"And must I, too, make such a promise, oh, my wife?"

"You too, my dearest," she said, with infinite yearning of pity in her voice and eyes. "You must not shrink. You are nearest and dearest and all the world to me; our souls are knit into one, for all life and all time. Think dear, that there have been times when brave men have killed their wives and their womenkind, to keep them from falling into the hands of the enemy. Their hands did not falter any the more because

hotch-pot: A legal term meaning to gather properties together so that they can be divided equally, especially when a person dies without a will (*OED* OL).

those that they loved implored them to slay them. It is men's duty towards those whom they love, in such times of sore trial! And oh, my dear, if it is to be that I must meet death at any hand, let it be at the hand of him that loves me best. Dr. Van Helsing, I have not forgotten your mercy in poor Lucy's case to him who loved" — she stopped with a flying blush, and changed her phrase — "to him who had best right to give her peace. If that time shall come again, I look to you to make it a happy memory of my husband's life that it was his loving hand which set me free from the awful thrall upon me."

"Again I swear!" came the Professor's resonant voice. Mrs. Harker smiled, positively smiled, as with a sigh of relief she leaned back and said: —

"And now one word of warning, a warning which you must never forget: this time, if it ever come, may come quickly and unexpectedly, and in such case you must lose no time in using your opportunity. At such a time I myself might be — nay! if the time ever comes, *shall* be — leagued with your enemy against you."

"One more request;" she became very solemn as she said this, "it is not vital and necessary like the other, but I want you to do one thing for me, if you will." We all acquiesced, but no one spoke; there was no need to speak: —

"I want you to read the Burial Service." She was interrupted by a deep groan from her husband; taking his hand in hers, she held it over her heart, and continued. "You must read it over me some day. Whatever may be the issue of all this fearful state of things, it will be a sweet thought to all or some of us. You, my dearest, will I hope read it, for then it will be in your voice in my memory for ever — come what may!"

"But oh, my dear one," he pleaded, "death is afar off from you."

"Nay," she said, holding up a warning hand. "I am deeper in death at this moment than if the weight of an earthly grave lay heavy upon me!"

"Oh, my wife, must I read it?" he said, before he began.

"It would comfort me, my husband!" was all she said; and he began to read when she had got the book ready.

How can I — how could any one — tell of that strange scene, its solemnity, its gloom, its sadness, its horror; and, withal, its sweetness. Even a sceptic, who can see nothing but a travesty of bitter truth in anything holy or emotional, would have been melted to the heart had he seen that little group of loving and devoted friends kneeling round that stricken and sorrowing lady; or heard the tender passion of her husband's voice, as in tones so broken with emotion that often he had to pause, he read the simple and beautiful service for the Burial of the Dead. I — I cannot go on — words — and — v-voice — f-fail m-me! . . . .

   She was right in her instinct. Strange as it all was, bizarre as it may hereafter seem even to us who felt its potent influence at the time, it comforted us much; and the silence, which showed Mrs. Harker's coming relapse from her freedom of soul, did not seem so full of despair to any of us as we had dreaded.

Jonathan Harker's Journal

   15 *October. Varna.* — We left Charing Cross° on the morning of the 12th, got to Paris the same night, and took the places secured for us in the Orient Express.° We travelled night and day, arriving here at about five o'clock. Lord Godalming went to the Consulate to see if any telegram had arrived for him, whilst the rest of us came on to this hotel — the Odessus. The journey may have had incidents; I was, however, too eager to get on, to care for them. Until the *Czarina Catherine* comes into port there will be no interest for me in anything in the wide world. Thank God! Mina is well, and looks to be getting stronger; her colour is coming back. She sleeps a great deal; throughout the journey she slept nearly all the time. Before sunrise and sunset, however, she is very wakeful and alert; and it has become a habit for Van Helsing to hypnotise her at such times. At first, some effort was needed, and he had to make many passes; but now, she seems to yield at once, as if by habit, and scarcely any action is needed. He seems to have power at these particular moments to simply will, and her thoughts obey him. He always asks her what she can see and hear. She answers to the first: —

   "Nothing; all is dark." And to the second: —

   "I can hear the waves lapping against the ship, and the water rushing by. Canvas and cordage strain and masts and yards creak. The wind is high — I can hear it in the shrouds, and the bow throws back the foam." It is evident that the *Czarina Catherine* is still at sea, hastening on her way to Varna. Lord Godalming has just returned. He had four telegrams, one each day since we started, and all to the same effect: that the *Czarina Catherine* had not been reported to Lloyd's from anywhere. He had arranged before leaving London that his agent should send him every day a telegram saying if the ship had been reported. He

---

Charing Cross: The location of Charing Cross Station, the terminus for the South-Eastern Railway (Black; *Baedeker* 1896).   *Orient Express:* A luxury train that began running from Paris to Varna in 1883 (*Enc. Brit.* OL).

was to have a message even if she were not reported, so that he might be sure that there was a watch being kept at the other end of the wire.

We had dinner and went to bed early. To-morrow we are to see the Vice-Consul, and to arrange, if we can, about getting on board the ship as soon as she arrives. Van Helsing says that our chance will be to get on board between sunrise and sunset. The Count, even if he takes the form of a bat, cannot cross the running water of his own volition, and so cannot leave the ship. As he dare not change to man's form without suspicion — which he evidently wishes to avoid — he must remain in the box. If, then, we can come on board after sunrise, he is at our mercy; for we can open the box and make sure of him, as we did of poor Lucy, before he wakes. What mercy he shall get from us will not count for much. We think that we shall not have much trouble with officials or the seamen. Thank God! this is the country where bribery can do anything, and we are well supplied with money. We have only to make sure that the ship cannot come into port between sunset and sunrise without our being warned, and we shall be safe. Judge Moneybag will settle this case, I think!

16 *October.* — Mina's report still the same: lapping waves and rushing water, darkness and favouring winds. We are evidently in good time, and when we hear of the *Czarina Catherine* we shall be ready. As she must pass the Dardanelles we are sure to have some report.

.   .   .

17 *October.* — Everything is pretty well fixed now, I think, to welcome the Count on his return from his tour. Godalming told the shippers that he fancied that the box sent aboard might contain something stolen from a friend of his, and got a half consent that he might open it at his own risk. The owner gave him a paper telling the Captain to give him every facility in doing whatever he chose on board the ship, and also a similar authorisation to his agent at Varna. We have seen the agent, who was much impressed with Godalming's kindly manner to him, and we are all satisfied that whatever he can do to aid our wishes will be done. We have already arranged what to do in case we get the box open. If the Count is there, Van Helsing and Seward will cut off his head at once and drive a stake through his heart. Morris and Godalming and I shall prevent interference, even if we have to use the arms which we shall have ready. The Professor says that if we can so treat the Count's body, it will soon after fall into dust. In such case there would be no evidence against us, in case any suspicion of murder were aroused. But even if it were not, we should stand or fall by our act and perhaps some day this very script may be evidence to come between

some of us and a rope. For myself, I should take the chance only too thankfully if it were to come. We mean to leave no stone upturned to carry out our intent. We have arranged with certain officials that the instant the *Czarina Catherine* is seen, we are to be informed by a special messenger.

24 *October.* — A whole week of waiting. Daily telegrams to Godalming, but only the same story: "Not yet reported." Mina's morning and evening hypnotic answer is unvaried: lapping waves, rushing water, and creaking masts.

Telegram, October 24th

Rufus Smith, Lloyd's, London, to Lord Godalming,
care of H.B.M. Vice-Consul,° Varna
"*Czarina Catherine* reported this morning from Dardanelles."

Dr. Seward's Diary

25 *October.* — How I miss my phonograph! To write diary with a pen is irksome to me; but Van Helsing says I must. We were all wild with excitement yesterday when Godalming got his telegram from Lloyd's. I know now what men feel in battle when the call to action is heard. Mrs. Harker, alone of our party, did not show any signs of emotion. After all, it is not strange that she did not; for we took special care not to let her know anything about it; and we all tried not to show any excitement when we were in her presence. In old days she would, I am sure, have noticed, no matter how we might have tried to conceal it; but in this way she is greatly changed during the past three weeks. The lethargy grows upon her, and though she seems strong and well, and is getting back some of her colour, Van Helsing and I are not satisfied. We talk of her often; we have not, however, said a word to the others. It would break poor Harker's heart — certainly his nerve — if he knew that we had even a suspicion on the subject. Van Helsing examines, he tells me, her teeth very carefully, whilst she is in the hypnotic condition, for he says that so long as they do not begin to sharpen there is no active danger of a change in her. If this change should come, it would be necessary to take steps! . . . . We both know what those steps would have to be, though we do not mention our thoughts to each other. We should neither of us shrink from the task — awful though it be to con-

---

H.B.M. *Vice-Consul:* Her Britannic Majesty's Vice-Consul, a consular official, deputy or assistant to the consul.

template. "Euthanasia" is is an excellent and a comforting word! I am grateful to whoever invented it.

It is only about 24 hours' sail from the Dardanelles to here, at the rate the *Czarina Catherine* has come from London. She should therefore arrive some time in the morning; but as she cannot possibly get in before then, we are all about to retire early. We shall get up at one o'clock, so as to be ready.

25 *October, Noon.* — No news yet of the ship's arrival. Mrs. Harker's hypnotic report this morning was the same as usual, so it is possible that we may get news at any moment. We men are all in fever of excitement, except Harker, who is calm; his hands are as cold as ice, and an hour ago I found him whetting the edge of the great Ghoorka knife which he now always carries with him. It will be a bad look out for the Count if the edge of that "Kukri" ever touches his throat, driven by that stern, ice-cold hand!

Van Helsing and I were a little alarmed about Mrs. Harker to-day. About noon she got into a sort of lethargy which we were neither of us happy about it. She had been restless all the morning, so that we were at first glad to know that she was sleeping. When, however, her husband mentioned casually that she was sleeping so soundly that he could not wake her, we went to her room to see for ourselves. She was breathing naturally and looked so well and peaceful that we agreed that the sleep was better for her than anything else. Poor girl, she has so much to forget that it is no wonder that sleep, if it brings oblivion to her, does her good.

Later. — Our opinion was justified, for when after a refreshing sleep of some hours she woke up, she seemed brighter and better than she has been for days. At sunset she made the usual hypnotic report. Wherever he may be in the Black Sea, the Count is hurrying to his destination. To his doom I trust!

26 *October.* — Another day and no tidings of the *Czarina Catherine*. She ought to be here by now. That she is still journeying *somewhere* is apparent, for Mrs. Harker's hypnotic report at sunrise was still the same. It is possible that the vessel may be lying by, at times, for fog; some of the streamers which came in last evening reported patches of fog both to north and south of the port. We must continue our watching, as the ship may now be signalled any moment.

27 *October, Noon.* — Most strange; no news yet of the ship we wait for. Mrs. Harker reported last night and this morning as usual: "lapping waves and rushing water." though she added that "the waves were very faint." The telegrams from London have been the same: "no further

report." Van Helsing is terribly anxious, and told me just now that he fears the Count is escaping us. He added significantly: —

"I did not like that lethargy of Madam Mina's. Souls and memories can do strange things during trance." I was about to ask him more, but Harker just then came in, and he held up a warning hand. We must try to-night, at sunset, to make her speak more fully when in her hypnotic state.

28 October. — Telegram

Rufus Smith, London, to Lord Godalming,
care of H.B.M. Vice-Consul, Varna

"*Czarina Catherine* reported entering Galatz° at one o'clock to-day."

Dr. Seward's Diary

28 *October.* — When the telegram came announcing the arrival in Galatz I do not think it was such a shock to any of us as might have been expected. True, we did not know whence, or how, or when, the bolt would come; but I think we all expected that something strange would happen. The delay of arrival at Varna made us individually satisfied that things would not be just as we had expected; we only waited to learn where the change would occur. None the less, however, was it a surprise. I supposed that nature works on such a hopeful basis that we believe against ourselves that things will be as they ought to be, not as we should know that they will be. Transcendentalism° is a beacon to the angels, even if it be a will-o'-the-wisp° to man. It was an odd experience, and we all took it differently. Van Helsing raised his hands over his head for a moment, as though in remonstrance with the Almighty; but he said not a word, and in a few seconds stood up with his face sternly set. Lord Godalming grew very pale, and sat breathing heavily. I was myself half stunned and looked in wonder at one after another. Quincey Morris tightened his belt with that quick movement which I knew so well; in our old wandering days it meant "action." Mrs. Harker grew ghastly white, so that the scar on her forehead seemed to burn,

---

Galatz: A city in Romania located on the Danube, about 120 miles northeast of Bucharest.   **Transcendentalism:** An idealistic nineteenth-century movement of New England writers and philosophers who believed in the innate goodness of human nature and attempted to improve the social institutions of their time by experimenting with reforms such as communal living, suffrage for women, and better conditions for workers (*Enc. Brit.* OL).   **will-o'-the-wisp:** A delusive or misleading hope.

but she folded her hands meekly and looked up in prayer. Harker smiled — actually smiled — the dark bitter smile of one who is without hope; but at the same time his action belied his words, for his hands instinctively sought the hilt of the great Kukri knife and rested there.

"When does the next train start for Galatz?" said Van Helsing to us generally.

"At 6.30 to-morrow morning!" We all stared, for the answer came from Mrs. Harker.

"How on earth do you know?" said Art.

"You forget — or perhaps you do not know, though Jonathan does and so does Dr. Van Helsing — that I am the train fiend. At home in Exeter I always used to make up the time-tables, so as to be helpful to my husband. I found it so useful sometimes, that I always make a study of the time-tables now. I knew that if anything were to take us to Castle Dracula we should go by Galatz, or at any rate through Bucharest,° so I learned the times very carefully. Unhappily there are not many to learn, as the only train to-morrow leaves as I say."

"Wonderful woman!" murmured the Professor.

"Can't we get a special?"° asked Lord Godalming. Van Helsing shook his head: "I fear not. This land is very different from your's or mine; even if we did have a special, it would probably not arrive as soon as our regular train. Moreover we have something to prepare. We must think. Now let us organize. You, friend Arthur, go to the train and get the tickets and arrange that all be ready for us to go in the morning. Do you, friend Jonathan, go to the agent of the ship and get from him letters to the agent in Galatz, with authority to make search the ship just as it was here. Morris Quincey, you see the Vice-Consul, and get his aid with his fellow in Galatz and all he can do to make our way smooth, so that no times be lost when over the Danube. John will stay with Madam Mina and me, and we shall consult. For so if time be long you may be delayed; and it will not matter when the sun set, since I am here with Madam to make report."

"And I," said Mrs. Harker brightly, and more like her old self than she had been for many a long day, "shall try to be of use in all ways, and shall think and write for you as I used to do. Something is shifting from me in some strange way, and I feel freer than I have been of late!" The three younger men looked happier at the moment as they seemed to realise the significance of her words; but Van Helsing and I, turning to

---

Bucharest: The capital of Romania.   *special:* A train hired privately for a specific journey.

each other, met each a grave and troubled glance. We said nothing at
the time however.

When the three men had gone out to their tasks Van Helsing asked
Mrs. Harker to look up the copy of the diaries and find him the part of
Harker's journal at the Castle. She went away to get it; when the door
was shut upon her he said to me: —

"We mean the same! speak out!"

"There is some change. It is a hope that makes me sick, for it may
deceive us."

"Quite so. Do you know why I asked her to get the manuscript?"

"No!" said I, "unless it was to get an opportunity of seeing me
alone."

"You are part right, friend John, but only in part. I want to tell you
something. And oh, my friend, I am taking a great — a terrible — risk;
but I believe it is right. In the moment when Madam Mina said those
words that arrest both our understanding, an inspiration come to me.
In the trance of three days ago the Count sent her his spirit to read her
mind; or more like he took her to see him in his earth-box in the ship
with water rushing, just as it go free at rise and set of sun. He learn then
that we are here; for she have more to tell in her open life with eyes to
see and ears to hear than he, shut, as he is, in his coffin-box. Now he
make his most effort to escape us. At present he want her not. He is
sure with his so great knowledge that she will come at his call; but he
cut her off — take her, as he can do, out of his own power, that so she
come not to him. Ah! there I have hope that our man-brains that have
been of man so long and that have not lost the grace of God, will come
higher than his child-brain that lie in his tomb for centuries, that grow
not yet to our stature, and that do only work selfish and therefore small.
Here comes Madam Mina; not a word to her of her trance! She know it
not; and it would overwhelm her and make despair just when we want
all her hope, all her courage; when most we want all her great brain
which is trained like man's brain, but is of sweet woman and have a
special power which the Count give her, and which he may not take
away altogether — though he think not so. Hush! let me speak, and
you shall learn. Oh John, my friend, we are in awful straits. I fear, as I
never feared before. We can only trust the good God. Silence! here she
comes!"

I thought that the Professor was going to break down and have hysterics, just as he had when Lucy died, but with a great effort he controlled himself and was at perfect nervous poise when Mrs. Harker
tripped into the room, bright and happy-looking and, in the doing of

work, seemingly forgetful of her misery. As she came in, she handed a number of sheets of typewriting to Van Helsing. He looked over them gravely, his face brightening up as he read. Then holding the pages between his finger and thumb he said: —

"Friend John, to you with so much of experience already — and you too, dear Madam Mina, that are young, — here is a lesson: do not fear ever to think. A half-thought has been buzzing often in my brain, but I fear to let him loose his wings. Here now, with more knowledge, I go back to where that half-thought come from, and I find that he be no half-thought at all; that be a whole thought, though so young that he is not yet strong to use his little wings. Nay, like the "Ugly Duck" of my friend Hans Andersen,° he be no duck-thought at all, but a big swan-thought that sail nobly on big wings, when the time come for him to try them. See I read here what Jonathan have written: —

" 'That other of his race who, in a later age, again and again, brought his forces over The Great River into Turkey Land; who, when he was beaten back, came again, and again, and again, though he had to come alone from the bloody field where his troops were being slaughtered, since he knew that he alone could ultimately triumph.'

"What does this tell us? Not much? no! The Count's child-thought see nothing; therefore he speak so free. Your man-thought see nothing; my man-thought see nothing, till just now. No! But there comes another word from some one who speak without thought because she too know not what it mean — what it *might* mean. Just as there are elements which rest, yet when in nature's course they move on their way and they touch — then pouf! and there comes a flash of light, heaven's wide, that blind and kill and destroy some; but that show up all earth below for leagues and leagues. Is it not so? Well, I shall explain. To begin have you ever study the philosophy of crime. 'Yes' and 'No.' You, John, yes; for it is a study of insanity. You, no, Madam Mina; for crime touch you not — not but once. Still, your mind works true, and argues not *a particulari ad universale.*° There is this peculiarity in criminals. It is so constant, in all countries and at all times, that even police, who know not much from philosophy, come to know it empirically, that *it is.* That is to be empiric. The criminal always work at one crime — that is the true criminal who seems predestinate to crime, and who will of none other. This criminal has not full man-brain. He is clever and cunning

Ugly Duck . . . Hans Andersen: In "The Ugly Duckling," a tale by the Danish writer Hans Christian Andersen (1805–1875), a duckling rejected for his ugliness turns out to be a swan.   *a particulari ad universale:* From the particular to the universal or general (Latin).

and resourceful; but he be not of man-stature as to brain. He be of child-brain in much. Now this criminal of ours is predestinate to crime also; he too have child-brain, and it is of the child to do what he have done. The little bird, the little fish, the little animal learn not by principle, but empirically; and when he learn to do, then there is to him the ground to start from to do more. '*Dos pou sto,*' said Archimedes. "Give me a fulcrum, and I shall move the world!"° To do once, is the fulcrum whereby child-brain become man-brain; and until he have the purpose to do more, he continue to do the same again every time, just as he have done before! Oh, my dear. I see that your eyes are opened, and that to you the lightning flash show all the leagues," for Mrs. Harker began to clap her hands, and her eyes sparkled. He went on: —

"Now you shall speak. Tell us two dry men of science what you see with those so bright eyes." He took her hand and held it whilst she spoke. His finger and thumb closed on her pulse, as I thought instinctively and unconsciously, as she spoke: —

"The Count is a criminal and of criminal type. Nordau° and Lombroso° would so classify him, and *quâ* criminal he is of imperfectly formed mind. Thus, in a difficulty he has to seek resource in habit. His past is a clue, and the one page of it that we know — and that from his own lips — tells that once before, when in what Mr. Morris would call a 'tight place,' he went back to his own country from the land he had tried to invade, and thence, without losing purpose, prepared himself for a new effort. He came again, better equipped for his work; and won. So he came to London to invade a new land. He was beaten, and when all hope of success was lost, and his existence in danger, he fled back over the sea to his home; just as formerly he had fled back over the Danube from Turkey land."

"Good, good! oh, you so clever lady!" said Van Helsing, enthusiastically, as he stooped and kissed her hand. A moment later he said to me, as calmly as though we had been having a sick room consultation: —

"Seventy-two only; and in all this excitement. I have hope." Turning to her again, he said with keen expectation: —

'*Dos pou sto,*' *said Archimedes. . . . move the world:* Archimedes (287–212 B.C.E.), a Greek mathematician and inventor, is reputed to have made this statement to Hiero, King of Syracuse (*Enc. Brit.* OL; *Enc. Brit.* 11th).   *Nordau:* Max Nordau (1849–1923), Hungarian physician and prominent Zionist, argued in his book *Degeneration* that civilized man was degenerating intellectually as well as physically and that the modern era was one of decadence and confusion (*Enc. Brit.* 11th).   *Lombroso:* Cesar Lombroso (1835–1909), Italian criminologist, proposed that criminal tendencies were inherited. He believed that criminals were throwbacks to earlier evolutionary stages and could be identified by physical characteristics (*Enc. Brit.* OL).

"But go on. Go on! there is more to tell if you will. Be not afraid; John and I know. I do in any case, and shall tell you if you are right. Speak, without fear!"

"I will try to; but you will forgive me if I seem egotistical."

"Nay! fear not, you must be egotist, for it is of you that we think."

"Then, as he is criminal he is selfish; and as his intellect is small and his action is based on selfishness, he confines himself to one purpose. That purpose is remorseless. As he fled back over the Danube, leaving his forces to be cut to pieces, so now he is intent on being safe, careless of all. So, his own selfishness frees my soul somewhat of the terrible power which he acquired over me on that dreadful night. I felt it, Oh! I felt it. Thank God, for His great mercy! My soul is freer than it has been since that awful hour; and all that haunts me is a fear lest in some trance or dream he may have used my knowledge for his ends." The Professor stood up: —

"He has so used your mind; and by it he has left us here in Varna, whilst the ship that carried him rushed through enveloping fog up to Galatz, where, doubtless, he had made preparation for escaping from us. But his child-mind only saw so far; and it may be that, as ever is in God's Providence, the very thing that the evil doer most reckoned on for his selfish good, turns out to be his chiefest harm. The hunter is taken in his own snare, as the great Psalmist says.° For now that he think he is free from every trace of us all, and that he has escaped us with so many hours to him, then his selfish child-brain will whisper him to sleep. He think, too, that as he cut himself off from knowing your mind, there can be no knowledge of him to you; there is where he fail! That terrible baptism of blood which he give you makes you free to go to him in spirit, as you have as yet done in your times of freedom, when the sun rise and set. At such times you go by my volition and not his; and this power to good of you and others, you have won from your suffering at his hands. This is now all more precious that he know it not, and to guard himself have even cut himself off from his knowledge of our where. We, however, are not all selfish, and we believe that God is with us through all this blackness, and these many dark hours. We shall follow him; and we shall not flinch; even if we peril ourselves that we become like him. Friend John, this has been a great hour; and it have done much to advance us on our way. You must be scribe and write him all down, so that when the others return from their work you can give it to them; then they shall know as we do."

The hunter is taken . . . Psalmist says: See Ps. 9.15–16.

And so I have written it whilst we wait their return, and Mrs. Harker has written with her typewriter all since she brought the MS. to us.

CHAPTER XXVI. DR. SEWARD'S DIARY

29 *October.* — This is written in the train from Varna to Galatz. Last night we all assembled a little before the time of sunset. Each of us had done his work as well as he could; so far as thought, and endeavour, and opportunity go, we are prepared to get to Galatz. When the usual time came round Mrs. Harker prepared herself for her hypnotic effort; and after a longer and more strenuous effort on the part of Van Helsing than has been usually necessary, she sank into the trance. Usually she speaks on a hint; but this time the Professor had to ask her questions, and to ask them pretty resolutely, before we could learn anything; at last her answer came: —

"I can see nothing; we are still; there are no waves lapping, but only a steady swirl of water softly running against the hawser.° I can hear men's voices calling, near and far, and the roll and creak of oars in the rowlocks. A gun is fired somewhere; the echo of it seems far away. There is tramping of feet overhead, and ropes and chains are dragged along. What is this? There is a gleam of light; I can feel the air blowing upon me."

Here she stopped. She had risen, as if impulsively, from where she lay on the sofa, and raised both her hands, palms upwards, as if lifting a weight. Van Helsing and I looked at each other with understanding. Quincey raised his eye-brows slightly and looked at her intently, whilst Harker's hand instinctively closed round the hilt of his Kukri. There was a long pause. We all knew that the time when she could speak was passing; but we felt it was useless to say anything. Suddenly she sat up, and, as she opened her eyes, said sweetly: —

"Would none of you like a cup of tea? You must all be so tired!" We could only make her happy, and so acquiesced. She bustled off to get tea; when she had gone Van Helsing said: —

"You see, my friends. *He* is close to land: he has left his earth-chest. But he has yet to get on shore. In the night he may lie hidden somewhere; but if he be not carried on shore, or if the ship do not touch it, he cannot achieve the land. In such case he can, if it be in the night, change his form and can jump or fly on shore, as he did at Whitby. But

hawser: A rope used to moor or tow a ship (*OED* OL).

if the day come before he get on shore, then, unless he be carried he cannot escape. And if he be carried, then the customs men may discover what the box contains. Thus, in fine, if he escape not on shore to-night, or before dawn, there will be the whole day lost to him. We may then arrive in time; for if he escape not at night we shall come on him in day-time, boxed up and at our mercy; for he dare not be his true self, awake and visible, lest he be discovered."

There was nor more to be said, so we waited in patience until the dawn; at which time we might learn more from Mrs. Harker.

Early this morning we listened, with breathless anxiety, for her response in her trance. The hypnotic stage was even longer in coming than before; and when it came the time remaining until full sunrise was so short that we began to despair. Van Helsing seemed to throw his whole soul into the effort; at last, in obedience to his will she made reply: —

"All is dark. I hear lapping water, level with me, and some creaking as of wood on wood." She paused, and the red sun shot up. We must wait till to-night.

And so it is that we are travelling towards Galatz in an agony of expectation. We are due to arrive between two and three in the morning; but already, at Bucharest, we are three hours late, so we cannot possibly get in till well after sun-up. Thus we shall have two more hypnotic messages from Mrs. Harker; either or both may possibly throw more light on what is happening.

Later. — Sunset had come and gone. Fortunately it came at a time when there was no distraction; for had it occurred whilst we were at a station, we might not have secured the necessary calm and isolation. Mrs. Harker yielded to the hypnotic influence even less readily than this morning. I am in fear that her power of reading the Count's sensations may die away, just when we want it most. It seems to me that her imagination is beginning to work. Whilst she has been in the trance hitherto she has confined herself to the simplest of facts. If this goes on it may ultimately mislead us. If I thought that the Count's power over her would die away equally with her power of knowledge it would be a happy thought; but I am afraid that it may not be so. When she did speak, her words were enigmatical: —

"Something is going out; I can feel it pass me like a cold wind. I can hear, far off, confused sounds — as of men talking in strange tongues, fierce-falling water, and the howling of wolves." She stopped and a shudder ran through her, increasing in intensity for a few seconds, till, at the end, she shook as though in a palsy. She said no more, even in answer to her Professor's imperative questioning. When she woke from the trance, she was cold, and exhausted, and languid; but her mind was all alert. She could not remember anything, but asked what she had said; when she was told, she pondered over it deeply, for a long time and in silence.

30 *October, 7 a.m.* — We are near Galatz now, and I may not have time to write later. Sunrise this morning was anxiously looked for by us all. Knowing of the increasing difficulty of procuring the hypnotic trance Van Helsing began his passes earlier than usual. They produced no effect, however, until the regular time when she yielded with a still greater difficulty, only a minute before the sun rose. The Professor lost no time in his questioning; her answer came with equal quickness: —

"All is dark. I hear water swirling by, level with my ears, and the creaking of wood on wood. Cattle low far off. There is another sound, a queer one like —" she stopped and grew white, and whiter still.

"Go on; Go on! Speak, I command you!" said Van Helsing in an agonized voice. At the same time there was despair in his eyes, for the risen sun was reddening even Mrs. Harker's pale face. She opened her eyes, and we all started as she said, sweetly and seemingly with the utmost unconcern: —

"Oh Professor why ask me to do what you know I can't? I don't remember anything." Then, seeing the look of amazement on our faces, she said, turning from one to the other with a troubled look: —

"What have I said? What have I done? I know nothing, only that I was lying here, half asleep, and I heard you say 'go on! speak, I command you!' It seemed so funny to hear you order me about, as if I were a bad child!"

"Oh, Madam Mina" he said, sadly, "it is proof, if proof be needed, of how I love and honour you, when a word for your good, spoken more earnest than ever, can seem so strange because it is to order her whom I am proud to obey!"

The whistles are sounding; we are nearing Galatz. We are on fire with anxiety and eagerness.

Mina Harker's Journal

30 *October.* — Mr. Morris took me to the hotel where our rooms had been ordered by telegraph, he being the one who could best be spared, since he does not speak any foreign language. The forces were distributed much as they had been at Varna, except that Lord Godalming went to the Vice-Consul as his rank might serve as an immediate

guarantee of some sort to the official, we being in extreme hurry. Jonathan and the two doctors went to the shipping agent to learn particulars of the arrival of the *Czarina Catherine.*

Later. — Lord Godalming has returned. The Consul is away, and the Vice-Consul sick; so the routine work has been attended by a clerk. He was very obliging, and offered to do anything in his power.

Jonathan Harker's Journal

30 October. — At nine o'clock Dr. Van Helsing, Dr. Seward, and I called on Messrs. Mackenzie & Steinkoff, the agents of the London firm of Hapgood. They had received a wire from London, in answer to Lord Godalming's telegraphed request, asking them to show us any civility in their power. They were more than kind and courteous, and took us at once on board the *Czarina Catherine* which lay at anchor out in the river harbour. There we saw the Captain, Donelson by name, who told us of his voyage. He said that in all his life he had never had so favourable a run.

"Man!" he said, "but it made us afeard, for we expeckit that we should have to pay for it wi' some rare piece o' ill luck, so as to keep up the average. It's no canny° to run frae London to the Black Sea wi' a wind ahint° ye, as though the Deil himself were blawin' on yer sail for his ain purpose. An' a' the time we could not speer° a thing. Gin° we were nigh a ship, or a port, or a headland, a fog fell on us and travelled wi' us, till when after it had lifted and we looked out, the deil a thing could we see. We ran by Gibraltar wi'oot bein' able to signal; an' till we came to the Dardanelles and had to wait to get our permit to pass, we never were within hail o' aught. At first I inclined to slack off sail and beat about till the fog was lifted; but whiles,° I tocht that if the Deil was minded to get us into the Black Sea quick, he was like to do it whether we would or no. If we had a quick voyage it would be no to our miscredit wi't he owners, or no hurt to our traffic; an' the Old Mon who had served his ain purpose wad be decently grateful to us for no hinderin' him." This mixture of simplicity and cunning, of superstition and commercial reasoning, aroused Van Helsing, who said: —

"Mine friend, that Devil is more clever than he is thought by some; and he know when he meet his match!" The skipper was not displeased with the compliment, and went on: —

---

no canny: Unnatural (dialect). *ahint:* Behind (dialect). *speer:* Though dictionaries of Scottish dialect give "ask" as the primary meaning, here the word seems to mean "see." *Gin:* When (dialect). *whiles:* Meanwhile (dialect).

"When we got past the Bosphorus the men began to grumble; some o' them, the Roumanians, came and asked me to heave overboard a big box which had been put on board by a queer lookin' old man just before we had started frae London. I had seen them speer at the fellow, and put out their twa fingers when they saw him, to guard against the evil eye. Man! but the supersteetion of foreigners is pairfectly rideeculous! I sent them aboot their business pretty quick; but as just after a fog closed in on us, I felt a wee bit as they did anent° something, though I wouldn't say it was agin° the bit box. Well, on we went, and as the fog didn't let up for five days I joost let the wind carry us; for if the Deil wanted to get somewheres — well, he would fetch it up a'reet. An' if he didn't, well we'd keep a sharp look out anyhow. Sure enuch, we had a fair way and deep water all the time; and two days ago, when the mornin' sun came through the fog, we found ourselves just in the river opposite Galatz. The Roumanians were wild, and wanted me right or wrong to take out the box and fling it in the river. I had to argy wi' them aboot it wi' a handspike;° an' when the last o' them rose off the deck, wi' his head in his hand, I had convinced them that, evil eye or no evil eye, the property and the trust of my owners were better in my hands than in the river Danube. They had, mind ye, taken the box on the deck ready to fling in, and as it was marked Galatz *viâ* Varna, I thocht I'd let it lie till we discharged in the port an' get rid o't athegither. We didn't do much clearin' that day, an' had to remain the nicht at anchor; but in the mornin', braw an' airly,° an hour before sun-up, a man came aboard wi' an order, written to him from England, to receive a box marked for one Count Dracula. Sure enuch the matter was one ready to his hand. He had his papers a' reet, an' glad I was to be rid o' the dam thing, for I was beginnin' masel' to feel uneasy at it. If the Deil did have any luggage aboord the ship, I'm thinkin' it was nane ither than that same!

"What was the name of the man who took it?" asked Dr. Van Helsing with restrained eagerness.

"I'll be tellin' ye' quick!" he answered, and, stepping down to his cabin, produced a receipt signed "Immanuel Hildesheim." Burgenstrasse 16 was the address. We found out that this was all the Captain knew; so with thanks we came away.

We found Hildesheim in his office, a Hebrew of rather the Adelphi Theatre° type, with a nose like a sheep, and a fez. His arguments were

---

anent: About (dialect).   **agin:** Concerning.   **handspike:** A wooden bar used as a lever.   **braw an' airly:** Bright and early, very early.   **Adelphi Theatre:** A London theater famous for melodrama, farce, and spectacular effects (Black; *Baedeker* 1896).

pointed with specie° — we doing the punctuation — and with a little bargaining he told us what he knew. This turned out to be simple but important. He had received a letter from Mr. de Ville of London, telling him to receive, if possible before sunrise so as to avoid customs, a box which would arrive at Galatz in the *Czarina Catherine*. This he was to give in charge to a certain Petrof Skinsky, who dealt with the Slovaks who traded down the river to the port. He had been paid for his work by an English bank note, which had been duly cashed for gold at the Danube International Bank. When Skinsky had come to him, he had taken him to the ship and handed over the box, so as to save porterage.° That was all he knew.

We then sought for Skinsky, but were unable to find him. One of his neighbours, who did not seem to bear him any affection, said that he had gone away two days before, no one knew whither. This was corroborated by his landlord who had received by messenger the key of the house together with the rent due, in English money. This had been between ten and eleven o'clock last night. We were at a standstill again.

Whilst we were talking one came running and breathlessly gasped out that the body of Skinsky had been found inside the wall of the churchyard of St. Peter, and that the throat had been torn open as if by some wild animal. Those we had been speaking with ran off to see the horror, the women crying out "This is the work of a Slovak!" We hurried away lest we should have been in some way drawn into the affair, and so detained.

As we came home we could arrive at no definite conclusion. We were all convinced that the box was on its way, by water, to somewhere; but where that might be we would have to discover. With heavy hearts we came home to the hotel to Mina.

When we met together, the first thing was to consult as to taking Mina again into our confidence. Things are getting desperate, and it is at least a chance, though a hazardous one. As a preliminary step, I was released from my promise to her.

Mina Harker's Journal

30 *October, evening.* — They were so tired and worn out and dispirited that there was nothing to be done till they had some rest; so I asked them all to lie down for half an hour whilst I should enter everything

---

specie: Money *(OED)*.   **porterage:** A charge for the transportation of goods *(OED* OL).

up to the moment. I feel so grateful to the man who invented the "Traveller's" typewriter, and to Mr. Morris for getting this one for me. I should have felt quite astray doing the work if I had to write with a pen. . . .

It is all done; poor dear, dear Jonathan, what he must have suffered, what must he be suffering now. He lies on the sofa hardly seeming to breathe, and his whole body appears in collapse. His brows are knit; his face is drawn with pain. Poor fellow, maybe he is thinking, and I can see his face all wrinkled up with the concentration of his thoughts. Oh! if I could only help at all. . . . I shall do what I can. . . .

I have asked Dr. Van Helsing, and he has got me all the papers that I have not yet seen. . . . Whilst they are resting, I shall go over all carefully, and perhaps I may arrive at some conclusion. I shall try to follow the Professor's example, and think without prejudice on the facts before me. . . .

I do believe that under God's providence I have made a discovery. I shall get the maps and look over them. . . .

I am more than ever sure that I am right. My new conclusion is ready, so I shall get our party together and read it. They can judge it; it is well to be accurate, and every minute is precious.

Mina Harker's Memorandum

(Entered in Her Journal)

Ground of inquiry. — Count Dracula's problem is to get back to his own place.

(*a*) He must be *brought back* by some one. This is evident; for had he power to move himself as he wished he could go either as man, or wolf, or bat, or in some other way. He evidently fears discovery or interference, in the state of helplessness in which he must be — confined as he is between dawn and sunset in his wooden box.

(*b*) *How is he to be taken?* — Here a process of exclusions may help us. By road, by rail, by water?

1. *By Road.* — There are endless difficulties, especially in leaving a city.

(*x*) There are people; and people are curious, and investigate. A hint, a surmise, a doubt as to what might be in the box, would destroy him.

(*y*) There are, or there might be, customs and octroi officers° to pass.

---

octroi officers: Officers collecting taxes on certain articles at the town borders *(OED).*

(*z*) His pursuers might follow. This is his greatest fear; and in order to prevent his being betrayed he has repelled, so far as he can, even his victim — me!

2. *By Rail.* — There is no one in charge of the box. It would have to take its chance of being delayed; and delay would be fatal, with enemies on the track. True, he might escape at night; but what would he be, if left in a strange place with no refuge that he could fly to. This is not what he intends; and he does not mean to risk it.

3. *By Water.* — Here is the safest way, in one respect, but with most danger in another. On the water he is powerless except at night; even then he can only summon fog and storm and snow and his wolves. But were he wrecked, the living water would engulf him, helpless; and he would indeed be lost. He could have the vessel drive to land; but if it were unfriendly land, wherein he was not free to move, his position would still be desperate.

We know from the record that he was on the water; so what we have to do is to ascertain *what* water.

The first thing is to realise exactly what he has done as yet; we may, then, get a light on what his later task is to be.

Firstly. — We must differentiate between what he did in London as part of his general plan of action, when he was pressed for moments and had to arrange as best he could.

Secondly we must see, as well as we can surmise it from the facts we know of, what he has done here.

As to the first, he evidently intended to arrive at Galatz, and sent invoice to Varna to deceive us lest we should ascertain his means of exit from England; his immediate and sole purpose then was to escape. The proof of this, is the letter of instructions sent to Immanuel Hildesheim to clear and take away the box *before sunrise.* There is also the instruction to Petrof Skinsky. These we must only guess at; but there must have been some letter or message, since Skinsky came to Hildesheim.

That, so far, his plans were successful we know. The *Czarina Catherine* made a phenomenally quick journey — so much so that Captain Donelson's suspicions were aroused; but his superstition united with his canniness played the Count's game for him, and he ran with his favouring wind through fogs and all till he brought up blindfold° at Galatz. That the Count's arrangements were well made, has been proved. Hildesheim cleared the box, took it off, and gave it to Skinsky.

blindfold: "Without forethought, heedless, reckless" (*OED* 2: 288).

Skinsky took it — and here we lose the trail. We only know that the box is somewhere on the water, moving along. The customs and the octroi, if there be any, have been avoided.

Now we come to what the Count must have done after his arrival — *on land,* at Galatz.

The box was given to Skinsky before sunrise. At sunrise the Count could appear in his own form. Here, we ask why Skinsky was chosen at all to aid in the work? In my husband's diary, Skinsky is mentioned as dealing with the Slovaks who trade down the river to the port; and the man's remark, that the murder was the work of a Slovak, showed the general feeling against his class. The Count wanted isolation.

My surmise is, this: that in London the Count decided to get back to his Castle by water, as the most safe and secret way. He was brought from the Castle by Szgany, and probably they delivered their cargo to Slovaks who took the boxes to Varna, for there they were shipped for London. Thus the Count had knowledge of the persons who could arrange this service. When the box was on land, before sunrise or after sunset, he came out from his box, met Skinsky and instructed him what to do as to arranging the carriage of the box up some river. When this was done, and he knew that all was in train, he blotted out his traces, as he thought, by murdering his agent.

I have examined the map and find that the river most suitable for the Slovaks to have ascended is either the Pruth or the Sereth.° I read in the typescript that in my trance I heard cows low and water swirling level with my ears and the creaking of wood. The Count in his box, then, was on a river in an open boat — propelled probably either by oars or poles, for the banks are near and it is working against stream. There would be no such sound if floating down stream.

Of course it may not be either the Sereth or the Pruth, but we may possibly investigate further. Now of these two, the Pruth is the more easily navigated, but the Sereth is, at Fundu,° joined by the Bistritza° which runs up round the Borgo pass. The loop it makes is manifestly as close to Dracula's Castle as can be got by water."

Pruth . . . Sereth: Two of Romania's principal rivers, both of which join the Danube close to Galatz. The Pruth formed the eastern boundary of Romania, separating the district of Moldavia from Russia. The Sereth originated in Transylvania, flowing through Moldavia until it reached the Danube (*Enc. Brit.* 11th).   **Fundu:** As with some of the geography of Hampstead Heath, this location seems to be fictitious.   **Bistritza:** A tributary of the Sereth (*Enc. Brit.* 11th).

Mina Harker's Journal *(Continued)*

When I had done reading, Jonathan took me in his arms and kissed me. The others kept shaking me by both hands, and Dr. Van Helsing said: —

"Our dear Madam Mina is once more our teacher. Her eyes have seen where we were blinded. Now we are on the track once again, and this time we may succeed. Our enemy is at his most·helpless; and if we can come on him by day, on the water, our task will be over. He has a start, but he is powerless to hasten, as he may not leave his box lest those who carry him may suspect; for them to suspect would be to prompt them to throw him in the stream where he perish. This he knows, and will not. Now men, to our Council of War; for, here and now, we must plan what each and all shall do."

"I shall get a steam launch and follow him" said Lord Godalming.

"And I, horses to follow on the bank lest by chance he land," said Mr. Morris.

"Good!" said the Professor, "both good. But neither must go alone. There must be force to overcome force if need be; the Slovak is strong and rough, and he carries rude arms." All the men smiled, for amongst them they carried a small arsenal. Said Mr. Morris: —

"I have brought some Winchesters; they are pretty handy in a crowd, and there may be wolves. The Count, if you remember, took some other precautions; he made some requisitions on others that Mrs. Harker could not quite hear or understand. We must be ready at all points." Dr. Seward said: —

"I think I had better go with Quincey. We have been accustomed to hunt together, and we two, well armed, will be a match for whatever may come along. You must not be alone Art. It may be necessary to fight the Slovaks, and a chance thrust — for I don't suppose these fellows carry guns — would undo all our plans. There must be no chances, this time; we shall not rest until the Count's head and body have been separated, and we are sure that he cannot re-incarnate." He looked at Jonathan as he spoke, and Jonathan looked at me. I could see that the poor dear was torn about in his mind. Of course he wanted to be with me; but then the boat service would, most likely, be the one which would destroy the . . . the . . . the . . . Vampire. (Why did I hesitate to write the word?) He was silent awhile, and during his silence Dr. Van Helsing spoke: —

"Friend Jonathan, this is to you for twice reasons. First, because you

are young and brave and can fight, and all energies may be needed at
the last; and again that it is your right to destroy him — that — which
has wrought such woe to you and yours. Be not afraid for Madam
Mina; she will be my care, if I may. I am old. My legs are not so quick to
run as once; and I am not used to ride so long or to pursue as need be,
or to fight with lethal weapons. But I can be of other service; I can fight
in other way. And I can die, if need be, as well as younger men. Now let
me say that what I would is this: while you, my Lord Godalming, and
friend Jonathan go in your so swift little steamboat up the river, and
whilst John and Quincey guard the bank where perchance he might be
landed, I will take Madam Mina right into the heart of the enemy's
country. Whilst the old fox is tied in his box, floating on the running
stream whence he cannot escape to land — where he dares not raise
the lid of his coffin-box lest his Slovak carriers should in fear leave
him to perish — we shall go in the track where Jonathan went, — from
Bistritz over the Borgo, and find our way to the Castle of Dracula.
Here, Madam Mina's hypnotic power will surely help, and we shall find
our way — all dark and unknown otherwise — after the first sunrise
when we are near that fateful place. There is much to be done, and
other places to be made sanctify, so that that nest of vipers be obliterated." Here Jonathan interrupted him hotly: —

"Do you mean to say, Professor Van Helsing, that you would bring
Mina, in her sad case and tainted as she is with that devil's illness, right
into the jaws of his death-trap? Not for the world! Not for Heaven or
Hell!" He became almost speechless for a minute, and then went on: —

"Do you know what the place is? Have you seen that awful den of
hellish infamy — with the very moonlight alive with grisly shapes, and
every speck of dust that whirls in the wind a devouring monster in
embryo? Have you felt the Vampire's lips upon your throat?" Here he
turned to me, and as his eyes lit on my forehead, he threw up his arms
with a cry: "Oh, my God, what have we done to have this terror upon
us!" and he sank down on the sofa in a collapse of misery. The Professor's voice, as he spoke in clear, sweet tones, which seemed to vibrate in
the air, calmed us all: —

"Oh my friend, it is because I would save Madam Mina from that
awful place that I would go. God forbid that I should take her into that
place. There is work — wild work — to be done there, that her eyes may
not see. We men here, all save Jonathan, have seen with their own eyes
what is to be done before that place can be purify. Remember that we are
in terrible straits. If the Count escape us this time — and he is strong

and subtle and cunning — he may choose to sleep him for a century; and then in time our dear one" — he took my hand — "would come to him to keep him company, and would be as those others that you, Jonathan, saw. You have told us of their gloating lips; you heard their ribald laugh as they clutched the moving bag that the Count threw to them. You shudder; and well may it be. Forgive me that I make you so much pain, but it is necessary. My friend, is it not a dire need for the which I am giving, if need me, my life? If it were that anyone went into that place to stay, it is I who would have to go, to keep them company."

"Do as you will;" said Jonathan, with a sob that shook him all over. "We are in the hands of God!"

Later. — Oh, it did me good to see the way that these brave men worked. How can women help loving men when they are so earnest, and so true, and so brave! And, too, it made me think of the wonderful power of money! What can it not do when it is properly applied; and what might it do when basely used. I felt so thankful that Lord Godalming is rich, and that both he and Mr. Morris, who also has plenty of money, are willing to spend it so freely. For it they did not, our little expedition could not start, either so promptly or so well equipped, as it will within another hour. It is not three hours since it was arranged what part each of us was to do; and now Lord Godalming and Jonathan have a lovely steam launch, with steam up ready to start at a moment's notice. Dr. Seward and Mr. Morris have half a dozen beautiful horses, well appointed. We have all the maps and appliances of various kinds that can be had. Professor Van Helsing and I are to leave by the 11.40 train to-night for Veresti, where we are to get a carriage to drive to the Borgo Pass. We are bringing a good deal of ready money, as we are to buy a carriage and horses. We shall drive ourselves, for we have no one whom we can trust in the matter. The Professor knows something of a great many languages, so we shall get on all right. We have all got arms, even for me a large-bore revolver; Jonathan would not be happy unless I was armed like the rest. Alas! I cannot carry one arm that the rest do; the scar on my forehead forbids that. Dear Dr. Van Helsing comforts me by telling me that I am fully armed as there may be wolves; the weather is getting colder every hour, and there are snow-flurries which come and go as warnings.

Later. — It took all my courage to say good-bye to my darling. We may never meet again. Courage, Mina! the Professor is looking at you keenly; his look is a warning. There must be no tears now — unless it may be that God will let them fall in gladness.

Jonathan Harker's Journal

October 30, *Night.* — I am writing this in the light from the furnace door of the steam launch; Lord Godalming is firing up. He is an experienced hand at the work, as he has had for years a launch of his own on the Thames, and another on the Norfolk Broads.° Regarding our plans, we finally decided that Mina's guess was correct, and that if any waterway was chosen for the Count's escape back to his Castle, the Sereth and then the Bistritza at its junction, would be the one. We took it, that somewhere about the 47th degree, north latitude, would be the place chosen for the crossing the country between the river and the Carpathians. We have no fear in running at good speed up the river at night; there is plenty of water, and the banks are wide enough apart to make steaming, even in the dark, easy enough. Lord Godalming tells me to sleep for a while, as it is enough for the present for one to be on watch. But I cannot sleep — how can I with the terrible danger hanging over my darling, and her going out into that awful place. . . . My only comfort is that we are in the hands of God. Only for that faith it would be easier to die than to live, and so be quit of all the trouble. Mr. Morris and Dr. Seward were off on their long ride before we started; they are to keep up the right bank, far enough off to get on higher lands where they can see a good stretch of river and avoid the following of its curves. They have, for the first stages, two men to ride and lead their spare horses — four in all, so as not to excite curiosity. When they dismiss the men, which shall be shortly, they shall themselves look after the horses. It may be necessary for us to join forces; if so they can mount our whole party. One of the saddles has a movable horn,° and can be easily adapted for Mina, if required.

It is a wild adventure we are on. Here, as we are rushing along through the darkness, with the cold from the river seeming to rise up and strike us; with all the mysterious voices of the night around us, it all comes home. We seem to be drifting into unknown places and unknown ways; into a whole world of dark and dreadful things. Godalming is shutting the furnace door. . . .

31 *October.* — Still hurrying along. The day has come, and Godalming is sleeping. I am on watch. The morning is bitterly cold; the furnace heat is grateful, though we have heavy fur coats. As yet we have passed only a few open boats, but none of them had on board any box or package of anything like the size of the one we seek. The men were

Norfolk Broads: A system of waterways in Norfolk, England (*Enc. Brit.* OL).   **saddles . . .**
movable horn: A saddle that can be converted for a woman to ride sidesaddle.

scared every time we turned our electric lamp on them, and fell on their knees and prayed.

1 November, evening. — No news all day; we have found nothing of the kind we seek. We have now passed into the Bistritza; and if we are wrong in our surmise our chance is gone. We have overhauled every boat, big and little. Early this morning, one crew took us for a Government boat, and treated us accordingly. We saw in this a way of smoothing matters, so at Fundu, where the Bistritza runs into the Sereth, we got a Roumanian flag which we now fly conspicuously. With every boat which we have overhauled since then this trick has succeeded; we have had every deference shown to us, and not once any objection to whatever we chose to ask or do. Some of the Slovaks tell us that a big boat passed them, going at more than usual speed as she had a double crew on board. This was before they came to Fundu, so they could not tell us whether the boat turned into the Bistritza or continued on up the Sereth. At Fundu we could not hear of any such boat, so she must have passed there in the night. I am feeling very sleepy; the cold is perhaps beginning to tell upon me, and nature must have rest some time. Godalming insists that he shall keep the first watch. God bless him for all his goodness to poor dear Mina and me.

2 November, morning. — It is broad daylight. That good fellow would not wake me. He says it would have been a sin to, for I slept so peacefully and was forgetting my trouble. It seems brutally selfish of me to have slept so long, and let him watch all night; but he was quite right. I am a new man this morning; and, as I sit here and watch him sleeping, I can do all that is necessary both as to minding the engine, steering, and keeping watch. I can feel that my strength and energy are coming back to me. I wonder where Mina is now, and Van Helsing. They should have got to Veresti about noon on Wednesday. It would take them some time to get the carriage and horses; so if they had started and travelled hard, they would be about now at the Borgo Pass. God guide and help them! I am afraid to think what may happen. If we could only go faster! but we cannot; the engines are throbbing and doing their utmost. I wonder how Dr. Seward and Mr. Morris are getting on. There seem to be endless streams running down from the mountains into this river, but as none of them are very large — at present, at all events, though they are terrible doubtless in winter and when the snow melts — the horsemen may not have met much obstruction. I hope that before we get to Strasba we may see them; for if by that time we have not overtaken the Count, it may be necessary to take counsel together what to do next.

Dr. Seward's Diary

2 *November.* — Three days on the road. No news, and no time to write it if there had been, for every moment is precious. We have had only the rest needful for the horses; but we are both bearing it wonderfully. Those adventurous days of ours are turning up useful. We must push on; we shall never feel happy till we get the launch in sight again.

3 *November.* — We heard at Fundu that the launch had gone up the Bistritza. I wish it wasn't so cold. There are signs of snow coming; and if it falls heavy it will stop us. In such case we must get a sledge and go on, Russian fashion.

4 *November.* — To-day we heard of the launch having been detained by an accident when trying to force a way up the rapid. The slovak boats get up all right, by aid of a rope, and steering with knowledge. Some went up only a few hours before. Godalming is an amateur fitter° himself, and evidently it was he who put the launch in trim again. Finally, they got up the Rapids all right, with local help, and are off on the chase afresh. I fear that the boat is not any better for the accident; the peasantry tell us that after she got upon the smooth water again, she kept stopping every now and again so long as she was in sight. We must push on harder than ever; our help may be wanted soon.

Mina Harker's Journal

31 *October.* — Arrived at Veresti at noon. The Professor tells me that this morning at dawn he could hardly hypnotize me at all, and that all I could say was: "dark and quiet." He is off now buying a carriage and horses. He says that he will later on try to buy additional horses, so that we may be able to change them on the way. We have something more than 70 miles before us. The country is lovely, and most interesting; if only we were under different conditions, how delightful it would be to see it all. If Jonathan and I were driving through it alone what a pleasure it would be. To stop and see people, and learn something of their life, and to fill our minds and memories with all the colour and picturesqueness of the whole wild, beautiful country and the quaint people! But, alas! —

Later. — Dr. Van Helsing has returned. He has got the carriage and horses; we are to have some dinner, and to start in an hour. The landlady is putting us up a huge basket of provisions; it seems enough for a company of soldiers. The Professor encourages her, and whispers to me

---

fitter: A person skilled in putting machine parts together.

that it may be a week before we can get any good food again. He has
been shopping too, and has sent home such a wonderful lot of fur coats
and wraps, and all sorts of warm things. There will not be any chance of
our being cold.

. . .

We shall soon be off. I am afraid to think what may happen to us. We
are truly in the hands of God. He alone knows what may be, and I pray
Him, with all the strength of my sad and humble soul, that He will
watch over my beloved husband; that whatever may happen, Jonathan
may know that I loved him and honoured him more than I can say, and
that my latest and truest thought will be always for him.

CHAPTER XXVII. MINA HARKER'S JOURNAL

1 *November.* — All day long we have travelled, and at a good speed.
The horses seem to know that they are being kindly treated, for they go
willingly their full stage at best speed. We have now had so many
changes and find the same thing so constantly that we are encouraged
to think that the journey will be an easy one. Dr. Van Helsing is laconic;
he tells the farmers that he is hurrying to Bistritz, and pays them well to
make the exchange of horses. We get hot soup, or coffee, or tea; and off
we go. It is a lovely country; full of beauties of all imaginable kinds, and
the people are brave, and strong, and simple, and seem full of nice qualities. They are *very, very* superstitious. In the first house where we
stopped, when the woman who served us saw the scar on my forehead,
she crossed herself and put out two fingers towards me, to keep off the
evil eye. I believe they went to the trouble of putting an extra amount
of garlic into our food; and I can't abide garlic. Ever since then I have
taken care not to take off my hat or veil, and so have escaped their suspicions. We are travelling fast, and as we have no driver with us to carry
tales, we go ahead of scandal; but I daresay that fear of the evil eye will
follow hard behind us all the way. The Professor seems tireless; all day
he would not take any rest, though he made me sleep for a long spell.
At sunset time he hypnotized me, and he says that I answered as usual
"darkness, lapping water and creaking wood;" so our enemy is still on
the river. I am afraid to think of Jonathan, but somehow I have now no
fear for him, or for myself. I write this whilst we wait in a farmhouse for
the horses to be got ready. Dr. Van Helsing is sleeping. Poor dear, he
looks very tired and old and grey, but his mouth is set as firmly as a conqueror's; even in his sleep he is instinct with resolution. When we have

well started I must make him rest whilst I drive. I shall tell him that we have days before us, and he must not break down when most of all his strength will be needed . . . . All is ready; we are off shortly.

2 *November, morning.* — I was successful, and we took turns driving all night; now the day is on us, bright though cold. There is a strange heaviness in the air — I say heaviness for want of a better word; I mean that it oppresses us both. It is very cold, and only our warm furs keep us comfortable. At dawn Van Helsing hypnotised me; he says I answered "darkness, creaking wood and roaring water," so the river is changing as they ascend. I do hope that my darling will not run any chance of danger — more than need be; but we are in God's hands.

2 *November, night.* — All day long driving. The country gets wilder as we go, and the great spurs of the Carpathians, which at Veresti seemed so far from us and so low on the horizon, now seem to gather round us and tower in front. We both seem in good spirits; I think we make an effort each to cheer the other; in the doing so we cheer ourselves. Dr. Van Helsing says that by morning we shall reach the Borgo Pass. The houses are very few here now, and the Professor says that the last horses we got will have to go on with us, as we may not be able to change. He got two in addition to the two we changed, so that now we have a rude four-in-hand. The dear horses are patient and good, and they give us no trouble. We are not worried with other travellers, and so even I can drive. We shall get to the Pass in daylight; we do not want to arrive before. So we take it easy, and have each a long rest in turn. Oh, what will to-morrow bring to us? We go to seek the place where my poor darling suffered so much. God grant that we may be guided aright, and that He will deign to watch over my husband and those dear to us both, and who are in such deadly peril. As for me, I am not worthy in His sight. Alas! I am unclean to His eyes, and shall be until He may deign to let me stand forth in His sight as one of those who have not incurred His wrath.

Memorandum by Abraham Van Helsing

4 *November.* — This is to my old and true friend John Seward, M.D., of Purfleet, London, in case I may not see him. It may explain. It is morning, and I write by a fire which all the night I have kept alive — Madam Mina aiding me. It is cold, cold; so cold that the grey heavy sky is full of snow, which when it falls will settle for all winter as the ground is hardening to receive it. It seems to have affected Madam Mina; she has been so heavy of head all day that she was not like herself. She

sleeps, and sleeps, and sleeps! She, who is usual so alert, have done literally nothing all the day; she even have lost her appetite. She make no entry into her little diary, she who write so faithful at every pause. Something whisper to me that all is not well. However, to-night she is more *vif*.° Her long sleep all day have refresh and restore her, for now she is all sweet and bright as ever. At sunset I try to hypnotise her, but alas! with no effect; the power has grown less and less with each day, and to-night it fail me altogether. Well, God's will be done — whatever it may be, and whithersoever it may lead!

Now to the historical, for as Madam Mina write not in her stenography, I must, in my cumbrous old fashion, that so each day of us may not go unrecorded.

We got to the Borgo Pass just after sunrise yesterday morning. When I saw the signs of the dawn I got ready for the hypnotism. We stopped our carriage, and got down so that there might be no disturbance. I made a couch with furs, and Madam Mina, lying down, yield herself as usual, but more slow and more short time than ever, to the hypnotic sleep. As before, came the answer: "darkness and the swirling of water." Then she woke, bright and radiant, and we go on our way and soon reach the Pass. At this time and place she become all on fire with zeal; some new guiding power be in her manifested, for she point to a road and say: —

"This is the way."

"How know you it?" I ask.

"Of course I know it," she answer, and with a pause, add: "Have not my Jonathan travel it and wrote of his travel?"

At first I think somewhat strange, but soon I see that there be only one such by-road. It is used but little, and very different from the coach road from the Bukovina to Bistritz, which is more wide and hard, and more of use.

So we came down this road; when we meet other ways — not always were we sure that they were roads at all, for they be neglect and light snow have fallen — the horses know and they only. I give rein to them, and they go on so patient. By-and-by we find all the things which Jonathan have note in that wonderful diary of him. Then we go on for long, long hours and hours. At the first, I tell Madam Mina to sleep; she try, and she succeed. She sleep all the time; till at the last, I feel myself to suspicious grow, and attempt to wake her. But she sleep on, and I may

---

vif: Lively (French). Van Helsing uses the masculine form of the adjective, rather than the feminine, *vive*.

not wake her though I try. I do not wish to try too hard lest I harm her; for I know that she have suffer much, and sleep at times be all-in-all to her. I think I drowse myself, for all of sudden I feel guilt, as though I have done something; I find myself bolt up, with the reins in my hand, and the good horses go along jog, jog, just as ever. I look down and find Madam Mina still sleep. It is now not far off sunset time, and over the snow the light of the sun flow in big yellow flood, so that we throw great long shadow on where the mountains rise so steep. For we are going up, and up; and all is oh! so wild and rocky, as though it were the end of the world.

Then I arouse Madam Mina. This time she wake with not much trouble, and then I try to put her to hypnotic sleep. But she sleep not, being as though I were not. Still I try and try, till all at once I find her and myself in dark; so I look round, and find that the sun have gone down. Madam Mina laugh, and I turn and look at her. She is now quite awake; and look so well as I never saw her since that night at Carfax when we first enter the Count's house. I am amaze, and not at ease then; but she is so bright and tender and thoughtful for me that I forget all fear. I light a fire, for we have brought supply of wood with us, and she prepare food while I undo the horses and set them, tethered in shelter, to feed. Then when I return to the fire she have my supper ready. I go to help her; but she smile, and tell me that she have eat already — that she was so hungry that she would not wait. I like it not, and I have grave doubts; but I fear to affright her, and so I am silent of it. She help me and I eat alone; and then we wrap in fur and lie beside the fire, and I tell her to sleep while I watch. But presently I forget all of watching; and when I sudden remember that I watch, I find her lying quiet, but awake, and looking at me with so bright eyes. Once, twice more the same occur, and I get much sleep till before morning. When I wake I try to hypnotise her; but alas! though she shut her eyes obedient, she may not sleep. The sun rise up, and up, and up; and then sleep come to her too late, but so heavy that she will not wake. I have to lift her up, and place her sleeping in the carriage when I have harnessed the horses and made all ready. Madam still sleep, and sleep; and she look in her sleep more healthy and more redder than before. And I like it not. And I am afraid, afraid, afraid! — I am afraid of all things — even to think; but I must go on my way. The stake we play for is life and death, or more than these, and we must not flinch.

5 *November, morning.* — Let me be accurate in everything, for though you and I have seen some strange things together, you may at

the first think that I, Van Helsing, am mad — that the many horrors and the so long strain on nerves has at the last turn my brain.

All yesterday we travel, ever getting closer to the mountains, and moving into a more and more wild and desert land. There are great, frowning precipices and much falling water, and Nature seem to have held sometime her carnival. Madam Mina still sleep and sleep; and though I did have hunger and appeased it, I could not waken her — even for food. I began to fear that the fatal spell of the place was upon her, tainted as she is with that Vampire baptism. "Well," said I to myself, "if it be that she sleep all the day, it shall also be that I do not sleep at night." As we travel on the rough road, for a road of an ancient and imperfect kind there was, I held down my head and slept. Again I waked with a sense of guilt and of time passed, and found Madam Mina still sleeping, and the sun low down. But all was indeed changed; the frowning mountains seemed further away, and we were near the top of a steep-rising hill, on summit of which was such a castle as Jonathan tell of in his diary. At once I exulted and feared; for now, for good or ill, the end was near. I woke Madam Mina, and again tried to hypnotise her; but alas! unavailing till too late. Then, ere the great dark came upon us — for even after down-sun the heavens reflected the gone sun on the snow, and all was for a time in a great twilight — I took out the horses and fed them in what shelter I could. Then I make a fire; and near it I make Madam Mina, now awake and more charming than ever, sit comfortable amid her rugs. I got ready food: but she would not eat, simply saying that she had not hunger. I did not press her, knowing her unavailingness. But I myself eat, for I must needs now be strong for all. Then, with the fear on me of what might be, I drew a ring so big for her comfort, round where Madam Mina sat; and over the ring I passed some of the wafer, and I broke it fine so that all was well guarded. She sat still all the time — so still as one dead; and she grew whiter and ever whiter till the snow was not more pale; and no word she said. But when I drew near, she clung to me, and I could know that the poor soul shook her from head to feet with a tremor that was pain to feel. I said to her presently, when she had grown more quiet: —

"Will you not come over to the fire?" for I wished to make a test of what she could. She rose obedient, but when she have made a step she stopped, and stood as one stricken.

"Why not go on?" I asked. She shook her head, and, coming back, sat down in her place. Then, looking at me with open eyes, as of one waked from sleep, she said simply: —

"I cannot!" and remained silent. I rejoiced, for I knew that what she could not, none of those that we dreaded could. Though there might be danger to her body, yet her soul was safe!

Presently the horses began to scream, and tore at their tethers till I came to them and quieted them. When they did feel my hands on them, they whinnied low as in joy, and licked at my hands and were quiet for a time. Many times through the night did I come to them, till it arrive to the cold hour when all nature is at lowest; and every time my coming was with quiet of them. In the cold hour the fire began to die, and I was about stepping forth to replenish it, for now the snow came in flying sweeps and with it a chill mist. Even in the dark there was a light of some kind, as there ever is over snow; and it seemed as though the snow-flurries and the wreaths of mist took shape as of women with trailing garments. All was in dead, grim silence only that the horses whinnied and cowered, as if in terror of the worst. I began to fear — horrible fears; but then came to me the sense of safety in that ring wherein I stood. I began, too, to think that my imaginings were of the night, and the gloom, and the unrest that I have gone through, and all the terrible anxiety. It was as though my memories of all Jonathan's horrid experience were befooling me; for the snow flakes and the mist began to wheel and circle round, till I could get as though a shadowy glimpse of those women that would have kissed him. And then the horses cowered lower and lower, and moaned in terror as men do in pain. Even the madness of fright was not to them, so that they could break away. I feared for my dear Madam Mina when these weird figures drew near and circled round. I looked at her, but she sat calm, and smiled at me; when I would have stepped to the fire to replenish it, she caught me and held me back, and whispered, like a voice that one hears in a dream, so low it was: —

"No! No! Do not go without. Here you are safe!" I turned to her, and looking in her eyes, said: —

"But you? It is for you that I fear! whereat she laughed — a laugh, low and unreal; and said: —

"Fear for *me*! Why fear for me? None safer in all the world from them than I am," and as I wondered at the meaning of her words, a puff of wind made the flame leap up, and I see the red scar on her forehead. Then, alas! I knew. Did I not, I would soon have learned, for the wheeling figures of mist and snow came closer, but keeping ever without the Holy circle. Then they began to materialise, till — if God have not take away my reason, for I saw it through my eyes — there were before me in actual flesh the same three women that Jonathan saw in the room, when they would have kissed his throat. I knew the swaying round forms, the bright hard eyes, the white teeth, the ruddy colour, the voluptuous lips. They smiled ever at poor dear Madam Mina; and as their laugh came through the silence of the night, they twined their arms and pointed to her, and said in those so sweet tingling tones that Jonathan said were of the intolerable sweetness of the water-glasses: —

"Come, sister. Come to us. Come! Come!" In fear I turned to my poor Madam Mina, and my heart with gladness leapt like flame; for oh! the terror in her sweet eyes, the repulsion, the horror, told a story to my heart that was all of hope. God be thanked she was not, yet, of them. I seized some of the firewood which was by me, and holding out some of the Wafer, advanced on them towards the fire. They drew back before me, and laughed their low horrid laugh. I fed the fire, and feared them not; for I knew that we were safe within our protections. They could not approach me, whilst so armed, nor Madam Mina whilst she remained within the ring, which she could not leave no more than they could enter. The horses had ceased to moan, and lay still on the ground; the snow fell on them softly, and they grew whiter. I knew that there was for the poor beasts no more of terror.

And so we remained till the red of the dawn began to fall through the snow-gloom. I was desolate and afraid, and full of woe and terror; but when that beautiful sun began to climb the horizon life was to me again. At the first coming of the dawn the horrid figures melted in the whirling mist and snow; the wreaths of transparent gloom moved away towards the castle, and were lost.

Instinctively, with the dawn coming, I turned to Madam Mina, intending to hypnotise her; but she lay in a deep and sudden sleep, from which I could not wake her. I tried to hypnotise through her sleep, but she made no response, none at all; and the day broke. I fear yet to stir. I have made my fire and have seen the horses, they are all dead. To-day I have much to do here, and I keep waiting till the sun is up high; for there may be places where I must go, where that sunlight, though snow and mist obscure it, will be to me a safety.

I will strengthen me with breakfast, and then I will to my terrible work. Madam Mina still sleeps; and, God be thanked! she is calm in her sleep. . . .

Jonathan Harker's Journal

4 *November, evening.* — The accident to the launch has been a terrible thing for us. Only for it we should have overtaken the boat long

ago; and by now my dear Mina would have been free. I fear to think of her, off on the wolds° near that horrid place. We have got horses, and we follow on the track. I note this whilst Godalming is getting ready. We have our arms. The Szgany must look out if they mean fight. Oh, if only Morris and Seward were with us. We must only hope! If I write no more Good bye, Mina! God bless and keep you.

Dr. Seward's Diary

5 *November.* — With the dawn we saw the body of Szgany before us dashing away from the river with their leiter-waggon. They surrounded it in a cluster, and hurried along as though beset. The snow is falling lightly and there is a strange excitement in the air. It may be our own excited feelings, but the depression is strange. Far off I hear the howling of wolves; the snow brings them down from the mountains, and there are dangers to all of us, and from all sides. The horses are nearly ready, and we are soon off. We ride to death of some one. God alone knows who, or where, or what, or when, or how it may be. . . .

Dr. Van Helsing's Memorandum

5 *November, afternoon.* — I am at least sane. Thank God for that mercy at all events, though the proving it has been dreadful. When I left Madam Mina sleeping within the Holy circle, I took my way to the castle. The blacksmith hammer which I took in the carriage from Veresti was useful; though the doors were all open I broke them off the rusty hinges, lest some ill-intent or ill-chance should close them, so that being entered I might not get out. Jonathan's bitter experience served me here. By memory of his diary I found my way to the old chapel, for I knew that here my work lay. The air was oppressive; it seemed as if there was some sulphurous fume, which at times made me dizzy. Either there was a roaring in my ears or I heard afar off the howl of wolves. Then I bethought me of my dear Madam Mina, and I was in terrible plight. The dilemma had me between his horns. Her, I had not dare to take into this place, but left safe from the Vampire in that Holy circle; and yet even there would be the wolf! I resolve me that my work lay here, and that as to the wolves we must submit, if it were God's Will. At any rate it was only death and freedom beyond. So did I choose for her. Had it but been for myself the choice had been easy; the maw of the

---

wolds: Rolling uplands (*OED*).

wolf were better to rest in than the grave of the Vampire! So I make my choice to go on with my work.

I knew that there were at least three graves to find — graves that are inhabit; so I search, and search, and I find one of them. She lay in her Vampire sleep, so full of life and voluptuous beauty that I shudder as though I have come to do murder. Ah, I doubt not that in old time, when such things were, many a man who set forth to do such a task as mine, found at the last his heart fail him, and then his nerve. So he delay, and delay, and delay, till the mere beauty and the fascination of the wanton Un-dead have hypnotise him; and he remain on, and on, till sunset come, and the Vampire sleep be over. Then the beautiful eyes of the fair woman open and look love, and the voluptuous mouth present to a kiss — and man is weak. And there remain one more victim in the Vampire fold; one more to swell the grim and grisly ranks of the Un-dead! . . . .

There is some fascination, surely, when I am moved by the mere presence of such an one, even lying as she lay in a tomb fretted with age and heavy with the dust of centuries, though there be that horrid odour such as the lairs of the Count have had. Yes, I was moved — I, Van Helsing, with all my purpose and with my motive for hate — I was moved to a yearning for delay which seemed to paralyse my faculties and to clog my very soul. It may have been that the need of natural sleep, and the strange oppression of the air were beginning to overcome me. Certain it was that I was lapsing into sleep, the open-eyed sleep of one who yields to a sweet fascination, when there came through the snow-stilled air a long, low wail, so full of woe and pity that it woke me like the sound of a clarion. For it was the voice of my dear Madam Mina that I heard.

Then I braced myself again to my horrid task, and found by wrenching away tomb-tops one other of the sisters, the other dark one. I dared not pause to look on her as I had on her sister, lest once more I should begin to be enthrall; but I go on searching until, presently, I find in a high great tomb as if made to one much beloved that other fair sister which, like Jonathan I had seen to gather herself out of the atoms of the mist. She was so fair to look on, so radiantly beautiful, so exquisitely voluptuous, that the very instinct of man in me, which calls some of my sex to love and to protect one of hers, made my head whirl with new emotion. But God be thanked, that soul-wail of my dear Madam Mina had not died out of my ears; and, before the spell could be wrought further upon me, I had nerved myself to my wild work. By this time I had searched all the tombs in the chapel, so far as I could tell; and as there had been only three of these Un-Dead phantoms around us in the night, I took it that there were no more of active Un-Dead existent. There was one great tomb more lordly than all the rest; huge it was, and nobly proportioned. On it was but one word.

DRACULA

This then was the Un-Dead home of the King-Vampire, to whom so many more were due. Its emptiness spoke eloquent to make certain what I knew. Before I began to restore these women to their dead selves through my awful work, I laid in Dracula's tomb some of the Wafer, and so banished him from it, Un-Dead, for ever.

Then began my terrible task, and, I dreaded it. Had it been but one, it had been easy, comparative. But three! To begin twice more after I had been through a deed of horror; for if it was terrible with the sweet Miss Lucy, what would it not be with these strange ones who had survived through centuries, and who had been strengthened by the passing of the years; who would, if they could, have fought for their foul lives. . . .

Oh, my friend John, but it was butcher work; had I not been nerved by thoughts of other dead, and of the living over whom hung such a pall of fear, I could not have gone on. I tremble and tremble even yet, though till all was over, God be thanked, my nerve did stand. Had I not seen the repose in the first face, and the gladness that stole over it just ere the final dissolution came, as realisation that the soul had been won, I could not have gone further with my butchery. I could not have endured the horrid screeching as the stake drove home; the plunging of writhing form, and the lips of bloody foam. I should have fled in terror and left my work undone. But it is over! And the poor souls, I can pity them now and weep, as I think of them placid each in her full sleep of death, for a short moment ere fading. For, friend John, hardly had my knife severed the head of each, before the whole body began to melt away and crumble into its native dust, as though the death that should have come centuries agone had at last assert himself and say at once and loud "I am here!"

Before I left the castle I so fixed its entrances that never more can the Count enter there Un-Dead.

When I stepped into the circle where Madam Mina slept, she woke from her sleep, and, seeing me, cried out in pain that I had endured too much.

"Come!" she said, "Come away from this awful place! Let us go to meet my husband who is, I know, coming towards us." She was looking thin and pale and weak; but her eyes were pure and glowed with fervour. I was glad to see her paleness and her illness, for my mind was full of the fresh horror of that ruddy vampire sleep.

And so with trust and hope, and yet full of fear, we go eastward to meet our friends — and *him* — whom Madam Mina tell me that she *know* are coming to meet us.

Mina Harker's Journal

6 *November.* — It was late in the afternoon when the Professor and I took our way towards the east whence I knew Jonathan was coming. We did not go fast, though the way was steeply downhill, for we had to take heavy rugs and wraps with us; we dared not face the possibility of being left without warmth in the cold and the snow. We had to take some of our provisions too, for we were in a perfect desolation, and, so far as we could see through the snow-fall, there was not even the sign of a habitation. When we had gone about a mile, I was tired with the heavy walking and sat down to rest. Then we looked back and saw where the clear line of Dracula's castle cut the sky; for we were so deep under the hill whereon it was set that the angle of perspective of the Carpathian mountains was far below it. We saw it in all its grandeur, perched a thousand feet on the summit of a sheer precipice, and with seemingly a great gap between it and the steep of the adjacent mountain on any side. There was something wild and uncanny about the place. We could hear the distant howling of wolves. They were far off, but the sound, even though coming muffled through the deadening snowfall, was full of terror. I knew from the way Dr. Van Helsing was searching about that he was trying to seek some strategic point, where we would be less exposed in case of attack. The rough roadway still led downwards; we could trace it through the drifted snow.

In a little while the Professor signalled to me, so I got up and joined him. He had found a wonderful spot, a sort of natural hollow in a rock, with an entrance like a doorway between two boulders. He took me by the hand and drew me in: "See!" he said, "here you will be in shelter; and if the wolves do come I can meet them one by one." He brought in our furs, and made a snug nest for me, and got out some provisions and forced them upon me. But I could not eat; to even try to do so was repulsive to me, and, much as I would have liked to please him, I could not bring myself to the attempt. He looked very sad, but did not reproach me. Taking his field-glasses from the case, he stood on the top of the rock, and began to search the horizon. Suddenly he called out: —

"Look! Madam Mina, look! look!" I sprang up and stood beside him on the rock; he handed me his glasses and pointed. The snow was now falling more heavily, and swirled about fiercely, for a high wind was beginning to blow. However there were times when there were pauses between the snow flurries and I could see a long way round. From the height where we were it was possible to see a great distance; and far off, beyond the white waste of snow, I could see the river lying like a black ribbon in kinks and curls as it wound its way. Straight in front of us and not far off — in fact so near that I wondered we had not noticed before — came a group of mounted men hurrying along. In the midst of them was a cart, a long leiter-waggon which swept from side to side, like a dog's tail wagging, with each stern inequality of the road. Outlined against the snow as they were, I could see from the men's clothes that they were peasants or gypsies of some kind.

On the cart was a great square chest. My heart leaped as I saw it, for I felt that the end was coming. The evening was now drawing close, and well I knew that at sunset the Thing, which was till then imprisoned there, would take new freedom and could in any of many forms elude all pursuit. In fear I turned to the Professor; to my consternation, however, he was not there. An instant later, I saw him below me. Round the rock he had drawn a circle, such as we had found shelter in last night. When he had completed it he stood beside me again, saying: —

"At least you shall be safe here from *him!*" He took the glasses from me, and at the next lull of the snow swept the whole space below us. "See," he said, "they come quickly; they are flogging the horses, and galloping as hard as they can." He paused and went on in a hollow voice: —

"They are racing for the sunset. We may be too late. God's will be done!" Down came another blinding rush of driving snow, and the whole landscape was blotted out. It soon passed, however, and once more his glasses were fixed on the plain. Then came a sudden cry: —

"Look! Look! Look! See, two horsemen follow fast, coming up from the south. It must be Quincey and John. Take the glass. Look, before the snow blots it all out!" I took it and looked. The two men might be Dr. Seward and Mr. Morris. I knew at all events that neither of them was Jonathan. At the same time I *knew* that Jonathan was not far off; looking around I saw on the north side of the coming party two other men, riding at break-neck speed. One of them I knew was Jonathan, and the other I took, of course, to be Lord Godalming. They, too, were pursuing the party with the cart. When I told the Professor he shouted in glee like a schoolboy, and, after looking intently till a snowfall made sight impossible, he laid his Winchester rifle ready for use against the boulder at the opening of our shelter. "They are all converging," he said. "When the time comes we shall have the gypsies on all sides." I got out my revolver ready to hand, for whilst we were speaking the howling of wolves came louder and closer. When the snowstorm abated a moment we looked again. It was strange to see the snow falling such heavy flakes close to us, and beyond, the sun shining more and more brightly as it sank down towards the far mountain tops. Sweeping the glass all around us I could see here and there dots moving singly and in twos and threes and larger numbers — the wolves were gathering for their prey.

Every instant seemed an age whilst we waited. The wind came now in fierce bursts, and the snow was driven with fury as it swept upon us in circling eddies. At times we could not see an arm's length before us; but at others as the hollow-sounding wind swept by us, it seemed to clear the air-space around us so that we could see afar off. We had of late been so accustomed to watch for sunrise and sunset, that we knew with fair accuracy when it would be; and we knew that before long the sun would set.

It was hard to believe that by our watches it was less than an hour that we waited in that rocky shelter before the various bodies began to converge close upon us. The wind came now with fiercer and more bitter sweeps, and more steadily from the north. It seemingly had driven the snow clouds from us, for, with only occasional bursts, the snow fell. We could distinguish clearly the individuals of each party, the pursued and the pursuers. Strangely enough those pursued did not seem to realize, or at least to care, that they were pursued; they seemed, however, to hasten with redoubled speed as the sun dropped lower and lower on the mountain tops.

Closer and closer they drew. The Professor and I crouched down behind our rock, and held our weapons ready; I could see that he was determined that they should not pass. One and all were quite unaware of our presence.

All at once two voices shouted out to: "Halt!" One was my Jonathan's, raised in a high key of passion; the other Mr. Morris' strong resolute tone of quiet command. The gypsies may not have known the language, but there was no mistaking the tone, in whatever tongue the words were spoken. Instinctively they reined in, and at the instant Lord Godalming and Jonathan dashed up at one side and Dr. Seward and Mr. Morris on the other. The leader of the gypsies, a splendid looking fellow who sat his horse like a centaur, waved them back, and in a fierce voice gave to his companions some word to proceed. They lashed the horses which sprang forward; but the four men raised their Winchester rifles, and in an unmistakeable way commanded them to stop. At the same moment Dr. Van Helsing and I rose behind the rock and pointed our weapons at them. Seeing that they were surrounded the men tightened their reins and drew up. The leader turned to them and gave a word at which every man of the gypsy party drew what weapon he carried, knife or pistol, and held himself in readiness to attack. Issue was joined in an instant.

The leader, with a quick movement of his rein, threw his horse out in front, and pointing first to the sun — now close down on the hill tops — and then to the castle, said something which I did not understand. For answer, all four men of our party threw themselves from their horses and dashed towards the cart. I should have felt terrible fear at seeing Jonathan in such danger, but that the ardour of battle must have been upon me as well as the rest of them; I felt no fear, but only a wild, surging desire to do something. Seeing the quick movement of our parties, the leader of the gypsies gave a command; his men instantly formed round the cart in a sort of undisciplined endeavour, each one shouldering and pushing the other in his eagerness to carry out the order.

In the midst of this I could see that Jonathan on one side of the ring of men, and Quincey on the other, were forcing a way to the cart; it was evident that they were bent on finishing their task before the sun should set. Nothing seemed to stop or even to hinder them. Neither the levelled weapons or the flashing knives of the gypsies in front, or the howling of the wolves behind, appeared to even attract their attention. Jonathan's impetuosity, and the manifest singleness of his purpose, seemed to overawe those in front of him; instinctively they cowered aside and let him pass. In an instant he had jumped upon the cart, and, with a strength which seemed incredible, raised the great box, and flung it over the wheel to the ground. In the meantime, Mr. Morris had had to use force to pass through his side of the ring of Szgany. All the time I had been breathlessly watching Jonathan I had, with the tail of my eye, seen him pressing desperately forward, and had seen the knives of the gypsies flash as he won a way through them, and they cut at him.

He had parried with his great bowie knife, and at first I thought that he too had come through in safety; but as he sprang beside Jonathan, who had by now jumped from the cart, I could see that with his left hand he was clutching at his side, and that the blood was spurting through his fingers. He did not delay notwithstanding this, for as Jonathan, with desperate energy, attacked one end of the chest, attempting to prize off the lid with his great Kukri knife, he attacked the other frantically with his bowie. Under the efforts of both men the lid began to yield; the nails drew with a quick screeching sound, and the top of the box was thrown back.

By this time the gypsies, seeing themselves covered by the Winchesters, and at the mercy of Lord Godalming and Dr. Seward, had given in and made no further resistance. The sun was almost down on the mountain tops, and the shadows of the whole group fell long upon the snow. I saw the Count lying within the box upon the earth, some of which the rude falling from the cart had scattered over him. He was deathly pale, just like a waxen image, and the red eyes glared with the horrible vindictive look which I knew too well.

As I looked, the eyes saw the sinking sun, and the look of hate in them turned to triumph.

But, on the instant, came the sweep and flash of Jonathan's great knife. I shrieked as I saw it shear through the throat; whilst at the same moment Mr. Morris's bowie knife plunged into the heart.

It was like a miracle; but before our very eyes, and almost in the drawing of a breath, the whole body crumbled into dust and passed from our sight.

I shall be glad as long as I live that even in that moment of final dissolution, there was in the face a look of peace, such as I never could have imagined might have rested there.

The Castle of Dracula now stood out against the red sky, and every stone of its broken battlements was articulated against the light of the setting sun.

The gypsies, taking us as in some way the cause of the extraordinary disappearance of the dead man, turned, without a word, and rode away as if for their lives. Those who were unmounted jumped upon the leiter-wagon and shouted to the horsemen not to desert them. The wolves, which had withdrawn to a safe distance, followed in their wake, leaving us alone.

Mr. Morris, who had sunk to the ground, leaned on his elbow, holding his hand pressed to his side; the blood still gushed through his fingers. I flew to him, for the Holy circle did not now keep me back; so did the two doctors. Jonathan knelt behind him and the wounded man laid back his head on his shoulder. With a sigh he took, with a feeble effort, my hand in that of his own which was unstained. He must have seen the anguish of my heart in my face, for he smiled at me and said: —

"I am only too happy to have been of any service! Oh, God!" he cried suddenly, struggling up to a sitting posture and pointing to me, "It was worth for this to die! Look! look!"

The sun was now right down upon the mountain top, and the red gleams fell upon my face, so that it was bathed in rosy light. With one impulse the men sank on their knees and a deep and earnest "Amen" broke from all as their eyes followed the pointing of his finger as the dying man spoke: —

"Now God be thanked that all has not been in vain! See! the snow is not more stainless than her forehead! The curse has passed away!"

And, to our bitter grief, with a smile and in silence, he died, a gallant gentleman.

———

NOTE

Seven years ago we all went through the flames; and the happiness of some of us since then is, we think, well worth the pain we endured. It is an added joy to Mina and to me that our boy's birthday is the same day as that on which Quincey Morris died. His mother holds, I know, the secret belief that some of our brave friend's spirit has passed into him. His bundle of names links all our little band of men together; but we call him Quincey.

In the summer of this year we made a journey to Transylvania, and went over the old ground which was, and is, to us so full of vivid and terrible memories. It was almost impossible to believe that the things which we had seen with our own eyes and heard with our own ears were living truths. Every trace of all that had been was blotted out. The castle stood as before, reared high above a waste of desolation.

When we got home we got to talking of the old time — which we could all look back on without despair, for Godalming and Seward are both happily married. I took the papers from the safe where they have been ever since our return so long ago. We were struck with the fact, that in all the mass of material of which the record is composed, there is hardly one authentic document; nothing but a mass of type-writing, except the later note-books of Mina and Seward and myself, and Van Helsing's memorandum. We could hardly ask any one, even did we wish to, to accept these as proofs of so wild a story. Van Helsing summed it all up as he said, with our boy on his knee: —

"We want no proofs; we ask none to believe us! This boy will some day know what a brave and gallant woman his mother is. Already he knows her sweetness and loving care; later on he will understand how some men so loved her, that they did dare much for her sake."

JONATHAN HARKER.

Contextual Illustrations
and Documents

The vampire has become familiar to us through its proliferation in film and popular culture during the twentieth century, often in forms influenced by Bram Stoker's narrative. Stoker captures the figure vividly, but the vampire has a significant history in the nineteenth century that largely antedates *Dracula* (1897). There were important literary precursors for *Dracula*, including John Polidori's story "The Vampyre" (1819) and J. Sheridan Le Fanu's novella "Carmilla" (1872). Earlier even than Polidori, Byron wrote "The Giaour" (1814), a poem in which a Turk curses the Giaour and condemns him to become a vampire who feasts on his own family: ". . . on earth as Vampire sent, / Thy corse shall from its tomb be rent: / Then ghastly haunt thy native place, / And suck the blood of all thy race . . ." At midcentury, the vampire appeared prominently in popular literature in James Malcolm Rymer's penny gothic serial *Varney The Vampire, Or the Feast of Blood* (serialized 1845–47; published in 3 vols., 1847).

In the texts and political cartoons reprinted here, nineteenth-century thinkers, writers, and artists use the image of the vampire memorably, in most cases before the publication of *Dracula*. Some of the documents express attitudes concerning criminality, race, and human degeneration that influenced Stoker and the British reading public of the 1890s. The image of the vampire in antagonistic expressions of political difference has a long history in England that begins in the eighteenth century with articles such as "Political Vampyres" (1732), in which ministers of state are compared to blood-sucking bats.[1] Because of its association with blood sucking, the vampire was used in the nineteenth century to signify national antagonism between the British and the Irish and political disagreements in Ireland between classes. In 1879, for example, the Irish activist Michael Davitt, one of the founders of the Land League, gave an inflammatory speech in which he called Irish landlords a "brood of cormorant vampires" (*Freeman's Journal*, October 18, 1879). The image of the vampire in political cartoons, which Stoker and his audience would have encountered, gives weight to readings of *Dracula* that take the political situation of the Irish centrally into account. It is unlikely that Stoker would have missed "**The Irish Vampire**" in *Punch* by the well-known illustrator and cartoonist John Tenniel, in which the Irish National Land League is presented as a vampire about to victimize Ireland, who lies sleeping (p. 376). Tenniel gives the vampire the face of Charles Stuart Parnell (1846–1891), the Irish political leader who worked aggressively for Home Rule, or limited autonomy, for Ireland. Parnell was president of the Land League, which advocated peasant control of the land but drew supporters with more revolutionary nationalistic goals. The response in the *Irish Pilot* reverses the images by presenting the English as a blood-sucking, but also cowardly, creature kept at bay by a militant National League representing Ireland ("**The English Vampire**," p. 377). A later cartoon shows Parnell doubled, like Jekyll and Hyde, with his evil self equipped with batlike wings ("**The Two Parnells**," p. 378). The vampire hunters in *Dracula* set out with an intensity that indicates a shared attitude among the British, the American, and the European who make up the group, but the attitude is centrally that of the English against a threatening outsider who is not English. (It is worth remarking, in this regard, that *Helsing* is an anagram of *English* and that Van Helsing, if it is a Dutch name at all, is not a common one.) In another *Punch* cartoon, "**The Irish Frankenstein**," Tenniel portrays the degenerate, murderous object of English hatred and fear as an Irish Gothic monster (p. 379). His version is a more grotesque rendition of a cartoon that had appeared in *Punch* decades earlier (November 4, 1843). Tenniel is responding to the Phoenix Park murders in Dublin, in which English officials were brutally murdered by nationalist extremists. Stoker's

---

[1]Anon., "Political Vampyres," *Gothic Documents: A sourcebook 1700–1820*, ed. E. J. Clery and Robert Miles (New York and Manchester, England: Manchster UP, 2000) 24–26.

presentation of the vampire, then, mingles images and implications that were prominently used by both the Irish and the English to express a mixture of anger and prejudice. The prejudice often includes attitudes that occur in the writings of the late-nineteenth-century criminal anthropologists and theorists of degeneration whose works are represented in this section.

As an alien creature, the vampire holds a place in the cultural imagination of the time involving broader issues than the political conflict between the English and the Irish. The association of the vampire with female power emerges in positive ways that are not obviously threatening when two of the most admired women performers at the turn of the century, Sarah Bernhardt (1844–1923) and Loïe Fuller (1862–1928), represented themselves as bats. The pre-eminent actress on the European stage at the end of the nineteenth century, Bernhardt was also a sculptor who created an image of herself as an inkwell that took the shape of a bat. The most influential dancer of the day, Fuller sometimes created in her performances the illusion that she was a large bat that had metamorphosed into a dancer.[2] The vampire was also part of an orientalizing imagination whose exotic tastes were fed by continuing encounters between European and non-Western peoples during the expansion of European empires. The excerpt from the translation of **Vikram and the Vampire, or Tales of Hindu Devilry** (p. 380), by the adventurer and linguist Sir Richard Francis Burton (1821–1890), locates the vampire within the exotic world that Burton represents more erotically in many of his other translations. *Vikram* served as a prelude for Burton's more ambitious and more famous unexpurgated translation of *The Arabian Nights* (1885–8). Like Scheherazade in the latter work, the Baital, or Vampire, is a storyteller whose fate depends on his ability to amuse and manipulate his audience by the tales that he tells. In the tales of *The Arabian Nights,* the woman turns out to be more clever than the powerful man who threatens her with death, and in *Vikram,* the vampire is at least as crafty as the man who has him provisionally and partially in his control. Stoker, who knew and admired Burton, would have been aware that *Vikram* was republished in the memorial edition of Burton's writings soon after Burton's death, when Stoker had just begun work on *Dracula*. Both the preface to the

[2]At the exhibition *Art Nouveau 1890–1914* (Victoria and Albert Museum, London, April 6–July 30, 2000; National Gallery of Art, Washington, D.C., October 8–January 28, 2001), Bernhardt's inkwell bust was on display, and a film of Fuller's metamorphosis from bat into female dancer was shown continuously. See Paul Greenhalgh, ed., *Art Nouveau 1890–1914* (London: V&A, 2000) 85.

Memorial Edition by Burton's widow and Burton's original preface claim *Vikram* to be the model for later narratives, including the European novel. Burton never ascribes a precise date to *Vikram,* but he asserts that the *Decameron* of Boccaccio, a series of tales with a frame written in Italian in the fourteenth century, was influenced by it. And he indicates that the title character was a ruler who gave his name to a system of dating that includes an initial event during the first century B.C.E. Like *Dracula,* though in a more emphatically comic and overtly exotic way, *Vikram* combines an apparently threatening, Gothic atmosphere (evident in the excerpt from the introduction to the tales) with laughable exaggerations.

A link between Stoker's narrative and the exotic East emerges in the excerpt from Major E. C. Johnson's **On the Track of the Crescent, Erratic Notes from the Paraeus to Pesth** (p. 383), a book that Stoker knew. Johnson writes about Turkey, Hungary, and Transylvania, an East less distant from England than the Indian subcontinent of Burton's *Vikram.* In the excerpt, Johnson compares the Irish to the Székelys, an apparently ethnically Turkic people that moved west into Transylvania. Dracula proudly claims descent from this Magyar-speaking people, whose language, deriving presumably from ancestors who lived in the Ural Mountains, the boundary between Asia and Europe, puts them in a small minority among European peoples. Johnson's comparison, then, identifies the Irish with these strange outsiders to the main groups within Europe. The Irish for him resembled invaders from the east. Johnson refers to the Irish in a derogatory way as "Paddy" (offensive British slang for "Patrick") when he compares them to the Wallachs, the group composing the majority of the Transylvanian population. Others writing in the second half of the nineteenth century linked the peoples of the eastern part of Europe to blood-thirsty practices and specifically to the vampire and related monsters of a bestial kind. In the excerpt from Sabine Baring-Gould's **The Book of Were-wolves** (p. 385), she reports the story of Elizabeth Bathory's bloodletting in Hungary. Emily Gerard's book **The Land Beyond the Forest** (p. 386), whose title is a literal translation of Transylvania, specifically mentions the vampire, or *nosferatu,* and some of the beliefs associated with it.

Stoker has his vampire hunters, especially Van Helsing, talk about the vampire in ways that identify this outsider from the East who takes animal forms as an example of the criminal and of degeneration. In doing so, Stoker drew on the thinking of contemporary theorists in social science, law, medicine, and related disciplines, many of whom were influenced by Charles Darwin's ideas concerning the animal origins of the human species. Prominent among these was Cesare Lombroso, an Italian social theorist who developed criminal anthropology. In *L'Uomo delinquente* or **Criminal Man** (p. 388), originally published in 1876 and later expanded with illustrations in a French translation shortly before *Dracula* appeared, Lombroso identifies socially deviant behavior, especially violent crime, with biological throwbacks to earlier stages of human evolution. In his introduction to *Criminal Man,* an adaptation of his work in English by his daughter, Gina Lombroso Ferrero, he comments on the apparently superhuman abilities of some criminals, their bestial physical characteristics, and their tendency toward cannibalism and the drinking of blood. Max Nordau dedicated his *Entartung,* translated into English as **Degeneration** (1895) (p. 389), to Lombroso. In the excerpts from the opening chapters of *Degeneration,* Nordau focuses on the decline of civilization at the end of the nineteenth century, or fin-de-siècle, as a process in which the few hold sway over the many, and he describes degeneration within a situation that he views as apocalyptic.

Richard von Krafft-Ebing's **Psychopathia Sexualis** (p. 394), a highly influential "medico-legal study" of aberrant sexuality, appeared in English translation while Stoker was working on *Dracula*. Like Van Helsing, Krafft-Ebing brings training and interests in law and medicine to his work. The excerpts from the lengthy section on "Sadism" cite vivid cases involving both men and women in which pathological sexuality and bloodletting combine in violent crimes and in domestic sexual relations. Krafft-Ebing compares both men and women to vampires.

The threatening power of the female with regard to sexuality and the vampire is expressed not only in medically oriented treatises in the latter part of the nineteenth century but also in literature and in writing about art. Rudyard Kipling's misogynistic poem "**The Vampire**" (p. 397) was written to accompany the exhibition of a painting of that title by his cousin, Philip Burne-Jones, and was published in the gallery catalogue and in the *Daily Mail,* a London newspaper. The most famous and influential description of a woman as vampiric published in Victorian England is Walter Pater's commentary on Leonardo's painting of Mona Lisa (**The Renaissance**, p. 398) in his essay on Leonardo in *Studies in the History of the Renaissance* (later called *The Renaissance*). The description was so widely admired that W. B. Yeats included the portion concerning the vampire as verse as the first item in his *Oxford Book of Modern Verse, 1892–1935* (1936), even though the passage is not verse and not within the chronological limits of the volume he was editing.

Two of the most influential philosophers of the nineteenth century, Karl Marx and Friedrich Nietzsche, use the image of the vampire vividly, in Marx's case as part of his commentary in the first volume of *Capital* **"The Limits of the Workday"** (p. 400) on the working day as a period in which the capitalist sucks as much as possible out of the worker. Nietzsche links the vampire not directly to the economic system but to philosophical idealism, which Marx and Engels identified in *The German Ideology* (1845–46) as the philosophical counterpart of capitalism. In section 372, **"Why We Are Not Idealists"** (p. 400), of the fifth book of *Joyful Wisdom,* Nietzsche appears to take the direction set by Marx and Engels, who, as materialist thinkers objected to the philosophical idealism of Hegel and others, because idealism with its emphasis on spirit tended to close its eyes willfully on the material basis of human existence. At the same time that Nietzsche links philosophical idealism with vampirism, however, he suggests that the kind of philosophy that thinks of itself as the wiser opposite of idealism may be just as wrongheaded.

Anthropology, the academic study of humankind and culture, had its origin in late-nineteenth-century comparative investigations of myth and religions from various cultures. Among the most influential and prolific of the scholars producing comparative studies was James Frazer, whose *The Golden Bough,* first published in two volumes in 1890, eventually appeared in a third edition (1906–15) as 12 volumes. The excerpt printed here from one of Frazer's early essays, **"On Certain Burial Customs as Illustrative of the Primitive Theory of the Soul"** (p. 401), concerns burial customs outside Western Europe that differ from British practices. Central among these are steps taken to prevent undead creatures, such as the vampire, from emerging after burial.

Stoker would have had access to the ninth edition (1888) of the *Encyclopædia Britannica* in the British Library while he was writing *Dracula.* The article entitled **"Vampire"** (p. 402), written by a scholar who died in 1895, before *Dracula* was published, presents authoritatively what was known and believed about the vampire as a bat and a myth when Stoker was writing *Dracula.*

The Irish Vampire, Punch *(October 24, 1885).*

The English Vampire, Irish Pilot *(November 7, 1885).*

The Two Parnells; or, The Man Beside Himself: Parnell the Patriot and Parnell the Traitor, Fun *(December 10, 1890).*

The Irish Frankenstein, Punch *(May 20, 1882)*.

RICHARD F. BURTON

From Vikram and the Vampire
or Tales of Hindu Devilry (1870)

*[Editor's Note: Burton, translator of the tale, writes in the preface to
the first edition of 1870:*

The Baital-Pachisi, *or* Twenty-five *(tales of a)* Baital — *a Vampire
or evil spirit which animates dead bodies — is an old and thoroughly
Hindu repertory. It is the rude beginning of that fictitious history
which ripened to the* Arabian Nights' Entertainments, *and which,
fostered by the genius of Boccaccio, produced the romance of the chivalrous days, and its last development, the novel — that prose-epic of
modern Europe. . . .*

*In her preface to the Memorial Edition of 1893, Burton's wife Isabel
elaborates:*

*The story turns chiefly on a great king named Vikram, the King
Arthur of the East, who in pursuance of his promise to a Jogi or Magician, brings to him the Baital (Vampire), who is hanging on a
tree. The difficulties King Vikram and his son have in bringing the
Vampire into the presence of the Jogi are truly laughable; and on this
thread is strung a series of Hindú fairy stories, which contain much
interesting information on Indian customs and manners. It also
alludes to that state, which induces Hindú devotees to allow themselves to be buried alive, and to appear dead for weeks or months,
and then to return to life again; a curious state of mesmeric cata-
lepsy, into which they work themselves by concentrating the mind
and abstaining from food. . . .*

*What follows is from the "Introduction," that is, the first, framing
segment of the tales.]*

The darkness of the night was frightful, the gloom deepened till it
was hardly possible to walk. The clouds opened their fountains, raining
so that you would say they could never rain again. Lightning blazed
forth with more than the light of day, and the roar of the thunder
caused the earth to shake. Baleful gleams tipped the black cones of the

From Richard Burton, trans., *Vikram and the Vampire or Tales of Hindu Devilry* (London: Tylston and Edwards, 1870). Excerpts from preface to the Memorial Edition
(1893) by Isabel Burton, preface to the first (1870) edition by Richard Burton, and
introduction.

trees and fitfully scampered like fireflies over the waste. Unclean goblins dogged the travellers and threw themselves upon the ground in their path and obstructed them in a thousand different ways. Huge snakes, whose mouths distilled blood and black venom, kept clinging around their legs in the roughest part of the road, till they were persuaded to loose their hold either by the sword or by reciting a spell. In fact, there were so many horrors and such a tumult and noise that even a brave man would have faltered, yet the king kept on his way.

At length having passed over, somehow or other, a very difficult road, the Raja arrived at the smashana, or burning place pointed out by the jogi. Suddenly he sighted the tree where from root to top every branch and leaf was in a blaze of crimson flame. And when he, still dauntless, advanced towards it, a clamour continued to be raised, and voices kept crying, "Kill them! kill them! seize them! seize them! take care that they do not get away! let them scorch themselves to cinders! let them suffer the pains of Patala.[1]"

Far from being terrified by this state of things the valiant Raja increased in boldness, seeing a prospect of an end to his adventure. Approaching the tree he felt that the fire did not burn him, and so he sat there for a while to observe the body, which hung, head downwards, from a branch a little above him.

Its eyes, which were wide open, were of a greenish-brown, and never twinkled; its hair also was brown,[2] and brown was its face — three several shades which, notwithstanding, approached one another in an unpleasant way, as in an over-dried cocoa-nut. Its body was thin and ribbed like a skeleton or a bamboo framework, and as it held on to a bough, like a flying fox,[3] by the toe-tips, its drawn muscles stood out as if they were ropes of coir.° Blood it appeared to have none, or there would have been a decided determination of that curious juice to the head; and as the Raja handled its skin, it felt icy cold and clammy as might a snake. The only sign of life was the whisking of a ragged little tail much resembling a goat's.

Judging from these signs the brave king at once determined the creature to be a Baital — a Vampire. For a short time he was puzzled to reconcile the appearance with the words of the giant, who informed

[1]The warm region below. [The notes in this selection are Burton's.]

[2]Hindus admire only glossy black hair: the "bonny brown hair" loved by our ballads is assigned by them to low-caste men, witches, and fiends.

[3]A large kind of bat; a popular and silly Anglo-Indian name. It almost justified the irate Scotchman in calling "prodigious leears" those who told him in India that foxes flew and trees were tapped for toddy.

°*coir:* Fiber from the husk of coconuts.

him that the anchorite had hung the oilman's son to a tree. But soon he explained to himself the difficulty, remembering the exceeding cunning of jogis and other reverend men, and determining that his enemy, the better to deceive him, had doubtless altered the shape and form of the young oilman's body.

With this idea, Vikram was pleased, saying, "My trouble has been productive of fruit." Remained the task of carrying the Vampire to Shanta-Shil the devotee. Having taken his sword, the Raja fearlessly climbed the tree, and ordering his son to stand away from below, clutched the Vampire's hair with one hand, and with the other struck such a blow of the sword, that the bough was cut and the thing fell heavily upon the ground. Immediately on falling it gnashed its teeth and began to utter a loud wailing cry like the screams of an infant in pain. Vikram having heard the sound of its lamentations, was pleased, and began to say to himself, "This devil must be alive." Then nimbly sliding down the trunk, he made a captive of the body, and asked "Who art thou?"

Scarcely, however, had the words passed the royal lips, when the Vampire slipped through the fingers like a worm, and uttering a loud shout of laughter, rose in the air with its legs uppermost, and as before suspended itself by its toes to another bough. And there it swung to and fro, moved by the violence of its cachinnation.

"Decidedly this is the young oilman!" exclaimed the Raja, after he had stood for a minute or two with mouth open, gazing upwards and wondering what he should do next. Presently he directed Dharma Dhwaj not to lose an instant in laying hands upon the thing when it next might touch the ground, and then he again swarmed up the tree. Having reached his former position, he once more seized the Baital's hair, and with all the force of his arms — for he was beginning to feel really angry — he tore it from its hold and dashed it to the ground, saying, "O wretch, tell me who thou art?"

Then, as before, the Raja slid deftly down the trunk, and hurried to the aid of his son, who in obedience to orders, had fixed his grasp upon the Vampire's neck. Then, too, as before, the Vampire, laughing aloud, slipped through their fingers and returned to its dangling-place.

To fail twice was too much for Raja Vikram's temper, which was right kingly and somewhat hot. This time he bade his son strike the Baital's head with his sword. Then, more like a wounded bear of Himalaya than a prince who had established an era, he hurried up the tree, and directed a furious blow with his sabre at the Vampire's lean and calfless legs. The violence of the stroke made its toes loose their hold of the bough, and when it touched the ground, Dharma Dhwaj's blade fell heavily upon its matted brown hair. But the blows appeared to have lighted on iron-wood — to judge at least from the behaviour of the Baital, who no sooner heard the question, "O wretch, who art thou?" than it returned in loud glee and merriment to its old position.

Five mortal times did Raja Vikram repeat this profitless labour. But so far from losing heart, he quite entered into the spirit of the adventure. Indeed he would have continued climbing up that tree and taking that corpse under his arm — he found his sword useless — and bringing it down, and asking it who it was, and seeing it slip through his fingers, six times sixty times, or till the end of the fourth and present age,[4] had such extreme resolution been required.

However, it was not necessary. On the seventh time of falling, the Baital, instead of eluding its capturer's grasp, allowed itself to be seized, merely remarking that "even the gods cannot resist a thoroughly obstinate man." And seeing that the stranger, for the better protection of his prize, had stripped off his waistcloth and was making it into a bag, the Vampire thought proper to seek the most favourable conditions for himself, and asked his conqueror who he was, and what he was about to do?

[4]The Hindus, like the European classics and other ancient peoples, reckon four ages: — The Satya Yug, or Golden Age, numbered 1,728,000 years; the second, or Treta Yug, comprised 1,290,000; the Dwapar Yug had 864,000; and the present, the Kali Yug, has shrunk to 832,000 years.

MAJOR E. C. JOHNSON

From On the Track of the Crescent, Erratic Notes from the Paraeus to Pesth (1885)

The next day, accompanied by a friend who is attached to the Turkish embassy here, I visited Dr. Schliemann's beautiful collection. The ornaments are identical in appearance with those found in the old mounds of Ireland, and seem to have been made by an identical people. Necklaces, earrings of fine gold, thin plates of the same metal, and the half-moon or 'two-horned' ornament, suggesting a Phœnician origin. Can the Tuatha te Danann, the early invaders of Ireland (said to have come from Greece), have taken with them Etruscan artificers in gold and silver, one of whom made the celebrated silver hand for King Nuada,

From Major E. C. Johnson, *On the Track of the Crescent, Eratic Notes from the Piraeus to Pesth* (London: Hurst and Blackett, 1885).

or are we to assign this strange resemblance merely to a simultaneous development of like art forms? I think the former hypothesis the most probable. . . .

The Székelys have played a very important part in the history of Hungary and Transylvania. They were recognised as kindred by the Magyars on their first entering Hungary, and the two races have remained allies ever since. The Székelys also received certain privileges in return for their having guarded the frontier towards Moldavia and 'Turkey-land.' They became also the guardians of the national language, for they speak the purest Hungarian. In the struggle for independence in 1848 they joined the national forces against the Austrians, and only yielded when Russian intervention rendered further resistance futile. . . .

The character of the Székelys seems to be a curious combination of the canny Scot and the imprudent Irishman. Like the former, they are plucky, industrious, and frugal. Like the latter, they are excitable, and, consequently, despondent under reverses. . . .

My host, the Count, returned in safety, gun and all, from Marosvásárhely, but he brought with him terrible news. He had encountered the inevitable 'man in the street,' and, from that authority, had learned that Ireland had risen in revolt, that the entire English army had been despatched to put down the rebellion, and, finally, that America was sending men and ships to help the rebels. This was terrible news indeed, and, if true, would materially shorten not only my stay in Hungary, but — a matter of more importance — my rent-roll. However, I received the statement *cum grano*, and did not hurry myself. . . .

The population of Transylvania is about 2,000,000, and of these some 1,200,000 are Wallachs, or, as they call themselves, Rummie. The Hungarians call them Oláhok. The Wallach has many points of resemblance to our friend Paddy. He is grossly superstitious, as the number of crosses by the roadside and on every eminence testify; and, like his prototype, he lives in abject terror of his priest, of whose powers he has the most exalted ideas. He believes that 'his rivirence' could turn him into a cow, or, as in Lover's famous anecdote, 'make him meander up and down in the form of an ould gander' for eternity, should he show any sign of having a will of his own. He is, too, a lazy, pleasant, good-natured, drunken, careless, improvident fellow; living like the grasshopper while the sun shines, and 'the divil may care for the morn.' His wife is, however, a marked contrast to him, and most emphatically his 'better' half, for she is never at rest, and does all the work, both in and out of the house; she is also very clever with her needle.

I have already described the Wallach costume, male and female; I will merely observe here that the women are very fond of show, and make themselves up, like any civilised lady of Western fashion. They rouge their cheeks, and paint their eyebrows; wear earrings and necklaces of beads and coins, and, when they can afford it, of gold and silver. These they hang sometimes down to the waist. They also embroider their chemises on the breast and sleeves with gaudy coloured threads. The girls wear netting on their heads, and the married women white cloths. The Wallach peasant is, of course, very fond of marrying early, and when asked why he marries, candidly replies 'to have somebody to work for him and to keep him clean.' He has one, or at most two rooms in his cottage, and here he and all his family live. He further resembles the Irish peasant in his hospitality to pigs, and his simplicity.

SABINE BARING-GOULD

From The Book of Were-wolves: Being an Account of a Terrible Superstition (1865)

Michael Wagener relates a horrible story which occurred in Hungary, suppressing the name of the person, as it was that of a still powerful family in the country. It illustrates what I have been saying, and shows how trifling a matter may develope the passion in its most hideous proportions.

Elizabeth ———— was wont to dress well in order to please her husband, and she spent half the day over her toilet. On one occasion, a lady's-maid saw something wrong in her head-dress, and as a recompence for observing it, received such a severe box on the ears that the blood gushed from her nose, and spirted on to her mistress's face. When the blood drops were washed off her face, her skin appeared much more beautiful — whiter and more transparent on the spots where the blood had been.

Elizabeth formed the resolution to bathe her face and her whole body in human blood so as to enhance her beauty. Two old women and a certain Fitzko assisted her in her undertaking. This monster used to kill the luckless victim, and the old women caught the blood, in which Elizabeth was wont to bathe at the

From Sabine Baring-Gould, *The Book of Were-wolves: Being an Account of a Terrible Superstition* (London: Smith, Elder, 1865).

hour of four in the morning. After the bath she appeared more beautiful than before.

She continued this habit after the death of her husband (1604) in the hopes of gaining new suitors. The unhappy girls who were allured to the castle, under the plea that they were to be taken into service there, were locked up in a cellar. Here they were beaten till their bodies were swollen. Elizabeth not unfrequently tortured the victims herself; often she changed their clothes which dripped with blood, and then renewed her cruelties. The swollen bodies were then cut up with razors.

Occasionally she had the girls burned, and then cut up, but the great majority were beaten to death.

At last her cruelty became so great, that she would stick needles into those who sat with her in a carriage, especially if they were of her own sex. One of her servant-girls she stripped naked, smeared her with honey, and so drove her out of the house.

When she was ill, and could not indulge her cruelty, she bit a person who came near her sick bed as though she were a wild beast.

She caused, in all, the death of 650 girls, some in Tscheita, on the neutral ground, where she had a cellar constructed for the purpose; others in different localities; for murder and bloodshed became with her a necessity.

When at last the parents of the lost children could no longer be cajoled, the castle was seized, and the traces of the murders were discovered. Her accomplices were executed, and she was imprisoned for life.

EMILY GERARD

From The Land Beyond the Forest: Facts, Figures, and Fancies from Transylvania (1888)

More decidedly evil is the *nosferatu,* or vampire, in which every Roumanian peasant believes as firmly as he does in heaven or hell. There are two sorts of vampires, living and dead. The living vampire is generally the illegitimate offspring of two illegitimate persons; but even a flawless pedigree will not insure any one against the intrusion of a

From Emily Gerard, *The Land Beyond the Forest: Facts, Figures and Fancies from Transylvania* (New York: Harper & Brothers, 1888).

vampire into their family vault, since every person killed by a nosferatu becomes likewise a vampire after death, and will continue to suck the blood of other innocent persons till the spirit has been exorcised by opening the grave of the suspected person, and either driving a stake through the corpse, or else firing a pistol-shot into the coffin. To walk smoking round the grave on each anniversary of the death is also supposed to be effective in confining the vampire. In very obstinate cases of vampirism it is recommended to cut off the head, and replace it in the coffin with the mouth filled with garlic, or to extract the heart and burn it, strewing its ashes over the grave.

That such remedies are often resorted to even now is a well-attested fact, and there are probably few Roumanian villages where such have not taken place within memory of the inhabitants. There is likewise no Roumanian village which does not count among its inhabitants some old woman (usually a midwife) versed in the precautions to be taken in order to counteract vampires, and who makes of this science a flourishing trade. She is frequently called in by the family who has lost a member, and requested to "settle" the corpse securely in its coffin, so as to insure it against wandering. The means by which she endeavors to counteract any vampire-like instincts which may be lurking are various. Sometimes she drives a nail through the forehead of the deceased, or else rubs the body with the fat of a pig which has been killed on the Feast of St. Ignatius, five days before Christmas. It is also very usual to lay the thorny branch of a wild-rose bush across the body to prevent it leaving the coffin. . . .

Perhaps the most important day in the Roumanian's year is that of St. George, April 24th (May 6th), the eve of which is said to be still frequently kept up by occult meetings taking place at night in lonely caverns or within ruined walls, and where all the ceremonies usual to the celebration of a witches' Sabbath are put into practice. This night is the great one to beware of witches, to counteract whose influence square-cut blocks of turf (to which are sometimes added thorny branches) are placed in front of each door and window. This is supposed effectually to bar their entrance to house or stables; but for still greater precaution it is usual for the peasants to keep watch all night near the sleeping cattle. This same night is likewise the best one for seeking treasures.

CESARE LOMBROSO

From Criminal Man (1911)

I began dimly to realise that the *a priori* studies on crime in the abstract, hitherto pursued by jurists, especially in Italy, with singular acumen, should be superseded by the direct analytical study of the criminal, compared with normal individuals and the insane.

I, therefore, began to study criminals in the Italian prisons, and, amongst others, I made the acquaintance of the famous brigand Vilella. This man possessed such extraordinary agility, that he had been known to scale steep mountain heights bearing a sheep on his shoulders. . . .

This was not merely an idea, but a revelation. At the sight of that skull, I seemed to see all of a sudden, lighted up as a vast plain under a flaming sky, the problem of the nature of the criminal — an atavistic being who reproduces in his person the ferocious instincts of primitive humanity and the inferior animals. Thus were explained anatomically the enormous jaws, high cheek-bones, prominent superciliary arches, solitary lines in the palms, extreme size of the orbits, handle-shaped or sessile ears found in criminals, savages, and apes, insensibility to pain, extremely acute sight, tattooing, excessive idleness, love of orgies, and the irresistible craving for evil for its own sake, the desire not only to extinguish life in the victim, but to mutilate the corpse, tear its flesh, and drink its blood.

I was further encouraged in this bold hypothesis by the results of my studies on Verzeni, a criminal convicted of sadism and rape, who showed the cannibalistic instincts of primitive anthropophagists and the ferocity of beasts of prey.

From Cesare Lombroso, "Introduction" to Gina Lombroso-Ferrero, *Criminal Man, According the Classification of Cesare Lombroso* (New York: G. P. Putnam's Sons, 1911).

MAX NORDAU

From Degeneration (1892)

Such is the notion underlying the word *fin-de-siècle*. It means a practical emancipation from traditional discipline, which theoretically is still in force. To the voluptuary this means unbridled lewdness, the unchaining of the beast in man; to the withered heart of the egoist, disdain of all consideration for his fellow-men, the trampling under foot of all barriers which enclose brutal greed of lucre and lust of pleasure; to the contemner of the world it means the shameless ascendency of base impulses and motives, which were, if not virtuously suppressed, at least hypocritically hidden; to the believer it means the repudiation of dogma, the negation of a super-sensuous world, the descent into flat phenomenalism; to the sensitive nature yearning for æsthetic thrills, it means the vanishing of ideals in art, and no more power in its accepted forms to arouse emotion. And to all, it means the end of an established order, which for thousands of years has satisfied logic, fettered depravity, and in every art matured something of beauty.

One epoch of history is unmistakably in its decline, and another is announcing its approach. There is a sound of rending in every tradition, and it is as though the morrow would not link itself with to-day. Things as they are totter and plunge, and they are suffered to reel and fall, because man is weary, and there is no faith that it is worth an effort to uphold them. Views that have hitherto governed minds are dead or driven hence like disenthroned kings, and for their inheritance they that hold the titles and they that would usurp are locked in struggle. Meanwhile interregnum in all its terrors prevails; there is confusion among the powers that be; the million, robbed of its leaders, knows not where to turn; the strong work their will; false prophets arise, and dominion is divided amongst those whose rod is the heavier because their time is short. Men look with longing for whatever new things are at hand, without presage whence they will come or what they will be. They have hope that in the chaos of thought, art may yield revelations of the order that is to follow on this tangled web. The poet, the musician, is to announce, or divine, or at least suggest in what forms civilization will further be evolved. What shall be considered good to-morrow — what

From Max Nordau, *Degeneration* (1895; reprint, New York: Fertig, 1968). Translation of the second German edition (1893).

shall be beautiful? What shall we know to-morrow — what believe in? What shall inspire us? How shall we enjoy? So rings the question from the thousand voices of the people, and where a market-vendor sets up his booth and claims to give an answer, where a fool or a knave suddenly begins to prophesy in verse or prose, in sound or colour, or professes to practise his art otherwise than his predecessors and competitors, there gathers a great concourse, crowding around him to seek in what he has wrought, as in oracles of the Pythia, some meaning to be divined and interpreted. And the more vague and insignificant they are, the more they seem to convey of the future to the poor gaping souls gasping for revelations, and the more greedily and passionately are they expounded.

Such is the spectacle presented by the doings of men in the reddened light of the Dusk of the Nations. Massed in the sky the clouds are aflame in the weirdly beautiful glow which was observed for the space of years after the eruption of Krakatoa. Over the earth the shadows creep with deepening gloom, wrapping all objects in a mysterious dimness, in which all certainty is destroyed and any guess seems plausible. Forms lose their outlines, and are dissolved in floating mist. The day is over, the night draws on. The old anxiously watch its approach, fearing they will not live to see the end. A few amongst the young and strong are conscious of the vigour of life in all their veins and nerves, and rejoice in the coming sunrise. Dreams, which fill up the hours of darkness till the breaking of the new day, bring to the former comfortless memories, to the latter high-souled hopes. And in the artistic products of the age we see the form in which these dreams become sensible.

Here is the place to forestall a possible misunderstanding, The great majority of the middle and lower classes is naturally not *fin-de-siècle*. It is true that the spirit of the times is stirring the nations down to their lowest depths, and awaking even in the most inchoate and rudimentary human being a wondrous feeling of stir and upheaval. But this more or less slight touch of moral sea-sickness does not excite in him the cravings of travailing women, nor express itself in new æsthetic needs. The Philistine or the Proletarian still finds undiluted satisfaction in the old and oldest forms of art and poetry, if he knows himself unwatched by the scornful eye of the votary of fashion, and is free to yield to his own inclinations. He prefers Ohnet's novels to all the symbolists, and Mascagni's *Cavalleria Rusticana* to all Wagnerians and to Wagner himself; he enjoys himself royally over slap-dash farces and music-hall melodies, and yawns or is angered at Ibsen; he contemplates gladly chromos of paintings depicting Munich beer-houses and rustic taverns, and passes the open-air painters without a glance. It is only a very small minority who honestly find pleasure in the new tendencies, and announce them with genuine conviction as that which alone is sound, a sure guide for the future, a pledge of pleasure and of moral benefit. But this minority has the gift of covering the whole visible surface of society, as a little oil extends over a large area of the surface of the sea. It consists chiefly of rich educated people, or of fanatics. The former give the *ton* to all the snobs, the fools, and the blockheads; the latter make an impression upon the weak and dependent, and intimidate the nervous. All snobs affect to have the same taste as the select and exclusive minority, who pass by everything that once was considered beautiful with an air of the greatest contempt. And thus it appears as if the whole of civilized humanity were converted to the æsthetics of the Dusk of the Nations. . . .

The conception of degeneracy, which, at this time, obtains throughout the science of mental disease, was first clearly grasped and formulated by Morel. In his principal work — often quoted, but, unfortunately, not sufficiently read — the following definition of what he wishes to be understood by 'degeneracy' is given by this distinguished expert in mental pathology, who was, for a short time, famous in Germany, even outside professional circles.

'The clearest notion we can form of degeneracy is to regard it as *a morbid deviation from an original type*. This deviation, even if, at the outset, it was ever so slight, contained transmissible elements of such a nature that anyone bearing in him the germs becomes more and more incapable of fulfilling his functions in the world; and mental progress, already checked in his own person, finds itself menaced also in his descendants.'

When under any kind of noxious influences an organism becomes debilitated, its successors will not resemble the healthy, normal type of the species, with capacities for development, but will form a new sub-species, which, like all others, possesses the capacity of transmitting to its offspring, in a continuously increasing degree, its peculiarities, these being morbid deviations from the normal form — gaps in development, malformations and infirmities. That which distinguishes degeneracy from the formation of new species (phylogeny) is, that the morbid variation does not continuously subsist and propagate itself, like one that is healthy, but, fortunately, is soon rendered sterile, and after a few generations often dies out before it reaches the lowest grade of organic degradation.

Degeneracy betrays itself among men in certain physical characteristics, which are denominated 'stigmata,' or brand-marks — an unfortunate term derived from a false idea, as if degeneracy were necessarily the consequence of a fault, and the indication of it a punishment. Such stigmata consist of deformities, multiple and stunted growths in the first line of asymmetry, the unequal development of the two halves of the face and cranium; then imperfection in the development of the external ear, which is conspicuous for its enormous size, or protrudes from the head, like a handle, and the lobe of which is either lacking or adhering to the head, and the helix of which is not involuted; further, squint-eyes, hare-lips, irregularities in the form and position of the teeth; pointed or flat palates, webbed or supernumerary fingers (syn- and poly-dactylia), etc. In the book from which I have quoted, Morel gives a list of the anatomical phenomena of degeneracy, which later observers have largely extended. In particular, Lombroso has conspicuously broadened our knowledge of stigmata, but he apportions them merely to his 'born criminals' — a limitation which from the very scientific standpoint of Lombroso himself cannot be justified, his 'born criminals' being nothing but a subdivision of degenerates. Féré expresses this very emphatically when he says, 'Vice, crime and madness are only distinguished from each other by social prejudices.'

There might be a sure means of proving that the application of the term 'degenerates' to the originators of all the *fin-de-siècle* movements in art and literature is not arbitrary, that it is no baseless conceit, but a fact; and that would be a careful physical examination of the persons concerned, and an inquiry into their pedigree. In almost all cases, relatives would be met with who were undoubtedly degenerate, and one or more stigmata discovered which would indisputably establish the diagnosis of 'Degeneration.' Of course, from human consideration, the result of such an inquiry could often not be made public; and he alone would be convinced who should be able to undertake it himself.

Science, however, has found, together with these physical stigmata, others of a mental order, which betoken degeneracy quite as clearly as the former; and they allow of an easy demonstration from all the vital manifestations, and, in particular, from all the works of degenerates, so that it is not necessary to measure the cranium of an author, or to see the lobe of a painter's ear, in order to recognise the fact that he belongs to the class of degenerates.

Quite a number of different designations have been found for these persons. Maudsley and Ball call them 'Borderland dwellers' — that is to say, dwellers on the borderland between reason and pronounced madness. Magnan gives to them the name of 'higher degenerates' (*dégénérés supérieurs*), and Lombroso speaks of 'mattoids' (from *matto*, the Italian for insane), and 'graphomaniacs,' under which he classifies those semi-insane persons who feel a strong impulse to write. In spite, however, of this variety of nomenclature, it is a question simply of one single species of individuals, who betray their fellowship by the similarity of their mental physiognomy.

In the mental development of degenerates, we meet with the same irregularity that we have observed in their physical growth. The asymmetry of face and cranium finds, as it were, its counterpart in their mental faculties. Some of the latter are completely stunted, others morbidly exaggerated. That which nearly all degenerates lack is the sense of morality and of right and wrong. For them there exists no law, no decency, no modesty. In order to satisfy any momentary impulse, or inclination, or caprice, they commit crimes and trespasses with the greatest calmness and self-complacency, and do not comprehend that other persons take offence thereat. When this phenomenon is present in a high degree, we speak of 'moral insanity' with Maudsley; there are, nevertheless, lower stages in which the degenerate does not, perhaps, himself commit any act which will bring him into conflict with the criminal code, but at least asserts the theoretical legitimacy of crime; seeks, with philosophically sounding fustian, to prove that 'good' and 'evil,' virtue and vice, are arbitrary distinctions; goes into raptures over evildoers and their deeds; professes to discover beauties in the lowest and most repulsive things; and tries to awaken interest in, and so-called 'comprehension' of, every bestiality. The two psychological roots of moral insanity, in all its degrees of development, are, firstly, unbounded egoism, and, secondly, impulsiveness — *i.e.,* inability to resist a sudden impulse to any deed; and these characteristics also constitute the chief intellectual stigmata of degenerates. In the following sections of this work, I shall find occasion to show on what organic grounds, and in consequence of what peculiarities of their brain and nervous system, degenerates are necessarily egoistical and impulsive.

RICHARD VON KRAFFT-EBING

From Psychopathia Sexualis, with Special Reference to Contrary Sexual Instinct: A Medico-Legal Study (1893)

(a) *Lust-Murder (Lust Potentiated as Cruelty, Murderous Lust Extending to Anthropophagy).* — The most horrible example, shows the connection between lust and a desire to kill. . . .

In such cases it may even happen that appetite for the flesh of the murdered victim arises, and, in consequence of this perverse coloring of the idea, parts of the body may be eaten. . . .

The Whitechapel murderer, who still eludes the vigilance of the police, probably belongs in this category of psycho-sexual monsters.[1] The constant absence of uterus, ovaries, and labia, in the victims (ten) of this modern Bluebeard, allows the presumption that he seeks and finds still further satisfaction in anthropophagy.

In other cases of lust-murder, for physical and mental reasons (*vide supra*), violation is omitted, and the sadistic crime alone becomes the equivalent of coitus. . . .

The cases in which the perpetrator injures and cuts up the corpse are clearer. Such cases come next to those of lust-murder, in that, in these individuals, cruelty, or at least an impulse to attack the female body, is connected with lust. It is possible that a remnant of moral sense deters from the cruel act on a living woman, and possibly the fancy passes beyond lust-murder and rests on its result, the corpse. Here, also, it is possible that the idea of defenselessness of the body plays a *rôle.*

Case 23. Sergeant Bertrand, a man of delicate physical constitution and of peculiar character; from childhood silent and inclined to solitude. . . .

In 1847 and 1848, during two weeks, as reported, the impulse, accompanied by violent headache, to commit brutalities on corpses, actuated him. Amidst the greatest dangers and difficulties, he satisfied this impulse some fifteen times. He dug up the bodies with his hands, in nowise sensible, in his excitement, to the injuries he thus inflicted on himself. When he had obtained the

From Richard von Krafft-Ebing, *Psychopathia Sexualis, with Special Reference to Contrary Sexual Instinct: A Medico-Legal Study,* trans. Charles Gilbert Chaddock, M.D. (Philadelphia and London: F. A. Davis Co. Publishers, 1893). Authorized translation of the seventh German edition.

[1]The Whitechapel murderer was more popularly known as Jack the Ripper.

body, he cut it up with a sword or pocket-knife, tore out the entrails, and then masturbated. The sex of the bodies is said to have been a matter of indifference to him, though it was ascertained that this modern vampire had dug up more female than male corpses. During these acts he declares himself to have been in an indescribable state of sexual excitement. After having cut them up, he had sometimes reinterred the bodies.

In July, 1848, he accidentally came across the body of a girl of sixteen. Then, for the first time, he experienced a desire to carry out coitus on a cadaver. "I covered it with kisses and pressed it wildly to my heart. All that one could enjoy with a living woman is nothing in comparison with the pleasure I experienced. After I had enjoyed it for about a quarter of an hour, I cut the body up, as usual, and tore out the entrails. Then I buried the cadaver again." Only after this, as B. declares, had he felt the impulse to use the bodies sexually before cutting them up, and thereafter he had done it in three instances. The actual motive of the exhuming of the bodies, however, was then, as before, to cut them up; and the enjoyment in so doing was greater than in using the bodies sexually. The latter act had always been nothing more than an episode of the principal one, and had never quieted his desires; therefore, he had always cut up the body afterward or mutilated another body. The medico-legal examiners gave an opinion of "monomania." Court-martial sentence to one year's imprisonment. (Michéa, *Union méd.*, 1849; Lunier, *Annal. méd.-psychol.*, 1849, p. 153; Tardieu, "Attentats aux moeurs," 1878, p. 114; Legrand, "La folie devant les tribun.," p. 524.)

(c) *Injury of Women (Stabbing, Flagellation, etc.)* — Following lust-murder and violation of corpses, come cases closely allied to the former, in which injury of the victim of lust and sight of the victim's blood are a delight and pleasure for degenerate men. The notorious Marquis de Sade, after whom the combination of lust and cruelty has been named, was such a monster. Coitus only excited him when he could prick the object of his desire until the blood came. His greatest pleasure was to injure prostitutes and then bind their wounds.

Here also belongs the case of a captain mentioned by Brierre de Boismont, who always compelled the object of his affection to place leeches ad pudenda before coitus, which was very frequent. Finally this woman became very anæmic and, as a result of this, insane. . . .

Cruelty arises from various sources, and is natural to primitive man. Compassion, in contrast with it, is a secondary manifestation, and acquired late. The instinct to fight and destroy, so important an endowment in prehistoric conditions, is long afterward operative; and, in the ideas engendered by civilization, like that of "the criminal," it finds new objects, even though its original object — "the enemy" — still exists. That not simply the death, but also torture, of the conquered is demanded, is in part explained by the sense of power, which satisfies itself in this way; and in part by the insatiableness of the impulse of vengeance. Thus all cruelty and all historical enormities may be explained without recourse to sadism (which may often have been in operation, but which cannot be assumed, since it is relatively an infrequent perversion).

At the same time, there is still another powerful psychical element to take into consideration, which explains the attraction that is still exerted by executions, etc.; and that is, the pleasure there is in intense and unusual impressions and rare sights, in contrast with which, in coarse and blunted beings, pity is silent.

But undoubtedly there are individuals for whom, in spite of, or even by reason of, their lively compassion, all that is connected with death and suffering has a mysterious attraction; who, with inward opposition, and yet following a dark impulse, occupy themselves with such things, or at least with pictures and notices of them. Still, this is not sadism, as long as no sexual element enters into consciousness; and yet it is possible that, in unconscious life, slender threads connect such manifestations with the hidden depths of sadism.

(h) *Sadism in Woman.* — That sadism — a perversion, as we have seen, frequent in men — is much less frequent in women, is easily explained. In the first place, sadism, in which the need of subjugation of the opposite sex forms a constituent element, in accordance with its nature, represents a pathological intensification of the masculine sexual character; in the second place, the obstacles which oppose the expression of this monstrous impulse are, of course, much greater for a woman than for a man. Yet sadism occurs in women; and it can only be explained by the primary constituent element, — the general hyperexcitation of the motor sphere. Only two cases have thus far been scientifically studied.

Case 42. A married man presented himself with numerous scars of cuts on his arms. He told their origin as follows: When he wished to approach his wife, who was young and somewhat "nervous," he first had to make a cut in his arm. Then she would suck the wound, and during the act become violently excited sexually.

This case recalls the wide-spread legend of the vampires, the origin of which may perhaps be referred to such sadistic facts.[2]

[2]The legend is especially spread throughout the Balkan peninsula. Among the Greeks it has its origin in the myth of the *lamiæ* and *marmolykes*, — blood-sucking women. Goethe made use of this in his "Bride of Corinth." The verses referring to vampirism, "suck thy heart's blood," etc., can be thoroughly understood only when compared with their ancient sources. [Krafft-Ebing's note.]

RUDYARD KIPLING

The Vampire (1897)

A FOOL there was and he made his prayer
(Even as you and I!)
To a rag and a bone and a hank of hair
(We called her the woman who did not care)
But the fool he called her his lady fair —
(Even as you and I!)

Oh, the years we waste and the tears we waste
And the work of our head and hand
Belong to the woman who did not know
(And now we know that she never could know)
And did not understand!

A fool there was and his goods he spent
(Even as you and I!)
Honour and faith and a sure intent
(And it wasn't the least what the lady meant)
But a fool must follow his natural bent
(Even as you and I!)

Oh, the toil we lost and the spoil we lost
And the excellent things we planned
Belong to the woman who didn't know why
(And now we know that she never knew why)
And did not understand!

The fool was stripped to his foolish hide
(Even as you and I!)

From *Rudyard Kipling's Verse: Inclusive Edition, 1885–1936* (London: Hodder and Stoughton, Ltd., 1940).

Which she might have seen when she threw him aside —
(But it isn't on record the lady tried)
So some of him lived but the most of him died —
(Even as you and I!)

And it isn't the shame and it isn't the blame
That stings like a white hot brand —
It's coming to know that she never knew why
(Seeing, at last, she could never know why)
And never could understand!

WALTER PATER

From The Renaissance (1894)

La Gioconda[1] is, in the truest sense, Leonardo's masterpiece, the revealing instance of his mode of thought and work. In suggestiveness, only the *Melancholia* of Dürer is comparable to it; and no crude symbolism disturbs the effect of its subdued and graceful mystery. We all know the face and hands of the figure, set in its marble chair, in that circle of fantastic rocks, as in some faint light under sea. Perhaps of all ancient pictures time has chilled it least. As often happens with works in which invention seems to reach its limit, there is an element in it given to, not invented by, the master. In that inestimable folio of drawings, once in the possession of Vasari, were certain designs by Verrocchio, faces of such impressive beauty that Leonardo in his boyhood copied them many times. It is hard not to connect with these designs of the elder, by-past master, as with its germinal principle, the unfathomable smile, always with a touch of something sinister in it, which plays over all Leonardo's work. Besides, the picture is a portrait. From childhood we see this image defining itself on the fabric of his dreams; and but for express historical testimony, we might fancy that this was but his ideal lady, embodied and beheld at last. What was the relationship of a living Florentine to this creature of his thought? By what strange affinities had the dream and the person grown up thus apart, and yet so closely together? Present from the first incorporeally in Leonardo's brain, dimly traced in the designs of Verrocchio, she is found present at last in

From Walter Pater, *The Renaissance,* 4th ed. (London: Macmillan, 1873; 4th ed. 1894).
[1]*La Gioconda* is Leonardo da Vinci's *Mona Lisa.*

Il Giocondo's house. That there is much of mere portraiture in the picture is attested by the legend that by artificial means, the presence of mimes and flute-players, that subtle expression was protracted on the face. Again, was it in four years and by renewed labour never really completed, or in four months and as by stroke of magic, that the image was projected?

The presence that rose thus so strangely beside the waters, is expressive of what in the ways of a thousand years men had come to desire. Hers is the head upon which all "the ends of the world are come," and the eyelids are a little weary. It is a beauty wrought out from within upon the flesh, the deposit, little cell by cell, of strange thoughts and fantastic reveries and exquisite passions. Set it for a moment beside one of those white Greek goddesses or beautiful women of antiquity, and how would they be troubled by this beauty, into which the soul with all its maladies has passed! All the thoughts and experience of the world have etched and moulded there, in that which they have of power to refine and make expressive the outward form, the animalism of Greece, the lust of Rome, the mysticism of the middle age with its spiritual ambition and imaginative loves, the return of the Pagan world, the sins of the Borgias. She is older than the rocks among which she sits; like the vampire, she has been dead many times, and learned the secrets of the grave; and has been a diver in deep seas, and keeps their fallen day about her; and trafficked for strange webs with Eastern merchants and, as Leda, was the mother of Helen of Troy, and, as Saint Anne, the mother of Mary; and all this has been to her but as the sound of lyres and flutes, and lives only in the delicacy with which it has moulded the changing lineaments, and tinged the eyelids and the hands. The fancy of a perpetual life, sweeping together ten thousand experiences, is an old one; and modern philosophy has conceived the idea of humanity as wrought upon by, and summing up in itself, all modes of thought and life. Certainly Lady Lisa might stand as the embodiment of the old fancy, the symbol of the modern idea.

KARL MARX

From The Limits of the Workday (1867)

The capitalist has bought labor power at its daily value. Its use value belongs to him during the workday. In this way he has obtained the right to make the worker work for him during that day. But what is a workday? In any case, shorter than a natural day of living. By how much? The capitalist has his own opinion about this extreme point, the necessary boundary of the workday. As a capitalist, he is only personified capital. His soul is capital's soul. Capital has, however, but a single driving force, the drive to increase its own value, to create surplus value, to absorb the largest possible amount of surplus labor by means of its unchanging part, the relations of production. Like a vampire, capital is dead labor that keeps itself alive only by drinking in living labor and that invigorates itself more the more labor it sucks in. During the period when the worker works, the capitalist consumes the labor power he has bought from him. If the worker uses up his available time for himself, then he steals from the capitalist.

From Karl Marx, *Capital*, vol. 1, trans. by J. P. Riquelme from Karl Marx and Friedrich Engels, *Werke, Band 23*, Karl Marx's *Das Kapital: Kritik der politischen Ökonomie, Erster Band, Buch I: Der Produktionsprozess des Kapitals* (Berlin: Dietz, 1968), 247.

FRIEDRICH NIETZSCHE

From Why We Are Not Idealists (1886)

Why we are not Idealists. — Formerly philosophers feared the senses: have we perhaps all too thoroughly unlearned this fear? These days we are all sensualists, we, the present and the future of philosophy, *not* with regard to theory, but with regard to *praxis*, in practice. . . . Those earlier philosophers held the view that the senses would tempt them away from their world, the cold realm of "ideas," to a dangerous southern island, where they feared their virtues as philosophers would melt away like snow in the sunshine. "Wax in the ears" was at that time virtually a condition for philosophizing; a true philosopher listened to life no longer; in so far as living is music, he *disavowed* that music, — it

From Friedrich Nietzsche, *Joyful Wisdom*, book 5, trans. by J. P. Riquelme from Friedrich Nietzsche, *Sämtliche Werke, Kritische Studienausgabe in 15 Bänden, Band 3* (Munich: Deutscher Taschenbuch, 1980), 623–24.

is an old philosophical superstition that all music is the music of Sirens. — Nowadays we might tend to decide precisely the reverse (which could be in itself just as wrong): namely that *ideas,* with their cold, anemic appearance, and not even despite this appearance, are more seductively misleading than the senses, — they always lived on the "blood" of the philosopher, they consumed his senses, yes, if you will credit me, also his "heart." These old-time philosophers were heartless: philosophizing was always a kind of vampirism. Do you not feel in response to such figures as even Spinoza something deeply enigmatic and uncanny? Do you not see the theatre piece that is playing here, the constantly *growing paleness* — , the always more ideally displayed spiritualizing? Don't you imagine in the background some long hidden female bloodsucker that makes its start with the senses and ultimately lets remain, leaves behind only bones and their rattling? — I mean categories, formulas, *words* (then, you will forgive me, what is *leftover* from Spinoza, *amor intellectualis dei,* is the rattling of bones, nothing more! what is love, what is god, if they have lost every drop of blood? . . .) In summary: all philosophical idealism has been up until now something like a sickness, where it has not been, as in Plato's case, the caution of an extremely rich and dangerous health, the fear of *overpowering* senses, the sagacity of a clever Socrates. — Perhaps we moderns are not sufficiently healthy to *require* Plato's idealism? And we do not fear the senses because — —

JAMES FRAZER

From On Certain Burial Customs as Illustrative of the Primitive Theory of the Soul (1886)

In his *Roman Questions,* that delightful storehouse of old-world lore, Plutarch asks — "When a man who has been falsely reported to have died abroad, returns home alive, why is he not admitted by the door, but gets up on the tiles and so lets himself down into the house?" The curious custom to which Plutarch here refers prevails in modern Persia, for we read in *Hajji Baba* (c. 18) of the man who went through "the ceremony of making his entrance over the roof, instead of through the door; for such is the custom when a man who has been thought dead

From James Frazer, *Garnered Sheaves: Essays, Addresses, and Reviews* (London: Macmillan and Co., 1931) 4–6.

returns home alive." From a passage in Agathias we may perhaps infer that the custom is at least as old as the sixth century of our era. A custom so remote from our modern ways must necessarily have its roots far back in the history of our race. Imagine a modern Englishman, whom his friends had given up for dead, rejoining the home circle by coming down the chimney, instead of entering by the front door. In this paper I propose to show that the custom originated in certain primitive beliefs and observances touching the dead — beliefs and observances by no means confined to Greece and Rome, but occurring in similar if not identical forms in many parts of the world. . . .

Another simple but effectual plan is to nail the dead man to the coffin (the Chuwash again) or to tie his feet together (among the Arabs), or his hands together (in Voigtland), or his neck to his legs (among the Troglodytes, Damaras, and New Zealanders). The Wallachians drive a long nail through the skull and lay the thorny stem of a wild rose bush on the shroud. The Californians and Damaras clinched matters by breaking his spine. The corpses of suicides and vampires had stakes run through them. Sometimes the heads of vampires are cut off, or their hearts torn out and hacked in pieces, and their bodies burned, or boiling water and vinegar are poured on their graves.

ENCYCLOPÆDIA BRITANNICA

Vampire (1888)

VAMPIRE, a term, apparently of Servian origin (*wampir*), originally applied in eastern Europe to blood-sucking ghosts, but in modern usage transferred to one or more species of blood-sucking bats inhabiting South America.

In the first-mentioned meaning a vampire is usually supposed to be the soul of a dead man which quits the buried body by night to suck the blood of living persons. Hence, when the vampire's grave is opened, his corpse is found to be fresh and rosy from the blood which he has thus absorbed. To put a stop to his ravages, a stake is driven through the corpse, or the head cut off, or the heart torn out and the body burned, or boiling water and vinegar are poured on the grave. The persons who turn vampires are generally wizards, witches, suicides and those who have come to a violent end or have been cursed by their parents or by

From *Encyclopædia Britannica*, 9th ed., vol. 24 (Edinburgh: Black, 1888) 52–53.

the church. But any one may become a vampire if an animal (especially a cat) leaps over his corpse or a bird flies over it. Sometimes the vampire is thought to be the soul of a living man which leaves his body in sleep, to go in the form of a straw or fluff of down and suck the blood of other sleepers. The belief in vampires chiefly prevails in Slavonic lands, as in Russia (especially White Russia and the Ukraine), Poland and Servia, and among the Czechs of Bohemia and the other Slavonic races of Austria. It became specially prevalent in Hungary between the years 1730 and 1735, whence all Europe was filled with reports of the exploits of vampires. Several treatises were written on the subject, among which may be mentioned Ranft's *De masticatione mortuorum in tumulis* (1734) and Calmet's *Dissertation on the Vampires of Hungary*, translated into English in 1750. It is probable that this superstition gained much ground from the reports of those who had examined the bodies of persons buried alive though believed to be dead, and was based on the twisted position of the corpse, the marks of blood on the shroud and on the face and hands — results of the frenzied struggle in the coffin before life became extinct. The belief in vampirism has also taken root among the Albanians and modern Greeks, but here it may be due to Slavonic influence.

Two species of blood-sucking bats (the only species known) — *Desmodus rufus* and *Diphylla ecaudata* — representing two genera (see CHIROPTERA), inhabit the tropical and part of the subtropical regions of the New World, and are restricted to South and Central America. They appear to be confined chiefly to the forest-clad parts, and their attacks on men and other warm-blooded animals were noticed by some of the earliest writers. Thus Peter Martyr (Anghiera), who wrote soon after the conquest of South America, says that in the Isthmus of Darien there were bats which sucked the blood of men and cattle when asleep to such a degree as to even kill them. Condamine, a writer of the 18th century, remarks that at Borja (Ecuador) and in other places they had entirely destroyed the cattle introduced by the missionaries. Sir Robert Schomburgk relates that at Wicki, on the river Berbice, no fowls could be kept on account of the ravages of these creatures, which attacked their combs, causing them to appear white from loss of blood. The present writer, when in South and Central America, had many accounts given him as to the attacks of the vampires, and it was agreed upon by most of his informants that these bats when attacking horses showed a decided preference for those of a grey colour. It is interesting to speculate how far the vampire bats may have been instrumental — when they were, perhaps, more abundant — in causing the destruction of the horse, which had disappeared from America previous to the discovery of that continent.

Although these bats were known thus early to Europeans, the species to which they belonged were not determined for a long time, several of the large frugivorous species having been wrongly set down as blood-suckers, and named accordingly. Thus the name *Vampyrus* was suggested to Geoffroy and adopted by Spix, who also considered that the long-tongued bats of the group *Glossophaga* were addicted to blood, and accordingly described *Glossophaga soricina* as a very cruel blood-sucker (*sanguisuga crudelissima*), believing that the long brush-tipped tongue was used to increase the flow of blood. *Vampyrus spectrum*, a large bat inhabiting Brazil, of sufficiently forbidding aspect, which was long considered by naturalists to be thoroughly sanguivorous in its habits, and named accordingly by Geoffroy, has been shown by the observations of travellers to be mainly frugivorous, and is considered by the inhabitants of the countries in which it is found to be perfectly harmless. Charles Waterton believed *Artibeus planirostris*, a common bat in British Guiana, usually found in the roofs of houses, and now known to be frugivorous, to be the veritable vampire; but neither he nor any of the naturalists that preceded him had succeeded in detecting any bat in the act of drawing blood. It fell to the lot of Charles Darwin to determine one of the blood-sucking species at least, and the following is his account of the circumstances under which the discovery of the sanguivorous habits of *Desmodus rufus* was made: "The vampire bat is often the cause of much trouble by biting the horses on their withers. The injury is generally not so much owing to the loss of blood as to the inflammation which the pressure of the saddle afterwards produces. The whole circumstance has lately been doubted in England; I was therefore fortunate in being present when one was actually caught on a horse's back. We were bivouacking late one evening near Coquimbo, in Chile, when my servant, noticing that one of the horses was very restive, went to see what was the matter, and, fancying he could detect something, suddenly put his hand on the beast's withers, and secured the vampire" (*Naturalist's Voyage Round the World*, p. 22).

Desmodus rufus, the common blood-sucking bat, is widely spread over the tropical and subtropical parts of Central and South America from Oaxaca to southern Brazil and Chile. It is a comparatively small bat, a little larger than the noctule, the head and body about 3 in. in length, the forearm 2½, with a remarkably long and strong thumb; it is destitute of a tail, and has a very peculiar physiognomy. The body is covered with rather short fur of a reddish-brown colour but varying in shade, the extremities of the hairs sometimes ashy. The teeth are peculiar and characteristic, admirably adapted for the purposes for which they are employed. The upper front teeth (incisors), of which there are only two, are enormously enlarged, and in shape obliquely triangular like small guillotines. The canines, though smaller than the incisors, are large and sharp; but the cheek-teeth, so well developed in other bats, are very small and reduced in number to two above and three below, on each side, with laterally compressed crowns rising but slightly above the level of the gum, their longitudinally disposed cutting edges (in the upper jaw) being continuous with the base of the canine and with each other. The lower front teeth (incisors) are small, bifid, in pairs, and separated from the canines, with a space in front. The lower cheek-teeth are narrow, like those in the upper jaw, but the anterior tooth is slightly larger than the others, and separated by a small space from the canines. Behind the lower incisors the jaw is deeply hollowed out to receive the extremities of the large upper incisors.

With this peculiar dentition there is associated as remarkable a departure from the general type in the form of the digestive apparatus. The exceedingly narrow oesophagus opens at right angles into a narrow, intestine-like stomach, which almost immediately terminates on the right, without a distinct pylorus, in the duodenum, but on the left forms a greatly elongated caecum, bent and folded upon itself, which appears at first sight like part of the intestines. This, the cardiac extremity of the stomach is, for a short distance to the left of the entrance of the oesophagus, still very narrow, but soon increases in size, till near its termination it attains a diameter quite three times that of the short pyloric portion. The length of this cardiac diverticulum of the stomach appears to vary from 2 to 6 in., the size in each specimen probably depending on the amount of food obtained by the animal before it was captured.

The only other known species of blood-sucking bat, *Diphylla ecaudata,* inhabits Brazil, and appears to be much less abundant than *Desmodus rufus,* from which it is distinguished by its slightly smaller size, by the absence of a groove in the front of the lower lip, the non-development of the interfemoral membrane in the centre, and the presence of a short calcaneum (absent in *D. rufus*), but more particularly by the presence of an additional rudimentary cheek-tooth (?molar) above and below, and the peculiar form of the lower incisors, which are much expanded in the direction of the jaws and pectinated, forming a semicircular row touching each other, the outer incisors being wider than the inner ones, with six notches, the inner incisors with three each.

Thus constituted, these bats present, in this extraordinary differentiation of the manducatory and digestive apparatus, a departure from the type of other species of the family (*Phyllostomidae*) to which they belong unparalleled in any of the other orders of *Mammalia,* standing apart from all other mammals as being fitted only for a diet of blood, and capable of sustaining life upon that alone.[1] Travellers describe the wounds inflicted by the large sharp-edged incisors as being similar to those caused by a razor when shaving: a portion of the skin is shaved off and, a large number of severed capillary vessels being thus exposed, a constant flow of blood is maintained. From this source the blood is drawn through the exceedingly narrow gullet — too narrow for anything solid to pass — into the intestine-like stomach, whence it is, probably, gradually drawn off during the slow progress of digestion, while the animal, sated with food, is hanging in a state of torpidity from the roof of its cave or from the inner sides of a hollow tree.

[1]This sentence was omitted from the 10th edition (1902) and from later editions, presumably because the statement was found to be erroneous. While he was writing *Dracula,* however, Stoker would have known only the entry as it was published in the 9th edition of the *Britannica* (1888).

PART TWO

Dracula:
A Case Study in
Contemporary Criticism

A Critical History
of *Dracula*

Dracula has spawned a rich progeny of speculative critical responses since its publication in 1897, so many and so various that a brief critical history can provide only an outline with examples of the main types that have emerged. The fact that the book does not conform to the conventions of realism helps account for the variety and intensity of the interpretive speculations, which a less fantastic, less allegorical narrative would likely not generate. Following the initial reviews, which were mixed in their judgments of the book's quality, *Dracula* attracted little attention from literary scholars and critics for much of the twentieth century. Beginning in the 1950s and increasingly since the 1970s, it has drawn responses from academic critics interested in a wide range of topics and perspectives, including historical and literary sources, narrative technique, psychoanalysis, gender roles, anthropology, Victorian culture, capitalism, the history of Gothic writing, poststructuralism, imperialism, postcolonialism, and Irish studies.[1] Broadly speaking, recent

[1]Many of the most suggestive and persuasive readings of *Dracula* through the mid-1990s have been reprinted in critical collections focused on the book or on Stoker's writings in general. Twenty-five essays on *Dracula* published before 1990, including many of the most influential ones, are available in two collections, *Dracula: The Vampire and the Critics* (1988), edited by Margaret L. Carter, and *The Critical Response to Bram Stoker* (1993), edited by Carol A. Senf. The latter volume also includes reviews of *Dracula* and essays and reviews about other works by Stoker. A more recent critical casebook, *Dracula: Bram Stoker* (1999), edited by Glennis Byron, complements these earlier volumes,

critics have responded to the book from two general orientations. Some have focused primarily on details that invite and support psychoanalytic readings, while others have staked out, explicitly or implicitly, a contrasting conceptual territory that emphasizes history or society rather than mind. Whether the specific approach gives precedence to issues of mind or issues of history, or tries to assign comparable weight to both, many critics read *Dracula* as either supporting values and tendencies of late-nineteenth-century British culture or reflecting on them with significant independence.

INITIAL REACTIONS AND DEVELOPING CRITICAL ACCEPTANCE

The psychological and social contours of critical writing about *Dracula* emerged only late in the twentieth century, after over half a century of dispute and, sometimes, disparagement concerning its literary quality. When *Dracula* appeared it was reviewed widely but with a mixed response in major British newspapers and periodicals, including the *Athenaeum,* the *Bookman,* the *Daily Mail,* the *Pall Mall Gazette, Punch,* and the *Spectator.* The reviewer in the *Bookman* compares the work to the popular tales of Wilkie Collins (1824–1889), a well-regarded writer of narratives involving mystery, crime, and suspense, but maintains that the audacity and horror of *Dracula* are distinctive. Like many later readers, the reviewer understands the narrative as a heroic, conservative tale "of human skill and courage pitted against inhuman wrong and superhuman strength" (Senf, *Critical,* 61). The *Athenaeum*'s review is less laudatory, claiming that Stoker's skill and imaginative conceptions are not sufficient to make his book high literature. From then until the 1950s critics treated *Dracula* as a minor but vivid and enduring piece of popular writing that had both contributed to and tapped a cultural fascination with the vampire. In *The Super-*

---

since the majority of the essays it reprints appeared originally in the 1990s. Commentators on the criticism of *Dracula* have framed their descriptions using sets of categories that differ from mine. Carter, for example, divides the critical responses into the following emphases: "historical, political, psychosexual, metaphysical, or structural (i.e., focusing on narrative technique, not necessarily adhering to a 'structuralist' school of criticism)" (2). Clive Leatherdale identifies five main emphases in the criticism: sexual repression, psychoanalysis, religious motifs, occult and mythic elements, and social and political tendencies (11 and "Part Three: Perspectives," 155–240). Byron organizes his selected bibliography of the criticism under the following headings: formalist, psychoanalytic, Marxist and historicist, and feminist and gender issues (219–20).

natural in Modern English Fiction (1917), Dorothy Scarborough, herself a writer of fiction involving Gothic motifs, singles out *Dracula* as "the tensest, most dreadful modern story of vampirism" (163), a book she warns against reading alone late at night. In *The Vampire: His Kith and Kin* (1928), Montague Summers includes *Dracula* in his chapter concerning "The Vampire in Literature," but he complains that Stoker's book is too long and prolix. For him, *Dracula*'s appeal arises from the vampire as subject, not Stoker's accomplishments as a writer. In *Supernatural Horror in Literature* (1939), H. P. Lovecraft, himself a well-published writer of strange tales, expresses a low opinion of Stoker's artistic achievement in any of his books, though he admits that *Dracula* is the best of them.

More extended and admiring treatments of *Dracula* began to appear when critics examined in detail the book's relation to folkloric and historical sources and its narrative techniques. Source studies and commentaries concerned with literary form provided a backdrop against which later critics could treat *Dracula* seriously from psychological and social perspectives. Significant source studies were first published in the 1950s. In one of the earliest of these, *"Dracula,* The Monastic Chronicles and Slavic Folklore"* (1956), Bacil F. Kirtley identifies Vlad the Impaler, Prince of Wallachia, as an important model for Count Dracula and discusses both Vlad's life and Romanian vampire legends. He also identifies Arminius Vambery, a famous Hungarian linguist and Orientalist scholar, whom Stoker met in London, as the model for Van Helsing's friend, Arminius. Kirtley's essay and the many later attempts to identify Stoker's sources and his transformations of them establish that the author of *Dracula* was a well-informed writer who had spent substantial time doing research for the book, which he wrote over a period of seven years, while also working as a theater manager. Grigore Nandris's "The Historical Dracula: The Theme of His Legend in the Western and in the Eastern Literatures of Europe" (1966) contains a more extensive discussion of Vlad and vampire legends. Raymond McNally and Radu Florescu provide the most elaborate historical study of Vlad in relation to Count Dracula, *In Search of Dracula* (1972), speculating that the bloody career of Countess Elizabeth Bathory also provided Stoker with a model.[2] These explorations of

---

[2]McNally and Florescu have together and separately published other volumes focusing on the history and legends that stand behind the figure of Dracula, including their *The Essential Dracula* (1979) and McNally's *Dracula Was a Woman* (1984). I have not included these books in the review of criticism, since their subjects are more historical than literary.

sources and related studies published in the 1970s and 1980s reflect the growing scholarly interest in *Dracula* and make available relevant historical, folkloric, and literary information.

Critics writing about narrative technique in *Dracula* eventually challenged the negative literary judgments in the reviews and the early criticism, which suggested that the book was not, in fact, literature. They did so by arguing that what had appeared to some early readers as stylistic flaws were instead marks of originality with significant implications. These defenses of *Dracula*'s artistic merit regularly maintain that some of the narration's dissonant, inconsistent aspects encourage us to question the vampire hunters' views. Among the earliest influential commentaries of this kind is Carol Senf's "*Dracula:* The Unseen Face in the Mirror" (1979). Senf brings out the self-interested motives of Stoker's narrators and catalogues resemblances between the vampire and the vampire hunters to establish similarities between the forces of "good" and "evil." She argues that the vampire hunters turn away from recognizing that the vampire is the unacknowledged self. In "The Narrative Method of *Dracula*" (1985), David Seed draws on Stoker's notes to describe his careful shaping of the material formally.[3] Identifying elements of the book's pervasive doubling structure, Alan P. Johnson argues for the significant ordering of the narrative in "Bent and Broken Necks: Signs of Design in Stoker's *Dracula*" (1987). Johnson focuses in particular on the doubling between male and female characters (Swales and Lucy; Renfield and Mina). He maintains as well that Dracula is the counterpart for the central female characters' unconscious rebellious desires and for the oppressive egotism of the male characters. Rebecca Pope describes *Dracula*'s narration as polyphonic, or multivocal, in "Writing and Biting in *Dracula*" (1990), a commentary that combines feminist and Marxist perspectives with reflections on narrative form. Relying on M. M. Bakhtin's ideas about the dialogical, open aspects of literature, she concentrates on Mina as the arranger of a text that refuses to conform to conventional social hierarchies of patriarchal power; instead, the book avoids the implications and illusions of a single continuous authorial voice. In this Bakhtinian reading, what some readers might regard as a flawed style becomes a virtue; because it is multiple and dialogical rather than singular and

---

[3]In their catalogue for an exhibition at the Rosenbach Museum and Library in Philadelphia celebrating the centenary of *Dracula*'s publication, Michael Barsanti and Wendy Good describe the prepublication material that Seed works with in his essay.

monological it can prevent narrative closure. Despite these and other defenses of the book's complex stylistic and conceptual achievements, some critics and editors still hesitate to acknowledge Stoker's artistic accomplishment.

The writings pertinent to *Dracula* by Devendra Varma during the 1970s and 1980s combine source studies with textual interpretation and, like the critical work concerned with narrative technique, argue for *Dracula*'s significance. He outlines briefly the book's sources in folklore, history, and Stoker's life in "The Genesis of Dracula: A Re-Visit" (1975). In "The Vampire in Legend, Lore, and Literature," his introduction to the reprinting (1970) of John Malcolm Rymer's Gothic serial, *Varney the Vampyre; or, The Feast of Blood* (1847), Varma places *Dracula* within the history of Oriental and European vampiric folklore and presents a more complicated, engaging evocation of the Count than do earlier critics. Varma celebrates Stoker's achievement in creating Dracula as an "essentially human" figure "not totally evil" in whom we recognize something that lives "within us all" (Varma xxviii). Varma's later essay "Dracula's Voyage: From Pontus to Hellespontus" (1986) interprets the Count's trip to England in relation to Coleridge's *The Rime of the Ancient Mariner*. Clive Leatherdale carries further Varma's work toward establishing *Dracula* as a text that warrants scholarly attention in *Dracula: The Novel and the Legend* (originally published 1985; revised ed., 1993). In the face of what he calls a lack of "serious critical study" (Leatherdale 9) for most of the century, Leatherdale champions *Dracula*'s importance by providing a lengthy review of the book's sources, a detailed commentary on the major characters, and a series of chapters concerning the most revealing trends in the criticism. Leatherdale's book marks an important moment in the study of *Dracula* because of its attempt to span the range of critical responses, beginning with Montague Summers in the 1920s, from whom Leatherdale takes his epigraph for part one, through David Punter in the 1980s, from whose well-regarded history of Gothic literature, *The Literature of Terror* (discussed below), Leatherdale chooses a passage to bring his own commentary to conclusion. Leatherdale's list of articles and books pertinent to interpreting *Dracula* in his "Select Bibliography," which later critics build on (see Carter 2), indicates that a significant critical response had already begun by the time of his own study, despite the comparative lack of attention to Stoker's writings. The catalogue of Stoker's sources, taken from his working notes for *Dracula*, in Leatherdale's bibliography confirms the range of Stoker's research and presents a reliable list of books that Stoker consulted.[4]

PSYCHOANALYTIC READINGS

Psychoanalytic interpretations of *Dracula* begin in the 1950s with readings that understand the book's details as symptoms of the author's psychic tendencies. By the 1980s, however, psychoanalytic critics develop textual interpretations that are largely independent of claims about the author. Maurice Richardson's essay "The Psychoanalysis of Ghost Stories" (1959) contains the first of many critical readings of *Dracula* based on psychoanalytic concepts. Relying on strategies developed from Freud, Richardson maintains that details of the narrative arise from the author's repressed fantasies concerning perverse sexuality and incest. He turns in particular to Freud's notion that the history of the human species involves a primal horde struggling in an Oedipal way against the father who wants to keep all the women to himself. Like many later critics, Richardson sees Dracula and Van Helsing as doubles, the bad father and the good one. In his reading, Van Helsing leads the younger men, as if they were the sons in Freud's psychoanalytic narrative, to defeat his evil antagonist and satisfy their sexual appetites in legitimate ways. In memorably extravagant statements that later critics cite or echo, Richardson says that Count Dracula proffers "a vast polymorph perverse bisexual oral-anal-genital sadomasochistic timeless orgy" (429) and that the narrative is "a kind of incestuous necrophilious, oral-anal-sadistic all-in wrestling match" located in "a sort of homicidal lunatic's brothel in a crypt" (427). One measure of Stoker's achievement is the surprising recurrence in the critical response beginning with Richardson of language and claims that are, like *Dracula*, simultaneously excessive and revealing. Essays less rhetorically extravagant than Richardson's but presenting related readings appeared in the journal *American Imago* in the 1970s and 1980s. In "*Dracula:* Pro-

---

[4]Alongside Leatherdale's work toward consolidating *Dracula*'s reputation have come various editions of the book with the elaborate annotations of a committed editor or with more succinct ones produced by established scholars of Victorian and modern literature. Leonard Wolf's edition of the book, *The Essential Dracula* (1993), provides extended glosses, and several editions by academic critics have appeared in the past decade. The increased availability of the book in reliable editions and the more frequent, more various scholarly writing about *Dracula* suggest that it has crossed into the canon of literature regularly taught and discussed in university classrooms, as Mary Shelley's *Frankenstein* did in the 1970s.

longed Childhood Illness and the Oral Triad" (1972), Joseph Bierman draws psychoanalytic conclusions about the author based on textual and biographical details. He reads the narrative as if it were a dream in which Stoker could fulfill his wish to undo a threat of loss by staging other men's loss of women. In "The Vampire Myth" (1980), James Twitchell follows Richardson by interpeting *Dracula* as an adolescent fantasy involving antagonism toward the possessive father.[5] While stressing the prevalence and significance of the vampire, Twitchell ascribes comparatively low artistic merit to *Dracula*.

The attractions and persistence of the psychoanalytic perspective for critics of *Dracula* are evident in several influential essays published in the journal *Literature and Psychology* during the 1970s and 1980s by Christopher Bentley, Thomas Byers, and Phyllis Roth. These commentators, however, rely on psychoanalytic concepts primarily to interpret the narrative rather than the author's psyche. In "The Monster in the Bedroom: Sexual Symbolism in Bram Stoker's *Dracula*" (1972), Bentley draws on the work of Freud and Ernest Jones as he catalogues at length what he considers the book's repressed displays of perverse sexuality, some of which tend, he suggests, toward the homoerotic. Incidental to the psychoanalytic interpretation, Bentley comments that the medicalizing of vampirism in Stoker's narrative is modern society's response to the threatening unknown by turning it into a disease amenable to treatment. In "Good Men and Monsters: The Defenses of *Dracula*" (1981), Byers argues that the Count and his relations with the vampire hunters represent a fear of male dependence and vulnerability that necessitates the destroying of the vampire in order to deny the dependence and protect the patriarchal hierarchy. He does so, however, without suggesting, as Bierman and others had earlier, that fears and wishes expressed in the narrative are symptoms of Stoker's psychic state.

Although psychoanalytic in its approach, Roth's influential "Suddenly Sexual Women in Bram Stoker's *Dracula*" (1977) considers the narrative's representations of gender roles in ways that make it also a feminist interpretation. Instead of describing the book as involving primarily an Oedipal struggle against the father to possess the mother,

---

[5]The essay anticipates Twitchell's books *The Living Dead: A Study of the Vampire in Romantic Literature* (1981), a survey of vampirism as an element in nineteenth-century representations of art and the artist beginning with literary Romanticism, and *Dreadful Pleasures: An Anatomy of Modern Horror* (1985), which includes chapters not only about the vampire but about other monsters important in popular culture, including the wolf man and Frankenstein.

Roth argues for a pre-Oedipal ambivalent drama of desire for the mother and for her destruction. The narrative's central ambivalences are, in her view, pre-Oedipal in their "hostility toward the mother" and "toward female sexuality" (113). She reads the parallel but contrasting stories of Lucy and Mina as two symbolic confrontations with the mother, in the first of which she is destroyed and in the second of which she is saved, as part of a structure that works through "the desire to destroy the threatening mother . . . who threatens by being desirable" (120). By means of her psychoanalytic method, Roth argues for antifeminist elements in *Dracula*, ones that invite the reader to accept the victimizing of women. In that regard, her essay complements a feminist reading published in the same year that bases its argument primarily on literary history rather than psychoanalytic concepts, Judith Weissman's "Women as Vampires: *Dracula* as a Victorian Novel." Weissman contrasts the largely comic portrayal of woman as sexually voracious in eighteenth-century fiction with the fearful presentation of women in *Dracula*. Stoker's narrative is, in Weissman's view, ultimately about male control over women and their terrifying appetites in the nineteenth century.

Later critics have brought the work of Jacques Lacan, the French psychoanalyst and reinterpreter of Freud, to bear on *Dracula*. In "Dracula as Totemic Monster: Lacan, Freud, Oedipus and History" (1979), Richard Astle presents in a post-Freudian way the determining place of Oedipal psychic tendencies in nineteenth-century British culture by mapping relations among the characters in light of one of Lacan's structures, *schéma R*. By contrast, Elisabeth Bronfen's Lacanian reading in "Hysteric and Obsessional Discourse: Responding to Death in *Dracula*" (1992) emphasizes neither Oedipal relations nor a pre-Oedipal antagonism toward the mother. Instead, she invokes Lacan's contrast between "hysteric" discourse, associated with the feminine and the fluidity of the unconscious, and "obsessional" discourse, associated with the masculine and the clarity of logical thought. Bronfen argues that the vampire's bite induces hysteric thinking and behavior that obsessional tendencies have to eradicate because the hysteric represents the threat of death. Like Roth, she sees a reassertion of stability in the narrative but argues that it is undermined by the unstable character of the documents as they are arranged into the book's own fluid discourse. Bronfen's turn to instabilities of style and structure emerges from a poststructuralist engagement with psychoanalytic thinking about the book's details.

Among the many other psychoanalytic readings and the longer

studies focusing on vampires, Laurence A. Rickels's *The Vampire Lectures* (1999) deserves special mention.[6] This lengthy volume is comprised of twenty-six lectures from Rickels's course "Vampirism in German Literature and Beyond," which is also an introduction to psychoanalytic theory (Rickels ix). Although Rickels is a scholar of German literature, he chooses not to present his views in a conventional academic form with a scholarly apparatus of detailed references and step-by-step argument. He proceeds instead by shifting, often rapidly, from text to text and from film to film, all relevant to *Dracula* through their influence on the text or their having been influenced by it, and from perspective to perspective within a wide range of psychoanalytic thought. The extravagant and fragmented aspects of the writing in *The Vampire Lectures* are in the spirit of pop culture in various forms, in the spirit of Richardson's description of *Dracula,* and in the spirit of *Dracula* itself. The book's title has dual implications, suggesting both lectures *about* the vampire and lectures *by* him. The first seven lectures are most directly relevant to *Dracula* and to early film versions of it, especially F. W. Murnau's *Nosferatu* (1922). In lectures four through six, Rickels orients us to the Oedipal, heroic interpretation of the vampire hunters. He challenges and displaces that reading by offering various speculative, often revealing correlations between vampirism, media technology, and psychoanalysis with respect to representations of women and to psychoanalytic meditations on mourning. Rickels brings out the multiple associations of the vampire hunters with developments in media and technology (as does Jennifer Wicke, without a psychoanalytic emphasis, in "Vampiric Typewriting," p. 577 in this volume). Based on those associations, he suggests that the vampire hunters constitute a "double of vampirism" (Rickels 51) pointing toward the future and implicating us. He moves beyond the Oedipal reading by suggesting the relevance of psychoanalytic writing about the uncanny and about melancholia for responses to *Dracula.*

CULTURAL, HISTORICAL, AND SOCIAL READINGS

Although some critical readings of *Dracula* that emphasize psychoanalytic concepts also engage historical and social issues, such as Roth's "Suddenly Sexual Women," more frequently psychoanalytic and social

---

[6]Recent longer studies that discuss *Dracula* extensively together with various films, monsters, and other phenomena of popular culture include the books by Auerbach and Glover mentioned below.

perspectives produce significantly different specific readings based on distinct general orientations. In "The Vampire in the Mirror: The Sexuality of *Dracula*" (1988), John Allen Stevenson attempts explicitly to develop an alternative to psychoanalytic interpretations of sexual conflict in the narrative by turning instead to anthropological concepts. By contrast with psychoanalytic descriptions of mind, anthropological descriptions of culture provide a conceptual vocabulary for understanding incest and miscegenation as a matter of racial differences, not just desire. In Stevenson's reading, Dracula's threat projects an undermining of the cultural rules for exogamy and endogamy, which determine how far out from the tribe and how close to the tribe men and women can find appropriate sexual partners. The concern about exogamy, or marriage with foreigners, does not have an obvious psychoanalytic source, or not only such a source, since it arises from Victorian constructions of racial difference, which occur in the historical situation of a white, European imperial society in regular contact abroad and increasingly at home with people from other cultures.

Although Stevenson relies in his essay on our taking historical contexts into account, he stops short of a historicist interpretation by claiming that the fears embodied in *Dracula* are more universal than they are historical. Generally speaking, historicist critics tend to avoid making universal claims, which they object to in psychoanalytic readings. The direction that Stevenson takes enables readings of the narrative that describe and interpret it not primarily with reference to incest, desire, and an intimate, forbidden family romance; for such a critic, the book reflects processes occurring on a large historical stage rather than in the theater of the mind. Further, the narrative need not be read as narrowly reflecting those processes in a deterministic way; it can be a reflection *on* the processes as well. Like psychoanalytic critics, those working from other assumptions regularly face the question of the extent to which *Dracula* is conservative or liberatory in its tendencies. Many critics emphasizing social relations argue that the narrative largely supports already existing structures, which have determined its shape and its attitudes, while some suggest that it enables the imagining, by contrast with its own social context, of quite different relations that have yet to come fully into being.

Franco Moretti's influential Marxist commentary on *Dracula*, "Dialectic of Fear" (Italian 1978; English 1983), argues that the book is politically conservative. Orienting his reading on Marx's description of the capitalist as vampiric, sucking the life out of labor, Moretti identifies Dracula with monopoly capitalism. According to Moretti, Count Dracula resembles the apparently long-buried money that Harker sees in the castle. The money that has come back from the grave is, according to Moretti, capital embarking "on the conquest of the world: . . . the story of Dracula the vampire" (91). At the same time that he resembles money, however, Dracula takes an ancient form that threatens the vampire hunters, bourgeois defenders of a status quo bound up with capitalism. For Moretti the book is an allegory of monopoly capital, whose "ambition is to subjugate the last vestiges of the liberal era and destroy all forms of economic independence" (92). He claims that Dracula as a monopolist is both the distant past and the foreign future of late Victorian capitalist competition, something that appears to be feudal but that will produce new forms of monopoly to displace and overwhelm the economic forms of the present. Moretti argues, in effect, that Stoker's narrative affirms the bourgeois delusion, described by Marx, that the self-destructive consequences of capitalism can be avoided. The effect on the reader, in his view, is to identify with the vampire hunters and to be grateful that the dominance of the indefensible, self-serving system Dracula threatened is reasserted.

Other critics who attempt to situate Stoker's narrative in relation to nineteenth-century social institutions and intellectual developments have argued for his reliance on Victorian science and for his critical reflections on it. In "Seward's Folly: *Dracula* as a Critique of 'Normal Science'" (1986), John L. Greenway brings out the deluded, ineffective character of Seward's science, which he sees as expressing "sentimental conventions" (220) in ways that amount to ignorance of a structured kind (230). Anne McWhir focuses more on the blurred structure of categories in the narrative than on specific debts to Victorian science in "Pollution and Redemption in *Dracula*" (1987). The constant breakdown of categories, such as science and myth, civilized and savage, she argues, reveals the primitive basis of modern scientific thinking. Despite the pervasive blurring of boundaries in *Dracula,* she finds a reassertion of clear boundaries in the book's ending.

In "Physical Immunity and Racial Destiny" from her *Somatic Fictions: Imagining Illness in Victorian Culture* (1995), a study of Victorian medical discourse and other Victorian representations of health and illness, Athena Vrettos interprets *Dracula* with reference to consumption, not as an economic matter but as a nutritional metaphor signifying imperial expansion. In comparison with Moretti, she reaches a mixed conclusion about the book's acceptance of a hierarchical status quo. Having established "correlations between racial fitness and imperial aggression" (163) in Victorian thinking, Vrettos points out a displacement of the correlations in *Dracula* onto a foreign intruder who seems to be from a superior species. In her view, Stoker pushes Victorian links between diet and evolutionary stage to the absurd conclusion that cannibalism indicates the highest level of evolution, with the vampire as the "'master' carnivore" (166). This development undermines the goal of evolutionary progress in a way that resembles the self-defeating contradiction that Marxists assert capitalism harbors. Vrettos also argues that *Dracula* reflects the contradictory connection between spirtualism and scientific inquiry, evident in Victorian theories of degeneration and criminal anthropology. Although Stoker's text makes the contradictions visible, it does so for her in a way that "legitimizes more than it attacks" (174). Like his society, Stoker was, Vrettos concludes, "deeply divided about the politics of empire and the morality of science" (174). David Glover's commentary on Stoker's entire writing career, *Vampires, Mummies, and Liberals: Bram Stoker and the Politics of Popular Fiction* (1996), takes a similar stand. He explores the interplay of fantasy and realism in Stoker's writings as evidence that Stoker was responding to the decline of progressive politics and to the disputed character of science in late Victorian England.

Other divisions in Victorian society that critics find reflected in *Dracula* concern the roles of men and women. Readings of *Dracula* that place primary emphasis on issues involving gender have, as we have seen, sometimes relied on psychoanalytic categories, but frequently they interpret the book largely in relation to categories and concepts involving society. In "*Dracula:* Stoker's Response to the New Woman" (1982), Carol Senf argues for the ambivalent character of Stoker's response to the New Woman novelists of the 1890s and to the political issues they raise concerning women's rights. In her view, Lucy and Mina split the unattractive and attractive aspects of the New Woman, with Lucy embodying the unattractive aggression. As a woman who works and who thinks independently, Mina also represents the New Woman, though in a form that is comparatively conservative and unthreatening. Many other suggestive feminist readings of *Dracula* have appeared that are not psychoanalytic in their orientation, including commentaries by Bram Dijkstra and Gail B. Griffin (see "Works Cited"). Often feminist readings argue that, rather than staging antifeminist tendencies for us to recognize and judge, the book embodies misogynistic Victorian attitudes in ways that invite us to accept or even enjoy the victimizing of women.

Among the most suggestive of the socially oriented interpretations focusing on issues of male gender and the crossing of gender boundaries is Christopher Craft's "'Kiss Me With Those Red Lips': Gender and Inversion in Bram Stoker's *Dracula*" (1984). Craft builds on earlier, psychoanalytic readings concerning the book's sexual implications by critics such as Roth and Bentley, but he focuses on the contrasts between cultural expectations concerning male and female behavior and the actions of Stoker's characters. Craft draws homoerotic implications from some of the book's prominent details. He argues that *Dracula* includes repeated instances of male homosexual desire displaced onto a heterosexual structure because of the fear of homosexuality. In his view the female characters mediate forbidden relations between males. In this reading, the monstrous heterosexuality of Lucy, Mina, and the three female vampires implicitly represents a forbidden homoerotic desire as an inversion of conventional gender relations. The female vampires seem to represent female sexuality, but they actually threaten penetration of the male. According to Craft, forbidden desire lies just below the narrative's surface in the relations of the Count and Harker and among the male vampire hunters. Craft links the narrative strategy of displacement to the nineteenth-century discourse of inversion, with its reliance on heterosexual paradigms to gloss male desire. For him, *Dracula* participates in a Victorian horror of fluid gender roles. Although Craft recognizes the crossing of gender boundaries in the book, he reads the ending as a conventionally Gothic rejection of the monstrous and reassertion of generally accepted values. Later essayists, including Marjorie Howes in "The Mediation of the Feminine" (1988) and Talia Schaffer in "'A Wilde Desire Took Me': The Homoerotic History of *Dracula*" (1994), extend Craft's reading of the book as an instance of "queer Gothic." Schaffer shifts the focus from parallels in the intellectual discourse of the time to an actual historical situation. Instead of associating Count Dracula with Henry Irving, Stoker's employer (as critics who read *Dracula* from the perspective of Stoker's biography have often done), Schaffer links the Count to Oscar Wilde, Stoker's younger Irish contemporary, and sees the narrative as responding to the notorious trial and conviction of Wilde in the mid-1890s on charges of illegal homosexual behavior.

In *Our Vampires, Ourselves* (1995), Nina Auerbach develops a critical position that challenges the socially and historically oriented commentaries described above. Her views are distinctly and provocatively at odds with many critics' characterizations of *Dracula*. She expressly opposes the historicist readings of Moretti and Craft (mentioned above) and those of Halberstam and Arata (mentioned below), which situate the book in relation to its historical context. Auerbach prefers instead to examine both material that antedates the book and later developments, including films and our own contemporary situation. Her commentary still responds to social and historical issues, but they are not those that interest new historicist critics. Auerbach's interpretation of earlier literary representations of vampires enables her to argue that Count Dracula is not a transgressive figure. She defends her refusal to confine him to his own century with the claim that he is "a harbinger of a world to come, a world that is our own" (63). Although Auerbach reads *Dracula*, necessarily, in retrospect, she insists on doing so not by reconstructing the context of the past but by keeping in view the future frame of reference that the book helps create, a world that we inhabit.

RECENT DEVELOPMENTS: HISTORY OF THE GOTHIC, POSTCOLONIAL PERSPECTIVES, AND IRISH STUDIES

Dracula's standing in literary criticism has changed in part because the standing and the critical descriptions of Gothic literature have also changed. The history of Gothic narrative has received more serious consideration by literary critics in the past three decades than at any earlier period. In the section "Gothic and Decadence" (Punter 2: 1–26) of his synoptic study, *The Literature of Terror* (1980; revised, expanded edition 1996), by contrast with many earlier critics of *Dracula*, David Punter assesses Stoker's work in a highly positive way. He argues that the violating of "taboo" in *Dracula* involves boundary crossings that raise the question of what it means to be human. His argument is part of his general reinterpretation of the Gothic, which he claims to be not escapist literature but a response to anxieties that are simultaneously psychological and social. Although Punter shifts the critical focus away from the author's psyche and toward social matters in his study, he does so while retaining his commitment to psychoanalytic concepts, which regularly inform his readings. He says memorably that from a Freudian perspective, Dracula is the "passion which never dies, endless desire of the unconscious for gratification" (2: 19), but that, at the same time, from a Marxist perspective, he is the "final aristocrat," who threatens the late-nineteenth-century bourgeois family (2: 17).

Many essays and books on either nineteenth- or twentieth-century Gothic narratives attend to the book's place in the history of Gothic writing. Kathleen Spencer reads *Dracula* as an important example of "urban gothic" in "Purity and Danger: *Dracula*, the Urban Gothic, and the Late Victorian Degeneracy Crisis" (1992). This kind of Gothic writing, which developed late in the nineteenth century, presents its strange events close to home and in the present. Spencer identifies Victorian concerns about degeneration in *Dracula*, as do Daniel Pick (1988) and Laura Croley (1995). In "Dangerous Discoveries and Mad Scientists: Some Late-Victorian Horrors" (1987), Chris Baldick sets *Dracula* briefly but incisively in a line of nineteenth-century writing stretching from Mary Shelley's *Frankenstein* (1818; revised 1831) through Robert Louis Stevenson's *The Strange Case of Dr Jekyll and Mr Hyde* (1886) and Oscar Wilde's *The Picture of Dorian Gray* (1891). He sketches the connection to *Frankenstein*, a text he is unwilling to classify as Gothic, and also to Conan Doyle's presentation of the antagonism between Sherlock Holmes and Moriarty by describing Van Helsing and Dracula as doubles, "twin halves of a single, perversely sexualized Frankensteinian transgressor" (Baldick 147). Baldick compares Van Helsing's violence to female bodies with Victor Frankenstein's destruction of the female monster he was creating. His comparison of *Dracula* to *Frankenstein*, a text that has achieved canonical status, indicates the increase in critical acceptance of *Dracula*, which began in the 1970s. Despite the evident irony in *Dracula*, which Baldick recognizes, that the chief vampire hunter is Count Dracula's double, he concludes that the book is conservative, since no perspective emerges to explicitly counter Van Helsing's militancy. He reads the ending as consonant with a Gothic tradition that antedates *Frankenstein*, in which the values of the bourgeoisie dominate.

In her essay "Technologies of Monstrosity" (1993) and her subsequent book *Skin Shows: Gothic Horror and the Technology of Monsters* (1995), Judith Halberstam puts *Dracula* at the center of her reconsidered history of the Gothic from *Frankenstein* to *The Silence of the Lambs*. Explicitly distancing herself from the frequent blindspot about society in psychoanalytic criticism, Halberstam challenges those who interpret *Dracula* as conservative and complicit. In a reading of *Dracula* that combines racial, sexual, and economic perspectives, she convincingly exams the relationship of Stoker's vampire to nineteenth-century anti-Semitic discourse. Halberstam defines the Gothic as a technology of monstrosity that creates the monstrous from fragments of class, race, and gender discourse not accepted by the dominant ideology, while simultaneously exposing the constructed character of what that dominant ideology labels the monstrous. The notion that the Gothic contains a critique of the culture it draws on for its elements, which it presents in exaggerated form, opens the possibility of interpreting *Dracula* as less determined by cultural expectations than many critics have allowed. In "Toward a History of Gothic and Modernism: Dark Modernity from Bram Stoker to Samuel Beckett" (2000), an essay influenced by poststructural and postcolonial writings, I draw conclusions that are at odds with conservative interpretations of the narrative, since I find in *Dracula* "a model, replicated in later works, for the emergence of hybridity as the character of the future and of modern experience" (Riquelme 591). By hybridity, I mean an in-between condition that tends to blur the clear distinctions between apparent opposites, distinctions on which hierarchies of value and power depend. I argue as well for the centrality of *Dracula* in the shift from Victorian to modernist writing.

In "Gothic Criticism" (2000), their metacritical commentary on critical writing about Gothic narratives, Chris Baldick and Robert Mighall, like Nina Auerbach, express their dissatisfaction with some prevalent strategies used by those who write about the Gothic. In particular, they object to a reductive tendency in historicist criticism of the Gothic to characterize British culture as anxiety-ridden and Stoker's narrative as subversive. Although they admit that David Punter's insights are often judicious, Baldick and Mighall cite his work on the Gothic as a prime example of the tendency to psychologize a historical situation without sufficient justification. Of special concern to them is the overuse of the word *subversive* in the service of political correctness, though they do not call it that. Focusing on responses to *Dracula*, they play on their category *Gothic criticism* by suggesting that the criticism has itself become *Gothic* since it projects a melodramatic conflict between the embattled outsider and social forces of repression. The strictures that Baldick and Mighall bring to bear are in many regards salutary, particularly as a warning to readers about some questionable tendencies in the response to *Dracula*. They complain that frequently critics claim to rely on historical knowledge to reverse the heroic reading of *Dracula* as the story of good people conquering an evil monster but that the historical framework for reading the narrative as the liberated monster's battle against repressive foes needs substantiating. In their view, the reversal says more about the critics' political views than about the book's implications. Baldick and Mighall's complaints, however, are less convincing about critical arguments that find mixed evidence in the narrative for its relation to cultural concerns and expectations and about interpretations that argue for the resemblances between the monster and those who struggle against him.

Mighall attempts to provide an alternative to the tendencies he and Baldick criticize in "Sex, History and the Vampire" (1998) and in the longer chapter on *Dracula* and the postscript of his *A Geography of Victorian Gothic Fiction* (1999). Setting the vampire in the late Victorian discourse concerning pathological sexuality, Mighall argues that Van Helsing is a sexologist in reverse, imputing supernatural meanings to events that a Victorian sexologist would interpret differently. He argues for keeping the discourses of sexology and horror fiction separate, rather than blurring the boundaries between discourses as new historicists do, in order to exclude the sexual reading of vampirism and see the vampire as literally a monster rather than a figure for something else. William Hughes also explores the cultural discourses of Stoker's time in *Beyond Dracula: Bram Stoker's Fiction in Its Cultural Context* (2000), in which he adduces religious contexts, depictions of masculinity and femininity, and medical writings to explain how they influenced Stoker's thinking and also how their collisions in Stoker's texts produce new meanings. His study is noteworthy for its reading of Stoker's writings in new frames of reference. In particular, Hughes's account of *Dracula* deals not with blood considered medically and racially, a topic treated by earlier critics, but with the symptoms the vampire's victims exhibit in relation to medical works of the time and with vampirism in relation to abnormal medical conditions.

Largely lacking from critical responses to *Dracula* before 1990 is a recognition of the narrative's relation to the history of the British Empire, especially with respect to the Irish situation. In recent decades attitudes toward British and Irish writings from the latter part of the nineteenth century, during the decline of the British Empire, have changed. Critics who use imperial and Irish contexts for interpreting literary texts now often invoke British views about nonwhite foreigners, the situation of the Irish under long-term British rule, and political issues involving empire. They tend to rely on the work of theorists such as Edward Said, Gayatri Spivak, and Homi Bhabha concerning colonialism's history and effects and concerning the character of post-colonialism. Patrick Brantlinger places *Dracula* in the context of the literature of empire when he identifies a strand of late-nineteenth-century Gothic narratives that he calls the "imperial Gothic" in an article of that title (1985) and in his later book, *The Rule of Darkness:*

British Literature and Imperialism, 1830–1914 (1988). He argues that British fears of atavism appear in adventure literature, including *Dracula*, as a Gothic dimension that includes occult elements. W. J. McCormack places *Dracula* in the history of Irish writing that he calls the "Irish Gothic" in his essay introducing a section of the second volume of *The Field Day Anthology of Irish Writing* (1991). Because of these and related critical developments, the previous lack of attention to imperial and Irish implications in the response to *Dracula* has begun to be filled.

Since *Dracula* stands at the intersection of literature with an imperial aspect, Gothic narratives, and Irish writing, the book's critics have begun linking in various ways concerns related to the decline of empire, motifs and structures characteristic of Gothic writing, aspects of the Irish situation, and Stoker's background as Anglo-Irish. Among the most influential readings of *Dracula* to take the history and literature of empire into consideration is Stephen Arata's "The Occidental Tourist: *Dracula* and the Anxiety of Reverse Colonization" (1990). For Arata, *Dracula* expresses the fear of reverse colonization, specifically the anxiety that the imperial homeland will be invaded by savage, foreign, colonized peoples. He draws on Edward Said's writings about Orientalism to describe the Count's traveling west as a reversal of Harker's traveling east that, by mimicking the prejudicial Orientalist attitudes of the West toward the East, redirects them as Occidentalist attitudes held by someone from the East toward the West. In an explicit turn away from psychoanalytic interpretation, Arata focuses on the book's fusing of the travel narrative with the Gothic for their mutual transformation. He argues compellingly that the expectations of the imperial tourist are turned upside down when the travel narrative becomes Gothic and that the usual Gothic reassertion of stability is undermined at the end of *Dracula*. Because the traveler's expectations are never convincingly restored, Arata suggests, the closing invites us to reject Van Helsing's concluding statement as hollow. Arata's reading of the ending as the undoing of a conventional Gothic closing sets his interpretation in opposition to the assertions by Craft, Baldick, and others who claim that the ending restores stability in a conservative way.

Writing in the wake of Arata's ground-breaking essay, Cannon Schmitt identifies the fear of invasion more narrowly than does Arata as English anxiety about the Irish and about miscegenation. In "Mother Dracula: Orientalism, Degeneration, and Anglo-Irish National Subjectivity at the Fin de Siècle" (1994), a commentary that relies on the work of Edward Said, Schmitt argues that *Dracula*'s Orientalism, its opposition of East to West, actually refers to another set of oppositions, Irish to English. Schmitt links the rise of the literary vampire with English imperial collapse, associating it with a fin de siècle discourse of degeneration and decline. For Schmitt, Stoker's text embodies an insistent rejection of racial impurity at a time when a civilization supposedly in decline needed rejuvenation from outside. In "Landlord and Soil: *Dracula*," attending to the concern with property in Gothic narratives and drawing on Terry Eagleton's characterization of Stoker's narrative, Seamus Deane identifies Count Dracula with an absentee Irish landlord "running out of soil" (90).[7] He argues that *Dracula* presents in terms of land, soil, and speech the overcoming of demons and deviations in a way that mystifies aspects of the Irish situation. Locating the book within "Gothic and Celtic twilights" (94), he asserts its relation to the cultural nationalism of the 1890s and to "a whole series of Irish nineteenth-century novels" (91).

In "The Irish Vampire: *Dracula*, Parnell, and the Troubled Dreams of Nationhood" (1997), Michael Valdez Moses elaborates at length the book's Irish connection. He argues for numerous echoes of late-nineteenth-century Irish history and culture in *Dracula*, in particular details from the life and political strategies of Charles Stuart Parnell (1846–1891), the Irish political leader who advocated Home Rule. Although his argument is more satisfying in general than in some of its specifics, Moses does present suggestively a mass of historical material that Stoker would have been aware of, material that might well have influenced the sometimes contradictory presentation of the Count, Van Helsing, and other major characters. One implication to be drawn from Moses's essay is indisputable: that part of the book's continuing fascination arises from its evocation of a conflicted political situation involving a clash of national identities, an evocation that resonates with a significant aspect of our own time, the conflicted constructing of national identities in the postcolonial aftermath of the fall of empires.

Joseph Valente's *Dracula's Crypt: Bram Stoker, Irishness and the Question of Blood* (2001) provides the first sustained critical commentary informed by postcolonial and poststructural thinking that persuasively addresses the Irish aspects of *Dracula*. Like Auerbach, Baldick, and Mighall, Valente takes issue with readings of *Dracula* from a historicist perspective, in particular, deterministic interpretations that

---

[7]Deane cites Terry Eagleton's *Heathcliff and the Great Hunger: Studies in Irish Culture* (215–16) as the source for his allegorizing of Count Dracula as an absentee landlord whose property is slipping away.

argue for a direct, causal relation between an Irish cultural situation that Stoker experienced and the details and implications of his narrative. Valente persuasively suggests that the Irish character of *Dracula* and its author are in need of more nuanced description than earlier critics have provided. Drawing on the work of the postcolonial theorist Homi Bhabha, Valente sketches the metrocolonial situation of Ireland at Stoker's time, marked by its proximity to the metropolitan center of the British Empire and by the racial identity its inhabitants shared with the British. Framing his reading of *Dracula* in the complex texture of Stoker's in-between status as Anglo-Irish but with a strong native Celtic dimension on his mother's side, Valente identifies various contradictions in the narrative. Those contradictions suggest that the Count frequently embodies antithetical perspectives while his antagonists are presented not as his opposites but as his doubles. By combining psychoanalytic and postcolonial insights, Valente is able to trace the contradictory implications of *Dracula* in ways that undermine readings of the book's Irish character that put Stoker on one side or the other of a two-way struggle for political control. Future critics will have to attend to Valente's rich formulations about the book's pervasive ambiguous doublings.

The recent developments in the response to *Dracula* carry forward the interests of earlier interpreters in psychological and social issues, but they frame them in new ways within a reconsidered history and conception of Gothic writing and within the dynamics of imperialism and postcolonialism. In these new readings, we recognize *Dracula* as a book whose continuing relevance to our modernity we are just beginning to understand.

WORKS CITED

Arata, Stephen D. "The Occidental Tourist: *Dracula* and the Anxiety of Reverse Colonization." *Victorian Studies* 33 (1990): 621–45. Rev. and rpt. in Arata's *Fictions of Loss in the Victorian Fin de Siècle*. Cambridge, England: Cambridge UP, 1996. 107–32. Rpt. in Senf 1993 84–99 and Byron 119–44.

Astle, Richard. "Dracula as Totemic Monster: Lacan, Freud, Oedipus and History." *Sub-Stance* 8.4 (1979): 98–105.

Auerbach, Nina. *Our Vampires, Ourselves*. Chicago and London: U of Chicago P, 1995.

Baldick, Chris. "Dangerous Discoveries and Mad Scientists: Some Late-Victorian Horrors." *In Frankenstein's Shadow: Myth, Monstrosity, and Nineteenth-Century Writing.* By Baldick. Oxford: Clarendon, 1987. 141–62.

Baldick, Chris, and Robert Mighall. "Gothic Criticism." *A Companion to the Gothic.* Ed. David Punter. Oxford, England, and Malden, MA: Blackwell, 2000. 209–28.

Barsanti, Michael J., and Wendy Van Wyck Good. *Bram Stoker's Dracula: A Centennial Exhibition at the Rosenbach Museum & Library, April 10–November 2, 1997.* Philadelphia: Rosenbach Museum & Library, 1997.

Bentley, Christopher F. "The Monster in the Bedroom: Sexual Symbolism in Bram Stoker's *Dracula.*" *Literature and Psychology* 22 (1972): 27–34. Rpt. in Carter 25–34.

Bierman, Joseph. "*Dracula:* Prolonged Childhood Illness and the Oral Triad." *American Imago* 29 (1972): 186–98. Rpt. in Senf 1993 46–51.

Brantlinger, Patrick. "Imperial Gothic: Atavism and the Occult in the British Adventure Novel, 1880–1914." *ELT* 28 (1985): 243–52. Elaborated in Brantlinger. *The Rule of Darkness: British Literature and Imperialism, 1830–1914.* Ithaca: Cornell UP, 1988.

Bronfen, Elisabeth. "Hysteric and Obsessional Discourse: Responding to Death in *Dracula.*" *Over Her Dead Body: Death, Femininity and the Aesthetic.* By Bronfen. New York: Routledge; Manchester, England: Manchester UP, 1992. 313–22. Rpt. in Byron 55–67.

Byers, Thomas B. "Good Men and Monsters: The Defenses of *Dracula.*" *Literature and Psychology* 31 (1981): 24–31. Rpt. in Carter 149–58.

Byron, Glennis, ed. *Dracula: Bram Stoker.* New Casebooks. New York: St. Martin's, 1999.

Carter, Margaret L., ed. *Dracula: The Vampire and the Critics.* Ann Arbor and London: UMI, 1988.

Craft, Christopher. " 'Kiss Me With Those Red Lips': Gender and Inversion in Bram Stoker's *Dracula.*" *Representations* 8 (1984): 107–33. Rev. and rpt. in Craft. *Another Kind of Love: Male Homosexual Desire in English Discourse, 1850–1920.* Berkeley: U of California P, 1994. Rpt. in Carter 167–94 and Byron 93–118.

Croley, Laura Sagella. "The Rhetoric of Reform in Stoker's *Dracula:* Depravity, Decline, and the Fin-de-Siècle 'Residuum.' " *Criticism: A Quarterly for Literature and the Arts* 37 (1995): 85–108.

Deane, Seamus. "Landlord and Soil: *Dracula.*" *Strange Country: Modernity and Nationhood in Irish Writing since 1790.* By Deane. Oxford: Clarendon, 1997. 89–94, and n. 212–15.

Dijkstra, Bram. "Metamorphoses of the Vampire: Dracula and His Daughters." *Idols of Perversity: Fantasies of Feminine Evil in Fin de Siècle Culture.* By Djikstra. Oxford: Oxford UP, 1987.

Eagleton, Terry. *Heathcliff and the Great Hunger: Studies in Irish Culture.* London and New York: Verso, 1995.

Glover, David. *Vampires, Mummies, and Liberals: Bram Stoker and the Politics of Popular Fiction.* Durham and London: Duke UP, 1996.

Greenway, John L. "Seward's Folly: *Dracula* as a Critique of 'Normal Science.'" *Stanford Literature Review* 3 (1986): 213–30. Rpt. in Senf *Critical* 73–84.

Griffin, Gail B. "'Your Girls That You All Love Are Mine': *Dracula* and the Victorian Male Sexual Imagination." *International Journal of Women's Studies* 3 (1980): 454–65. Rpt. in Carter 137–48.

Halberstam, Judith. "Technologies of Monstrosity: Bram Stoker's *Dracula.*" *Victorian Studies* 36 (1993): 333–52. Rpt. in rev. form in Halberstam. *Skin Shows: Gothic Horror and the Technology of Monsters.* Durham: Duke UP, 1995. 86–106. Rpt. in Byron 173–96.

Howes, Marjorie. "The Mediation of the Feminine: Bisexuality, Homoerotic Desire, and Self-Expression in Bram Stoker's *Dracula.*" *Texas Studies in Literature and Language* 30 (1988): 104–19.

Hughes, William. *Beyond Dracula: Bram Stoker's Fiction in Its Cultural Context.* New York: St. Martin's, 2000.

Johnson, Alan P. "Bent and Broken Necks: Signs of Design in Stoker's *Dracula.*" *Victorian Newsletter* 72 (1987): 17–24. Rpt. in Carter 231–46.

Kirtley, Bacil F. "*Dracula*, The Monastic Chronicles and Slavic Folklore." *Midwest Folklore* 6 (1956): 133–39. Rpt. in Carter 11–18.

Leatherdale, Clive. *Dracula: The Novel and the Legend, A Study of Bram Stoker's Gothic Masterpiece.* 1985. Rev. ed. Brighton, England: Desert Island, 1993.

Lovecraft, H. P. *Supernatural Horror in Literature.* 1939. New York: Dover, 1973.

McCormack, W. J. "Irish Gothic and After." *The Field Day Anthology of Irish Writing*. Ed. Seamus Deane. Vol. 2. Derry: Field Day, 1991. 831–54.

McNally, Raymond. *Dracula Was a Woman*. London: Hale, 1984.

McNally, Raymond, and Radu Florescu. *The Essential Dracula*. New York: Mayflower, 1979.

———. *In Search of Dracula*. New York: Graphic Society, 1972.

McWhir, Anne. "Pollution and Redemption in *Dracula*." *Modern Language Studies* 17.3 (1987). 31–40.

Mighall, Robert. *A Geography of Victorian Gothic Fiction: Mapping History's Nightmares*. Oxford and New York: Oxford UP, 1999.

———. "Sex, History and the Vampire." *Bram Stoker: History, Psychoanalysis and the Gothic*. Ed. William Hughes and Andrew Smith. New York: St. Martin's, 1998. Rpt. in rev. form in Mighall 1999.

Moretti, Franco. "Dialectic of Fear." *Signs Taken for Wonders: Essays in the Sociology of Literary Forms*. By Moretti. Trans. Susan Fischer, David Forgas, and David Miller. London: Verso, 1983. 83–108. Orig. pub. in Italian in *calibano* 2 (1978). Rpt. in Byron 43–54.

Moses, Michael Valdez. "The Irish Vampire: *Dracula*, Parnell, and the Troubled Dreams of Nationhood," *Journal x:* 2.1 (Autumn 1997): 67–111.

Nandris, Grigore. "The Historical Dracula: The Theme of His Legend in the Western and in the Eastern Literatures of Europe." *Comparative Literature Studies* 3 (1966): 367–96.

Pick, Daniel. " 'Terrors of the Night': *Dracula* and 'Degeneration' in the Late Nineteenth Century." *Critical Quarterly* 30.4 (1988): 72–87. Rpt. in Pick. *Faces of Degeneration: A European Disorder, c.1848–1918*. Cambridge: Cambridge UP, 1989. 167–75.

Pope, Rebecca A. "Writing and Biting in *Dracula*." *Lit: Literature, Interpretation, Theory* 1 (1990): 199–216. Rpt. in Byron 68–92.

Punter, David. *The Literature of Terror: A History of Gothic Fictions from 1765 to the Present Day. Volume I: The Gothic Tradition; Volume II: The Modern Gothic*. 1980. Rev. ed. London and New York: Longman, 1996.

Rev. of *Dracula*. *Athenaeum* 109 June 26, 1897: 835. Rpt. in Senf *Critical* 59–60.

Rev. of *Dracula*. *Bookman* 12 August 1897: 129. Rpt. in Senf *Critical* 61.

Rev. of *Dracula*. *Spectator* 79 July 31, 1897: 150. Rpt. in Senf *Critical* 60–61.

Richardson, Maurice. "The Psychoanalysis of Ghost Stories." *The Twentieth Century* 166 (1959): 419–31.

Rickels, Laurence A. *The Vampire Lectures.* Minneapolis: U of Minnesota P, 1999.

Riquelme, John Paul. "Toward a History of Gothic and Modernism: Dark Modernity from Bram Stoker to Samuel Beckett." *Modern Fiction Studies* 46.3 (Fall 2000): 585–605.

Roth, Phyllis. "Suddenly Sexual Women in Bram Stoker's *Dracula.*" *Literature and Psychology* 27 (1977): 113–21. Rpt. in rev. form in Roth. *Bram Stoker.* Boston: Twayne, 1982. 111–26. Rpt. in Carter 57–68 and Byron 30–42.

Scarborough, Dorothy. *The Supernatural in Modern English Fiction.* New York: Putnam's, 1917.

Schaffer, Talia. "'A Wilde Desire Took Me': The Homoerotic History of *Dracula.*" *ELH* 61 (1994): 381–425.

Schmitt, Cannon. "Mother Dracula: Orientalism, Degeneration, and Anglo-Irish National Subjectivity at the Fin de Siècle." *Irishness and (Post)Modernism.* Ed. John S. Rickard. London: Associated UP, 1994. 25–43.

Seed, David. "The Narrative Method of *Dracula.*" *Nineteenth Century Fiction* 40 (1985): 61–75. Rpt. in Carter 195–206.

Senf, Carol A., ed. *The Critical Response to Bram Stoker.* Westport, CT, and London: Greenwood, 1993.

———. "*Dracula:* Stoker's Response to the New Woman." *Victorian Studies* 26 (1982): 33–49.

———. "*Dracula:* The Unseen Face in the Mirror." *Journal of Narrative Technique* 9 (1979): 160–70. Rpt. in Carter 93–104.

Spencer, Kathleen L. "Purity and Danger: *Dracula,* the Urban Gothic, and the Late Victorian Degeneracy Crisis." *ELH* 59 (1992): 197–225.

Stevenson, John Allen. "The Vampire in the Mirror: The Sexuality of *Dracula.*" *PMLA* 103 (1988): 139–49.

Summers, Montague. *The Vampire: His Kith and Kin.* London: Routledge and Kegan Paul, 1928.

Twitchell, James. *Dreadful Pleasures: An Anatomy of Modern Horror.* New York and Oxford: Oxford UP, 1985.

———. *The Living Dead: A Study of the Vampire in Romantic Literature.* Durham: Duke UP, 1981.

———. "The Vampire Myth." *American Imago* 37 (1980): 83–92. Rpt. in Carter 109–16.

Valente, Joseph. *Dracula's Crypt: Bram Stoker, Irishness and the Question of Blood.* Urbana: U of Illinois P, 2002.

Varma, Devendra P. "Dracula's Voyage: From Pontus to Hellespontus." In Carter 207–14.

———. "The Genesis of Dracula: A Re-Visit." *The Vampire's Bedside Companion.* Ed. Peter Underwood. London: Leslie Frewin, 1975. Rpt. in Carter 39–50.

———. "The Vampire in Legend, Lore, and Literature." Introduction to *Varney the Vampyre; or, The Feast of Blood.* By John Malcolm Rymer. 3 vols. New York: Arno, 1970. I.xiii–xxx.

Vrettos, Athena. "Physical Immunity and Racial Destiny: Stoker and Haggard." *Somatic Fictions: Imagining Illness in Victorian Culture.* By Vrettos. Stanford: Stanford UP, 1995: 154–76.

Weissman, Judith. "Women as Vampires: *Dracula* as a Victorian Novel." *Midwest Quarterly* 18 (1977): 392–405. Rpt. in Carter 69–78.

Wicke, Jennifer. "Vampiric Typewriting: *Dracula* and Its Media." *ELH* 59 (1992): 467–93. Rpt. in this volume, pp. 577–99.

Wolf, Leonard. *The Essential Dracula.* New York: Plume, 1993.

Gender Criticism
and *Dracula*

WHAT IS GENDER CRITICISM?

Feminist criticism was accorded academic legitimacy in American universities "around 1981," Jane Gallop claims in her book *Around 1981: Academic Feminist Literary Theory*. With Gallop's title and amusing approximation in mind, Naomi Schor has since estimated that, "around 1985, feminism began to give way to what has come to be called gender studies" (Schor 275).

In explaining her reason for saying that feminism began to give way to gender studies "around 1985," Schor says that she chose that date "in part because it marks the publication of *Between Men*," a book whose author, the influential gender critic Eve Kosofsky Sedgwick, "articulates the insights of feminist criticism onto those of gay-male studies, which had up to then pursued often parallel but separate courses (affirming the existence of a homosexual or female imagination, recovering lost traditions, decoding the cryptic discourse of works already in the canon by homosexual or feminist authors)" (Schor 276). Today, gay and lesbian criticism is so much a part of gender criticism that some people equate "sexualities criticism" with the gender approach.

Many would quarrel with the notion that feminist criticism and women's studies have been giving way to gender criticism and gender studies — and with the either/or distinction that such a claim implies.

Some would argue that feminist criticism is by definition gender criticism. (When Simone de Beauvoir declared in 1949 that "one is not born a woman, one becomes one" [301], she was talking about the way in which individuals of the female sex assume the feminine gender — that is, that elaborate set of restrictive, socially prescribed attitudes and behaviors that we associate with femininity.) Others would point out that one critic whose work *everyone* associates with feminism (Julia Kristeva) has problems with the feminist label, while another critic whose name, like Sedgwick's, is continually linked with the gender approach (Teresa de Lauretis) continues to refer to herself and her work as feminist.

Certainly, feminist and gender criticism are not polar opposites but, rather, exist along a continuum of attitudes toward sex and sexism, sexuality and gender, language and the literary canon. There are, however, a few distinctions to be made between those critics whose writings are inevitably identified as being toward one end of the continuum or the other.

One distinction is based on focus: as the word implies, "feminists" have concentrated their efforts on the study of women and women's issues. Gender criticism, by contrast, has not been woman centered. It has tended to view the male and female sexes — and the masculine and feminine genders — in terms of a complicated continuum, much as we are viewing feminist and gender criticism. Critics like Diane K. Lewis have raised the possibility that black women may be more like white men in terms of familial and economic roles, like black men in terms of their relationships with whites, and like white women in terms of their relationships with men. Lesbian gender critics have asked whether lesbian women are really more like straight women than they are like gay (or for that matter straight) men. That we refer to gay and lesbian studies as gender studies has led some to suggest that gender studies is a misnomer; after all, homosexuality is not a gender. This objection may easily be answered once we realize that one purpose of gender criticism is to criticize gender as we commonly conceive of it, to expose its insufficiency and inadequacy as a category.

Another distinction between feminist and gender criticism is based on the terms *gender* and *sex*. As de Lauretis suggests in *Technologies of Gender* (1987), feminists of the 1970s tended to equate gender with sex, gender difference with sexual difference. But that equation doesn't help us explain "the differences among women, . . . the differences *within women*." After positing that "we need a notion of gender that is not so bound up with sexual difference," de Lauretis provides just such a notion by arguing that "gender is not a property of bodies or something originally existent in human beings"; rather, it is "the product of various social technologies, such as cinema" (2). Gender is, in other words, a construct, an effect of language, culture, and its institutions. It is gender, not sex, that causes a weak old man to open a door for an athletic young woman. And it is gender, not sex, that may cause one young woman to expect old men to behave in this way, another to view this kind of behavior as chauvinistic and insulting, and still another to have mixed feelings (hence de Lauretis's phrase "differences *within women*") about "gentlemanly gallantry."

Still another, related distinction between feminist and gender criticism is based on the *essentialist* views of many feminist critics and the *constructionist* views of many gender critics (both those who would call themselves feminists and those who would not). Stated simply and perhaps too reductively, the term *essentialist* refers to the view that women are essentially different from men. *Constructionist,* by contrast, refers to the view that most of those differences are characteristics not of the male and female sex (nature) but, rather, of the masculine and feminine genders (nurture). Because of its essentialist tendencies, "radical feminism," according to Sedgwick, "tends to deny that the meaning of gender or sexuality has ever significantly changed; and more damagingly, it can make future change appear impossible" (*Between Men* 13).

Most obviously essentialist would be those feminists who emphasize the female body, its difference, and the manifold implications of that difference. The equation made by some avant-garde French feminists between the female body and the *maternal* body has proved especially troubling to some gender critics, who worry that it may paradoxically play into the hands of extreme conservatives and fundamentalists seeking to reestablish patriarchal family values. In her book *The Reproduction of Mothering* (1978), Nancy Chodorow, a sociologist of gender, admits that what we call "mothering"— not having or nursing babies but mothering more broadly conceived — is commonly associated not just with the feminine gender but also with the female sex, often considered nurturing by nature. But she critically interrogates the common assumption that it is in women's nature or biological destiny to "mother" in this broader sense, arguing that the separation of home and workplace brought about by the development of capitalism and the ensuing industrial revolution made mothering *appear* to be essentially a woman's job in modern Western society.

If sex turns out to be gender where mothering is concerned, what differences *are* grounded in sex — that is, nature? *Are* there *essential* differences between men and women — other than those that are purely anatomical and anatomically determined (for example, a man can exclusively take on the job of feeding an infant milk, but he may not do so from his own breast)? A growing number of gender critics would answer the question in the negative. Sometimes referred to as "extreme constructionists" and "postfeminists," these critics have adopted the viewpoint of philosopher Judith Butler, who in her book *Gender Trouble* (1990) predicts that "sex, by definition, will be shown to have been gender all along" (8). As Naomi Schor explains their position, "there is nothing outside or before culture, no nature that is not always and already enculturated" (278).

Whereas a number of feminists celebrate women's difference, post-feminist gender critics would agree with Chodorow's statement that men have an "investment in difference that women do not have" (Eisenstein and Jardine 14). They see difference as a symptom of oppression, not a cause for celebration, and would abolish it by disman-tling gender categories and, ultimately, destroying gender itself. Because gender categories and distinctions are embedded in and per-petuated through language, gender critics like Monique Wittig have called for the wholesale transformation of language into a nonsexist, and nonheterosexist, medium.

Language has proved the site of important debates between femi-nist and gender critics, essentialists and constructionists. Gender critics have taken issue with those French feminists who have spoken of a fem-inine language and writing and who have grounded differences in lan-guage and writing in the female body.[1] For much the same reason, they have disagreed with those French-influenced Anglo-American critics who, like Toril Moi and Nancy K. Miller, have posited an essential rela-tionship between sexuality and textuality. (In an essentialist sense, such critics have suggested that when women write, they tend to break the rules of plausibility and verisimilitude that men have created to evaluate fiction.) Gender critics like Peggy Kamuf posit a relationship only between *gender* and textuality, between what most men and women *become* after they are born and the way in which they write. They are

---

[1]Because feminist/gender studies, not unlike sex/gender, should be thought of as existing along a continuum of attitudes and not in terms of simple opposition, attempts to highlight the difference between feminist and gender criticism are inevitably prone to reductive overgeneralization and occasional distortion. Here, for instance, French femi-nism is made out to be more monolithic than it actually is. Hélène Cixous has said that a few men (such as Jean Genet) have produced "feminine writing," although she suggests that these are exceptional men who have acknowledged their own bisexuality.

therefore less interested in the author's sexual "signature"— in whether
the author was a woman writing — than in whether the author was (to
borrow from Kamuf) "Writing like a Woman."

Feminists such as Miller have suggested that no man could write the
"female anger, desire, and selfhood" that Emily Brontë, for instance,
inscribed in her poetry and in *Wuthering Heights* (*Subject* 72). In the
view of gender critics, it is and has been possible for a man to write like
a woman, a woman to write like a man. Shari Benstock, a noted feminist
critic whose investigations into psychoanalytic and poststructuralist
theory have led her increasingly to adopt the gender approach, poses
the following question to herself in *Textualizing the Feminine* (1991):
"Isn't it precisely 'the feminine' in Joyce's writings and Derrida's that
carries me along?" (45). In an essay entitled "Unsexing Language:
Pronominal Protest in Emily Dickinson's 'Lay This Laurel,'" Anna Shannon Elfenbein has argued that "like Walt Whitman, Emily Dickinson
crossed the gender barrier in some remarkable poems," such as "We
learned to like the Fire / By playing Glaciers — when a Boy —" (215).

It is also possible, in the view of most gender critics, for women to
read as men, men as women. The view that women can, and indeed
have been forced to, read as men has been fairly noncontroversial.
Everyone agrees that the literary canon is largely "androcentric" and
that writings by men have tended to "immasculate" women, forcing
them to see the world from a masculine viewpoint. But the question of
whether men can read as women has proved to be yet another issue
dividing feminist and gender critics. Some feminists suggest that men
and women have some essentially different reading strategies and outcomes, while gender critics maintain that such differences arise entirely
out of social training and cultural norms. One interesting outcome of
recent attention to gender and reading is Elizabeth A. Flynn's argument that women in fact make the best interpreters of imaginative literature. Based on a study of how male and female students read works of
fiction, she concludes that women come up with more imaginative,
open-ended readings of stories. Quite possibly the imputed hedging
and tentativeness of women's speech, often seen by men as disadvan-
tages, are transformed into useful interpretive strategies — receptivity
combined with critical assessment of the text — in the act of reading
(Flynn and Schweickart 286).

In singling out a catalyst of gender studies, many historians of criticism have pointed to Michel Foucault. In his *History of Sexuality*
(1976, trans. 1978), Foucault distinguished sexuality from sex, calling

the former a "technology of sex." De Lauretis, who has deliberately developed her theory of gender "along the lines of . . . Foucault's theory of sexuality," explains his use of "technology" this way: "sexuality, commonly thought to be a natural as well as a private matter, is in fact completely constructed in culture according to the political aims of the society's dominant class" (*Technologies* 2, 12).

Foucault suggests that homosexuality as we now think of it was to a great extent an invention of the nineteenth century. In earlier periods there had been "acts of sodomy" and individuals who committed them, but the "sodomite" was, according to Foucault, "a temporary aberration," not the "species" he became with the advent of the modern concept of homosexuality (42–43). According to Foucault, in other words, sodomitic acts did not define people so markedly as the word *homosexual* tags and marks people now. Sodomitic *acts* have been replaced by homosexual *persons*, and in the process the range of acceptable relationships between individuals of the same gender has been restrictively altered. As Sedgwick writes, "to specify someone's sexuality [today] is not to locate her or him on a map teeming with zoophiles, gynecomasts, sexoesthetic inverts, and so forth. . . . In the late twentieth century, if I ask you what your sexual orientation or sexual preference is, you will understand me to be asking precisely one thing: whether you are homosexual or heterosexual" ("Gender" 282).

By historicizing sexuality, Foucault made it possible for his successors to consider the possibility that all of the categories and assumptions that currently come to mind when we think about sex, sexual difference, gender, and sexuality are social artifacts, the products of cultural discourses. Following Foucault's lead, some gay and lesbian critics have argued that the heterosexual/homosexual distinction is as much a cultural construct as is the masculine/feminine dichotomy.

Arguing that sexuality is a continuum, not a fixed and static set of binary oppositions, a number of gay and lesbian critics have critiqued heterosexuality arguing that it has been an enforced corollary and consequence of what Gayle Rubin has referred to as the "sex/gender system" ("Traffic"). According to this system, persons of the male sex are assumed to be masculine, masculine men are assumed to be attracted to women, and therefore it is supposedly natural for men to be attracted to women and unnatural for them to be attracted to men. Lesbian critics have also taken issue with some feminists on the grounds that they proceed from fundamentally heterosexual and even heterosexist assumptions. Particularly offensive to lesbians have been those feminists

who, following Doris Lessing, have implied that to affirm a lesbian identity is to act out feminist hostility against men. According to poet-critic
Adrienne Rich:

> The fact is that women in every culture throughout history have
> undertaken the task of independent, nonheterosexual, women-
> centered existence, to the extent made possible by their context,
> often in the belief that they were the "only ones" ever to have
> done so. They have undertaken it even though few women have
> been in an economic position to resist marriage altogether; and
> even though attacks against [them] have ranged from aspersions
> and mockery to deliberate gynocide. ("Compulsory" 141)

Rich goes on to suggest, in her essay entitled "Compulsory Heterosexuality and Lesbian Existence," that "heterosexuality [is] a beachhead of
male dominance," and that, "like motherhood, [it] needs to be recognized and studied as a political institution" (143, 145).

If there is such a thing as reading like a woman and such a thing as
reading like a man, how then do lesbians read? Are there gay and lesbian ways of reading? Many would say that there are. Rich, by reading
Emily Dickinson's poetry as a lesbian — by not assuming that "heterosexual romance is the key to a woman's life and work"— has introduced us to a poet somewhat different from the one heterosexual critics
have made familiar (*Lies* 158). As for gay reading, Wayne Koestenbaum
has defined "the (male twentieth-century first world) gay reader" as
one who "reads resistantly for inscriptions of his condition, for texts
that will confirm a social and private identity founded on a desire for
other men. . . . Reading becomes a hunt for histories that deliberately
foreknow or unwittingly trace a desire felt not by author but by reader,
who is most acute when searching for signs of himself" (176–77).

Lesbian critics have produced a number of compelling reinterpreta-
tions, or inscriptions, of works by authors as diverse as Emily Dickinson,
Virginia Woolf, and Toni Morrison. As a result of these provocative
readings, significant disagreements have arisen between straight and
lesbian critics and among lesbian critics as well. Perhaps the most famous and interesting example of this kind of interpretive controversy
involves the claim by Barbara Smith and Adrienne Rich that Morrison's
novel *Sula* can be read as a lesbian text — and author Toni Morrison's
counterclaim that it cannot.

Gay male critics have produced a body of readings no less revisionist
and controversial, focusing on writers as staidly classic as Henry James
and Wallace Stevens. In Melville's *Billy Budd* and *Moby-Dick*, Robert K.

Martin suggests, a triangle of homosexual desire exists. In the latter novel, the hero must choose between a captain who represents "the imposition of the male on the female" and a "Dark Stranger" (Queequeg) who "offers the possibility of an alternate sexuality, one that is less dependent upon performance and conquest" (5).

Masculinity as a complex construct producing and reproducing a constellation of behaviors and goals, many of them destructive (like performance and conquest) and most of them injurious to women, has become the object of an unprecedented number of gender studies. A 1983 issue of *Feminist Review* contained an essay entitled "Anti-Porn: Soft Issue, Hard World," in which B. Ruby Rich suggested that the "legions of feminist men" who examine and deplore the effects of pornography on women might better "undertake the analysis that can tell us why men like porn (not, piously, why this or that exceptional man does *not*)" (Clark 185). The advent of gender criticism makes precisely that kind of analysis possible. Stephen H. Clark, who alludes to Ruby Rich's challenge, reads T. S. Eliot "as a man." Responding to "Eliot's implicit appeal to a specifically masculine audience — 'You! hypocrite lecteur! — mon semblable, — mon *frère!*'"— Clark concludes that poems such as "Sweeney among the Nightingales" and "Gerontion," rather than offering what they are usually said to offer — "a social critique into which a misogynistic language accidentally seeps"— instead articulate a masculine "psychology of sexual fear and desired retaliation" (Clark 173).

Some gender critics focusing on masculinity have analyzed "the anthropology of boyhood," a phrase coined by Mark Seltzer in an article in which he comparatively reads, among other things, Stephen Crane's *Red Badge of Courage,* Jack London's *White Fang,* and the first *Boy Scouts of America* handbook (150). Others have examined the fear men have that artistry is unmasculine, a guilty worry that surfaces perhaps most obviously in "The Custom-House," Hawthorne's lengthy preface to *The Scarlet Letter.* Still others have studied the representation in literature of subtly erotic disciple-patron relationships, relationships like the ones between Nick Carraway and Jay Gatsby, Charlie Marlow and Lord Jim, Doctor Watson and Sherlock Holmes, and any number of characters in Henry James's stories. Not all of these studies have focused on literary texts. Because the movies have played a primary role in gender construction during our lifetimes, gender critics have analyzed the dynamics of masculinity (vis-à-vis femininity and androgyny) in films from *Rebel without a Cause* to *Tootsie* to last year's Best Picture. One of the "social technologies" most influential in (re)constructing gender, film is one of the media in which today's sexual politics is most evident.

Necessary as it is, in an introduction such as this one, to define the difference between feminist and gender criticism, it is equally necessary to conclude by unmaking the distinction, at least partially. The two topics just discussed (film theory and so-called queer theory) give us grounds for undertaking that necessary deconstruction. The alliance I have been creating between gay and lesbian criticism on the one hand and gender criticism on the other is complicated greatly by the fact that not all gay and lesbian critics are constructionists. Indeed, a number of them (Robert K. Martin included) share with many feminists the *essentialist* point of view; that is, they believe homosexuals and heterosexuals to be essentially different, different by nature, just as a number of feminists believe men and women to be different.

In film theory and criticism, feminist and gender critics have so influenced one another that their differences would be difficult to define based on any available criteria, including the ones just outlined. Cinema has been of special interest to contemporary feminists like Trinh T. Minh-ha (herself a filmmaker) and Gayatri Chakravorty Spivak (whose critical eye has focused on movies including *My Beautiful Laundrette* and *Sammie and Rosie Get Laid*). Teresa de Lauretis, whose *Technologies of Gender* (1987) has proved influential in the area of gender studies, continues to publish film criticism consistent with earlier, unambiguously feminist works in which she argued that "the representation of woman as spectacle — body to be looked at, place of sexuality, and object of desire — so pervasive in our culture, finds in narrative cinema its most complex expression and widest circulation" (*Alice* 4).

Feminist film theory has developed alongside a feminist performance theory grounded in Joan Riviere's recently rediscovered essay "Womanliness as a Masquerade" (1929), in which the author argues that there is no femininity that is *not* masquerade. Marjorie Garber, a contemporary cultural critic with an interest in gender, has analyzed the constructed nature of femininity by focusing on men who have apparently achieved it — through the transvestism, transsexualism, and other forms of "cross-dressing" evident in cultural productions from Shakespeare to Elvis, from "Little Red Riding Hood" to *La Cage aux Folles*. The future of feminist and gender criticism, it would seem, is not one of further bifurcation but one involving a refocusing on femininity, masculinity, and related sexualities, not only as represented in poems, novels, and films but also as manifested and developed in video, on television, and along the almost infinite number of waystations rapidly being developed on the information highways running through an exponentially expanding cyberspace.

In the essay that follows, Sos Eltis argues that *Dracula* was written in a period when the categories *masculine* and *feminine* were being challenged and redefined. Consequently, it was also a period in which conservative factions sought to reestablish or "reinscribe" the old norms. Even studies in fields such as pathology and psychology performed this culturally conservative work by defining, describing, and documenting "deviant" forms of sexuality, thereby reinforcing the notion that only monogamous heterosexuality is "normal."

Bram Stoker, Eltis goes on to argue, "deliberately located the gothic horror of *Dracula* in this late-nineteenth-century world of . . . gender instability and proliferating discourses" about sexuality (p. 451 in this volume). Quoting a case history written by a "sexologist" about a woman who has to suck her husband's blood to become sexually excited, Eltis says that the woman's sexual history "prefigures that of Stoker's Lucy." She proceeds by discussing Dr. John Seward's case history of R. M. Renfield (whom Seward classifies as a "life-eating maniac") and by reminding us that "Count Dracula himself is neatly filed [by Van Helsing] under a recently identified category, that of the 'criminal type' as classified by Max Nordau and Cesare Lombroso, two contemporary documenters of the outcasts, delinquents, and perverts of modern society" (p. 451).

Eltis grounds the period's "unprecedented anxiety and uncertainty about the social roles, sexual nature, and natural spheres of activity of men and women" in "Victorian feminism," which had brought about changes in property and marriage laws that "gave wives legal status independent from their spouses, enabling them to own and inherit wealth" (p. 452). The independence of the "New Woman" (a term coined by the radical feminist novelist Sarah Grand) threatened the status quo, raising questions about "the compatibility of . . . maternal functions, intellectual development and social emancipation" (p. 453). In the meantime, "concomitant questions" were also being asked about masculinity and, especially, about the new-style, decadent young men who were generally supportive of women's liberation. And amidst all the questions regarding new women, new men, and "the future of healthy civilization," a "new discourse grew up, based on an inverted interpretation of the Darwinian science of evolution." It "portrayed civilization as degenerating" and suggested that, increasingly, "it was the 'unfit' who were surviving" (p. 454).

Dracula, Eltis admits, "seems to express . . . these contemporary fears of degeneration and the dangers of the New Woman" (p. 455). Harker's frightening vision of Dracula's "degenerate race inheriting the future reproduces visions of hereditary decay," the vampire women "infected by [his] corrupting kiss" seem like "monstrous embodiments of Nordau's nymphomaniacal New Women," and even the Count's personal appearance tends to identify him with the gender-confused new man (p. 456). (His "red lips, long pointed nails, and his house-keeping skills . . . are suggestively effeminate" [p. 456]). But Dracula, Eltis goes on to argue, expresses a contrasting viewpoint as well. For instance, the "staking of Lucy" episode would seem to represent "masculine dominance" designed to restore a young woman who has become "the Thing" to "sweetness and purity." But there is another way of viewing it, for the "Un-Dead Lucy" who is staked — in her vulnerability, faithful monogamy, and need to be rescued — is as much like "the traditional feminine, defenseless and frivolous Victorian lady" as she is like the New Woman (p. 457).

Similarly thought-provoking, in Eltis's view, is the novel's treatment of Dracula's "sternly masculine opponents" (p. 458). Surely men like Van Helsing, Arthur Holmwood, and Quincey Morris could be represented unambiguously by a novelist attempting to reassert the masculinist ideology of patriarchal society. Yet these men, "their strapping masculine appearance" notwithstanding, often display "conventionally feminine behavior," sobbing on and sympathizing with one another even while being praised for their manliness. "The recurrence of these declarations of the manliness of emotional outpourings," Eltis proposes, "suggests an anxiety about gender boundaries," but it also shows the extent to which the text represents a masculinity that "may include a number of more traditionally feminine elements" (p. 459).

But of all the characters in Dracula that problematize gender identity and relationship, that of Mina proves most interesting to Eltis. "[C]areful to separate herself from the misguided New Women of her day," Mina supposes that her "healthy appetite would horrify the apparently bodiless New Woman" (p. 459). Yet, for all her critical and even derisive references, Mina is herself a collection of attributes and characteristics associated with "the modern professional woman." (She "travels fearlessly across Europe to nurse her fiancé," is "learned and well informed about contemporary debates," and "reasons, calculates, and deduces" with the best of men [pp. 459–60].) Both like and unlike the kind of woman perceived by many as a threat to civilization, Mina is a character with "a conventionally feminine appearance" and "modern New Woman skills" that, rather than contributing to "the rot of degeneration as envisioned by Max Nordau," prove to effect "part of its cure" (p. 461). (It is Mina's "masculine-trained brain that, by deducing the Count's return route to Transylvania, makes his arrest possible" [p. 461].)

In Mina, Eltis suggests, Stoker creates a character who challenges the either/or construct commonly used in his day in conjunction with masculine/feminine. Just as Mina's "brain" doesn't render her masculine (or threaten the future of civilization), so her traditionally female body and reproductive role fail to render her conventionally feminine. She becomes a mother, but her child, according to Eltis, never becomes a "symbol of his mother's reappropriation by Victorian gender norms," a marker proving that she has been "properly chastized and cleansed of her New Womanly aspirations" (p. 462). Indeed, Quincey is proof that "the New Woman's manly skills did not damage her womanly virtues." Thus, Mina's New Woman qualities "pos[e] no threat to her femininity and maternal potential," and "the novel actually portrays her professional skills as another way of expressing her feminine nature" (p. 462). Even more than through Lucy, her suitors, and the Count, through Mina *Dracula* "engages with contemporary worries about sexuality and gender roles" but also "offers an alternative solution to the regressive prescriptions of more conservative commentators" (p. 464).

Eltis provides an excellent example of contemporary gender criticism. Her focus on the nineteenth-century association of "domesticity" with "feminine," her interest in rediscovering literature by women of the period (like Mona Caird, who critiqued that association), and her willingness to track the effects of those associations and critiques in such things as "changing property and marriage laws" make her essay a broadly representative example of Anglo-American feminist criticism. Her position that gender differences thought of within a given culture as "natural" or "essential" may, in fact, be constructs of the culture in question allies her with gender criticism (of a type affirmed by most feminists). Even more representative of gender criticism is the way in which the debate about changing women's roles "inevitably extend[s] to include masculinity" (p. 450) and — beyond that — sexuality more generally. Her interest in the representation of "divergent and 'deviant' sexuality" (p. 450) in such things as the trial of Oscar Wilde for his homosexuality shows an awareness of issues important to gay and lesbian criticism and so-called queer theory.

Ross C Murfin

GENDER CRITICISM: A SELECTED BIBLIOGRAPHY

Studies of Gender and Sexuality

Berg, Temma F., ed., and Anna Shannon Elfenbein, Jeanne Larsen, and Elisa K. Sparks, co-eds. *Engendering the Word: Feminist Essays in Psychosexual Poetics.* Urbana: U of Illinois P, 1989.

Boone, Joseph A., and Michael Cadden, eds. *Engendering Men: The Question of Male Feminist Criticism.* New York: Routledge, 1990.

Butler, Judith. *Gender Trouble: Feminism and the Subversion of Identity.* New York: Routledge, 1990.

Chodorow, Nancy. *The Reproduction of Mothering: Psychoanalysis and the Sociology of Gender.* Berkeley: U of California P, 1978.

Claridge, Laura, and Elizabeth Langland, eds. *Out of Bounds: Male Writing and Gender(ed) Criticism.* Amherst: U of Massachusetts P, 1990.

de Lauretis, Teresa. *Technologies of Gender: Essays on Theory, Film, and Fiction.* Bloomington: Indiana UP, 1987.

Doane, Mary Ann. "Masquerade Reconsidered: Further Thoughts on the Female Spectator." *Discourse* 11 (1988–89): 42–54.

Eisenstein, Hester, and Alice Jardine, eds. *The Future of Difference.* Boston: G. K. Hall, 1980.

Flynn, Elizabeth A., and Patrocinio P. Schweickart, eds. *Gender and Reading: Essays on Readers, Texts, and Contexts.* Baltimore: Johns Hopkins UP, 1986.

Foucault, Michel. *The History of Sexuality.* Vol. 1. Trans. Robert Hurley. New York: Random, 1978.

Kamuf, Peggy. "Writing Like a Woman." *Women and Language in Literature and Society.* Ed. Sally McConnell-Ginet et al. New York: Praeger, 1980. 284–99.

Laqueur, Thomas. *Making Sex: Body and Gender from the Greeks to Freud.* Cambridge: Harvard UP, 1990.

Riviere, Joan. "Womanliness as a Masquerade." 1929. Rpt. in *Formations of Fantasy*. Ed. Victor Burgin, James Donald, and Cora Kaplan. London: Methuen, 1986. 35–44.

Rubin, Gayle. "Thinking Sex: Notes for a Radical Theory of the Politics of Sexuality." Abelove et al. 3–44.

———. "The Traffic in Women: Notes on the 'Political Economy' of Sex." *Toward an Anthropology of Women*. Ed. Rayna R. Reiter. New York: Monthly Review, 1975. 157–210.

Schor, Naomi. "Feminist and Gender Studies." *Introduction to Scholarship in Modern Languages and Literatures*. Ed. Joseph Gibaldi. New York: MLA, 1992. 262–87.

Sedgwick, Eve Kosofsky. *Between Men: English Literature and Male Homosocial Desire*. New York: Columbia UP, 1988.

———. "Gender Criticism." *Redrawing the Boundaries: The Transformation of English and American Literary Studies*. Ed. Stephen Greenblatt and Giles Gunn. New York: MLA, 1992. 271–302.

Lesbian and Gay Criticism

Abelove, Henry, Michèle Aina Barale, and David Halperin, eds. *The Lesbian and Gay Studies Reader*. New York: Routledge, 1993.

Butters, Ronald, John M. Clum, and Michael Moon, eds. *Displacing Homophobia: Gay Male Perspectives in Literature and Culture*. Durham: Duke UP, 1989.

Clark, Stephen H. "Testing the Razor: T. S. Eliot's Poems." Berg et al. 167–89.

Craft, Christopher. *Another Kind of Love: Male Homosexual Desire in English Discourse, 1850–1920*. Berkeley: U of California P, 1994.

de Lauretis, Teresa. *The Practice of Love: Lesbian Sexuality and Perverse Desire*. Bloomington: Indiana UP, 1994.

Dollimore, Jonathan. *Sexual Dissidence: Augustine to Wilde, Freud to Foucault*. Oxford: Clarendon, 1991.

Elfenbein, Anna Shannon. "Unsexing Language: Pronominal Protest in Emily Dickenson's 'Lay This Laurel.'" Berg et al. 208–23.

Fuss, Diana, ed. *Inside/Out: Lesbian Theories, Gay Theories*. New York: Routledge, 1991.

Garber, Marjorie. *Vested Interests: Cross-Dressing and Cultural Anxiety*. New York: Routledge, 1992.

Halperin, David M. *One Hundred Years of Homosexuality and Other Essays on Greek Love*. New York: Routledge, 1990.

Koestenbaum, Wayne. "Wilde's Hard Labour and the Birth of Gay Reading." Boone and Cadden 176–89.

The Lesbian Issue. Spec. issue of *Signs* 9 (1984).

Martin, Robert K. *Hero, Captain, and Stranger: Male Friendship, Social Critique, and Literary Form in the Sea Novels of Herman Melville.* Chapel Hill: U of North Carolina P, 1986.

Munt, Sally, ed. *New Lesbian Criticism: Literary and Cultural Readings.* New York: Harvester Wheatsheaf, 1992.

Rich, Adrienne. "Compulsory Heterosexuality and Lesbian Existence." *The "Signs" Reader: Women, Gender, and Scholarship.* Ed. Elizabeth Abel and Emily K. Abel. Chicago: U of Chicago P, 1983. 139–68.

Seltzer, Mark. "The Love Master." Boone and Cadden 140–58.

Smith, Barbara. "Toward a Black Feminist Criticism." *The New Feminist Criticism.* Ed. Elaine Showalter. New York: Pantheon, 1985. 168–85.

Stimpson, Catherine R. "Zero Degree Deviancy: The Lesbian Novel in English." *Critical Inquiry* 8 (1981): 363–79.

Weeks, Jeffrey. *Sexuality and Its Discontents: Meanings, Myths, and Modern Sexualities.* London: Routledge, 1985.

Wittig, Monique. "The Mark of Gender." *The Poetics of Gender.* Ed. Nancy K. Miller. New York: Columbia UP, 1986. 63–73.

———. "One Is Not Born a Woman." *Feminist Issues* 1.2 (1981): 47–54.

———. *The Straight Mind and Other Essays.* Boston: Beacon, 1992.

Queer Theory

Butler, Judith. *Bodies That Matter: On the Discursive Limits of "Sex."* New York: Routledge, 1993.

Cohen, Ed. *Talk on the Wilde Side: Towards a Genealogy of Discourse on Male Sexualities.* New York: Routledge, 1993.

de Lauretis, Teresa, ed. Spec. issue on queer theory, *Differences* 3.2 (1991).

Sedgwick, Eve Kosofsky. *Epistemology of the Closet.* Berkeley: U of California P, 1991.

———. *Tendencies.* Durham: Duke UP, 1993.

Sinfield, Alan. *Cultural Politics — Queer Reading.* Philadelphia: U of Pennsylvania P, 1994.

———. *The Wilde Century: Effeminacy, Oscar Wilde, and the Queer Moment.* New York: Columbia UP, 1994.

Other Works Referred to in
"What Is Gender Criticism?"

Benstock, Shari. *Textualizing the Feminine: On the Limits of Genre.* Norman: U of Oklahoma P, 1991.

de Beauvoir, Simone. *The Second Sex.* 1949. Ed. and trans. H. M. Parshley. New York: Modern Library, 1952.

de Lauretis, Teresa. *Alice Doesn't: Feminism, Semiotics, Cinema.* Bloomington: Indiana UP, 1989.

Gallop, Jane. *Around 1981: Academic Feminist Literary Theory.* New York: Routledge, 1992.

Miller, D. A. *The Novel and the Police.* Berkeley: U of California P, 1988.

Miller, Nancy K. *Subject to Change: Reading Feminist Writing.* New York: Columbia UP, 1988.

Rich, Adrienne. *On Lies, Secrets, and Silence: Selected Prose, 1966–1979.* New York: Norton, 1979.

Tate, Claudia. *Black Women Writers at Work.* New York: Continuum, 1983.

Gender Criticism of *Dracula*

Craft, Christopher. "'Kiss Me With Those Red Lips': Gender and Inversion in Bram Stoker's *Dracula*." *Representations* 8 (1984): 107–33. Rev. and rpt. in Craft. *Another Kind of Love: Male Homosexual Desire in English Discourse, 1850–1920.* Berkeley: U of California P, 1994.

Roth, Phyllis. "Suddenly Sexual Women in Bram Stoker's *Dracula*." *Literature and Psychology* 27 (1977): 113–21. Rev. and rpt. in Roth. *Bram Stoker.* Boston: Twayne, 1982. 111–26.

Senf, Carol. "*Dracula:* Stoker's Response to the New Woman." *Victorian Studies* 26 (1982): 33–49.

Weissman, Judith. "Women as Vampires: *Dracula* as a Victorian Novel." *Midwest Quarterly* 18 (1977): 392–405.

A GENDER STUDIES PERSPECTIVE

SOS ELTIS

Corruption of the Blood and Degeneration of the Race: *Dracula* and Policing the Borders of Gender

The decade in which Bram Stoker wrote and published *Dracula* was one of unprecedented anxiety and uncertainty about the social roles, sexual nature, and natural spheres of activity of men and women. As numerous women fought for a larger role in public life and challenged the traditions that defined women's nature as naturally submissive, passive, self-sacrificing, and domestic, so the debate inevitably extended to include masculinity and man's natural role. While Victorian feminists encroached on previously male preserves, crossing borders and redefining categories, the more conservative press reacted by reinscribing gender norms, insisting on the essential differences between the sexes and their consequently separate duties.

Closely connected to this debate, the 1880s and 1890s also saw the publication of numerous studies in pathology, psychology, and sexology. In his "medico-legal study," *Psychopathia Sexualis*, for example, the German sexologist Dr. Krafft-Ebing (p. 394 in this volume) documented hundreds of case studies of divergent and "deviant" sexuality, exhaustively listing, cataloguing, and typing each individual. Under "Sadism in Women," he described "Case 42," a woman whose sexual history prefigures that of Stoker's Lucy:

> A married man presented himself with numerous scars of cuts on his arms. He told their origin as follows: When he wished to approach his wife, who was young and somewhat 'nervous,' he first had to make a cut in his arm. Then she would suck the wound, and during the act become violently excited sexually.[1]

Krafft-Ebing's study exemplifies the late-nineteenth-century's methods of policing sexuality. As Michel Foucault argued, in his influential *History of Sexuality*, heterosexual monogamy's status as the central

---

[1]Dr. R. von Krafft-Ebing, *Psychopathia Sexualis, with Especial Reference to Contrary Sexual Instinct: A Medico-Legal Study.* Authorized translation of 7th enlarged and revised German edition, by Charles Gilbert Chaddock (Philadelphia and London: F. A. Davis, 1892), 87.

standard became assumed, unstated, while around it was established an ever-growing discourse of "perverse" sexualities: the sensuality of those who did not like the opposite sex, obsessions, petty manias, fantasies, and acts of sexual violence.[2] Classified and typed according to their acts and modes of conduct, individuals were both contained and marginalized by a discourse that simultaneously asserted the normality of those who did not share their "aberrant" proclivities.

Stoker deliberately located the gothic horror of *Dracula* in this late-nineteenth-century world of technological advance, gender instability and proliferating discourses. Mina travels with a portable typewriter; Dr. John Seward records his medical notes on a phonographic wax cylinder. In writing his case history of "R. M. Renfield, ætat 59 — Sanguine temperament," like Krafft-Ebing, Seward constructs a category to contain Renfield's peculiarity: "I shall have to invent a new classification for him, and call him a zoophagous (life-eating) maniac" (p. 92). Count Dracula himself is neatly filed under a recently identified category, that of the "criminal type" as classified by Max Nordau and Cesare Lombroso, two contemporary documenters of the outcasts, delinquents, and perverts of modern society.[3] In Stoker's novel the Other is categorized, identified as monstrous, and then exterminated, in the ritual staking and beheading perpetrated on Lucy and the three vampire women, and intended for the Count.

But Stoker's Count will not remain stable and fixed within a category, any more than the novel will accept such a simple pattern of interpretation. Before Jonathan Harker meets Dracula he confidently reports his impression of crossing from West to East, but such assured belief in the presence of clear borders is swiftly undermined in his dealings with the Count, for Dracula is the master of shape-shifting and boundary crossing. He is both dead and Un-Dead; young and old; man, bat, and wolf. He is a Transylvanian aristocrat who can pass in Hyde Park as an English gentleman, and an ancient warrior who deals with solicitors, clerks, and customs men. *Dracula*'s engagement with the late-Victorian debate on gender roles and differences is similarly complex and hard to categorize. The end of the novel does not offer a

[2]Michel Foucault, *The Will to Knowledge: The History of Sexuality*, vol.1. Trans. Robert Hurley (Penguin: London, 1978), Part II, "The Perverse Implantation."

[3]Max Nordau, *Entartung* (1892; second edition Berlin: C. Duncker, 1893); translated as *Degeneration* (New York: D. Appleton, 1895). Cesare Lombroso, *La donna delinquente* (Torino: Roux, 1893); translated as *The Female Offender* (London: T. F. Unwin, 1895). *L'uomo delinquente* (Torino: Bocca, 1889); published in summary form in English translation by Gina Lombroso as *Criminal Man* (New York: Putnam, 1911).

straightforward resolution to the gender confusion that is generated by
Dracula's incursions into civilized London. Though Dracula himself is
finally pinned down by Quincey Morris's bowie knife, the baby that
bears Quincey's name does not necessarily fix Mina in a traditionally
conservative female role.[4]

The second half of the nineteenth century was a period of upheaval
in the social and legal position of women in Britain. Changes in property and marriage laws gave wives a legal status independent of their
husbands, enabling them to own and inherit wealth separate from their
spouses and, in limited circumstances, to be awarded custody of their
children. The foundation of new women's colleges gave access to
higher education for the first time, and the professions available to
women were slowly extended from the nursery, the stage, and the
three-volume novel to include such male bastions as medicine and journalism. The campaign for women's rights finally became most strongly
focused on the demand for suffrage, and "Votes for Women" was the
rallying cry of late-Victorian feminism.

In 1894 the radical feminist novelist Sarah Grand coined the term
"New Woman" in an article entitled "The New Aspect of the Woman
Question" in the *North American Review,* and the label stuck, being
adopted by both the champions of sexual equality and by the conservative press to mock these misguided and unbecomingly manly women.[5]
Cartoonists portrayed the New Woman as a plain bespectacled spinster,
clutching a latchkey and a copy of Ibsen's plays, or as a rash young
thing, with a cigarette and a glass of whisky in her hand, sporting a
divided skirt or bloomers in ludicrous imitation of male dress.[6] But,
though the popular press found it easy to caricature the New Woman,
there was in fact no such single coherent figure, nor was there consen-

---

[4]Even this final confining of Dracula is, perhaps, doubtful. I am inclined to agree
with Phyllis Roth's students in their skepticism as to the final destruction of the Count.
His throat is cut, but no actual beheading is mentioned, and the piercing of his heart does
not necessarily constitute staking. Dracula's death falls flat after the violent deaths of Lucy
and the other vampire women, and Stoker's excision of the orgasmic explosion of the
castle denies the Count a similarly climactic ending. See Phyllis A. Roth, "Suddenly Sexual Women in Bram Stoker's *Dracula,*" *Literature and Psychology* 27 (1977). 113–21.

[5]Grand, "The New Aspect of the Woman Question," *North American Review* 158
(1894), 271–3.

[6]See for example *Life* 13 June 1895, p. 395 and 8 July 1897, pp. 30–31; *Punch,* 10
April 1894, p. 194 and 11 September 1897, p. 110. Ibsen's *A Doll's House* was first performed in London in 1889, and Nora Helmer's abandoning of husband and child to find
herself was soon used as a prime example of the selfishness of the would-be liberated
woman.

sus as to the right way forward for emancipated womanhood. The area of most heated debate and least agreement was that of woman's relation to the family, and the compatibility of her maternal functions, intellectual development, and social emancipation. So, for example, Grant Allen, author of the New Woman novel *The Woman Who Did* (1895), argued that women were misguided in seeking access to male professions, when the real issue was the need for higher status and better rights for mothers, whether inside or outside of marriage.[7] Millicent Garrett Fawcett, a leader of the women's suffrage campaign, ridiculed Allen's novel and its free-love-advocating heroine, declaring of Allen: "He is not a friend, but an enemy [of the women's movement], and it is as an enemy that he endeavours to link together the claim of women to citizenship and social and industrial independence with attacks upon marriage and the family."[8] However, Mona Caird devoted extended passages of her novel *The Daughters of Danaus* (1894) to railing against society's demand that women sacrifice themselves to husband and children, and harshly condemned the institution of marriage as it stood.[9] Sarah Grand, by contrast, championed sexual purity and motherhood in her 1893 novel on the Woman Question, *The Heavenly Twins*.

Challenges to definitions of woman's nature and role brought concomitant questions and anxieties about masculinity. Eliza Lynn Linton, for example, characterized all male supporters of women's emancipation as infected by the weakness of the opposite sex: "Like the Wild Women whose claims they advocate, they are hysterically susceptible to outside influences; they prefer emotion to reason; they champion the individual as against the law and the community; they like faith better than demonstration." As she scornfully concluded, "the unsexed woman pleases the unsexed man."[10] The trials and conviction of Oscar Wilde in 1895, for acts of so-called gross indecency involving young men, confirmed many of these fears, and *Punch* was predictably quick to voice conservative anxieties about gender confusion. On the day

---

[7] Allen, "Plain Words on the Woman Question," *Fortnightly Review*, 52 (Oct. 1889), 448–58.

[8] Fawcett, "The Woman Who Did," *Contemporary Review* (1895), 630. Qtd. in Sally Ledger, "The New Woman and the Crisis of Victorianism," in Ledger and Scott McCracken (eds), *Cultural Politics at the Fin de Siecle* (Cambridge: Cambridge University Press, 1995), p. 33.

[9] Caird, *The Daughters of Danaus* (London, 1894). See also Caird, "A Defence of the So-Called 'Wild Women,'" *Nineteenth Century* 31 (May 1892), 811–29.

[10] Linton, "The Partisans of the Wild Women," *Nineteenth Century*, 31 (March 1892), 457 and 461.

after the second Wilde trial began, the magazine published an attack on "Sexomania" "By an Angry Old Buffer":

> When Adam delved and Eve span
> No one need ask which was the man.
> Bicycling, footballing, scarcely human,
> All wonder now, "Which is the woman?"
> But a new fear my bosom vexes;
> Tomorrow there may be no sexes!
> Unless, as end to all the pother,
> Each one in fact become the other.[11]

The most commercially successful expression of society's fears about the New Woman and her companion the male decadent was probably Marie Corelli's novel, *The Sorrows of Satan*, which was first published in 1895 and went through thirty-seven editions in the next three years. The novel charts the downfall of an idle, vain, and effete dandy, and his New Woman wife, Sibyl. Both become enamored of the Devil who is visiting London in human guise. Sibyl attempts to commit adultery with the Devil before her husband's very eyes, and justifies herself by declaring: "You have only to read the 'new' fiction, and indeed all 'new' literature generally, to be assured that your ideas of domestic virtue are quite out of date. Both men and women are, according to certain accepted writers of the day, at equal liberty to love where they will, and where they may. Polygamous liberty is the 'new' creed!"[12] The Devil himself recoils in horror from her liberated corruption.

The greatest danger of the New Woman, however, was her supposed threat to the future of healthy civilization and the human race. The last decades of the nineteenth century, with their unavoidable evidence of urban overcrowding, extreme poverty, and industrial pollution, together with challenges to religious belief, moral codes, attitudes to class and sexual roles, resulted in the erosion of any easy optimistic belief in progress. A new discourse grew up, based on an inverted interpretation of the Darwinian science of evolution, which portrayed civilization as degenerating. It diagnosed a social decay in which it was the "unfit" who were surviving; hoards of the uneducated, debased, diseased, and neurotic were reproducing at a terrifying rate, and their

---

[11] *Punch*, (27 April 1895), 203. Quoted in Ledger, p.26. For other examples of satire on gender confusion see, for example, *Pick-Me-Up* 11 Jan 1896, p.236; and *Punch* (23 July 1898) p.34.

[12] Corelli, *The Sorrows of Satan* (Oxford: Oxford University Press, 1996), 297.

defects were being genetically transmitted and exaggerated from generation to generation. A phenomenal outcrop of books by doctors, scientists, and social commentators analyzed this decay, and it is to this group of works that Lombroso's studies in criminality and Max Nordau's *Degeneration* belong, as both authors identify criminal and degenerate types and find their roots in hereditary defects.[13] The New Woman was seen as both a symptom of and a contributor to this decay. Nordau condemned the modern women who applauded the radical heroines of Ibsen's plays, denouncing them as "women who in the viragoes of Ibsen's drama — hysterical, nymphomaniacal, perverted in maternal instinct — recognise their own portrait or the ideal of development of their degenerate imagination."[14] According to these specialists, not only radical feminism but the very fact of women studying could endanger the future health of the species. Menstruation and childbearing were such a drain on women's resources that they would only overstrain their systems if they were to attempt mental exercise as well. In 1874, for example, Henry Maudsley warned that the price of "female intellectual work" would be "a puny, enfeebled and sickly race," and Charles Harper declared that unsexed New Women would bring about "the degradation and ultimate extinction of the race."[15]

Dracula at first glance seems to express with precision these contemporary fears of degeneration and the dangers of the New Woman. Harker's nightmare vision of Dracula's degenerate race inheriting the future reproduces visions of hereditary decay: "This was the being I was helping to transfer to London, where, perhaps for centuries to come he might, amongst its teeming millions, satiate his lust for blood, and create a new and ever-widening circle of semi-demons to batten on the helpless" (p. 74). Count Dracula is not just identified as a Lombrosian criminal type, his very features mark him out as criminally degenerate: his protruding teeth, pointed ears, and hairy hands are telling signs.[16]

[13]See, for example, B. A. Morel, *Traité des dégénérescences physiques, intellectuelles et morales de l'éspèce humaine* (Paris: J. B. Bailliere; New York: H. Bailliere, 1857); Charles Fréré, *Dégénérescence et criminalité* (Paris: F. Alcan, 1888); Edwin Lankester, *Degeneration* (New York: Humboldt, 1891); Henry Maudsley, *Body and Will* (London: Kegan Paul, Trench, 1883).

[14]Max Nordau, *Degeneration* (Heinemann: London, 1895), 413.

[15]Maudsley, "Sex in Mind and Education," *Fortnightly Review* 21 (April 1874). Quoted in Sally Ledger, *The New Woman: Fiction and Feminism at the fin de siècle* (Manchester University Press: Manchester, 1997). Charles G. Harper, *Revolted Woman: Past, Present and To Come* (Elkin Mathews: London, 1894), 27. See also, Grant Allen, "Plain Words on the Woman Question," 453.

[16]Gina Lombroso Ferrero, *Criminal Man, according to the Classification of Cesare Lombroso* (Putnam's Sons; New York and London, 1911) xv, 15, 17 & 40.

Furthermore, Dracula's red lips, long pointed nails, and his housekeeping skills — making Harker's bed and preparing his meals with invisible ease — are suggestively effeminate. The hint of sexual deviancy, which underlines Jonathan Harker's instinctive shudder at the touch of Dracula's hand, is confirmed when Dracula throws his female accomplice aside to declare his exclusive proprietorial claim: "This man belongs to me!"[17] (p. 62).

Similarly, the vampire women, infected by Dracula's corrupting kiss, are monstrous embodiments of Nordau's nymphomaniacal New Women. Traditional gender roles are reversed, as Harker lies prone on the sofa in "an agony of delightful anticipation," followed by "languorous ecstacy," while the female vampire gloats over him, preparing to pierce his flesh with her teeth (p. 62). Vampirism infects women with masculine sexual aggression and perverts their maternal instincts into an appetite for infant blood; the three vampire women are fed babies in a bag by Dracula, and the newly risen Un-Dead Lucy clutches her latest child-victim to her bosom in an obscene inversion of maternal suckling. Their degeneration to the level of the animal is clear; Lucy growls over her infant prey "as a dog growls over a bone," and the fair vampire woman licks her lips over Jonathan and then proceeds to devour a child, just as the wolves lick their lips after feasting on the baby's mother (pp. 219, 61–62, 68).

Like the sadistic blood-sucking woman catalogued by Krafft-Ebing as "Case 42," Lucy is identified as deviant; but more violent means than simple categorization are needed to control her sexuality. The staking of Lucy is described in overtly sexual terms, as a reassertion of masculine dominance and sexual aggression:

> Arthur placed the point over the heart, and as I looked I could see its dint in the white flesh. Then he struck with all his might.
>
> The Thing in the coffin writhed. . . . The body shook and quivered and twisted in wild contortions; the sharp white teeth champed together till the lips were cut, and the mouth was smeared with a crimson foam. But Arthur never faltered. He looked like a figure of Thor. . . . (p. 223)

Arthur Holmwood becomes the embodiment of determined, self-controlled masculinity as he drives his fiancé into the orgasmic throes of death. Lucy is restored from "the Thing," devoid of gender or

---

[17]For a highly suggestive analysis of the homosexual subtext of *Dracula*, see Christopher Craft, "'Kiss Me with those Red Lips': Gender and Inversion in Bram Stoker's *Dracula*," *Representations* 8 (1984), 107–33.

humanity, to the "sweetness and purity" of the woman they recognize. The band of male friends have reasserted the proper order of things, and the nymphomaniac vampire, who threatened to infect her lover and devour the children of the city, is put back in her box.

Yet the neatness of this scheme, with its easy identification and expulsion of the New Woman's threat, and its clear antithesis between sexually deviant vampires and the band of healthy opponents who defend the straightforward division of gender roles, simply does not fit with the complex contradictions of the text as a whole. Some critics have identified Lucy as a New Woman, as manifested in her sleepwalking desire to escape from the home and her aberrant sexual appetite, complaining to Mina, "Why can't they let a girl marry three men, or as many as want her, and save all this trouble?"[18] (p. 80). But, taken as a whole, Lucy is far more reminiscent of the traditional feminine, defenseless and frivolous Victorian lady. Her first letter is full of parties, "Pops," and beaux, and she clearly has no occupations or concerns beyond her social engagements and amours. She has known Mina since they were children together, but such is her childish vulnerability that not only the men in the novel, but her female friend too, become her protectors; as Mina writes: "It was my privilege to be your friend and guide when you came from the schoolroom to prepare for the world of life" (p. 124). Lucy Westenra is not an 1890s feminist like Grant Allen's Herminia Barton or Mona Caird's Hadria Fullerton; she is far more closely related to Laura Fairley, the passive mid-Victorian heroine of Wilkie Collins's *The Woman in White* (1860), who is protected and rescued not only by men but by her resourceful, intelligent and determined cousin, Marion.[19] Nor is the contrast between the rampant sexuality of the female vampire and the normality of "untainted" woman that clear-cut. As Nina Auerbach has pointed out, the Un-Dead Lucy is faithfully monogamous in directing her sexual attentions to Arthur Holmwood alone.[20] Once vampirized, Lucy is unfaithful only through the blood transfusions, given to her while she is unconscious,

[18]See, for example, Elaine Showalter, *Sexual Anarchy: Gender and Culture at the Fin de Siècle* (Virago: London, 1992), 179–84; Carol A. Senf, "*Dracula:* Stoker's response to the New Woman," *Victorian Studies* 26 (Autumn 1982), 33–49.

[19]Grant Allen, *The Woman Who Did* (Boston: Roberts Brothers; London: J. Lane, 1895); Mona Caird, *The Daughters of Danaus* (London: Bliss, Sands & Foster, 1894); Wilkie Collins, *The Woman in White* (London: Sampson Low, 1860). Collins's novel was probably a model for *Dracula*, being based on a similar patchwork of multiple narrative and giving a similar importance to details and dates recorded in a (woman's) journal.

[20]Nina Auerbach, *Our Vampires, Ourselves* (University of Chicago Press: Chicago, 1995), 79–80.

which, as Van Helsing observes, render her a "polyandrist" (p. 186). A similar blurring of distinctions occurs when one notes that Lucy's frail and loving mother does her child more harm by removing the protective garlic flowers from her daughter's neck and by stunning Lucy in her panicking death throes, than the vampirized Lucy does to any of the tiny tots who are mesmerised by the "bloofer lady" (p. 189).

The juxtaposition of Dracula and his sternly masculine opponents is equally ambiguous. Van Helsing, the father/mentor/tutor who heads the trio of Lucy's admirers, is bound to John Seward through his gratitude for an act that both mimics and inverts the poisonous vampiric kiss. So Van Helsing writes to Seward, offering Arthur his help:

> Tell your friend that when that time you suck from my wound so swiftly the poison of the gangrene from that knife that our other friend, too nervous, let slip, you did more for him when he wants my aids and you call for them than all his great fortune could do.[21] (p. 130)

The manliness of these men is frequently asserted and emphasized throughout the text. Van Helsing needs only a second's glance to recognize Arthur Holmwood's "strong young manhood," and he greets Quincey Morris with similar approval: "You're a man and no mistake" (p. 162). Their strapping masculine appearance is significant as an indicator of how much blood they can donate to the anemic Lucy, but the appraising gaze necessarily contains aesthetic as well as practical standards of assessment.

Other assertions of the men's manliness are prompted by displays of what would more conventionally be typed as feminine behavior. When Arthur Holmwood breaks down, throws his arms round John Seward's shoulders, and lays his sobbing head on his breast, Seward remarks that, "I comforted him as well as I could. In such cases men do not need much expression. A grip of the hand, the tightening of an arm over the shoulder, a sob in unison, are expressions of sympathy dear to a man's heart" (p. 180). John Seward's faith in the silent and restrained communication of masculine sympathy soon falters when he is faced with "a regular fit of hysterics" from Professor Van Helsing after Lucy's funeral:

> He laughed till he cried, and I had to draw the blinds down lest anyone should see us and misjudge; and then he cried till he laughed again; and laughed and cried together, just as a woman

---

[21]Another curious parallel is to be found between the description of Dracula throwing the female vampire off Jonathan Harker, and that of Van Helsing dragging Arthur Holmwood off the dying Lucy.

does. I tried to be stern with him, as one is to a woman under the circumstances; but it had no effect. Men and women are so different in manifestations of nervous strength or weakness! (p. 185)

Clearly disturbed by Van Helsing's loss of control, and skeptical at his attempt to explain it as the expression of a strong sense of humor, Seward looks for reassurance from the essential difference between male and female behavior — though the significant difference here appears to be the relative recalcitrance of masculine hysteria. Mina also turns to ideas of gender difference to dispel her sense of discomfort when Arthur falls sobbing on her bosom within minutes of their first being introduced: "I suppose there is something in woman's nature that makes a man free to break down before her and express his feelings on the tender or emotional side without feeling it derogatory to his manhood" (p. 235). The recurrence of these declarations of the manliness of emotional outpourings suggests an anxiety about gender boundaries, and all the characters respond by asserting that true masculinity may include a number of more traditionally feminine elements. Their insistence on separate categories responds and yields to the fluidity of gendered behavior within the text.

Mina is the character who most clearly subverts traditional gender categories. She is careful to separate herself from the misguided New Women of her day, musing that her healthy appetite would horrify the apparently bodiless New Woman. While she watches Lucy sleeping, she speculates that New Women writers will some day suggest that men and women should see each other sleeping before they propose or accept, if, that is, New Women let men do the proposing rather than foolishly taking the initiative themselves.[22] A lack of appetite was not commonly taken to be a primary trait of the New Woman, though sexual aggression was certainly attributed to her by a number of critics. Yet, despite these mocking references to the New Woman, Mina herself is possessed of a number of her commonly recognized attributes. Employed as a schoolmistress, she extends her skills by learning shorthand and typing, the accomplishments of the modern professional woman. Mina travels fearlessly across Europe to nurse her fiancé, and her journal is not intended as a record of her girlish emotions, but rather "an exercise book," in which she will try to train herself in describing the world as "lady journalists do" (p. 76). She is learned and well informed about contemporary debates; she has read Nordau and Lombroso, and quickly

---

[22]Mina does not see Jonathan Harker sleeping before accepting his proposal, but she does nurse him and watch over his sleep before she marries him.

picks up on Van Helsing's references. Above all, she reasons, calculates, and deduces with "her great brain which is trained like man's brain, but is of sweet woman," as Van Helsing puts it (p. 334).

Her emotional restraint, courage, and nervous strength often surpass those of the men around her. Jonathan Harker is prostrated by a nervous collapse, Van Helsing breaks down in hysterics, and Arthur Holmwood sobs on male and female shoulders, but it is only once Mina has been weakened by Dracula's drinking of her blood that she gives in to tears: "I, who never cried on my own account" (p. 260). Having read the terrible account of Lucy's staking and beheading, she is offered brandy by Dr. Seward, but she is "[f]ortunately . . . not of a fainting disposition" (p. 230). Reversing the more conventional relation of husband and wife, Jonathan Harker is struck down by brain fever, but in the words of Sister Agatha, "has won all hearts by his sweetness and gentleness"[23] (p. 118). It is Mina who travels to his rescue, and who later carefully protects him from troublesome thoughts by transcribing his diary, because, "then, perhaps, if I am ready, poor Jonathan may not be upset, for I can speak for him and never let him be troubled or worried with it at all" (pp. 189–90).

Mina's appearance is deceptive. She frequently takes on a masculine role, but still maintains a conventionally feminine appearance. When she ventures out to East Cliff in search of the sleepwalking Lucy, she automatically assumes the role of protector, giving the more fragile woman her shoes as she walks home barefoot over the gravel. But before walking back in the dark, Mina is careful to daub her feet with mud from a puddle, so as not to arouse suspicions. The action is a perfect image for Mina's behavior throughout the novel, combining propriety with ingenuity, concealing her toughness with decorous modesty. Mina constantly defies expectations. Jonathan Harker's memos to send Transylvanian cooking recipes back to Mina hardly prepare the reader for his fiancé's professional skills. Seward, Morris, and Holmwood are all similarly misled by, in the words of John Seward, this "sweet-faced, dainty-looking girl" (p. 226). In contradiction to the characters' reliance on physiognomy, she is not to be known or understood by her appearance but through her writing. On first encountering Mina, Seward, Morris, and Holmwood all hesitate to talk explicitly in the presence of a protected lady, and in each case Mina presents them with typewritten transcripts in order to reveal her true, resilient character.

---

[23]Havelock Ellis, for example, in his study of sexual differences, identifies neuraesthenia, hysteria, and nervous collapse as predominantly female maladies, *Man and Woman: A Study of Human Secondary Sexual Characters* (Walter Scott: London, 1894), 278–80.

Mina's New Woman talents are the outward expression of the inner strength, courage, and resilience that defy her male colleagues' expectations of frail and nervous womanhood. More important, her modern New Woman skills are not part of the rot of degeneration as envisioned by Max Nordau, but part of its cure. Without Mina's shorthand records, typed transcripts, and journalistic construction of the narrative, Dracula's intentions and methods could never have been traced. It is Mina's masculine-trained brain that, by deducing the Count's return route to Transylvania, makes his arrest possible.

Yet, despite all they learn of Mina's unconventional strength, the men are still plagued by fears of her overstraining her system. Like Henry Maudsley and Charles Harper, they are concerned about the effects such expense of nervous energy will have on her female constitution. John Seward relies on his medical training in declaring that, "it is no place for a woman, and if she had remained in touch with the affair, it would in time infallibly have wrecked her" (p. 259). Professor Van Helsing similarly worries that, "it is no part for a woman," quite explicitly referring this to concerns about her maternal functions as a "young woman and not so long married," for whom "there may be other things to think of some time" (p. 240). The men therefore exclude Mina from their meetings, leaving her at home while they venture out to examine the old chapel and to burgle one of the Count's London residences. They frequently and ironically congratulate themselves on their wisdom in recognizing Mina's womanly weakness and the necessity of preserving her in the safe and proper location of the home. Having feasted uninterrupted on the home-bound Mina, Dracula mocks the *men* for having strayed too far from their proper domestic sphere: "They should have kept their energies for use closer to home" (p. 288). Having endangered Mina by casting her in a narrow gender role, the men learn their lesson and reintegrate her into their activities. When they falter, and exclude her once more from their councils, she earns her readmittance by offering hypnosis as a means of tracking Dracula's presence and by deducing his chosen route. She wins her reward, and in the final shoot-out is armed with a large-bore revolver like the others — a gun that she seems to need no lessons in using.[24]

Mina's baby, the boy who is named after the entire band but is called Quincey, is thus not the symbol of his mother's reappropriation

[24]Women using firearms was the subject of particular outrage in the writings of some critics of the New Woman — see, for example, Eliza Lynn Linton, "The Wild Woman as Social Insurgent," *Nineteenth Century* 30 (Oct. 1891), 597–9, and Harper, *Revolted Woman*, chap.1.

by Victorian gender norms. Mina's maternal status does not mark her
out as properly chastized and cleansed of her New Womanly aspirations. On the contrary, it validates her masculine courage and enterprise, her trained mind, and the dangers she bravely encounters, as in
no way incompatible with the valuable female functions on which the
future of the race depends. Mina can study and think like a man, face
hideous dangers, *and* happily fulfill her maternal function. Mina's
maternal status contradicts writers like Grant Allen, who declared that
giving masculine training to women only served to destroy their female
instincts: "The result was that many women became unsexed in the
process, and many others acquired a distaste, an unnatural distaste, for
the functions which nature intended them to perform," with the end
result that, "many of the most cultivated and able families of the
English-speaking race will have become extinct."[25] Dr. Seward's and
Professor Van Helsing's fears about Mina's future maternal functions
clearly result from reading too much Allen, Maudsley, and Nordau, but
such anxieties are contradicted by the healthy presence of young
Quincey.

   Mina's role in *Dracula* goes beyond a defence of her New Woman
qualities as posing no threat to her femininity and maternal potential;
the novel actually portrays her professional skills as another way of
expressing her feminine nature. When Van Helsing first asks to see her
journal, Mina flirts with him, teasing the Professor with her shorthand
skills:

> I could not resist the temptation of mystifying him a bit — I sup-
> pose it is some taste of the original apple that remains still in our
> mouths — so I handed him the shorthand diary. He took it with a
> grateful bow, and said:
>   "May I read it?"
>   "If you wish," I answered as demurely as I could. (p. 193)

Mina likens herself to Eve in her immodest flaunting of her shorthand
skills. Similarly, she uses her typewriting abilities to soothe and protect
John Seward's pain, helping him to keep his agony private by transcribing the wax cylinder recordings of his "soul crying out" into the more
emotionally neutral medium of print.

   In one of his most enthusiastic paeans of praise to Mina, Van Helsing celebrates her God-given fusion of the best of both genders:

---

[25] Allen, "Plain Words on the Woman Question," 455–6.

Ah, that wonderful Madam Mina! She has man's brain — a brain
that a man should have were he much gifted — and woman's
heart. The good God fashioned her for a purpose, believe me,
when He made that so good combination. (p. 240)

This androgynous mixture offers a strong echo of a letter Bram Stoker
wrote to Walt Whitman in 1872. Stoker exclaimed to the American
poet, "How sweet it is for a strong healthy man with a woman's eyes
and a child's wishes to feel that he can speak to a man who can be if he
wishes father, and brother and wife to his soul."[26] In both descriptions,
a fusion of masculinity and femininity is viewed admiringly as an ideal
for men and women. So Van Helsing takes care to brush Lucy's hair as
she lies dying; and Jonathan Harker, when Dracula's assault on his wife
is narrated, displays both aspects of manhood: ". . . whilst the face of
white set passion worked convulsively over the bowed head, the hands
tenderly and lovingly stroked the ruffled hair" (p. 285). At their
noblest, each character combines elements of both traditional masculinity and femininity; the men become stronger and more determined after their cathartic expressions of grief and compassion, and
Mina's womanly tenderness finds expression through her shorthand
and typing skills. The manliness that the narrators constantly reassert
whenever the men act in traditionally "unmanly" ways is not narrowly
restrictive, but unusually all-embracing. Any attempt to assert narrow
gender boundaries, as when Mina is confined to the home, only serves
to weaken the band's efforts.

Bram Stoker carefully placed *Dracula* in the context of fin de siècle
instability and anxiety, and so sought to exploit the fears that had
helped to make *The Sorrows of Satan* and *The Woman Who Did* so extra-
ordinarily popular. The unrestrained sexual appetite and aggression displayed by the vampiric Lucy offer a nightmare vision of animal sexuality
and the loss of all restraint. It is an extreme horror that calls for equally
extreme measures to contain it — the unsettling violence of Lucy's
staking and decapitation. Yet it is not female sexuality per se that is
being punished but its uncontrolled excess. Vampire sexuality is sinis-
terly attractive to the uninfected humans, and seems to exist at the
opposite end of a continuum from "healthy" sexuality. Jonathan
Harker eagerly anticipates the fair vampire's bite despite his horror, and
Mina similarly confesses that she did not want to hinder Dracula as he

[26]Quoted in Barbara Belford, *Bram Stoker: A Biography of the Author of* Dracula
(Phoenix Giant: London, 1997), 43.

bared her throat. Van Helsing too finds "the very instinct of man in me" draws him toward the voluptuous beauty of the female vampires in their tombs. The physical lure of the vampire, the animal sensuality that Dracula's blood unleashes, is not monstrously "other" than ordinary human sexuality, but an unrestrained manifestation of the same. Dracula invades the Harkers' very marriage bed and Mina's horror reaches a peak when she sees her husband's nightshirt stained with blood and realizes that their own sexual relations are now poisoned: "Unclean, unclean! I must touch him or kiss him no more. Oh that it should be that it is I who am now his worst enemy, and whom he may have most cause to fear" (p. 285). This taint is removed with Dracula's death, and with it the threat that Mina, like Lucy and the other vampire women, will become sexually aggressive and predatory, and that her spiritual purity will be displaced by purely animal appetite. The novel's moral scheme is more complex than a dichotomy of opposites: the "good" characters burgle houses, bribe officials, and break into tombs, and their sexuality is different from the vampires' only in degree. Men and women resist becoming vampires by controlling and containing their sexual urges.[27]

Dracula engages with contemporary worries about sexuality and gender roles, but offers an alternative solution to the regressive prescriptions of more conservative commentators. Contemporary writers such as Nordau, Linton, and Allen linked together sexual incontinence, ambiguous gender roles, and the degeneration of the race, in order to argue that women should resist the temptation to leave their proper domestic sphere. Stoker exploited the same fears but offered a less restrictive solution, while separating the issues other writers presented as inherently connected. Aggressive female sexuality is a source of terror in *Dracula,* but it is the old-fashioned Lucy who becomes a predatory vampire, while the professionally skilled Mina remains demurely monogamous. The men in the novel react to the vampires' threat by trying to confine Mina within a traditionally limited gender role. They are, as they learn, misguided; Mina's masculine skills and intelligence, like the men's feminine compassion and tenderness, are a vital part of the struggle against the debased vampire breed. These expanded gender roles and fluid boundaries are part of a healthy future. Stoker's

---

[27]This emphasis on sexual restraint is reproduced in a number of Stoker's other novels, in which even marital consummation is deferred — see e.g., *The Snake's Pass* (1890), *The Mystery of the Sea* (1902) and *The Lady of the Shroud* (1909).

effeminate Count and sexually predatory vampiric women vividly enact a fin de siècle cultural panic, but they are defeated by a fluid and surprisingly modern combination of masculine and feminine qualities. Mina's child is held up as the crowning glory of the story, joining together the band's names, and proving that the New Woman's manly skills did not damage her womanly virtues. He is the healthy harbinger of a regenerate future.

Psychoanalytic Criticism
and *Dracula*

WHAT IS PSYCHOANALYTIC CRITICISM?

It seems natural to think about novels in terms of dreams. Like dreams, literary works are fictions, inventions of the mind that, although based on reality, are by definition not literally true. Like a literary work, a dream may have some truth to tell, but, like a literary work, it may need to be interpreted before that truth can be grasped. We can live vicariously through romantic fictions, much as we can through daydreams. Terrifying novels and nightmares affect us in much the same way, plunging us into an atmosphere that continues to cling, even after the last chapter has been read — or the alarm clock has sounded.

The notion that dreams allow such psychic explorations, of course, like the analogy between literary works and dreams, owes a great deal to the thinking of Sigmund Freud, the famous Austrian psychoanalyst who in 1900 published a seminal essay, *The Interpretation of Dreams.* But is the reader who feels that Emily Brontë's *Wuthering Heights* is dreamlike — who feels that Mary Shelley's *Frankenstein* is nightmarish — necessarily a Freudian literary critic? To some extent the answer has to be yes. We are all Freudians, really, whether or not we have read a single work by Freud. At one time or another, most of us have referred to ego, libido, complexes, unconscious desires, and sexual repression. The premises of Freud's thought have changed the way the Western world thinks about itself. Psychoanalytic criticism has influenced the teachers our teachers studied with, the works of scholarship and criticism they read, and the critical and creative writers *we* read as well.

What Freud did was develop a language that described, a model that explained, a theory that encompassed human psychology. Many of the elements of psychology he sought to describe and explain are present in the literary works of various ages and cultures, from Sophocles' *Oedipus Rex* to Shakespeare's *Hamlet* to works being written in our own day. When the great novel of the twenty-first century is written, many of these same elements of psychology will probably inform its discourse as well. If, by understanding human psychology according to Freud, we can appreciate literature on a new level, then we should acquaint ourselves with his insights.

Freud's theories are either directly or indirectly concerned with the nature of the unconscious mind. Freud didn't invent the notion of the unconscious; others before him had suggested that even the supposedly "sane" human mind was conscious and rational only at times, and even then at possibly only one level. But Freud went further, suggesting that the powers motivating men and women are *mainly* and *normally* unconscious.

Freud, then, powerfully developed an old idea: that the human mind is essentially dual in nature. He called the predominantly passional, irrational, unknown, and unconscious part of the psyche the *id,* or "it." The *ego,* or "I," was his term for the predominantly rational, logical, orderly, conscious part. Another aspect of the psyche, which he called the *superego,* is really a projection of the ego. The superego almost seems to be outside of the self, making moral judgments, telling us to make sacrifices for good causes even though self-sacrifice may not be quite logical or rational. And, in a sense, the superego *is* "outside," since much of what it tells us to do or think we have learned from our parents, our schools, or our religious institutions.

What the ego and superego tell us *not* to do or think is repressed, forced into the unconscious mind. One of Freud's most important contributions to the study of the psyche, the theory of repression, goes something like this: much of what lies in the unconscious mind has been put there by consciousness, which acts as a censor, driving underground unconscious or conscious thoughts or instincts that it deems unacceptable. Censored materials often involve infantile sexual desires, Freud postulated. Repressed to an unconscious state, they emerge only in disguised forms: in dreams, in language (so-called Freudian slips), in creative activity that may produce art (including literature), and in neurotic behavior.

According to Freud, all of us have repressed wishes and fears; we all have dreams in which repressed feelings and memories emerge disguised, and thus we are all potential candidates for dream analysis. One of the unconscious desires most commonly repressed is the childhood wish to displace the parent of our own sex and take his or her place in the affections of the parent of the opposite sex. This desire really involves a number of different but related wishes and fears. (A boy — and it should be remarked in passing that Freud here concerns himself mainly with the male — may fear that his father will castrate him, and he may wish that his mother would return to nursing him.) Freud referred to the whole complex of feelings by the word *oedipal,* naming the complex after the Greek tragic hero Oedipus, who unwittingly killed his father and married his mother.

Why are oedipal wishes and fears repressed by the conscious side of the mind? And what happens to them after they have been censored? As Roy P. Basler puts it in *Sex, Symbolism, and Psychology in Literature* (1975), "from the beginning of recorded history such wishes have been restrained by the most powerful religious and social taboos, and as a result have come to be regarded as 'unnatural,'" even though "Freud found that such wishes are more or less characteristic of normal human development":

> In dreams, particularly, Freud found ample evidence that such wishes persisted. . . . Hence he conceived that natural urges, when identified as "wrong," may be repressed but not obliterated. . . . In the unconscious, these urges take on symbolic garb, regarded as nonsense by the waking mind that does not recognize their significance. (14)

Freud's belief in the significance of dreams, of course, was no more original than his belief that there is an unconscious side to the psyche. Again, it was the extent to which he developed a theory of how dreams work — and the extent to which that theory helped him, by analogy, to understand far more than just dreams — that made him unusual, important, and influential beyond the perimeters of medical schools and psychiatrists' offices.

The psychoanalytic approach to literature not only rests on the theories of Freud; it may even be said to have *begun* with Freud, who was interested in writers, especially those who relied heavily on symbols. Such writers regularly cloak or mystify ideas in figures that make sense only when interpreted, much as the unconscious mind of a neurotic disguises secret thoughts in dream stories or bizarre actions that need to be interpreted by an analyst. Freud's interest in literary artists led him to make some unfortunate generalizations about creativity; for example, in the twenty-third lecture in *Introductory Lectures on Psycho-Analysis* (1922), he defined the artist as "one urged on by instinctive needs that are too clamorous" (314). But it also led him to write creative literary criticism of his own, including an influential essay on "The Relation of a Poet to Daydreaming" (1908) and "The Uncanny" (1919), a provocative psychoanalytic reading of E. T. A. Hoffman's supernatural tale "The Sandman."

Freud's application of psychoanalytic theory to literature quickly caught on. In 1909, only a year after Freud had published "The Relation of a Poet to Daydreaming," the psychoanalyst Otto Rank published *The Myth of the Birth of the Hero*. In that work, Rank subscribes to the notion that the artist turns a powerful, secret wish into a literary fantasy, and he uses Freud's notion about the "oedipal" complex to explain why the popular stories of so many heroes in literature are so similar. A year after Rank had published his psychoanalytic account of heroic texts, Ernest Jones, Freud's student and eventual biographer, turned his attention to a tragic text: Shakespeare's *Hamlet*. In an essay first published in the *American Journal of Psychology,* Jones, like Rank, makes use of the oedipal concept: he suggests that Hamlet is a victim of strong feelings toward his mother, the queen.

Between 1909 and 1949, numerous other critics decided that psychological and psychoanalytic theory could assist in the understanding of literature. I. A. Richards, Kenneth Burke, and Edmund Wilson were among the most influential to become interested in the new approach. Not all of the early critics were committed to the approach; neither were all of them Freudians. Some followed Alfred Adler, who believed that writers wrote out of inferiority complexes, and others applied the ideas of Carl Gustav Jung, who had broken with Freud over Freud's emphasis on sex and who had developed a theory of the *collective* unconscious. According to Jungian theory, a great work of literature is not a disguised expression of its author's personal, repressed wishes; rather, it is a manifestation of desires once held by the whole human race but now repressed because of the advent of civilization.

It is important to point out that among those who relied on Freud's models were a number of critics who were poets and novelists as well. Conrad Aiken wrote a Freudian study of American literature, and poets such as Robert Graves and W. H. Auden applied Freudian insights when writing critical prose. William Faulkner, Henry James, James Joyce, D. H. Lawrence, Marcel Proust, and Toni Morrison are only a few of the novelists who have either written criticism influenced by Freud or who have written novels that conceive of character, conflict, and creative writing itself in Freudian terms. The poet H. D. (Hilda Doolittle) was actually a patient of Freud's and provided an account of her analysis in her book *Tribute to Freud.* By giving Freudian theory credibility among students of literature that only they could bestow, such writers helped to endow earlier psychoanalytic criticism with a largely Freudian orientation that has begun to be challenged only in the last two decades.

The willingness, even eagerness, of writers to use Freudian models in producing literature and criticism of their own consummated a relationship that, to Freud and other pioneering psychoanalytic theorists, had seemed fated from the beginning; after all, therapy involves the close analysis of language. René Wellek and Austin Warren included "psychological" criticism as one of the five "extrinsic" approaches to literature described in their influential book *Theory of Literature* (1942). Psychological criticism, they suggest, typically attempts to do at least one of the following: provide a psychological study of an individual writer; explore the nature of the creative process; generalize about "types and laws present within works of literature"; or theorize about the psychological "effects of literature upon its readers" (81). Entire books on psychoanalytic criticism began to appear, such as Frederick J. Hoffman's *Freudianism and the Literary Mind* (1945).

Probably because of Freud's characterization of the creative mind as "clamorous" if not ill, psychoanalytic criticism written before 1950 tended to psychoanalyze the individual author. Poems were read as fantasies that allowed authors to indulge repressed wishes, to protect themselves from deep-seated anxieties, or both. A perfect example of author analysis would be Marie Bonaparte's 1933 study of Edgar Allan Poe. Bonaparte found Poe to be so fixated on his mother that his repressed longing emerges in his stories in images such as the white spot on a black cat's breast, said to represent mother's milk.

A later generation of psychoanalytic critics often paused to analyze the characters in novels and plays before proceeding to their authors. But not for long, since characters, both evil and good, tended to be seen by these critics as the author's potential selves, or projections of various repressed aspects of his or her psyche. For instance, in *A Psychoanalytic Study of the Double in Literature* (1970), Robert Rogers begins with the view that human beings are double or multiple in nature. Using this assumption, along with the psychoanalytic concept of "dissociation" (best known by its result, the dual or multiple personality), Rogers concludes that writers reveal instinctual or repressed selves in their books, often without realizing that they have done so.

In the view of critics attempting to arrive at more psychological insights into an author than biographical materials can provide, a work of literature is a fantasy or a dream — or at least so analogous to daydream or dream that Freudian analysis can help explain the nature of the mind that produced it. The author's purpose in writing is to gratify secretly some forbidden wish, in particular an infantile wish or desire that has been repressed into the unconscious mind. To discover what the wish is, the psychoanalytic critic employs many of the terms and procedures developed by Freud to analyze dreams.

The literal surface of a work is sometimes spoken of as its "manifest content" and treated as a "manifest dream" or "dream story" would be treated by a Freudian analyst. Just as the analyst tries to figure out the "dream thought" behind the dream story — that is, the latent or hidden content of the manifest dream — so the psychoanalytic literary critic tries to expose the latent, underlying content of a work. Freud used the words *condensation* and *displacement* to explain two of the mental processes whereby the mind disguises its wishes and fears in dream stories. In condensation, several thoughts or persons may be condensed into a single manifestation or image in a dream story; in displacement, an anxiety, a wish, or a person may be displaced onto the image of another, with which or whom it is loosely connected through a string of associations that only an analyst can untangle. Psychoanalytic critics treat metaphors as if they were dream condensations; they treat metonyms — figures of speech based on extremely loose, arbitrary associations — as if they were dream displacements. Thus figurative literary language in general is treated as something that evolves as the writer's conscious mind resists what the unconscious tells it to picture or describe. A symbol is, in Daniel Weiss's words, "a meaningful concealment of truth as the truth promises to emerge as some frightening or forbidden idea" (20).

In a 1970 article entitled "The 'Unconscious' of Literature," Norman Holland, a literary critic trained in psychoanalysis, succinctly sums up the attitudes held by critics who would psychoanalyze authors, but without quite saying that it is the *author* that is being analyzed by the psychoanalytic critic. "When one looks at a poem psychoanalytically," he writes, "one considers it as though it were a dream or as though some ideal patient [were speaking] from the couch in iambic pentameter." One "looks for the general level or levels of fantasy associated with the language. By level I mean the familiar stages of childhood development — oral [when desires for nourishment and infantile sexual desires overlap], anal [when infants receive their primary pleasure from defecation], urethral [when urinary functions are the locus of sexual pleasure], phallic [when the penis or, in girls, some penis substitute is of primary interest], oedipal." Holland continues by analyzing not Robert Frost but Frost's poem "Mending Wall" as a specifically oral fantasy that is not unique to its author. "Mending Wall" is "about breaking down the wall which marks the separated or individuated self so as to return to a state of closeness to some Other"— including and perhaps essentially the nursing mother ("'Unconscious'" 136, 139).

While not denying the idea that the unconscious plays a role in creativity, psychoanalytic critics such as Holland began to focus more on the ways in which authors create works that appeal to *our* repressed wishes and fantasies. Consequently, they shifted their focus away from the psyche of the author and toward the psychology of the reader and the text. Holland's theories, which have concerned themselves more with the reader than with the text, have helped to establish another school of critical theory: reader-response criticism. Elizabeth Wright explains Holland's brand of modern psychoanalytic criticism in this way: "What draws us as readers to a text is the secret expression of what we desire to hear, much as we protest we do not. The disguise must be good enough to fool the censor into thinking that the text is respectable, but bad enough to allow the unconscious to glimpse the unrespectable" (117).

Holland is one of dozens of critics who have revised Freud significantly in the process of revitalizing psychoanalytic criticism. Another such critic is R. D. Laing, whose controversial and often poetical writings about personality, repression, masks, and the double or "schizoid" self have (re)blurred the boundary between creative writing and psychoanalytic discourse. Yet another is D. W. Winnicott, an "object relations" theorist who has had a significant impact on literary criticism. Critics influenced by Winnicott and his school have questioned the tendency to see reader/text as an either/or construct; instead, they have seen reader and text (or audience and play) in terms of a *relationship* taking place in what Winnicott calls a "transitional" or "potential" space — space in which binary terms such as *real* and *illusory, objective* and *subjective,* have little or no meaning.

Psychoanalytic theorists influenced by Winnicott see the transitional or potential reader/text (or audience/play) space as being *like* the space entered into by psychoanalyst and patient. More important, they also see it as being similar to the space between mother and infant: a space characterized by trust in which categorizing terms such as *knowing* and *feeling* mix and merge and have little meaning apart from one another.

Whereas Freud saw the mother-son relationship in terms of the son and his repressed oedipal complex (and saw the analyst-patient relationship in terms of the patient and the repressed "truth" that the analyst could scientifically extract), object-relations analysts see both relationships as *dyadic* — that is, as being dynamic in both directions. Consequently, they don't depersonalize analysis or their analyses. It is hardly surprising, therefore, that contemporary literary critics who apply object-relations theory to the texts they discuss don't depersonalize critics or categorize their interpretations as "truthful," at least not in any objective or scientific sense. In the view of such critics, interpretations are made of language — itself a transitional object — and are themselves the mediating terms or transitional objects of a relationship.

Like critics of the Winnicottian school, the French structuralist theorist Jacques Lacan focused on language and language-related issues. He treated the unconscious *as* a language and, consequently, viewed the dream not as Freud did (that is, as a form and symptom of repression) but rather as a form of discourse. Thus we may study dreams psychoanalytically to learn about literature, even as we may study literature to learn more about the unconscious. In Lacan's seminar on Poe's "The Purloined Letter," a pattern of repetition like that used by psychoanalysts in their analyses is used to arrive at a reading of the story. According to Wright, "the new psychoanalytic structural approach to literature" employs "analogies from psychoanalysis . . . to explain the workings of the text as distinct from the workings of a particular author's, character's, or even reader's mind" (125).

Lacan, however, did far more than extend Freud's theory of dreams, literature, and the interpretation of both. More significantly, he took Freud's whole theory of psyche and gender and added to it a crucial third term — that of language. In the process, he both used and significantly developed Freud's ideas about the oedipal stage and complex.

Lacan pointed out that the pre-oedipal stage, in which the child at first does not even recognize its independence from its mother, is also a pre*verbal* stage, one in which the child communicates without the medium of language, or — if we insist on calling the child's communications a language — in a language that can only be called *literal*. ("Coos," certainly, cannot be said to be figurative or symbolic.) Then, while still in the pre-oedipal stage, the child enters the *mirror* stage.

During the mirror period, the child comes to view itself and its mother, later other people as well, *as* independent selves. This is the stage in which the child is first able to fear the aggressions of another, to desire what is recognizably beyond the self (initially the mother), and, finally, to want to compete with another for the same desired object. This is also the stage at which the child first becomes able to feel sympathy with another being who is being hurt by a third, to cry when another cries. All of these developments, of course, involve projecting beyond the self and, by extension, constructing one's own self (or "ego" or "I") as others view one — that is, as *another*. Such constructions, according to Lacan, are just that: constructs, products, artifacts — fictions of coherence that in fact hide what Lacan called the "absence" or "lack" of being.

The mirror stage, which Lacan also referred to as the *imaginary* stage, is fairly quickly succeeded by the oedipal stage. As in Freud, this stage begins when the child, having come to view itself as self and the father and mother as separate selves, perceives gender and gender differences between its parents and between itself and one of its parents. For boys, gender awareness involves another, more powerful recognition, for the recognition of the father's phallus as the mark of his difference from the mother involves, at the same time, the recognition that his older and more powerful father is also his rival. That, in turn, leads to the understanding that what once seemed wholly his and even indistinguishable from himself is in fact someone else's: something properly desired only at a distance and in the form of socially acceptable *substitutes*.

The fact that the oedipal stage roughly coincides with the entry of the child into language is extremely important for Lacan. For the linguistic order is essentially a figurative or "Symbolic" order; words are not the things they stand for but are, rather stand-ins or substitutes for those things. Hence boys, who in the most critical period of their development have had to submit to what Lacan called the "Law of the Father"— a law that prohibits direct desire for and communicative intimacy with what has been the boy's whole world — enter more easily into the realm of language and the Symbolic order than do girls, who have never really had to renounce that which once seemed continuous with the self: the mother. The gap that has been opened up for boys, which includes the gap between signs and what they substitute — the gap marked by the phallus and encoded with the boy's sense of his maleness — has not opened up for girls, or has not opened up in the same way, to the same degree.

For Lacan, the father need not be present to trigger the oedipal stage; nor does his phallus have to be seen to catalyze the boy's (easier) transition into the Symbolic order. Rather, Lacan argued, a child's recognition of its gender is intricately tied up with a growing recognition of the system of names and naming, part of the larger system of substitutions we call language. A child has little doubt about who its mother is, but who is its father, and how would one know? The father's claim rests on the mother's *word* that he is in fact the father; the father's relationship to the child is thus established through language and a system of marriage and kinship — names — that in turn is basic to rules of everything from property to law. The name of the father (*nom du père*, which in French sounds like *non du père*) involves, in a sense, nothing of the father — nothing, that is, except his word or name.

Lacan's development of Freud has had several important results. First, his sexist-seeming association of maleness with the Symbolic order, together with his claim that women cannot therefore enter easily into the order, has prompted feminists not to reject his theory out of hand but, rather, to look more closely at the relation between language and gender, language and women's inequality. Some feminists have gone so far as to suggest that the social and political relationships between male and female will not be fundamentally altered until language itself has been radically changed. (That change might begin dialectically, with the development of some kind of "feminine language" grounded in the presymbolic, literal-to-imaginary communication between mother and child.)

Second, Lacan's theory has proved of interest to deconstructors and other poststructuralists, in part because it holds that the ego (which in Freud's view is as necessary as it is natural) is a product or construct.

The ego-artifact, produced during the mirror stage, *seems* at once unified, consistent, and organized around a determinate center. But the unified self, or ego, is a fiction, according to Lacan. The yoking together of fragments and destructively dissimilar elements takes its psychic toll, and it is the job of the Lacanian psychoanalyst to "deconstruct," as it were, the ego, to show its continuities to be contradictions as well.

In the essay that follows, Dennis Foster explains "the ambivalent experience of desiring something that will terrify us" by invoking Freud's theory that we are "fundamentally divided on a psychic level"— that is to say, that we contain an adult, rational self and another self, a "bad child" we bury deep in the unconscious (p. 483 in this volume). According to Freud, the "bluntly mechanical oral impulse"— the "enjoyments of mouthing, ingesting, incorporating, and destroying that are satisfied by the oral impulse"— is one of the primitive desires the developing child represses or, at least, restrains as it divides itself off from "the other person, the Not-me," the "other child, who becomes the wild, perverse, desiring, violent creature of our nightmares" (p. 483). Stoker's *Dracula,* Foster goes on to argue, "embodies . . . this most primitive of our vital drives" (p. 484), the desire to suck, eat, consume, consume utterly — even inappropriately — which in its most extreme form involves the appetite to eat (and destroy by eating) human flesh.

As figured in Dracula, this horrible hunger that we would psychically repress turns out to be an infectious, communicable appetite. First Lucy, then Mina, is subject to "vampiric conversion" thanks to the carelessness of four suitors: Dr. Seward, Quincey Morris, Arthur Holmwood, and Jonathan Harker — men who thus become, in Foster's view, "accomplices of Dracula." These otherwise "upright, honorable, defenders of womanhood" become accomplices, Foster suggests, because they fear the sexual implications of marriage *and* because they themselves, at some level, sympathize with the vampire's insatiable oral desire. (Harker descriptively dwells on the food he eats in the Count's castle, and Dr. Seward lavishes journal space on R. M. Renfield, a patient who eats a bird that ate spiders that ate flies in order to "absorb as many lives as he can.")

The women in the novel, too, experience primitive oral desires. In the scene in which Dracula holds Mina's mouth to his chest, urging her to "drink from an open wound," Mina is both the "sucking child," the "child drinking at her mother's breast," and "a vampire: in drinking

Dracula's blood, she enjoys the pleasure normally reserved for the vampire" (p. 489). Lucy, after being bitten, preys exclusively on children, who are drawn to her by their hunger for maternal nourishment and then consumed by her hunger to be fed.

Having suggested that the men are vampiric accomplices out of their aversion to heterosexual experience, Foster subsequently "expose[s] the link between the oral and erotic" (p. 488). We begin life experiencing the erotic orally; over time, other experiences supplement and substitute for sucking and eating, after which point mature sexuality itself may also be sublimated, i.e., by desires for money, success, or some type of moral purity. Dracula, by contrast, is stuck at an early stage of development where the desire for sex — indeed, all desire — is undifferentiated from the desire for nourishment. And he is childlike in another sense, namely, that he does not know death. Children only think they are immortal: eventually they come to know that they will die and consequently become more careful in what they desire and do. Vampires unlearn their mortality and regain, though at no little cost, the voracious "rage for pleasure that we see in the child" (p. 492). The attraction of vampires, as Foster points out, is their negation of death; "Stoker's term, 'Un-Dead,' suggests that desire to be freed from the limits of human satisfaction, yet not to be dead" (p. 492). Of course, in being freed from the limits of human satisfaction we would be free to experience many things — many of them seductive — of which we have learned to be afraid.

We would even be free to desire fear itself. In making this point, Foster implicitly takes us back to his original remark about the "ambivalent experience of desiring something that will terrify us" (p. 483). When we see horror movies like *Scream*, we are afraid the teenage girl will open a door that we would be disappointed if she didn't open. The pleasure of reading *Dracula* is a similar pleasure, one that allows us, momentarily, the freedom to desire, experience, and enjoy experiencing the forbidden or taboo.

To summarize all of Foster's points would be to spoil the pleasure afforded by his carefully constructed argument. Suffice it to say two things in conclusion. One: that Foster views *Dracula* as a "morality tale that . . . ultimately grants us access to the hunger of Dracula" (p. 498). (Thus, it not only carries us across our own psychic divide to where we can flirt with forbidden interests and urges but also is, itself, "fundamentally divided," containing a conventionally moral voice and another, subliminal one analogous to "the other person" or "Not-me" that each of us contains and sometimes hears from afar.) Two: that Foster's essay impressively exemplifies the best of contemporary psychoanalytic criticism. Informed by Lacan, it is grounded in Freud, using not only his ideas about psychic division but also those involving the oral (and anal) stage, the death instinct, and the sublimation of primitive desire entailed by development and acculturation — submission to what Lacan has called the Law of the Father.

Ross C Murfin

PSYCHOANALYTIC CRITICISM:
A SELECTED BIBLIOGRAPHY

Some Short Introductions to Psychological and Psychoanalytic Theory

Holland, Norman. "The 'Unconscious' of Literature: The Psychoanalytic Approach." *Contemporary Criticism*. Ed. Malcolm Bradbury and David Palmer. Stratford-Upon-Avon Studies 12. New York: St. Martin's, 1971. 131–53.

Natoli, Joseph, and Frederik L. Rusch, comps. *Psychocriticism: An Annotated Bibliography*. Westport: Greenwood, 1984.

Scott, Wilbur. *Five Approaches to Literary Criticism*. London: Collier-Macmillan, 1962. See the essays by Burke and Gorer as well as Scott's introduction to the section "The Psychological Approach: Literature in the Light of Psychological Theory."

Wellek, Rene, and Austin Warren. *Theory of Literature*. New York: Harcourt, 1942. See the chapter "Literature and Psychology" in pt. 3, "The Extrinsic Approach to the Study of Literature."

Wright, Elizabeth. "Modern Psychoanalytic Criticism." *Modern Literary Theory: A Comparative Introduction*. Ed. Ann Jefferson and David Robey. Totowa: Barnes, 1982. 113–33.

Freud, Lacan, and Their Influence

Althusser, Louis. *Writings on Psychoanalysis: Freud and Lacan*. Ed. Olivier Corpet and Francois Matheron. Trans. Jeffrey Mehlman. New York: Columbia UP, 1996.

Basler, Roy P. *Sex, Symbolism, and Psychology in Literature*. New York: Octagon, 1975. See especially 13–19.

Clement, Catherine. *The Lives and Legends of Jacques Lacan*. Trans. Arthur Goldhammer. New York: Columbia UP, 1983.

Copjec, Joan. *Read My Desire: Lacan Against the Historicists.* Cambridge: MIT P, 1994.

Feldstein, Richard, Bruce Fink, and Maire Jaanus, eds. *Reading Seminar XI: Lacan's Four Fundamental Concepts of Psychoanalysis.* Albany: State U of New York P, 1995.

Fink, Bruce. *The Lacanian Subject: Between Language and Jouissance.* Princeton: Princeton UP, 1995.

Freud, Sigmund. *Introductory Lectures on Psycho-Analysis.* Trans. Joan Riviere. London: Allen, 1922.

Hill, Philip. *Lacan For Beginners.* New York: Writers and Readers, 1997.

Lacan, Jacques. *Ecrits: A Selection.* Trans. Alan Sheridan. New York: Norton, 1977.

———. *The Ego in Freud's Theory and in the Technique of Psychoanalysis 1954–1955.* Ed. Jacques-Alain Miller. Trans. Sylvana Tomaselli. The Seminar of Jacques Lacan Book II. New York: Norton, 1988.

———. *The Ethics of Psychoanalysis: 1959–1960.* Ed. Jacques-Alain Miller. Trans. Dennis Porter. The Seminar of Jacques Lacan Book VII. New York: Norton, 1992.

———. *Feminine Sexuality: Lacan and the ecole freudienne.* Ed. Juliet Mitchell and Jacqueline Rose. Trans. Rose. New York: Norton, 1982.

———. *The Four Fundamental Concepts of Psychoanalysis.* Trans. Alan Sheridan. London: Penguin, 1980.

———. *Freud's Papers on Technique 1953–1954.* Ed. Jacques-Alain Miller. Trans. John Forrester. The Seminar of Jacques Lacan Book I. New York: Norton, 1988.

———. *On Feminine Sexuality: The Limits of Love and Knowledge.* Ed. Jacques-Alain Miller. Trans. Bruce Fink. The Seminar of Jacques Lacan Book XX: Encore 1972–1973. New York: Norton, 1998.

Lee, Jonathan Scott. *Jacques Lacan.* Boston: Twayne, 1990.

Ragland-Sullivan, Ellie. *Essays on the Pleasures of Death: From Freud to Lacan.* New York: Routledge, 1995.

Roudinesco, Elisabeth. *Jacques Lacan.* Trans. Barbara Bray. New York: Columbia UP, 1997.

Schneiderman, Stuart. *Jacques Lacan: The Death of an Intellectual Hero.* Cambridge: Harvard UP, 1983.

Zizek, Slavoj. *Enjoy Your Symptom: Jacques Lacan in Hollywood and Out.* New York: Routledge, 1992.

————. *The Metastases of Enjoyment: Six Essays on Woman and Causality.* New York: Verso, 1994.

————. *The Sublime Object of Ideology.* New York: Verso, 1989.

Psychoanalysis, Feminism, and Literature

Barr, Marleen S., and Richard Feldstein. *Discontented Discourses: Feminism/Textual Intervention/Psychoanalysis.* Urbana: U of Illinois P, 1989.

Benjamin, Jessica. *The Bonds of Love: Psychoanalysis, Feminism and the Problem of Domination.* New York: Pantheon, 1988.

Bernheimer, Charles, and Claire Kahane, eds. *In Dora's Case: Freud-Hysteria-Feminism.* New York: Columbia UP, 1985.

de Lauretis, Teresa. *The Practice of Love: Lesbian Sexuality and Perverse Desire.* Bloomington: Indiana UP, 1994.

Elliott, Patricia. *From Mastery to Analysis: Theories of Gender in Psychoanalytic Criticism.* Ithaca: Cornell UP, 1991.

Felman, Shoshana. *What Does a Woman Want? Reading and Sexual Difference.* Baltimore: Johns Hopkins UP, 1993.

Gallop, Jane. *The Daughter's Seduction: Feminism and Psychoanalysis.* Ithaca: Cornell UP, 1982.

————. *Thinking Through the Body.* New York: Columbia UP, 1988.

Garner, Shirley Nelson, Claire Kahane, and Madelon Sprengnether. *The (M)other Tongue: Essays in Feminist Psychoanalytic Interpretation.* Ithaca: Cornell UP, 1985.

Grosz, Elizabeth. *Jacques Lacan: A Feminist Introduction.* New York: Routledge, 1990.

Irigaray, Luce. *This Sex Which Is Not One.* Trans. Catherine Porter. Ithaca: Cornell UP, 1985.

————. *Speculum of the Other Woman.* Trans. Gillian C. Gill. Ithaca: Cornell UP, 1985.

Jacobus, Mary. "Is There a Woman in This Text?" *New Literary History* 14 (1982): 117–41.

Kristeva, Julia. *The Kristeva Reader.* Ed. Toril Moi. New York: Columbia UP, 1986. See especially the selection from *Revolution in Poetic Language* 89–136.

MacCannell, Juliet Flower. *The Regime of the Brother: After the Patriarchy.* New York: Routledge, 1991.

Mitchell, Juliet. *Psychoanalysis and Feminism.* New York: Random, 1974.

Mitchell, Juliet, and Jacqueline Rose, Introduction I and Introduction II. Lacan, *Feminine Sexuality: Jacques Lacan and the ecole freudienne* 1–26, 27–57.

Rose, Jacqueline. *Sexuality in the Field of Vision.* New York: Verso, 1986.

Sprengnether, Madelon. *The Spectral Mother: Freud, Feminism, and Psychoanalysis.* Ithaca: Cornell UP, 1990.

Psychological and Psychoanalytic Studies of Literature, Culture, and the Arts

Apollon, Willy, and Richard Feldstein, eds. *Lacan. Politics, Aesthetics.* Albany: State U of New York P, 1996.

Bersani, Leo. *Baudelaire and Freud.* Berkeley: U of California P, 1977.

———. *The Freudian Body: Psychoanalysis and Art.* New York: Columbia UP, 1986.

Bettelheim, Bruno. *The Uses of Enchantment: The Meaning and Importance of Fairy Tales.* New York: Knopf, 1976.

Bracher, Mark. *Lacan, Discourse, and Social Change: A Psychoanalytic Cultural Criticism.* Ithaca: Cornell UP, 1993.

Grosz, Elizabeth. *Space, Time, and Perversion: Essays on the Politics of Bodies.* New York: Routledge, 1995.

Hartman, Geoffrey, ed. *Psychoanalysis and the Question of the Text.* Baltimore: Johns Hopkins UP, 1978.

Hertz, Neil. *The End of the Line: Essays on Psychoanalysis and the Sublime.* New York: Columbia UP, 1985.

Jacobus, Mary. *First Things: The Maternal Imaginary in Literature, Art, and Psychoanalysis.* New York: Routledge, 1995.

Krauss, Rosalind. *The Optical Unconscious.* Cambridge: MIT P, 1994.

Poizat, Michel. *The Angel's Cry: Beyond the Pleasure Principle in Opera.* Trans. Arthur Denner. Ithaca: Cornell UP, 1992.

Salecl, Renata, and Slavoj Zizek, eds. *Gaze and Voice as Love Objects.* Durham: Duke UP, 1996.

Silverman, Kaja. *The Threshold of the Visible World.* New York: Routledge, 1996.

Lacanian Psychoanalytic Studies of Literature

Booker, M. Keith. "Notes Toward a Lacanian Reading of Wallace Stevens." *Journal of Modern Literature* 16 (1990): 493–509.

Davis, Robert Con, ed. *The Fictional Father: Lacanian Readings of the Text*. Amherst: U of Massachusetts P, 1981.

———. *Lacan and Narration: The Psychoanalytic Difference in Narrative Theory*. Baltimore: Johns Hopkins UP, 1984.

Devlin, Kim. "Castration and Its Discontents: A Lacanian Approach to *Ulysses*." *James Joyce Quarterly* 29 (1991): 117–44.

Felman, Shoshana, ed. *Literature and Psychoanalysis: The Question of Reading: Otherwise*. Baltimore: Johns Hopkins UP, 1982. Includes Lacan's seminar on Shakespeare's *Hamlet*.

Homans, Margaret. *Bearing the Word: Language and Female Experience in Nineteenth-Century Women's Writing*. Chicago: U of Chicago P, 1986.

Lacan, Jacques. "The Essence of Tragedy: A Commentary on Sophocles's *Antigone*." Lacan, *The Ethics of Psychoanalysis* 243–87.

Mellard, James M. *Using Lacan, Reading Fiction*. Urbana: U of Illinois P, 1991.

Miller, David Lee. "Writing the Specular Son: Jonson, Freud, Lacan, and the (K)not of Masculinity." *Desire in the Renaissance: Psychoanalysis and Literature*. Ed. Valeria Finucci and Regina Schwartz. Princeton: Princeton UP, 1994. 233–60.

Muller, John P., and William J. Richardson, eds. *The Purloined Poe: Lacan, Derrida. and Psychoanalytic Reading*. Baltimore: Johns Hopkins UP, 1988. Includes Lacan's seminar on Poe's "The Purloined Letter."

Netto, Jeffrey A. "Dickens with Kant and Sade." *Style* 29 (1995): 441–58.

Rapaport, Herman. *Between the Sign & the Gaze*. Ithaca: Cornell UP, 1994.

Schad, John. "'No One Dreams': Hopkins, Lacan, and the Unconscious." *Victorian Poetry* 32 (1994): 141–56.

Psychoanalytic Readings of *Dracula*

Bronfen, Elisabeth. "Hysteric and Obsessional Discourse: Responding to Death in *Dracula*." *Over Her Dead Body: Death, Femininity and the Aesthetic*. By Bronfen. New York: Routledge; Manchester, England: Manchester UP, 1992. 313–22.

Dundes, Alan. "The Vampire as Bloodthirsty Revenant: A Psychoanalytic Post Mortem." *The Vampire: A Casebook*. Ed. Dundes. Madison: U of Wisconsin P, 1998. 159–75.

Kahane, Claire. "The Gothic Mirror." *The (M)other Tongue: Essays in Feminist Psychoanalytic Interpretation*. Shirley Nelson Garner,

Claire Kahane, and Madelon Sprengnether, eds. Ithaca: Cornell UP, 1985. 334–51.

Rickels, Laurence A. *The Vampire Lectures.* Minneapolis: U of Minnesota P, 1999.

A PSYCHOANALYTIC PERSPECTIVE

DENNIS FOSTER

"The little children can be bitten": A Hunger for Dracula

We are all familiar with that moment of dreamlike suspension in movies when the monster, the killer, or some swarming, vital mass of birds, worms, or spiders waits somewhere just out of sight. The protagonist, who should know better, moves steadily, stupidly toward an encounter everyone else can see coming. "Don't, don't open that door," we scream, and yet how disappointed we would be if the victim turned away, leaving the nightmare behind the door. After all, for the audience, that encounter with the horrid thing is the life of the party, the difference between a good scare and another yawner: we want to experience the agonizing thrill of knowing the worst, even though our better selves would warn the victim. But oddly, the characters do not see what they are walking into. And their refusing to know what would spare them, keep them from the consuming horror, only stimulates our hunger for the event.

The ambivalent experience of desiring something that will terrify us can be understood psychoanalytically. At the heart of psychoanalysis is the claim that we are fundamentally divided on a psychic level. We become who we are — we take on our subjective identities — by denying, refusing, or negating the other person we might have been: the male or female we are not, the sibling we envy, the bad child who has all the fun. We become ourselves, good instead of bad. And considering the dangers of being bad, one could say we decide to live rather than die, although living comes at a great cost. Psychoanalysis then goes on to say something more troubling: the other person, the Not-me, does not die off, but lives on within our psyches, beyond the reach of the rational, reflective, articulate mind. We abandon that other child, who becomes the wild, perverse, desiring, violent creature of our nightmares.

It remains what cannot be spoken, but its reemergence constantly threatens our peace in the form, for example, of dreams, slips of the tongue, fantasies, and depression.

Sigmund Freud emerged on the Western scene at about the same moment as Bram Stoker's novel of the seductive, hungry force of darkness. On a trip to America, Freud made a claim that oddly evokes Dracula: "They don't realize we're bringing them the plague" (qtd. in *Ecrits* Lacan, 116). The story Freud tells, with its themes of violence, sexuality, and death, in which women and children figure shockingly as both heroes and victims, horrified many of his contemporaries even as it began to turn them into Freudians. He seems to threaten that after hearing his story, his audience will no longer live in a simple sunny world, a world like the one Lucy Westenra inhabited prior to her encounter with Dracula. Like Dracula, he sails out of the east bearing a cargo that will infect a population, arousing that unconscious other. The Enlightenment, the movement that replaced faith and obedience with reason and individual liberty, a movement to which Freud is indebted, may have opened a window to let in the sunshine of free rational enquiry, but it also produced a shadow. We knowers, as Friedrich Nietzsche called us, remain unknown to ourselves (149). We remain ignorant because the fruit of self-knowledge would be, as Nietzsche put it, "unpalatable": we prefer to think ourselves good and refuse evidence to the contrary. Freud provided us with the language to see ourselves as possessed by an other, uncanny self who stands behind us but casts no reflection in the mirror of consciousness. And yet, he knew that once he had taught us to look with his eyes, we would not be able to turn away from the missing image: we would forever want to know and not to know. We would hunger for that unpalatable fruit.

At the heart of *Dracula* is hunger, that blindly mechanical oral impulse that each of us discovers in the first days after birth.[1] In maturing, we go beyond that impulse into the more complex desires of civilized life, but we never transcend the simple, sometimes shameful enjoyments of mouthing, ingesting, incorporating, and destroying that are satisfied by the oral impulse. Think of how scrupulously parents police the oral habits of their children, repeatedly taking from them the parts of the world that they would inappropriately consume. The monster Dracula, I will argue, embodies the reemergence of this most primitive of our vital drives in an unaging form. The book *Dracula*, so

---

[1]This oral dimension has been often noted. For example, Maggie Kilgore comments on the prevalence of the oral phase in *Dracula* and other gothic tales. And Alan Dundes notes that the vampire's victim "regresses to an oral sadistic infantile level" (169).

deliberately presented as a moral tale where good defeats evil, allows us to revile the self-serving perversion of the vampire's hunger. Sustained by this stance of moral superiority, we repudiate the impulses we share with the monster and are allowed the guilt-free enjoyment of condemning and destroying the evil one. These are pleasures readers share with most of the characters.

To condemn, however, does not imply that the oral impulses various characters face will be overcome. Dracula's enemies, in fact, are surprisingly ineffective at stopping either Dracula or themselves from satisfying their appetites. No one reading *Dracula* can miss, for example, the obvious signs that Lucy Westenra receives nightly visits from the Count. A modern reader, knowing in the ways of vampires, immediately sees the symptoms: Lucy's pallor, her exhaustion, and those two fang-sized wounds on her neck. Her protectors see them as well, and they are all alarmed, particularly Van Helsing, who is full of vampire lore. Van Helsing even makes arrangements to protect Lucy from vampires, although without informing the others of the nature of her danger. He tells Dr. Seward, "You keep watch all night; see that she is well fed, and that nothing disturbs her" (p. 140 in this volume). Rather than telling him to keep vampires out of the room, he mentions only that she might be disturbed by hunger, which turns out, oddly, to be the problem. Of course, Dracula's appetite directly threatens her (which Van Helsing might have mentioned), but since her encounter with the vampire, she is infected by his hunger: she has "an appetite like a cormorant" (p. 124). The sleepwalking that had afflicted her since childhood turns her steps toward her meetings with Dracula. Van Helsing cryptically warns Seward, "If you leave her, and harm befall, you shall not sleep easy hereafter" (p. 140), which also alludes to the real, unspoken problem: in the hereafter, vampires do not rest but walk the nights, and if Dr. Seward is careless, he will become one of them, driven as they are by a hunger he can't yet name. Although Van Helsing may know what is going on, he seems unable to say it, as if he is trapped in metaphor and indirection, characteristic strategies of the unconscious.

Notice that on nights following Van Helsing's warning, Dr. Seward does leave Lucy alone, and Dracula comes to her repeatedly. In their inexperience, Dr. Seward and his friends might be excused for failing to deal properly with their first vampire attack. Even suspecting that Lucy is in danger, they don't move her to a safer place, but lay her out on her bed, asleep and vulnerable, as if laying a table. In their carelessness, the men become accomplices to Lucy's vampiric conversion. Subsequently, they make the same mistake with Mina. They leave her alone in

Dr. Seward's house even after Renfield's terrified pleas not to be left in the house overnight might have alerted them to the house's danger, and the presence of great bats at the windows might have reminded them of Lucy's experience. The next day they notice Mina's pallor, yet fail to link it to Lucy's identical symptoms, even though they are thinking of nothing but vampires. Van Helsing and his band of men, these upright, honorable, defenders of womanhood and other virtues, regularly, blindly submit their women to Dracula's kiss: we should ask, what do these men want?

We might begin by looking at what they do not want. As much as they all long to be married to Lucy or Mina, they manage to arrange things so that none of them actually risks having sex. Three of the men propose to Lucy (Quincey Morris, Dr. Seward, and Arthur Holmwood, soon to be Lord Godalming), and the two whom she rejects, Morris and Seward, seem thereafter to resign themselves to celibacy. Holmwood wins the lady, but despite the fact that Lucy is eager to be married, he is slow to wed and Dracula takes her first. The fourth lover, Jonathan Harker, seems to be deeply in love with Mina, but he is so incapacitated by his visit to Dracula's castle that, when he does marry her, simply staying alive takes all his energy. And soon thereafter, Mina becomes vampiric and too dangerous even to kiss. Unless you want to conclude that these men all suffer from bad timing, you might think that they do not want sex with these women. Or if they do, some other desire or fear stands in the way of their acting effectively.

The first several chapters of the book do, however, give us an indication of what interests Mina's fiancé, Jonathan Harker. As he makes his way to Dracula's castle, he writes an account of his travels, including with surprising detail the meals he eats. In the first two pages of the book, he writes two memoranda to himself to get the recipe for a tasty dish. He tells us that "there are many odd things" to write about, but among the exotic curiosities of Transylvania, he makes room to "put down my dinner exactly," a horrible meal with meat suitable only for cats and with a wine merely "not disagreeable" (p. 31). And when he eats well at Dracula's castle, he writes that he had an "excellent roast chicken. This, with some cheese and a salad and a bottle of old Tokay" (p. 42). The wine was improving: his food is important to him. Harker continues to discuss eating arrangements in some detail while he stays in the castle, though his eating is marked by its contrast to Dracula's apparent abstinence. Once the action returns to England, meals are less prominent in the characters' accounts of their own activities (although nothing is ever done without breakfast, a meal that is mentioned twenty-eight times in the book), but Dr. Seward's journal returns frequently to the eating habits of Renfield. Rather than eating roast chickens, Renfield consumes flies and spiders intending, he says, to "absorb as many lives as he can" (p. 92); this disgusting habit appears to Dr. Seward unrelated to his own consumption of fish, flesh, and fowl. Eating is on everyone's mind, but of course eating is the central activity of the book: Dracula intends to feed on the oblivious population of London. Whatever other desires the vampire hunters have, then, they share with Dracula a preference for eating when it comes to carnal pleasures, for the oral over the genital.

Oral pleasures are among our first, combining the vital necessity of eating with the pleasing activity of sucking. Freud, commenting on this pleasure, writes: "No one who has seen a baby sinking back satiated from the breast and falling asleep with flushed cheeks and a blissful smile can escape the reflection that this picture persists as a prototype of the expression of sexual satisfaction in later life" (*Three Essays,* 182). The infant's intermittent happiness in being a consumer of a mother's breast (or so it must seem to the child who has never actually seen milk) must be left behind as one grows, as must most of the behaviors of childhood. Psychoanalysis describes in varying ways the processes by which infancy's most intense and reliable sources of satisfaction are displaced to other objects, people, practices: we take up toys, jobs, and lovers throughout life, hoping for happiness. But bliss does not come, not in toys, in work, nor in the sadly fickle satisfactions of sex. In large part because sex does not put an end to desire, the energy behind sexual desire becomes the engine for work, art, conquest, in short, for civilization.[2] Still, we imagine that once upon a time we were really happy, and that someday we will be really happy again. Although we have lost the paradise of childhood (a childhood more fantasy than reality), we accept loss as the price we pay to become productive (and reproductive) members of society. Psychoanalysis argues, however, that the dream of such early pleasures continues to haunt us, fixating some of us on a real or imagined loss of something from childhood. Vampires may express that haunting.

Consider the case of Lucy following her first death. Having moved from sleepwalking fiancé to night-walking undead, Lucy goes out for nightly feedings and preys exclusively on young children whose common speech deficiency identifies her as the "bloofer" lady. Whether

[2]Freud writes at length about the combination of accomplishment and unhappiness that characterizes civilization in *Civilization and Its Discontents* (1930).

beautiful or bloody, the bloofer lady does not frighten the children. Rather, they follow her willingly when she calls. One child bitten by Lucy tells the nurse that he wants to leave her care "to play with the 'bloofer lady'" (p. 204). The newspaper reports that a "favourite game of the little ones at present is luring each other away by wiles" (p. 188), with all of them eager to play the part of Lucy. She has something they aspire to: "even Ellen Terry could not be so winningly attractive as some of these grubby-faced little children pretend — and even imagine themselves — to be" (p. 188). The children, like the men before them, are drawn to this motherly, erotically charged woman, giving themselves to her while they also identify with her. Reciprocally, she, like the children, needs herself to be fed, but in this respect she is like all mothers: they are fed by their children, deriving comfort, meaning, companionship, and pleasure from them, even as they feed them. She is the source of both joy and horror to her child, since she is the one who can both give and take life. Lucy's vampiric relations with the children expose the link between the oral and the erotic in the era of childhood and the mutual haunting of mother and child.

The vampire's capacity for evoking these lost pleasures is displayed even more dramatically in Dracula, who, oddly, is the only male vampire in the book. Despite the representation of the Count as a masculine figure with a history of leadership and violence, he also appears in the ambiguous position of both mother and child. He is the master, the father of vampires, but as the one who brings new vampires into the world, he exhibits some distinctly motherly qualities. In one of the most explicitly sexualized scenes in *Dracula,* the Count is depicted holding Mina's mouth to his breast where she is compelled to drink from an open wound (p. 283). As in all of Dracula's encounters with his victims, Mina falls into a dreamy state in which she is unable to resist Dracula's advances. If this were an openly sexual advance, it would be clear what is happening: unable to take an active interest in sexual pleasure, horrified by sexual desire (his or hers) the women of nineteenth-century fiction finding themselves on the verge of a sexual encounter had the option of fainting and thereby escaping the guilt of active participation and pleasure.[3] Nevertheless, Mina's swoon should alert us to her experience of some fearful desire. In this scene, Mina is both the child drinking at her mother's breast and, in an inversion of the

[3]Heinrich von Kleist's *The Marquise of O* — (1809) provides a classic example of stunned unknowing. The Marquise, daughter of a painter and mother of two well-bred children, manages, following the fall of her castle, not to know with whom she had sex or even that she had sex at all.

expected vampiric embrace, a vampire: in drinking Dracula's blood, she enjoys the pleasure normally reserved for the vampire. We see in this image that the suckling child, though helpless to control her own limbs, is not passive in her pleasure. Rather, she actively seeks to consume the mother she depends on. And Dracula as mother, rather than simply destroying his victims, teaches the women he assaults to be as vigorous in their pursuit of enjoyment as men usually are. (Recall Lucy reaching out to Arthur: "My arms are hungry for you" [p. 219].) Mina, then, gets a literal taste of what it is like not only to be a vampire but to desire. It is no wonder she grows faint before the act and wipes her lips afterwards in telling the story "as though to cleanse them from pollution" (p. 288) — or is it the memory of a good meal?

As odd as it is to see Dracula in the position of a mother, it is even more curious to see Van Helsing comparing Dracula — the ancient, sophisticated warrior — to a child who is unable to grasp the more mature calculations of the men. Just as the men are despairing about the possibility of catching up with Dracula once he flees London, Van Helsing points out that "In some faculties of mind he has been, and is, only a child" (p. 300). Although Van Helsing's point is that Dracula's intellectual and moral immaturity gives the men an advantage over him, Van Helsing is also acknowledging a quality in Dracula that has contributed to the enduring appeal of this figure to readers. Insofar as he is a child, Dracula embodies something of the drives and compulsions that we adults have tamed and diminished. Dracula knows what he wants (unlike the men who can't quite figure out what to do with their women) and moves relentlessly toward it, incarnating some fundamental drive to enjoyment. Compare him, for example, to the child, the human animal at the breast, driven by organic bodily forces to possess the one thing it wants. In order to mature, that child must learn to substitute other objects for that fantastic breast in an increasing, flowering complexity that allows him to desire, say, a good grade on an essay or a hot stock for his portfolio.

Culture depends on this capacity for substitution, which Freud calls "sublimation." Dracula, however, appears to be arrested at an early (oral?) stage, unable, unwilling, or simply not needing to move ahead like an ordinary mortal into the tangled world of adult sexuality with its compromises and restrictions. Generally (for there are always exceptions), we each must choose either males or females to be our sexual partners, foregoing the other; we exclude from our desiring glance those parents, siblings, and children we otherwise love passionately; one lover is never quite enough, and yet many is too many; flesh in its weakness never matches the aspirations of spirit. In Dracula's case, however, things are otherwise. He still lives out enjoyments that Van Helsing and his crew no longer have such direct access to: he is the Peter Pan of the undead, one of the lost boys.[4] And as in *Peter Pan,* there is an ambivalence about the lost boys' condition: as fine as it may be to never have to grow up, never grow old, Wendy finds that they miss their mothers. Because they don't mature, they cannot find comfort in an age-appropriate woman's arms; neither do they ever have to shift their affection from a mother to what Freud, with his odd gift for phrasing, refers to as "strange and unloved women" (i.e. those not in their own families). In a similar moment of sympathetic understanding, Van Helsing pities Dracula for having fallen from noble maturity into his pathetic vampire state and would bring him back from "Never Never Land," even if it means putting a stake through his heart. But since Dracula never complains about being a vampire, living forever, and feeding on a fresh woman every night, we might see in Van Helsing's pity (as well as in Wendy's) the spice of envy and resentment.

If we look again at Harker's account of his trip to Castle Dracula in the first four chapters of the book, we might ask to what extent he is also reluctant to leave the pleasures of childhood. On the verge of wedded bliss, he leaves Mina and the sexual obligations that would follow from marriage for his Transylvanian adventure: "to explain the purchase of a London estate to a foreigner" (p. 40), a job even he finds suspiciously trivial. He has just passed his exams and should be a "full-blown solicitor," someone in a mature, responsible position, but in Dracula's castle he is reduced to a passive guest or prisoner whose only duty seems to be to chatter (yet another oral task) while Dracula waits on him. Like a parent speaking to a child, Dracula warns Harker not to venture out of his room at night, and when he disobeys, he encounters the three female vampires, at whose approach he, like Lucy and Mina, falls into a stupor of "languorous ecstacy" (p. 62) and sexual irresponsibility. As those "thrilling and repulsive" women lean over him, he is filled with a "wicked, burning desire that they would kiss me with those red lips" (p. 62), but can only "[wait] with beating heart." Although his desires are fierce, he is passive before them, as helpless as an infant dandled by a gigantic mother to pursue or resist satisfaction. Dracula's victims throughout the rest of the book are mostly women,

---

[4]The film titled *The Lost Boys* (1987) also makes this connection between vampirism and Peter Pan. The leader of the vampire boys wants to find a mother for them so that they can become a complete vampire family.

but here at the beginning is the anxiety, for male readers, at least that any man can find himself infantilized.

We have many fantasies about childhood, the main one being that it is a stage of innocence, without knowledge of the fierce demands of sexuality that we attribute to the adult body. Clearly, the drives for pleasure are present in children, announced with screams when they are frustrated and pursued with a concentrated focus when the means for satisfaction are available. What children do lack is a knowledge of death, not just that a mouse or kitten or grandparent can die, but that they themselves inevitably must die: there is something in the way we are made that does not suit us for immortality. Freud argues that earth's original protozoan creatures that reproduce through division are effectively immortal, the offspring indistinguishable from the parent organisms. But once life depends on sexual reproduction, "an unlimited duration of individual life would become a quite pointless luxury. . . . death became possible and expedient" (*Beyond* 46). Death is implied in our sexual being. The French psychoanalyst Jacques Lacan argues that sexual desire is ultimately a desire for that missing thing that would make us immortal.[5] Leaving childhood implies our discovering that we lack something in our being: we are divided into male and female, and so we will never be whole.[6] Our most intense pleasures, of which the orgasmic climax of intercourse is only the most obvious, are in some fashion a more or less momentary overcoming of that sense of being divided, separated. Sexuality is what we have instead of being complete, immortal, but for that reason our sexuality leads us inevitably to a confrontation with our mortality. Because we lack that immortal thing, we die. Because we lack, we desire — but not happily. Part of the appeal of children, I suspect, is that they are still immortal (the reason we are born "trailing clouds of glory" as William Wordsworth says in "Ode: Intimations of Immortality") and remind us of what we have lost in maturing, in eating of the tree of knowledge. We know the children will age and die, but since they don't know this, they can simply want what they want. Why shouldn't we envy them? They are like the explorers Nick Carraway at the end of F. Scott Fitzgerald's *The Great Gatsby*

[5]Writing of the relation of sex to mortality, Lacan says: "It is the libido, *qua* pure life instinct, that is to say, immortal life, or irrepressible life, life that has need of no organ, simplified, indestructible life. It is precisely what is subtracted from the living being by virtue of the fact that it is subject to the cycle of sexed reproduction." (*Four* 198)

[6]Freud, who is always willing to acknowledge the wisdom of poets, invokes Plato's myth of sexual division and a similar account in the Upanishads, in both of which an originally whole human is split into separate, desiring male and female parts (*Beyond* 57–58).

imagines first seeing America as the "fresh, green breast of the new world" and thinking they would be able to drink their fill forever.

Perhaps this is the vampire, then, the projection of the childlike immortality onto an adult body: vampires experience the rage for pleasure that we see in the child, but they suffer from neither the child's incapacity nor the adult's sentence of death. And in their capacity for sexless reproduction that does not carry the inevitability of replacement, they are outside the binary of life and death. They are undead, the negation of death, and though Van Helsing may pity them for being trapped on earth and hence deprived of eternal life beyond death, the undead do not lament their condition; rather, they fight fiercely to preserve themselves.

Our human prejudice, like Van Helsing's, favors life, but our actions frequently express a contrary longing. One of Freud's most enigmatic and profound insights is that we all ultimately strive to "return" to an earlier, inorganic state of being (*Beyond* 36). We humans suffer from "unlust," unpleasure, the tension between what we need and our ability to find satisfaction; we suffer from desire. Some desires are simple: when we are hungry we want food, when we are cold we want warmth. But our human desires are also more complex, condemning us to impossible desires for lost things — call it Eden, the Golden Age, or Mother — that we will never have again, and that we never really had. In striving to fulfill our desires, we are literally moving toward a place before desire, before loss, before life. This is the "death drive," not a drive to *be* dead (as Freud points out, none of us has been dead, and so the term has no meaning for the individual unconscious), but to be freed from the painful separation that is life. Stoker's term, "Un-Dead," suggests that desire to be freed from the limits of human satisfaction, yet not to be dead.

Humans live in the midst of death. Of course, we know we will die. But in addition we live surrounded by our dead, both in the architectural monuments and cemeteries that house them in our cities, and in the culture that we live within and pass on to the next generation. It can be unsettling to realize that our ideas, our language, and our history are not our own but are transmitted through us unconsciously, largely independent of that conscious self which we esteem so highly. Even more unsettling at times is the realization that not even our bodies are our own. We are shaped by our DNA: it is the undead thing that constructs our bodies, and our minds and culture exist for the sole purpose (in evolutionary terms) of allowing DNA to replicate itself. Compared to our immortal DNA, we humans are ephemeral creatures, mere hosts for this unconscious molecule. But we don't often have to think about our servitude to the molecule: some fundamental repression conceals from us the drives and motives of our undead selves.

There is something fundamentally "inhuman" to our being: however "noble in reason" humans are, however "like an angel in apprehension" (Shakespeare, *Hamlet,* II.ii.305), at our core we are linked to that ancient, inorganic state, never born, and hence not dead: undead.[7] We see an expression of this insight into our construction in the tales of zombies (recall again Lucy's sleepwalking), where people are reduced to automatons, laboring with machinelike persistence to fulfill the will of some master. On a genetic level, we could call the master "evolution"— in all of our daily busyness, in all of the complexity of our civilization, we work like zombies to produce the next set of human genes, even when we know rationally that such replication serves the world and humanity ill, destroying our water, land, and air. On the level of the individual psyche, we see the master at work in the wealth of incomprehensible, contradictory, compulsive, irrational behaviors that constitute our lives.[8] Most of us, no matter how old, have had the uncanny and unpleasant experience of feeling once more like the child we thought we had outgrown, just as we recognize in a facial or vocal expression, in a gesture or attitude the parent we couldn't imagine becoming. We don't have to look to the supernatural to see the persistence within us of something that is not us.

Dracula speaks to some unconscious, undead drive in Lucy and Mina when he goes to them. Consider his encounter with Mina. When Dracula comes to her, Mina is at home and in her bed because the men deemed her too weak to join them in the final pursuit of the monster. They think this despite the fact that Harker had recently noticed that Mina's labors had left her more "absolutely strong and well" (p. 251) than he had ever seen her before. She has been independent, resourceful, and tireless, but now she withdraws in obedience to her "husband's great love and from the good, good wishes of those other strong men" (p. 260). The first night Dracula visits her, she goes to bed "simply because they told me to" (p. 260) and is reduced to a weeping, anxious, mindless creature of the men's will, one incapable of action or pleasure.

[7]I derive my understanding of the inhuman from Lyotard's book *The Inhuman,* an idea I discuss in chapter 2 of *Sublime Enjoyment.* You will also find a discussion of DNA and vampirism in my chapter on W. S. Burroughs in chapter 7 of that book.

[8]Freud collected everyday, nonneurotic examples of such behavior in *The Interpretation of Dreams* (1900) and *The Psychopathology of Everyday Life* (1901). Here you will find the examples of dreams, denials, and "Freudian slips" that make us all Freudians despite ourselves.

But once she has drunk from Dracula's breast, she begins to share his thoughts, warning her men that when Dracula calls, she will have no choice but to do his bidding. Mina, the chaste, faithful, courageous Mina, may become yet another of those vampire tramps who came so near to ravishing Harker. (Naturally, the men promise to kill her first, before she goes too far.) The worst danger posed by Dracula, then, is not death, but the possibility that the women whom he touches will begin to act in ways that escape the wishes of the good, good men. This brings us then closer to the psychoanalytic problem at the heart of *Dracula:* the real fear is not that some unslakable thirst will produce monsters, but that some master could command any one of us to fulfill some horrible drive that had been repressed with the greatest diligence.

We must, however, recall reality: there are no vampires. Perhaps we should see this fear as being, in fact, a wish: no one would fear a seducer if one did not think he might be seduced, wish he would be seduced. Talia Schaffer's argument that *Dracula* is about the fear of homosexual seduction following the trial of Oscar Wilde points to a similar "fear" surrounding Wilde: there would be no danger of seduction ("recruitment" in today's militarized language) if there were no temptation. For Stoker's characters, temptation waits behind every dark door. Or they wish it did. The fact is that temptations can come to seem wildly satisfying only if the Law, the Father, has said "No": in placing something beyond reach, the No produces the fantasy that it is what the child wants. And if he only waits long enough (until he grows up, until the Father dies), he'll get it. But that fantasy is in serious trouble for the characters in *Dracula:* the fathers in this book are all dead (Mina's and Lucy's fathers) or dying (Lord Godalming and Mr. Hawkins), taking the promise of future enjoyment with them when they take away the prohibition. Lucy is available and willing to provide some healthy sex, but none of the men seems eager to test his capacity for bliss in an encounter with her. It is as if they know that there is no real object that will satisfy them, and all they can do is delay the realization of that knowledge.

Dracula, however, like the suckling child, knows what delights him. Blood is the sure thing, the endlessly repeatable object that fulfills his only need, for he has only the one need. Like the pervert who knows that his particular fetish will always arouse him, Dracula knows what he wants. Few of us, the normal neurotics, desire so simply: satisfy a craving with this food, this lover, this car, and soon the craving will return for some different meat/neighbor/sports utility vehicle. After all, those are not the things we lost and hope to find again. Those lost objects belong to what Lacan calls the Real, that category of things that cannot be named or represented, and hence cannot be asked for.[9] Every attempt to grasp something in the Real results in a missed encounter that leads to repetition, to one more attempt at satisfaction (Lacan, *Four*, ch. 5). But for Dracula, blood is the Real Thing. Consequently, Dracula seems to restore to the English the promise that had been the payoff for obeying the fathers, for agreeing to wait, which is the response to the anxiety of loss termed "castration."[10] As Van Helsing puts it, if Dracula succeeds, he will become "the father or furtherer of a new order of beings, whose road must lead through Death, not Life" (p. 300). But unlike the Fathers who said No, Dracula demonstrates that there is something Real that will enable them to have full enjoyment. And the horrifying command Dracula brings is this: enjoy![11]

Unlike the pleasures most of us pursue, which are tied to the endless permutations of fashion, advertising, television, and celebrity, there is something mechanical about Dracula's demands, despite the elaborate trappings of civilization he exhibits. It is as if his culture, his mastery of languages and manners, is simply a set of devices to enable the mechanical drive to function. We see something of this machine at work after Dracula passes the vampiric infection to Lucy: she returns sleepwalking to the East Cliff where she met him, and she would go again were her door not locked. At first this appearance of an irrational, unconscious (but unsleeping?) mechanism in her suggests her total servitude to the master, but it also brings an increasingly robust appearance, as if the loss of an autonomous self led to a vibrant physical presence. And once she is "dead," she appears "more radiantly beautiful

---

[9]In Lacan's terms, this means that the Real belongs neither to the Symbolic (the realm of symbolization and representation) nor the Imaginary (the realm of the image, the visible). Consequently, the Real is evoked by the sense that something is left out, missing but necessary to the wholeness of the world.

[10]Lacan defines castration to mean "that *jouissance* [enjoyment] must be refused, so that it can be reached on the inverted ladder . . . of the Law of desire" (*Ecrits* 324). Enjoyment, this implies, cannot be attained directly, but only through a detour that obeys the father's No: do not pass this way.

[11]Zizek describes this idea of the father: "What emerges under the guise of the phantom-like 'living-dead' — of the specter which hinders 'normal' sexual relationship — is, however, the reverse of the Name of the Father, namely the 'anal father' who definitely *does* enjoy" (125). Although the normal "No" of the Father may lead to an attenuated, dissatisfying sexual relationship, the "anal father's" yes leads to a compelling, yet terrible enjoyment. This undead father instructs you to pursue the Real Thing, even though it takes you away from Life. Such a turn occurs in David Lynch's film *Blue Velvet* (1986) when the hero, returning home to Lumberton to visit his ailing father, finds himself dissatisfied with the affection of a sweetly perfect girlfriend and becomes entangled in the sadomasochistic affair of the horrific anal father (played by Dennis Hopper at his scariest) and his mistress. Lumberton never looks the same again.

than ever. . . . The lips were red, nay redder than before; and on the cheeks was a delicate bloom" (p. 209). But the more striking change in Lucy is that she is no longer the frustrated maiden in white waiting for some man to release her from her situation of constrained femininity, a release that would bring the inevitable physical and psychological burdens of children. Rather, she becomes literally a woman of the night who takes what she wants. Van Helsing notes her sharp teeth: with these, "'little children can be bitten'" (p. 209). A mother's fierce love of children ("You're so cute I could just eat you up") reveals itself in Lucy's perverse feeding on the bodies of children who, had she by chance conceived them, would have fed on her. So she bites, enjoying the pleasure of children without the suffering of motherhood. Under the influence of the vampiric master, she feels no human ambivalence but enjoys, rather, a relentless drive to consume.

When Lucy encounters her fiancé on one of her nightly walks, she drops the child she has been sucking and invites her man into her arms: "Come to me, Arthur. Leave these others and come to me. My arms are hungry for you. Come, and we can rest together. Come, my husband, come!" (p. 219). This creature, the men think, only looks like Lucy: "The sweetness was turned to adamantine, heartless cruelty, and the purity to voluptuous wantonness" (p. 218). Hard, heartless, wanton: this Lucy has been condensed into a pure manifestation of drive. "May I cut off the head of the dead Miss Lucy?" (p. 214) asks Van Helsing, as if to save her true self by separating it from her monstrous body ("the whole carnal and unspiritual appearance" [p. 221]). We might, however, invert the terms and wish for Lucy's sake that her body had been released from the repressive head. She disgusts the men because as the undead, she is undeadened, unrestrained. The men look for the "unequalled sweetness and purity" they identified with Lucy, but they can find it in her face only following her second, final death. They see "her truth" in the "traces of care and pain and waste" left on her face, not in traces of pleasure or happiness. The Lucy they loved was always the deadened woman they imagined her to be.

It is not just the women, however, who fall under the reign of a master. If there is a figurative Father in the book, it is Van Helsing. And yet this trustworthy father figure, the man who embodies the Law all others should serve, pushes the other men toward an enjoyment more horrific than that offered by Dracula. When he asks to cut off Lucy's head, Holmwood replies "in a storm of passion": "Heavens and earth, no!" (p. 214). The intensity of Holmwood's response suggests that he recognizes a disturbing and improper desire in Van Helsing's doubt-

lessly pragmatic request. But Van Helsing is the leader of these servants of the Law and will save them from their own improper desires:
when Lucy invites Holmwood to "rest together" with her, for example,
Holmwood "opened wide his arms" (p. 219) and would have succumbed to her if Van Helsing had not intervened. He obeys Van Helsing's "No," turning away from this display of female sexuality and
toward his duty. But Holmwood's adherence to duty also leads him to
his most intense enjoyment in the book: he places a huge stake on
Lucy's bare breast ("I could see its dint in the white flesh") and ham-
mers it through her body while she "quivered and twisted in wild contortions" (p. 223). Just like those indentured to Dracula, he acts
robotically, "never [faltering]. He looked like a figure of Thor as his
trembling arm rose and fell, driving deeper and deeper the mercy-
bearing stake." This pile-driving man could behave this way, we are
told, only because he was "forced to his task by more than human considerations" (p. 223): only in duty, that is, in doing good, can he justify
such violence and such perverse satisfaction.

But as is often the case, the more than human is also less than
human, as the brightest angel becomes the darkest devil. In all passionate commitment to duty, we should hear the command "Enjoy!," the
directive to take pleasure precisely in renouncing conventional pleasure
in the name of the higher law. The odd overlap between Dracula and
Van Helsing, then, arises from the function of the Father in both
restraining and giving access to pleasure. Behind the good Father of the
Law is the horror of what Freud in *Totem and Taboo* calls the "primal
father"[12] and Slavoj Zizek calls the "anal father" (see n.11, p. 495). The
anal father, the monster who has no restraint and whose excessive
enjoyment threatens everyone, is the still living, undead residue of the
murdered primal father's awful freedom. Nina Schwartz argues that our
"ambivalence . . . toward the anal father derives from [his] simultaneously calling forth both the possibility for enjoyment and the revulsion
we have learned to feel toward such pleasure" (14). The only possibility
of overcoming that ambivalence is to mask the anal father with the face
of the good Father of the Law. Van Helsing, then, represents the Law,

---

[12]Freud speculates that society began with the killing of that father: "One day the
brothers who had been driven out came together, killed and devoured their father and so
made an end of the patriarchal horde. United, they had the courage to do and succeeded
in doing what would have been impossible for them individually" (*Totem,* 141). In order
to remain united in society, the brothers must both constantly evoke that father, more
mythic than real, lest any one of them rise up to become him. But that evocation is also a
reminder of what was lost, not just the primal father, but the enjoyment available to him.

saving the men from their revolting desires, but paradoxically freeing them to act on the lingering demand of the anal father. That is, Van Helsing tells the good men he leads that their enjoyment will come through renunciation, not indulgence; but in service to that renunciation, no extremity will be denied.

Our interest in Dracula and vampires is not, I think, that many would want to join his crew. *Dracula,* that is, does not directly invite us to take that "road . . . through Death" (p. 300). Jeffrey Dahlmer and Hannibal Lecter[13] not withstanding, we cannot return to that infant state of oral gratification: we take it on faith, willingly suspending disbelief, that in fictive settings eating children and driving stakes through young women can impart a certain wild enjoyment, and Bram Stoker has given us a fantasy of such enjoyment cloaked in a morality tale. But it is the morality tale itself that ultimately grants us access to something like the hunger of Dracula. The moral voice in *Dracula* points to the monster and to the voluptuous wantonness of Lucy and tells us that it is true, some people do attain pure enjoyment, but that our duty is to destroy them, the evil ones. Lacking real vampires to condemn in our daily lives, the Van Helsings and other masters find the monsters of enjoyment elsewhere, in sullen teens, in the pungent foods and irritating music of ethnic populations, in the sordid sexuality of almost any identifiable group who, in their otherness, seem to enjoy too much. Just as Dracula's huge appetite threatened that band of men with the loss of all pleasure, these various others in their apparent enjoyment (no matter how miserable their real economic circumstances) can be seen as the thieves of the good, good people's happiness, as creatures worthy of the stake. Here, finally, is the real horror of *Dracula:* that there are always spiritual and political leaders, like Van Helsing, ready to stage a blood feast founded on the call of duty, and that our neighbors, who only yesterday were our friends, will join them, a band of soldiers beneath a moral banner ready to serve the latest master.

WORKS CITED

Dundes, Alan. "The Vampire as Bloodthirsty Revenant: A
    Psychoanalytic Post Mortem." *The Vampire: A Casebook.* By
    Dundes. Madison: U Wisconsin P, 1998. 159–75.

[13]Two famous anthropophagites of the 1990s, one real, the other invented by the writer Thomas Harris.

Foster, Dennis. *Sublime Enjoyment: On the Perverse Motive in American Literature*. New York: Cambridge UP, 1997.

Freud, Sigmund. *Beyond the Pleasure Principle*. 1920. *The Standard Edition of the Complete Psychological Works of Sigmund Freud*. Ed. and trans. James Strachey. Vol. 18. London: Hogarth, 1953. 24 vols.

———. *Civilization and Its Discontents*. 1930. Vol. 21.

———. *Three Essays on the Theory of Sexuality*. 1905. Vol. 7.

———. *Totem and Taboo*. 1913. Vol. 13.

Kilgore, Maggie. *The Rise of the Gothic Novel*. New York: Routledge, 1995.

Lacan, Jacques. *Ecrits: A Selection*. Trans. Alan Sheridan. New York: Norton, 1977.

———. *The Four Fundamental Concepts of Psycho-Analysis*. 1973. Trams. Alan Sheridan. New York: Norton, 1978.

Lyotard, Jean-François. *The Inhuman: Reflections on Time*. Trans. Geoffrey Bennington and Rachel Bowlby. Stanford: Stanford UP, 1991.

Nietzsche, Friedrich. *The Birth of Tragedy and The Genealogy of Morals*. 1887. Trans. Francis Golffing. Garden City: Doubleday, 1956.

Schaffer, Talia. "'A Wilde Desire Took Me': The Homoerotic History of *Dracula*." *ELH* 61.2 (1994): 381–425.

Schwartz, Nina. "The Absent One in 'Apartment Zero'." *Camera Obscura*. 37 (1996): 7–30.

Zizek, Slavoj. *Enjoy Your Symptom: Jacques Lacan in Hollywood and Out*. New York: Routledge, 1992.

The New Historicism
and *Dracula*

WHAT IS THE NEW HISTORICISM?

The title of Brook Thomas's *The New Historicism and Other Old-Fashioned Topics* (1991) is telling. Whenever an emergent theory, movement, method, approach, or group gets labeled with the adjective "new," trouble is bound to ensue, for what is new today is either established, old, or forgotten tomorrow. Few of you will have heard of the band called The New Kids on the Block. New Age bookshops and jewelry may seem "old hat" by the time this introduction is published. The New Criticism, or formalism, is just about the oldest approach to literature and literary study currently being practiced. The new historicism, by contrast, is *not* as old-fashioned as formalism, but it is hardly new, either. The term *new* eventually and inevitably requires some explanation. In the case of the new historicism, the best explanation is historical.

Although a number of influential critics working between 1920 and 1950 wrote about literature from a psychoanalytic perspective, the majority took what might generally be referred to as the historical approach. With the advent of the New Criticism, however, historically oriented critics almost seemed to disappear from the face of the earth. The dominant New Critics, or formalists, tended to treat literary works as if they were self-contained, self-referential objects. Rather than basing their interpretations on parallels between the text and historical contexts (such as the author's life or stated intentions in writing the work), these critics concentrated on the relationships *within* the text that give it its form and meaning. During the heyday of the New Criticism, concern about the interplay between literature and history virtually disappeared from literary discourse. In its place was a concern about intratextual repetition, particularly of images or symbols but also of rhythms and sound effect.

About 1970 the New Criticism came under attack by reader-response critics (who believe that the meaning of a work is not inherent in its internal form but rather is cooperatively produced by the reader and the text) and poststructuralists (who, following the philosophy of Jacques Derrida, argue that texts are inevitably self-contradictory and that we can find form in them only by ignoring or suppressing conflicting details or elements). In retrospect it is clear that, their outspoken opposition to the New Criticism notwithstanding, the reader-response critics and poststructuralists of the 1970s were very much *like* their formalist predecessors in two important respects: for the most part, they ignored the world beyond the text and its reader, and, for the most part, they ignored the historical contexts within which literary works are written and read.

Jerome McGann first articulated this retrospective insight in 1985, writing that "a text-only approach has been so vigorously promoted during the last thirty-five years that most historical critics have been driven from the field, and have raised the flag of their surrender by yielding the title 'critic,' and accepting the title 'scholar' for themselves" (*Inflections* 17). Most, but not all. The American Marxist Fredric Jameson had begun his 1981 book *The Political Unconscious* with the following two-word challenge: "Always historicize!" (9). Beginning about 1980, a form of historical criticism practiced by Louis Montrose and Stephen Greenblatt had transformed the field of Renaissance studies and begun to influence the study of American and English Romantic literature as well. And by the mid-1980s, Brook Thomas was working on an essay in which he suggests that classroom discussions of Keats's "Ode on a Grecian Urn" might begin with questions such as the following: Where would Keats have seen such an urn? How did a Grecian urn end up in a museum in England? Some very important historical and political realities, Thomas suggests, lie behind and inform Keats's definitions of art, truth, beauty, the past, and timelessness.

When McGann lamented the surrender of "most historical critics," he no doubt realized what is now clear to everyone involved in the study of literature. Those who have *not* yet surrendered — had not yet "yield[ed] the title 'critic'" to the formalist, reader-response, and post-structuralist "victors" — were armed with powerful new arguments and intent on winning back long-lost ground. Indeed, at about the same time that McGann was deploring the near-complete dominance of critics advocating the text-only approach, Herbert Lindenberger was sounding a more hopeful note: "It comes as something of a surprise," he wrote in 1984, "to find that history is making a powerful comeback" ("New History" 16).

We now know that history was indeed making a powerful comeback in the 1980s, although the word is misleading if it causes us to imagine that the historical criticism being practiced in the 1980s by Greenblatt and Montrose, McGann and Thomas, was the same as the historical criticism that had been practiced in the 1930s and 1940s. Indeed, if the word *new* still serves any useful purpose in defining the historical criticism of today, it is in distinguishing it from the old historicism. The new historicism is informed by the poststructuralist and reader-response theory of the 1970s, plus the thinking of feminist, cultural, and Marxist critics whose work was also "new" in the 1980s. New historicist critics are less fact- and event-oriented than historical critics used to be, perhaps because they have come to wonder whether the truth about what really happened can ever be purely and objectively known. They are less likely to see history as linear and progressive, as something developing toward the present or the future ("teleological"), and they are also less likely to think of it in terms of specific eras, each with a definite, persistent, and consistent Zeitgeist ("spirit of the times"). Consequently, they are unlikely to suggest that a literary text has a single or easily identifiable historical context.

New historicist critics also tend to define the discipline of history more broadly than it was defined before the advent of formalism. They view history as a social science and the social sciences as being properly historical. In *Historical Studies and Literary Criticism* (1985), McGann speaks of the need to make "sociohistorical" subjects and methods central to literary studies; in *The Beauty of Inflections: Literary Investigations in Historical Method and Theory* (1985), he links sociology and the future of historical criticism. "A sociological poetics," he writes, "must be recognized not only as relevant to the analysis of poetry, but in fact as central to the analysis" (62). Lindenberger cites anthropology as particularly useful in the new historical analysis of literature, especially anthropology as practiced by Victor Turner and Clifford Geertz.

Geertz, who has related theatrical traditions in nineteenth-century Bali to forms of political organization that developed during the same period, has influenced some of the most important critics writing the new kind of historical criticism. Due in large part to Geertz's anthropological influence, new historicists such as Greenblatt have asserted that literature is not a sphere apart or distinct from the history that is relevant to it. That is what the old criticism tended to do: present the background information you needed to know before you could fully appreciate the separate world of art. The new historicists have used what Geertz would call "thick description" to blur distinctions, not only between history and the other social sciences but also between background and foreground, historical and literary materials, political and poetical events. They have erased the old boundary line dividing historical and literary materials, showing that the production of one of Shakespeare's historical plays was a political act and historical event, while at the same time showing that the coronation of Elizabeth I was carried out with the same care for staging and symbol lavished on works of dramatic art.

In addition to breaking down barriers that separate literature and history, history and the social sciences, new historicists have reminded us that it is treacherously difficult to reconstruct the past as it really was, rather than as we have been conditioned by our own place and time to believe that it was. And they know that the job is utterly impossible for those who are unaware of that difficulty and insensitive to the bent or bias of their own historical vantage point. Historical criticism must be "conscious of its status as interpretation," Greenblatt has written (*Renaissance* 4). McGann obviously concurs, writing that "historical criticism can no longer make any part of [its] sweeping picture unselfconsciously, or treat any of its details in an untheorized way" (*Studies* 11).

Unselfconsciously and *untheorized* are the key words in McGann's statement. When new historicist critics of literature describe a historical change, they are highly conscious of, and even likely to discuss, the *theory* of historical change that informs their account. They know that the changes they happen to see and describe are the ones that their theory of change allows or helps them to see and describe. And they know, too, that their theory of change is historically determined. They seek to minimize the distortion inherent in their perceptions and representations by admitting that they see through preconceived notions; in other words, they learn to reveal the color of the lenses in the glasses that they wear.

Nearly everyone who wrote on the new historicism during the 1980s cited the importance of the late Michel Foucault. A French philosophical historian who liked to think of himself as an archaeologist of human knowledge, Foucault brought together incidents and phenomena from areas of inquiry and orders of life that we normally regard as being unconnected. As much as anyone, he encouraged the new historicist critic of literature to redefine the boundaries of historical inquiry.

Foucault's views of history were influenced by the philosopher Friedrich Nietzsche's concept, *wirkliche* ("real" or "true") history that is neither melioristic (that is, "getting better all the time") nor metaphysical. Like Nietzsche, Foucault didn't see history in terms of a continuous development toward the present. Neither did he view it as an abstraction, idea, or ideal, as something that began "In the beginning" and that will come to THE END, a moment of definite closure, a Day of Judgment. In his own words, Foucault "abandoned [the old history's] attempts to understand events in terms of . . . some great evolutionary process" (*Discipline and Punish* 129). He warned a new generation of historians to be aware of the fact that investigators are themselves "situated." It is difficult, he reminded them, to see present cultural practices critically from within them, and because of the same cultural practices, it is extremely difficult to enter bygone ages. In *Discipline and Punish: The Birth of the Prison* (1975), Foucault admitted that his own interest in the past was fueled by a passion to write the history of the present.

Like Marx, Foucault saw history in terms of power, but his view of power probably owed more to Nietzsche than to Marx. Foucault seldom viewed power as a repressive force. He certainly did not view it as a tool of conspiracy used by one specific individual or institution against another. Rather, power represents a whole web or complex of forces; it is that which produces what happens. Not even a tyrannical aristocrat simply wields power, for the aristocrat is himself formed and empowered by a network of discourses and practices that constitute power. Viewed by Foucault, power is "positive and productive," not "repressive" and "prohibitive" (Smart 63). Furthermore, no historical event, according to Foucault, has a single cause; rather, it is intricately connected with a vast web of economic, social, and political factors.

A brief sketch of one of Foucault's major works may help clarify some of his ideas. *Discipline and Punish* begins with a shocking but accurate description of the public drawing and quartering of a Frenchman who had botched his attempt to assassinate King Louis XV in 1757. Foucault proceeds by describing rules governing the daily life of modern Parisian felons. What happened to torture, to punishment as public spectacle? he asks. What complex network of forces made it disappear? In working toward a picture of this "power," Foucault turns up many interesting puzzle pieces, such as the fact that in the early years of the nineteenth century, crowds would sometimes identify with the prisoner and treat the executioner as if *he* were the guilty party. But Foucault sets forth a related reason for keeping prisoners alive, moving punishment indoors, and changing discipline from physical torture into mental rehabilitation: colonization. In this historical period, people were needed to establish colonies and trade, and prisoners could be used for that purpose. Also, because these were politically unsettled times, governments needed infiltrators and informers. Who better to fill those roles than prisoners pardoned or released early for showing a willingness to be rehabilitated? As for rehabilitation itself, Foucault compares it to the old form of punishment, which began with a torturer extracting a confession. In more modern, "reasonable" times, psychologists probe the minds of prisoners with a scientific rigor that Foucault sees as a different kind of torture, a kind that our modern perspective does not allow us to see as such.

Thus, a change took place, but perhaps not as great a change as we generally assume. It may have been for the better or for the worse; the point is that agents of power didn't make the change because mankind is evolving and, therefore, more prone to perform good-hearted deeds. Rather, different objectives arose, including those of a new class of doctors and scientists bent on studying aberrant examples of the human mind. And where do we stand vis-à-vis the history Foucault tells? We are implicated by it, for the evolution of discipline as punishment into the study of the human mind includes the evolution of the "disciplines" as we now understand that word, including the discipline of history, the discipline of literary study, and now a discipline that is neither and both, a form of historical criticism that from the vantage point of the 1980s looked "new."

Foucault's type of analysis has been practiced by a number of literary critics at the vanguard of the back-to-history movement. One of them is Greenblatt, who along with Montrose was to a great extent responsible for transforming Renaissance studies in the early 1980s and revitalizing historical criticism in the process. Greenblatt follows Foucault's lead in interpreting literary devices as if they were continuous with all other representational devices in a culture; he therefore turns to scholars in other fields in order to better understand the workings of literature. "We wall off literary symbolism from the symbolic structures operative elsewhere," he writes, "as if art alone were a human creation, as if humans themselves were not, in Clifford Geertz's phrase, cultural artifacts" (*Renaissance* 4).

Greenblatt's name, more than anyone else's, is synonymous with the new historicism; his essay entitled "Invisible Bullets" (1981) has been said by Patrick Brantlinger to be "perhaps the most frequently cited example of New Historicist work" (45). An English professor at the University of California, Berkeley — the early academic home of the new historicism — Greenblatt was a founding editor of *Representations,* a journal published by the University of California Press that is still considered today to be *the* mouthpiece of the new historicism.

In *Learning to Curse* (1990), Greenblatt cites as central to his own intellectual development his decision to interrupt his literary education at Yale University by accepting a Fulbright fellowship to study in England at Cambridge University. There he came under the influence of the great Marxist cultural critic Raymond Williams, who made Greenblatt realize how much — and what — was missing from his Yale education. "In Williams' lectures," Greenblatt writes, "all that had been carefully excluded from the literary criticism in which I had been trained — who controlled access to the printing press, who owned the land and the factories, whose voices were being repressed as well as represented in literary texts, what social strategies were being served by the aesthetic values we constructed — came pressing back in upon the act of interpretation" (2).

Greenblatt returned to the United States determined not to exclude such matters from his own literary investigations. Blending what he had learned from Williams with poststructuralist thought about the indeterminacy or "undecidability" of meaning, he eventually developed a critical method that he now calls "cultural poetics." More tentative and less overtly political than cultural criticism, it involves what Thomas calls "the technique of montage. Starting with the analysis of a particular historical event, it cuts to the analysis of a particular literary text. The point is not to show that the literary text reflects the historical event but to create a field of energy between the two so that we come to see the event as a social text and the literary text as a social event" ("New Literary Historicism" 490). Alluding to deconstructor Jacques Derrida's assertion that "there is nothing outside the text," Montrose explains that the goal of this new historicist criticism is to show the "historicity of texts and the textuality of history" (Veeser 20).

The relationship between the cultural poetics practiced by a number of new historicists and the cultural criticism associated with Marxism is important, not only because of the proximity of the two approaches but also because one must recognize the difference between the two to understand the new historicism. Still very much a part of the contemporary critical scene, cultural criticism (sometimes called "cultural studies" or "cultural critique") nonetheless involves several tendencies more compatible with the old historicism than with the thinking of new historicists such as Greenblatt. These include the tendency to believe that history is driven by economics; that it is determinable even as it determines the lives of individuals; and that it is progressive, its dialectic one that will bring about justice and equality.

Greenblatt does not privilege economics in his analyses and views individuals as agents possessing considerable productive power. (He says that "the work of art is the product of a negotiation between a creator or class of creators . . . and the institutions and practices of a society" [*Learning* 158]: he also acknowledges that artistic productions are "intensely marked by the private obsessions of individuals," however much they may result from "collective negotiation and exchange" [*Negotiations* vii].) His optimism about the individual, however, should not be confused with optimism about either history's direction or any historian's capacity to foretell it. Like a work of art, a work of history is the negotiated product of a private creator and the public practices of a given society.

This does not mean that Greenblatt does not discern historical change, or that he is uninterested in describing it. Indeed, in works from *Renaissance Self-Fashioning* (1980) to *Shakespearean Negotiations* (1988), he has written about Renaissance changes in the development of both literary characters and real people. But his view of change — like his view of the individual — is more Foucauldian than Marxist. That is to say, it is not melioristic or teleological. And, like Foucault, Greenblatt is careful to point out that any one change is connected with a host of others, no one of which may simply be identified as cause or effect, progressive or regressive, repressive or enabling.

Not all of the critics trying to lead students of literature back to history are as Foucauldian as Greenblatt. Some even owe more to Marx than to Foucault. Others, like Thomas, have clearly been more influenced by Walter Benjamin, best known for essays such as "Theses on the Philosophy of History" and "The Work of Art in the Age of Mechanical Reproduction." Still others — McGann, for example — have followed the lead of Soviet critic M. M. Bakhtin, who viewed literary works in terms of discourses and dialogues between the official, legitimate voices of a society and other, more challenging or critical voices echoing popular or traditional culture. In the "polyphonic" writings of Rabelais, for instance, Bakhtin found that the profane language of Carnival and other popular festivals offsets and parodies the "legitimate" discourses representing the outlook of the king, church, and socially powerful intellectuals of the day.

Moreover, there are other reasons not to consider Foucault the single or even central influence on the new historicism. First, he critiqued the old-style historicism to such an extent that he ended up being antihistorical, or at least ahistorical, in the view of a number of new historicists. Second, his commitment to a radical remapping of the relations of power and influence, cause and effect, may have led him to adopt too cavalier an attitude toward chronology and facts. Finally, the very act of identifying and labeling *any* primary influence goes against the grain of the new historicism. Its practitioners have sought to "decenter" the study of literature, not only by overlapping it with historical studies (broadly defined to include anthropology and sociology) but also by struggling to see history from a decentered perspective. That struggle has involved recognizing (1) that the historian's cultural and historical position may not afford the best purview of a given set of events and (2) that events seldom have any single or central cause. In keeping with these principles, it may be appropriate to acknowledge Foucault as just one of several powerful, interactive intellectual forces rather than to declare him the single, master influence.

Throughout the 1980s it seemed to many that the ongoing debates about the sources of the new historicist movement, the importance of Marx or Foucault, Walter Benjamin or Mikhail Bakhtin, and the exact locations of all the complex boundaries between the new historicism and other "isms" (Marxism and poststructuralism, to name only two), were historically contingent functions of the new historicism *newness*. In the initial stages of their development, new intellectual movements are difficult to outline clearly because, like partially developed photographic images, they are themselves fuzzy and lacking in definition. They respond to disparate influences and include thinkers who represent a wide range of backgrounds; like movements that are disintegrating, they inevitably include a broad spectrum of opinions and positions.

From the present vantage point, however, it seems that the inchoate quality of the new historicism is characteristic rather than a function of newness. The boundaries around the new historicism remain fuzzy, not because it hasn't reached its full maturity but because, if it is to live up to its name, it must always be subject to revision and redefinition as historical circumstances change. The fact that so many critics we label new historicist are working right at the border of Marxist, poststructuralist, cultural, postcolonial, feminist, and now even a new form of reader-response (or at least reader-oriented) criticism is evidence of the new historicism's multiple interests and motivations, rather than of its embryonic state.

New historicists themselves advocate and even stress the need to perpetually redefine categories and boundaries — whether they be disciplinary, generic, national, or racial — not because definitions are unimportant but because they are historically constructed and thus subject to revision. If new historicists like Thomas and reader-oriented critics like Steven Mailloux and Peter Rabinowitz seem to spend most of their time talking over the low wall separating their respective fields, then maybe the wall is in the wrong place. As Catherine Gallagher has suggested, the boundary between new historicists and feminists studying "people and phenomena that once seemed insignificant, indeed outside of history: women, criminals, the insane" often turns out to be shifting or even nonexistent (Veeser 43).

If the fact that new historicists all seem to be working on the border of another school should not be viewed as a symptom of the new historicism's newness (or disintegration), neither should it be viewed as evidence that new historicists are intellectual loners or divisive outriders who enjoy talking over walls to people in other fields but who share no common views among themselves. Greenblatt, McGann, and Thomas all started with the assumption that works of literature are simultaneously influenced by and influencing reality, broadly defined. Whatever their disagreements, they share a belief in referentiality — a belief that literature refers to and is referred to by things outside itself — stronger than that found in the works of formalist, poststructuralist, and even reader-response critics. They believe with Greenblatt that the "central concerns" of criticism "should prevent it from permanently sealing off one type of discourse from another or decisively separating works of art from the minds and lives of their creators and their audiences" (*Renaissance* 5).

McGann, in his introduction to *Historical Studies and Literary Criticism,* turns referentiality into a rallying cry:

> What will not be found in these essays . . . is the assumption, so common in text-centered studies of every type, that literary works are self-enclosed verbal constructs, or looped intertextual fields of autonomous signifiers and signifieds. In these essays, the question of referentiality is once again brought to the fore. (3)

In "Keats and the Historical Method in Literary Criticism," he suggests a set of basic, scholarly procedures to be followed by those who have rallied to the cry. These procedures, which he claims are "practical derivatives of the Bakhtin school," assume that historicist critics will study a literary work's "point of origin" by studying biography and bibliography. The critic must then consider the expressed intentions of the author, because, if printed, these intentions have also modified the developing history of the work. Next, the new historicist must learn the history of the work's reception, as that body of opinion has become part of the platform on which we are situated when we study the work at our own particular "point of reception." Finally, McGann urges the new historicist critic to point toward the future, toward his or her *own* audience, defining for its members the aims and limits of the critical project and injecting the analysis with a degree of self-consciousness that alone can give it credibility (*Inflections* 62).

In his introduction to a collection of new historical writings on *The New Historicism* (1989), H. Aram Veeser stresses the unity among new historicists, not by focusing on common critical procedures but, rather, by outlining five "key assumptions" that "continually reappear and bind together the avowed practitioners and even some of their critics":

1. that every expressive act is embedded in a network of material practices;
2. that every act of unmasking, critique, and opposition uses the tools it condemns and risks falling prey to the practice it exposes;
3. that literary and nonliterary texts circulate inseparably;
4. that no discourse, imaginative or archival, gives access to unchanging truths nor expresses inalterable human nature;
5. finally, . . . that a critical method and a language adequate to describe culture under capitalism participate in the economy they describe. (xi)

These same assumptions are shared by a group of historians practicing what is now commonly referred to as "the new cultural history." Influenced by *Annales*-school historians in France, post-Althusserian Marxists, and Foucault, these historians share with their new historicist counterparts not only many of the same influences and assumptions but also the following: an interest in anthropological and sociological subjects and methods; a creative way of weaving stories and anecdotes about the past into revealing thick descriptions; a tendency to focus on nontraditional, noncanonical subjects and relations (historian Thomas

Laqueur is best known for *Making Sex: Body and Gender from the Greeks to Freud* [1990]); and some of the same journals and projects.

Thus, in addition to being significantly unified by their own interests, assumptions, and procedures, new historicist literary critics have participated in a broader, interdisciplinary movement toward unification virtually unprecedented within and across academic disciplines. Their tendency to work along disciplinary borderlines, far from being evidence of their factious or fractious tendencies, has been precisely what has allowed them to engage historians in a conversation certain to revolutionize the way in which we understand the past, present, and future.

In beginning "Ambivalence and Ascendancy in Bram Stoker's *Dracula*," Gregory Castle places the text of the novel within the context of the Anglo-Irish ruling class (the so-called Ascendancy) and the "Catholic-Irish 'natives'" (p. 518 in this volume). Quoting Terry Eagleton's assertion that the Ascendancy was "parasitic" (p. 519), Castle reveals that Eagleton was hardly the first to suggest that the Anglo-Protestant rulers were — metaphorically speaking — bloodsuckers. Eagleton's view that "Dracula is a ghoulish type of the absentee Ascendancy landlord" (p. 520) merely develops an analogy made by Michael Davitt, the nineteenth-century Irish Land Leaguer who referred to members of the ascendancy as "cormorant vampires" (p. 519).

Borrowing another interesting analogy from Eagleton, Castle suggests that just as the Anglo-Irish ruling class never ruled effectively and thus never achieved "cultural hegemony," so "realism, the dominant mode of literary expression in nineteenth-century Britain," never achieved ascendancy in Ireland either (p. 520). Like the Ascendancy, realism never really ruled; it was always unstable, allowing Irish fiction to evolve into a modernist form able to critique the false impression realism gives of transparency, disinterest, and neutrality. "Colonized writers," in Castle's words, tended "to create unrealistic (that is to say fantastic) representations of unbearable social conditions," and even Irish Protestant novelists (such as Stoker) created "macabre or ghostly allegories of their feelings of displacement and disempowerment" (p. 520). (Watching the rise of the Catholic middle class and of Catholic power more generally, these writers reasonably feared a "reverse" in the "power dynamic of colonialism" [p. 521]), one that would cause their absorption by the Catholic Irish or, alternatively, by the English, from whom they were also and equally, physically and culturally, distant.)

Thus, given the position of the Ascendancy at the time of *Dracula*'s writing, "the threat represented by [the vampire] could be read as emanating not only from a foreign source, a primitive Catholic Other, but from the English themselves." This "double threat," Castle argues, "places the Anglo-Irish as a class on both sides of the colonial divide" (p. 522). In Stoker's novel, this double placement can be seen in the fact that Count Dracula is primitive but also polite (thereby symbolizing the Catholic and English threats, respectively). "Though it is set in London and Transylvania and features no Irish characters," Castle writes, "it is possible, even inevitable, to read Stoker's novel as an expression of the Protestant Ascendancy's most deeply rooted fears" (p. 522).

Castle admits that, "for many readers of *Dracula*, the Irish historical context may not seem relevant to their understanding of a man [Stoker] who had become an important player in the English theater community and whose sensibilities, judging from characters like Jonathan Harker, John Seward, and Arthur Holmwood, are British imperialist" (pp. 523–24). Nonetheless, he argues, "Stoker was the quintessential Irish Protestant," and, like many of his class, he felt "contradictory feelings of estrangement and entitlement" where Catholic Ireland *and* Protestant Britain were concerned (p. 524).

Stoker also, Castle maintains, had developed "an uneasy dependency on the very Catholicism, with its sacramental magic, that the Protestant Ascendancy was reputed to fear" (p. 524). He "borrows and refashions the sacramental icons, rituals, and prayers," not to advance or mock Catholicism but, rather, to "forestall the decline of an ineffectual Ascendancy" by appropriating and Gothicizing the sacraments and all they represent (p. 524). "Reading *Dracula* in the context of Irish Protestant occultism" — referred to by one historian as "Protestant magic" — can "help us understand why, in this Gothic drama of the return of the repressed, Dracula wears an Englishman's clothes and Van Helsing, the protector of English women and English values, brandishes a Roman Catholic cross" (p. 525).

Taken "in the context of the 1890s," Castle argues, the appropriation of the sacramental by Protestant intellectuals may be seen as an attempt to make up for their own lack of "national and spiritual vision" — in other words, as "the desire of a marginalized elite to appropriate religious rituals in order to invigorate itself" (p. 526). Castle goes on to list some specifically "sacramental elements" in *Dracula* — the scene in which a peasant woman offers Harker a crucifix, Mina's use of a ribbon and her wedding ring to express devotion to and trust in her husband, and Van Helsing's implausible claim that he has an Indulgence. (Van Helsing is said to forge an "uneasy . . . unconscious, link between Protestant and sacramental magic" and indeed to use the linked powers of "science and the supernatural . . . Catholic sacraments against a demonized Catholic foe" [p. 530].)

Castle maintains that Stoker wrote *Dracula* from an uncomfortably in-between vantage point, one allowing him to stake out an intellectual position simultaneously at odds with the inflexible Irish nationalists and their English antagonists. In reaching this conclusion, Castle's essay — which ranges far beyond what can be suggested in this introduction — provides a telling contemporary example of the new historicism insofar as it considers everything from politics to religion, science to magic, and the relationship between colonizer and colonized while focusing on the way in which literature at once reflects, reflects on, and critiques those informing situations and institutions. Finally, Castle's use of Eagleton shows the influence of Marxist interpretations of history on new historicist readings of literature, as does his reflection on the way in which literary texts stand in relationship to hegemonic imperatives — or their absence.

Ross C Murfin

THE NEW HISTORICISM:
A SELECTED BIBLIOGRAPHY

The New Historicism: Further Reading

Brantlinger, Patrick. "Cultural Studies vs. the New Historicism." *English Studies/Cultural Studies: Institutionalizing Dissent*. Ed. Isaiah Smithson and Nancy Ruff. Urbana: U of Illinois P, 1994. 43–58.

Cox, Jeffrey N., and Larry J. Reynolds, eds. *New Historical Literary Study*. Princeton: Princeton UP, 1993.

Dimock, Wai-chee. "Feminism, New Historicism, and the Reader." *American Literature* 63 (1991): 601–22.

Gallagher, Catherine, and Stephen Greenblatt. *Practicing New Historicism*. Chicago: U of Chicago P, 2000.

Howard, Jean. "The New Historicism in Renaissance Studies." *English Literary Renaissance* 16 (1986): 13–43.

Lindenberger, Herbert. *The History in Literature: On Value, Genre, Institutions*. New York: Columbia UP, 1990.

————. "Toward a New History in Literary Study." *Profession: Selected Articles from the Bulletins of the Association of Departments of English and the Association of the Departments of Foreign Languages.* New York: MLA, 1984. 16–23.

Liu, Alan. "The Power of Formalism: The New Historicism." *English Literary History* 56 (1989): 721–71.

McGann, Jerome. *The Beauty of Inflections: Literary Investigations in Historical Method and Theory.* Oxford: Clarendon, 1985.

————. *Historical Studies and Literary Criticism.* Madison: U of Wisconsin P, 1985. See especially the introduction and the essays in the following sections: "Historical Methods and Literary Interpretations" and "Biographical Contexts and the Critical Object."

Montrose, Louis Adrian. "Renaissance Literary Studies and the Subject of History." *English Literary Renaissance* 16 (1986): 5–12.

Morris, Wesley. *Toward a New Historicism.* Princeton: Princeton UP, 1972.

New Literary History 21 (1990). "History and . . ." (special issue). See especially the essays by Carolyn Porter, Rena Fraden, Clifford Geertz, and Renato Rosaldo.

Representations. This quarterly journal, printed by the University of California Press, regularly publishes new historicist studies and cultural criticism.

Thomas, Brook. "The Historical Necessity for — and Difficulties with — New Historical Analysis in Introductory Courses." *College English* 49 (1987): 509–22.

————. *The New Historicism and Other Old-Fashioned Topics.* Princeton: Princeton UP, 1991.

————. "The New Literary Historicism." *A Companion to American Thought.* Ed. Richard Wightman Fox and James T. Klappenberg. New York: Basil Blackwell, 1995.

————. "Walter Benn Michaels and the New Historicism: Where's the Difference?" *Boundary* 2.18 (1991): 118–59.

Veeser, H. Aram, ed. *The New Historicism.* New York: Routledge, 1989. See especially Veeser's introduction, Louise Montrose's "Professing the Renaissance," Catherine Gallagher's "Marxism and the New Historicism," and Frank Lentricchia's "Foucault's Legacy: A New Historicism?"

Wayne, Don E. "Power, Politics and the Shakespearean Text: Recent Criticism in England and the United States." *Shakespeare Reproduced: The Text in History and Ideology.* Ed. Jean Howard and Marion O'Connor. New York: Methuen, 1987. 47–67.

Winn, James A. "An Old Historian Looks at the New Historicism."
    Comparative Studies in Society and History 35 (1993): 859–70.

The New Historicism: Influential Examples

The new historicism has taken its present form less through the
elaboration of basic theoretical postulates and more through certain
influential examples. The works listed represent some of the most
important contributions guiding research in this area.

Bercovitch, Sacvan. *The Rites of Assent: Transformations in the
    Symbolic Construction of America.* New York: Routledge, 1993.

Brown, Gillian. *Domestic Individualism: Imagining Self in
    Nineteenth-Century America.* Berkeley: U of California P,
    1990.

Dollimore, Jonathan. *Radical Tragedy: Religion, Ideology and Power
    in the Drama of Shakespeare and His Contemporaries.* Brighton:
    Harvester, 1984.

Dollimore, Jonathan, and Alan Sinfield, eds. *Political Shakespeare:
    New Essays in Cultural Materialism.* Manchester: Manchester UP,
    1985. This volume occupies the borderline between new histori-
    cist and cultural criticism. See especially the essays by Dollimore,
    Greenblatt, and Tennenhouse.

Gallagher, Catherine. *The Industrial Reformation of English Fiction.*
    Chicago: U of Chicago P, 1985.

Goldberg, Jonathan. *James I and the Politics of Literature.* Baltimore:
    Johns Hopkins UP, 1983.

Greenblatt, Stephen J. *Learning to Curse: Essays in Early Modern
    Culture.* New York: Routledge, 1990.

———. *Marvelous Possessions: The Wonder of the New World.* Chicago:
    U of Chicago P, 1991.

———. *Renaissance Self-Fashioning from More to Shakespeare.*
    Chicago: U of Chicago P, 1980. See chapter 1 and the chapter on
    Othello titled "The Improvisation of Power."

———. *Shakespearean Negotiations: The Circulation of Social Energy
    in Renaissance England.* Berkeley: U of California P, 1988. See
    especially "The Circulation of Social Energy" and "Invisible
    Bullets."

Liu, Alan. *Wordsworth, the Sense of History.* Stanford: Stanford UP,
    1989.

Marcus, Leah. *Puzzling Shakespeare: Local Reading and Its
    Discontents.* Berkeley: U of California P, 1988.

McGann, Jerome. *The Romantic Ideology.* Chicago: U of Chicago P, 1983.

Michaels, Walter Benn. *The Gold Standard and the Logic of Naturalism: American Literature at the Turn of the Century.* Berkeley: U of California P, 1987.

Montrose, Louis Adrian. "'Shaping Fantasies': Figurations of Gender and Power in Elizabethan Culture." *Representations* 2 (1983): 61–94. One of the most influential early new historicist essays.

Mullaney, Steven. *The Place of the Stage: License, Play, and Power in Renaissance England.* Chicago: U of Chicago P, 1987.

Orgel, Stephen. *The Illusion of Power: Political Theater in the English Renaissance.* Berkeley: U of California P, 1975.

Sinfield, Alan. *Literature, Politics, and Culture in Postwar Britain.* Berkeley: U of California P, 1989.

Tennenhouse, Leonard. *Power on Display: The Politics of Shakespeare's Genres.* New York: Methuen, 1986.

Foucault and His Influence

As I point out in the introduction to the new historicism, some new historicists would question the "privileging" of Foucault implicit in this section heading ("Foucault and His Influence") and the following one ("Other Writers and Works"). They might cite the greater importance of one of those other writers or point out that to cite a central influence or a definitive cause runs against the very spirit of the movement.

Dreyfus, Hubert L., and Paul Rabinow. *Michel Foucault: Beyond Structuralism and Hermeneutics.* Chicago: U of Chicago P, 1983.

Foucault, Michel. *The Archaeology of Knowledge.* Trans. A. M. Sheridan Smith. New York: Harper, 1972.

———. *Discipline and Punish: The Birth of the Prison.* 1975. Trans. Alan Sheridan. New York: Pantheon, 1978.

———. *The History of Sexuality.* Trans. Robert Hurley. Vol. 1. New York: Pantheon, 1978.

———. *Language, Counter-Memory, Practice.* Ed. Donald F. Bouchard. Trans. Donald F. Bouchard and Sherry Simon. Ithaca: Cornell UP, 1977.

———. *The Order of Things: An Archaeology of the Human Sciences.* New York: Vintage, 1973.

———. *Politics, Philosophy, Culture.* Ed. Lawrence D. Kritzman. Trans. Alan Sheridan et al. New York: Routledge, 1988.

———. *Power/Knowledge.* Ed. Colin Gordon. Trans. Colin Gordon et al. New York: Pantheon, 1980.

———. *Technologies of the Self.* Ed. Luther H. Martin, Huck Gutman, and Patrick H. Hutton. Amherst: U of Massachusetts P, 1988.

Sheridan, Alan. *Michel Foucault: The Will to Truth.* New York: Tavistock, 1980.

Smart, Barry. *Michel Foucault.* New York: Travistock, 1985.

Other Writers and Works of Interest to New Historical Critics

Bakhtin, M. M. *The Dialogic Imagination: Four Essays.* Ed. Michael Holquist. Trans. Caryl Emerson. Austin: U of Texas P, 1981. Bakhtin wrote many influential studies on subjects as varied as Dostoyevsky, Rabelais, and formalist criticism. But this book, in part due to Holquist's helpful introduction, is probably the best place to begin reading Bakhtin.

Benjamin, Walter. "The Work of Art in the Age of Mechanical Reproduction." 1936. *Illuminations.* Ed. Hannah Arendt. Trans. Harry Zohn. New York: Harcourt, 1968.

Fried, Michael. *Absorption and Theatricality: Painting and Beholder in the Works of Diderot.* Berkeley: U of California P, 1980.

Geertz, Clifford. *The Interpretation of Cultures.* New York: Basic, 1973.

———. *Negara: The Theatre State in Nineteenth-Century Bali.* Princeton: Princeton UP, 1980.

Goffman, Erving. *Frame Analysis.* New York: Harper, 1974.

Jameson, Fredric. *The Political Unconscious.* Ithaca: Cornell UP, 1981.

Koselleck, Reinhart. *Futures Past.* Trans. Keith Tribe. Cambridge: MIT P, 1985.

Said, Edward. *Orientalism.* New York: Columbia UP, 1978.

Turner, Victor. *The Ritual Process: Structure and Anti-Structure.* Chicago: Aldine, 1969.

Young, Robert. *White Mythologies: Writing History and the West.* New York: Routledge, 1990.

New Historical Studies of *Dracula*

Arata, Stephen D. "The Occidental Tourist: *Dracula* and the Anxiety of Reverse Colonization." *Victorian Studies* 33 (1990): 621–45. Rev. and rpt. in Arata's *Fictions of Loss in the Victorian Fin de Siècle.* Cambridge, England: Cambridge UP, 1996. 107–32.

Gagnier, Regenia. "Evolution and Information, or Eroticism and
    Everyday Life, in *Dracula* and Late Victorian Aestheticism." *Sex
    and Death in Victorian Literature*. Ed. Regina Barreca.
    Bloomington: Indiana UP, 1990. 140–57.

Halberstam, Judith. "Technologies of Monstrosity: Bram Stoker's
    Dracula." *Victorian Studies* 36 (1993): 333–52. Rpt. in rev. form
    in Halberstam. *Skin Shows: Gothic Horror and the Technology of
    Monsters*. Durham: Duke UP, 1995. 86–106.

Spencer, Kathleen L. "Purity and Danger: *Dracula*, the Urban
    Gothic, and the Late Victorian Degeneracy Crisis." *ELH* 59
    (1992): 197–225.

Warwick, Alexandra. "Vampires and the Empire: Fears and Fictions of
    the 1890s." *Cultural Politics at the Fin de Siècle*. Eds. Sally Ledger
    and Scott McCracken. Cambridge: Cambridge UP, 1995.
    202–20.

A NEW HISTORICAL PERSPECTIVE

GREGORY CASTLE

Ambivalence and Ascendancy
in Bram Stoker's *Dracula*

Ascendancy in Decline

Historical approaches to literature have become increasingly
appealing to many readers in the past two decades, and nowhere is this
more apparent than in Irish studies, where revisionist writing about history and a literary criticism informed by new thinking about postcolonial situations have altered our way of looking at Irish culture and
politics. It is within this context that we have seen a reconsideration of
the relationship between the Anglo-Irish ruling class (the Irish Protestant Ascendancy) and the Catholic-Irish "natives." In *Heathcliff and
the Great Hunger* (1995), Terry Eagleton maps the failure of the
Ascendancy elite to achieve political and cultural hegemony. The perspective he provides enables us to see in *Dracula* the effect of social dis-
location and loss of power, which Stoker would have experienced as an
Anglo-Irishman.

Though the Anglo-Irish considered themselves a client of the British state, their ineffectual rule of Ireland — marked by absentee landlordism that drained Ireland of its capital and many of its goods, "rack-rent" policies that often bordered on extortion, and social and political ineptitude — ultimately guaranteed that they would never achieve the kind of political and social dominance required by any ruling class. "Hegemony is not just a psychological matter," writes Eagleton. "[I]t is also a question of economic incentives and social techniques, religious practices and electoral routines" (28). In his description of the economic and social basis of the Ascendancy, the Irish historian J. C. Beckett hits upon one reason for its failure to achieve hegemony: its social insularity. "To entertain their neighbors, and be entertained by them, at drinking and field-sports was almost the sum-total of their activities, and probably formed a fair index of their notions of social responsibility and public duty" (182). Still, like R. F. Foster and other Irish historians, Beckett concedes that the Ascendancy did contain individuals who overcame selfishness and improvidence in order to champion the efforts of their more reform-minded peers. This attitude toward the Anglo-Irish Ascendancy indicates that even those who wish to see it in the best possible light cannot avoid noting its utter failure to achieve dominance, despite its advantageous connections to the British empire. Its "half-hearted" attempts at social reform only underscored this failure and, ultimately, helped create the social and political conditions for a Catholic nationalist middle class to rise and express their own political and social power.

"Taken as a whole," writes Eagleton, "the Ascendancy represented a backward, unmannerly sector of the British governing class; and their ability to win the loyalty of their tenants was seriously disabled by the ethnic, religious and cultural abyss which yawned between them" (59). He goes on to claim that, at its worst, the Ascendancy was a "parasitic social formation" (66).[1] Some historians, like R. F. Foster, play down the parasitical or vampiric side of the Ascendancy. Citing Michael Davitt, the nineteenth-century Irish Land Leaguer who called the Ascendancy "cormorant vampires," Foster writes that this "picture . . . has long been disproved; if the post-Famine Irish landlords were vampires, they were not very good at it" (*Modern Ireland* 375). Anyone

---

[1]Elsewhere, Foster talks of the "'vampirizing' tendency of the Irish Parliamentary Party" (*Modern Ireland* 468), a largely Irish Protestant group. For a generally more charitable view of the Ascendancy, see 167–94.

expecting a Manichaean dualism,[2] in which the Ascendancy sits squarely on the side of the British Empire against a common Catholic Irish foe, is frustrated by the ambivalent social position of the Irish Protestant, marked as both colonizer and colonized, "caught on the hop between conflicting cultural norms, whose whole existence is a barely tolerable in-betweenness" (Eagleton 160). For Eagleton, the failure of the Anglo-Irish political elite to achieve control over the political and social life of Ireland and to maintain close allegiances with the British state corresponds to a development in literature in which realism, the dominant mode of literary expression in nineteenth-century Britain, becomes unstable and ambiguous in the work of Irish writers. For a number of reasons having to do with Ireland's colonial status — especially the absence of a strong middle class and a "native" language — Irish fiction develops in a direction that "lends itself more obviously to modernism" (Eagleton 148). By this Eagleton means that Irish fiction anticipates the modernist critique of a form of realism that concealed its aesthetic operations. In this way, realism creates an impression of transparency, of a neutral, disinterested mode of depicting social life ideally suited to the development of a bourgeois class seeking to legitimize and naturalize its ideological commitments. It claims to permit us to see the otherwise unseen causes of social events and to understand the "stealthy effect" (Eagleton 201) of social conditions on character.

The Irish Protestant novelistic tradition lays claim to no such transparency. Realism fails to take hold, in part because the Ascendancy intelligentsia had occluded or mythologized their own involvement in the causes of social events. Moreover, the causal relationship between social conditions and the individual in realistic literature, which might be said to reflect a bourgeois social compact, does not obtain under conditions of colonial domination. As Eagleton suggests, the pressures of the "real" in colonial societies produces social consequences that are not always explicable in terms of cause and effect and drive colonized writers to create unrealistic (that is to say, fantastic) representations of unbearable social conditions. We see this throughout the nineteenth century in the tendency of Irish Protestant Gothic novelists such as Charles Maturin, Sheridan Le Fanu, and Bram Stoker to create macabre or ghostly allegories of their feelings of social displacement and disempowerment. Eagleton's brief characterization of Dracula as a ghoulish type of the absentee Ascendancy landlord (215) suggests a direction for

---

[2]Manichaeanism refers to a binary situation, in this case one in which the colonizer and colonized are locked in a pitched battle for domination. Manichaeanism originally referred to a religious dualistic philosophy in Persia in the third century C.E.

analysis that has been largely ignored in recent historical criticism of *Dracula*. Much of this criticism is concerned with Stoker's ambivalent sexuality and his response to the threat of absorption by a rising Catholic middle class. In this criticism, Dracula represents the "return of the repressed," and this return is especially threatening when it appears to reverse the power dynamic of colonialism or to foretell the absorption, both socially and politically, of the Ascendancy by the Catholic Irish. Though the fears of absorption were quite real, the fear of "reverse colonization" emerges more obviously from English anxieties than from Anglo-Irish concerns. The Ascendancy had perhaps more to fear from the English than they did from the Catholic Irish.[3]

Many of the social issues alluded to in *Dracula* — social decadence, racial degeneration, poverty, disease (especially syphilis), the fear of immigration from the colonies[4] — were very much English concerns. Critics who analyze the significance of these issues in *Dracula* take their cue from Mina Harker, who identifies Dracula as "a criminal and of criminal type. Nordau and Lombroso would so classify him"(p. 336 in this volume). Max Nordau's *Degeneration,* published in German in 1892 and in English in 1895, constituted the leading edge of criticism leveled against the excesses of "civilized" culture at the fin de siècle. In overheated rhetoric, Nordau excoriates the decay of a sick culture:

> [T]he *fin-de-siècle* mood . . . is the impotent despair of a sick man, who feels himself dying by inches in the midst of an eternally living nature blooming insolently for ever. It is the envy of a rich, hoary voluptuary, who sees a pair of young lovers making for a sequestered forest nook; it is the mortification of the exhausted and impotent refugee from a Florentine plague, seeking in an enchanted garden the experiences of a Decamerone, but striving in vain to snatch one more pleasure of sense from the uncertain hour. (3)

Nordau's rhetoric is not far from that of English social reformers in the 1890s, such as Charles and William Booth. Charles Booth's census of London's East End created new categories of the urban poor. In addition to creating the Salvation Army, his brother William published an influential book in 1890, *Darkest England and the Way Out,* which set forth a plan for the segregation and, ultimately, forced emigration of

---

[3]On the threat of "reverse colonization," that is the process by which natives of the colonies make their way to the metropolitan center, see Arata; on the threat of absorption, see Schmitt.

[4]See Boone, Craft, Croley, Glover, Halberstam, McWhir, Pick, Spencer, and Warwick.

the most degenerate members of the urban population.[5] Against this English background, argues Daniel Pick, Stoker's *Dracula* presents "a vision of the bio-medical degeneration of the race" that "at once sensationalized the horrors of degeneration and charted reassuringly the process of their confinement and containment" (75, 83). In this view, the threat is to the *English* race, and Stoker's narrative structure, which allocates narrative authority to exclusively English characters who produce their own version of events, reinforces this national emphasis.

But it is clear, given the destiny of the Ascendancy in the nineteenth century, that Anglo-Irish anxieties were not the same as English ones and that the threat represented by Dracula could be read as emanating not only from a foreign source, a primitive Catholic Other, but from the English themselves who, for all intents and purposes, abandoned their Anglo-Irish clients. This double threat — and double fear — marks a congenital instability in terms of political and cultural identity, an instability that places the Anglo-Irish as a class on both sides of the colonial divide. In *Dracula,* this double placement results in anomalous, hybrid figures: a primitive, atavistic Dracula is nonetheless civilized while the civilized, rational English are dependent on primitive superstition. If we read *Dracula* as "a kind of allegory, which properly interpreted lays bare the historical forces at its heart" (Eagleton 183), these forces — which blur the line between civilized and primitive, national and transnational — need to be recognized and explained. By staging this allegory in London, the heart of the empire, Stoker invites us to consider the threat of Dracula within the binary structure of imperialism (which makes an absolute distinction between the primitive or premodern colonized and the civilized or modern colonizer), a structure in which Dracula represents the return of the repressed colonial subject. But when we read *Dracula* with an awareness of Stoker's ambivalent Anglo-Irishness, the emphasis shifts from a binary structure in which a Protestant England is invaded by Catholic vampires to an ambivalent structure in which Anglo-Irish Protestants must negotiate between the Catholic peasantry they mistreated and the English politicians who hold their future in their hands. Though it is set in London and Transylvania and features no Irish characters, it is possible, even inevitable, to read Stoker's novel as an expression of the Protestant Ascendancy's most deeply rooted fears.

Dracula responds to these fears and the cultural displacement of the Ascendancy class. By projecting an ambivalent Anglo-Irish subjec-

---

[5]On the Booths and the "rhetoric of reform," see Croley.

tivity onto two highly ambivalent fictional characters, Abraham Van Helsing and Count Dracula, it expresses the social "reality" of an elite ruling class that has lost its legitimacy and become "homeless." Stoker's text is thus a reflection of a particular historical process in which the Ascendancy descended from its stable position as a ruling class to "a form of cultural displacement" (Eagleton 63). As many critics have noted, this shift became apparent to the Ascendancy in the closing decades of the nineteenth century, when Land League agitation in Ireland and land legislation in England resulted in the virtual disestablishment of the Anglo-Irish land-owning class.[6] By the time Stoker published *Dracula* in 1897, the threat of absorption by a politically powerful Catholic middle class was palpable, despite the success of the Catholic church in its campaign in 1890 to topple Charles Stewart Parnell, an Anglo-Irish politician whose affair with a married woman, Mrs. Kitty O'Shea, cost him the leadership of the Irish Parliamentary Party. The Ascendancy had cause for alarm, especially given the rhetoric of Irish-Ireland nationalists like D. P. Moran, who could write, in 1905, at the peak of the Literary Revival, "the Gael must be the element that absorbs" (37).[7] The "clerical-national alliance" continued unabated after Parnell's fall, with some Irish political allegiances shifting to Gladstone's Liberal party, which drafted the 1886 and 1893 Home Rule Bills.[8] By the late 1890s, increasingly virulent protestations from what Foster calls "irreconcilable elements left out of the Parnellite equation," together with a dwindling of Anglo-Irish support for Home Rule, created a climate of paranoia and deracination (*Modern Ireland* 427). The prospect of absorption by a growing Catholic middle class led the Ascendancy into an "obsessive, hierarchical subculture" (Foster, *Modern Ireland* 427) in which self-perceptions were colored by the double threat of Catholic political power and English indifference.

For many readers of *Dracula*, the Irish historical context may not seem relevant to their understanding of a man who had become an important player in the English theater community and whose sensibilities, judging from characters like Jonathan Harker, John Seward, and

Arthur Holmwood, are British and imperialist. But it is worth noting that before he went to work for Henry Irving at the Lyceum Theatre, Stoker was the quintessential Irish Protestant: the star student of Edward Dowden, professor of English at Trinity College, Dublin (the pinnacle of Protestant education in Ireland), "the brilliant son of a professional Dublin Protestant Family, Trinity Gold Medallist, Auditor of the College Philosophical Society, Double First and civil servant" (Foster, "Protestant Magic" 259).[9] Though not a land-owning member of the Ascendancy class, he nevertheless enjoyed the privileges of that class as well as the sense of ambivalence with respect to the British government, which had, for all intents and purposes, abandoned the Anglo-Irish. Like many of his class, he developed modes of "escapism motivated by the threat of a take-over by the Catholic middle classes — a threat all the more inexorable because it is being accomplished by peaceful means and with the free legal aid of British governments" ("Protestant Magic" 251). Reading *Dracula* with an awareness of this ambivalence and the social crisis that follows from it, we find a displaced expression of Stoker's — and the Ascendancy's — contradictory feelings of estrangement and entitlement. But the ambivalence encrypted in *Dracula* involves something more than a mixed feeling with regard to the British government's policy of appeasing an increasingly restive and politically potent Catholic middle class; indeed, it seems to involve an uneasy dependency on the very Catholicism, with its sacramental magic, that the Protestant Ascendancy was reputed to fear.

Like Oscar Wilde before him and James Joyce after, Stoker borrows and refashions the sacramental icons, rituals, and prayers; but unlike them, he does not do so in order to advance an ethical or artistic program that stands in defiance of Church or State authority. Rather, Stoker is more interested in using sacramental elements in order to protect Church and State from a threat that is, paradoxically, marked as Catholic. His recourse to sacramentalism amounts to a preemptive tactic, one in which the Irish Catholic's sacramental desire and the rituals that express it are appropriated. His intention is to exert a symbolic domination over Catholic Ireland and thus to forestall the decline of an ineffectual Ascendancy class and to fend off the reverse colonization or absorption that events in fin de siècle Ireland seemed ominously to foreshadow. Stoker's reaction to political realities like land expropria-

---

[9]Foster goes on to note of Stoker's first book, *Duties of Clerks of the Petty Sessions,* that "[o]nly an Irish Protestant could have graduated so easily from that to *Dracula*" ("Protestant Magic" 259).

tion, Catholic democracy, and, inevitably, Home Rule — all of which, by 1897, would have been regarded as serious threats to Ascendancy privilege — was not merely to appropriate but also to Gothicize sacramental desire. Reading *Dracula* in the context of Irish Protestant occultism, what Foster calls "Protestant magic," can help us understand why, in this Gothic drama of the return of the repressed, Dracula wears an Englishman's clothes and Van Helsing, the protector of English women and English values, brandishes a Roman Catholic cross.

Sacramental Magic

Reading the Anglo-Irish plot of *Dracula* involves recognizing the tensions, ambiguities, and contradictions that marked the Ascendancy's ambivalent, compromised position. In Stoker's use of sacramental elements, we find a contradiction: the fight against the atavistic horror of vampirism, the cutting-edge technology deployed by Van Helsing and his Crew of Light,[10] is useless without recourse to occult and sacramental practices. Critics typically interpret the contradictory interdependence of superstition and modernity in *Dracula* as a reflection of the ambivalence generated by competing ideologies of gender, race, class, and nationalism within modernity.[11] Geoffrey Wall puts the matter plainly when he writes that in *Dracula* we find a "contradiction between the archaic stuff of its narrative and the contemporary techniques which allow that narrative to emerge" (15).[12] However, Stoker's use of sacramental ritual and icons to ward off a demonized Catholic threat is less paradoxical and enigmatic if taken in the context of the Irish 1890s. During that decade, the threat of the Catholic middle class provoked Protestant intellectuals to embrace occult knowledge, to Gothicize their alienation, to engage in a ritualistic self-fashioning that, paradoxically, appropriates the sacramental in order to make up for a paucity of national and spiritual vision. What we discover is a text deeply ambivalent about the Catholicism it impugns: in order to compensate for the increasing political power of the Catholic Irish, Stoker

[10]The phrase "Crew of Light" (referring to Van Helsing, Seward, Holmwood, Morris, and the Harkers) is Craft's invention, though he takes his cue from Stoker: "Lucy, *lux*, light" (208, n. 7).

[11]See Wicke, who notes that "it is not merely the atavism of Dracula that makes his appearance in England so frightful; it is his relative modernity" (p. 598). Others — notably McWhir (31), Glover (249) and Spencer (200) — note the blurring of line between modern and premodern.

[12]See Craft (101), Gagnier (147, 153), Greenway, Jann, and Wicke.

symbolically transforms them into Transylvanian peasants and into the Count, both occupying a primitive landscape where their sacramental desire is recoded as superstition, ignorance, monstrosity, and atavism. But this displacement and disavowal of the Catholic Other does not prevent scientists like the Dutchman Van Helsing from taking up sacramental rituals in order to supply what the rationalism and materialism of modernity had repudiated: a way of seeing beyond the limits of a "normal" scientific paradigm and the "sentimental" social truths that legitimate and sustain it (Greenway 218ff).

Stoker's and his characters' ambivalent attitude toward Catholicism and sacramentalism reflects to some degree a colonialist desire to disavow the Irish Catholic; but it also reflects the desire of a marginalized elite to appropriate religious ritual in order to invigorate itself. From the Gothic romanticism of Charles Maturin and Sheridan Le Fanu to the occult esotericism of the Literary Revivalists, Irish Protestant intellectuals turned to mysticism and the occult in order to solemnize and ritualize their otherwise impoverished social condition. Foster's description of W. B. Yeats's Protestant subculture fits Stoker's: "an insecure middle-class, with a race-memory of elitism and a predisposition towards seeking refuge in the occult" ("Protestant Magic" 265–6). Stoker probably shared Yeats's "exasperation with Catholic demos, and a refusal to allow that element the monopoly of being 'Irish'" (246). This strain of "Protestant magic" is, as Foster indicates, part of a long Ascendancy tradition of "occult preoccupations." The interest in secretive or esoteric societies counteracted both scientific positivism and Roman Catholicism. The popularity of Freemasonry and occult orders reflects a desire for access to spiritual and irrational experiences that provided a compensatory escape from social and cultural displacement and a balm for anxieties concerning the threat of a powerful Catholic middle class. For many Ascendancy intellectuals, this kind of access offered a powerful alternative both to Catholicism and to conventional modes of historical and social analysis emanating from Britain.[13]

Sacramental elements manifest themselves on a number of levels in Stoker's text. On one level, we find references to an array of sacramental practices including marriage, baptism, confession, the Eucharist, extreme unction, and even, if we regard vampiric induction in this light, the taking of (un)holy orders.[14] Stoker's descriptions of these practices

---

[13]On "occult preoccupations" see Foster, "Protestant Magic" (251, 261–3), and Jann (274).

[14]On the seven principle sacraments, see "Theology of Sacraments" in *The New Catholic Encyclopedia* (12: 806–15, esp. 811).

are anthropological in so far as they correspond to the actual conditions of religious life in Transylvania. But on another level, the sacraments become an element of a Gothic fantasy in which they become vulnerable to Van Helsing's (and Dracula's) occult resignification. We can trace the change from an anthropological to a Gothic representation in Stoker's shifting treatment of sacramental elements. In the opening chapters, which detail Jonathan Harker's journey to and sojourn in Dracula's castle, the accoutrements of Catholicism are regarded with an ethnographic distance and disdain.[15] Upon his arrival in Transylvania, Harker notes the frequency with which the local peasants cross themselves reverently and describes them in the style of the imperial travelogue:

> Here and there we passed Cszeks and Slovaks, all in picturesque attire, but I noticed that goitre was painfully prevalent. By the roadside were many crosses, and as we swept by, my companions all crossed themselves. Here and there was a peasant man or woman kneeling before a shrine who did not even turn round as we approached, but seemed in the self-surrender of devotion to have neither eyes nor ears for the outer world. (p. 33)

Stoker's depiction of the Transylvanian peasants draws on a source, Major E. C. Johnson's *On the Track of the Crescent* (1885), which compares them to Irish and Scottish peasants.[16] We see reflected quite clearly in Jonathan Harker's depictions of the Transylvanian peasants the attitude of the Ascendancy toward the Irish Catholic. It is one he would have found seconded in his source material, where the "grossly superstitious" Roman Catholic Székely peasants are described as exhibiting "a curious combination of the canny Scot and the imprudent Irishman" (p. 384). Johnson's description of the Greek Orthodox Wallachians typifies the imperial travelogues of the period. The Wallachians, he notes, have

> many points of resemblance to our friend Paddy. He is grossly superstitious, as the number of crosses by the roadside and on every eminence testify; and, like his prototype, he lives in abject terror of his priest, of whose powers he has the most exalted ideas.

[15]On the imperial travelogue, see Arata; on ethnography see Gagnier, who notes "Stoker's ethnographic obsessions, such as dialect" (150), and Foster, who writes that Stoker's working notes for *Dracula* reflect "seven years of Yeats-style research into folklore, myth, armchair anthropology, medieval history, and magic" ("Protestant Magic" 259).

[16]As far as I can tell, only Foster notes this aspect of Stoker's source; unfortunately, he does not pursue the point: "The Irishness of Dracula must be left aside here" (259).

He believes that 'his rivirence' could turn him into a cow, or, as in Lover's famous anecdote, 'make him meander up and down in the form of an ould gander' for eternity, should he show any sign of having a will of his own. (105)

In a less overt manner, Stoker performs a similar displacement by which the Eastern European Other takes on the characteristics of a latently Irish primitive. An early scene between Jonathan and a peasant woman sets an imperial English tone: "She then rose and dried her eyes, and taking a crucifix from her neck offered it to me. I did not know what to do, for as an English Churchman, I have been taught to regard such things as in some measure idolatrous, and yet it seemed so ungracious to refuse an old lady meaning so well and in such a state of mind" (p. 31). Harker's attitude here is typical of the imperious Englishman; more surprising is the way in which this attitude, a kinder and gentler version of Johnson's, is transformed as the narrative moves beyond Harker's travelogue, with its generic commitments to a colonialist attitude, and begins to record the disturbing events back home in the metropolis.

The gradual approach of Dracula, with his ambiguous identity — noble and base, civilized and monstrous — appears to weaken the resistance of Englishmen and Englishwomen and to make them susceptible to the vampiric desire that is one of the secrets contained in Harker's notebook. In a section preceded by a "[s]trange and sudden change in Renfield" (p. 119), the madman who is "mixed up with the Count in an indexy kind of way" (p. 252), Mina artlessly and perhaps unconsciously borrows the sacramental language to express her devotion to and trust in her husband. She ties his notebook with ribbon and seals it with her wedding ring. She then kisses it and shows it to Jonathan: "[I] told him that I would keep it so, and then it would be an outward and visible sign for us all our lives that we trusted each other; that I would never open it unless it were for his own dear sake or for the sake of some stern duty" (p. 123). Mina's paraphrase of Catholic theology — in which the sacraments are "visible signs chosen by Christ to bring mankind the grace of His paschal mystery"[17] — sets the stage for a later development: the intervention of Van Helsing, who performs the work of synthesis, unthinkable to Jonathan and only imagined by Mina, of

[17] *The New Catholic Encyclopedia* (12: 806). "Sacraments are signs of faith in a twofold sense. On the one hand, they are objective expressions of the faith as it is professed and lived in the Church. . . . On the other hand, they express the personal faith of the recipient. 'All sacraments are certain protestations of faith' (Aquinas *ST* 3a, 72.5 ad 2)" (12: 813–14).

reason and superstition, of the Churchman and the idolatrous Catholic peasant. As a scientist, lawyer, and European, Van Helsing shares common ground with the English characters. But his Catholicism and his belief in occult knowledge and practices link him with the peasant Other, particularly as it was represented by Irish Protestant Revivalists, including Yeats, J. M. Synge, Lady Augusta Gregory, and Standish O'Grady, who were profoundly ambivalent toward Catholicism. Van Helsing introduces the sacramental as occult practice among his rationalist English friends, even claiming, implausibly, that he has an Indulgence. His use of the sacraments is, professedly, a sacred one, done in the name of God for the good of humanity, but his professions should not blind us to the impact his intervention has on his English friends.

Van Helsing, nevertheless, has a distinctly Anglo-Irish coloration, because he embodies the easy familiarity with the mystical and the occult of Irish Protestants who sought secret wisdom in order to overcome social deracination. But so too does Count Dracula. When we consider the relation between him and the culture of which he is seemingly an integral part, we find another displaced Anglo-Irishman, this one a monstrous parody of the rack-rent absentee landlord, parasitical and haughty. Dracula wears the "monstrous" face that the Ascendancy wore at some periods of Irish history, particularly during the famine. His decrepit castle, the lack of servants, the mingling of fear and respect accorded him by Catholic peasants who seem to stand to him in a relation of subservience — all of this suggests the social milieu of the Ascendancy Big House. He resembles the irredeemable gentry, helpless, isolated, and fallen into decay, found in the stories of Sheridan Le Fanu, one of Stoker's models as a writer.[18]

Van Helsing and Dracula each embodies an aspect of Stoker's split and compromised Anglo-Irish identity in a double projection that allegorizes social anxieties and offers symbolic consolation for feelings of political illegitimacy and spiritual and cultural homelessness. On the one hand, Dracula represents the monstrous "parasitic social formation," as Eagleton describes the Ascendancy, which is brought down by rational and scientific Englishmen. The Ascendancy's political inadequacy is thus played out in Dracula's vampirism and the Crew of Light's heroic protection of English values and English women. On the other hand, we have something like the Protestant magician in Van Helsing,

[18]"[T]hough ostensibly set in Derbyshire, [Le Fanu's "authentic masterpiece" *Uncle Silas*] was long ago spotted by Elizabeth Bowen as an Irish story in disguise, dealing with exploitation, imprisonment, fractured identity, and hauntings" (Foster, "Protestant Magic" 251).

whose mystified science disrupts the binary opposition between the heartless, eminently rational English and the victimized, powerless Catholic Irish. Van Helsing "infects" English values and rational science when he supplements both with sacramental magic, which he authoritatively declares necessary in combating a threat that he depicts as demonically Catholic. "'And now, my friends,'" Van Helsing says solemnly, "'we have a duty here to do. We must sterilise this earth, so sacred of holy memories, that he has brought from a far distant land for such fell use. He has chosen this earth because it has been holy. Thus we defeat him with his own weapon, for we make it more holy still'" (p. 297). But the symbolic triumph embodied in Van Helsing's exorcism of Dracula is offset by Jonathan Harker's note that concludes the novel. The ambiguity of the note, which Steven Arata calls "troubled and qualified," suggests that Dracula's attempt to penetrate English society may have succeeded after all.[19] The Harkers' son, Quincey, named after the man who died while bringing Dracula down, "links all our little band of men together" (p. 368). Jonathan refers to spiritual links, of course. But there are blood connections as well, for Mina's unholy sacramental union with Dracula suggests that her son may carry Dracula's blood in his veins. Reading the Anglo-Irish plot of *Dracula* reveals that even symbolic triumphs are ambivalent, since it is unclear whether Quincey represents the corruption or the revitalization of the English race.

A Priestly Science

Like many of the productions of the Irish Literary Revival, in which Irish Protestant intellectuals invented an occult peasantry, Stoker's *Dracula* effects an uneasy, because partly unconscious, link between Protestant and sacramental magic. We see this most vividly in Van Helsing's sacramental occultism, which brings to bear a "foreign" synthesis of science and the rituals and supernatural powers of the Catholic sacraments against a demonized Catholic foe. Van Helsing's arrival in England comes shortly after Mina's sacramental ritual of sealing Jonathan's notebook. Seward describes him to Holmwood as a man on the cutting edge of science: "He is a seemingly arbitrary man, but this

---

[19]Arata goes on to note that "Harker unwittingly calls attention to the fact that the positions of vampire and victim have been reversed. Now it is Dracula whose blood is appropriated and transformed to nourish a faltering race" (643). Halberstam makes the opposite point: "In *Dracula*, vampires are precisely a race and a family that weakens the stock of Englishness by passing on degeneracy and the disease of blood lust" (340).

is because he knows what he is talking about better than any one else. He is a philosopher and a metaphysician, and one of the most advanced scientists of his day; and he has, I believe, an absolutely open mind" (p. 129). The master/disciple relation between Seward and Van Helsing underscores the distinction between the self-assured conventionality of the former and the enigmatic authority of the latter. Van Helsing is presented from the first as enigmatic, a rationalist who presents his knowledge in parables or withholds it in portentous silences. In defending his strategy to keep Lucy Westenra's condition from Holmwood, he tells Seward: "I have sown my corn, and Nature has her work to do in making it sprout" (p. 135). He is arbitrary and imperious, consistently holding back what he knows and controlling who finally comes to know it. His skepticism with respect to conventional science comports easily with a deep knowledge of and respect for the occult. His authority comes not from Seward's conventional science, but from an occulted, priestly version of it: "There is grim purpose in all I do; and I warn you that you do not thwart me" (p. 146). Part of his power is directly attributable to his unorthodox assumption of sacramental authority (he is, after all, *not* a priest). The sacramental paraphernalia, particularly "a little golden crucifix" (p. 176) brought in to save Lucy after science has failed, provokes no discernible response from those gathered around her bed who have come to trust implicitly in Van Helsing's methods. The mystery that he imparts to the crucifix and the Host — which he can barely name, calling them the "other things which [the Un-Dead] shun" (p. 216) — is a hybrid one, compounded of the awesome power of the priest and the pagan superstitiousness of the peasant.[20] His heterodoxy is commented on, ironically enough, by the conventional scientist, Seward, who quotes Van Helsing's justification for using the supreme sacrament: "'The Host. I brought it from Amsterdam. I have an Indulgence.' It was an answer that appalled the most sceptical of us, and we felt individually that in the presence of such earnest purpose as the Professor's, a purpose which could thus use the to him most sacred of things, it was impossible to distrust" (p. 217).

Seward, of course, can only grasp Van Helsing's recourse to the unscientific in strictly religious terms, citing his "earnest purpose" as sufficient justification for an illegitimate use of the sacraments. What

[20]See Anne McWhir: "Between the familiarity and reasonableness of prayer-book religion [i.e., Anglicanism] and the superstitious rituals and beliefs of foreign Catholicism there is Van Helsing's use of ritual magic derived from Catholicism to preserve an Anglican world" (McWhir 33).

Seward fails to see is the extent to which Van Helsing mystifies conventional science, for example, when he says: " 'You do not let your eyes see nor your ears hear, and that which is outside your daily life is not of account to you. . . . But yet we see around us every day the growth of new beliefs, which think themselves new; and which are yet but the old, which pretend to be young — like the fine ladies at the opera. . . . There are always mysteries in life'" (pp. 201–02). When asked if he could believe in such paranormal concepts as "corporeal transference" or "astral bodies," Seward demurs. Only "hypnotism" is "accountable." Van Helsing, in seeking to wean Seward from his limitations, prepares him for a much more disturbing message: "that science does not always validate social truth" (Greenway 227). Van Helsing's paradoxical conjoining of the rational and the supernatural, governed by a prophylactic use of the sacraments, brings together two conflicting imperatives. One is the rational desire for an ordered account, exemplified by Seward's clinical approach to Renfield and Mina Harker's archival foresight: "[T]he whole story is put together in such a way that every point tells." (pp. 251–52). The other is the necessity for occult knowledge and practices that will enable the technologies of writing to represent what is *unaccountable*. In his role as a progressive scientist, Van Helsing champions paranormal approaches to experience; but his acceptance of superstition and folklore places him well outside the bounds of empirical science. Through his influence, the Crew of Light, conventionally pious and valiant, at bottom rational, nevertheless become caught up in the ambiguous conjunction of science and occult knowledge and fall in with his plan to "restore Lucy to [them] as a holy, and not an unholy, memory" (p. 222). To that end they say the prayer for the dead over her somnambulant body and heartily destroy her. By the time Seward confronts Dracula in his London house, he is "[i]nstinctively" brandishing a crucifix and the Host (p. 304).

When we read the sacramental elements in *Dracula* as reflecting anxiety over the loss of Ascendancy power, Van Helsing's priestly scientism emerges as a critique that aims not to denigrate Catholicism but rather to implicate conventional science and English rationality in an indictment of its own origins and limitations. He invigorates rational scientific inquiry with a Gothicized sacramentalism, in an act that suggests the impotence of both science and the established Church of England. His odd marriage of rationality and sacramental ritual resembles the decadent Catholicism that flourished in Dublin at the fin de siècle, which involved the potent mixture of sexuality and occult knowledge that we find in Yeats's mystical stories and Wilde's *The Picture of*

Dorian Gray.[21] When he places a "little golden crucifix" on Lucy's dead lips to protect her from the ghastly transformation into a wanton vampire that he knows will take place (p. 176), he supplements medical science with an occult protection against Lucy's vampiric sexuality. We see a similar use of sacramental elements in his resignification of the Host. When Van Helsing inspects Carfax the first time, intoning "*In manus tuas, Domine*" and crossing himself before entering, he warns his Crew that they "must not desecrate needless" the Sacred Wafer he has passed out to them for protection (p. 253); yet he is willing to appropriate the sanctifying powers of the Host into an *ad hoc* ritual on the authority of a bogus Indulgence. When they return to Carfax to "cleanse" Dracula's crates of earth, Van Helsing remarks that Dracula "has chosen this earth because it has been holy. Thus we defeat him with his own weapon, for we make it more holy still" (p. 297). Orthodox or not, the brandishing of crucifixes and sacred wafers does little more than temporarily daunt Dracula, who turns into a "great black cloud" and sails away after being caught vamping Mina Harker (p. 283). Moreover, when the Host sears its image onto Mina's forehead, she seems to bear a reminder not just of her "uncleanliness" but also of the inefficacy of the Host, which has proven powerless to protect Mina's soul even as it proves successful in warding off Dracula's diabolical advances. The "'Vampire's baptism of blood'" (p. 318) occurs in spite of Van Helsing's trappings of sacramental authority, which plays no major role in the final, victorious struggle to destroy Dracula. The crucifix can make Dracula cringe and the Host can contaminate his earth boxes, but what defeats him in the end is hypnotism, telepathy and other "new science" procedures that Van Helsing advocates and that enable the Crew of Light to trap and execute him. There is nothing ambiguous or occult about the "great kukri knife" that Jonathan Harker uses to dispatch Dracula or his "impetuosity, and the manifest singleness of his purpose" (p. 367).

Understood as an allegory of Ascendancy deracination, Stoker's narrative evokes a déclassé ruling elite filled with resentment over a sense of lost privilege that turns to occultism and sacramentalism in order to spiritualize its social and political displacement. Dracula performs a grotesque parody of "Protestant magic" within that allegory, his vampirism mocking both the sacramental desire of the Irish Catholic and the hybridizing impulse of the Irish Protestant occultist.

---

[21]On decadent Catholicism, see Hanson, especially the chapter on Wilde, "The Temptation of St. Oscar," (229–96).

In Stoker's working papers, we find notes indicating that the Count "has an ambivalent attitude towards the icons of religion: he can be moved only by relics older than his own *real* date or century (that is, when he actually lived) — more recent relics leave him unmoved" (qtd. in Frayling 343). Frayling goes on to note, however, that "the idea that vampires could be moved only by relics older than their own *real* date sounds ancient and folkloric, but appears to have been invented by Stoker" (344–5). In a process of creative cultural translation, Stoker augments his research into Transylvania folklore concerning the vampire myth by inventing sacramental elements for it, much as the Anglo-Irish Revivalists translated Irish folklore, giving to it an occult significance that reflects their own desire for a magical conception of the world. Dracula becomes the embodiment of the deracinated native intellectual, caught between two national identities — the Catholic Irish and the English — neither of which appears to offer any hope for the future of the Ascendancy.

Mediating these national extremes is the Catholic "foreigner" Van Helsing, the scientist whose sacerdotal knowledge challenges the assumptions of an imperial class without himself having to abdicate from that class. Like the "Protestant magician," who sought spiritual authority to make up for the failure of political power, Van Helsing seeks to make up for the failures of science by adopting sacramental rituals. Some critics have noted that Van Helsing's medical procedures resemble Dracula's vampirism. Arata puts it well when he writes that "Van Helsing and his tradition have polished teeth into hypodermic needles, a cultural refinement that masks violation as healing" (87). But Dracula has likewise refined his predatory vampirism into a subtle strategy of revenge and seduction, in which Englishwomen like Mina Harker are countermined, transformed into his "kin" and, incestuously, his "bountiful wine-press[es]" (p. 288). *Dracula* presents Anglo-Irish anxiety displaced onto opposed characters: on the one hand, Van Helsing represents the alienated Anglo-Irish intellectual dabbling in the occult; on the other hand, Dracula represents the deracinated landlord class that resents the empire for abandoning it and that holds the Catholic peasants in thrall. This double projection of a compromised identity upsets any attempt to read *Dracula* in a Manichaean or binary way, for though the Crew of Light emerge victorious, the worldview that made the victory possible may have been fatally undermined in the process. Like Yeats in the 1890s, Stoker envisioned a world in which binary opposites — good and evil, male and female, spirit and matter — struggle for supremacy. But Stoker anticipates Yeats's vision of a "rough beast slouching toward Bethlehem" when he depicts a struggle that is confused or multiplied by a force that threatens to undermine the very foundations of binary thinking. This peculiar binary struggle captures the position of the Anglo-Irish caught between the poles of English colonizer and Catholic colonized, never quite secure in their role as a *native* ruling class ambiguously supported from outside. At the end of the novel, Van Helsing is secure in the bosom of his adopted and adoptive English family and Dracula is never quite contained or defeated, for his blood courses still in the veins of Jonathan Harker's child. This conclusion drives home the point that ambivalence marks the compromised history and social position of the Irish Protestant Ascendancy.

WORKS CITED

Arata, Stephen D. "The Occidental Tourist: *Dracula* and the Anxiety of Reverse Colonization." *Victorian Studies* 33 (Summer 1990): 621–45.

Beckett, J. C. *The Making of Modern Ireland, 1603–1923.* London: Faber, 1966.

Boone, Troy. " 'He is English and therefore adventurous': Politics, Decadence, and *Dracula.*" *Studies in the Novel* 25.1 (Spring 1993): 76–91.

Craft, Christopher. *Another Kind of Love: Male Homosexual Desire in English Discourse 1850–1920.* Berkeley: U of California P, 1994. 71–105.

Croley, Laura Sagolla. "The Rhetoric of Reform in Stoker's *Dracula:* Depravity, Decline, and the Fin-de-Siècle 'Residuum.'" *Criticism* 37.1 (Winter 1995): 85–108.

Eagleton, Terry. *Heathcliff and the Great Hunger: Studies in Irish Culture.* London: Verso, 1995.

Foster, R. F. *Modern Ireland 1600–1972.* London: Penguin, 1989.

———. "Protestant Magic: W. B. Yeats and the Spell of Irish History." *Proceedings of the British Academy* 75 (1989): 243–66.

Frayling, Christopher. "Bram Stoker's Working Papers for *Dracula.*" *Dracula.* By Bram Stoker. Ed. Nina Auerbach and David J. Skal. New York: Norton, 1997. 339–50.

Gagnier, Regenia. "Evolution and Information, or Eroticism and Everyday Life, in *Dracula* and Late Victorian Aestheticism." *Sex and Death in Victorian Literature.* Ed. Regina Barreca. London: Macmillan, 1990. 140–57.

Glover, David. "'Our enemy is not merely spiritual': Degeneration and Modernity in Bram Stoker's *Dracula.*" *Victorian Literature and Culture* 22 (1994): 249–65.

Greenway, John L. "Seward's Folly: *Dracula* as a Critique of 'Normal Science.'" *Stanford Literature Review* 3 (Fall 1986): 213–30.

Halberstam, Judith. "Technologies of Monstrosity: Bram Stoker's *Dracula.*" *Victorian Studies* 36 (Spring 93): 333–52.

Hanson, Ellis. *Decadence and Catholicism.* Cambridge: Harvard UP, 1997.

Hyde, Douglas. "The Necessity for De-Anglicizing Ireland." *The Revival of Irish Literature: Addresses by Sir Charles Gavan Duffy, K.C.M.G., Dr. George Sigerson, and Dr. Douglas Hyde.* London: Fisher Unwin, 1894. 115–61.

Jann, Rosemary. "Saved by Science? The Mixed Messages of Stoker's *Dracula.*" *Texas Studies in Literature and Language* 31 (Summer 1989): 273–87.

Johnson, Major E. C. "On the Track of Transylvania." *The Origins of* Dracula: *The Background to Bram Stoker's Gothic Masterpiece.* Ed. Clive Leatherdale. London: William Kimber, 1987. 97–108.

Larkin, Emmet. *The Roman Catholic Church in Ireland and the Fall of Parnell, 1888–1891.* Chapel Hill: U of North Carolina P, 1979.

McWhir, Anne. "Pollution and Redemption in *Dracula.*" *Modern Language Studies* 27.3 (Summer 1987): 31–40.

Moran, D. P. *The Philosophy of Irish Ireland.* Dublin: Duffy, 1905.

The New Catholic Encyclopedia. New York: McGraw-Hill, 1967–79.

Nordau, Max. *Degeneration.* New York: D. Appleton, 1895.

Pick, Daniel. "'Terrors of the night': *Dracula* and 'Degeneration' in the Late-Nineteenth Century." *Critical Quarterly* 30.4 (1988): 71–87.

Schaffer, Talia. "'A wilde desire took me': The Homoerotic History of *Dracula.*" *ELH* 61 (1994): 381–425.

Schmitt, Cannon. "Mother Dracula: Orientalism, Degeneration, and Anglo-Irish National Subjectivity at the Fin de Siècle." *Bucknell Review* 38.1 (1994): 25–43.

Spencer, Kathleen L. "Purity and Danger: *Dracula,* the Urban Gothic, and the Late Victorian Degeneracy Crisis." *ELH* 59 (1992): 197–225.

Warwick, Alexandra. "Vampires and the Empire: Fears and Fictions of the 1890s." *Cultural Politics at the Fin De Siècle*. Eds. Sally Ledger and Scott McCracken. Cambridge: Cambridge UP, 1995, 202–20.

Wicke, Jennifer. "Vampiric Typewriting: *Dracula* and Its Media." *ELH* 59 (1992): 467–93. Rpt. in this volume, pp. 577–99.

Deconstruction and *Dracula*

WHAT IS DECONSTRUCTION?

Deconstruction has a reputation for being the most complex and forbidding of contemporary critical approaches to literature, but in fact
almost all of us have, at one time, either deconstructed a text or badly
wanted to deconstruct one. Sometimes when we hear a lecturer effectively
marshal evidence to show that a book means primarily one thing, we long
to interrupt and ask what he or she would make of other, conveniently
overlooked passages that seem to contradict the lecturer's thesis. Sometimes, after reading a provocative critical article that *almost* convinces us
that a familiar work means the opposite of what we assumed it meant, we
may wish to make an equally convincing case for our former reading of the
text. We may not think that the poem or novel in question better supports
our interpretation, but we may recognize that the text can be used to support *both* readings. And sometimes we simply want to make that point:
texts can be used to support seemingly irreconcilable positions.

To reach this conclusion is to feel the deconstructive itch. J. Hillis
Miller, the preeminent American deconstructor, puts it this way:
"Deconstruction is not a dismantling of the structure of a text, but a
demonstration that it has already dismantled itself. Its apparently solid
ground is no rock but thin air" ("Stevens' Rock" 341). To deconstruct
a text isn't to show that all the high old themes aren't there to be found

in it. Rather, it is to show that a text — not unlike DNA with its double helix — can have intertwined, opposite "discourses" — strands of narrative, threads of meaning.

Ultimately, of course, deconstruction refers to a larger and more complex enterprise than the practice of demonstrating that a text can have contradictory meanings. The term refers to a way of reading texts practiced by critics who have been influenced by the writings of the French philosopher Jacques Derrida. It is important to gain some understanding of Derrida's project and of the historical backgrounds of his work before reading the deconstruction that follows, let alone attempting to deconstruct a text.

Derrida, a philosopher of language who coined the term *deconstruction*, argues that we tend to think and express our thoughts in terms of opposites. Something is black but not white, masculine and therefore not feminine, a cause rather than an effect, and so forth. These mutually exclusive pairs or dichotomies are too numerous to list, but would include beginning/end, conscious/unconscious, presence/ absence, and speech/writing. If we think hard about these dichotomies, Derrida suggests, we will realize that they are not simply oppositions; they are also hierarchies in miniature. In other words, they contain one term that our culture views as being superior and one term viewed as negative or inferior. Sometimes the superior term seems only subtly superior (*speech, cause*), whereas sometimes we know immediately which term is culturally preferable (*presence, beginning*, and *consciousness* are easy choices). But the hierarchy always exists.

Of particular interest to Derrida, perhaps because it involves the language in which all the other dichotomies are expressed, is the hierarchical opposition "speech/writing." Derrida argues that the "privileging" of speech, that is, the tendency to regard speech in positive terms and writing in negative terms, cannot be disentangled from the privileging of presence. (Postcards are written by absent friends; we read Plato because he cannot speak from beyond the grave.) Furthermore, according to Derrida, the tendency to privilege both speech and presence is part of the Western tradition of *logocentrism*, the belief that in some ideal beginning were creative *spoken* words, words such as "Let there be light," spoken by an ideal, *present* God.[1] According to logocentric tradition, these

[1]Derrida sometimes uses the word *phallogocentrism* to indicate that there is "a certain indissociability" between logocentrism and the "phallocentrism" (Derrida, *Acts* 57) of a culture whose God created light, the world, and man before creating woman — from Adam's rib. "Phallocentrism" is another name for patriarchy. The role that deconstruction has played in feminist analysis will be discussed later.

words can now only be represented in unoriginal speech or writing (such as the written phrase in quotation marks above). Derrida doesn't seek to reverse the hierarchized opposition between speech and writing, or presence and absence, or early and late, for to do so would be to fall into a trap of perpetuating the same forms of thought and expression that he seeks to deconstruct. Rather, his goal is to erase the boundary between oppositions such as speech and writing, and to do so in such a way as to throw the order and values implied by the opposition into question.

Returning to the theories of Ferdinand de Saussure, who invented the modern science of linguistics, Derrida reminds us that the association of speech with present, obvious, and ideal meaning — and writing with absent, merely pictured, and therefore less reliable meaning — is suspect, to say the least. As Saussure demonstrated, words are *not* the things they name and, indeed, they are only arbitrarily associated with those things. A word, like any sign, is what Derrida has called a "deferred presence"; that is to say, "the signified concept is never present in itself," and "every concept is necessarily . . . inscribed in a chain or system, within which it refers to another and to other concepts" ("Différance" 138, 140). Neither spoken nor written words have present, positive, identifiable attributes themselves. They have meaning only by virtue of their difference from other words (*red, read, reed*) and, at the same time, their contextual relationship to those words. Take *read* as an example. To know whether it is the present or past tense of the verb — whether it rhymes with *red* or *reed* — we need to see it in relation to some other words (for example, *yesterday*).

Because the meanings of words lie in the differences between them and in the differences between them and the things they name, Derrida suggests that all language is constituted by *différance,* a word he has coined that puns on two French words meaning "to differ" and "to defer": words are the deferred presences of the things they "mean," and their meaning is grounded in difference. Derrida, by the way, changes the *e* in the French word *différence* to an *a* in his neologism *différance;* the change, which can be seen in writing but cannot be heard in spoken French, is itself a playful, witty challenge to the notion that writing is inferior or "fallen" speech.

In *Dissemination* (1972) and *De la grammatologie* [*Of Grammatology*] (1967), Derrida begins to redefine writing by deconstructing some old definitions. In *Dissemination,* he traces logocentrism back to Plato, who in the *Phaedrus* has Socrates condemn writing and who, in all the great dialogues, powerfully postulates that metaphysical longing for origins and ideals that permeates Western thought. "What Derrida does in his reading of Plato," Barbara Johnson points out in her translator's introduction to *Dissemination*, "is to unfold dimensions of Plato's *text* that work against the grain of (Plato's own) Platonism" (xxiv). Remember: that is what deconstruction does according to Miller; it shows a text dismantling itself.

In *Of Grammatology*, Derrida turns to the *Confessions* of Jean-Jacques Rousseau and exposes a grain running against the grain. Rousseau — who has often been seen as another great Western idealist and believer in innocent, noble origins — on one hand condemned writing as mere representation, a corruption of the more natural, childlike, direct, and therefore undevious speech. On the other hand, Rousseau acknowledged his own tendency to lose self-presence and blurt out exactly the wrong thing in public. He confesses that, by writing at a distance from his audience, he often expressed himself better: "If I were present, one would never know what I was worth," Rousseau admitted (Derrida, *Of Grammatology* 142). Thus, Derrida shows that one strand of Rousseau's discourse made writing seem a secondary, even treacherous supplement, while another made it seem necessary to communication.

Have Derrida's deconstructions of *Confessions* and the *Phaedrus* explained these texts, interpreted them, opened them up and shown us what they mean? Not in any traditional sense. Derrida would say that anyone attempting to find a single, homogeneous or universal meaning in a text is simply imprisoned by the structure of thought that would oppose two readings and declare one to be right and not wrong, correct rather than incorrect. In fact, any work of literature that we interpret defies the laws of Western logic, the laws of opposition and noncontradiction. From deconstruction's point of view, texts don't say "A and not B." They say "A and not-A." "Instead of a simple 'either/or' structure," Johnson explains, "deconstruction attempts to elaborate a discourse that says *neither* 'either/or' *nor* 'both/and' nor even 'neither/nor,' while at the same time not totally abandoning these logics either. The word *deconstruction* is meant to undermine the either/or logic of the opposition 'construction/destruction.' Deconstruction is both, it is neither, and it reveals the way in which both construction and destruction are themselves not what they appear to be" (Johnson, *World* 12–13).

Although its ultimate aim may be to criticize Western idealism and logic, deconstruction began as a response to structuralism and to formalism, another structure-oriented theory of reading. Using Saussure's theory as Derrida was to do later, European structuralists attempted to create a *semiology*, or science of signs, that would give humankind at once a scientific and a holistic way of studying the world and its human inhabitants. Roland Barthes, a structuralist who later shifted toward poststructuralism, hoped to recover literary language from the isolation in which it had been studied and to show that the laws that govern it govern all signs, from road signs to articles of clothing. Claude Lévi-Strauss, a structural anthropologist who studied everything from village structure to the structure of myths, found in myths what he called *mythemes,* or building blocks, such as basic plot elements. Recognizing that the same mythemes occur in similar myths from different cultures, he suggested that all myths may be elements of one great myth being written by the collective human mind.

Derrida did not believe that structuralists had the concepts that would someday explain the laws governing human signification and thus provide the key to understanding the form and meaning of everything from an African village to Greek myth to Rousseau's *Confessions.* In his view, the scientific search by structural anthropologists for what unifies humankind amounts to a new version of the old search for the lost ideal, whether that ideal be Plato's bright realm of the Idea or the Paradise of Genesis or Rousseau's unspoiled Nature. As for the structuralist belief that texts have "centers" of meaning, in Derrida's view that derives from the logocentric belief that there is a reading of the text that accords with "the book as seen by God." Jonathan Culler, who thus translates a difficult phrase from Derrida's *L'Écriture et la différence* [*Writing and Difference*] (1967) in his book *Structuralist Poetics* (1975), goes on to explain what Derrida objects to in structuralist literary criticism:

> [When] one speaks of the structure of a literary work, one does so from a certain vantage point: one starts with notions of the meaning or effects of a poem and tries to identify the structures responsible for those effects. Possible configurations or patterns that make no contribution are rejected as irrelevant. That is to say, an intuitive understanding of the poem functions as the "centre" . . . : it is both a starting point and a limiting principle. (244)

Deconstruction calls into question assumptions made about literature by formalist, as well as by structuralist, critics. Formalism, or the New Criticism as it was once commonly called, assumes a work of literature to be a freestanding, self-contained object, its meanings found in the complex network of relations that constitute its parts (images, sounds, rhythms, allusions, and so on). To be sure, deconstruction is somewhat like formalism in several ways. Both formalism and deconstruction are text-oriented approaches whose practitioners pay a great deal of attention to rhetorical *tropes* (forms of figurative language including allegory, symbol, metaphor, and metonymy). And formalists, long before deconstructors, discovered counterpatterns of meaning in the same text. Formalists find ambiguity: deconstructors find undecidability. On close inspection, however the formalist understanding of rhetorical tropes or figures is quite different from that of deconstruction, and undecidability turns out to be different from the ambiguity formalists find in texts.

Formalists, who associated literary with figurative language, made qualitative distinctions between types of figures of speech; for instance, they valued symbols and metaphors over metonyms. (A metonym is a term standing for something with which it is commonly associated or contiguous; we use metonymy when we say we had "the cold plate" for lunch.) From the formalist perspective, metaphors and symbols are less arbitrary figures than metonyms and thus rank more highly in the hierarchy of tropes: a metaphor ("I'm feeling blue") supposedly involves a special, intrinsic, nonarbitrary relationship between its two terms (the feeling of melancholy and the color blue); a symbol ("the river of life") allegedly involves a unique fusion of image and idea.

From the perspective of deconstruction, however, these distinctions are suspect. In "The Rhetoric of Temporality," Paul de Man deconstructs the distinction between symbol and allegory; elsewhere, he, Derrida, and Miller have similarly questioned the metaphor/metonymy distinction, arguing that all figuration is a process of linguistic substitution. In the case of a metaphor (or symbol), they claim, we have forgotten what juxtaposition or contiguity gave rise to the association that now seems mysteriously special. Derrida, in "White Mythology," and de Man, in "Metaphor (*Second Discourse*)," have also challenged the priority of literal over figurative language, and Miller has gone so far as to deny the validity of the literal/figurative distinction, arguing that all words are figures because all language involves *catachresis*, "the violent, forced, or abusive importation of a term from another realm to name something which has no proper name" (Miller, *Ariadne* 21).

The difference between the formalist concept of literary ambiguity and the deconstructive concept of undecidability is as significant as the gap between formalist and deconstructive understandings of figurative language. Undecidability, as de Man came to define it, is a complex notion easily misunderstood. There is a tendency to assume that it refers to readers who, when forced to decide between two or more equally plausible and conflicting readings, throw up their hands and decide that the choice can't be made. But undecidability in fact debunks this whole notion of reading as a decision-making process carried out on texts by readers. To say we are forced to choose or decide, or that we are unable to do so, is to locate the problem of undecidability falsely within ourselves, rather than recognizing that it is an intrinsic feature of the text.

Undecidability is thus different from ambiguity, as understood by formalists. Formalists believe that a complete understanding of a literary work is possible, an understanding in which ambiguities will be resolved objectively by the reader, even if only in the sense that they will be shown to have definite, meaningful functions. Deconstructors do not share that belief. They do not accept the formalist view that a work of literary art is demonstrably unified from beginning to end, in one certain way, or that it is organized around a single center that ultimately can be identified and defined. Neither do they accept the concept of irony as simply saying one thing and meaning another thing that will be understood with certainty by the reader. As a result, deconstructors tend to see texts as more radically heterogeneous than do formalists. The formalist critic ultimately makes sense of ambiguity; undecidability, by contrast, is never reduced, let alone mastered by deconstructive reading, although the incompatible possibilities between which it is impossible to decide can be identified with certainty.

For critics practicing deconstruction, a literary text is neither a sphere with a center nor an unbroken line with a definite beginning and end. In fact, many assumptions about the nature of texts have been put in question by deconstruction, which in Derrida's words "dislocates the borders, the framing of texts, everything which should preserve their immanence and make possible an internal reading or merely reading in the classical sense of the term" ("Some Statements" 86). A text consists of words inscribed in and inextricable from the myriad discourses that inform it; from the point of view of deconstruction, the boundaries between any given text and that larger text we call language are always shifting.

It was that larger text that Derrida was referring to when he made his famous statement *"there is nothing outside the text"* (*Grammatology* 158). To understand what Derrida meant by that statement, consider the following: we know the world through language, and the acts and practices that constitute that "real world" (the Oklahoma City bombing, the decision to marry) are inseparable from the discourses out of which they arise and as open to interpretation as any work of literature. Derrida is not alone in deconstructing the world/text opposition. De Man viewed language as something that has great power in individual, social, and political life. Geoffrey Hartman, who was closely associated with deconstruction during the 1970s, wrote that "nothing can lift us out of language" (xii).

Once we understand deconstruction's view of the literary text — as words that are part of and that resonate with an immense linguistic structure in which we live and move and have our being — we are in a better position to understand why deconstructors reach points in their readings at which they reveal, but cannot decide between, incompatible interpretive possibilities. A text is not a unique, hermetically sealed space. Perpetually open to being seen in the light of new contexts, any given text has the potential to be different each time it is read. Furthermore, as Miller has shown in *Ariadne's Thread: Story Lines* (1992), the various "terms" and "famil[ies] of terms" we use in performing our readings invariably affect the results. Whether we choose to focus on a novel's characters or its realism, for instance, leads us to different views of the same text. "No one thread," Miller asserts, "can be followed to a central point where it provides a means of overseeing, controlling, and understanding the whole" (21).

Complicating matters still further is the fact that the individual words making up narratives — the words out of which we make our mental picture of a character or place — usually have several (and often have conflicting) meanings due to the complex histories of their usage. (If your professor tells the class that you have written a "fulsome report" and you look up the word *fulsome* in a contemporary dictionary, you will learn that it can mean either "elaborate" or "offensive"; if, for some reason, you don't know what *offensive* means, you will find out that it can equally well describe your favorite quarterback and a racist joke.) "Each word," as Miller puts it, "inheres in a labyrinth of branching interverbal relationships"; often there are "forks in the etymological line leading to bifurcated or trifurcated roots." Deconstructors often turn to etymology, not to help them decide whether a statement means this or that, but rather as a way of revealing the coincidence of several meanings in the same text. "The effect of etymological retracing," Miller writes, "is not to ground the work solidly but to render it unstable, equivocal, wavering, groundless" (*Ariadne* 19).

Deconstruction is not really interpretation, the act of choosing between or among possible meanings. Derrida has glossed de Man's statement that "there is no need to deconstruct Rousseau" by saying that "this was another way of saying: there is always already deconstruction, at work *in* works, especially *literary* works. It cannot be applied, after the fact and from outside, as a technical instrument. Texts deconstruct *themselves* by themselves" (Derrida, *Memoires* 123). If deconstruction is not interpretation, then what is it? Deconstruction may be defined as reading, as long as reading is defined as de Man defined it — as a process involving moments of what he called *aporia* or terminal uncertainty, and as an act performed with full knowledge of the fact that all texts are ultimately unreadable (if reading means reducing a text to a single, homogeneous meaning). Miller explains unreadability by saying that although there are moments of great lucidity in reading, each "lucidity will in principle contain its own blind spot requiring a further elucidation and exposure of error, and so on, ad infinitum. . . . One should not underestimate, however, the productive illumination produced as one moves through these various stages of reading" (*Ethics* 42, 44).

Miller's point is important because, in a sense, it deconstructs or erases the boundary between the readings of deconstructors and the interpretations of more traditional critics. It suggests that all kinds of critics have had their moments of lucidity; it also suggests that critics practicing deconstruction know that their *own* insights — even their insights into what is or isn't contradictory, undecidable, or unreadable in a text — are hardly the last word. As Art Berman writes, "In *Blindness and Insight* de Man demonstrates that the apparently well-reasoned arguments of literary critics contain contradiction at their core; yet there is no alternative path to insight. . . . The readers of criticism recognize the blindness of their predecessors, reorganize it, and thereby gain both the insight of the critics and a knowledge of the contradiction that brings forth insight. Each reader, of course, has his own blindness; and the criticism of criticism is not a matter of rectifying someone else's mistakes" (Berman 239–40).

When de Man spoke of the resistance to theory he referred generally to the antitheoretical bias in literary studies. But he might as well have been speaking specifically of the resistance to deconstruction, as expressed not only in academic books and journals but also in popular magazines such as *Newsweek*. Attacks on deconstruction became more common and more personal some four years after de Man's death in 1983. That was the year that a Belgian scholar working on a doctoral thesis discovered ninety-two articles that de Man had written during World War II for the Brussels newspaper *Le Soir,* a widely read French-language daily that had fallen under Nazi control during the German occupation of Belgium. Ultimately, one hundred seventy articles by de Man were found in *Le Soir;* another ten were discovered in *Het Vlaamsche Land,* a collaborationist newspaper published in Flemish. These writings, which date from 1941 (when de Man was twenty-one years old), ceased to appear before 1943, by which time it had become clear to most Belgians that Jews were being shipped to death camps such as Auschwitz.

De Man's wartime journalism consists mainly, but not entirely, of inoffensive literary pieces. In one article de Man takes Germany's triumph in World War II as a given, places the German people at the center of Western civilization, and foresees a mystical era involving suffering but also faith, exaltation, and rapture. In another article, entitled *"Les Juifs dans la littérature actuelle"* ["Jews in Present-day Literature"], de Man scoffs at the notion that Jewish writers have significantly influenced the literature of his day and, worse, considers the merits of creating a separate Jewish colony that would be isolated from Europe.

No one who had known de Man since his immigration to the United States in 1948 had found him to be illiberal or anti-Semitic. Furthermore, de Man had spent his career in the United States demystifying or, as he would have said, "debunking" the kind of ideological assumptions (about the relationship between aesthetics and national cultures) that lie behind his most offensive Belgian newspaper writings. The critic who in *The Resistance to Theory* (1986) argued that literature must not become "a substitute for theology, ethics, etc." (de Man 24) had either changed radically since writing of the magical integrity and wholeness of the German nation and its culture or had not deeply believed what he had written as a young journalist.

These points have been made in various ways by de Man's former friends and colleagues. Geoffrey Hartman has said that de Man's later work, the work we associate with deconstruction, "looks like a belated, but still powerful, act of conscience" (26–31). Derrida, who like Hartman is a Jew, has read carefully de Man's wartime discourse, showing it to be "split, disjointed, engaged in incessant conflicts" (Hamacher, Hertz, and Keenan 135). "On the one hand," Derrida finds *"unpardonable"* de Man's suggestion that a separate Jewish colony be set up; "on the other hand," he notes that of the four writers de Man praises in the same article (André Gide, Franz Kafka, D. H. Lawrence, and Ernest Hemingway), not one was German, one (Kafka) *was* Jewish, and all four "represent everything that Nazism . . . would have liked to extirpate from history and the great tradition" (Hamacher, Hertz, and Keenan 145).

While friends asserted that some of de Man's statements were unpardonable, deconstruction's severest critics tried to use a young man's sometimes deplorable statements as evidence that a whole critical

movement was somehow morally as well as intellectually flawed. As
Andrej Warminski summed it up, "the 'discovery' of the 1941–42 writings is being used to perpetuate the old myths about so-called 'deconstruction'" (Hamacher, Hertz, and Keenan 389). Knowing what some
of those myths are — and why, in fact, they *are* myths — aids our
understanding in an indirect, contrapuntal way that is in keeping with
the spirit of deconstruction.

In his book *The Ethics of Reading* (1987), Miller refutes two
notions commonly repeated by deconstruction's detractors. One is the
idea that deconstructors believe a text means nothing in the sense that
it means whatever the playful reader *wants* it to mean. The other is the
idea that deconstruction is "immoral" insofar as it refuses to view literature in the way it has traditionally been viewed, namely, "as the foundation and embodiment, the means of preserving and transmitting, the
basic humanistic values of our culture" (9). Responding to the first
notion, Miller points out that neither Derrida nor de Man "has ever
asserted the freedom of the reader to make the text mean anything he
or she wants it to mean. Each has in fact asserted the reverse" (10). As
for the second notion — that deconstructors are guilty of shirking an
ethical responsibility because their purpose is not to (re)discover and
(re)assert the transcendent and timeless values contained in great
books — Miller argues that "this line of thought" rests "on a basic misunderstanding of the way the ethical moment enters into the act of
reading" (9). That "ethical moment," Miller goes on to argue, "is not a
matter of response to a thematic content asserting this or that idea
about morality. It is a much more fundamental 'I must' responding to
the language of literature in itself. . . . Deconstruction is nothing more
or less than good reading as such" (9–10). Reading itself, in other
words, is an act that leads to further ethical acts, decisions, and behaviors in a real world involving relations to other people and to society at
large. For these, the reader must take responsibility, as for any other
ethical act.

A third commonly voiced objection to deconstruction is to its playfulness, to the evident pleasure its practitioners take in teasing out all
the contradictory interpretive possibilities generated by the words in a
text, their complex etymologies and contexts, and their potential to be
read figuratively or even ironically. Certainly, playfulness and pleasure
are aspects of deconstruction. In his book *The Post Card* (1987), Derrida specifically associates deconstruction with pleasure; in an interview
published in a collection of his essays entitled *Acts of Literature* (1992),
he speculates that "it is perhaps this *jouissance* which most irritates the

all-out adversaries of deconstruction" (56). But such adversaries misread deconstruction's "jouissance," its pleasurable playfulness. Whereas they see it as evidence that deconstructors view texts as tightly enclosed fields on which they can play delightfully useless little word games, Derrida has said that the "subtle and intense pleasure" of deconstruction arises from the "dismantl[ing]" of repressive assumptions, representations and ideas — in short, from the "lifting of repression" (*Acts* 56–57). As Gregory S. Jay explains in his book *America the Scrivener: Deconstruction and the Subject of Literary History* (1990), "Deconstruction has been not only a matter of reversing binary oppositions but also a matter of disabling the hierarchy of values they enable and of speculating on alternative modes of knowing and of acting" (xii).

Far from viewing literature as a word-playground, Derrida, in Derek Attridge's words, "emphasizes . . . literature as an institution," one "not given in nature or the brain but brought into being by processes that are social, legal, and political, and that can be mapped historically and geographically" (*Acts* 23). By thus characterizing Derrida's emphasis, Attridge counters the commonest of the charges that have been leveled at deconstructors, namely, that they divorce literary texts from historical, political, and legal institutions.

In *Memoirs for Paul de Man* (1986), Derrida argues that, where history is concerned, "deconstructive discourses" have pointedly and effectively questioned "the classical assurances of history, the genealogical narrative, and periodizations of all sorts" (15) — in other words, the tendency of historians to view the past as the source of (lost) truth and value, to look for explanations in origins, and to view as unified epochs (for example, the Victorian period, 1837–1901) what are in fact complex and heterogeneous times in history. As for politics, Derrida points out that de Man invariably "says something about institutional structures and the political stakes of hermeneutic conflicts," which is to say that de Man's commentaries acknowledge that conflicting interpretations reflect and are reflected in the politics of institutions (such as the North American university).

In addition to history and politics, the law has been a subject on which deconstruction has had much to say of late. In an essay on Franz Kafka's story "Before the Law," Derrida has shown that for Kafka the law as such exists but can never be confronted by those who would do so and fulfill its commands. Miller has pointed out that the law "may only be confronted in its delegates or representatives or by its effects on us or others" (*Ethics* 20). What or where, then, is the law itself? The law's presence, Miller suggests, is continually deferred by narrative, that is, writing about or on the law which constantly reinterprets the law in the attempt to reveal what it really is and means. This very act of (re)interpretation, however, serves to "defer" or distance the law even further from the case at hand, since the (re)interpretation takes precedence (and assumes prominence) over the law itself. (As Miller defines it, narrative would include everything from a Victorian novel that promises to reveal moral law to the opinion of a Supreme Court justice regarding the constitutionality of a given action, however different these two documents are in the conventions they follow and the uses to which they are put.) Miller likens the law to a promise, "the validity of [which] does not lie in itself but in its future fulfillment," and to a story "divided against itself" that in the end "leaves its readers . . . still in expectation" (*Ethics* 33).

Because the facts about deconstruction are very different from the myth of its playful irreverence and irrelevance, a number of contemporary thinkers have found it useful to adapt and apply deconstruction in their work. For instance, a deconstructive theology has been developed. Architects have designed and built buildings grounded, as it were, in deconstructive architectural theory. In the area of law, the Critical Legal Studies movement has, in Christopher Norris's words, effectively used "deconstructive-thinking" of the kind de Man used in analyzing Rousseau's *Social Contract* "to point up the blind spots, conflicts, and antinomies that plague the discourse of received legal wisdom." Critical legal theorists have debunked "the formalist view of law," that is, the "view which holds law to be a system of neutral precepts and principles," showing instead how the law "gives rise to various disabling contradictions," such as "the problematic distinction between 'private' and 'public' domains." They have turned deconstruction into "a sophisticated means of making the point that all legal discourse is performative in character, i.e., designed to secure assent through its rhetorical power to convince or persuade" (Norris, *Deconstruction and the Interests* 17). Courtroom persuasion, Gerald Lopez has argued in a 1989 article in the *Michigan Law Review,* consists of storytelling as much as argument (Clayton 13).

In the field of literary studies, the influence of deconstruction may be seen in the work of critics ostensibly taking some other, more political approach. Barbara Johnson has put deconstruction to work for the feminist cause. She and Shoshana Felman have argued that chief among those binary oppositions "based on repression of differences with entities" is the opposition man/woman (Johnson, *Critical* x). In a reading of the "undecidability" of "femininity" in Balzac's story "The Girl with

the Golden Eyes," Felman puts it this way: "the rhetorical hierarchization of the . . . opposition between the sexes is . . . such that woman's
difference is suppressed, being totally subsumed by the reference of the
feminine to masculine identity" ("Rereading" 25).

Elsewhere, Johnson, Felman, and Gayatri Spivak have combined
Derrida's theories with the psychoanalytic theory of Jacques Lacan to
analyze the way in which gender and sexuality are ultimately textual,
grounded in language and rhetoric. In an essay on Edmund Wilson's
reading of Henry James's story *The Turn of the Screw*, Felman has
treated sexuality as a form of rhetoric that can be deconstructed, shown
to contain contradictions and ambiguities that more traditional readings of sexuality have masked. Gay and lesbian critics have seen the
positive implications of this kind of analysis, hence Eve Kosofsky Sedgwick's admission in the early pages of her book *Epistemology of the
Closet* (1990): "One main strand of argument in this book is deconstructive, in a fairly specific sense. The analytic move it makes is to
demonstrate that categories presented in a culture as symmetrical
binary oppositions . . . actually subsist in a more unsettled and dynamic
tacit relation" (9–10).

In telling "The Story of Deconstruction" in his book on contemporary American literature and theory, Jay Clayton assesses the current status of this unique approach. Although he notes how frequently
deconstructive critics have been cited for their lack of political engagement, he concludes that deconstruction, "a movement accused of
formalism and intellectualism, participates in the political turn of contemporary culture" (34). He suggests that what began as theory in the
late 1960s and 1970s has, over time, developed into a method employed
by critics taking a wide range of approaches to literature — ethnic, feminist, new historicist, Marxist — in addition to critics outside of literary
studies per se who are involved in such areas as Critical Legal Studies and
Critical Race Theory, which seeks to "sustain a complementary relationship between the deconstructive energies of Critical Legal Studies and
the constructive energies of civil rights activism" (58).

Clayton cites the work of Edward Said as a case in point. Through
1975, the year that his *Beginnings: Intention and Method* was published, Said was employing a form of deconstructive criticism that, in
Clayton's words, emphasized the "power" of texts "to initiate projects
in the real world" (45–46). Said became identified with cultural and postcolonial criticism, however, beginning in 1978 with the publication of
his book *Orientalism*, in which he deconstructs the East/West, Orient/
Occident opposition. Said argues that Eastern and Middle Eastern

peoples have for centuries been stereotyped by the Western discourses of "orientalism," a textuality that in no way reflects the diversity and differences that exist among the peoples it claims to represent. According to Said, that stereotyping not only facilitated the colonization of vast areas of the globe by the so-called West but also still governs, to a great extent, relations with the Arab and the so-called Eastern world. The expansion of Said's field of vision to include not just literary texts but international relations is powerfully indicative of the expanding role that deconstruction currently plays in developing contemporary understandings of politics and culture, as well as in active attempts to intervene in these fields.

Deconstructors would say that, in realistic works of fiction, repetition — or "doubling" — generally serves to provides the reader with a familiar sense of binary order, a familiar set of either-or values. For instance, In D. H. Lawrence's *Sons and Lovers,* Paul Morel's spiritual girlfriend Miriam "repeats" Paul's pious mother, whereas a later, more physical lover named Clara Dawes harkens back to Walter, Paul's more sensuous, coal-mining father. In the essay that follows, John Paul Riquelme argues that *Dracula* — like other works in the *anti*realistic, Gothic tradition — contains "repetitions and doublings" that "blur the boundaries" between — and even "undermine" — socially accepted distinctions and oppositions (p. 559 in this volume).

Riquelme sees the novel as an "antirealistic work" in part because it continually suggests that things commonly understood to be distinct or even opposite (human and animal, living and dead, external and internal monsters, etc.) in fact bear an uncanny resemblance to one another. Stoker even manages to depict seemingly opposite characters (e.g., Jonathan Harker and Count Dracula, Dr. Seward and Renfield, Van Helsing and Dracula) as "counterparts, or even collaborators" (p. 561), thereby suggesting a different vision of human nature and possibility than is found in so-called realistic fiction. Both in "story and style," Riquelme writes, *Dracula* "counters realism's clarity and sanity," questioning distinctions commonly taken for granted and, in the process, presenting characters quite different from the "seemingly real" people we encounter in realistic texts: recognizably distinct entities "behaving and thinking in a manner we find believable" (p. 560).

Jonathan Harker, upon seeing Count Dracula climb, lizardlike, down a castle wall, wonders, "What manner of man is this, or what manner of creature is it in the semblance of man?" (p. 58). When he later claims to have duplicated this subhuman/superhuman act (thus repeating or doubling Dracula through his actions), we must either ask what manner of man *he* is — either that, or we must assume that he has gone insane. And yet if he is insane, who in the novel *is* a consistently credible source of information? In posing questions such as this one, Riquelme suggests, the novel undermines its own authority or credibility while, simultaneously and implicitly, raising similarly serious questions about realism. Is realism's "appearance of accurate rendering" only a "pose of sanity and clear vision" (p. 562)? The "journal writing throughout" *Dracula* offers "apparently objective reportage," and yet it is reportage on "unbelievable events" (p. 562).

In arguing that Stoker tends to blur distinctions and to bring differences into unexpected alignment, Riquelme focuses not only on the novel's characters but also on its language. For instance, a single word may be repeated in different ways to refer to entirely different things that, nonetheless, however we explain it, turn out to have bearing upon one another. (Harker travels in a literal "trap" [i.e., carriage] toward the figurative trap that is Dracula's castle.) Single phrases similarly invite different readings ("knowledge of the brain"), as can single sentences. (Does Van Helsing's statement "I am at least sane" mean "at least *I* am sane" or "I have at *least* held onto my sanity"?) Similarly, names and symbols are often used in ways that vex conventional sense making. ("Helsing" is supposedly a Dutch name but suggests "English" anagrammatically. And what do a rosary and crucifix signify when hung around the neck of Harker, a Protestant?)

Again and again, the novel's language yokes differences and blurs distinctions; repeatedly, it "suggests different meanings that can neither be easily separated nor readily reconciled" (p. 563). Riquelme's best example may be the poetry quoted by Seward with Lucy in mind: "We thought her dying whilst she slept, / And sleeping when she died." The two lines not only link things presumed to be different (sleep and death) but also highlight distinctions (between deathlike sleep and sleeplike death) through a repetition involving word-order reversal (dying . . . slept, / sleeping . . . died").

In developing his argument, Riquelme suggests that the unlikely yoking of different- or opposite-seeming characters is not merely like or parallel to the conjunction of different- or opposite-seeming meanings in words, names, symbols, phrases, sentences, or lines. Rather, these unexpected character alignments are made possible by the fact that the novel's characters — like its central ideas and plot elements — are grounded in and arise from its antirealistic, ambiguous language. For instance, the concept of the undead can hardly be separated from the odd, antirealistic *word* "undead," which suggests the opposite of death but does not mean "life" in any conventional sense. When Van Helsing reports that Mina "cried out in pain that I had suffered too much" (p. 362), the ambiguous or even "indeterminate" nature of the text invites opposite interpretive possibilities that, by extension, blur distinctions relevant both to character and to plot. (Is it Mina — or is it Van Helsing — who has "endured too much" by this point in the story? Or, alternatively, are these very different characters united by their suffering?)

Toward the end of his essay, Riquelme broadens his view of the novel's "indeterminacy" and "unreliability" still further to include its mode of narration, in which a "transcriber" (such as Mina) is typing something that she once told someone else — and is typing it as if she doesn't know what happened later (to her, no less!). Thus, Riquelme concludes, "[t]he issue of the narration's reliability is bottomless" (p. 569).

Riquelme's approach to *Dracula* is representative of deconstruction in any number of ways. First, and perhaps most obviously, it is interested in the way in which its subject text blurs boundaries between what Western culture assumes to be hierarchal oppositions (superhuman/subhuman, civilized/savage). Like other deconstructors, Riquelme focuses closely on the text, viewing the (confused) oppositions between characters, concepts, and interpretive possibilities where plot and narrative are concerned as a result of language's indeterminacy. His interest in the maddening labyrinth of meanings into which a single word may lead — thanks not only to etymological complexity but also to the (questionable) opposition between literal and figurative possibilities — parallels that of Derrida and de Man, who spoke of the text's "undecidability." His elucidation of the way in which repetitions, whether of words or character traits, undermine rather than reinforce the reader's sense that the text offers a reliable representation of stable similarities and determinate differences is anticipated by J. Hillis Miller's book *Fiction and Repetition: Seven English Novels* (1982). Much as Miller argues (while focusing on novels other than Stoker's), Riquelme maintains that *Dracula*'s "pervasive doublings . . . undermine the impression of clarity, intelligibility, and certainty that . . . readers want to retain" (p. 560). Typical of numerous deconstructions of literary texts, Riquelme's fine essay teases out tendencies in a "book's language" that continually "[challenge] the possibility of clarity and interpretive closure" (p. 561).

Ross C Murfin

DECONSTRUCTION:
A SELECTED BIBLIOGRAPHY

Writings on Deconstruction

Arac, Jonathan, Wlad Godzich, and Wallace Martin, eds. *The Yale Critics: Deconstruction in America*. Minneapolis: U of Minnesota P, 1983. See especially the essays by Bové, Godzich, Pease, and Corngold.

Berman, Art. *From the New Criticism to Deconstruction: The Reception of Structuralism and Post-Structuralism*. Urbana: U of Illinois P, 1988.

Butler, Christopher. *Interpretation, Deconstruction, and Ideology: An Introduction to Some Current Issues in Literary Theory*. Oxford: Oxford UP, 1984.

Clayton, Jay. *The Pleasure of Babel: Contemporary American Literature and Theory*. New York: Oxford UP, 1993.

Culler, Jonathan. *On Deconstruction: Theory and Criticism After Structuralism*. Ithaca: Cornell UP, 1982.

———. *Structuralist Poetics: Structuralism, Linguistics and the Study of Literature*. Ithaca: Cornell UP, 1975. See especially ch. 10.

Esch, Deborah. "Deconstruction." *Redrawing the Boundaries: The Transformation of English and American Literary Studies*. Ed. Stephen Greenblatt and Giles Gunn. New York: MLA, 1992. 374–91.

Feminist Studies 14 (1988). Special issue on deconstruction and feminism.

Hamacher, Werner, Neil Hertz, and Thomas Keenan. *Responses: On Paul de Man's Wartime Journalism*. Lincoln: U of Nebraska P, 1989.

Hartman, Geoffrey. "Blindness and Insight." *The New Republic*, 7 Mar. 1988.

Jay, Gregory S. *America the Scrivener: Deconstruction and the Subject of Literary History*. Ithaca: Cornell UP, 1990.

Leitch, Vincent B. *American Literary Criticism from the Thirties to the Eighties*. New York: Columbia UP, 1988. See especially ch. 10, "Deconstructive Criticism."

———. *Cultural Criticism, Literary Theory, Poststructuralism*. New York: Columbia UP, 1992.

Loesberg, Jonathan. *Aestheticism and Deconstruction: Pater, Derrida, and de Man*. Princeton: Princeton UP, 1991.

Melville, Stephen W. *Philosophy Beside Itself: On Deconstruction and Modernism*. Theory and History of Lit. 27. Minneapolis: U of Minnesota P, 1986.

Norris, Christopher. *Deconstruction and the Interests of Theory*. Oklahoma Project for Discourse and Theory 4. Norman: U of Oklahoma P, 1989.

————. *Deconstruction: Theory and Practice*. London: Methuen, 1982. Rev. ed. London: Routledge, 1991.

————. *Paul de Man, Deconstruction and the Critique of Aesthetic Ideology*. New York: Routledge, 1988.

Weber, Samuel. *Institution and Interpretation*. Minneapolis: U of Minnesota P, 1987.

Works by de Man, Derrida, and Miller

de Man, Paul. *Allegories of Reading*. New Haven: Yale UP, 1979. See especially ch. 1 "Semiology and Rhetoric," and ch. 7, "Metaphor (*Second Discourse*)."

————. *Blindness and Insight*. New York: Oxford UP, 1971. Minneapolis: U of Minnesota P, 1983. The 1983 edition contains essays not included in the original edition. See especially "Rhetoric of Temporality."

————. "Phenomenality and Materiality in Kant." *Hermeneutics: Questions and Prospects*. Ed. Gary Shapiro and Alan Sica. Amherst: U of Massachusetts P, 1984. 121–44.

————. *The Resistance to Theory*. Minneapolis: U of Minnesota P, 1986.

————. *Romanticism and Contemporary Culture*. Ed. E. S. Burt, Kevin Newmarkj, and Andrzej Warminski. Baltimore: Johns Hopkins UP, 1993.

————. *Wartime Journalism, 1939–1943*. Lincoln: U of Nebraska P, 1989.

Derrida, Jacques. *Acts of Literature*. Ed. Derek Attridge. New York: Routledge, 1992.

————. "Différance." *Speech and Phenomena*. Trans. David B. Alison. Evanston: Northwestern UP, 1973.

————. *Dissemination*. 1972. Trans. Barbara Johnson. Chicago: U of Chicago P, 1981. See especially the concise, incisive "Translator's Introduction," which provides a useful point of entry into this work and others by Derrida.

———. "Force of Law: The 'Mystical Foundation of Authority.'" Trans. Mary Quaintance. *Deconstruction and the Possibility of Justice.* Ed. Drucilla Cornell, Michel Rosenfeld, and David Gray Carlson. New York: Routledge, 1992. 3–67.

———. *Given Time. 1, Counterfeit Money.* Trans. Peggy Kamuf. Chicago: U of Chicago P, 1992.

———. *Margins of Philosophy.* Trans. Alan Bass. Chicago: U of Chicago P, 1982. Contains the essay "White Mythology: Metaphor in the Text of Philosophy."

———. *Memoires for Paul de Man.* Wellek Library Lectures. Trans. Cecile Lindsay, Jonathan Culler, and Eduardo Cadava. New York: Columbia UP, 1986.

———. *Of Grammatology.* Trans. Gayatri C. Spivak. Baltimore: Johns Hopkins UP, 1976. Trans. of *De la grammatologie.* 1967.

———. "Passions." *Derrida: A Critical Reader.* Ed. David Wood. Cambridge: Basil Blackwell, 1992.

———. *The Post Card: From Socrates to Freud and Beyond.* Trans. with intro. Alan Bass. Chicago: U of Chicago P, 1987.

———. "Some Statements and Truisms about Neo-logisms, Newisms, Postisms, and Other Small Seisisms." *The States of "Theory."* New York: Columbia UP, 1990. 63–94.

———. *Specters of Marx.* Trans. Peggy Kamuf. New York: Routledge, 1994.

———. *Writing and Difference.* 1967. Trans. Alan Bass. Chicago: U of Chicago P, 1978.

Miller, J. Hillis. *Ariadne's Thread: Story Lines.* New Haven: Yale UP, 1992.

———. *The Ethics of Reading: Kant, de Man, Eliot, Trollope, James, and Benjamin.* New York: Columbia UP, 1987.

———. *Fiction and Repetition: Seven English Novels.* Cambridge: Harvard UP, 1982.

———. *Hawthorne and History: Defacing It.* Cambridge: Basil Blackwell, 1991. Contains a bibliography of Miller's work from 1955 to 1990.

———. *Illustrations.* Cambridge: Harvard UP, 1992.

———. "Stevens' Rock and Criticism as Cure." *Georgia Review* 30 (1976): 3–31, 330–48.

———. *Typographies.* Stanford: Stanford UP, 1994.

———. *Versions of Pygmalion.* Cambridge: Harvard UP, 1990.

Essays on Deconstruction
and Poststructuralism

Barthes, Roland. *S/Z*. Trans. Richard Miller. New York: Hill, 1974.
In this influential work, Barthes turns from a structuralist to a
poststructuralist approach.

Benstock, Shari. *Textualizing the Feminine: On the Limits of Genre.*
Norman: U of Oklahoma P, 1991.

Bloom, Harold, et al., eds. *Deconstruction and Criticism.* New York:
Seabury, 1979. Includes essays by Bloom, de Man, Derrida, and
Hartman.

Chase, Cynthia. *Decomposing Figures.* Baltimore: Johns Hopkins UP,
1986.

Cohen, Tom. *Anti-Mimesis: From Plato to Hitchcock.* Cambridge:
Cambridge UP, 1994.

Elam, Diane. *Feminism and Deconstruction: Ms. en Abyme.* New York:
Routledge, 1994.

Felman, Shoshana. "Rereading Femininity." Special Issue on
"Feminist Readings: French Texts/American Contexts," *Yale
French Studies* 62 (1981): 19–44.

———. "Turning the Screw of Interpretation." *Literature and
Psychoanalysis: The Question of Reading: Otherwise.* Special issue,
Yale French Studies 55–56 (1978): 3–508. Baltimore: Johns
Hopkins UP, 1982.

Harari, Josué, ed. *Textual Strategies: Perspectives in Post-Structuralist
Criticism.* Ithaca: Cornell UP, 1979.

Johnson, Barbara. *The Critical Difference: Essays in the Contemporary
Rhetoric of Reading.* Baltimore: Johns Hopkins UP, 1980.

———. *A World of Difference.* Baltimore: Johns Hopkins UP,
1987.

Krupnick, Mark, ed. *Displacement: Derrida and After.* Bloomington:
Indiana UP, 1987.

Meese, Elizabeth, and Alice Parker, eds. *The Difference Within:
Feminism and Critical Theory.* Philadelphia: Benjamins, 1989.

Sedgwick, Eva Kosofsky. *Epistemology of the Closet.* Berkeley: U of
California P, 1990.

Ulmer, Gregory L. *Applied Grammatology.* Baltimore: Johns Hopkins
UP, 1985.

———. *Teletheory: Grammatology in the Age of Video.* New York:
Routledge, 1989.

Deconstruction and *Dracula*

Boone, Troy. "'He is English and Therefore Adventurous': Politics, Decadence, and *Dracula*." *Studies in the Novel* 25 (1993): 76–91.

Kilgour, Maggie. "Vampiric Arts: Bram Stoker's Defense of Poetry." *Bram Stoker: History, Psychoanalysis and the Gothic*. Eds. William Hughes and Andrew Smith. London: Macmillan, 1998. 47–61.

McWhir, Anne. "Pollution and Redemption in *Dracula*." *Modern Language Studies* 17.3 (1987): 31–40.

Valente, Joseph. *Dracula's Crypt: Bram Stoker, Irishness and the Question of Blood*. Urbana: U of Illinois P, 2002.

A DECONSTRUCTIVE PERSPECTIVE

JOHN PAUL RIQUELME

Doubling and Repetition/ Realism and Closure in *Dracula*

"Truly there is no such thing as finality."
— Dr. Seward, page 199

Like its primary precursors in the tradition of Gothic narrative, *Dracula* is an antirealistic work filled with doubling and repetition. It resembles in this regard Mary Shelley's *Frankenstein, or the Modern Prometheus* (1819; revised 1831), Robert Louis Stevenson's *The Strange Case of Dr. Jekyll and Mr. Hyde* (1886), and Oscar Wilde's *The Picture of Dorian Gray* (1891). The doublings and repetitions in all these works blur the boundaries that inform the principles of coherence we associate with sanity and that regulate the limits and distinctions of our social world: boundaries between animal and human, female and male, child and adult, savage and civilized, living and dead, among other ostensibly contrasting pairs that underlie our confidence in hierarchies of order, value, and power. Those hierarchies include social arrangements in which some groups, whether defined by class, national origin, ethnicity, or gender, exercise power over others who are ostensibly different from them. It is not surprising that a book by an Irish author would respond in significant ways to the logic and the effects of such arrangements. The doublings in *Dracula* tend to undermine the putative differences that help maintain social hierarchies because those doublings frequently suggest that the supposedly contrasting groups and individuals resemble each other.[1]

The book's pervasive doublings emerge regularly in the narration during arresting scenes and passages that undermine the impression of clarity, intelligibility, and certainty that some characters and readers want to retain. This is not to say that the book is unclear or unintelligible. Instead, it is quite clear and direct in the presentation of abiding enigmas within the narrative that suggest stability and closure are not possible. Vivid passages and enigmatic details that are difficult to ignore press us to consider the bases on which we think of our world and ourselves as well-ordered, sane, and safe. By suggesting that the monster is not outside but within, they create alternatives for self-understanding. Stability of an inflexible kind limits what can be thought, experienced, and created. The instabilities and uncertainties in *Dracula* are simultaneously threatening and potentially liberating.

I have placed *Dracula* in an antirealistic tradition because it differs emphatically from English and American realistic fiction, which presents, in continuous narrative and in a readily intelligible style, seemingly real characters behaving and thinking in a manner we find believable. Count Dracula, Van Helsing, Renfield, and others are far from realistically presented. In both story and style, through doubling and repetition, *Dracula* counters realism's clarity and sanity, raising instead questions that suggest a different vision of ourselves and the future than seems possible in realistic writing. Such questions arise during the scene in Chapter 21 in which Mina drinks Dracula's blood (p. 283 in this volume). The scene's language and its staging of the crossing of various boundaries provide one memorable culmination for some of the book's major tendencies. Those tendencies are visible from the begin-

---

[1]For a contrasting discussion of doubling in Stoker's fiction, including *Dracula,* see Phyllis Roth, *Bram Stoker,* esp. 127–28. My argument, that Stoker evokes through doublings the enemy within, is at odds with the reading fielded by Roth, who claims that "throughout Stoker's fiction, the best in the human spirit always triumphs over an evil" (128). I pursue my argument in another form and with reference to a range of Gothic texts, including *Dracula,* in "Toward a History of Gothic and Modernism: Dark Modernity from Bram Stoker to Samuel Beckett," particularly in the section, "The 1890s: Mona Lisa, Other Vampires, and Dark Doubles" (590–96). For an interpretation of doubling in Stoker's writing that takes postcolonial issues into account, see Joseph Valente, " 'Double Born': Bram Stoker and the Metrocolonial Gothic"; Valente's *Dracula's Crypt: Bram Stoker, Irishness and the Question of Blood* (forthcoming, U of Illinois P, 2002) provides a book-length treatment of Stoker's works, especially *Dracula,* along the lines he sets out in his essay, which focuses on one of Stoker's short stories.

ning, when details of the narration and the narrative create an eddying in the book's language that challenges the possibility of clarity and interpretive closure. The challenge comes in small but telling details of style and narrative and in larger elements of plot and structure, including the continuing contrasts and connections between characters: Harker and Dracula, Dr. Seward and his patient Renfield, Mina and her friend Lucy, Van Helsing and Dracula, and Mina and Dracula, all of whom are in salient, surprising ways counterparts, or even collaborators.

In the opening chapters, we discover that Jonathan Harker is both Dracula's instrument and his double, just as he is the agent but also the protegé of his employer, Mr. Hawkins, whom he eventually replaces. By standing in parallel but subservient relation to both Dracula and a British employer, Harker provides an important structural element that bridges two apparently antithetical worlds. Later, his spouse, Mina, also provides a bridge between the vampire and his opponents because of her close relations, amounting to collaboration, with both. Her role as the conduit between worlds is pervasive in the story, since it is through her work that the tale has been transcribed and, presumably, edited. She composes the link between the world of the readers and that of the vampire and his antagonists. Her future husband's role begins to become clear in Chapter 3, when Harker realizes that, as Mr. Hawkins' agent, he must do Dracula's bidding, especially since he has become "a prisoner" who has "no choice" in the face of Dracula's "mastery" (p. 56). He has lost his human agency, or free will, by becoming the agent of Dracula and Hawkins. For business reasons, he collaborates with Hawkins and Dracula to sell a piece of real estate, a part of home, to a dangerous foreigner. This act eventually results in Harker's sharing his wife with the vampire.

The story of Count Dracula and his victims, potential and actual, is a narrative concerning choice. In the history of his family that the Count reveals to Harker in Chapter 3, he presents himself and his people as freedom fighters who resist the attempts of foreign powers to conquer them. In effect, he has fought to maintain his freedom of choice. But the vampire is a creature who appears to have no choice in its need for blood as nourishment, and its victims lose their human agency when they also succumb to that need. Loss of the power to choose is the reality, as well, for Harker, an ordinary person, because of his business obligations independent of the vampire's bite. The bizarre behavior of the vampire hunters later in the narrative also involves their assuming that they have no choice but to take the steps that they do, even when those steps involve breaking laws and mutilating the body of a woman. They will protect their homes and values, as the vampire says he has protected his. The intensity and the excessive character of the commitment on both sides result in the apparent elimination of options and in actions that no longer involve choice. The apparent loss of freedom to choose points to a disturbing parallel between Harker's world of work, the vampire's behavior, and the actions of those who are intent on destroying him.

In Harker's case, the disturbing character of the resemblance becomes evident early on, in Chapter 4, when Harker decides to "imitate" Dracula, whom he has seen several times crawling lizardlike down the castle wall (p. 58). The last time he observes Dracula performing this feat, Harker notices, to his shock, that Dracula is wearing Harker's own "suit of clothes" (p. 67). When he sees Dracula climb down the wall for the first time in Chapter 3, Harker asks "What manner of man is this, or what manner of creature is it in the semblance of man?" (p. 58). Uncannily, Dracula has become for Harker a semblance of the human that may, in fact, not be human at all, since it has the ability of a nonhuman creature, a fly or a lizard, to move up and down on vertical surfaces. A conventional hierarchy of understanding has been violated when the superhuman turns out to resemble something less than human. Contradictions of this sort undermine Harker's stability. His similarity to Dracula grows maddeningly close when Dracula dresses in Harker's clothing and when Harker successfully duplicates Dracula's seemingly impossible act. Because Harker begins to resemble Dracula in his ability to scale walls, the question "what manner of man is this?" becomes pertinent for them both. It would be reasonable to conclude that Harker's report of events has to be discounted because he has lost his sanity. It is, however, difficult to discount what he says, since so many others report similarly bizarre details concerning Dracula in the remaining twenty-four chapters. The threat of madness is mentioned or implied early in the narrative and regularly later. Harker is aware of it in the third chapter, when he counsels himself to be calm and tells himself that by writing in his journal, "The habit of entering accurately must help to soothe me" (p. 60). The *must* suggests that Harker hopes it will, not that it actually does. There is an implicit reflection here on realism, whose appearance of accurate rendering may also have the effect of soothing the writer or the reader and contributing to a pose of sanity and clear vision. As apparently objective reportage about unbelievable events, the journal writing throughout the narrative keeps realism's commitment to a semblance of accuracy in view as a defense either against madness or against admitting that madness already holds sway. The threat or reality of madness that Harker experiences derives in part from the uncertainty he feels about his situation and surroundings, an uncertainty that involves enigmas, ambiguities, and doubling. As readers we are in a position sometimes immediately, sometimes retrospectively, to understand details that evoke the situation Harker is facing in ways that are not immediately available to the character. That is, we can recognize meaningful implications for some details in the text that Harker understands differently. Because these details sometimes involve multiple meanings of words or multiple implications of references, the book's readers experience instances of doubling, ambiguity, and transformation not as the characters do but as matters of style and implication. At the end of the first chapter, for example, Harker describes himself as making noises in order to startle the wolves who have attacked his coach and to allow the coachman to reach the "trap" (p. 39). As readers of Stoker's time would have known, the word *trap* is a name for the vehicle in which Harker rides. Three paragraphs later, at the beginning of Chapter 2, he mentions that the coachman takes his "traps" out of the vehicle. This time, the word *trap* refers to his luggage. The quick repetition of the word brings to the fore that it can carry different meanings in different contexts. In Harker's situation, the word suggests different meanings simultaneously, since we know that he is entering a trap set by Dracula and Harker's unknowingly complicit employer. By the beginning of Chapter 3, Harker uses the word in a third way when he describes his response to being a prisoner as "mad" behavior like that of "a rat . . . in a trap" (p. 51). Harker traveled in a trap, and he brought traps with him to his own imprisonment, but only belatedly does he discover that he has walked willingly into a trap, in a sequence of repetitions of a single syllable that turns out to have pointed all along to the meaning that emerges explicitly only in its final occurrence.

The dating of Harker's trip in Dracula's trap to Dracula's trap on "the eve of St George's Day" (p. 30) suggests different meanings that can neither be easily separated nor readily reconciled. The old woman who gives Harker a rosary and crucifix to protect him explains that the people in the region believe that at midnight before St. George's Day "all the evil things in the world will have full sway" (p. 30). Within the events of the narrative, the evil refers explicitly to Dracula, but because of their familiarity with British culture Stoker's readers would have known that St. George is the patron saint of England, famous for being the slayer of a monster. The night, then, evokes England as well as Dracula, specifically an England that thinks of itself as taking action against evil creatures. The same night is closely associated with antithetical figures and events: the slaying of the dragon and the advent of the monster, the knight as emblem of England and the creature of the night who is associated with the East.

On this night, Jonathan Harker, who identifies himself as a Protestant, specifically a member of the Church of England, wears around his neck a rosary with a crucifix. These items are obviously part of a Roman Catholic system of practices and beliefs that English Protestants, as well as other Protestants, sometimes characterize prejudicially as superstitious, by contrast with their own beliefs and practices. In eighteenth-century Gothic narratives, villainous actions are often set in Catholic countries far from England and perpetrated or abetted by Catholic clergy, as if England and Protestant belief were immune from such evil. English prejudicial attitudes toward the Irish have also often merged with anti-Catholic attitudes. In *Dracula* the scene of Gothic action shifts from a Catholic region in eastern Europe to the island that is home to the English. Not just abroad but at home, English Protestant characters, including Harker and other vampire hunters, accept the use of objects from Catholic ritual, including the host and the cross, against the vampire, and they proceed under a leader who is Catholic. When they do so, they adopt attitudes that are as irrational and superstitious as any that the British complain about in the Irish or that earlier Gothic narratives project onto the people of Catholic countries. In light of the crossing or softening of the boundary between Catholic and Protestant in *Dracula*, the superiority of the mostly English vampire hunters becomes impossible to maintain. Stoker implicitly identifies in a humorous way even the chief vampire hunter, the Dutchman, Van Helsing, with the British by choosing for his surname an anagram of the word *English*. If *Van Helsing* is a genuine Dutch name, it is not one commonly encountered. Stoker's choice depends on the anagram that suggests that Van Helsing, though he may be Dutch, is essentially English.

No action makes it more difficult to admire and identify with the vampire hunters than their handling of Lucy's body at Van Helsing's insistence and direction when they disinter her at the end of Chapter 16. Dracula is never described in such bloody detail committing the kind of gruesome violence against a woman's body that the vampire hunters perpetrate. It is difficult even to give a name to their actions. Are they saving Lucy's soul, protecting English society from alien invasion, desecrating a grave, practicing a superstitious ritual of a misogynist kind, or mutilating a woman's body in a highly erotic, enraged way? Because of the details of language and scene, the reader can understand the act in a way that differs radically from the perpetrators' self-understanding. It is difficult to exclude or ignore the alternative interpretations. The vampire hunters themselves express the difficulty of distinguishing opposites in Lucy's case when Seward quotes in his diary at the end of Chapter 12 lines of poetry that constitute a rhetorical chiasmus, a statement in which words are repeated but in reversed positions:

> "We thought her dying whilst she slept,
> And sleeping when she died." (p. 174)

The repetition in reversed order, "dying . . . slept, / sleeping . . . dead," in which the verbs switch both positions and conjugated forms, captures the conundrum of the vampire's dual status as *undead*, neither living nor dead, that is the book's abiding, challenging enigma.[2] It is a meaningful coincidence that the name for the rhetorical figure of repetition in reversed order, *chiasmus*, comes from a Greek root meaning "cross." The cross in *Dracula* is a religious artifact used against the vampire, but the rhetorical crossings in the style efface the distinctions between apparent opposites. Immediately after citing the chiastic lines in his diary, Seward reports a remark by Van Helsing that repeats the blurring of opposites: that "the end" is in this case "only the beginning" (p. 174). Van Helsing reiterates the sentiment in other words at the start of Chapter 17 after Lucy has been dealt with.

Curiously, Lucy largely disappears from the narrative once she has been dispatched. As if she does not matter any longer to the vampire hunters, she is hardly mentioned. But we are unlikely to forget the violence done to her body, especially in the book's closing when Van Helsing commits similar acts against the female vampires in Chapter 27. He explicitly reminds us that the "terrible task" of his "butcher work" at

---

[2]In his seminal essay "The Structural Study of Myth," Claude Lévi-Strauss explains, in a way that is relevant for understanding the crossovers in *Dracula* and the concept of the *undead*, the persistence and the power of myths in culture as an attempt to deal with real contradictions in human experience. He asserts that "the purpose of myth is to provide a logical model capable of overcoming a contradiction" but that this is "an impossible achievement if, as it happens, the contradiction is real" (193). Because of the impossibility, "the logic of myth" involves "a double, reciprocal exchange" (191). He focuses in particular on a Zuni myth that attempts to provide "a mediation between life and death" (185), that is, a mediation for a contradiction that is also captured by the concept of the *undead*.

this point in the hunt resembles what had to be done to "the sweet Miss Lucy" (p. 362). At the beginning of the memorandum in which Van Helsing describes the scene of destruction at the female vampires' tomb, he comments on having retained his own sanity: "I am at least sane" (p. 360). Because of Van Helsing's weak grasp of idiomatic English, he could be distinguishing himself from others by suggesting that "I," "at least," am "sane." Or he could be asserting that whatever psychic damage he has sustained in the battle against Dracula, he still has his sanity. Van Helsing's statement leaves the impression that, like Harker in the early chapters, he is trying to retain his mental equilibrium. His statement is followed soon by his fantasizing about the female vampires in a sexual way and by acts of violence that can reasonably cause us to wonder about his motives and his stability. This Dutch incarnation of St. George, the slayer of the monster and representative hero for the English, appears to have two sides, one of which is dark. The demon, or enemy, to be exorcised appears to be within, most obviously within those who claim that their acts of violence are not indications of mad barbarity.

The resemblance between the vampire and his antagonists is matched in one recurring way by the similarities between Renfield and Dr. Seward. Those similarities constitute a reciprocally defining relationship between characters who appear to be quite different: the one mad, the other sane; the one a patient, the other a doctor. The details linking the two are abundant and various. Seward is particularly important in the narrative as a certified expert on sanity. His role in the culture, as well as his business, is to distinguish between the sane and the mad and, we assume, to restore insane patients to sanity. He is central to the narration, since he reports a great deal of the action by making recordings that Mina later turns into typescript. Like Harker and Van Helsing, Seward is concerned about his own mental health in ways that can make us wonder about the doctor's mental stability. In Chapter 5, he describes the "empty feeling" (p. 82) of being lovelorn that robs him of appetite and interest after Lucy refuses his marriage proposal. In Chapter 8, he counsels himself not to become habituated to the drugs to which he has easy access (p. 120). As Seward reports in Chapter 10, one of the first things Van Helsing says to him after arriving is that "All men are mad in some way or the other," though some are "your madmen" and some are "God's madmen," "the rest of the world" (p. 135). For Van Helsing, the mad who march under God's banner are somehow different. In the case of Renfield and Dr. Seward, the resemblance obscures the difference.

Renfield's zoophagous commitment to a hierarchical food chain (reported in Seward's diary, pp. 89–93) in which he occupies the top position (above cat-bird-spider-fly) is the counterpart of Seward's feeling that he stands above his subordinates and his patients. Renfield's careful keeping of accounts concerning his pets, to whom he does what he wants, matches Seward's assiduous recording of thoughts and events, including details about his patients, over whom he exercises control. Like Harker, Seward has a commitment to tracing events "*accurately*" (p. 82; his italics). When he first comments on Renfield's unusual case in Chapter 5, Seward mentions that his attempt to shake the emptiness of disappointed love leads him to make himself "master" of the facts of his patient's "hallucination," but that he has gone too far: "In my manner of doing it there was, I now see, something of cruelty. I seemed to wish to keep him to the point of his madness — a thing which I avoid with the patients as I would the mouth of hell. (*Mem.*, under what circumstances would I *not* avoid the pit of hell?) . . . Hell has its price!" (p. 82). Seward's confession is disturbing and his rhetoric excessive. He clearly shares with his patient a sadistic tendency.

When Seward describes Renfield's behavior toward the insects and animals he collects, he again conjoins matters of "love" and "cruelty," not his own, but Renfield's. Renfield displays a "love of animals" that is hard to distinguish from the patient's being "only abnormally cruel" (p. 90). The fly that Renfield caught and ate after it "buzzed into the room" (p. 90) has one counterpart in what Seward terms "[t]he thought that has been buzzing about my brain" (p. 92). This thought follows from the conclusion that Renfield is trying to absorb as many lives as possible by moving up the hierarchy of living beings from insects through animals toward human beings. It includes Seward's temptation "to complete the experiment" in a way that he compares to the criticized practice of "vivisection" in order to "advance science in . . . the knowledge of the brain" (p. 92). Seward presents himself here as the mad scientist, since he seems to be suggesting that he might allow Renfield to continue the chain of consumption with human beings. Seward's phrasing involves a genitive construction, "knowledge of the brain," that is both subjective and objective; it suggests in an undecidable way both furthering what we know *about* the brain and increasing what the brain, specifically what Seward calls his own "exceptional brain," *itself* knows. In the latter reading, Seward is formulating the goal of absorbing as many buzzing thoughts into his brain as he possibly can. In this regard, the doctor takes his lead from the patient, especially when his intellectual appetite results in his considering the

sacrifice of human beings as a means to reach his goal. The resemblance
is emphasized in this segment of the narration when Seward's rhetoric,
which includes a triple commitment to "work. Work! work!" (p. 93)
echoes his report of Renfield's triply expressed desire to "feed — and
feed — and feed!" (p. 91).

Renfield's behavior and speech are often puzzling, including his
denial in Chapter 9 that he would ever harm Seward, who is the object
of his attack. Seward responds by wondering, "Am I to take it that I
have anything in common with him, so that we are, as it were, to stand
together . . . ?" (p. 125). Part of what they have in common is a delusion of grandeur concerning their resemblance to divinity, a delusion
that is one with their hierarchical views. As Renfield explains in Chapter
18 during a moment of lucidity, his goal is immortality, to "prolong
life" "indefinitely" "by consuming a multitude of live things" (p. 239).
In the linking of these two characters, Stoker stages cultural attitudes
that justify the ill treatment of other creatures and other people,
whether individuals or groups, who, because they are assumed to be
inferior, become subject to incarceration, enslavement, or extermina-
tion. Both of the characters strive for mastery, but they simultaneously
submit to more powerful masters, Dracula and Van Helsing. By giving
us a dual representation of the attitudes at work, Stoker is able to bring
out the self-delusion that prevents the participants from recognizing in
themselves the madness they can sometimes recognize in others.

Though Seward does not grasp, or perhaps only does not admit, his
kinship with Renfield, the reader has a point of vantage for recognizing
it. Their common delusion of superiority is particularly evident in
Seward's odd report about Renfield's peculiar behavior in Chapter 8.
Having been alerted by the attendant that Renfield refused to deal with
him and spoke condescendingly, Seward visits Renfield and receives the
same treatment. He concludes that his patient is suffering from a religious mania that involves his thinking of himself as an "Omnipotent
Being," and he quotes Renfield's biblical-sounding statement about
bride-maidens rejoicing. But as he does so, the doctor expresses his
own scorn for both the attendant and Renfield in language that is also
biblical sounding. When Seward asserts that "the God created from
human vanity," meaning Renfield, "sees no difference between an eagle
and a sparrow" (p. 119), he uses language that resembles Renfield's to
identify himself with the stronger, more powerful bird. Such a predator
might well eat a sparrow, as Renfield already has. The doctor wants to
see differences between his own attitudes and position and those of
Renfield, but they are, at most, differences of degree, not kind.

Seward's recordings result in a crucial, lengthy part of the narration. It is through him that we hear about two of the narrative's most vivid moments: the violence that the vampire hunters do to Lucy's body in Chapter 16 and Mina's ingesting of Dracula's blood in Chapter 21. The scene involving Mina and Dracula is considerably less violent than the earlier scene involving Lucy. The style, however, is memorable and enigmatic, particularly when Seward describes the act in which the human woman and the male vampire engage:

> His face was turned from us, but the instant we saw we all recognized the Count — in every way, even to the scar on his forehead. With his left hand he held both Mrs. Harker's hands, keeping them away from her arms at full tension; his right hand gripped her by the back of the neck, forcing her face down on his bosom. Her white nightdress was smeared with blood, and a thin stream trickled down the man's bare breast which was shown by his torn-open dress. The attitude of the two had a terrible resemblance to a child forcing a kitten's nose into a saucer of milk to compel it to drink. (p. 283)

The question of reliability arises emphatically in this passage. It is difficult to imagine how the group could have seen Dracula's scar if they could not see his face. This particular instance of a questionable detail contributes to the larger issue of the book's narration as a whole, since Mina has transcribed everything from a variety of sources and media. The result is a fragmented, episodic, textualized narration, rather than a narration that, as in many realistic narratives, presents a continuous sequence of action in a style that gives the impression of the reliable voice of a single narrator.

This scene complicates our impression of the status of the telling, since the transcriber, who is, in effect, the author, is the woman who has sucked blood from Dracula's breast as part of an embrace she admits later in the chapter she "did not want to hinder" (p. 287). The book provides no guidance about how we should take Mina's transforming experience into account as we read her transcription of events that turn out to be otherwise unverifiable. The issue of the narration's reliability is bottomless. When she transcribes Seward's report of her embrace with Dracula, Mina is both subject and object. She is the subject who writes, the person ultimately responsible for making the representation available to us in the aftermath of her experience with Dracula. In this role, she resembles the mythological figure, Echo, who creates a distinctive voice for herself by repeating and reconfiguring the language of others. In the representation Mina makes available, during her experience with Dracula, she is the object of Seward's observation and the object of Dracula's desire and his manipulations. Even so, since she admits that she did not resist Dracula's advances, Mina is not only the object of a male's desire but also a subject with desires of her own, on which she acts. Temporally, she stands in two places, as the later transcriber of a story that involves centrally her own past experiences. While Mina is presenting what happened to her in the past, she knows already what her future in the narrative will be.

The scene between Mina and Dracula is as resistant to being characterized in a determinate way as is the earlier dispatching of Lucy. Is it an attack, a scene of feeding that gives Mina new abilities, or a perverse moment of sexual congress? The sentence in which Seward compares the scene to a kitten's nose being forced into a saucer of milk captures the simultaneous crossing of several boundaries in a way that undoes the distinctions necessary for realistic narration of intelligible events and for maintaining hierarchies of power. Seward may think the resemblance is "terrible" because it undoes the logic of conventional understanding. It may sometimes be necessary to push a kitten's nose into milk in order to encourage it to drink a liquid that does not come from its own species, but "force" and "compel" suggest violence and mastery. Seward may have Renfield's cruelty to animals on his mind, and he may be drawing on experiences from his own childhood about which we have not heard, ones involving his own treatment of animals. The comparison turns an adult woman into a young animal while it also puts the male who seems to be attacking her in the position of an adult woman who is breastfeeding an infant. Van Helsing claims that the vampire is actually childlike in his thinking, but here it stands as an adult in relation to the infantalized Mina. But this adult male who suckles is also compared to a child. Animal and human, male and female, child and adult, perverse sexuality and breastfeeding have simultaneously exchanged places, as if they were interchangeable rather than different and distinct. The threat that the distinctions by which we order our identities and our lives are not absolute and not sustainable comes through vividly when Mina as Dracula's sexual partner becomes an infant animal at the androgynous breast of a childlike creature.

Like Leda in W. B. Yeats's "Leda and the Swan" after her embrace with Zeus, who has incarnated himself as a swan, Mina takes something away from the embrace that may not have been intended. As a result of her telepathic contact with Dracula, she can be both his partner and one of the vampire hunters. In her role as medium, she is a collaborator in both senses, working together with one side but also involved with the enemy. Her oddly dual position emerges in the ambiguous language of the passage that presents her awakening after Van Helsing returns from his butchery. The ambiguities embody the climactic convergence of the narrative, in which the hunters and their quarry are coming together. Mina reports Van Helsing's outcry that " 'They are all converging'" as part of a scene involving conjoined opposites: there is both "snow falling" and "sun shining," and the gypsy leader on horseback looks "like a centaur" (p. 366), a merger of human and beast. The centaurlike gypsy is matched on the other side by Jonathan Harker, who exhibits superhuman strength and wields a "great Kukri knife" (p. 367), a weapon associated not with Europeans but with fierce indigenous people from Nepal, some of whom served the British as soldiers.

The book's style in these closing pages, in which a "look of hate" is transformed into "a look of peace" (p. 367), reaches a high point of indeterminacy. As Mina awakens, Van Helsing reports that she "cried out in pain that I had endured too much" (p. 362). It is impossible to know whether this is an ambiguous instance of indirect discourse (his assertion that she actually said either "You have endured too much" or "I have endured too much"), or a statement that he has suffered too much contact with her pain of this kind, or a statement that he has himself suffered too much of the same pain he recognizes in Mina. The last of those readings suggests a sharing of consciousness between Van Helsing and Mina like her telepathic link to Dracula. We cannot know with certainty whose pain is evoked. When Mina urges Van Helsing to come with her " 'to meet my husband who is, I know, coming towards us,' " he describes her as a compound creature, pale, thin, and weak but with eyes that "glowed with fervour" (p. 363). Van Helsing does not seem to recognize, however, that her statement about her husband's coming toward them can refer either to Harker or to Dracula. If she knows that Harker is coming, it is only because she is in telepathic contact with the vampire. She may, in fact, consider Dracula to be her husband.

That Mina has had conjugal relations of a strange kind with Dracula affects our understanding of the book's closing. She has given birth not only to the story we have just read from "a mass of type-writing" (p. 368) but also to a child who carries a "bundle of names" that Jonathan Harker feels "links all our little band of men together." The child may well literally do that, since the blood of its mother is a mixture of her own with the blood she ingests at the vampire's breast, and his blood includes that of Lucy, who had transfusions from the vampire hunters. Harker does not mention and would surely not want to admit that the link also includes Dracula, whose blood Mina tasted. The narration does not make it unambiguously clear that the vampire hunters actually did away with Dracula, but even if they did, Mina's child preserves something from Dracula in a living form that has a future. A repetition of what has happened becomes possible through Mina's act of doubling herself in childbirth. The question that Harker posed about Dracula, "what manner of man is this?," will need to be posed again about Harker's own child in the story's sequel. Although Dr. Seward sets no standard of reliability and sanity in *Dracula,* his assertion about closure is confirmed by this narrative: "Truly there is no such thing as finality." (p. 199) As Van Helsing realized about Lucy's apparent death, what looks like the end is only the beginning.

WORKS CITED

Lévi-Strauss, Claude. "The Structural Study of Myth." *The Structuralists: From Marx to Lévi-Strauss.* Ed. Richard T. and Fernande M. De George. Garden City: Doubleday, 1972. 169–94.

Riquelme, John Paul. "Toward a History of Gothic and Modernism: Dark Modernity from Bram Stoker to Samuel Beckett." *Modern Fiction Studies* 43.3 (Fall 2000): 585–605. Special issue on *Gothic & Modernism.*

Roth, Phyllis. *Bram Stoker.* Boston: Twayne, 1982.

Valente, Joseph. "'Double Born': Bram Stoker and the Metrocolonial Gothic." *Modern Fiction Studies* 43.3 (Fall 2000): 632–45. Special issue on *Gothic & Modernism.*

Combining Perspectives on *Dracula*

So far, this volume's emphasis has been on mapping the boundaries of particular contemporary critical approaches and traditions. In presenting this final essay, by Jennifer Wicke, the emphasis is reversed, for the intention is to demonstrate the permeability of such approaches, traditions, and boundaries. The goal is to suggest how supposedly disparate assumptions can be held simultaneously — and how supposedly diverse rhetorical conventions can mix, merge, and metamorphose. To put it more plainly, Wicke's essay allows us to see how a critic can draw on the insights of *several* critical traditions (in effect, combining perspectives) to present a view of a work unavailable from any one window, any single critical perspective.

Toward the beginning of her essay, Wicke points out that many critics have taken a psychoanalytic approach to *Dracula* rather than the Marxist or "materialist," socioeconomic one she has mainly chosen. Her approach promises to focus on such subjects as stenography and typewriting, thereby taking us into the "shabby, dusty corners" of the novel rather than into "its more delicious excesses" (p. 578 in this volume). Wicke goes on to suggest, however, that the psychological and economic components of Stoker's text are not as bifurcated and disparate as are the assumptions and vocabularies of critics performing "materialist and psychosexual readings," both of which have heretofore ignored what she calls the "category of consumption." Consumption, which lies on the "cusp" of the erotic and economic, is in Wicke's view the "crux," not only of *Dracula* but also of "the modernist divide for both theory and literature" (p. 578).

Wicke sees in Count Dracula a representation of "mass culture, the developing technologies of the media in its many forms, . . . mass transport, tourism, photography and lithography in image production, and mass-produced narrative" (p. 579). And she views *Dracula* as a self-conscious, self-referential example of technology-driven, mass-produced narrative. A "narrative patchwork" made up of the "journal entries, letters, professional records, and newspaper clippings" collected by a "band of vampire hunters," the manuscript is "textually completely au courant," a "motley fusion of speech and writing, recording and transcribing, image and typography" (p. 579).

Dr. Seward, for instance, keeps his journal by making gramophone recordings of his voice and then having Mina transcribe his words into typewritten form. Textual confusions and possible inconsistencies are created when, midway through the text, we begin reading Mina's transcriptions rather than "hearing" Seward "speaking to us from out of the text" (p. 580). Thus, *Dracula* represents its own "means of production" as one involving speech that has been taken over and "*vampirized*" (emphasis added) via transcription and "typewriting," both of which "strip away" the emotional nuances and power latent in voice (p. 581). Similarly, Jonathan Harker's journal has been consumed, "colonized," and transformed by the technologies of mass culture. We read a version that has been "uncoded by Mina's act of typewriting" the original, which was in "stenographic form." But stenography, or shorthand, has already bled and changed "Jonathan's hot inner monologue," turning a swooning vision into bureaucratic squiggles that later transcode and translate into "'kiss me with those red lips'" (p. 581).

Having linked the novel's psychosexual content to its means of narrative production, Wicke returns her focus to the broader cultural context, connecting the vampiric consumption of content via shorthand to the vampiric transformation of cultural labor of which stenography was symptomatic. This transformation occurred due to the combined influence of a number of late-nineteenth-century developments, including the "rationalization (in [Max] Weber's sense) of the procedures of bureaucracy and business, the feminization of the clerical workforce, [and] the standardization of mass business writing" (p. 581).

Thus, stenography and other developments and procedures that came to define the modern office are not, in Wicke's view, what Karl Marx might have seen them as: dehumanizing modes of production threatening the ancient, mythic mysteries represented by vampirism. Rather, they are the modern face of vampirism, modes of consumption intimately intertwined with their subject, the translated translation of practices with which they are intimately linked. They themselves suggest the way back to "Transylvania, the doomed castle, and the ghastly doings Jonathan experiences there" (p. 581).

In the last analysis, moreover, even those experiences prove more uncannily modern than mysteriously medieval. Jonathan, as Wicke points out, travels as a "tourist," drinking in local culture, writing down recipes, and carrying a gift of photographs for the Count. Thus, Wicke writes, "[P]hotography joins the list of new techniques or processes juxtaposed with the story of the medieval aristocratic vampire, but the Kodak snapshot camera . . . is really also a celluloid analog of vampirism in action, the extraction out of an essence in the act of consumption" (pp. 582–83). So is the telegraph, as is the "[m]anifold" typewriter function that makes textual replicas via a process that reminds Wicke of the way vampires replicate themselves. "Here we step into the age of mechanical reproduction with a vengeance," she writes, "since the reproductive process that makes vampires is so closely allied to the mechanical replication of culture" (p. 586).

Wicke begins her essay by quoting Marx, and she often views *Dracula* from the perspective of Marxist criticism, that is, in terms of materialist mass culture and its modes of production and consumption. (See the Glossary definition of *Marxist Criticism*.) One of the classics of Marxist criticism is Walter Benjamin's "The Work of Art in the Age of Mechanical Reproduction" (1936), an essay to which Wicke makes explicit reference.

But Wicke also begins by declaring her intent to relate consumption to the novel's psychosexual content, thereby bringing together the vocabularies and interests of materialist and psychoanalytic criticism (see "What Is Psychoanalytic Criticism?" p. 466). In the process, she adeptly employs the assumptions and terminology of Freudian analysis. (She even at one point reads Van Helsing's hypnosis of Mina in terms of Sigmund Freud's famous psychoanalysis of a patient named Dora.)

But to find in Wicke's analysis only a combination of Marxist and psychoanalytic perspectives would be to miss the richness of the critical mix she employs. Throughout, she offers the insights of feminist criticism (see the Glossary definition) and gender criticism (see "What Is Gender Criticism?" p. 434), finding evidence in the novel of the commodification of women, describing the feminization of the clerical workplace (and a related, broader "gender division of labor"), viewing vampire women like Lucy as symptoms of the Victorian fear of erotic female sexuality, and analyzing the cultural association of women with domesticity and the home — the site of mass culture's inimical invasion. Wicke even manages to combine feminist, gender, and new historicist criticism (see "What Is New Historicism?" p. 500) when she argues that the modern discourse of sexuality is based on the culture of consumption — and that mass culture has reasserted culture's historic control of sexuality through the media that define it.

The inevitable repetition of the word *culture* in any introduction to Wicke's essay also attests to its proximity to so-called cultural criticism. Defined at some length in the Glossary, *cultural criticism* — briefly — is an approach to literature that defines literature broadly; insists on the significance of mass culture (as opposed to culture with a capital *C*); and looks for its reflection in, impact on, and reproduction through literature (in the way that Wicke foregrounds such things as shorthand and typewriting, photography and newspaper articles). And, like those cultural critics who practice so-called postcolonial criticism (see *postcolonial criticism* in the Glossary) Wicke extends her analysis of practices that develop within a dominant culture to those performed *by* that culture on others outside it. She deftly links her notion that the standardization and commodification involved in a vampiric mass media culture are a form of "imperialism" within Western European society to the idea that the desire to destroy Count Dracula signifies the imperialistic drive to triumph over "racial otherness" (a desire paradoxically shared by Count Dracula, an unlikely "partner in imperialism" who is quickly "conquering the eastern territory" of Europe and making inroads in England) (p. 597).

Wicke is also aware of narratology and reader-response criticism (see Glossary), the former focusing on the way texts produce meaning, the latter viewing readers as producers as well as consumers of meaning. She constantly refers to the text as a "collage or bricolage" of "inserted" narrative, as involving "textual mechanics" that raise questions about how reliable certain "voices" are — and whether they are as "authoritative as the other voices in the text" (pp. 583–84).

Finally, Wicke's related interest in the way in which Stoker's text represents the "colonization" of speech by writing — and, more important, her view that the speech-writing distinction is one of several "dizzy contradictions" that "fissure . . . the text" (p. 578) — draws on insights from deconstruction (see "What Is Deconstruction?" p. 538). Deconstructors since Jacques Derrida have blurred the speech-writing distinction and questioned the privileging of speech over writing in

Western culture. They have also related the (un)reliability of texts identified by certain reader-response critics to textual contradictions that flow from words' multiple meanings and that make textual meaning "indeterminate."

Ross C Murfin

COMBINING PERSPECTIVES

JENNIFER WICKE

Vampiric Typewriting: *Dracula* and Its Media

In the Introduction to the *Grundrisse* Marx asks, thinking about the relation of Greek art to the present day: "What chance has Vulcan against Roberts & Co., Jupiter against the lightning-rod and Hermes against the Credit-Mobilier? All mythology overcomes and dominates and shapes the forces of nature . . . it therefore vanishes with the advent of real mastery over them. What becomes of Fama alongside Printing House Square?"[1] The incongruity — and mastery — of *Dracula* lies in its willingness to set the mythological, Gothic, medieval mystery of Count Dracula squarely in the midst of Printing House Square. The *Grundrisse* is Marx's complex meditation on the intertwined fates of production, consumption and distribution, prefaced by these worries about the place of the aesthetic in the modern socioeconomic landscape. Within its novelistic form, *Dracula* too could be said to pose and to enact the occultation of those three processes, by its privileging of consumption, which subsumes the other two. This engorgement is staged by the collision of ancient mythologies with contemporary modes of production.

Miss Mina Murray writes to Miss Lucy Westenra about her current preoccupations: "I have been working very hard lately, because I want to keep up with Jonathan's studies, and I have been practising shorthand very assiduously. When we are married I shall be able to be very useful to Jonathan, and if I can stenograph well enough I can take down what he wants to say in this way and write it out for him on the typewriter, which I am also practicing very hard. He and I sometimes write letters in shorthand, and he is keeping a stenographic journal of

---

[1] Karl Marx, *Grundrisse,* trans. Martin Nicolaus (London: Penguin, 1973) 110.

his travels abroad" (pp. 75–76 in this volume). While such girlish pursuits, if slavishly dutiful, scarcely seem ominous, it is Mina's very prowess with the typewriter that brings down Dracula on unsuspecting British necks, even including her very own. In what follows I want to propose that as radically different as the sexy act of vamping and such prosaic labor on the typewriter appear, there are underlying ties between them that can ultimately make sense of the oxymoron of vampiric typewriting. The argument will turn attention to the technologies that underpin vampirism, making for the dizzy contradictions of this book, and permitting it to be read as the first great *modern* novel in British literature. In doing so, I will be concentrating on the shabby, dusty corners of *Dracula*, inspecting its pockets for lint rather than examining its more delicious excesses, and putting pressure on the aspects of *Dracula* that have received less attention because they, like practicing shorthand, don't immediately seem as pleasurable. *Dracula* cannot help but be a heady cocktail, even under inauspiciously stringent critical circumstances, and part of what I hope to show in so pursuing its media are its connections to the everyday life of typewriters, neon, advertisement, and neoimperialism we are still living today. To drain *Dracula* of some of its obvious terrors may help to highlight the more banal terrors of modern life. . . .

[The longer essay from which this commentary is extracted contains at this point a discussion of Franco Moretti's double reading of *Dracula*, from a Marxist perspective and from a psychoanalytic perspective, which he considers discrete analyses. Moretti's reading appears in "Dialectic of Fear" in his *Signs Taken for Wonders* (London: Verso, 1983): 83–108.]

. . . [M]y choice of *Dracula* rests on a desire to investigate the uncoupled chain of materialist and psychosexual readings, because I see *Dracula* lodged at the site of that difficulty, at a crux that marks the modernist divide for both theory and literature. It is necessary to juggle several balls in the air at once, to force a collision between these vocabularies. What causes Moretti's economic and sexual allegories to diverge so thoroughly, in my view, is the paradoxical absence of the category of consumption; what I will work through here is the uneasy status of consumption as it is poised between two seemingly exclusionary vocabularies that nonetheless intersect (often invisibly) precisely there.

In considering *Dracula*, I am turning the text to face forward into the twentieth century, rather than assessing its status as Victorian mythography, since what I want to give is a reading that opens up into a thesis about the modernity we can then read off the wildly voluptuous, and even Medusan, *volte face* thereby revealed. This is not to discount the probing and incisive readings that do annex *Dracula* to its very real Victorian contexts, but rather to shift the agenda in critical terms to the work that the text can do as a liminal modernist artifact, an exemplary text that then lies hauntingly behind the uncanny creations of modernism, at the borders of what is accepted as "high modernism," the high art tradition of its literature.[2] The vampirism this text articulates is crucial to the dynamics of modernity, as well as to giving a name to our current theoretical predicaments. *Dracula* is not a coherent text; it refracts hysterical images of modernity. One could call it a chaotic reaction-formation in advance of modernism, wildly taking on the imprintings of mass culture.

To begin by eliminating all the suspense of my own theoretical trajectory: the social force most analogous to Count Dracula's as depicted in the novel is none other than mass culture, the developing technologies of the media in its many forms, as mass transport, tourism, photography and lithography in image production, and mass-produced narrative. To take seriously the status of mass culture in an incipiently mass cultural artifact is to have a privileged vantage on the dislocations and transformations it occasions, especially because *Dracula* has been so successful in hiding the pervasiveness of the mass cultural within itself, foregrounding instead its exotic otherness.

What has been little remarked about the structure of *Dracula* is precisely how its narrative is ostensibly produced, its means of production. A narrative patchwork made up out of the combined journal entries, letters, professional records, and newspaper clippings that the doughty band of vampire hunters had separately written or collected, it is then collated and typed by the industrious Mina, wife of the first vampire target and ultimately a quasi-vampire herself.[3] The multiplicity of narrative viewpoints has been well discussed, but the crucial fact is that all of these narrative pieces eventually comprising the manuscript we are said to have in our hands emanate from radically dissimilar and even state-of-the-art media forms. *Dracula,* draped in all its feudalism and medieval gore, is textually completely au courant. Nineteenth-century

[2]Among the best treatments of the Victorian legacy to be discovered, in one form or another, in the book are Nina Auerbach's commentary on the text in her *Woman and the Demon: The Life of Victorian Myth* (Cambridge: Harvard Univ. Press, 1982); John Stevenson's essay "A Vampire in the Mirror: The Sexuality of *Dracula.*" *PMLA* 103 (1988): 139–49; and Daniel Pick's essay "'Terrors of the Night': Dracula and 'Degeneration,'" *Critical Quarterly* 30 (Winter 1988): 71–87.

[3]David Seed touches on this in his "The Narrative Method of Dracula," *Nineteenth Century Fiction* 40 (June 1985): 61–75.

diaristic and epistolary effusion is invaded by cutting edge technology, in a transformation of the generic materials of the text into a motley fusion of speech and writing, recording and transcribing, image and typography.

Dr. Seward, for example, the young alienist who operates the private insane asylum so fortuitously located next to Count Dracula's London property, produces his voluminous journal not by writing it, but by recording his own words on gramophone records, which then must be transcribed. Since the gramophone is in 1897 an extremely recently invented device, even Dr. Seward is confused by some of its properties; his worst realization is that in order to find some important gem of recorded insight, he will have to listen to all the records again.[4] Never fear, since the incomparable Madame Mina offers to transcribe all the cylinders to typewritten form after she has listened to them, realizing their value as part of the puzzle of tracking the vampire. "I put the forked metal to my ears and listened," she writes. And later, "that is a wonderful machine, but it is cruelly true . . . No one must hear them (his words) spoken ever again! I have copied out the words on my typewriter." Despite the apparent loss of "aura," in Benjamin's sense, ostensibly found in the mechanical reproduction of Seward's diary, what Mina is struck by is the latent emotional power of the recorded voice, whose spectacular emotion the typewriter can strip away. Her transcription of Dr. Seward's wax cylinders occurs mid-way in the text, when the search for Dracula in London is begun in earnest. What that timing implies is that all Dr. Seward's previous entries, and there are many, are recordings, as it were, voicings coded in the most up-to-date inscription, speaking to us from out of the text. There is ample textual confusion swirling about this point, and much inconsistency, since Dr. Seward's diary includes abbreviations and chemical formulas that do not have meaning "orally"; moreover, when the machine is used by others, there is a vampiric exchange involved — a chapter title tells us, "Dr. Seward's Phonograph Diary, spoken by Van Helsing." The burden this mode of production puts on narration is expressed when Dr. Seward reacts to hearing the burial service read over Mina, a prophylactic act in case they have to kill her. "I — I cannot go on — words — and — v-voice — fail m-me!" (p. 328). Such doughty sentimentality cannot mask the fact that Seward's diary constitutes the immaterialization of a voice, a technologized zone of the novel, inserted at a histori-

---

[4]Dr. Seward follows recent medical practice in this, as Leonard Wolf's *The Annotated Dracula* (New York: Ballantine Books, 1975) notes (118).

cal point where phonography was not widespread, because still quite expensive, but indicative of things to come. We are not dealing here with pure speech in opposition to writing, but instead with speech already colonized, or vampirized, by mass mediation.

The other materials forming the narrative's typed body are equally mass-culturally produced. Jonathan Harker's journal, which begins the novel and recounts the fateful discovery of Count Dracula as a vampire, only to have the memory of this insupportable revelation wiped out by a bout of brain fever, is "actually" a document in stenographic form, later itself uncoded by Mina's act of typewriting. Stenography is a fortuitous code for Jonathan, since Dracula, who seems to know everything else, does not take shorthand, and doesn't confiscate the journal, an act that would deprive us of the first-hand frisson of narrative in progress. We as readers don't see on the page the little swirls and abbreviations we might expect from a manuscript in shorthand, since that would keep us from reading; it would produce cognitive dissonance for readers to be reminded that the terrifying narrative his diary unfolds is meant to be inscribed in that elliptical, bureaucratized form of writing known as shorthand. What, after all, is the stenographic version of "kiss me with those red lips," Jonathan's hot inner monologue as he lies swooning on the couch surrounded by his version of Dracula's angels? Shorthand may seem to fall innocently outside the sphere of mass cultural media, but in fact it participates in one of the most thoroughgoing transformations of cultural labor of the twentieth-century, the rationalization (in Weber's[5] sense) of the procedures of bureaucracy and business, the feminization of the clerical work force, the standardization of mass business writing. The modern office is very far afield from Transylvania, the doomed castle, and the ghastly doings Jonathan experiences there, but shorthand is utterly material to the ramifications of vampirism. Vampirism springs up, or takes command, at the behest of shorthand. Although the pages we open to start our reading of the book look like any printed pages, there is a crucial sense in which we are inducted into Count Dracula lore by the insinuation of this invisible, or translated, stenography. This submerged writing is the modern, or mass cultural, cryptogram; the linkage of this mode of abbreviated writing with the consumption process is made apparent by our willingness to

---

[5]Max Weber (1864–1920), German philosophical sociologist and historian, used the term *Rationalization* to refer to the displacement of traditional, value-oriented forms of social organization by institutions and behavior based on efficiency, profit, and self-interest. [Editor's note.]

invest these abbreviations with the fully-fleshed body of typed and printed writing. Shorthand flows through us, as readers, to be transubstantiated as modern, indeterminate, writing.

Jonathan has begun his journey to that foreboding place as a tourist of sorts; the impressions he jots down with most relish initially are the recipes for strange foods he would like Mina to try — the "national dishes," as he calls them: "(*Mem.*, get recipe for Mina)" (p. 27). He first tastes a chicken dish made with red pepper that, insidiously enough, makes him thirsty; even the red peppers are suspicious in a text with such a fixed color scheme of red and white. Count Dracula, of course, has a national dish as well, only it is comprised of the bodies not yet belonging to his nation, and Mina, who was going to get the chance to whip up the national dish of the Carpathians, is to become his food for thought. The local color Jonathan drinks in, as recipes and customs and costumes, has the form of regularized tourism; Dracula's castle becomes an unwonted departure from the Transylvanian Baedeker. This may be the point at which to broach the larger argument that will dog the more local one I am making. I am trying to give a reading of the society of consumption and its refraction in *Dracula,* but that society rests on, is impossible without, the imperial economy. It is overly glib to talk about commodity culture without this insistent awareness; what particularly draws me to *Dracula,* and what makes it a modern text, is the embeddedness there of consumption, gender, and empire. Jonathan's travels are made not to a specific British colonial or imperial possession, but to a place with a dense history of conquest and appropriation. He is funneled into this history by means of the accoutrements of modern travel and leisure; Jonathan, who is on business, is nonetheless a tourist *manqué.* In this instance too, Count Dracula and his extraordinary logic of production are encountered through the lens of mass cultural preoccupations and techniques.

Jonathan bears a gift of sorts for Dracula, a set of Kodak pictures of the British house the latter is interested in purchasing, although Dracula in fact has another motive for having brought the rather drab young law clerk so far from England: he wants to borrow his speech, to learn English perfectly from his captive, Harker Jonathan, as he occasionally slips in addressing him. The presence of the Kodak camera in the midst of such goings on is unexpected and yet far from accidental. Photography joins the list of new cultural techniques or processes juxtaposed with the story of the medieval aristocratic vampire, but the Kodak snapshot camera so many people were wielding at the time is really also a celluloid analog of vampirism in action, the extraction out of an essence in an act of consumption. For a time at the turn of the century, "kodak" meant eye-witness proof; a testimony to the accuracy of Joseph Conrad's portrayal of circumstances in the Belgian Congo was headed "A Kodak on the Congo." The photographic evidence Jonathan brings to Count Dracula is also a talismanic offering, a simulacrum of the communion wafer Professor Van Helsing will put to Mina's forehead with such disastrously scarring results. In the latter case, the alembic contamination of vampire blood produces the "image" of vampirism as a red mark on white skin; photography makes its images in a similarly alchemical, if less liturgical, fashion. Jonathan Harker and Count Dracula come into a relation of exchange with one another through the mediation of the photographic image; more than that, the untoward aspects of vampirism are first signaled by the mention of the Kodak, which precedes the Count's version of vampirism by several pages. Both the history of photography as a domestic practice, as well as photography's connection to ethnography and travel, are summoned up textually by Jonathan's kodaks. Even the subsequent descriptions of what the Count looks like are altered by these initial references to photography, since his frightful looks bear such resemblance to the photographically cataloged "deviants" of Lombroso and others, and his quaint alterity seems to cry out for immortalization by the National Geographic (that is, photographic) touch. It is possible to speculate that if a vampire's image cannot be captured in a mirror, photographs of a vampire might prove equally disappointing. That scary absence from the sphere of the photographable shunts the anxiety back onto vampirism itself: vampirism as a stand-in for the uncanny procedures of modern life.

The consumption of journalism's anonymous textuality marks the book's dialectic with mass culture as well. Large sections of the putatively typewritten manuscript derive from newspaper articles salvaged by the haggard participants in this dark tale — a reader is asked to imagine either that Mina's transcript has redundantly retyped the newsprint, or that the newspaper pieces are literally collated with those typewritten pages, a collage or bricolage of versions of print. Mina, for example, preserves the newspaper accounts of the shipwreck that, it later emerges, has brought Dracula to Britain's shores, there to wreak his havoc on Lucy Westenra, who has already begun to go into an insomniac decline. These extensive mass-mediated narrations are uncannily inserted amongst the other, purportedly "first-hand" reports of Jonathan, Mina, Lucy, Dr. Seward, and Professor Van Helsing. Clearly there is a pragmatic narrative reason for this, since otherwise the exposition of such events would be highly suspect — how would Mina on her own have managed to gather the deceased ship captain's log and find out about the mysterious cargo of boxes of earth the tragic ship carried? Beyond textual mechanics, however, lies the more intriguing fact that the anonymously-authored newspaper reports are coextensive with, and equally authoritative as, the other voices of the text. The text's action absolutely depends on the inclusion of mass-produced testimony; it absorbs these extraneous pieces within itself just as Dracula assimilates the life-blood of his victims. Even at the narrative level *Dracula* requires an immersion into mass-cultural discourse; its singular voices, however technologically-assisted, are in themselves not sufficient to exorcise an event which is unfolding at the level of collective consumption.

The transmogrification of the narrative's nominal events into mass cultural shards reaches its height when the posthumous whereabouts of Lucy Westenra, now a vampire in earnest, are revealed to the alert Professor Van Helsing and Dr. Seward by her mass-cultural incarnation as the "bloofer lady" of tabloid fame. Lucy has been preying on the lower-class children of London in her role as un-dead, stalking them after dark in the large London parks where they are left unaccountably alone. Her upper-middle class beauty is so miraculous to these waifs that she has achieved legendary status and a mass-cultural name. Without her tabloidization the men would have no chance to eliminate her with their ritualistic objects that can succeed in exorcising her — necklaces of garlic, doughy paste made up of communion wafers, stakes driven through the heart. As much as Lucy is taken up into the pantheon of Dracula's girls ("your girls that you love are mine"), she is also become currency within mass culture, where she circulates in the mass blood stream with a delicious thrill as the "bloofer lady." Lucy becomes an object of the mass press simultaneously with her assimilation into the vampiric fold; the two phenomena are intertwined in the logic of this vampirism. Unless and until Lucy is commoditized out over an adoring, and titillated, public by virtue of her exciting vampiric identity, she cannot be said to have consummated that identity in the terms of the text. While her vamping by Count Dracula precedes her "bloofer lady" role and indeed causes it, the un-dead Lucy is similarly vamped by the press, and vamps all those who come under her thrall by just reading about her in the morning newspaper. *Dracula* does not make distinctions among these consuming ontologies.

Other peculiar newspaper moments in the text include the Pall Mall Gazette account of a zookeeper whose wolf has escaped. We as readers are aware that Dracula has taken over its body for a night of rampaging, but the newspaper story is excitedly fixated on the raffish Cockney persona of the zookeeper, and on including his diction in the piece about this strange disappearance. Here as elsewhere the text pauses for a sustained entry into mass cultural territory; in this case there is not even the excuse of plot description, just the need to filter the vampiric through the mesh of a mediated response. Inclusion of the newspaper story also keeps up the pressure on the distinction between speech and writing that so fissures the text, because the point of the article seems as much to be transcribing the loquacious dialect of the zookeeper as adding to anyone's knowledge of the habits of Dracula. The newspaper page serves as a theater for the staging of class differences when its "standard" written English can erupt with the quoted, vigorous orality of lower-class modes of speech. Lucy breaks the charmed circle of class by becoming a twilight apparition of interest to all classes, as they read about her in the newspaper. The zookeeper perhaps occupies so much textual space in *Dracula* because vampirization, or consumption, originally seems to threaten class distinctions.

A final irony in a novel so deranged by the mass voice of journalism is the fact that the band of fearless vampire killers manages to keep any notice of vampirism out of the papers, reserving that for its own "truthful" pages; the mass cultural forms skirt the knowledge of Dracula but never come to be in possession of it — in my argument, because *Dracula* himself is an articulation of, a figuration for, that same mass culture, as a consequence supervening any of its individual media, which are shown to be limited in scope unless taken together. Dracula's individual powers all have their analogue in the field of the mass cultural; he comprises the techniques of consumption.

Consider all the media technologies the novel so incessantly displays and names: the telegraph that figures so largely in the communicative strategies that allow the band to defeat Dracula is an equivalent to the telephathic, telekinetic communication Dracula is able to have with Mina after sealing her into his race with her enforced drinking of his blood. The phonographic records Dr. Seward uses are the reproduction of a voice, of a being, without any body needing to be present, just as Dracula can insinuate himself as a voice into the heads of his followers, or call them from afar. The Kodak camera captures an image and then allows it to be moved elsewhere, freezing a moment of temporality and sending it across space, in a parallel to Dracula's insubstantiality and his vitiation of temporality. Like such images, he continues to circulate even when separated from his source; in other words, his blood can circulate and have its drastic effects even when he is not bodily present. Dracula also vitiates space, of course, and in this shares the very ubiquity of the mass media: advertising's anticipation of its readers into all the corners and matchbooks of their lives, the mass ceremonial of the press, a daily bestseller that has no shelf life and must be consumed immediately. Mass culture is protean, with the same horrific propensity to mutate that also defines Dracula's anarchic power, as he becomes a bat or a white mist at will. Even the subway, the Underground used by Mina and Dr. Seward in the novel, has its fearsome vampiric echoes, since like Dracula the subway uses an underground place for transport across space, a subterranean vault encrypted by modern transportation.

When Madame Mina, "pearl among women," provides the typescript that resolves the incommensurabilities of the assorted documents, phonographic records and so on, she is able to do this because, as she tells Dr. Seward with rightful pride, her typewriter has a function called "Manifold" that allows it to make multiple copies in threes. This function is positively vampiric, even to the name it has been given, reverberating with the multiplicity of men Dracula is, the manifold guises of the vampire, and the copying procedure which itself produces vampires, each of which is in a sense a replica of all the others. Here we step into the age of mechanical reproduction with a vengeance, since the reproductive process that makes vampires is so closely allied to the mechanical replication of culture. The perverse reversals of human reproduction that vampirism entails, making a crazy salad of gender roles and even of anatomical destiny, have been well discussed, and assuredly impinge on the terrors of *Dracula*. The ties to cultural reproduction and to cultural consumption need to be acknowledged as well, to place the book in its genuine context of modernity. Because Mina operates the manifold function her relation to Dracula is as close as it is later perverse. Typewriting itself partakes of the vampiric, although paradoxically in this text it can serve also as an instrument used to destroy it.[6]

The gender division of labor in consumption strongly pervades the representation of this mass cultural vampire and helps to situate Dra-

---

[6]See in this connection of course Walter Benjamin's "The Work of Art in an Age of Mechanical Reproduction." *Illuminations*, trans. Harry Zohn (New York: Schocken, 1969) 212–51, since despite its Brechtian utopianism, this essay forges the vocabulary for apprehending the mass cultural in modern critical theory.

cula unmistakably as a figure for consumption. Dracula cannot enter your home and molest you unless invited in; that same invitation is the one extended to the mass cultural, in the sense that it is its seductive invasion of the home that allows the domestic to become the site, the opening puncture wound, for all the techniques of mass culture. Mass culture or consumption can be said to transform culture from within the home, despite the obvious fact that many of its cultural technologies are encountered elsewhere, in the department store, on the billboard, in the nickelodeon parlor, at the newsstand or the telegraph office. The book is obsessed with all these technological and cultural modalities, with the newest of the new cultural phenomena, and yet it is they that shatter the fixed and circumscribed world the novel seems designed to protect through those very means, as the home is opened up to the instabilities of authority and the pleasures that lie outside the family as a unit of social reproduction. The same science, rationality and technologies of social control relied on to defend against the encroachments of Dracula are the source of the vampiric powers of the mass cultural with which Dracula, in my reading, is allied. Homes are the most permeable membrane possible for this transfusion, since by installing the middle-class and even the lower-class woman in economic isolation there by the end of the nineteenth century, a captive audience for the vampiric ministrations of commoditized culture, consumption and so-called "leisure," in the case of upper-class women, is thereby created.[7] Women are the ones who ineluctably let Dracula in.

It may seem that I accept the text's ambivalence about mass cultural transformation in connecting Dracula to it, but what I want to propose is a very different spin on the notion of consumption — the need to see it as, as Pierre Bourdieu calls it, "the production that is consumption." These changes are extraordinary and have powerful political effects; they are also, as I have claimed, premised on a cannibalization of resources from invisible places "elsewhere," in global economic terms. The contradictions of consumption run like fault lines through this text, and correspondingly in our own contemporary theory. It should be underscored, however, that consumption is always a labor — I don't at all mean the work of shopping, but a form of cultural labor,

[7]Fine accounts of the relation of women to mass culture can be found in Andreas Hussen's *After the Great Divide: Modernism and Mass Culture* (New York: Columbia Univ. Press, 1987), and in Tania Modleski's essay "Femininity and Mas(s)querade," in *Feminism Without Women: Culture and Criticism in a "Post Feminist" Age* (New York: Routledge, 1991) 23–34.

including the producing of meanings.[8] Because *Dracula* focuses on the entry into mass culture, it becomes one of our primary cultural expressions of that swooning relation and thus has needed to be revived incessantly, in films, books, and other cultural forms. The vampiric embrace is now a primary locus for our culture's self-reflexive assessment of its cultural being, since that being is fixed in the embrace of material consumption.

In the madman Renfield, Dr. Seward's star patient as an example of "zoophagy," we have a gloss on the psychic interiorizations of consumption. He is of course finally shown to be a disciple of Dracula, his master, in a theological partnership that runs roughshod over the psychoanalytic diagnoses Dr. Seward has been trying to make. Renfield's underlying sanity seems to inhere in his acceptance of racial and class differences as a matter of blood, his stalwartly hierarchical common sense, and in his staunch support for imperialist projects. He praises the country of the Texan Quincey Morris: "Mr. Morris, you should be proud of your great state. Its reception into the Union was a precedent which may have far-reaching effects hereafter, when the Pole and the Tropics may hold allegiance to the Stars and Stripes. The power of Treaty may yet prove a vast engine of enlargement, when the Monroe doctrine takes its true place as a political fable" (p. 248). Renfield actually adheres to an imperialism that has the vastest engine of enlargement in Dracula, but he is also able to admire a rival imperialism of great promise. The imperial nexus is also tied to the mass cultural through Renfield. When Mina Harker asks to meet this bizarre inmate, he agrees to converse with her, and he speaks about his own desire to devour living things as if it were in the remote past: "The doctor here will bear me out that on one occasion I tried to kill him for the purpose of strengthening my vital powers by the assimilation with my own body of his life through the medium of his blood — relying, of course, upon the Scriptural phrase, 'For the blood is the life'" (p. 239). The theological monologue represents vampirism's literalization of Christian practices, so embedded that it will require equivalent literalizations to supercede it. But Renfield goes on to reflect on a new cultural instance: "Though indeed, the vendor of a certain nostrum has vulgarised the truism to the

[8]I have argued for the revisionary nature of consumption elsewhere; some of the theorists who provide ballast for the rethinking of the process of consumption include Pierre Bourdieu, especially in his *Distinction: A Social Critique of the Judgment of Taste* (Cambridge: Harvard Univ. Press, 1984), Michel de Certeau's work, especially *The Practice of Everyday Life* (Berkeley, Univ. of California Press, 1984), and John Fiske's *Understanding Popular Culture* (Boston: Unwin Hyman, 1989).

very point of contempt. Isn't that true, doctor?" (p. 239) There was a British blood tonic that had adopted this phrase in its advertisements in "real life," but what Renfield objects to is amusingly crazy: advertising's debasement of the religious signification when Dracula, the original blood tonic man, is on his way to give the phrase his own supernally horrific debasement. This denigration of the popularizing and secularizing rhetoric of advertisement serves to underscore the conflation of Dracula with the world of advertisement and mass media made by the text, even where Renfield may make an invidious distinction. Advertisement itself, among many other forms, was a powerful recasting of the religious vocabulary, its translation into the promises of a salvational commodity culture; that language was, in a manner of speaking, lying around loose in a secularizing culture, and advertisement appropriated it for its own uses, as it recirculates all evacuated social languages.[9] This may often look like a vulgarization, when it is additionally a resurrection; the vampire enters into this circulatory economy as well. Count Dracula's more pointedly terrifying manifestation covers over the lurking fears, as well as pleasures, found in the deflating of spiritual rhetoric as it is recirculated as the currency of advertisement. Renfield's erratic "madness," his eating of live animals, is itself almost a pun on the tremors of consumption. He is unvampirized in the literal sense, only vampirized from afar, so at a double remove Renfield hypostatizes the consumer, directed by invisible longings and compelled by ghostly commands to absorb everything in sight. His is one cautionary tale of the "phagous" nature of consumption.

Dracula's own biorhythms are, paradoxically, very much those of everyday life under the altered conditions of the mass cultural; Dracula *must* consume on a daily basis. The outlandishness of Dracula's behavior is simultaneously made quotidian, regularized, indeed, everyday. . . . It can be no accident that the overwhelming trope of this novel is also the word for this new social economy — consumption. Dracula drinks his victims dry, takes all their blood and *consumes* it, rather than ingesting it. Ingesting or digesting these sanguinary meals would imply a rather more stolid, alimentary process than the one we witness. Van Helsing tactlessly reminds Mina that the previous night Dracula

---

[9]I argue for this in *Advertising Fictions: Literature, Advertising, and Social Reading* (New York: Columbia Univ. Press, 1988); the classic essay is Leo Spitzer's "American Advertising Explained as Popular Art." *Leo Spitzer: Representative Essays*, ed. Alban K. Forcione, Herbert Lindenberger, and Madeline Sutherland (Stanford: Stanford Univ. Press, 1988), wherein Spitzer shows the relation of the Protestant spirit of capitalism, as it were, to the language of advertising.

"banqueted" on her, but this word too has some of the baroque bravura of consumption. . . .

The vampire yokes himself to the feminine because the mass cultural creeps in on little female feet, invades the home and turns it inside out, making it a palace of consumption. . . . The connection between mass culture and the feminine has been made since its beginnings, and is arrestingly refigured in *Dracula,* since mass culture is appraised as feminizing, passive, voluptuous, carnal and anti-imperial, in the case of Lucy, and labor-intensive, productive and properly imperial where Mina is involved.

Lucy and Mina have shown themselves to be appetitive even before the attacks Dracula makes on them. The very day of Lucy's vamping by Dracula, who as a secret stowaway on the ship that has wrecked against the coast has just arrived at the seaside town of Whitby where the two are staying, the women go out to share that very British meal of "tea," a meal defined as a beverage. Mina says: "I believe we should have shocked the New Women with our appetites. Men are more tolerant, God bless them." The tea that they devour so sensually, in defiance of the putative austerity of the New Women, is a foreshadowing of their exposure to vampiric lust, but also an index of their placement in the chain of consumption. Another striking detail of the text attests to the propriety and discipline of Mina, yet also hints at unexplored depths of commodity desire. She rescues Lucy, although too late, from her vamping by Dracula as she sits in a zombie state by the sea. Since Lucy has walked out to meet Dracula in a somnambulant trance, she has neglected to put on shoes, so Mina gives hers over to Lucy upon hastening to her side. This leaves Mina with an awkward predicament: if she is seen by any townspeople on the midnight trip back to the relative safety of bourgeois girlhood's boudoir, they will draw inferences from her lack of footgear. Mina hits upon a startling trick, but one in keeping with her plucky pragmatism. She daubs her feet with mud, so that no reflection of white foot or ankle twinkling in the night can alert any sleepy voyeur who might be looking out a window. So Mina makes the trip back with her feet coated in mud; that expedient is a brilliant one, but also presents us subliminally with the image of a Mina thoroughly earth-bound, enmired. The scandal occurs for the reader's eyes alone, so that Mina's earthiness will be underscored even in her hour of intense decorum. The text's surface establishes the two women's purity and asexuality, yet slips in a glimpse of their susceptibility to consumption — a consumption that also demarcates them favorably in opposition to the New Women who eschew marriage and home. You're damned if you do, and damned if you don't consume.

Lucy has given signs that she is not utterly passive prior to her vampirization; she has been proposed to by three men on one day — by Dr. Seward, the gallant Texan Quincey Morris, and by the Honorable Arthur Holmwood, whom she does indeed accept. Yet in her letter to Mina recounting all this she bursts out: "Why can't they let a girl marry three men, or as many as want her, and save all this trouble? But this is heresy, and I must not say it" (p. 80). Lucy gets her wish, in one way: all of these men, with the addition of Professor Van Helsing, will have to give her a blood transfusion, thus becoming her husbands, as Van Helsing piquantly points out: "Ho, ho! Then this so sweet maid is a polyandrist, and me, with my poor wife dead to me, but alive by Church's law, though no wits, all gone — even I, who am faithful husband to this now-no-wife, am bigamist" (p. 186). Lucy is so metaphorized by the text, in contrast to Mina, typist extraordinaire, that the wavering boundary of her sexual appetite has serious consequences. If one considers her name, Luce, light and illumination, emanating out of the West-enra, she is clearly an overdetermined being, more than a woman, a civilizational cause. The sexual torque put on her vamping is indeed amazing, but I would claim that this must be considered beyond the level of the fear of women's sexuality and examined also as a very particular convergence of questions. Lucy stands in for the project of empire; it is her ineffable whiteness that is so valuable an icon to her male protectors — these are men who, as Quincey Morris points out, have served together in exotic places of danger and violence, in some inexplicable blend of Indiana Jones-style ethnographic adventure and military colonial exploits (p. 83). Their devotion to Lucy continues to unite them, and she becomes a kind of allegory of their mutual project in taming the rest of the world. Mina does not have this resonance, since she is resolutely plain and intelligent, and has not been sought over by a trio of explorers; her sole proposal was from Jonathan Harker, and he a home-bound lawyer. Lucy's white westernness becomes totemic in her vamping; the crepuscular universe she inhabits is a twilight of the gods of Western hegemony. An advertisement for Pear's soap of 1887, showing the legend "Pear's Soap is the Best" spelled out in shining white against a glowering dark rock, as astonished natives fall in awe before the handwriting on the wall, also reads, "The Formula of British Conquest," and in glossing its own trope, quotes the words of Phil Robinson, a war correspondent to the London Daily Telegraph, as follows: "Even if our invasion of the Soudan has done nothing else it has at any rate left the Arab something to puzzle his fuzzy head over, for the legend Pear's Soap is the Best, inscribed in white characters on the rock which marks the farthest point of our advance toward Berber, will tax all the wits of the Dervishes of the Desert to translate."[10] Lucy's vampirization comments directly on the dark side of that boast and its certainty, since even the joint ministrations of her band of admirers are ineffective in staving off the return of the imperial repressed. It would be far too reductive to read Dracula as a transposition of the fear of a massive colonial uprising, a revenge taken on the imperial seat by those so dominated, in the person of Count Dracula. To extirpate the imperial context, however, makes even the sexuality of the text denatured, decontextualized, since Lucy's iconic presence has as much to do with extended cultural preoccupations of the discourse of imperialism as it does with the "anxiety" about women's changing roles. These aspects can be made to mesh, without reductive narrowing, through the complex of consumption, a process equally invoked and implicated by imperial discourse and psychosexual representation.

All the more shocking, then, when the living, female impetus for imperial energies succumbs to the lures of consumption. Van Helsing has to convince the other men that their Miss Lucy could indeed be doing such a thing as biting children, and to do that he takes them to a park where they watch her in action. This scene is renowned for its excesses; although Lucy is out for children's blood, she's described as wantonly voluptuous, red-lipped and voluptuous, extremely voluptuous — they've never seen her this way before, flushed with desire and flaunting her sexual charms. She actually offers Arthur a taste of the delights he has missed, since she was snatched away on the eve of the wedding: "Come to me, Arthur. Leave these others and come to me. My arms are hungry for you. Come, and we can rest together" (p. 219). Arthur has to be restrained, of course, and when they prevent Lucy from getting into her tomb by the application of the communion wafer weather-stripping, there is a hilarious pun as she is compared to Medusa, the archetype of destructive female sexuality, giving them a hideous grimace as if, Dr. Seward says, "looks could kill." Medusa's "look" could turn men to stone; here it's really Lucy's *looks*, her voluptuous looks — her appearance, not her *regard* — that are so appalling and must be expunged. It should not seem trivializing to suggest that at

[10]See E. J. Hobsbawm. *The Age of Empire 1875–1914* (New York: Pantheon Books, 1987), Illustration Number 21.

least some of the fixation on carmine lips and cheeks is actually cosmetic — that Miss Lucy has been made over cosmetically by the pleasures of these new feminine products, the "paint" beginning to be available, if not worn by the middle-class virgin — in her posthumous state. Her sexuality is indeed excessive per se, but a large measure of its horror is yoked to its consumerist incarnadine as well, as if Lucy had availed herself of the rouge pot and the rice powder in dressing herself to kill. Such widely read "manuals" as Lily Langtry's treatise on the art of cosmetic use seem to have found their way into the lascivious descriptions of Lucy's unwonted sex appeal, and are consequently references to an arena of choice for women, however dimly articulated. Note too that the early Lucy of the text writes to Mina of her absence of interest in fashion, which actually displeases Arthur at that innocent stage! This strange irony reverberates with Lucy's love of fashionable slang.

That these men are on a sex hunt is borne out from the beginning, when Van Helsing tells Dr. Seward that Lucy has become a vampire and then must take the enraged doctor to the cemetery to show him proof. Van Helsing is holding a candle in order to light up the coffin to be able to drill a hole in it; the text says that his "sperm" dropped in "white patches" which congeal on the coffin plate bearing her name. Even if we know that sperm is short for the spermaceti still used in making the candle wax, this is a vivid description of Van Helsing's premature ejaculation onto Lucy, a prelude of things to come. Arthur does the honors when the group of adventurers has agreed that this Un-Dead must be dispatched, even especially because she has the body of a provocative Lucy — a "carnal" appearance, the text says. As the men surround the coffin, Arthur puts the point of the stake to her heart, "and as I [Dr. Seward] looked I could see its dint in the white flesh. Then he struck with all his might. The Thing in the coffin writhed; and a hideous, blood-curdling screech came from the opened red lips. The body shook and quivered and twisted in wild contortions; the sharp white teeth champed together till the lips were cut, and the mouth was smeared with crimson foam. But Arthur never faltered. He looked like a figure of Thor . . ." (p. 223). John Stevenson and others rightly view this as the picture of orgasm. It can't be denied that the text is fascinated with this spectacle of sexual violation, and Lucy is undeniably being punished for her sexuality as a vampire; as the imperturbable Van Helsing asks Arthur after this, with postcoital nonchalance, "May I cut off Miss Lucy's head?" The punishment is additionally inflicted for the separation of sexuality from reproduction, or its amalgamation; Lucy only procreates in the sense that vampiric attacks produce more vampires from the liaison. If this were all the text did with the cataclysm of female sexuality it would become yet another symptomatic document of sexual hierarchization. Yet more is entertained here than just the effacement of Lucy as a female character; what I want to urge is that there is a dialectical intertwining of the racial and national on the one hand, and consumption and femaleness on the other, that roughens such tidy analyses. It makes a difference that Lucy is the victim, so to speak, of the group of men who accompanied one another on their colonial voyages and who, as Quincey Morris puts it, "told yarns by the camp-fire in the prairies; and dressed one another's wounds after trying a landing at the Marquesas; and drunk healths on the shore of Titicaca" (p. 83). Their investment in expunging Lucy the vampire is inflected by this mutual history, and by Lucy's emblematic status as Western icon.

The textual investment shifts when Mina is vamped. For one thing, as Van Helsing has already pointed out, Madame Mina "has man-brain," so her relation to the equilibration of consumption and empire alters. Mina is an anomaly in evolutionary terms, and as such is affiliated to Dracula; her brain is not a female one, but instead is white, male and European, according to the brain science not merely of this book but of Western racial science generally until it peters out in the 1930s, to persist in Schockley and the sociobiologies. On that evolutionary scale the female brain, the criminal brain and the so-called savage or primitive brain are on a par; the adult white male brain is the evolutionary summit.[11] By leaping over this divide Mina occupies unclear territory, and one way of reading what happens to her is to assume that she is set up as Dracula's next victim as a means of establishing her femininity. With lavish abandon and extravagant bad faith her so-called protectors leave her alone in the insane asylum to spend the night, and congratulate themselves at every turn on having shielded her from unbearably painful knowledge; this, of the woman who has typed all the previous vampire documents, and is therefore the most fully in the know.

Having been imprinted with vampirism in a uniquely mediated way, by nursing from and fellating Dracula at the same moment, as she is forced to suck his blood from a wound in his breast, Mina becomes his telepathic double. There's a kinky notion of cerebral sex involved in this, to be sure; at the same time, it begins to make perfect sense that

[11]Stephen Jay Gould's *The Mismeasure of Man* (New York: Norton, 1981) effectively synopsizes these developments. Anne McWhir interestingly approaches the anthropological background in her essay "Pollution and Redemption in *Dracula.*" *Modern Language Studies* 17 (Summer 1987): 31–40.

Dracula would have this intimate cognitive relationship with Mina. If it is the case that at least part of *Dracula*'s marshaling of fear has to do with assigning a status to the mass cultural, and working through the anxieties it evokes, then the gender slippage that surrounds the characterization of Mina helps account for this. Consumption is psychosexual, yet also socioeconomic. Mina occupies a strange niche between the two, since she is consumed by Dracula, who banquets on her, and also consumes him, but without longing, without desire, and with all her cognitive faculties intact. She could be said to be a perfect replica of the labor of consumption in this regard: she is always doing something with it, always is consciously co-present with the act, unlike Lucy's white zombiedom. The text wants to protect itself from Mina's brain, from her knowledge. After her vamping, the men alternately need to tell her everything, and want to tell her nothing. Oscillating back and forth between these positions, Mina becomes more and more the author of the text; she takes over huge stretches of its narration, she is responsible for giving her vampire-hunting colleagues all information on Dracula's whereabouts, and she is still the one who coordinates and collates the manuscripts, although she has pledged the men to kill her if she becomes too vampiric in the course of time. Her act of collation is by no means strictly secretarial, either; Mina is the one who has the idea of looking back over the assembled manuscripts for clues to Dracula's habits and his future plans. Despite the continual attempts both consciously by the characters and unconsciously by the text itself to view Mina as a medium of transmission, it continually emerges that there is no such thing as passive transmission — invariably, intelligent knowledge is involved, and Mina goes to the heart of things analytically and structurally.

Mina is treated as a medium when Professor Van Helsing hypnotizes her repeatedly to allow her to reveal Dracula's whereabouts; of course we recognize in this a version of the psychoanalytic "cures" beginning to be effected through hypnotism, by Freud and others.[12] The woman is placed in a state where she does not know her own knowledge, she simply relates it as it is drawn from her by a man who knows what to make of it. All the reverberations to Freud's Dora are in place; the mesmeric and hypnotic world of Charcot is an open intertext of the novel. On all these grounds, including the professional activities

---

[12]Often mentioned, this link to a nascent psychoanalysis is laid out in John L. Greenway. "Seward's Folly: *Dracula* as a Critique of 'Normal Science.'" *Stanford Literature Review* 3 (Fall 1986): 213–30. Greenway concentrates on the historical forms of science *Dracula* is able to enact.

of Dr. Seward and the psychoanalytic mutterings of Van Helsing as he repudiates surface meanings for deeper trance states and hysterical body signs, psychoanalysis does a duet with *Dracula*. This should point us to Dracula's role in making vivid the split nature of consciousness and the predatory energies of the libidinal unconscious, and yet it should also be an alert that psychoanalysis and the novel *Dracula* are up against the same problematic: describing or figuring a process that is both productive and consumptive, contradictorily placed both psychically and socially. Mina does tell what her shared or double consciousness is up to, as if she were in the enviable and dangerous position of having her unconscious, which she has in a sense swallowed, speak to her with an audible voice, absent the condensations and displacements of lesser mortals. And yet she is not a controllable medium for Van Helsing, nor just a transparent recording device of the id within, Count Dracula. She is productive in her consumptive possession: Mina essentially becomes the detective of the final segment of the story.

The situation has gotten desperate in London; the men have found all but one of the Count's magic boxes and consecrated them, but he only needs one, and he has obviously departed in it from London. As the men fall prostrate in one or another ways, Mina sends them to lie down and vigorously applies herself to deducing the precise route Dracula must take to get himself carried back in his box to the Castle. For the first time an entry reads "Mina Harker's Memorandum" (p. 344). With relentless logic, the keen use of maps, geometrical calculations and brilliant speculation, she provides them all with a plan of attack, deciding which river Dracula will need to use to get home and how he can best be countered. "Our dear Madam Mina is once more our teacher," Van Helsing cries out. "Her eyes have been where ours were blinded" (p. 347). In a text that claims again and again that women need to be shielded from the reality of vampirism, a woman is responsible for seeing the way out. Yet Mina's prescience and logical ability are predicated on her proximity to the mass cultural forms she has mastered: for example, her hobby is memorizing the train schedule, since she is, in her own words, "a train fiend," which allows her to recreate Dracula's line of escape. Additionally, she is a typist with a portfolio. "I feel so grateful to the man who invented the 'Traveller's' typewriter," she testifies in eerie simulation of the traveling count (p. 344). Mina is that hybrid creature, the consumed woman whose consumption is a mode of knowledge. . . .

When Dracula comes to press his attentions on Mina he criticizes her for having played her brain against his, and he warns her that her male companions should feel grateful to him: "They should have kept their energies for use closer to home. Whilst they played wits against me — against me who commanded nations, and intrigued for them, and fought for them, hundreds of years before they were born — I was countermining them. And you, their best beloved one, are now to me, flesh of my flesh; blood of my blood; kin of my kin; my bountiful wine-press for a while; and shall be later on my companion and my helper" (p. 288). It is worth remarking that this extended speech by Dracula is recounted by Mina herself, not available first-hand from the eyewitness to the vamping. Here is the paradox of Dracula. While he is perforce racially other, of the alien vampire race, and while he has as a result of his racial otherness what Van Helsing calls a "child-brain" and a criminal brain, making him vulnerable to the tactics of the European adult male brain at its peak, he is also a partner in imperialism. In the "whirlpool of races" he describes to Jonathan at the beginning of the text, it is his race that emerges as the purest European, a noble race that in conquering this eastern territory in fact makes it historically possible to acquire the fruits of empire for the British, Dutch and Texan men who hunt him. One can readily imagine that the imperial situation produced a fear of that unspecified otherness coming for retaliation, but Dracula is not simply that apparition; he is an ally of imperial forces, and in some ways annexes his own project to that of imperial Britain's, as an extension to it or an elaboration of it. This is why he is not content with any vampiric empire that would take shape in archaic ways — even the Oriental despotism Marx speaks of is too *recherché* for the Count. He must come to London to modernize the terms of his conquest, to master the new imperial forms and to learn how to supplement his considerable personal powers by the most contemporary understanding of the metropolis. Dracula has, in short, felt himself to be on the periphery, however powerful he might be there, and by coming to England he has an opportunity to meld vampirism to the modern forces of imperial control. . . .

[At this point in the essay from which this commentary is taken, Wicke discusses the concept of nation in relation to language with attention to the polyglot nature of the text. Her discussion includes a comparison of Count Dracula's use of language with Van Helsing's.]

As Van Helsing sees it, Dracula's appetite is not for blood, but for a kind of knowledge and power he has become aware of as the attributes of modern, consumer capitalist culture. His "desire is keen" surely not just to enlarge the vampire dominions, but to transform vampiredom, to take it to the heart of the metropolis, where it feeds on the forces already set in motion by technological development. "What more may he not do when the greater world of thought is open to him," the professor muses, imagining Dracula's feelings as he lies on the periphery in his moldy Carpathian tomb. This should make it clear that it is not merely the atavism of Dracula that makes his appearance in England so frightful; it is his relative modernity, his attempt to be more British than the British in consolidating his goals. Franco Moretti interestingly hypothesizes Dracula as the figure for the circulation of money in late capitalism; Dracula does have a vivid scene where coins shower out of his clothes. Nonetheless, that symbology may take too literally the meaning of the "economic," since Dracula's economy is so mediated by its relation to consumption and to the forces of empire.

Understandably, *Dracula* concludes haltingly, and can only end by letting the modern, urban world of technology and consumption recede altogether. The final confrontation with the vampire takes place on horseback in the countryside, Dracula's coffin protected by a group of gypsy cart drivers. This low-tech ending allows the religiosity the text nervously relies on to resurface with less apparent anachronism, but the ancient and the modern cannot be made to converge. They each move on separate curves, asymptotically, never coalescing. Mina, the typist, has lost all her office equipment by the end, although she does narrate Dracula's death and records his last look of peace — a far cry from the orgasmic turbulence that passes over Lucy's visage. Mina's vampire mark, the red scar burned into her forehead by its contact with a holy wafer, recedes with the setting sun, and Mina is free to become a mother, to reproduce what she has heretofore only copied.

The novel doesn't forget its complex relation to the techniques of modernity, however; the religious apotheosis is not its last gasp. *Dracula* is an unstable brew, because it is made up out of mass cultural forms, and yet tries to use this loose collection to mount a retrogressive search and destroy mission against itself. Only the Bible seems to be a text with enough authority to confront Count Dracula — a text that seems (although it is not) to be unscathed by the market forces of commodity culture, a written assemblage of the spoken holy word, as composite and palimpsestic as the textual production this novel itself claims. It would appear that Mina's sudden unscarring would be proof of those powers, but the novel has already shown us again and again that these sacred words are not powerful enough, do not address the conditions of modern life, are not sufficiently passed through the crucible of mass culture to answer the problems of foreignness, otherness, and the unstable self. The baptismal font of language in this book has to be the typewriter, and it seems blasphemous to direct attention to the printed nature of the Bible, its role as the first printed book of Western culture, by Gutenberg's hand.

As a final proof of the divisions within the text, divisions that fruitfully and fearfully show us the dislocations in cultural authority that prompt its new world of language, consider the last and then the first words of the text. The group gets together years later, huddling around the boy who is, through Lucy's transfusions and the passage of her blood to Dracula, and hence to Mina, the putative son of all of the men and all the women, the "sexual history" going back to Dracula and his three brides, and "[w]e were struck with the fact that, in all the masses of material of which the record is composed, there is hardly one authentic document; nothing but a mass of type-writing" (p. 368). The only proof of the ravages of Dracula is the existence of the boy, young Quincey, named after the gallant Texan who gave his life for Mina's unvamping, and while he may constitute bodily proof for the friends, his unmarked state would represent the opposite to most people. But the first thing we read as we begin the text is this: "How these papers have been placed in sequence will be made manifest in the reading of them . . . there is throughout no statement of past things wherein memory may err, for all the records chosen are exactly contemporary, given from the standpoints and within the range of knowledge of those who made them." Which is it, truth, origin, the authority of knowledge, or a "mass of typewriting"? What makes this text so modern, not to say modernist, is that it knows that it will be consumed — it stages the very act of its own consumption, and problematizes it. The energies of modernity flow out of these same ineluctable wounds, and the undecidable nature of consumption. Most of all, the modernist text follows *Dracula* in acknowledging, however repressedly, the necessary relation of the modern world to its dialectical other, the rest of the globe. In that encounter, which *Dracula* enacts, a modernist writing begins.

The reading of the mass of typewriting is the labor of consumption the text requires of us. This mass is vampiric typewriting, this vampire is mass typewriting, this typewriting is mass vampirism. Under the sign of modernity we are vampires at a banquet of ourselves, we are Dracula and Madame Mina, the one who bites and the one who is bitten, the one who types and the one who is typewritten.

Glossary of Critical
and Theoretical Terms

ABSENCE The idea, advanced by French theorist Jacques Derrida, that authors are not present in texts and that meaning arises in the absence of any authority guaranteeing the correctness of any one interpretation.

See **Presence and Absence** for a more complete discussion of the concepts of presence and absence.

AFFECTIVE FALLACY *See* **New Criticism; Reader-Response Criticism.**

BASE *See* **Marxist Criticism.**

CANON A term used since the fourth century to refer to those books of the Bible that the Christian church accepts as being Holy Scripture — that is, divinely inspired. Books outside the canon (noncanonical books) are referred to as *apocryphal. Canon* has also been used to refer to the Saints Canon, the group of people officially recognized by the Catholic Church as saints. More recently, it has been employed to refer to the body of works generally attributed by scholars to a particular author (for example, the Shakespearean canon is currently believed to consist of thirty-seven plays that scholars feel can be definitively attributed to him). Works sometimes attributed to an author, but whose authorship is disputed or otherwise uncertain, are called apocryphal. *Canon* may also refer more generally to those literary works that are "privileged," or given special status, by a culture. Works we tend to think of as classics or as "Great Books" — texts that are repeatedly reprinted in anthologies of literature — may be said to constitute the canon.

Note: The following definitions are adapted and/or abridged versions of ones found in *The Bedford Glossary of Critical and Literary Terms,* by Ross Murfin and Supryia M. Ray (© Bedford Books 1997).

Contemporary **Marxist, feminist,** minority, and **postcolonial** critics have argued that, for political reasons, many excellent works never enter the canon. Canonized works, they claim, are those that reflect — and respect — the culture's dominant ideology or perform some socially acceptable or even necessary form of "cultural work." Attempts have been made to broaden or redefine the canon by discovering valuable texts, or versions of texts, that were repressed or ignored for political reasons. These have been published both in traditional and in nontraditional anthologies. The most outspoken critics of the canon, especially certain critics practicing **cultural criticism,** have called into question the whole concept of canon or "canonicity." Privileging no form of artistic expression, these critics treat cartoons, comics, and soap operas with the same cogency and respect they accord novels, poems, and plays.

CULTURAL CRITICISM, CULTURAL STUDIES Critical approaches with roots in the British cultural studies movement of the 1960s. A movement that reflected and contributed to the unrest of that decade, it both fueled and was fueled by the challenges to tradition and authority apparent in everything from the antiwar movement to the emergence of "hard rock" music. Birmingham University's Centre for Contemporary Cultural Studies, founded by Stuart Hall and Richard Hoggart in 1964, quickly became the locus of the movement, which both critiqued elitist definitions of culture and drew upon a wide variety of disciplines and perspectives.

In Great Britain, the terms *cultural criticism* and *cultural studies* have been used more or less interchangeably, and, to add to the confusion, both terms have been used to refer to two different things. On one hand, they have been used to refer to the analysis of literature (including popular literature) and other art forms in their social, political, or economic contexts; on the other hand, they have been used to refer to the much broader interdisciplinary study of the interrelationships between a variety of cultural **discourses** and practices (such as advertising, gift-giving, and racial categorization). In North America, the term *cultural studies* is usually reserved for this broader type of analysis, whereas *cultural criticism* typically refers to work with a predominantly literary or artistic focus.

Cultural critics examine how literature emerges from, influences, and competes with other forms of discourse (such as religion, science, or advertising) within a given culture. They analyze the social contexts in which a given text was written, and under what conditions it was — and is — produced, disseminated, and read. Like practitioners of cultural studies, they oppose the view that culture refers exclusively to high culture, culture with a capital *C,* seeking to make the term refer to popular, folk, urban, and mass (mass-produced, disseminated, mediated, and consumed) culture, as well as to that culture we associate with so-called great literature. In other words, cultural critics argue that what we refer to as a culture is in fact a set of interactive *cultures,* alive and changing, rather than static or monolithic. They favor analyzing literary works not as aesthetic objects complete in themselves but as works to be seen in terms of their relationships to other works, to economic conditions, or to broad social discourses (about childbirth, women's education, rural decay, etc.). Cultural critics have emphasized what Michel de Certeau, a French theorist, has called "the practice of everyday life," approaching literature more as an anthropologist than as a traditional "elitist" literary critic.

Several thinkers influenced by **Marxist** theory have powerfully affected the development of cultural criticism and cultural studies. The French philosophical historial Michel Foucault has perhaps had the strongest influence on cultural criticism and **the new historicism**, a type of literary criticism whose evolution has often paralleled that of North American cultural criticism. In works such as *Discipline and Punish* (1975) and *The History of Sexuality* (1976), Foucault studies cultures in terms of power relationships, a focus typical of Marxist thought. Unlike Marxists, however, Foucault did not see power as something exerted by a dominant **class** over a subservient one. For Foucault, power was more than repressive power: it was a complex of forces generated by the confluence — or conflict — of discourses; it was that which produces what happens. British critic Raymond Williams, best known for his book *Culture and Society: 1780–1950* (1958), influenced the development of cultural studies by arguing that culture is living and evolving rather than fixed and finished, further stating in *The Long Revolution* (1961) that "art and culture are ordinary." Although Williams did not define himself as a Marxist throughout his entire career, he always followed the Marxist practice of viewing culture in relation to **ideologies**, which he defined as the "residual," "dominant," or "emerging" ways in which individuals or social classes view the world.

Recent practitioners of cultural criticism and cultural studies have focused on issues of nationality, race, gender, and sexuality, in addition to those of power, ideology, and class. As a result, there is a significant overlap between cultural criticism and **feminist criticism**, and between cultural studies and African-American studies. This overlap can be seen in the work of contemporary feminists such as Gayatri Chakravorty Spivak, Trinh T. Minh-ha, and Gloria Anzaldua, who stress that although all women are female, they are something else as well (working-class, lesbian, Native American), a facet that must be considered in analyzing their writings. It can also be seen in the writings of Henry Louis Gates, who has shown how black American writers, to avoid being culturally marginalized, have prduced texts that fuse the language and traditions of the white Western **canon** with a black vernacular and tradition derived from African and Caribbean cultures.

Interest in race and ethnicity has accompanied a new, interdisciplinary focus on colonial and postcolonial societies, in which issues of race, class, and ethnicity loom large. Practitioners of **postcolonial studies**, another form of cultural studies inaugurated by Edward Said's book *Orientalism* (1978), have, according to Homi K. Bhabha, revealed the way in which certain cultures (mis)represent others in order to achieve and extend political and social domination in the modern world order. Thanks to the work of scholars like Bhabha and Said, education in general and literary study in particular is becoming more democratic, multicultural, and "decentered" (less patriarchal and Eurocentric) in its interests and emphases.

DECONSTRUCTION *See* "What Is Deconstruction?" pp. 538–59.

DIALECTIC Originally developed by Greek philosophers, mainly Socrates and Plato (in *The Republic* and *Phaedrus* [c. 360 B.C.E.]), a form and method of logical argumentation that typically addresses conflicting ideas or positions. When used in the plural, dialectics refers to any mode of argumentation that attempts to resolve the contradictions between opposing ideas.

The German philosopher G. W. F. Hegel described dialectic as a process whereby a *thesis*, when countered by an *antithesis*, leads to the *synthesis* of a new idea. Karl Marx and Friedrich Engels, adapting Hegel's idealist theory, used the phrase *dialectical materialism* to discuss the way in which a revolutionary class war might lead to the synthesis of a new socioeconomic order.

In literary criticism, *dialectic* typically refers to the oppositional ideas and/or mediatory reasoning that pervade and unify a given work or group of works. Critics may thus speak of the dialectic of head and heart (reason and passion) in William Shakespeare's plays. The American **Marxist critic** Fredric Jameson has coined the phrase "dialectical criticism" to refer to a Marxist critical approach that synthesizes **structuralist** and **poststructuralist** methodologies.

DIALOGIC CRITICISM A method of literary criticism based on theories developed by Soviet critic Mikhail Bakhtin. Bakhtin developed his theories in the 1920s and 1930s, but they did not enter the mainstream of Western literary critical thought until the 1980s, when they were translated from Russian.

In *Problems of Dostoevski's Poetics* (1929), Bakhtin spoke of works as being either comparatively monologic or *dialogic*. A monologic work, according to Bakhtin, is one that is clearly dominated by a single, controlling voice or **discourse**, even though it may contain characters representing a multitude of viewpoints. Contrary voices are subordinated to the authorial (and authoritative) voice, which is usually, though not always, representative of the dominant or "official" **ideology** of the author's culture. A dialogic work, by contrast, is one that permits numerous voices or discourses to emerge and to engage in dialogue with one another. In dialogic works, the culture's dominant social or cultural ideology may vie with the discourses of popular culture.

Having made the distinction between monologic and dialogic works, Bakhtin also argued that no work can be completely monologic. That is because the narrator, no matter how authorial and representative of the "official" culture, cannot avoid representing differing and even contrary viewpoints in the process of relating the thoughts and remarks of the diverse group of literary characters that inevitably populate a credibly fictional world. These other voices, which make any work *polyphonic* to some degree, inevitably disrupt the authoritative voice, even though it may remain dominant. Thus, for Bakhtin, the monologic/dialogic opposition was not an absolute; some works are more monologic, others more dialogic.

DISCOURSE Used specifically, (1) the thoughts, statements, or dialogue of individuals, especially of characters in a literary work; (2) the words in, or text of, a **narrative** as opposed to its story line; or (3) a "strand" within a given narrative that argues a certain point or defends a given value system. Discourse of the first type is sometimes categorized as *direct* or *indirect*. Direct discourse relates the thoughts and utterances of individuals and literary characters to the reader unfiltered by a third-person narrator. ("Take me home this instant!" she insisted.) Indirect discourse (also referred to as free indirect discourse) is more impersonal, involving the reportage of thoughts, statements, or dialogue by a third-person narrator. (She told him to take her home immediately.)

More generally, *discourse* refers to the language in which a subject or area of knowledge is discussed or a certain kind of business is transacted. Human knowledge is collected and structured in discourses. Theology and medicine are defined by their discourses, as are politics, sexuality, and literary criticism.

Contemporary literary critics have maintained that society is generally made up of a number of different discourses or *discourse communities,* one or more of which may be dominant or serve the dominant ideology. Each discourse has its own vocabulary, concepts, and rules — knowledge of which constitutes power. The psychoanalyst and **psychoanalytic critic** Jacques Lacan has treated the unconscious as a form of discourse, the patterns of which are repeated in literature. **Cultural critics,** following Soviet critic Mikhail Bakhtin, use the word *dialogic* to discuss the dialogue between discourses that takes place within language or, more specifically, a literary text. Some **poststructuralists** have used *discourse* in lieu of **text** to refer to any verbal structure, whether literary or not.

FEMINIST CRITICISM A type of literary criticism that became a dominant force in Western literary studies in the late 1970s, when feminist theory more broadly conceived was applied to linguistic and literary matters. Since the early 1980s, feminist literary criticism has developed and diversified in a number of ways and is now characterized by a global perspective.

French feminist criticism garnered much of its inspiration from Simone de Beauvoir's seminal book, *Le Deuxiéme Sexe* (*The Second Sex*) (1949). Beauvoir argued that associating men with humanity more generally (as many cultures do) relegates women to an inferior position in society. Subsequent French feminist critics writing during the 1970s acknowledged Beauvoir's critique but focused on language as a tool of male domination, analyzing the ways in which it represents the world from the male point of view and arguing for the development of a feminine language and writing.

Though interested in the subject of feminine language and writing, North American feminist critics of the 1970s and early 1980s began by analyzing literary texts — not by abstractly discussing language — via close textual reading and historical scholarship. One group practiced "feminist critique," examining how women characters are portrayed, exposing the patriarchal **ideology** implicit in the so-called classics, and demonstrating that attitudes and traditions reinforcing systematic masculine dominance are inscribed in the literary canon. Another group practiced what came to be called "gynocriticism," studying writings by women and examining the female literary tradition to find out how women writers across the ages have perceived themselves and imagined reality.

While it gradually became customary to refer to an Anglo-American tradition of feminist criticism, British feminist critics of the 1970s and early 1980s criticized the tendency of some North American critics to find universal or "essential" feminine attributes, arguing that differences of race, class, and culture gave rise to crucial differences among women across space and time. British feminist critics regarded their own critical practice as more political than that of North American feminists, emphasizing an engagement with historical process in order to promote social change.

By the early 1990s, the French, American, and British approaches had so thoroughly critiqued, influenced, and assimilated one another that nationality no longer automatically signaled a practitioner's approach. Today's critics seldom focus on "woman" as a relatively monolithic category; rather, they view "women" as members of different societies with different concerns. Feminists of color, Third World (preferably called **postcolonial**) feminists, and lesbian feminists stressed that women are not defined solely by the fact that they are female; other attributes (such as religion, class, and sexual orientation) are also important, making the problems and goals of one group of women different from those of another.

Many commentators have argued that feminist criticism is by definition **gender criticism** because of its focus on the feminine gender. But the relationship between feminist and gender criticism is, in fact, complex; the two approaches are certainly not polar opposites but, rather, exist along a continuum of attitudes toward sex, sexuality, gender, and language.

FIGURE, FIGURE OF SPEECH *See* **Trope.**

FORMALISM A general term covering several similar types of literary criticism that arose in the 1920s and 1930s, flourished during the 1940s and 1950s, and are still in evidence today. Formalists see the literary work as an object in its own right. Thus, they tend to devote their attention to its intrinsic nature, concentrating their analyses on the interplay and relationships between the text's essential verbal elements. They study the form of the work (as opposed to its content), although form to a formalist can connote anything from **genre** (for example, one may speak of "the sonnet form") to grammatical or rhetorical structure to the "emotional imperative" that engenders the work's (more mechanical) structure. No matter which connotation of form pertains, however, formalists seek to be objective in their analysis, focusing on the work itself and eschewing external considerations. They pay particular attention to literary devices used in the work and to the patterns these devices establish.

Formalism developed largely in reaction to the practice of interpreting literary **texts** by relating them to "extrinsic" issues, such as the historical circumstances and politics of the era in which the work was written, its philosophical or theological milieu, or the experiences and frame of mind of its author. Although the term formalism was coined by critics to disparage the movement, it is now used simply as a descriptive term.

Formalists have generally suggested that everyday language, which serves simply to communicate information, is stale and unimaginative. They argue that "literariness" has the capacity to overturn common and expected patterns (of grammar, of story line), thereby rejuvenating language. Such novel uses of language supposedly enable readers to experience not only language but also the world in an entirely new way.

A number of schools of literary criticism have adopted a formalist orientation, or at least make use of formalist concepts. **The New Criticism**, an American approach to literature that reached its height in the 1940s and 1950s, is perhaps the most famous type of formalism. But Russian formalism was the first major formalist movement; after the Stalinist regime suppressed it in the early 1930s, the Prague Linguistic Circle adopted its analytical methods. The Chicago School has also been classified as formalist insofar as the Chicago Critics examined and analyzed works on an individual basis; their interest in historical material, on the other hand, was clearly not formalist.

GAPS When used by **reader-response critics** familiar with the theories of Wolfgang Iser, the term refers to "blanks" in **texts** that must be filled in by readers. A gap may be said to exist whenever and wherever a reader perceives something to be missing between words, sentences, paragraphs, stanzas, or chapters. Readers respond to gaps actively and creatively, explaining apparent inconsistencies in point of view, accounting for jumps in chronology, speculatively supplying information missing from plots, and resolving problems or issues left ambiguous or "indeterminate" in the text.

Reader-response critics sometimes speak as if a gap actually exists in a text; a gap, of course, is to some extent a product of readers' perceptions. One reader may find a given text to be riddled with gaps while another reader may view that text as comparatively consistent and complete; different readers may find different gaps in the same text. Furthermore, they may fill in the gaps they find in different ways, which is why, a reader-response critic might argue, works are interpreted in different ways.

Although the concept of the gap has been used mainly by reader-response critics, it has also been used by critics taking other theoretical approaches. Practitioners of **deconstruction** might use *gap* when explaining that every text contains opposing and even contradictory **discourses** that cannot be reconciled. **Marxist critics** have used the term *gap* to speak of everything from the gap that opens up between economic **base** and cultural **superstructure** to two kinds of conflicts or contradictions found in literary texts. The first of these conflicts or contradictions, they would argue, results from the fact that even realistic texts reflect an **ideology**, within which there are inevitably subjects and attitudes that cannot be represented or even recognized. As a result, readers at the edge or outside of that ideology perceive that something is missing. The second kind of conflict or contradiction within a text results from the fact that works do more than reflect ideology; they are also fictions that, consciously or unconsciously, distance themselves from that ideology.

GAY AND LESBIAN CRITICISM sometimes referred to as *queer theory*, an approach to literature currently viewed as a form of **gender criticism**; *See* **Gender Criticism**.

GENDER CRITICISM *See* "What Is Gender Criticism?" pp. 434–49.

GENRE From the French *genre* for "kind" or "type," the classification of literary works on the basis of their content, form, or technique. The term also refers to individual classifications. For centuries works have been grouped and associated according to a number of classificatory schemes and distinctions, such as prose /poem /fiction /drama /lyric, and the traditional classical divisions: comedy /tragedy /lyric /pastoral /epic /satire. More recently, Northrop Frye has suggested that all literary works may be grouped with one of four sets of archetypal myths that are in turn associated with the four seasons; for Frye, the four main genre classifications are comedy (spring), romance (summer), tragedy (fall), and satire (winter). Many more specific genre categories exist as well, including autobiography, the essay, Gothic, the picaresque novel, and the sentimental novel. Current usage is thus broad enough to permit varieties of a given genre (such as the novel) as well as the novel in general to be legitimately denoted by the term *genre*.

Traditional thinking about genre has been revised and even roundly criticized by contemporary critics. For example, the prose /poem dichotomy has been largely discarded in favor of a lyric /drama /fiction (or narrative) scheme. The more general idea that works of imaginative literature can be solidly and satisfactorily classified according to set, specific categories has also come under attack in recent times.

HEGEMONY Most commonly, one nation's dominance or dominant influence over another. The term was adopted (and adapted) by the Italian **Marxist critic** Antonio Gramsci to refer to the process of consensus formation and to the pervasive system of assumptions, meanings, and values — the web of **ideologies**, in other words — that shapes the way things look, what they mean, and therefore what reality is for the majority of people within a given culture. Although Gramsci viewed hegemony as being powerful and persuasive, he did not believe that extant systems were immune to change; rather, he encouraged people to resist prevailing ideologies, to form a new consensus, and thereby to alter hegemony.

Hegemony is a term commonly used by **cultural critics** as well as by Marxist critics.

IDEOLOGY A set of beliefs underlying the customs, habits, and practices common to a given social group. To members of that group, the beliefs seem obviously true, natural, and even universally applicable. They may seem just as obviously arbitrary, idiosyncratic, and even false to those who adhere to another ideology. Within a society, several ideologies may coexist; one or more of these may be dominant.

Ideologies may be forcefully imposed or willingly subscribed to. Their component beliefs may be held consciously or unconsciously. In either case, they come to form what Johanna M. Smith has called "the unexamined ground of our experience." Ideology governs our perceptions, judgments, and prejudices — our sense of what is acceptable, normal, and deviant. Ideology may cause a revolution; it may also allow discrimination and even exploitation.

Ideologies are of special interest to politically oriented critics of literature because of the way in which authors reflect or resist prevailing views in their texts. Some **Marxist critics** have argued that literary texts reflect and reproduce the ideologies that produced them; most, however, have shown how ideologies are riven with contradictions that works of literature manage to expose and widen. Other Marxist critics have focused on the way in which texts themselves are characterized by gaps, conflicts, and contradictions between their ideological and anti-ideological functions.

Fredric Jameson, an American Marxist critic, argues that all thought is ideological, but that ideological thought that knows itself as such stands the chance of seeing through and transcending ideology.

Not all of the politically oriented critics interested in ideology have been Marxists. Certain non-Marxist **feminist critics** have addressed the question of ideology by seeking to expose (and thereby call into question) the patriarchal ideology mirrored or inscribed in works written by men — even men who have sought to counter sexism and break down sexual stereotypes. **New historicists** have been interested in demonstrating the ideological underpinnings not only of literary representations but also of our interpretations of them.

IMAGINARY ORDER *See* **Psychological Criticism and Psychoanalytic Criticism.**

IMPLIED READER *See* **Reader-Response Criticism.**

INTENTIONAL FALLACY *See* **New Criticism.**

INTERTEXTUALITY The condition of interconnectedness among texts, or the concept that any text is an amalgam of others, either because it exhibits signs of influence or because its language inevitably contains common points of reference with other texts through such things as allusion, quotation, genre, stylistic features, and even revisions. The critic Julia Kristeva, who popularized and is often credited with coining this term, views any given work as part of a larger fabric of literary **discourse**, part of a continuum including the future as well as the past. Other critics have argued for an even broader use and understanding of the term *intertextuality*, maintaining that literary history per se is too narrow a context within which to read and understand a literary text. When understood this way, *intertextuality* could be used by a **new historicist** or **cultural critic** to refer to the significant interconnectedness between a literary text and contemporary, nonliterary discussions of the issues represented in the literary text. Or it could be used by a **poststructuralist** to suggest that a work of literature can only be recognized and read within a vast field of signs and **tropes** that is like a text and that makes any single text self-contradictory and **undecidable**.

MARXIST CRITICISM A type of criticism in which literary works are viewed as the product of work and whose practitioners emphasize the role of class and ideology as they reflect, propagate, and even challenge the prevailing social order. Rather than viewing texts as repositories for hidden meanings, Marxist critics view texts as material products to be understood in broadly historical terms. In short, literary works are viewed as a product of work (and hence of the realm of production and consumption we call economics).

Marxism began with Karl Marx, the nineteenth-century German philosopher best known for writing *Das Kapital* (*Capital*) (1867), the seminal work of the communist movement. Marx was also the first Marxist literary critic, writing critical essays in the 1830s on writers such as Johann Wolfgang von Goethe and William Shakespeare. Even after Marx met Friedrich Engels in 1843 and began collaborating on overtly political works such as *The German Ideology* (1846) and *The Communist Manifesto* (1848), he maintained a keen interest in literature. In *The German Ideology*, Marx and Engels discussed the relationship between the arts, politics, and basic economic reality in terms of a general social theory. Economics, they argued, provides the *base*, or infrastructure, of society, from which a *superstructure* consisting of law, politics, philosophy, religion, and art emerges.

The revolution anticipated by Marx and Engels did not occur in their century, let alone in their lifetime. When it did occur, in 1917, it did so in a place unimagined by either theorist: Russia, a country long ruled by despotic czars but also enlightened by the works of powerful novelists and playwrights including Anton Chekhov, Alexander Pushkin, Leo Tolstoy, and Fyodor Dostoyevsky. Russia produced revolutionaries such as Vladimir Lenin, who shared not only Marx's interest in literature but also his belief in its ultimate importance. Leon Trotsky, Lenin's comrade in revolution, took a strong interest in literary matters as well, publishing a book called *Literature and Revolution* (1924) that is still viewed as a classic of Marxist literary criticism.

Of those critics active in the USSR after the expulsion of Trotsky and the triumph of Stalin, two stand out: Mikhail Bakhtin and Georg Lukács. Bakhtin viewed language — especially literary texts — in terms of discourses and **dialogues**. A novel written in a society in flux, for instance, might include an official, legitimate discourse, as well as one infiltrated by challenging comments. Lukács, a Hungarian who converted to Marxism in 1919, appreciated prerevolutionary, realistic novels that broadly reflected cultural "totalities" and were populated with characters representing human "types" of the author's place and time.

Perhaps because Lukács was the best of the Soviet communists writing Marxist criticism in the 1930s and 1940s, non-Soviet Marxists tended to develop their ideas by publicly opposing his. In Germany, dramatist and critic Bertolt Brecht criticized Lukács for his attempt to enshrine realism at the expense not only of the other "isms" but also of poetry and drama, which Lukács had largely ignored. Walter Benjamin praised new art forms ushered in by the age of mechanical reproduction, and Theodor Adorno attacked Lukács for his dogmatic rejection of nonrealist modern literature and for his elevation of content over form.

In addition to opposing Lukács and his overly constrictive **canon**, non-Soviet Marxists took advantage of insights generated by non-Marxist critical theories being developed in post-World War II Europe. Lucien Goldmann, a Romanian critic living in Paris, combined structuralist principles with Marx's base-superstructure model in order to show how economics determines the mental structures of social groups, which are reflected in literary texts. Goldmann rejected the idea of individual human genius, choosing instead to see works as the "collective" products of "trans-individual" mental structures. French Marxist Louis Althusser drew on the ideas of the **psychoanalytic** theorist Jacques Lacan and the Italian communist Antonio Gramsci, who discussed the relationship between ideology and **hegemony**, the pervasive system of assumptions and values that shapes the perception of reality for people in a given culture. Althusser's followers included Pierre Macherey, who in *A Theory of Literary Production* (1966) developed Althusser's concept of the relationship between literature and ideology; Terry Eagleton, who proposes an elaborate theory about how history enters texts, which in turn may alter history; and Fredric Jameson, who has argued that form is "but the working out" of content "in the realm of superstructure."

METAPHOR A **figure of speech** (more specifically a **trope**) that associates two unlike things; the representation of one thing by another. The image (or activity or concept) used to represent or "figure" something else is known as the **vehicle** of the metaphor; the thing represented is called the **tenor**. For instance, in the sentence "That child is a mouse," the child is the tenor, whereas the mouse is the vehicle. The image of a mouse is being used to represent the child, perhaps to emphasize his or her timidity.

Metaphor should be distinguished from **simile**, another figure of speech with which it is sometimes confused. Similes compare two unlike things by using a connective word such as *like* or *as*. Metaphors use no connective word to make their comparison. Furthermore, critics ranging from Aristotle to I. A. Richards have argued that metaphors equate the vehicle with the tenor instead of simply comparing the two.

This identification of vehicle and tenor can provide much additional meaning. For instance, instead of saying, "Last night I read a book," we might say, "Last night I plowed through a book." "Plowed through" (or the activity of plowing) is the vehicle of our metaphor; "read" (or the act of reading) is the tenor, the thing being figured. (As this example shows, neither vehicle nor tenor need be a noun; metaphors may employ other parts of speech.) The increment in meaning through metaphor is fairly obvious. Our audience knows not only *that* we read but also *how* we read, because to read a book in the way that a plow rips through earth is surely to read in a relentless, unreflective way. Note that in the sentence above, a new metaphor — "rips through" — has been used to explain an old one. This serves (which is a metaphor) as an example of just how thick (another metaphor) language is with metaphors!

Metaphors may be classified as *direct* or *implied*. A direct metaphor, such as "That child is a mouse" (or "He is such a doormat!"), specifies both tenor and vehicle. An implied metaphor, by contrast, mentions only the vehicle; the tenor is implied by the context of the sentence or passage. For instance, in the sentence "Last night I plowed through a book" (or "She sliced through traffic"), the tenor — the act of reading (or driving) — can be inferred.

Traditionally, metaphor has been viewed as the principal trope. Other figures of speech include simile, **symbol**, personification, allegory, **metonymy**, synecdoche, and conceit. **Deconstructors** have questioned the distinction between metaphor and metonymy.

METONYMY A **figure of speech** (more specifically a **trope**), in which one thing is represented by another that is commonly and often physically associated with it. To refer to a writer's handwriting as his or her "hand" is to use a metonymic figure.

Like other figures of speech (such as **metaphor**), metonymy involves the replacement of one word or phrase by another; thus, a monarch might be referred to as "the crown." As narrowly defined by certain contemporary critics, particularly those associated with **deconstruction**, the **vehicle** of a metonym is arbitrarily, not intrinsically, associated with the **tenor**. (There is no special, intrinsic likeness between a crown and a monarch; it's just that crowns traditionally sit on monarchs' heads and not on the heads of university professors.)

More broadly, metonym and metonymy have been used by recent critics to refer to a wide range of figures. **Structuralists** such as Roman Jakobson, who emphasized the difference between metonymy and metaphor, have recently been challenged by deconstructors, who have further argued that *all* figuration is arbitrary. Deconstructors such as Paul de Man and J. Hillis Miller have questioned the "privilege" granted to metaphor and the metaphor/metonymy distinction or "opposition," suggesting instead that all metaphors are really metonyms.

MODERNISM *See* **Postmodernism.**

NARRATIVE A story or a telling of a story, or an account of a situation or events. Narratives may be fictional or true; they may be written in prose or verse. Some critics use the term even more generally; Brook Thomas, a **new historicist**, has critiqued "narratives of human history that neglect the role human labor has played."

NARRATOLOGY The analysis of the **structural** components of a **narrative**, the way in which those components interrelate, and the relationship between this complex of elements and the narrative's basic story line. Narratology incorporates techniques developed by other critics, most notably Russian **formalists** and French **structuralists**, applying in addition numerous traditional methods of analyzing narrative fiction (for instance, those methods outlined in the "Showing as Telling" chapter of Wayne Booth's *The Rhetoric of*

Fiction [1961]). Narratologists treat narratives as explicitly, intentionally, and meticulously constructed systems rather than as simple or natural vehicles for an author's representation of life. They seek to analyze and explain how authors transforms a chronologically organized story line into a literary plot. (Story is the raw material from which plot is selectively arranged and constructed.)

Narratologists pay particular attention to such elements as point of view; the relations among story, teller, and audience; and the levels and types of **discourse** used in narratives. Certain narratologists concentrate on the question of whether any narrative can actually be neutral (like a clear pane of glass through which some subject is objectively seen) and on how the practices of a given culture influence the shape, content, and impact of "historical" narratives. Mieke Bal's *Narratology: Introduction to the Theory of Narrative* (1980) is a standard introduction to the narratological approach.

NEW CRITICISM, THE A type of **formalist** literary criticism that reached its height during the 1940s and 1950s, and that received its name from John Crowe Ransom's 1941 book *The New Criticism*. New Critics treat a work of literary art as if it were a self-contained, self-referential object. Rather than basing their interpretations of a **text** on the reader's response, the author's stated intentions, or parallels between the text and historical contexts (such as the author's life), New Critics perform a close reading of the text, concentrating on the internal relationships that give it its own distinctive character or form. New Critics emphasize that the structure of a work should not be divorced from meaning, viewing the two as constituting a quasi-organic unity. Special attention is paid to repetition, particularly of images or symbols, but also of sound effects and rhythms in poetry. New Critics especially appreciate the use of literary devices, such as irony and paradox, to achieve a balance or reconciliation between dissimilar, even conflicting, elements in a text.

Because of the importance placed on close textual analysis and the stress on the text as a carefully crafted, orderly object containing observable formal patterns, the New Criticism has sometimes been called an "objective" approach to literature. New Critics are more likely than certain other critics to believe and say that the meaning of a text can be known objectively. For instance, **reader-response critics** see meaning as a function either of each reader's experience or of the norms that govern a particular interpretive community, and **deconstructors** argue that texts mean opposite things at the same time.

The foundations of the New Criticism were laid in books and essays written during the 1920s and 1930s by I. A. Richards (*Practical Criticism* [1929]), William Empson (*Seven Types of Ambiguity* [1930]), and T. S. Eliot ("The Function of Criticism" [1933]). The approach was significantly developed later, however, by a group of American poets and critics, including R. P. Blackmur, Cleanth Brooks, John Crowe Ransom, Allen Tate, Robert Penn Warren, and William K. Wimsatt. Although we associate the New Criticism with certain principles and terms (such as the *affective fallacy* — the notion that the reader's response is relevant to the meaning of a work — and the *intentional fallacy* — the notion that the author's intention determines the work's meaning — the New Critics were trying to make a cultural statement rather than to establish a critical dogma. Generally Southern, religious, and culturally conservative, they advocated the inherent value of literary works (particularly of literary works regarded as beautiful art objects) because they were sick of the growing ugliness of modern life and contemporary events. Some recent theorists even link the rising popularity after World War II of the New Criticism (and other types of formalist literary criticism such as the Chicago School) to American isolationism. These critics tend to view the formalist tendency to isolate literature from biography and history as symptomatic of American fatigue with wider involvements. Whatever the source of the New Criticism's popularity (or the reason for its eventual decline), its practitioners and the textbooks they wrote were so influential in American academia that the approach became standard in college and even high school curricula through the 1960s and well into the 1970s.

NEW HISTORICISM, THE *See* "What Is The New Historicism?" pp. 500–18.

POSTCOLONIAL CRITICISM, POSTCOLONIAL STUDIES A type of **cultural criticism**, *postcolonial criticism* usually involves the analysis of literary texts produced in countries and cultures that have come under the control of European colonial powers at some point in their history. Alternatively, it can refer to the analysis of texts written about colonized places by writers hailing from the colonizing culture. In *Orientalism* (1978), Edward Said, a pioneer of postcolonial criticism and studies, has focused on the way in which the colonizing First World has invented false images and myths of the Third (postcolonial) World, stereotypical images and myths which have conveniently justified Western exploitation and domination of Eastern and Middle Eastern cultures and peoples. In an essay entitled "Postcolonial Criticism" (1992), Homi K. Bhabha has shown how certain cultures (mis)represent other cultures, thereby extending their political and social domination in the modern world order.

Postcolonial studies, a type of **cultural studies**, refers more broadly to the study of cultural groups, practices, and **discourses** — including but not limited to literary discourses — in the colonized world. The term *postcolonial* is usually used broadly to refer to the study of works written at any point after colonization first occurred in a given country, although it is sometimes used more specifically to refer to the analysis of texts and other cultural discourses that emerged after the end of the colonial period (after the success of liberation and independence movements). Among **feminist critics**, the postcolonial perspective has inspired an attempt to recover whole cultures of women heretofore ignored or marginalized, women who speak not only from colonized places but also from the colonizing places to which many of them fled.

Postcolonial criticism has been influenced by **Marxist** thought, by the work of Michel Foucault — whose theories about the power of discourses have influenced **the new historicism** — and by **deconstruction**, which has challenged not only hierarchical, **binary oppositions** such as west/east and north/south but also the notions of superiority associated with the first term of each opposition.

POSTMODERNISM A term referring to certain radically experimental works of literature and art produced after World War II. *Postmodernism* is distinguished from *modernism,* which generally refers to the revolution in art and literature that occurred during the period 1910–1930, particularly following the disillusioning experience of World War I. The postmodern era, with its potential for mass destruction and its shocking history of genocide, has evoked a continuing disillusionment similar to that widely experienced during the modern period. Much of postmodernist writing reveals and highlights the alienation of individuals and the meaninglessness of human existence. Post-modernists frequently stress that humans desperately (and ultimately unsuc-cessfully) cling to illusions of security to conceal and forget the void on which their lives are perched.

Not surprisingly, postmodernists have shared with their modernist precur-sors the goal of breaking away from traditions (including certain modernist tra-ditions, which, over time, had become institutionalized and conventional to some degree) through experimentation with new literary devices, forms, and styles. While preserving the spirit and even some of the themes of modernist lit-erature (the alienation of humanity, historical discontinuity, etc.), postmod-ernists have rejected the order that a number of modernists attempted to instill in their work through patterns of allusion, symbol, and myth. They have also taken some of the meanings and methods found in modernist works to extremes that most modernists would have deplored. For instance, whereas modernists such as T. S. Eliot perceived the world as fragmented and repre-sented that fragmentation through poetic language, many also viewed art as a potentially integrating, restorative force, a hedge against the cacophony and chaos that postmodernist works often imitate (or even celebrate) but do not attempt to counter or correct.

Because postmodernist works frequently combine aspects of diverse **gen-res**, they can be difficult to classify — at least according to traditional schemes of classification. Postmodernists, revolting against a certain modernist tendency toward elitist "high art," have also generally made a concerted effort to appeal to popular culture. Cartoons, music, "pop art," and television have thus become acceptable and even common media for postmodernist artistic expres-sion. Postmodernist literary developments include such genres as the Absurd, the antinovel, concrete poetry, and other forms of avant-garde poetry written in free verse and challenging the **ideological** assumptions of contemporary soci-ety. What postmodernist theater, fiction, and poetry have in common is the view (explicit or implicit) that literary language is its own reality, not a means of representing reality.

Postmodernist critical schools include **deconstruction**, whose practitioners explore the **undecidability** of texts, and **cultural criticism**, which erases the boundary between "high" and "low" culture. The foremost theorist of post-modernism is Francois Lyotard, best known for his book *La Condition post-moderne* (*The Postmodern Condition*) (1979).

POSTSTRUCTURALISM The general attempt to contest and subvert **structuralism** and to formulate new theories regarding interpretation and meaning, initiated particularly by **deconstructors** but also associated with cer-tain aspects and practitioners of **psychoanalytic**, **Marxist**, **cultural**, **feminist**, and **gender criticism**. Poststructuralism, which arose in the late 1960s, includes such a wide variety of perspectives that no unified poststructuralist the-ory can be identified. Rather, poststructuralists are distinguished from other contemporary critics by their opposition to structuralism and by certain con-cepts they embrace.

Structuralists typically believe that meaning(s) in a text, as well as the mean-ing of a text, can be determined with reference to the system of signification —

the "codes" and **conventions** that governed the text's production and that operate in its reception. Poststructuralists reject the possibility of such "determinate" knowledge. They believe that signification is an interminable and intricate web of associations that continually defers a determinate assessment of meaning. The numerous possible meanings of any word lead to contradictions and ultimately to the dissemination of meaning itself. Thus, poststructuralists contend that texts contradict not only structuralist accounts of them but also themselves.

To elaborate, poststructuralists have suggested that structuralism rests on a number of distinctions — between signifier and signified, self and language (or text), texts and other texts, and text and world — that are overly simplistic, if not patently inaccurate, and they have made a concerted effort to discredit these oppositions. For instance, poststructuralists have viewed the self as the subject, as well as the user, of language, claiming that although we may speak through and shape language, it also shapes and speaks through us. In addition, poststructuralists have demonstrated that in the grand scheme of signification, all "signifieds" are also signifiers, for each word exists in a complex web of language and has such a variety of denotations and connotations that no one meaning can be said to be final, stable, and invulnerable to reconsideration and substitution. Signification is unstable and indeterminate, and thus so is meaning. Poststructuralists, who have generally followed their structuralist predecessors in rejecting the traditional concept of the literary "work" (as the work of an individual and purposeful author) in favor of the impersonal "text," have gone structuralists one better by treating texts as "intertexts": crisscrossed strands within the infinitely larger text called language, that weblike system of denotation, connotation, and signification in which the individual text is inscribed and read and through which its myriad. possible meanings are ascribed and assigned. (Poststructuralist **psychoanalytic critic** Julia Kristeva coined the term **intertextuality** to refer to the fact that a text is a "mosaic" of preexisting texts whose meanings it reworks and transforms.)

Although poststructuralism has drawn from numerous critical perspectives developed in Europe and in North America, it relies most heavily on the work of French theorists, especially Jacques Derrida, Kristeva, Jacques Lacan, Michel Foucault, and Roland Barthes. Derrida's 1966 paper "Structure, Sign and Play in the Discourse of the Human Sciences" inaugurated poststructuralism as a coherent challenge to structuralism. Derrida rejected the structuralist presupposition that texts (or other structures) have self-referential centers that govern their language (or signifying system) without being in any way determined, governed, co-opted, or problematized by that language (or signifying system). Having rejected the structuralist concept of a self-referential center, Derrida also rejected its corollary: that a text's meaning is thereby rendered determinable (capable of being determined) as well as determinate (fixed and reliably correct). Lacan, Kristeva, Foucault, and Barthes have all, in diverse ways, arrived at similarly "antifoundational" conclusions, positing that no foundation or "center" exists that can ensure correct interpretation.

Poststructuralism continues to flourish today. In fact, one might reasonably say that poststructuralism serves as the overall paradigm for many of the most prominent contemporary critical perspectives. Approaches ranging from

reader-response criticism to the new historicism assume the "an~~ ~~tionalist" bias of poststructuralism. Many approaches also incorporate th~~ ~~structuralist position that texts do not have clear and definite meanin~~g~~ argument pushed to the extreme by those poststructuralists identified deconstruction. But unlike deconstructors, who argue that the process signification itself produces irreconcilable contradictions, contemporary criti~~c~~ oriented toward other poststructuralist approaches (**discourse** analysis or Lacanian psychoanalytic theory, for instance) maintain that texts do have real meanings underlying their apparent or "manifest" meanings (which often contradict or cancel out one another). These underlying meanings have been distorted, disguised, or repressed for psychological or **ideological** reasons but can be discovered through poststructuralist ways of reading.

PRESENCE AND ABSENCE Words given a special literary application by French theorist of **deconstruction** Jacques Derrida when he used them to make a distinction between speech and writing. An individual speaking words must actually be present at the time they are heard, Derrida pointed out, whereas an individual writing words is absent at the time they are read. Derrida, who associates presence with "logos" (the creating spoken Word of a present God who "In the beginning" said "Let there be light"), argued that the Western concept of language is *logocentric.* That is, it is grounded in "the metaphysics of presence," the belief that any linguistic system has a basic foundation (what Derrida terms an "ultimate referent"), making possible an identifiable and correct meaning or meanings for any potential statement that can be made within that system. Far from supporting this common Western view of language as logocentric, however, Derrida in fact argues that presence is not an ultimate referent" and that it does not guarantee determinable (capable of being determined) — much less determinate (fixed and reliably correct) — meaning. Derrida in fact calls into question the "privileging" of speech and presence over writing and absence in Western thought.

PSYCHOLOGICAL CRITICISM AND PSYCHOANALYTIC CRITICISM *See* "What Is Psychoanalytic Criticism?" pp. 466–83.

QUEER THEORY *See* **Gay and Lesbian Criticism; Gender Criticism.**

READER-RESPONSE CRITICISM A critical approach encompassing various approaches to literature that explore and seek to explain the diversity (and often divergence) of readers' responses to literary works.

Louise Rosenblatt is often credited with pioneering the approaches in *Literature as Exploration* (1938). In a 1969 essay entitled "Towards a Transactional Theory of Reading," she summed up her position as follows: "a poem is what the reader lives through under the guidance of the text and experiences as relevant to the text." Recognizing that many critics would reject this definition, Rosenblatt wrote: "The idea that a *poem* presupposes a *reader* actively involved with a *text is* particularly shocking to those seeking to emphasize the objectivity of their interpretations." Rosenblatt implicitly and generally refers to formalists (the most influential of whom are the **New Critics**) when she speaks of supposedly objective interpreters shocked by the notion that a "*poem*" is cooperatively produced by a "*reader*" and a "*text.*" Formalists spoke of "the poem itself," the "concrete work of art," the "real poem." They had no interest in what a work of literature makes a reader "live through." In fact, in *The Verbal Icon* (1954),

William K. Wimsatt and Monroe C. Beardsley used the term **affective fallacy** to define as erroneous the very idea that a reader's response is relevant to the meaning of a literary work.

Stanley Fish, whose early work is seen by some as marking the true beginning of contemporary reader-response criticism, also took issue with the tenets of formalism. In "Literature in the Reader: Affective Stylistics" (1970), he argued that any school of criticism that sees a literary work as an object, claiming to describe what it is and never what it does, misconstrues the very essence of literature and reading. Literature exists and signifies when it is read, Fish suggests, and its force is an affective force. Furthermore, reading is a temporal process, not a spatial one as formalists assume when they step back and survey the literary work as if it were an object spread out before them. The German critic Wolfgang Iser has described that process in his books *The Implied Reader: Patterns of Communication in Prose Fiction from Bunyan to Beckett* (1974) and *The Act of Reading: A Theory of Aesthetic Response* (1976). Iser argues that texts contain **gaps** (or blanks) that powerfully affect the reader, who must explain them, connect what they separate, and create in his or her mind aspects of a work that aren't *in* the text but that the text incites.

With the redefinition of literature as something that only exists meaningfully in the mind of the reader, with the redefinition of the literary work as a catalyst of mental events, comes a redefinition of the reader. No longer is the reader the passive recipient of those ideas that an author has planted in a text. "The reader is *active*," Rosenblatt had insisted. Fish makes the same point in "Literature in the Reader": "reading is . . . something you *do*." Iser, in focusing critical interest on the gaps in texts, on the blanks that readers have to fill in, similarly redefines the reader as an active maker of meaning. Other reader-response critics define the reader differently. Wayne Booth uses the phrase *the implied reader* to mean the reader "created by the work." Like Booth, Iser employs the term *the implied reader,* but he also uses "the educated reader" when he refers to what Fish calls the "intended reader."

Since the mid-1970s, reader-response criticism has evolved into a variety of new forms. Subjectivists such as David Bleich, Norman Holland, and Robert Crosman have viewed the reader's response not as one "guided" by the text but rather as one motivated by deep-seated, personal, psychological needs. Holland has suggested that, when we read, we find our own "identity theme" in the text using "the literary work to symbolize and finally to replicate ourselves. We work out through the text our own characteristic patterns of desire." Even Fish has moved away from reader-response criticism as he had initially helped define it, focusing on "interpretive strategies" held in common by "interpretive communities" — such as the one comprised by American college students reading a novel as a class assignment.

Fish's shift in focus is in many ways typical of changes that have taken place within the field of reader-response criticism — a field that, because of those changes, is increasingly being referred to as *reader-oriented criticism.* Recent reader-oriented critics, responding to Fish's emphasis on interpretive communities and also to the historically oriented perception theory of Hans Robert Jauss, have studied the way a given reading public's "horizons of expectations" change over time. Many of these contemporary critics view themselves as reader-oriented critics and as practitioners of some other critical approach as well. Certain **feminist** and **gender critics** with an interest in reader response have asked whether there is such a thing as "reading like a woman." Reading-oriented **new historicists** have looked at the way in which racism affects and is affected by reading and, more generally, the way in which politics can affect reading practices and outcomes. **Gay and lesbian critics**, such as Wayne Koestenbaum, have argued that sexualities have been similarly constructed within and by social **discourses** and that there may even be a homosexual way of reading.

REAL, THE *See* **Psychoanalytic Criticism and Psychological Criticism.**

SEMIOLOGY Another word for **semiotics**, created by Swiss linguist Ferdinand de Saussure in his 1915 book *Course in General Linguistics.* *See* **Semiotics.**

SEMIOTICS A term coined by Charles Sanders Peirce to refer to the study of signs, sign systems, and the way meaning is derived from them. **Structuralist** anthropologists, psychoanalysts, and literary critics developed semiotics during the decades following 1950, but much of the pioneering work had been done at the turn of the century by Pierce and by the founder of modem linguistics, Ferdinand de Saussure.

To a semiotician, a sign is not simply a direct means of communication, such as a stop sign or a restaurant sign or language itself. Rather, signs encompass body language (crossed arms, slouching), ways of greeting and parting (handshakes, hugs, waves), artifacts, and even articles of clothing. A sign is anything that conveys information to others who understand it based upon a system of codes and conventions that they have consciously learned or unconsciously internalized as members of a certain culture. Semioticians have often used concepts derived specifically from linguistics, which focuses on language, to analyze all types of signs.

Although Saussure viewed linguistics as a division of semiotics (semiotics, after all, involves the study of all signs, not just linguistic ones), much semiotic theory rests on Saussure's linguistic terms, concepts, and distinctions. Semioticians subscribe to Saussure's basic concept of the linguistic sign as containing a *signifier* (a linguistic "sound image" used to represent some more abstract concept) and *signified* (the abstract concept being represented). They have also found generally useful his notion that the relationship between signifiers and signified is arbitrary; that is, no intrinsic or natural relationship exists between them, and meanings we derive from signifiers are grounded in the differences among signifiers themselves. Particularly useful are Saussure's concept of the *phoneme* (the smallest basic speech sound or unit of pronunciation) and his idea that phonemes exist in two kinds of relationships: diachronic and synchronic.

A phoneme has a diachronic, or "horizontal," relationship with those other phonemes that precede and follow it (as the words appear, left to right, on this page) in a particular usage, utterance, or **narrative** — what Saussure called *parole* (French for "word"). A phoneme has a synchronic, or "vertical," relationship with the entire system of language within which individual usages, utterances, or narratives have meaning — what Saussure called *langue* (French for "tongue," as in "native tongue," meaning language). *An* means what it means in English because those of us who speak the language are plugged in to the same system (think of it as a computer network where different individuals access the same information in the same way at a given time). A principal tenet of semiotics is that signs, like words, are not significant in themselves, but instead have meaning only in relation to other signs and the entire system of signs, or *langue*. Meaning is not inherent in the signs themselves, but is derived from the differences among signs.

Given that semiotic theory underlies structuralism, it is not surprising that many semioticians have taken a broad, structuralist approach to signs, studying a variety of phenomena ranging from rites of passage to methods of preparing and consuming food to understand the cultural codes and conventions they reveal. Because of the broad-based applicability of semiotics, furthermore, structuralist anthropologists such as Claude Lévi-Strauss, literary critics such as Roland Barthes, and **psychoanalytic theorists** such as Jacques Lacan and Julia Kristeva, have made use of semiotic theories and practices. Kristeva, who is generally considered a pioneer of feminism although she eschews the feminist label, has argued that there is such a thing as *femine language* and that it is semiotic, not **symbolic** in nature. She thus employs both terms in an unusual way, using *semiotic* to refer to language that is rythmic, unifying, and fluid, and *symbolic* to refer to the more rigid associations redefined in the Western **canon**. The affinity between semiotics and structuralist literary criticism derives from the emphasis placed on *langue*, or system. Structuralist critics were reacting against **formalists** and their method of focusing on individual words as if meanings did not depend on anything external to the text.

SIMILE *See* **Metaphor; Trope.**

STRUCTURALISM A theory of humankind whose proponents attempted to show systematically, even scientifically, that all elements of human culture, including literature, may be understood as parts of a system of **signs**. Critic Robert Scholes has described structuralism as a reaction to " 'modernist' alienation and despair."

European structuralists such as Roman Jakobson, Claude Lévi-Strauss, and Roland Barthes (before his shift toward poststructuralism) attempted to develop a **semiology**, or **semiotics** (science of signs). Barthes, among others, sought to recover literature and even language from the isolation in which they had been studied and to show that the laws that govern them govern all signs, from road signs to articles of clothing.

Structuralism was heavily influenced by linguistics, especially by the pioneering work of linguist Ferdinand de Saussure. Particularly useful to structuralists were Saussure's concept of the phoneme (the smallest basic speech sound or unit of pronunciation) and his idea that phonemes exist in two kinds of relationships: diachronic and synchronic. A phoneme has a diachronic, or "horizontal," relationship with those other phonemes that precede and follow it (as the words appear, left to right, on this page) in a particular usage, utterance, or **narrative** — what Saussure called *parole* (French for "word"). A phoneme has a synchronic, or "vertical," relationship with the entire system of language within which individual usages, utterances, or narratives have meaning — what Saussure called *langue* (French for "tongue," as in "native tongue," meaning language). *An* means what it means in English because those of us who speak the language are plugged in to the same system (think of it as a computer network where different individuals can access the same information in the same way at a given time).

Following Saussure, Lévi-Strauss, an anthropologist, studied hundreds of myths, breaking them into their smallest meaningful units, which he called "mythemes." Removing each from its diachronic relations with other mythemes in a single myth (such as the myth of Oedipus and his mother), he vertically aligned those mythemes that he found to be homologous (structurally correspondent). He then studied the relationships within as well as between vertically aligned columns, in an attempt to understand scientifically, through ratios and proportions, those thoughts and processes that humankind has shared, both at one particular time and across time. Whether Lévi-Strauss was studying the structure of myths or the structure of villages, he looked for recurring, common elements that transcended the differences within and among cultures.

Structuralists followed Saussure in preferring to think about the overriding *langue,* or language of myth, in which each mytheme and mytheme-constituted myth fits meaningfully, rather than about isolated individual *paroles,* or narratives. Structuralists also followed Saussure's lead in believing that sign systems must be understood in terms of **binary oppositions** (a proposition later disputed by poststructuralist Jacques Derrida). In analyzing myths and texts to find basic structures, structuralists found that opposite terms modulate until they are finally resolved or reconciled by some intermediary third term. Thus a structuralist reading of Milton's *Paradise Lost* (1667) might show that the war between God and the rebellious angels becomes a rift between God and sinful, fallen man, a rift that is healed by the Son of God, the mediating third term.

Although structuralism was largely a European phenomenon in its origin and development, it was influenced by American thinkers as well. Noam Chomsky, for instance, who powerfully influenced structuralism through works such as *Reflections on Language* (1975), identified and distinguished between "surface structures" and "deep structures" in language and linguistic literatures, including **texts**.

SYMBOL Something that, although it is of interest in its own right, stands for or suggests something larger and more complex — often an idea or a range of interrelated ideas, attitudes, and practices.

Within a given culture, some things are understood to be symbols: the flag of the United States is an obvious example, as are the five intertwined Olympic rings. More subtle cultural symbols might be the river as a symbol of time and the journey as a symbol of life and its manifold experiences. Instead of appropriating symbols generally used and understood within their culture, writers often create their own symbols by setting up a complex but identifiable web of associations in their works. As a result, one object, image, person, place, or action suggests others, and may ultimately suggest a range of ideas.

A symbol may thus be defined as a **metaphor** in which the **vehicle** — the image, activity, or concept used to represent something else — represents many related things (or **tenors**), or is broadly suggestive. The urn in Keats's "Ode on a Grecian Urn" (1820) suggests many interrelated concepts, including art, truth, beauty, and timelessness.

Symbols have been of particular interest to **formalists**, who study how meanings emerge from the complex, patterned relationships among images in a work, and **psychoanalytic critics**, who are interested in how individual authors

and the larger culture both disguise and reveal unconscious fears and desires
through symbols. Recently, French **feminist critics** have also focused on the
symbolic. They have suggested that, as wide-ranging as it seems, symbolic language is ultimately rigid and restrictive. They favor **semiotic** language and writing — writing that neither opposes nor hierarchically ranks qualities or
elements of reality nor symbolizes one thing but not another in terms of a
third — contending that semiotic language is at once more fluid, rhythmic,
unifying, and feminine.

SYMBOLIC ORDER *See* **Psychological Criticism and Psychoanalytic
Criticism; Symbol.**

TENOR *See* **Metaphor; Metonymy; Symbol.**

TEXT From the Latin *texere,* meaning "to weave," a term that may be
defined in a number of ways. Some critics restrict its use to the written word,
although they may apply the term to objects ranging from a poem to the words
in a book to a book itself to a biblical passage used in a sermon to a written transcript of an oral statement or interview. Other critics include nonwritten material in the designation text, as long as that material has been isolated for analysis.

French **structuralist** critics took issue with the traditional view of literary
compositions as "works" with a form intentionally imposed by the author and a
meaning identifiable through analysis of the author's use of language. These
critics argued that literary compositions are texts rather than works, texts being
the product of a social institution they called *écriture* (writing). By identifying
compositions as texts rather than works, structuralists denied them the person-
alized character attributed to works wrought by a particular, unique author.
Structuralists believed not only that a text was essentially impersonal, the confluence of certain preexisting attributes of the social institution of writing, but
that any interpretation of the text should result from an impersonal *lecture*
(reading). This *lecture* included reading with an active awareness of how the linguistic system functions.

The French writer and theorist Roland Barthes, a structuralist who later
turned toward **poststructuralism**, distinguished text from *work* in a different
way, characterizing a text as open and a work as closed. According to Barthes,
works are bounded entities, conventionally classified in the **canon**, whereas
texts engage readers in an ongoing relationship of interpretation and reinterpretation. Barthes further divided texts into two categories: *lisible* (readerly)
and *scriptible* (writerly). Texts that are *lisible* depend more heavily on convention, making their interpretation easier and more predictable. Texts that are
scriptible are generally experimental, flouting or seriously modifying traditional
rules. Such texts cannot be interpreted according to standard conventions.

TROPE One of the two major divisions of **figures of speech** (the other
being *rhetorical figures*). Trope comes from a word that literally means "turning"; to trope (with figures of speech) is, figuratively speaking, to turn or twist
some word or phrase to make it mean something else. **Metaphor, metonymy,
simile,** personification, and synecdoche are sometimes referred to as the principal tropes.

UNDECIDABILITY *See* **Deconstruction.**

VEHICLE *See* **Metaphor; Metonymy; Symbol.**

About the Contributors

THE VOLUME EDITOR

John Paul Riquelme is professor of English at Boston University. Author of *Teller and Tale in Joyce's Fiction: Oscillating Perspectives* (1983) and *Harmony of Dissonances: T. S. Eliot, Romanticism, and Imagination* (1991), he has also edited numerous books and issues of journals, including an issue of *Modern Fiction Studies* focusing on "The Gothic and Modernism" (2000). He has edited a Case Study Edition of Hardy's *Tess of the d'Urbervilles* for Bedford/St. Martin's (1998), and is currently working on a study of Oscar Wilde's aesthetic politics and the origins of literary modernism in 1890s Britain.

THE CRITICS

Gregory Castle is an associate professor of English at Arizona State University. He was awarded the Gerald Kahan Scholar's Prize in 1998 by the American Society for Theater Research for an essay on John M. Synge's *Playboy of the Western World*. His scholarly articles have appeared in *James Joyce Quarterly, Genre, Twentieth-Century Literature, European Joyce Studies,* and *Theatre Journal,* and his most recent publications include *Modernism and the Celtic Revival* (2001) and *Postcolonial Discourses: An Anthology* (2001).

Sos Eltis is a fellow and tutor in English at Brasenose College of Oxford University, where she teaches nineteenth- and twentieth-century literature. Her interests include Victorian and modern drama, performance studies, and theater history. Author of *Revising Wilde: Society and Subversion in the Plays of Oscar Wilde* (1996), she is currently working on an article on the fallen woman in Victorian and Edwardian drama, as well as a book on themes in modern drama.

Dennis Foster is a professor of English at Southern Methodist University, where he has taught courses in critical theory, contemporary literature, nineteenth-century American literature, psychoanalysis and literature, and contemporary fiction. In addition to numerous essays and reviews, his publications include *Confession and Complicity in Narrative* (1987) and *Sublime Enjoyment: On the Perverse Motive in American Literature* (1997).

Jennifer Wicke is a professor of English at the University of Virginia, where she teaches nineteenth- and twentieth-century British and American literature, critical theory, and film and media studies. One of the editors of the *Longman Anthology of British Literature* (1999), she has also coedited *Feminism and Postmodernism* (1994). Her book *Advertising Fictions: Literature, Advertisement and Social Reading* (1988) focuses on the work of Charles Dickens, Henry James, and James Joyce.

THE SERIES EDITOR

Ross C Murfin, general editor of the series, is provost of Southern Methodist University. He has taught literature at Yale University and the University of Virginia and has published scholarly studies on Joseph Conrad, Thomas Hardy, and D. H. Lawrence. With Supryia M. Ray, he is the author of *The Bedford Glossary of Critical and Literary Terms*.